Financial Reporting and Analysis

CFA® PROGRAM CURRICULUM • VOLUME 3

LEVEL I
2011

CFA INSTITUTE

Learning Solutions

New York   Boston   San Francisco
London   Toronto   Sydney   Tokyo   Singapore   Madrid
Mexico City   Munich   Paris   Cape Town   Hong Kong   Montreal

1 2 3 4 5 6 7 8 9 10 V313 15 14 13 12 11 10

0999000000270552061

AG/JW

Please visit our website at *www.pearsoned.com*

ISBN 10: 0-558-52183-5
ISBN 13: 978-0-558-52183-7

CONTENTS

HOW TO USE THE CFA PROGRAM CURRICULUM

Congratulations on your decision to enter the Chartered Financial Analyst (CFA®) Program. This exciting and rewarding program of study reflects your desire to become a serious investment professional. You are embarking on a program noted for its high ethical standards and the breadth of knowledge, skills, and abilities it develops. Your commitment to the CFA Program should be educationally and professionally rewarding.

The credential you seek is respected around the world as a mark of accomplishment and dedication. Each level of the program represents a distinct achievement in professional development. Successful completion of the program is rewarded with membership in a prestigious global community of investment professionals. CFA charterholders are dedicated to life-long learning and maintaining currency with the ever-changing dynamics of a challenging profession. The CFA Program represents the first step towards a career-long commitment to professional education.

The CFA examination measures your degree of mastery of the assigned CFA Program curriculum. Therefore, the key to your success on the examination is reading and studying the CFA Program curriculum. The remaining sections provide background on the Candidate Body of Knowledge (CBOK™), the organization of the curriculum and tips for developing an effective study program.

Curriculum Development

The CFA Program curriculum is grounded in the practice of the investment profession. Utilizing the Global Body of Investment Knowledge (GBIK) collaborative website, CFA Institute performs a continuous practice analysis with investment professionals around the world to determine the knowledge, skills, and abilities that are relevant to the profession. Regional panels and targeted surveys are conducted annually to verify and reinforce the continuous feedback. The practice analysis process ultimately defines the Candidate Body of Knowledge (CBOK). The CBOK consists of four components:

► A broad topic outline that lists the major knowledge areas

► Topic area weights that indicate the relative exam weightings of the top-level topic areas

► Learning Outcome Statements (LOS) that advise candidates as to what they should be able to do with this knowledge (LOS are provided in candidate study sessions and at the beginning of each reading)

► The curriculum of material that candidates receive upon exam registration and are expected to master

A committee made up of practicing charterholders, in conjunction with CFA Institute staff, designs the CFA Program curriculum to deliver the CBOK to candidates. The examinations, also written by practicing charterholders, are designed to allow you to demonstrate your mastery of the CBOK as set forth in the CFA Program curriculum. As you structure your personal study program, you should emphasize mastery of the CBOK and the practical application of that knowledge. For more information on the practice analysis, CBOK, and development of the CFA Program curriculum, please visit www.cfainstitute.org/toolkit.

Organization of the Curriculum

The Level I CFA Program curriculum is organized into 10 topic areas. Each topic area begins with a brief statement of the material and the depth of knowledge expected.

Each topic area is then divided into one or more study sessions. These study sessions—18 sessions in the Level I curriculum—should form the basic structure of your reading and preparation.

Each study session includes a statement of its structure and objective, and is further divided into specific reading assignments. The outline on the inside front cover of each volume illustrates the organization of these 18 study sessions.

The reading assignments are the basis for all examination questions, and are selected or developed specifically to teach the CBOK. These readings are drawn from CFA Program-commissioned content, textbook chapters, professional journal articles, research analyst reports, and cases. Readings include problems and solutions as well as appendices to help you learn.

Reading-specific Learning Outcome Statements (LOS) are listed at the beginning of each reading. These LOS indicate what you should be able to accomplish after studying the reading. We encourage you to review how to properly use LOS, and the descriptions of commonly used LOS "command words," at www.cfainstitute.org/toolkit. The command words signal the depth of learning you are expected to achieve from the reading. You should use the LOS to guide and focus your study, as each examination question is based on an assigned reading and one or more LOS. However, the readings provide context for the LOS and enable you to apply a principle or concept in a variety of scenarios. The candidate is responsible for the entirety of all of the required material in a study session, the assigned readings as well as the end-of-reading questions and problems.

Features of the Curriculum

▶ **Required vs. Optional Segments** - You should read all of the pages for an assigned reading. In some cases, however, we have reprinted an entire chapter or article and marked those parts of the reading that are not required as "optional." The CFA examination is based only on the required segments, and the optional segments are included only when they might help you to better understand the required segments (by seeing the required material in its full context). When an optional segment begins, you will see an icon and a solid vertical bar in the outside margin that will continue until the optional segment ends, accompanied by another icon. *Unless the material is specifically marked as optional, you should assume it is required.* Keep in mind that the optional material is provided strictly for your convenience and will not be tested. You should rely on the required segments and the reading-specific LOS in preparing for the examination.

▶ **Problems/Solutions** - *All questions and problems in the readings as well as their solutions (which are provided directly following the problems) are part of the curriculum and required material for the exam.* When appropriate, we have included problems within and after the readings to demonstrate practical application and reinforce your understanding of the concepts presented. The questions and problems are designed to help you learn these concepts and may serve as a basis for exam questions. Many of the questions are adapted from past CFA examinations.

▶ **Margins** - The wide margins in each volume provide space for your note-taking.

▶ **Two-Color Format** - To enrich the visual appeal and clarity of the exhibits, tables, and text, the curriculum is printed in a two-color format.

▶ **Six-Volume Structure** - For portability of the curriculum, the material is spread over six volumes.

▶ **Glossary and Index** - For your convenience, we have printed a glossary and index in each volume. Throughout the curriculum, a **bolded blue** word in a reading denotes a term defined in the glossary.

▶ **Source Material** - The authorship, publisher, and copyright owners are given for each reading for your reference. We recommend that you use this CFA Institute curriculum rather than the original source materials because the curriculum may include only selected pages from outside readings, updated sections within the readings, and has problems and solutions tailored to the CFA Program.

▶ **LOS Self-Check** - We have inserted checkboxes next to each LOS that you can use to track your progress in mastering the concepts in each reading.

Designing Your Personal Study Program

Create a Schedule - An orderly, systematic approach to examination preparation is critical. You should dedicate a consistent block of time every week to reading and studying. Complete all reading assignments and the associated problems and solutions in each study session. Review the LOS both before and after you study each reading to ensure that you have mastered the applicable content and can demonstrate the knowledge, skill, or ability described by the LOS and the assigned reading. Use the new LOS self-check to track your progress and highlight areas of weakness for later review.

You will receive periodic e-mail communications that contain important study tips and preparation strategies. Be sure to read these carefully.

CFA Institute estimates that you will need to devote a minimum of 10–15 hours per week for 18 weeks to study the assigned readings. Allow a minimum of one week for each study session, and plan to complete them all at least 30–45 days prior to the examination. This schedule will allow you to spend the final four to six weeks before the examination reviewing the assigned material and taking online sample and mock examinations.

At CFA Institute, we believe that candidates need to commit to a *minimum* of 270–300 hours reading and reviewing the curriculum and end-of-reading questions and problems. Many candidates have also incorporated the online sample examinations into their preparations during the final weeks before the exam. This recommendation, however, may substantially underestimate the hours needed for appropriate examination preparation depending on your individual circumstances, relevant experience, and academic background. You will undoubtedly adjust your study time to conform to your own strengths and weaknesses, and your educational and professional background.

You will probably spend more time on some study sessions than on others, but on average you should plan on devoting 15 hours per study session. You should allow ample time for both in-depth study of all topic areas and additional concentration on those topic areas for which you feel least prepared.

Preliminary Readings - The reading assignments in Economics assume candidates already have a basic mastery of the concepts typically presented in introductory university-level economics courses. Information on suggested readings to improve your knowledge of these topics precedes the relevant study sessions.

Candidate Preparation Toolkit - We have created the online toolkit to provide a single comprehensive location with resources and guidance for candidate preparation. In addition to in-depth information on study program planning, the CFA Program curriculum, and the online sample and mock examinations, the toolkit also contains curriculum errata, printable study session outlines, sample examination questions, and more. Errata that we have identified in the curriculum are corrected and listed periodically in the errata listing in the toolkit. We encourage you to use the toolkit as your central preparation resource during your tenure as a candidate. Visit the toolkit at www.cfainstitute.org/toolkit.

Online Sample Examinations - CFA Institute online sample examinations are intended to assess your exam preparation as you progress toward the end of your study. After each question, you will receive immediate feedback noting the correct response and indicating the relevant assigned reading, so you'll be able to identify areas of weakness for further study. The 120-minute sample examinations reflect the question formats, topics, and level of difficulty of the actual CFA examinations. Aggregate data indicate that the CFA examination pass rate was higher among candidates who took one or more online sample examinations than among candidates who did not take the online sample examinations. For more information on the online sample examinations, please visit www.cfainstitute.org/toolkit.

Online Mock Examinations - In response to candidate requests, CFA Institute has developed mock examinations that mimic the actual CFA examinations not only in question format and level of difficulty, but also in length. The three-hour online mock exams are intended to be taken after you complete your study of the full curriculum, so you can test your understanding of the CBOK and your readiness for the exam. To further differentiate, feedback is provided at the end of the exam, rather than after each question as with the sample exams. CFA Institute recommends that you take these mock exams at the final stage of your preparation toward the actual CFA examination. For more information on the online mock examinations, please visit www.cfainstitute.org/toolkit.

Tools to Measure Your Comprehension of the Curriculum

With the addition of the online mock exams, CFA Institute now provides three distinct ways you can practice for the actual CFA exam. The full descriptions are above, but below is a brief summary of each:

End-of-Reading Questions and Problems - These are found at the end of each reading in the printed curriculum, and should be used to test your understanding of the concepts.

Online Sample Exams - Available in Fall 2010, online sample exams are designed to assess your exam preparation, and can help you target areas of weakness for further study.

Online Mock Exams - In contrast to the sample exams, mock exams will be available in Spring 2011. Mock exams are designed to replicate the exam day experience, and should be taken near the end of your study period to prepare for exam day.

Preparatory Providers - After you enroll in the CFA Program, you may receive numerous solicitations for preparatory courses and review materials. When considering a prep course, make sure the provider is in compliance with the CFA Institute Prep Provider Guidelines Program. Just remember, there are no shortcuts to success on the CFA examinations; reading and studying the CFA curriculum is the key to success on the examination. The CFA examinations reference only the CFA Institute assigned curriculum—no preparatory course or review course materials are consulted or referenced. For more information on the Prep Provider Guidelines Program, visit www.cfainstitute.org/cfaprog/resources/prepcourse.html.

SUMMARY

Every question on the CFA examination is based on specific pages in the required readings and on one or more LOS. Frequently, an examination question is also tied to a specific example highlighted within a reading or to a specific end-of-reading question and/or problem and its solution. To make effective use of the curriculum, please remember these key points:

1. All pages printed in the Custom Curriculum are required reading for the examination except for occasional sections marked as optional. You may read optional pages as background, but you will not be tested on them.

2. All questions, problems, and their solutions - printed at the end of readings - are part of the curriculum and required study material for the examination.

3. You should make appropriate use of the CFA Candidate Toolkit and the online sample/mock examinations.

4. You should schedule and commit sufficient study time to cover the 18 study sessions, review the materials, and take sample/mock examinations.

5. **Note:** Some of the concepts in the study sessions may be superseded by updated rulings and/or pronouncements issued after a reading was published. Candidates are expected to be familiar with the overall analytical framework contained in the assigned readings. Candidates are not responsible for changes that occur after the material was written.

Feedback

At CFA Institute, we are committed to delivering a comprehensive and rigorous curriculum for the development of competent, ethically grounded investment professionals. We rely on candidate and member feedback as we work to incorporate content, design, and packaging improvements. You can be assured that we will continue to listen to your suggestions. Please send any comments or feedback to curriculum@cfainstitute.org. Ongoing improvements in the curriculum will help you prepare for success on the upcoming examinations, and for a lifetime of learning as a serious investment professional.

FINANCIAL REPORTING AND ANALYSIS

STUDY SESSIONS

TOPIC LEVEL LEARNING OUTCOME

The candidate should be able to demonstrate a thorough knowledge of financial accounting procedures and the rules that govern disclosure. Emphasis is on basic financial statements and how alternative accounting methods affect those statements and the analysis of financial statement relationships.

Note:
In 2009, the Financial Accounting Standards Board (FASB) released the FASB Accounting Standards Codification™. The Codification is the single source of authoritative nongovernmental U.S. generally accepted accounting principles (U.S. GAAP) effective for periods ending after 15 September 2009. The Codification supersedes all previous U.S. GAAP standards. We have attempted to update the readings to reference or cross-reference the Codification as appropriate. Candidates are responsible for the content of accounting standards as addressed in the readings, not for the actual reference numbers.

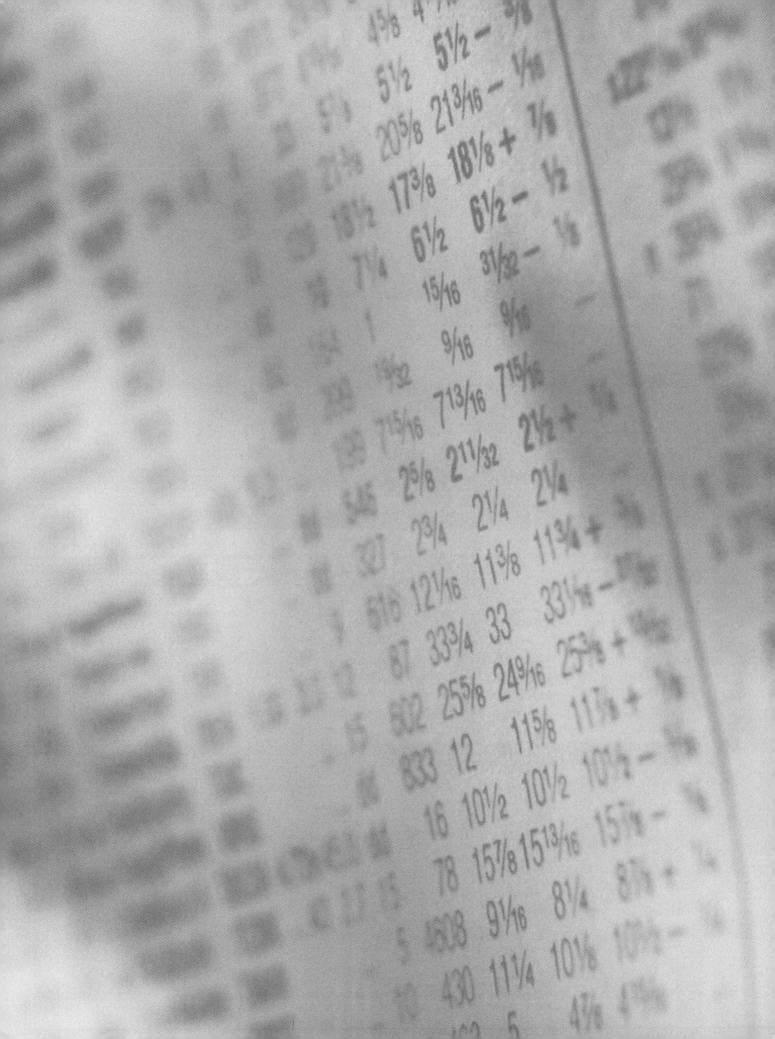

STUDY SESSION 7
FINANCIAL REPORTING AND ANALYSIS:
An Introduction

The readings in this study session discuss the general principles of the financial reporting system, underscoring the critical role of the analysis of financial reports in investment decision making.

The first reading introduces the range of information that an analyst may use in analyzing the financial performance of a company, including the principal financial statements (the income statement, balance sheet, statement of cash flows, and statement of changes in owners' equity), notes to those statements, and management's discussion and analysis of results. A general framework for addressing most financial statement analysis tasks is also presented.

A company's financial statements are the end-products of a process for recording the business transactions of the company. The second reading illustrates this process, introducing such basic concepts as the accounting equation and accounting accruals.

The presentation of financial information to the public by a company must conform to applicable financial reporting standards based on factors such as the jurisdiction in which the information is released. The final reading in this study explores the role of financial reporting standard-setting bodies worldwide and the International Financial Reporting Standards framework promulgated by the International Accounting Standards Board. The movement towards worldwide convergence of financial reporting standards is also introduced.

Note:
New rulings and/or pronouncements issued after the publication of the readings on financial reporting and analysis may cause some of the information in these readings to become dated. Candidates are expected to be familiar with the overall analytical framework contained in the study session readings, as well as the implications of alternative accounting methods for financial analysis and valuation, as provided in the assigned readings. Candidates are not responsible for changes that occur after the material was written.

For the purpose of Level I questions on financial reporting and analysis, when a ratio is defined and calculated differently in various texts, candidates should use the definitions given in the CFA Institute copyrighted readings by Robinson, et al. Variations in ratio definitions are part of the nature of practical financial analysis.

READING ASSIGNMENTS

FINANCIAL STATEMENT ANALYSIS: AN INTRODUCTION

by Thomas R. Robinson, CFA, Jan Hendrik van Greuning, CFA, Elaine Henry, CFA, and Michael A. Broihahn, CFA

LEARNING OUTCOMES

The candidate should be able to:	Mastery
a. discuss the roles of financial reporting and financial statement analysis;	☐
b. discuss the role of key financial statements (income statement, balance sheet, statement of cash flows, and statement of changes in owners' equity) in evaluating a company's performance and financial position;	☐
c. discuss the importance of financial statement notes and supplementary information, including disclosures of accounting methods, estimates, and assumptions, and management's discussion and analysis;	☐
d. discuss the objective of audits of financial statements, the types of audit reports, and the importance of effective internal controls;	☐
e. identify and explain information sources other than annual financial statements and supplementary information that analysts use in financial statement analysis;	☐
f. describe the steps in the financial statement analysis framework.	☐

INTRODUCTION 1

Analysts are employed in a number of functional areas. Commonly, analysts evaluate an investment in some type of security that has characteristics of equity (representing an ownership position) or debt (representing a lending position). In arriving at investment decisions or recommendations, analysts need to evaluate the performance, financial position, and value of the company issuing the securities. Company financial reports, which include financial statements and other data, provide the information necessary to evaluate the company and its securities. Consequently, the analyst must have a firm understanding of the

Note:
New rulings and/or pronouncements issued after the publication of the readings on financial reporting and analysis may cause some of the information in these readings to become dated. Candidates are expected to be familiar with the overall analytical framework contained in the study session readings, as well as the implications of alternative accounting methods for financial analysis and valuation, as provided in the assigned readings. Candidates are not responsible for changes that occur after the material was written.

information provided in each company's financial reports, including the financial notes and other forms of supplementary information.

This reading is organized as follows: Section 2 discusses the scope of financial statement analysis. Section 3 describes the sources of information used in financial statement analysis, including the primary financial statements (income statement, balance sheet, and statement of cash flows). Section 4 provides a framework for guiding the financial statement analysis process. A summary of the key points and practice problems in the CFA Institute multiple-choice format conclude the reading.

2   SCOPE OF FINANCIAL STATEMENT ANALYSIS

The role of financial reporting by companies is to provide information about their performance, financial position, and changes in financial position that is useful to a wide range of users in making economic decisions.[1] The role of financial statement analysis is to take financial reports prepared by companies, combined with other information, to evaluate the past, current, and prospective performance and financial position of a company for the purpose of making investment, credit, and other economic decisions.

In evaluating financial reports, analysts typically have an economic decision in mind. Examples include the following:

▶ Evaluating an equity investment for inclusion in a portfolio.
▶ Evaluating a merger or acquisition candidate.
▶ Evaluating a subsidiary or operating division of a parent company.
▶ Deciding whether to make a venture capital or other private equity investment.
▶ Determining the credit-worthiness of a company that has made a loan request.
▶ Extending credit to a customer.
▶ Examining compliance with debt covenants or other contractual arrangements.
▶ Assigning a debt rating to a company or bond issue.
▶ Valuing a security for making an investment recommendation to others.
▶ Forecasting future net income and cash flow.

There are certain themes in financial analysis. In general, analysts seek to examine the performance and financial position of companies as well as forecast future performance and financial position. Analysts are also concerned about factors that affect risks to the company's future performance and financial position. An examination of performance can include an assessment of a company's profitability (the ability to earn a profit from delivering goods and services) and

---

[1] See paragraph 12 of the "Framework for the Preparation and Presentation of Financial Statements," originally published by the International Accounting Standards Committee in 1989 and then adopted by the International Accounting Standards Board in 2001.

its cash flow generating ability (the ability to produce cash receipts in excess of cash disbursements). Profit and cash flow are not equivalent. Profit represents the excess of the prices at which goods or services are sold over all the costs of providing those goods and services (regardless of when cash is received or paid). Example 1 illustrates the distinction between profit and cash flow.

EXAMPLE 1

Profit versus Cash Flow

Sennett Designs (SD) sells imported furniture on a retail basis. SD began operations during December 2006 and sold furniture for cash of €250,000. The furniture that was sold by SD was delivered by the supplier during December, but the supplier has granted SD credit terms according to which payment is not due until January 2007. SD is obligated to pay €220,000 in January for the furniture it sold during December.

1. How much is SD's profit for December 2006 if no other transactions occurred?

2. How much is SD's cash flow for December 2006?

Solution to 1: SD's profit for December 2006 is the excess of the sales price (€250,000) over the cost of the goods that were sold (€220,000), or €30,000.

Solution to 2: The December 2006 cash flow is €250,000.

Although profitability is important, so is the ability to generate positive cash flow. Cash flow is important because, ultimately, cash is needed to pay employees, suppliers, and others to continue as a going concern. A company that generates positive cash flow from operations has more flexibility in funding needed investments and taking advantage of attractive business opportunities than an otherwise comparable company without positive cash flow. Additionally, cash flow is the source of returns to providers of capital. Therefore, the expected magnitude of future cash flows is important in valuing corporate securities and in determining the company's ability to meet its obligations. The ability to meet short-term obligations is generally referred to as **liquidity**, and the ability to meet long-term obligations is generally referred to as **solvency**. However, as shown in Example 1, cash flow in a given period is not a complete measure of performance in that period; for example, a company may be obligated to make future cash payments as a result of a transaction generating positive cash flow in the current period.

As noted earlier, profits reflect the ability of a company to deliver goods and services at prices in excess of the costs of delivering the goods and services. Profits also provide useful information about future (and past) cash flows. If the transaction of Example 1 were repeated year after year, the long-term average annual cash flow of SD would be €30,000, its annual profit. Many analysts not only evaluate past profitability but also forecast future profitability.

Exhibit 1 shows how news media coverage of corporate earnings announcements places corporate results in the context of analysts' expectations. Furthermore, analysts frequently use earnings in valuation, for example, when they value shares of a company on the basis of the price-to-earnings ratio (P/E) in relation to peer companies' P/Es or when they use a present value model of valuation that is based on forecasted future earnings.

EXHIBIT 1	An Earnings Release and Analyst Reaction

Panel A. Excerpt from Apple Earnings Release

Apple Reports Third Quarter Results
Posts Second Highest Quarterly Revenue and Earnings in Company's History

CUPERTINO, California—July 19, 2006—Apple® today announced financial results for its fiscal 2006 third quarter ended July 1, 2006. The Company posted revenue of $4.37 billion and a net quarterly profit of $472 million, or $.54 per diluted share. These results compare to revenue of $3.52 billion and a net profit of $320 million, or $.37 per diluted share, in the year-ago quarter. Gross margin was 30.3 percent, up from 29.7 percent in the year-ago quarter. International sales accounted for 39 percent of the quarter's revenue.

Apple shipped 1,327,000 Macintosh® computers and 8,111,000 iPods during the quarter, representing 12 percent growth in Macs and 32 percent growth in iPods over the year-ago quarter. . . .

Panel B. Excerpt from CNET News.com Report

"Mac Sales Up 12 Percent as Apple Profits Soar" by Tom Krazit

Apple Computer's third-quarter revenue fell a little short of expectations, but profitability was far higher than expected and Mac sales increased at a healthy clip.

. . . Net income was $472 million, or 54 cents per share, an improvement of 48 percent compared with last year's results of $320 million in net income and 37 cents per share. Analysts surveyed by Thomson First Call had been expecting Apple to report $4.4 billion in revenue and earn 44 cents per share.

. . . The outlook for the next period will probably disappoint some investors. The company predicted fourth-quarter revenue would be about $4.5 billion to $4.6 billion, less than the $4.9 billion analysts had been expecting. Apple executives will hold a conference call later Wednesday to discuss results.

Sources: www.apple.com/pr/library/2006/jul/19results.html and http://news.com.com/Mac+sales+up+12+percent+as+Apple+profits+soar/2100-1047_3-6096116.html.

Analysts are also interested in the current financial position of a company. The financial position can be measured by comparing the resources controlled by the company in relation to the claims against those resources. An example of a resource is cash. In Example 1, if no other transactions occur, the company should have cash at 31 December 2006 of €250,000. This cash can be used by the company to pay the obligation to the supplier (a claim against the company) and may also be used to make distributions to the owner (who also has a claim against the company for any profits that have been earned). Financial position is particularly important in credit analysis, as depicted in Exhibit 2.

| EXHIBIT 2 | Grupo Imsa Press Release Dated 18 January 2005 |

Standard & Poor's and Fitch Upgrade Grupo Imsa's Credit Rating

MONTERREY, Mexico: Grupo Imsa (NYSE:IMY) (BMV:IMSA) announces that Standard & Poor's has recently upgraded the Company's local currency corporate credit rating from BBB− to BBB and its national scale rating from mxAA to mxAA+. Fitch Mexico also increased Grupo Imsa's domestic rating from AA(mex) to AA+(mex). These rating upgrades reflect the positive results of Grupo Imsa's main businesses and the strengthening of its financial position, combined with the Company's geographic diversification, market leadership, state-of-the-art technology and high operational efficiency.

Mr. Marcelo Canales, Grupo Imsa's CFO, explained: "Grupo Imsa follows a policy of maintaining a solid financial position that ensures the Company's continuity for the benefit of our employees, shareholders and creditors. We take our financial commitments very seriously, as can be seen from the fact that during our 70 years of existence we have always complied with our financial obligations. The change in rating also reflects the strength of our business model and its capacity to generate cash." Mr. Canales added: "These upgrades in credit rating should translate into a better valuation of our debt to reflect Grupo Imsa's new financial reality."

Grupo Imsa, a holding company, dates back to 1936 and is today one of Mexico's leading diversified industrial companies, operating in three core businesses: steel processed products; steel and plastic construction products; and aluminum and other related products. With manufacturing and distribution facilities in Mexico, the United States, Europe and throughout Central and South America, Grupo Imsa currently exports to all five continents. Grupo Imsa's shares trade on the Mexican Stock Exchange (IMSA) and, in the United States, on the NYSE (IMY).

This document contains forward-looking statements relating to Grupo Imsa's future performance or its current expectations or beliefs, including statements regarding the intent, belief or current expectations of the Company and its management. Investors are cautioned that any such forward-looking statements are not guarantees of future performance and involve a number of risks and uncertainties pertaining to the industries in which the Company participates. Grupo Imsa does not intend, and does not assume any obligation, to update these forward-looking statements.

Source: Business Wire, 18 January 2005.

In conducting a financial analysis of a company, the analyst will regularly refer to the company's financial statements, financial notes and supplementary schedules, and a variety of other information sources. The next section introduces the major financial statements and most commonly used information sources.

3 MAJOR FINANCIAL STATEMENTS AND OTHER INFORMATION SOURCES

In order to perform an equity or credit analysis of a company, an analyst must collect a great deal of information. The nature of the information will vary based on the individual task but will typically include information about the economy, industry, and company as well as information about comparable peer companies. Much of this information will come from outside the company, such as economic statistics, industry reports, trade publications, and databases containing information on competitors. The company itself provides some of the core information for analysis in its financial reports, press releases, and conference calls and webcasts.

Companies prepare financial reports to report to investors and creditors on financial performance and financial strength at regular intervals (annually, semi-annually, and/or quarterly). Financial reports include financial statements and supplemental information necessary to assess the performance and financial position of the company. Financial statements are the end results of an accounting recordkeeping process that records the economic activities of a company. They summarize this information for use by investors, creditors, analysts, and others interested in a company's performance and financial position. In order to provide some assurances as to the information provided in the financial statements and related notes, the financial statements are audited by independent accountants who express an opinion on whether the financial statements fairly portray the company's performance and financial position.

3.1 Financial Statements and Supplementary Information

The key financial statements that are the focus of analysis are the income statement, balance sheet, statement of cash flows, and statement of changes in owners' equity. The income statement and statement of cash flows portray different aspects of a company's performance over a period of time. The balance sheet portrays the company's financial position at a given point in time. The statement of changes in owners' equity provides additional information regarding the changes in a company's financial position. In addition to the financial statements, a company provides other information in its financial reports that is useful to the financial analyst. As part of his or her analysis, the financial analyst should read and assess this additional information, which includes:

▶ notes to the financial statements (also known as footnotes) and supplementary schedules;

▶ management's discussion and analysis (MD&A); and

▶ the external auditor's report(s).

The following sections illustrate the major financial statements.

3.1.1 Income Statement

The income statement presents information on the financial results of a company's business activities over a period of time. The income statement communicates how much revenue the company generated during a period and what costs it incurred in connection with generating that revenue. Net income (revenue minus all costs) on the income statement is often referred to as the "bottom line" because of its proximity to the bottom of the income statement.[2] Income statements are reported on a consolidated basis, meaning that they include the revenues and expenses of affiliated companies under the control of the parent (reporting) company. The income statement is sometimes referred to as a **statement of operations** or **profit and loss** (P&L) **statement**. The basic equation underlying the income statement is Revenue − Expenses = Net income.

In Exhibit 3, the income statement is presented with the most recent year in the first column and the earliest year in the last column. Although this is a common presentation, analysts should be careful when reading an income statement because in other cases, the years may be listed from most distant to most recent.

Exhibit 3 shows that Wal-Mart's total revenue for the fiscal year ended 31 January 2005 was (in millions) $287,989. Wal-Mart then subtracted its operating costs and expenses to arrive at an operating income (profit) of $17,091. Operating income reflects a company's profits from its usual business activities, before deducting interest expense or taxes. Operating income is thus often referred to as EBIT, or earnings before interest and taxes. Operating income reflects the company's underlying performance independent of the use of financial leverage. Wal-Mart's total interest cost (net of the interest income that was earned from investments) for 2005 was $986; its earnings before taxes were, therefore, $16,105. Total income tax expense for 2005 was $5,589, and the minority interest expense (income earned by the minority shareholders from Wal-Mart subsidiary companies) was $249. After deducting these final expenses, Wal-Mart's net income for fiscal 2005 was $10,267.

Companies present their basic and diluted earnings per share on the face of the income statement. Earnings per share represents the net income divided by the number of shares of stock outstanding during the period. Basic earnings per share uses the weighted-average number of common shares that were actually outstanding during the period, whereas diluted earnings per share uses diluted shares—the number of shares that would be outstanding if potentially dilutive claims on common shares (e.g., stock options) were exercised by their holders. Wal-Mart's basic earning per share for 2005 was $2.41 ($10,267 net income ÷ 4,259 basic shares outstanding). Likewise, Wal-Mart's diluted earnings per share for 2005 was also $2.41 ($10,267 net income ÷ 4,266 diluted shares).

An analyst examining the income statement might note that Wal-Mart was profitable in each year and that revenue, operating income, net income, and earnings per share—all measures of profitability—increased over the three-year period. The analyst might formulate questions related to profitability, such as the following:

▶ Is the growth in revenue related to an increase in units sold, an increase in prices, or some combination?

▶ After adjusting for growth in the number of stores, is the company still more profitable over time?

▶ How does the company compare with other companies in the industry?

---

[2] "Net income" is also referred to as "net earnings" or "net profit." In the event that costs exceed revenues, it is referred to as "net loss."

EXHIBIT 3	Wal-Mart Consolidated Statements of Income (in Millions except Per Share Data)		

Fiscal Years Ended 31 January	2005	2004	2003
Revenues:			
Net sales	$285,222	$256,329	$229,616
Other income, net	2,767	2,352	1,961
	287,989	258,681	231,577
Costs and expenses:			
Cost of sales	219,793	198,747	178,299
Operating, selling, general, and administrative expenses	51,105	44,909	39,983
Operating income	17,091	15,025	13,295
Interest:			
Debt	934	729	799
Capital lease	253	267	260
Interest income	(201)	(164)	(132)
Interest, net	986	832	927
Income from continuing operations before income taxes and minority interest	16,105	14,193	12,368
Provision for income taxes:			
Current	5,326	4,941	3,883
Deferred	263	177	474
Total	5,589	5,118	4,357
Income from continuing operations before minority interest	10,516	9,075	8,011
Minority interest	(249)	(214)	(193)
Income from continuing operations	10,267	8,861	7,818
Income from discontinued operations, net of tax	–	193	137
Net income	$ 10,267	$ 9,054	$ 7,955
Basic net income per common share:			
Income from continuing operations	$ 2.41	$ 2.03	$ 1.77
Income from discontinued operations	–	0.05	0.03
Basic net income per common share	$ 2.41	$ 2.08	$ 1.80
Diluted net income per common share:			
Income from continuing operations	$ 2.41	$ 2.03	$ 1.76
Income from discontinued operations	–	0.04	0.03
Diluted net income per common share	$ 2.41	$ 2.07	$ 1.79
Weighted-average number of common shares:			
Basic	4,259	4,363	4,430
Diluted	4,266	4,373	4,446
Dividends per common share	$ 0.52	$ 0.36	$ 0.30

Answering such questions requires the analyst to gather, analyze, and interpret facts from a number of sources, including the income statement. The reading on understanding the income statement will explain the income statement in greater detail. The next section illustrates the balance sheet, the second major financial statement.

3.1.2 Balance Sheet

The **balance sheet** (also known as the **statement of financial position** or **statement of financial condition**) presents a company's current financial position by disclosing resources the company controls (assets) and what it owes (liabilities) at a specific point in time. **Owners' equity** represents the excess of assets over liabilities. This amount is attributable to the owners or shareholders of the business; it is the residual interest in the assets of an entity after deducting its liabilities. The three parts of the balance sheet are formulated in an accounting relationship known as the accounting equation: Assets = Liabilities + Owners' equity (that is, the total amount for assets must *balance* to the combined total amounts for liabilities and owners' equity). Alternatively, the three parts of the balance sheet of the accounting relationship may be formulated as Assets − Liabilities = Owners' equity. Depending on the form of the organization, owners' equity also goes by several alternative titles, such as "partners' capital" or "shareholders' equity."

Exhibit 4 presents Wal-Mart's consolidated balance sheets for the fiscal years ended 31 January 2004 and 2005.

EXHIBIT 4	Wal-Mart Consolidated Balance Sheets (in Millions except Per Share Data)	
Fiscal Years Ended 31 January	**2005**	**2004**
Assets		
Current assets:		
Cash and cash equivalents	$ 5,488	$ 5,199
Receivables	1,715	1,254
Inventories	29,447	26,612
Prepaid expenses and other	1,841	1,356
Total current assets	38,491	34,421
Property and equipment, at cost:		
Land	14,472	12,699
Buildings and improvements	46,582	40,192
Fixtures and equipment	21,461	17,934
Transportation equipment	1,530	1,269
Property and equipment, at cost	84,045	72,094
Less accumulated depreciation	18,637	15,684
Property and equipment, net	65,408	56,410

(Exhibit continued on next page . . .)

EXHIBIT 4	(continued)		

Property under capital lease:

Property under capital lease		4,997	4,286
Less accumulated amortization		1,838	1,673
Property under capital lease, net		3,159	2,613
Goodwill		10,803	9,882
Other assets and deferred charges		2,362	2,079
Total assets		**$120,223**	**$105,405**

Liabilities and shareholders' equity

Current liabilities:

Commercial paper		$ 3,812	$ 3,267
Accounts payable		21,671	19,425
Accrued liabilities		12,155	10,671
Accrued income taxes		1,281	1,377
Long-term debt due within one year		3,759	2,904
Obligations under capital leases due within one year		210	196
Total current liabilities		42,888	37,840
Long-term debt		20,087	17,102
Long-term obligations under capital leases		3,582	2,997
Deferred income taxes and other		2,947	2,359
Minority interest		1,323	1,484

Shareholders' equity:

Preferred stock ($0.10 par value; 100 shares authorized, none issued)		–	–
Common stock ($0.10 par value; 11,000 shares authorized, 4,234 and 4,311 issued and outstanding in 2005 and 2004, respectively)		423	431
Capital in excess of par value		2,425	2,135
Other accumulated comprehensive income		2,694	851
Retained earnings		43,854	40,206
Total shareholders' equity		49,396	43,623
Total liabilities and shareholders' equity		**$120,223**	**$105,405**

At 31 January 2005, Wal-Mart's total resources or assets were $120,223 (in millions). Shareholders' equity (in millions) was $49,396. Although Wal-Mart does not give a total amount for all the balance sheet liabilities, it may be determined from the accounting relationship as Total assets − Total shareholders' equity or $120,223 − $49,396 = $70,827.[3] Using the balance sheet and applying financial statement analysis, the analyst will be able to answer such questions as:

---

[3] Note that this computation includes an amount labeled "minority interest in liabilities." Minority (or non-controlling) interest represents an ownership in a subsidiary company by others (not the parent company). IFRS and U.S. GAAP (effective 15 December 2008) require that non-controlling interests in consolidated subsidiaries be presented on the consolidated balance sheet as a separate component of stockholders' equity. The minority interest must be clearly identified and labeled. Any entity with non-controlling interests in more than one subsidiary may present those interests in aggregate in the consolidated financial statements.

► Has the company's liquidity (ability to meet short-term obligations) improved?

► Is the company solvent (does it have sufficient resources to cover its obligations)?

► What is the company's financial position relative to the industry?

The reading on understanding the balance sheet will cover the analysis of the balance sheet in more depth. The next section illustrates the statement of cash flows.

3.1.3 Statement of Cash Flows

Although the income statement and balance sheet provide a measure of a company's success in terms of performance and financial position, cash flow is also vital to a company's long-term success. Disclosing the sources and uses of cash helps creditors, investors, and other statement users evaluate the company's liquidity, solvency, and financial flexibility. **Financial flexibility** is the ability to react and adapt to financial adversities and opportunities. The statement of cash flows classifies all company cash flows into operating, investing, and financing activity cash flows. **Operating activities** involve transactions that enter into the determination of net income and are primarily activities that comprise the day-to-day business functions of a company. **Investing activities** are those activities associated with the acquisition and disposal of long-term assets, such as equipment. **Financing activities** are those activities related to obtaining or repaying capital to be used in the business.

Exhibit 5 presents Wal-Mart's consolidated statement of cash flows for the fiscal years ended 31 January 2003, 2004, and 2005.

EXHIBIT 5	Wal-Mart Consolidated Statements of Cash Flows (in Millions)		
Fiscal Years Ended 31 January	**2005**	**2004**	**2003**
Cash flows from operating activities:			
Income from continuing operations	$ 10,267	$ 8,861	$ 7,818
Adjustments to reconcile net income to net cash provided by operating activities:			
Depreciation and amortization	4,405	3,852	3,364
Deferred income taxes	263	177	474
Other operating activities	378	173	685
Changes in certain assets and liabilities, net of effects of acquisitions:			
Decrease (increase) in accounts receivable	(304)	373	(159)
Increase in inventories	(2,635)	(1,973)	(2,219)
Increase in accounts payable	1,694	2,587	1,748
Increase in accrued liabilities	976	1,896	1,212
Net cash provided by operating activities of continuing operations	15,044	15,946	12,923
Net cash provided by operating activities of discontinued operations	–	50	82
Net cash provided by operating activities	15,044	15,996	13,005

(Exhibit continued on next page . . .)

EXHIBIT 5 (continued)			
Cash flows from investing activities:			
Payments for property and equipment	(12,893)	(10,308)	(9,245)
Investment in international operations	(315)	(38)	(749)
Proceeds from the disposal of fixed assets	953	481	311
Proceeds from the sale of McLane	–	1,500	–
Other investing activities	(96)	78	(73)
Net cash used in investing activities of continuing operations	(12,351)	(8,287)	(9,756)
Net cash used in investing activities of discontinued operations	–	(25)	(83)
Net cash used in investing activities	(12,351)	(8,312)	(9,839)
Cash flows from financing activities:			
Increase in commercial paper	544	688	1,836
Proceeds from issuance of long-term debt	5,832	4,099	2,044
Purchase of company stock	(4,549)	(5,046)	(3,383)
Dividends paid	(2,214)	(1,569)	(1,328)
Payment of long-term debt	(2,131)	(3,541)	(1,261)
Payment of capital lease obligations	(204)	(305)	(216)
Other financing activities	113	111	(62)
Net cash used in financing activities	(2,609)	(5,563)	(2,370)
Effect of exchange rate changes on cash	205	320	(199)
Net increase in cash and cash equivalents	289	2,441	597
Cash and cash equivalents at beginning of year	5,199	2,758	2,161
Cash and cash equivalents at end of year	$ 5,488	$ 5,199	$ 2,758
Supplemental disclosure of cash flow information:			
Income tax paid	$ 5,593	$ 4,358	$ 4,539
Interest paid	1,163	1,024	1,085
Capital lease obligations incurred	377	252	381

In the cash flows from operating activities section of Wal-Mart's statement of cash flows, the company reconciles its net income to net cash provided by operating activities. This emphasizes the different perspectives of the income statement and statement of cash flows. Income is reported when earned, not necessarily when cash is received. The statement of cash flows presents another aspect of performance: the ability of a company to generate cash flow from running its business. Ideally, the analyst would like to see that the primary source of cash flow is from operating activities (as opposed to investing or financing activities). Note that Wal-Mart had a large amount of operating cash flow, which increased from 2003 to 2004 but decreased slightly in 2005. Although operating cash flow was high, an analyst might question why net income increased but operating cash flow decreased in 2005.

The summation of the net cash flows from operating, investing, and financing activities and the effect of exchange rates on cash equals the net change in cash during the fiscal year. For Wal-Mart, the summation of these four cash flow activities in 2005 was $289, which thus increased the company's cash from $5,199 at 31 January 2004 (beginning cash balance) to $5,488 at 31 January 2005 (ending cash balance). Note that these beginning and ending cash balances agree with the cash reported on Wal-Mart's balance sheets in Exhibit 4.

The statement of cash flows will be treated in more depth in the reading on understanding the statement of cash flows.

3.1.4 Statement of Changes in Owners' Equity

The income statement, balance sheet, and statement of cash flows represent the primary financial statements used to assess a company's performance and financial position. A fourth financial statement is also available; this can be a "statement of changes in owners' equity," "statement of shareholders' equity," or "statement of retained earnings." This fourth statement, regardless of format chosen, primarily serves to report changes in the owners' investment in the business over time and assists the analyst in understanding the changes in financial position reflected on the balance sheet.

3.1.5 Financial Notes and Supplementary Schedules

Financial notes and supplementary schedules are an integral part of the financial statements. By way of example, the financial notes and supplemental schedules provide explanatory information about the following:

► business acquisitions and disposals;

► commitments and contingencies;

► legal proceedings;

► stock option and other employee benefit plans;

► related-party transactions;

► significant customers;

► subsequent events;

► business and geographic segments; and

► quarterly financial data.

Additionally, the footnotes contain information about the methods and assumptions used to prepare the financial statements. Comparability of financial statements is a critical requirement for objective financial analysis. Financial statement comparability occurs when information is measured and reported in a similar manner over time and for different companies. Comparability allows the analyst to identify and analyze the real economic substance differences and similarities between companies. The International Accounting Standards Board based in London sets forth standards under which international financial statements should be prepared. These are referred to as international financial reporting standards (IFRS). Similarly, the Financial Accounting Standards Board (FASB) in the United States sets forth standards (called statements of financial accounting standards[4]) that constitute the key part of the body of principles known as generally accepted accounting principles (U.S. GAAP). These two organizations are working to make their standards similar, but there are key differences. When

---

[4] In 2009, the Financial Accounting Standards Board (FASB) released the FASB Accounting Standards Codification™. The Codification is the single source of authoritative nongovernmental U.S. generally accepted accounting principles (U.S. GAAP) effective for periods ending after 15 September 2009. The Codification supersedes all previous U.S. GAAP standards. We have attempted to update the readings to reference or cross-reference the Codification as appropriate. Candidates are responsible for the content of international and U.S. accounting standards, not the actual reference numbers.

comparing a U.S. company with a European company, an analyst must understand differences in these standards, which can relate, for example, to the period in which to report revenue.

Even within each of these sets of standards there can be choices for management to make that can reduce comparability between companies. Both IFRS and U.S. GAAP allow the use of alternative accounting methods to measure company financial performance and financial condition where there are differences in economic environments between companies. Additionally, some principles require the use of estimates and assumptions in measuring performance and financial condition. This flexibility is necessary because, ideally, a company will select those methods, estimates, and assumptions within the principles that fairly reflect the unique economic environment of the company's business and industry. Although this flexibility in accounting principles ostensibly meets the divergent needs of many businesses, it creates a problem for the analyst because comparability is lost when flexibility occurs. For example, if a company acquires a piece of equipment to use in its operations, accounting standards require that the cost of the asset be reported as an expense in a systematic manner over the life of the equipment (estimating the process of the equipment wearing out). This allocation of the cost is known as **depreciation**. The standards permit a great deal of flexibility, however, in determining the manner in which each year's expense is determined. Two companies may acquire similar equipment but use different methods and assumptions to record the expense over time. Comparing the companies' performance directly is then impaired by this difference.

A company's accounting policies (methods, estimates, and assumptions) are generally presented in the notes to the financial statements. A note containing a summary of significant accounting policies reveals, for example, how the company recognizes its revenues and depreciates its capital assets. Analysts must be aware of the methods, estimates, and assumptions used by a company to determine if they are similar to those of other companies that are being used as benchmarks. If they are not similar, the analyst who understands accounting techniques can make adjustments to make the financial statements more comparable.

3.1.6 Management's Discussion and Analysis

Under U.S. GAAP, publicly held companies are often required to include in their financial reports a section called management's discussion and analysis (MD&A). A similar section may be included by companies reporting IFRS. In the MD&A, management must highlight any favorable or unfavorable trends and identify significant events and uncertainties that affect the company's liquidity, capital resources, and results of operations. The MD&A must also provide information about the effects of inflation, changing prices, or other material events and uncertainties that may cause the future operating results and financial condition to materially depart from the current reported financial information. Companies should also provide disclosure in the MD&A that discusses the critical accounting policies that require management to make subjective judgments and that have a significant impact on reported financial results. The MD&A section of a company's report, or a similar section for companies reporting under IFRS, provides a good starting place for understanding what is going on in the financial statements. Nevertheless, it is only one input for the analyst in seeking an objective and independent perspective on a company's performance and prospects.

3.1.7 Auditor's Reports

Financial statements presented in company annual financial reports are often required to be audited (examined) by an independent accounting firm that then expresses an opinion on the financial statements. Audits may be required by contractual arrangement, law, or regulation. Just as there are standards for preparing financial statements, there are standards for auditing and for expressing the resulting auditor's opinion. International standards for auditing have been developed by the International Auditing and Assurance Standards Board of the International Federation of Accountants. These standards have been adopted by many countries. Other countries, such as the United States, have developed their own standards. With the enactment of the Sarbanes–Oxley Act in the United States, auditing standards are being promulgated by the Public Company Accounting Oversight Board (PCAOB). Under International Standard on Auditing 200:

> The objective of an audit of financial statements is to enable the auditor to express an opinion whether the financial statements are prepared, in all material respects, in accordance with an applicable financial reporting framework.[5]

Publicly traded companies may also have requirements set by regulators or stock exchanges, such as appointing an independent audit committee of the board of directors to oversee the audit process. The audit process provides a basis for the independent auditor to express an audit opinion on the fairness of the financial statements that were audited. Because audits are designed and conducted by using audit sampling techniques, independent auditors cannot express an opinion that provides absolute assurance about the accuracy or precision of the financial statements. Instead, the independent audit report provides *reasonable assurance* that the financial statements are *fairly presented*, meaning that there is a high degree of probability that the audited financial statements are free from *material* error, fraud, or illegal acts that have a direct effect on the financial statements.

The standard independent audit report for a publicly traded company normally has several paragraphs under both the international and U.S. auditing standards. The first or "introductory" paragraph describes the financial statements that were audited and the responsibilities of both management and the independent auditor. The second or "scope" paragraph describes the nature of the audit process and provides the basis for the auditor's expression about reasonable assurance on the fairness of the financial statements. The third or "opinion" paragraph expresses the auditor's opinion on the fairness of the audited financial statements. An *unqualified* audit opinion states that the financial statements give a "true and fair view" (international) or are "fairly presented" (international and U.S.) in accordance with applicable accounting standards. This is often referred to as a "clean" opinion and is the one that analysts would like to see in a financial report. There are several other types of opinions. A *qualified* audit opinion is one in which there is some limitation or exception to accounting standards. Exceptions are described in the audit report with additional explanatory paragraphs so that the analyst can determine the importance of the exception. An *adverse* audit opinion occurs when the financial statements materially depart from accounting standards and are not fairly presented. An adverse opinion makes analysis of the financial statements easy: Don't bother, because the company's financial statements cannot be relied upon. Finally, a *disclaimer of opinion* occurs when, for some reason, the auditors are unable to issue an opinion. Exhibit 6 presents the independent auditor's report for Wal-Mart. Note that Wal-Mart received a "clean" or unqualified audit opinion from Ernst & Young LLP for the company's fiscal year ended 31 January 2005.

---

[5] International Federation of Accountants, *Handbook of International Auditing, Assurance, and Ethics Pronouncements*, 2006 edition, p. 230, available at www.ifac.org.

EXHIBIT 6	Wal-Mart's Independent Audit Report

Report of Independent Registered Accounting Firm
WAL-MART

The Board of Directors and Shareholders,
Wal-Mart Stores, Inc.

We have audited the accompanying consolidated balance sheets of Wal-Mart Stores, Inc. as of January 31, 2005 and 2004, and the related consolidated statements of income, shareholders' equity and cash flows for each of the three years in the period ended January 31, 2005. These financial statements are the responsibility of the company's management. Our responsibility is to express an opinion on these financial statements based on our audits.

We conducted our audits in accordance with the standards of the Public Company Accounting Oversight Board (United States). Those standards require that we plan and perform the audit to obtain reasonable assurance about whether the financial statements are free of material misstatement. An audit includes examining on a test basis, evidence supporting the amounts and disclosures in the financial statements. An audit also includes assessing the accounting principles used and significant estimates made by management, as well as evaluating the overall financial statement presentation. We believe that our audits provide a reasonable basis for our opinion.

In our opinion, the financial statements referred to above present fairly, in all material respects, the consolidated financial position of Wal-Mart Stores, Inc. at January 31, 2005 and 2004, and the consolidated results of its operations and its cash flows for each of the three years in the period ended January 31, 2005, in conformity with U.S. generally accepted accounting principles.

We also have audited, in accordance with the standards of the Public Accounting Oversight Board (United States), the effectiveness of Wal-Mart Stores, Inc.'s internal control over financial reporting as of January 31, 2005, based on criteria established in *Internal Control—Integrated Framework* issued by the Committee of Sponsoring Organizations of the Treadway Committee and our report dated March 25, 2005 expressed an unqualified opinion thereon.

Ernst & Young LLP
Rogers, Arkansas
March 25, 2005

Source: 2005 Wal-Mart Stores, Inc., Annual Report.

In the United States, under the Sarbanes–Oxley Act, the auditors must also express an opinion on the company's internal control systems. This information may be provided in a separate opinion or incorporated as a fourth paragraph in the opinion related to the financial statements. The internal control system is the company's internal system that is designed, among other things, to ensure that the company's process for generating financial reports is sound.

Although management has always been responsible for maintaining effective internal control, the Sarbanes–Oxley Act greatly increases management's responsibility for demonstrating that the company's internal controls are effective. Publicly traded companies in the United States are now required by securities regulators to:

▶ accept responsibility for the effectiveness of internal control;

▶ evaluate the effectiveness of internal control using suitable control criteria;

▶ support the evaluation with sufficient competent evidence; and

▶ provide a report on internal control.

The Sarbanes–Oxley Act specifically requires management's report on internal control to:

▶ state that it is management's responsibility to establish and maintain adequate internal control;

▶ identify management's framework for evaluating internal control;

▶ include management's assessment of the effectiveness of the company's internal control over financial reporting as of the end of the most recent year, including a statement as to whether internal control over financial reporting is effective;

▶ include a statement that the company's auditors have issued an attestation report on management's assessment; and

▶ certify that the company's financial statements are fairly presented.

Exhibit 7 presents Wal-Mart management's report on internal control to its company's shareholders. Note that Wal-Mart has fully complied with each of the reporting criterion that were discussed in the preceding paragraph.

EXHIBIT 7	Wal-Mart's Report to Shareholders on Corporate Governance and Internal Control

Management's Report to Our Shareholders
WAL-MART

Management of Wal-Mart Stores, Inc. ("Wal-Mart") is responsible for the preparation, integrity and objectivity of Wal-Mart's consolidated financial statements and other financial information contained in this Annual Report to Shareholders. Those consolidated financial statements were prepared in conformity with accounting principles generally accepted in the United States. In preparing those consolidated financial statements, Management was required to make certain estimates and judgments, which are based upon currently available information and Management's view of current conditions and circumstances.

The Audit Committee of the Board of Directors, which consists solely of independent directors, oversees our process of reporting financial information and the audit of our consolidated financial statements. The Audit Committee stays informed of the financial condition of Wal-Mart and regularly reviews Management's financial policies and procedures, the independence of our independent auditors, our internal control and the objectivity of our financial reporting. Both the independent financial auditors and the internal auditors have free access to the Audit Committee and meet with the Audit Committee periodically, both with and without Management present.

(Exhibit continued on next page . . .)

EXHIBIT 7   (continued)

We have retained Ernst & Young LLP, an independent registered public accounting firm, to audit our consolidated financial statements found in this annual report. We have made available to Ernst & Young LLP all of our financial records and related data in connection with their audit of our consolidated financial statements.

We have filed with the Securities and Exchange Commission the required certifications related to our consolidated financial statements as of and for the year ended January 31, 2005. These certifications are attached as exhibits to our Annual Report on Form 10-K for the year ended January 31, 2005. Additionally, we have also provided to the New York Stock Exchange the required annual certification of our Chief Executive Officer regarding our compliance with the New York Stock Exchange's corporate governance listing standards.

Report on Internal Control over Financial Reporting

Management has responsibility for establishing and maintaining adequate internal control over financial reporting. Internal control over financial reporting is a process designed to provide reasonable assurance regarding the reliability of financial reporting and the preparation of financial statements for external reporting purposes in accordance with accounting principles generally accepted in the United States. Because of its inherent limitations, internal control over financial reporting may not prevent or detect misstatements. Management has assessed the effectiveness of the company's internal control over financial reporting as of January 31, 2005. In making its assessment, Management has utilized the criteria set forth by the Committee of Sponsoring Organizations ("COSO") of the Treadway Commission in *Internal Control – Integrated Framework*. Management concluded that based on its assessment, Wal-Mart's internal control over financial reporting was effective as of January 31, 2005. Management's assessment of the effectiveness of the company's internal control over financial reporting as of January 31, 2005 has been audited by Ernst & Young LLP, an independent registered public accounting firm, as stated in their report which appears in this Annual Report to Shareholders.

Evaluation of Disclosure Controls and Procedures

We maintain disclosure controls and procedures designed to provide reasonable assurance that information, which is required to be timely disclosed, is accumulated and communicated to Management in a timely fashion. Management has assessed the effectiveness of these disclosure controls and procedures as of January 31, 2005 and determined that they were effective as of that date to provide reasonable assurance that information required to be disclosed by us in the reports we file or submit under the Securities Exchange Act of 1934, as amended, is accumulated and communicated to Management, as appropriate, to allow timely decisions regarding required disclosure and are effective to provide reasonable assurance that such information is recorded, processed, summarized and reported within the time periods specified by the SEC's rules and forms.

Report on Ethical Standards

Our company was founded on the belief that open communications and the highest standard of ethics are necessary to be successful. Our long-standing "Open Door" communication policy helps Management be aware of and address issues in a timely and effective manner. Through the open door policy all associates are encouraged to inform Management at the appropriate level when they are concerned about any matter pertaining to Wal-Mart.

Wal-Mart has adopted a Statement of Ethics to guide our associates in the continued observance of high ethical standards such as honesty, integrity and compliance with the law in the conduct of Wal-Mart's business. Familiarity and compliance with the Statement of Ethics is required of all associates who are part of Management. The company also maintains a separate Code of Ethics for our senior financial officers. Wal-Mart also has in

(Exhibit continued on next page . . .)

EXHIBIT 7	(continued)

place a Related-Party Transaction Policy. This policy applies to all of Wal-Mart's Officers and Directors and requires material related-party transactions to be reviewed by the Audit Committee. The Officers and Directors are required to report material related-party transactions to Wal-Mart. We maintain an ethics office which oversees and administers an ethics hotline. The ethics hotline provides a channel for associates to make confidential and anonymous complaints regarding potential violations of our statement of ethics, including violations related to financial or accounting matters.

H. Lee Scott
President and Chief Executive Officer

Thomas M. Schoewe
Executive Vice President and Chief Financial Officer

Source: 2005 Wal-Mart Stores, Inc., Annual Report.

Although these reports provide some assurances to analysts, they are not infallible. The analyst must always use a degree of healthy skepticism when analyzing financial statements.

3.2 Other Sources of Information

The information described in the previous section is generally provided to shareholders on an annual basis. Interim reports are also provided by the company either semiannually or quarterly. Interim reports generally present the four key financial statements and footnotes but are not audited. These interim reports provide updated information on a company's performance and financial position since the last annual period. Companies also prepare proxy statements for distribution to shareholders on matters that are to be put to a vote at the company's annual (or special) meeting of shareholders. The proxy statement typically provides useful information regarding management and director compensation and company stock performance and discloses any potential conflicts of interest that may exist between management, the board, and shareholders. Companies also provide relevant current information on their websites and in press releases and as part of conference calls. When performing financial statement analysis, analysts should review all these company sources of information as well as information from external sources regarding the economy, the industry, the company, and peer (comparable) companies. Information on the economy, industry, and peer companies is useful in putting the company's financial performance and position in perspective and in assessing the company's future. The next section presents a framework for using all this information in financial statement analysis.

4   FINANCIAL STATEMENT ANALYSIS FRAMEWORK

Analysts work in a variety of positions. Some are equity analysts whose main objective is to evaluate potential equity (share) investments to determine whether a prospective investment is attractive and what an appropriate purchase price might be. Others are credit analysts who evaluate the credit-worthiness of a company to decide whether (and with what terms) a loan should be made or what credit rating should be assigned. Analysts may also be involved in a variety of other tasks, such as evaluating the performance of a subsidiary company, evaluating a private equity investment, or finding stocks that are overvalued for purposes of taking a short position. This section presents a generic framework for financial statement analysis that can be used in these various tasks. The framework is summarized in Exhibit 8.[6]

The following sections discuss the individual phases of financial statement analysis.

4.1   Articulate the Purpose and Context of Analysis

Prior to undertaking any analysis, it is essential to understand the purpose of the analysis. An understanding of the purpose is particularly important in financial statement analysis because of the numerous available techniques and the substantial amount of data.

Some analytical tasks are well defined, in which case articulating the purpose of the analysis requires little decision making by the analyst. For example, a periodic credit review of an investment-grade debt portfolio or an equity analyst's report on a particular company may be guided by institutional norms such that the purpose of the analysis is given. Furthermore, the format, procedures, and/or sources of information may also be given.

For other analytical tasks, articulating the purpose of the analysis requires the analyst to make decisions. The purpose of an analysis guides further decisions about the approach, the tools, the data sources, the format in which to report results of the analysis, and the relative importance of different aspects of the analysis.

When facing a substantial amount of data, a less experienced analyst may be tempted to just start crunching numbers and creating output. It is generally advisable to resist the temptation and thus avoid the black hole of pointless number crunching. Consider the questions: If you could wave a magic wand and have all the numbers crunched, what conclusion would you be able to draw? What question would you be able to answer? What decision would your answer support?

The analyst should also define the context at this stage. Who is the intended audience? What is the end product—for example, a final report explaining conclusions and recommendations? What is the time frame (i.e., when is the report due)? What resources and resource constraints are relevant to completion of the analysis? Again, the context may be predefined (i.e., standard and guided by institutional norms).

Having clarified the purpose and context of the financial statement analysis, the analyst should next compile the specific questions to be answered by the

---

[6] Components of this framework have been adapted from van Greuning and Bratanovic (2003, p. 300) and from Benninga and Sarig (1997, pp. 134–156).

EXHIBIT 8	Financial Statement Analysis Framework	
Phase	**Sources of Information**	**Output**
1. Articulate the purpose and context of the analysis.	▶ The nature of the analyst's function, such as evaluating an equity or debt investment or issuing a credit rating. ▶ Communication with client or supervisor on needs and concerns. ▶ Institutional guidelines related to developing specific work product.	▶ Statement of the purpose or objective of analysis. ▶ A list (written or unwritten) of specific questions to be answered by the analysis. ▶ Nature and content of report to be provided. ▶ Timetable and budgeted resources for completion.
2. Collect data.	▶ Financial statements, other financial data, questionnaires, and industry/economic data. ▶ Discussions with management, suppliers, customers, and competitors. ▶ Company site visits (e.g., to production facilities or retail stores).	▶ Organized financial statements. ▶ Financial data tables. ▶ Completed questionnaires, if applicable.
3. Process data.	▶ Data from the previous phase.	▶ Adjusted financial statements. ▶ Common-size statements. ▶ Ratios and graphs. ▶ Forecasts.
4. Analyze/interpret the processed data.	▶ Input data as well as processed data.	▶ Analytical results.
5. Develop and communicate conclusions and recommendations (e.g., with an analysis report).	▶ Analytical results and previous reports. ▶ Institutional guidelines for published reports.	▶ Analytical report answering questions posed in Phase 1. ▶ Recommendation regarding the purpose of the analysis, such as whether to make an investment or grant credit.
6. Follow-up.	▶ Information gathered by periodically repeating above steps as necessary to determine whether changes to holdings or recommendations are necessary.	▶ Updated reports and recommendations.

analysis. For example, if the purpose of the financial statement analysis (or, more likely, the particular stage of a larger analysis) is to compare the historical performance of three companies operating in a particular industry, specific questions would include: What has been the relative growth rate of the companies and what has been the relative profitability of the companies?

4.2 Collect Data

Next, the analyst obtains the data required to answer the specific questions. A key part of this step is obtaining an understanding of the company's business, financial performance, and financial position (including trends over time and in comparison with peer companies). For historical analyses, financial statement data alone are adequate in some cases. For example, to screen a large number of alternative companies for those with a minimum level of profitability, financial statement data alone would be adequate. But to address more in-depth questions, such as why and how one company performed better or worse than its competitors, additional information would be required. As another example, to compare the historical performance of two companies in a particular industry, the historical financial statements would be sufficient to determine which had faster growing sales or earnings and which was more profitable; however, a broader comparison with overall industry growth and profitability would obviously require industry data.

Furthermore, information on the economy and industry is necessary to understand the environment in which the company operates. Analysts often take a top-down approach whereby they 1) gain an understanding of the macroeconomic environment, such as prospects for growth in the economy and inflation, 2) analyze the prospects of the industry in which the subject company operates based on the expected macroeconomic environment, and 3) determine the prospects for the company in the expected industry and macroeconomic environments. For example, an analyst may need to forecast future growth in earnings for a company. To project future growth, past company data provide one basis for statistical forecasting; however, an understanding of economic and industry conditions can improve the analyst's ability to forecast a company's earnings based on forecasts of overall economic and industry activity.

4.3 Process Data

After obtaining the requisite financial statement and other information, the analyst processes this data using appropriate analytical tools. For example, processing the data may involve computing ratios or growth rates; preparing common-size financial statements; creating charts; performing statistical analyses, such as regressions or Monte Carlo simulations; performing equity valuation; performing sensitivity analyses; or using any other analytical tools or combination of tools that are available and appropriate to the task. A comprehensive financial analysis at this stage would include the following:

► Reading and evaluating financial statements for each company subject to analysis. This includes reading the footnotes and understanding what accounting standards have been used (for example, IFRS or U.S. GAAP), what accounting choices have been made (for example, when to report revenue on the income statement), and what operating decisions have been made that affect reported financial statements (for example, leasing versus purchasing equipment).

► Making any needed adjustments to the financial statements to facilitate comparison, when the unadjusted statements of the subject companies reflect differences in accounting standards, accounting choices, or operating decisions. Note that commonly used databases do not make such analyst adjustments.

▶ Preparing or collecting common-size financial statement data [which scale data to directly reflect percentages (e.g., of sales) or changes (e.g., from the prior year)] and financial ratios (which are measures of various aspects of corporate performance based on financial statement elements). On the basis of common-size financial statements and financial ratios, analysts can evaluate a company's relative profitability, liquidity, leverage, efficiency, and valuation in relation to past results and/or peers' results.

4.4 Analyze/Interpret the Processed Data

Once the data have been processed, the next step—critical to any analysis—is to interpret the output. The answer to a specific financial analysis question is seldom the numerical answer alone; the answer to the analytical question relies on the interpretation of the output and the use of this interpreted output to support a conclusion or recommendation. The answers to the specific analytical questions may themselves achieve the underlying purpose of the analysis, but usually, a conclusion or recommendation is required. For example, an equity analysis may require a buy, hold, or sell decision or a conclusion about the value of a share of stock. In support of the decision, the analysis would cite such information as target value, relative performance, expected future performance given a company's strategic position, quality of management, and whatever other information was important in reaching the decision.

4.5 Develop and Communicate Conclusions/Recommendations

Communicating the conclusion or recommendation in an appropriate format is the next step in an analysis. The appropriate format will vary by analytical task, by institution, and/or by audience. For example, an equity analyst report would typically include the following components:[7]

▶ summary and investment conclusion;

▶ business summary;

▶ risks;

▶ valuation; and

▶ historical and pro forma tables.

The contents of reports may also be specified by regulatory agencies or professional standards. For example, the CFA Institute *Standards of Practice Handbook* (*Handbook*) dictates standards that must be followed in communicating recommendations. The *Handbook* provides, in part:

> Standard V(B) states the responsibility of members and candidates to include in their communications those key factors that are instrumental to the investment recommendation presented. A critical part of this requirement is to distinguish clearly between opinions and facts. In preparing a research report, the member or candidate must present the basic characteristics of the security being analyzed, which will allow the reader to evaluate the report and incorporate information the reader deems relevant to his or her investment decision making process.[8]

---

[7] Stowe, Robinson, Pinto, and McLeavey (2002, p. 27).

[8] *Standards of Practice Handbook* (2006, p. 105).

The *Handbook* requires that limitations to the analysis and any risks inherent to the investment be disclosed. Furthermore, the *Handbook* requires that any report include elements important to the analysis and conclusions so that readers can evaluate the conclusions themselves.

4.6 Follow-Up

The process does not end with the report. If an equity investment is made or a credit rating assigned, periodic review is required to determine if the original conclusions and recommendations are still valid. In the case of a rejected investment, follow-up may not be necessary but may be appropriate to determine if the analysis process should be refined (for example, if a rejected investment turns out to be successful in the market). Follow-up may involve repeating all the above steps in the process on a periodic basis.

SUMMARY

This reading has presented an overview of financial statement analysis. Among the major points covered are the following:

▶ The primary purpose of financial reports is to provide information and data about a company's financial position and performance, including profitability and cash flows. The information presented in financial reports—including the financial statements, financial notes, and management's discussion and analysis—allows the financial analyst to assess a company's financial position and performance and trends in that performance.

▶ Key financial statements that are a primary focus of analysis include the income statement, balance sheet, statement of cash flows, and statement of owners' equity.

▶ The income statement presents information on the financial results of a company's business activities over a period of time. The income statement communicates how much revenue the company generated during a period and what costs it incurred in connection with generating that revenue. The basic equation underlying the income statement is Revenue − Expense = Net income.

▶ The balance sheet discloses what a company owns (assets) and what it owes (liabilities) at a specific point in time. Owners' equity represents the portion belonging to the owners or shareholders of the business; it is the residual interest in the assets of an entity after deducting its liabilities. The three parts of the balance sheet are formulated in the accounting relationship of Assets = Liabilities + Owners' equity.

▶ Although the income statement and balance sheet provide a measure of a company's success, cash and cash flow are also vital to a company's long-term success. Disclosing the sources and uses of cash in the statement of cash flows helps creditors, investors, and other statement users evaluate the company's liquidity, solvency, and financial flexibility.

▶ The statement of changes in owners' equity reflects information about the increases or decreases to a company's owners' equity.

▶ In addition to the financial statements, a company provides other sources of financial information that are useful to the financial analyst. As part of his or her analysis, the financial analyst should read and assess the information presented in the company's financial note disclosures and supplementary schedules as well as the information contained in the management's discussion and analysis (MD&A). Analysts must also evaluate footnote disclosures regarding the use of alternative accounting methods, estimates, and assumptions.

▶ A publicly traded company must have an independent audit performed on its year-end financial statements. The auditor's opinion provides some assurance about whether the financial statements fairly reflect a company's performance and financial position. In addition, for U.S. publicly traded companies, management must demonstrate that the company's internal controls are effective.

► The financial statement analysis framework provides steps that can be followed in any financial statement analysis project, including the following:

  ► articulate the purpose and context of the analysis;

  ► collect input data;

  ► process data;

  ► analyze/interpret the processed data;

  ► develop and communicate conclusions and recommendations; and

  ► follow-up.

PRACTICE PROBLEMS FOR READING 29

1. Providing information about the performance and financial position of companies so that users can make economic decisions best describes the role of:

   A. auditing.

   B. financial reporting.

   C. financial statement analysis.

2. A company's current financial position would *best* be evaluated using the:

   A. balance sheet.

   B. income statement.

   C. statement of cash flows.

3. A company's profitability for a period would *best* be evaluated using the:

   A. balance sheet.

   B. income statement.

   C. statement of cash flows.

4. Accounting methods, estimates, and assumptions used in preparing financial statements are found in:

   A. footnotes.

   B. the auditor's report.

   C. the proxy statement.

5. Information about management and director compensation would *best* be found in:

   A. footnotes.

   B. the auditor's report.

   C. the proxy statement.

6. Information about material events and uncertainties would *best* be found in:

   A. footnotes.

   B. the proxy statement.

   C. management's discussion and analysis.

7. What type of audit opinion is preferred when analyzing financial statements?

   A. Qualified.

   B. Adverse.

   C. Unqualified.

8. Ratios are an input into which step in the financial analysis framework?

   A. Process data.

   B. Collect input data.

   C. Analyze/interpret the processed data.

SOLUTIONS FOR READING 29

1. B is correct. This is the role of financial reporting. The role of financial statement analysis is to evaluate the financial reports.

2. A is correct. The balance sheet portrays the current financial position. The income statement and statement of cash flows present different aspects of performance.

3. B is correct. Profitability is the performance aspect measured by the income statement. The balance sheet portrays the current financial position. The statement of cash flows presents a different aspect of performance.

4. A is correct. The footnotes disclose choices in accounting methods, estimates, and assumptions.

5. C is correct. Although some aspects of management compensation would be found in the footnotes, this is a required disclosure in the proxy statement.

6. C is correct. This is a component of management's discussion and analysis.

7. C is correct. An unqualified opinion is a "clean" opinion and indicates that the financial statements present the company's performance and financial position fairly.

8. C is correct. Ratios are an output of the process data step but are an input into the analyze/interpret data step.

FINANCIAL REPORTING MECHANICS

by Thomas R. Robinson, CFA, Jan Hendrik van Greuning, CFA,
Karen O'Connor Rubsam, CFA, Elaine Henry, CFA, and
Michael A. Broihahn, CFA

LEARNING OUTCOMES

The candidate should be able to:	Mastery
a. explain the relationship of financial statement elements and accounts, and classify accounts into the financial statement elements;	☐
b. explain the accounting equation in its basic and expanded forms;	☐
c. explain the process of recording business transactions using an accounting system based on the accounting equations;	☐
d. explain the need for accruals and other adjustments in preparing financial statements;	☐
e. explain the relationships among the income statement, balance sheet, statement of cash flows, and statement of owners' equity;	☐
f. describe the flow of information in an accounting system;	☐
g. explain the use of the results of the accounting process in security analysis.	☐

INTRODUCTION 〔 1 〕

The financial statements of a company are end-products of a process for recording transactions of the company related to operations, financing, and investment. The structures of financial statements themselves reflect the system of recording and organizing transactions. To be an informed user of financial statements, the analyst must be knowledgeable about the principles of this system. This reading will supply that essential knowledge, taking the perspective of the user rather than the preparer. Learning the process from this perspective will enable an analyst to grasp the critical concepts without being overwhelmed by the detailed technical skills required by the accountants who prepare financial statements that are a major component of financial reports.

Note:
New rulings and/or pronouncements issued after the publication of the readings on financial reporting and analysis may cause some of the information in these readings to become dated. Candidates are expected to be familiar with the overall analytical framework contained in the study session readings, as well as the implications of alternative accounting methods for financial analysis and valuation, as provided in the assigned readings. Candidates are not responsible for changes that occur after the material was written.

This reading is organized as follows: Section 2 describes the three groups into which business activities are classified for financial reporting purposes. Any transaction affects one or more of these groups. Section 3 describes how the elements of financial statements relate to accounts, the basic content unit of classifying transactions. The section is also an introduction to the linkages among the financial statements. Section 4 provides a step-by-step illustration of the accounting process. Section 5 explains the consequences of timing differences between the elements of a transaction. Section 6 provides an overview of how information flows through a business's accounting system. Section 7 introduces the use of financial reporting in security analysis. A summary of the key points and practice problems in the CFA Institute multiple-choice format conclude the reading.

2 THE CLASSIFICATION OF BUSINESS ACTIVITIES

Accountants give similar accounting treatment to similar types of business transactions. Therefore, a first step in understanding financial reporting mechanics is to understand how business activities are classified for financial reporting purposes.

Business activities may be classified into three groups for financial reporting purposes: operating, investing, and financing activities.

► **Operating activities** are those activities that are part of the day-to-day business functioning of an entity. Examples include the sale of meals by a restaurant, the sale of services by a consulting firm, the manufacture and sale of ovens by an oven-manufacturing company, and taking deposits and making loans by a bank.

► **Investing activities** are those activities associated with acquisition and disposal of long-term assets. Examples include the purchase of equipment or sale of surplus equipment (such as an oven) by a restaurant (contrast this to the sale of an oven by an oven manufacturer, which would be an operating activity), and the purchase or sale of an office building, a retail store, or a factory.

► **Financing activities** are those activities related to obtaining or repaying capital. The two primary sources for such funds are owners (shareholders) or creditors. Examples include issuing common shares, taking out a bank loan, and issuing bonds.

Understanding the nature of activities helps the analyst understand where the company is doing well and where it is not doing so well. Ideally, an analyst would prefer that most of a company's profits (and cash flow) come from its operating activities. Exhibit 1 provides examples of typical business activities and how these activities relate to the elements of financial statements described in the following section.

EXHIBIT 1	Typical Business Activities and Financial Statement Elements Affected

Operating activities	▶ Sales of goods and services to customers: (R)
	▶ Costs of providing the goods and services: (X)
	▶ Income tax expense: (X)
	▶ Holding short-term assets or incurring short-term liabilities directly related to operating activities: (A), (L)
Investing activities	▶ Purchase or sale of assets, such as property, plant, and equipment: (A)
	▶ Purchase or sale of other entities' equity and debt securities: (A)
Financing activities	▶ Issuance or repurchase of the company's own preferred or common stock: (E)
	▶ Issuance or repayment of debt: (L)
	▶ Payment of distributions (i.e., dividends to preferred or common stockholders): (E)

Accounting elements: Assets (A), Liabilities (L), Owners' Equity (E), Revenue (R), and Expenses (X).

Not all transactions fit neatly in this framework for purposes of financial statement presentation. For example, interest received by a bank on one of its loans would be considered part of operating activities because a bank is in the business of lending money. In contrast, interest received on a bond investment by a restaurant may be more appropriately classified as an investing activity because the restaurant is not in the business of lending money.

The next section discusses how transactions resulting from these business activities are reflected in a company's financial records.

ACCOUNTS AND FINANCIAL STATEMENTS

3

Business activities resulting in transactions are reflected in the broad groupings of financial statement elements: Assets, Liabilities, Owners' Equity, Revenue, and Expenses.[1] In general terms, these elements can be defined as follows: **assets** are the economic resources of a company; **liabilities** are the creditors' claims on the resources of a company; **owners' equity** is the residual claim on those resources;

---

[1] International Financial Reporting Standards use the term "income" to include revenue and gains. Gains are similar to revenue; however, they arise from secondary or peripheral activities rather than from a company's primary business activities. For example, for a restaurant, the sale of surplus restaurant equipment for more than its cost is referred to as a gain rather than revenue. Similarly, a loss is like an expense but arises from secondary activities. Gains and losses may be considered part of operations on the income statement (for example, a loss due to a decline in value of inventory) or may be part of nonoperating activities (for example, the sale of nontrading investments). Under U.S. GAAP, financial statement elements are defined to include assets, liabilities, owners' equity, revenue, expenses, gains, and losses. To illustrate business transactions in this reading, we will use the simple classification of revenues and expenses. All gains and revenue will be aggregated in revenue, and all losses and expenses will be aggregated in expenses.

revenues are inflows of economic resources to the company; and **expenses** are outflows of economic resources or increases in liabilities.[2]

Accounts provide individual records of increases and decreases in a *specific* asset, liability, component of owners' equity, revenue, or expense. The financial statements are constructed using these elements.

3.1 Financial Statement Elements and Accounts

Within the financial statement elements, accounts are subclassifications. **Accounts** are individual records of increases and decreases in a specific asset, liability, component of owners' equity, revenue, or expense. For financial statements, amounts recorded in every individual account are summarized and grouped appropriately within a financial statement element. Exhibit 2 provides a listing of common accounts. These accounts will be described throughout this reading or in following readings. Unlike the financial statement elements, there is no standard set of accounts applicable to all companies. Although almost every company has certain accounts, such as cash, each company specifies the accounts in its accounting system based on its particular needs and circumstances. For example, a company in the restaurant business may not be involved in trading securities and, therefore, may not need an account to record such an activity. Furthermore, each company names its accounts based on its business. A company in the restaurant business might have an asset account for each of its ovens, with the accounts named "Oven-1" and "Oven-2." In its financial statements, these accounts would likely be grouped within long-term assets as a single line item called "Property, plant, and equipment."

A company's challenge is to establish accounts and account groupings that provide meaningful summarization of voluminous data but retain enough detail to facilitate decision making and preparation of the financial statements. The actual accounts used in a company's accounting system will be set forth in a **chart of accounts**. Generally, the chart of accounts is far more detailed than the information presented in financial statements.

Certain accounts are used to offset other accounts. For example, a common asset account is accounts receivable, also known as "trade accounts receivable" or "trade receivables." A company uses this account to record the amounts it is owed by its customers. In other words, sales made on credit are reflected in accounts receivable. In connection with its receivables, a company often expects some amount of uncollectible accounts and, therefore, records an estimate of the amount that may not be collected. The estimated uncollectible amount is recorded in an account called **allowance for bad debts**. Because the effect of the allowance for bad debts account is to reduce the balance of the company's accounts receivable, it is known as a "contra asset account." Any account that is offset or deducted from another account is called a "**contra account**." Common contra asset accounts include allowance for bad debts (an offset to accounts receivable for the amount of accounts receivable that are estimated to be uncollectible), **accumulated depreciation** (an offset to property, plant, and equipment reflecting the amount of the cost of property, plant, and equipment that has been allocated to current and previous accounting periods), and **sales returns**

---

[2] The authoritative accounting standards provide significantly more detailed definitions of the accounting elements. Also note that "owners' equity" is a generic term and more specific titles are often used such as "shareholders' equity," "stockholders' equity," or "partners' capital." The broader terms "equity" and "capital" are also used on occasion.

and allowances (an offset to revenue reflecting any cash refunds, credits on account, and discounts from sales prices given to customers who purchased defective or unsatisfactory items).

EXHIBIT 2	Common Accounts

Assets	▶ Cash and cash equivalents
	▶ Accounts receivable, trade receivables
	▶ Prepaid expenses
	▶ Inventory
	▶ Property, plant, and equipment
	▶ Investment property
	▶ Intangible assets (patents, trademarks, licenses, copyright, goodwill)
	▶ Financial assets, trading securities, investment securities
	▶ Investments accounted for by the equity method
	▶ Current and deferred tax assets
	▶ [for banks, Loans (receivable)]
Liabilities	▶ Accounts payable, trade payables
	▶ Provisions or accrued liabilities
	▶ Financial liabilities
	▶ Current and deferred tax liabilities
	▶ Reserves
	▶ Minority interest
	▶ Unearned revenue
	▶ Debt payable
	▶ Bonds (payable)
	▶ [for banks, Deposits]
Owners' equity	▶ Capital, such as common stock par value
	▶ Additional paid-in capital
	▶ Retained earnings
	▶ Other comprehensive income
Revenue	▶ Revenue, sales
	▶ Gains
	▶ Investment income (e.g., interest and dividends)
Expense	▶ Cost of goods sold
	▶ Selling, general, and administrative expenses "SG&A" (e.g., rent, utilities, salaries, advertising)
	▶ Depreciation and amortization
	▶ Interest expense
	▶ Tax expense
	▶ Losses

For presentation purposes, assets are sometimes categorized as "current" or "noncurrent." For example, Tesco (a large European retailer) presents the following major asset accounts in its 2006 financial reports:

Noncurrent assets:

▶ Intangible assets including goodwill;

▶ Property, plant, and equipment;

▶ Investment property;

▶ Investments in joint ventures and associates.

Current assets:

▶ Inventories;

▶ Trade and other receivables;

▶ Cash and cash equivalents.

Noncurrent assets are assets that are expected to benefit the company over an extended period of time (usually more than one year). For Tesco, these include the following: intangible assets, such as goodwill;[3] property, plant, and equipment used in operations (e.g., land and buildings); other property held for investment, and investments in the securities of other companies.

Current assets are those that are expected to be consumed or converted into cash in the near future, typically one year or less. **Inventories** are the unsold units of product on hand (sometimes referred to as inventory stock). **Trade receivables** (also referred to as **commercial receivables**, or simply **accounts receivable**) are amounts customers owe the company for products that have been sold as well as amounts that may be due from suppliers (such as for returns of merchandise). **Other receivables** represent amounts owed to the company from parties other than customers. **Cash** refers to cash on hand (e.g., petty cash and cash not yet deposited to the bank) and in the bank. **Cash equivalents** are very liquid short-term investments, usually maturing in 90 days or less. The presentation of assets as current or noncurrent will vary from industry to industry and from country to country. Some industries present current assets first, whereas others list noncurrent assets first. This is discussed further in later readings.

3.2 Accounting Equations

The five financial statement elements noted previously serve as the inputs for equations that underlie the financial statements. This section describes the equations for three of the financial statements: balance sheet, income statement, and statement of retained earnings. A statement of retained earnings can be viewed as a component of the statement of stockholders' equity, which shows *all* changes to owners' equity, both changes resulting from retained earnings and changes resulting from share issuance or repurchase. The fourth basic financial statement, the statement of cash flows, will be discussed in a later section.

The **balance sheet** presents a company's financial position at a *particular point in time*. It provides a listing of a company's assets and the claims on those assets (liabilities and equity claims). The equation that underlies the balance

---

[3] **Goodwill** is an intangible asset that represents the excess of the purchase price of an acquired company over the value of the net assets acquired.

sheet is also known as the "basic accounting equation." A company's financial position is reflected using the following equation:

$$\text{Assets} = \text{Liabilities} + \text{Owners' equity} \tag{1a}$$

Presented in this form, it is clear that claims on assets are from two sources: liabilities or owners' equity. Owners' equity is the **residual claim** of the owners (i.e., the owners' remaining claim on the company's assets after the liabilities are deducted). The concept of the owners' residual claim is well illustrated by the slightly rearranged balance sheet equation, roughly equivalent to the structure commonly seen in the balance sheets of U.K. companies:

$$\text{Assets} - \text{Liabilities} = \text{Owners' equity} \tag{1b}$$

Other terms are used to denote owners' equity, including shareholders' equity, stockholders' equity, net assets, equity, net worth, net book value, and partners' capital. The exact titles depend upon the type of entity, but the equation remains the same. Owners' equity at a given date can be further classified by its origin: capital contributed by owners, and earnings retained in the business up to that date: [4]

$$\text{Owners' equity} = \text{Contributed capital} + \text{Retained earnings} \tag{2}$$

The **income statement** presents the performance of a business for a *specific period of time*. The equation reflected in the income statement is the following:

$$\text{Revenue} - \text{Expenses} = \text{Net income (loss)} \tag{3}$$

Note that **net income (loss)** is the difference between two of the elements: revenue and expenses. When a company's revenue exceeds its expenses, it reports net income; when a company's revenues are less than its expenses, it reports a net loss. Other terms are used synonymously with revenue, including sales and turnover (in the United Kingdom). Other terms used synonymously with net income include net profit and net earnings.

Also, as noted earlier, revenue and expenses generally relate to providing goods or services in a company's primary business activities. In contrast, gains (losses) relate to increases (decreases) in resources that are not part of a company's primary business activities. Distinguishing a company's primary business activities from other business activities is important in financial analysis; however, for purposes of the accounting equation, gains are included in revenue and losses are included in expenses.

The balance sheet and income statement are two of the primary financial statements. Although these are the common terms for these statements, some variations in the names occur. A balance sheet can be referred to as a "statement of financial position" or some similar term that indicates it contains balances at a point in time. Income statements can be titled "statement of operations,"

---

[4] This formula reflects the fundamental origins of owners' equity and reflects the basic principles of accounting. The presentation is somewhat simplified. In practice, the owners' equity section of a company's balance sheet may include other items, such as treasury stock (which arises when a company repurchases and holds its own stock) or other comprehensive income. **Comprehensive income** includes all income of the company. Some items of comprehensive income are not reported on the income statement. These items as a group are called **other comprehensive income**; such items arise, for example, when there are changes in the value of assets or liabilities that are not reflected in the income statement.

"statement of income," "statement of profit and loss," or some other similar term showing that it reflects the company's operating activity for a period of time. A simplified balance sheet and income statement are shown in Exhibit 3.

EXHIBIT 3	Simplified Balance Sheet and Income Statement

ABC Company, Inc. Balance Sheet As of 31 December 20X1		ABC Company, Inc. Income Statement For the Year Ended 31 December 20X1	
Assets	2,000	Revenue	250
Liabilities	500	Expense	50
Owners' equity	1,500	Net income	200
	2,000		

The balance sheet represents a company's financial position at a point in time, and the income statement represents a company's activity over a period of time. The two statements are linked together through the retained earnings component of owners' equity. Beginning retained earnings is the balance in this account at the beginning of the accounting period, and ending retained earnings is the balance at the end of the period. A company's ending retained earnings is composed of the beginning balance (if any), plus net income, less any distributions to owners (dividends). Accordingly, the equation underlying retained earnings is:

$$\text{Ending retained earnings} = \text{Beginning retained earnings} + \text{Net income} - \text{Dividends} \qquad \textbf{(4a)}$$

Or, substituting Equation 3 for Net income, equivalently:

$$\text{Ending retained earnings} = \text{Beginning retained earnings} + \text{Revenues} - \text{Expenses} - \text{Dividends} \qquad \textbf{(4b)}$$

As its name suggests, retained earnings represent the earnings (i.e., net income) that are retained by the company—in other words, the amount not distributed as dividends to owners. Retained earnings is a component of owners' equity and links the "as of" balance sheet equation with the "activity" equation of the income statement. To provide a combined representation of the balance sheet and income statement, we can substitute Equation 2 into Equation 1a. This becomes the expanded accounting equation:

$$\text{Assets} = \text{Liabilities} + \text{Contributed capital} + \text{Ending retained earnings} \qquad \textbf{(5a)}$$

Or equivalently, substituting Equation 4b into Equation 5a, we can write:

$$\text{Assets} = \text{Liabilities} + \text{Contributed capital} + \text{Beginning retained earnings} + \text{Revenue} - \text{Expenses} - \text{Dividends} \qquad \textbf{(5b)}$$

The last five items, beginning with contributed capital, are components of owners' equity.

The **statement of retained earnings** shows the linkage between the balance sheet and income statement. Exhibit 4 shows a simplified example of financial statements for a company that began the year with retained earnings of $250 and recognized $200 of net income during the period. The example assumes the company paid no dividends and, therefore, had ending retained earnings of $450.

The basic accounting equation reflected in the balance sheet (Assets = Liabilities + Owners' equity) implies that every recorded transaction affects at least two accounts in order to keep the equation in balance, hence the term **double-entry accounting** that is sometimes used to describe the accounting process. For example, the use of cash to purchase equipment affects two accounts (both asset accounts): cash decreases and equipment increases. As another example, the use of cash to pay off a liability also affects two accounts (one asset account and one liability account): cash decreases and the liability decreases. With each transaction, the accounting equation remains in balance, which is a fundamental accounting concept. Example 1 presents a partial balance sheet for an actual company and an application of the accounting equation. Examples 2 and 3 provide further practice for applying the accounting equations.

EXHIBIT 4	Simplified Balance Sheet, Income Statement, and Statement of Retained Earnings

Point in Time: Beginning of Period Balance Sheet	Change over Time: Income Statement *and* Changes in Retained Earnings	Point in Time: End of Period Balance Sheet

ABC Company, Inc.
(Beginning) Balance Sheet
As of 31 December 20X0

Assets	2,000
Liabilities	500
Contributed equity	1,250
Retained earnings	**250**
Owners' equity	1,500
	2,000

ABC Company, Inc.
Income Statement
Year Ended 31 December 20X1

Revenue	250
Expense	50
Net income	200

ABC Company, Inc.
(Ending) Balance Sheet
As of 31 December 20X1

Assets	2,200
Liabilities	500
Contributed equity	1,250
Retained earnings	**450**
Owners' equity	1,700
	2,200

ABC Company, Inc.
Statement of Retained Earnings
Year Ended 31 December 20X1

Beginning retained earnings	**250**
Plus net income	200
Minus dividends	0
Ending retained earnings	**450**

EXAMPLE 1

Using Accounting Equations (1)

Canon is a manufacturer of copy machines and other electronic equipment. Abbreviated balance sheets as of 31 December 2004 and 2005 are presented below.

Canon and Subsidiaries
Consolidated Balance Sheets
(Millions of Yen)

	31 Dec 2005	31 Dec 2004
Assets		
Total assets	¥4,043,553	¥3,587,021
Liabilities and stockholders' equity		
Total liabilities	1,238,535	1,190,331
Total stockholders' equity	?	2,396,690
Total liabilities and stockholders' equity	¥4,043,553	¥3,587,021

Using Equation 1a, address the following:

1. Determine the amount of stockholders' equity as of 31 December 2005.
2. **A.** Calculate and contrast the absolute change in total assets in 2005 with the absolute change in total stockholders' equity in 2005.
   B. Based on your answer to 2A, state and justify the relative importance of growth in stockholders' equity and growth in liabilities in financing the growth of assets over the two years.

Solution to 1: Total stockholders' equity is equal to assets minus liabilities; in other words, it is the residual claim to the company's assets after deducting liabilities. For 2005, the amount of Canon's total stockholders' equity was thus ¥4,043,553 million − ¥1,238,535 million = ¥2,805,018 million in 2005.

Solution to 2:

A. Total assets increased by ¥4,043,553 million − ¥3,587,021 million = ¥456,532 million. Total stockholders' equity increased by ¥2,805,018 million − ¥2,396,690 million = ¥408,328 million. Thus, in 2005, total assets grew by more than total stockholders' equity (¥456,532 million is larger than ¥408,328 million).

B. Using the relationship Assets = Liabilities + Owners' equity, the solution to 2A implies that total liabilities increased by the difference between the increase in total assets and the increase in total stockholders' equity, that is, by ¥456,532 million − ¥408,328 million = ¥48,204 million. (If liabilities had not increased by ¥48,204 million, the accounting equation would not be in balance.) Contrasting the growth in total stockholders' equity (¥408,328 million) with the growth in total liabilities (¥48,204 million), we see that the growth in stockholders' equity was relatively much more important than the growth in liabilities in financing total asset growth in 2005.

EXAMPLE 2

Using Accounting Equations (2)

An analyst has collected the following information regarding a company in advance of its year-end earnings announcement (amounts in millions):

Estimated net income	$ 150
Beginning retained earnings	$2,000
Estimated distributions to owners	$ 50

The analyst's estimate of ending retained earnings (in millions) should be closest to:

A. $2,000.
B. $2,100.
C. $2,150.
D. $2,200.

Solution: B is correct. Beginning retained earnings is increased by net income and reduced by distributions to owners: $2,000 + $150 − $50 = $2,100.

EXAMPLE 3

Using Accounting Equations (3)

An analyst has compiled the following information regarding RDZ, Inc.

Liabilities at year-end	€1,000
Contributed capital at year-end	€1,000
Beginning retained earnings	€500
Revenue during the year	€4,000
Expenses during the year	€3,800

There have been no distributions to owners. The analyst's estimate of total assets at year-end should be closest to:

A. €2,000.
B. €2,300.
C. €2,500.
D. €2,700.

Solution: D is correct. Ending retained earnings is first determined by adding revenue minus expenses to beginning retained earnings to obtain €700. Total assets would be equal to the sum of liabilities, contributed capital, and ending retained earnings: €1,000 + €1,000 + €700 = €2,700.

Having described the components and linkages of financial statements in abstract terms, we now examine more concretely how business activities are recorded. The next section illustrates the accounting process with a simple step-by-step example.

4   THE ACCOUNTING PROCESS

The accounting process involves recording business transactions such that periodic financial statements can be prepared. This section illustrates how business transactions are recorded in a simplified accounting system.

4.1 An Illustration

Key concepts of the accounting process can be more easily explained using a simple illustration. We look at an illustration in which three friends decide to start a business, Investment Advisers, Ltd. (IAL). They plan to issue a monthly newsletter of securities trading advice and to sell investment books. Although they do not plan to manage any clients' funds, they will manage a trading portfolio of the owners' funds to demonstrate the success of the recommended strategies from the newsletter. Because this illustration is meant to present accounting concepts, any regulatory implications will not be addressed. Additionally, for this illustration, we will assume that the entity will not be subject to income taxes; any income or loss will be passed through to the owners and be subject to tax on their personal income tax returns.

As the business commences, various business activities occur. Exhibit 5 provides a listing of the business activities that have taken place in the early stages of operations. Note that these activities encompass the types of operating, investing, and financing business activities discussed above.

4.2 The Accounting Records

If the owners want to evaluate the business at the end of January 2006, Exhibit 5 does not provide a sufficiently meaningful report of what transpired or where the company currently stands. It is clear that a system is needed to track this information and to address three objectives:

▶ Identify those activities requiring further action (e.g., collection of outstanding receivable balances).

▶ Assess the profitability of the operations over the month.

▶ Evaluate the current financial position of the company (such as cash on hand).

| EXHIBIT 5 | Business Activities for Investment Advisers, Ltd. |

#	Date	Business Activity
1	31 December 2005	▶ File documents with regulatory authorities to establish a separate legal entity. Initially capitalize the company through deposit of $150,000 from the three owners.
2	2 January 2006	▶ Set up a $100,000 investment account and purchase a portfolio of equities and fixed-income securities.
3	2 January 2006	▶ Pay $3,000 to landlord for office/warehouse. $2,000 represents a refundable deposit, and $1,000 represents the first month's rent.
4	3 January 2006	▶ Purchase office equipment for $6,000. The equipment has an estimated life of two years with no salvage value.[5]
5	3 January 2006	▶ Receive $1,200 cash for a one-year subscription to the monthly newsletter.
6	10 January 2006	▶ Purchase and receive 500 books at a cost of $20 per book for a total of $10,000. Invoice terms are that payment from IAL is due in 30 days. No cash changes hands. These books are intended for resale.
7	10 January 2006	▶ Spend $600 on newspaper and trade magazine advertising for the month.
8	15 January 2006	▶ Borrow $12,000 from a bank for working capital. Interest is payable annually at 10 percent. The principal is due in two years.
9	15 January 2006	▶ Ship first order to a customer consisting of five books at $25 per book. Invoice terms are that payment is due in 30 days. No cash changes hands.
10	15 January 2006	▶ Sell for cash 10 books at $25 per book at an investment conference.
11	30 January 2006	▶ Hire a part-time clerk. The clerk is hired through an agency that also handles all payroll taxes. The company is to pay $15 per hour to the agency. The clerk works six hours prior to 31 January, but no cash will be paid until February.
12	31 January 2006	▶ Mail out the first month's newsletter to customer. This subscription had been sold on 3 January. See item 5.
13	31 January 2006	▶ Review of the investment portfolio shows that $100 of interest income was earned and the market value of the portfolio has increased by $2,000. The balance in the investment account is now $102,100. The securities are classified as "trading" securities.

An accounting system will translate the company's business activities into usable financial records. The basic system for recording transactions in this illustration is a spreadsheet with each of the different types of accounts represented by a column. The accounting equation provides a basis for setting up this system. Recall the accounting Equation 5b:

$$\text{Assets} = \text{Liabilities} + \text{Contributed capital} + \text{Beginning retained earnings} + \text{Revenue} - \text{Expenses} - \text{Dividends}$$

[5] **Salvage value** (residual value) is the amount the company estimates that it can sell the asset for at the end of its useful life.

The specific accounts to be used for IAL's system include the following:

► Asset Accounts:

  Cash

  Investments

  Prepaid rent (cash paid for rent in advance of recognizing the expense)

  Rent deposit (cash deposited with the landlord, but returnable to the company)

  Office equipment

  Inventory

  Accounts receivable

► Liability Accounts:

  Unearned fees (fees that have not been earned yet, even though cash has been received)

  Accounts payable (amounts owed to suppliers)

  Bank debt

► Equity Accounts:

  Contributed capital

  Retained earnings

      Income

          Revenue

          Expenses

      Dividends

Exhibit 6 presents the spreadsheet representing IAL's accounting system for the first 10 transactions. Each event is entered on a new row of the spreadsheet as it occurs. To record events in the spreadsheet, the financial impact of each needs to be assessed and the activity expressed as an accounting transaction. In assessing the financial impact of each event and converting these events into accounting transactions, the following steps are taken:

1. Identify which accounts are affected, by what amount, and whether the accounts are increased or decreased.

2. Determine the element type for each account identified in Step 1 (e.g., cash is an asset) and where it fits in the basic accounting equation. Rely on the economic characteristics of the account and the basic definitions of the elements to make this determination.

3. Using the information from Steps 1 and 2, enter the amounts in the appropriate column of the spreadsheet.

4. Verify that the accounting equation is still in balance.

At any point in time, basic financial statements can be prepared based on the subtotals in each column.

EXHIBIT 6   Accounting System for Investment Advisers, Ltd.

		Assets =		Liabilities		+	Owners' Equity			
#	Cash	Other Assets	Account	Amount	Account	Contributed Capital	Beginning Retained Earnings	Revenue	Expense	Dividends
Beg. Balance	0	0		0		0	0	0	0	0
1 Capitalize	150,000					150,000				
2 Investments	(100,000)	100,000	Investments							
3 Pay landlord	(3,000)	1,000	Prepaid rent							
		2,000	Rent deposit							
4 Buy equipment	(6,000)	6,000	Office equipment							
5 Sell subscription	1,200			1,200	Unearned fees					
6 Buy books		10,000	Inventory	10,000	Accounts payable					
7 Advertise	(600)								(600)	
8 Borrow	12,000			12,000	Bank debt					
9 Sell books on account		125	Accounts receivable					125	(100)	
		(100)	Inventory							
10 Cash sale	250	(200)	Inventory					250	(200)	
Subtotal	53,850	118,825		23,200		150,000	150,000	375	(900)	

The following discussion identifies the accounts affected and the related element (Steps 1 and 2) for the first 10 events listed in Exhibit 5. The accounting treatment shows the account affected in bold and the related element in brackets. The recording of these entries into a basic accounting system (Steps 3 and 4) is depicted on the spreadsheet in Exhibit 6.

Because this is a new business, the accounting equation begins at zero on both sides. There is a zero beginning balance in all accounts.

---

31 December 2005

#	Business Activity	Accounting Treatment
1	▶ File documents with regulatory authorities to establish a separate legal entity. Initially capitalize the company through deposit of $150,000 from the three owners.	▶ **Cash [A]** is increased by $150,000, and **contributed capital [E]**[6] is increased by $150,000.

Accounting elements: Assets (A), Liabilities (L), Equity (E), Revenue (R), and Expenses (X).

This transaction affects two elements: assets and equity. Exhibit 6 demonstrates this effect on the accounting equation. The company's balance sheet at this point in time would be presented by subtotaling the columns in Exhibit 6:

Investment Advisers, Ltd.
Balance Sheet
As of 31 December 2005

Assets	
Cash	$150,000
Total assets	$150,000
Liabilities and owners' equity	
Contributed capital	$150,000
Total liabilities and owners' equity	$150,000

The company has assets (resources) of $150,000, and the owners' claim on the resources equals $150,000 (their contributed capital) as there are no liabilities at this point.

---

[6] The account title will vary depending upon the type of entity (incorporated or not) and jurisdiction. Alternative account titles are "common shares," "common stock," "members' capital," "partners' capital," etc.

For this illustration, we present an unclassified balance sheet. An **unclassified balance sheet** is one that does not show subtotals for current assets and current liabilities. Assets are simply listed in order of liquidity (how quickly they are expected to be converted into cash). Similarly, liabilities are listed in the order in which they are expected to be satisfied (or paid off).

2 January 2006

#	Business Activity	Accounting Treatment
2	▶ Set up a $100,000 investment account and purchase a portfolio of equities and fixed-income securities.	▶ **Investments [A]** were increased by $100,000, and **cash [A]** was decreased by $100,000.

Accounting elements: Assets (A), Liabilities (L), Equity (E), Revenue (R), and Expenses (X).

This transaction affects two accounts, but only one element (assets) and one side of the accounting equation, as depicted in Exhibit 6. Cash is reduced when the securities are purchased. Another type of asset, investments, increases. We examine the other transaction from 2 January before taking another look at the company's balance sheet.

2 January 2006

#	Business Activity	Accounting Treatment
3	▶ Pay $3,000 to landlord for office/warehouse. $2,000 represents a refundable deposit, and $1,000 represents the first month's rent.	▶ **Cash [A]** was decreased by $3,000, **deposits [A]** were increased by $2,000, and **prepaid rent [A]** was increased by $1,000.

Accounting elements: Assets (A), Liabilities (L), Equity (E), Revenue (R), and Expenses (X).

Once again, this transaction affects only asset accounts. Note that the first month's rent is initially recorded as an asset, prepaid rent. As time passes, the company will incur rent expense, so a portion of this prepaid asset will be transferred to expenses and thus will appear on the income statement as an expense.[7] This will require a later adjustment in our accounting system. Note that the

---

[7] An argument can be made for treating this $1,000 as an immediate expense. We adopt the approach of recording a prepaid asset in order to illustrate accrual accounting. A situation in which a company prepays rent (or insurance or any similar expense) for a time span covering multiple accounting periods more clearly requires the use of accrual accounting.

transactions so far have had no impact on the income statement. At this point in time, the company's balance sheet would be:

Investment Advisers, Ltd.
Balance Sheet
As of 2 January 2006

Assets	
Cash	$ 47,000
Investments	100,000
Prepaid rent	1,000
Deposits	2,000
Total assets	$150,000
Liabilities and owners' equity	
Contributed capital	$150,000
Total liabilities and owners' equity	$150,000

Note that the items in the balance sheet have changed, but it remains in balance; the amount of total assets equals total liabilities plus owners' equity. The company still has $150,000 in resources, but the assets now comprise cash, investments, prepaid rent, and deposits. Each asset is listed separately because they are different in terms of their ability to be used by the company. Note also that the owners' equity claim on these assets remains $150,000 because the company still has no liabilities.

---

3 January 2006

#	Business Activity	Accounting Treatment
4	▶ Purchase office equipment for $6,000 in cash. The equipment has an estimated life of two years with no salvage value.	▶ **Cash [A]** was decreased by $6,000, and **office equipment [A]** was increased by $6,000.

Accounting elements: Assets (A), Liabilities (L), Equity (E), Revenue (R), and Expenses (X).

The company has once again exchanged one asset for another. Cash has decreased while office equipment has increased. Office equipment is a resource that will provide benefits over multiple future periods and, therefore, its cost must also be spread over multiple future periods. This will require adjustments to our accounting records as time passes. **Depreciation** is the term for the process of spreading this cost over multiple periods.

3 January 2006

#	Business Activity	Accounting Treatment
5	▶ Receive $1,200 cash for a one-year subscription to the monthly newsletter.	▶ **Cash [A]** was increased by $1,200, and **unearned fees [L]** was increased by $1,200.

Accounting elements: Assets (A), Liabilities (L), Equity (E), Revenue (R), and Expenses (X).

In this transaction, the company has received cash related to the sale of subscriptions. However, the company has not yet actually earned the subscription fees because it has an obligation to deliver newsletters in the future. So, this amount is recorded as a liability called **unearned fees** (or **unearned revenue**). In the future, as the company delivers the newsletters and thus fulfills its obligation, this amount will be transferred to revenue. If the company fails to deliver the newsletters, the fees will need to be returned to the customer. As of 3 January 2006, the company's balance sheet would appear as

Investment Advisers, Ltd.
Balance Sheet
As of 3 January 2006

Assets	
Cash	$ 42,200
Investments	100,000
Prepaid rent	1,000
Deposits	2,000
Office equipment	6,000
Total assets	$151,200
Liabilities and owners' equity	
Liabilities	
Unearned fees	$ 1,200
Equity	
Contributed capital	$150,000
Total liabilities and owners' equity	$151,200

The company now has $151,200 of resources, against which there is a claim by the subscription customer of $1,200 and a residual claim by the owners of $150,000. Again, the balance sheet remains in balance, with total assets equal to total liabilities plus equity.

10 January 2006

#	Business Activity	Accounting Treatment
6	▶ Purchase and receive 500 books at a cost of $20 per book for a total of $10,000. Invoice terms are that payment from IAL is due in 30 days. No cash changes hands. These books are intended for resale.	▶ **Inventory [A]** is increased by $10,000, and **accounts payable [L]** is increased by $10,000.

Accounting elements: Assets (A), Liabilities (L), Equity (E), Revenue (R), and Expenses (X).

The company has obtained an asset, inventory, which can be sold to customers at a later date. Rather than paying cash to the supplier currently, the company has incurred an obligation to do so in 30 days. This represents a liability to the supplier that is termed accounts payable.

10 January 2006

#	Business Activity	Accounting Treatment
7	▶ Spend $600 on newspaper and trade magazine advertising for the month.	▶ **Cash [A]** was decreased by $600, and **advertising expense [X]** was increased by $600.

Accounting elements: Assets (A), Liabilities (L), Equity (E), Revenue (R), and Expenses (X).

Unlike the previous expenditures, advertising is an expense, not an asset. Its benefits relate to the current period. Expenditures such as advertising are recorded as an expense when they are incurred. Contrast this expenditure with that for equipment, which is expected to be useful over multiple periods and thus is initially recorded as an asset, and then reflected as an expense over time. Also, contrast this treatment with that for rent expense, which was paid in advance and can be clearly allocated over time, and thus is initially recorded as a prepaid asset and then reflected as an expense over time. The advertising expenditure in this example relates to the current period. If the company had paid in advance for several years worth of advertising, then a portion would be capitalized (i.e., recorded as an asset), similar to the treatment of equipment or prepaid rent and expensed in future periods. We can now prepare a partial income statement for the company reflecting this expense:

Investment Advisers, Ltd.
Income Statement
For the Period 1 January through 10 January 2006

Total revenue		$ 0
Expenses		
Advertising	600	
Total expense		600
Net income (loss)		$ (600)

Because the company has incurred a $600 expense but has not recorded any revenue (the subscription revenue has not been earned yet), an income statement for Transactions 1 through 7 would show net income of minus $600 (i.e., a net loss). To prepare a balance sheet for the company, we need to update the retained earnings account. Beginning retained earnings was $0 (zero). Adding the net loss of $600 (made up of $0 revenue minus $600 expense) and deducting any dividend ($0 in this illustration) gives ending retained earnings of minus $600. The ending retained earnings covering Transactions 1–7 is included in the interim balance sheet:

Investment Advisers, Ltd.
Balance Sheet
As of 10 January 2006

Assets	
Cash	$ 41,600
Investments	100,000
Inventory	10,000
Prepaid rent	1,000
Deposits	2,000
Office equipment	6,000
Total assets	$160,600
Liabilities and owners' equity	
Liabilities	
Accounts payable	$ 10,000
Unearned fees	1,200
Total liabilities	11,200
Equity	
Contributed capital	150,000
Retained earnings	(600)
Total equity	149,400
Total liabilities and owners' equity	$160,600

As with all balance sheets, the amount of total assets equals total liabilities plus owners' equity—both are $160,600. The owners' claim on the business has been reduced to $149,400. This is due to the negative retained earnings (sometimes referred to as a retained "deficit"). As noted, the company has a net loss after the first seven transactions, a result of incurring $600 of advertising expenses but not yet producing any revenue.

15 January 2006

#	Business Activity	Accounting Treatment
8	▶ Borrow $12,000 from a bank for working capital. Interest is payable annually at 10 percent. The principal is due in two years.	▶ **Cash [A]** is increased by $12,000, and **bank debt [L]** is increased by $12,000.

Accounting elements: Assets (A), Liabilities (L), Equity (E), Revenue (R), and Expenses (X).

Cash is increased, and a corresponding liability is recorded to reflect the amount owed to the bank. Initially, no entry is made for interest that is expected to be paid on the loan. In the future, interest will be recorded as time passes and interest accrues (accumulates) on the loan.

15 January 2006

#	Business Activity	Accounting Treatment
9	▶ Ship first order to a customer consisting of five books at $25 per book. Invoice terms are that payment is due in 30 days. No cash changes hands.	▶ **Accounts receivable [A]** increased by $125, and **revenue [R]** increased by $125. Additionally, **inventory [A]** decreased by $100, and **cost of goods sold [X]** increased by $100.

Accounting elements: Assets (A), Liabilities (L), Equity (E), Revenue (R), and Expenses (X).

The company has now made a sale. Sale transaction records have two parts. One part represents the $125 revenue to be received from the customer, and the other part represents the $100 cost of the goods that have been sold. Although payment has not yet been received from the customer in payment for the goods, the company has delivered the goods (five books) and so revenue is recorded. A corresponding asset, accounts receivable, is recorded to reflect amounts due from the customer. Simultaneously, the company reduces its inventory balance by the cost of the five books sold and also records this amount as an expense termed **cost of goods sold**.

15 January 2006

#	Business Activity	Accounting Treatment
10	► Sell for cash 10 books at $25 per book at an investment conference.	► **Cash [A]** is increased by $250, and **revenue [R]** is increased by $250. Additionally, **inventory [A]** is decreased by $200, and **cost of goods sold [X]** is increased by $200.

Accounting elements: Assets (A), Liabilities (L), Equity (E), Revenue (R), and Expenses (X).

Similar to the previous sale transaction, both the $250 sales proceeds and the $200 cost of the goods sold must be recorded. In contrast with the previous sale, however, the sales proceeds are received in cash. Subtotals from Exhibit 6 can once again be used to prepare a preliminary income statement and balance sheet to evaluate the business to date:

Investment Advisers, Ltd.
Income Statement
For the Period 1 January through 15 January 2006

Total revenue		$ 375
Expenses		
Cost of goods sold	300	
Advertising	600	
Total expenses		900
Net income (loss)		$ (525)

Investment Advisers, Ltd.
Balance Sheet
As of 15 January 2006

Assets	
Cash	$ 53,850
Accounts receivable	125
Investments	100,000
Inventory	9,700
Prepaid rent	1,000
Deposits	2,000
Office equipment	6,000
Total assets	$172,675

(Continued on next page . . .)

(continued)

Liabilities and owners' equity	
Liabilities	
Accounts payable	$ 10,000
Unearned fees	1,200
Bank debt	12,000
Total liabilities	23,200
Equity	
Contributed capital	150,000
Retained earnings	(525)
Total equity	149,475
Total liabilities and owners' equity	$172,675

An income statement covering Transactions 1–10 would reflect revenue to date of $375 for the sale of books minus the $300 cost of those books and minus the $600 advertising expense. The net loss is $525, which is shown in the income statement as $(525) using the accounting convention that indicates a negative number using parentheses. This net loss is also reflected on the balance sheet in retained earnings. The amount in retained earnings at this point equals the net loss of $525 because retained earnings had $0 beginning balance and no dividends have been distributed. The balance sheet reflects total assets of $172,675 and claims on the assets of $23,200 in liabilities and $149,475 owners' equity. Within assets, the inventory balance represents the cost of the 485 remaining books (a total of 15 have been sold) at $20 each.

Transactions 1–10 occurred throughout the month and involved cash, accounts receivable, or accounts payable; accordingly, these transactions clearly required an entry into the accounting system. The other transactions, items 11–13, have also occurred and need to be reflected in the financial statements, but these transactions may not be so obvious. In order to prepare complete financial statements at the end of a reporting period, an entity needs to review its operations to determine whether any accruals or other adjustments are required. A more complete discussion of accruals and adjustments is set forth in the next section, but generally speaking, such entries serve to allocate revenue and expense items into the correct accounting period. In practice, companies may also make adjustments to correct erroneous entries or to update inventory balances to reflect a physical count.

In this illustration, adjustments are needed for a number of transactions in order to allocate amounts across accounting periods. The accounting treatment for these transactions is shown in Exhibit 7. Transactions are numbered sequentially, and an "a" is added to a transaction number to denote an adjustment relating to a previous transaction. Exhibit 8 presents the completed spreadsheet reflecting these additional entries in the accounting system.

EXHIBIT 7	Investment Advisers, Ltd., Accruals and Other Adjusting Entries on 31 January 2006

#	Business Activity	Accounting Treatment
11	▶ Hire a part-time clerk. The clerk is hired through an agency that also handles all payroll taxes. The company is to pay $15 per hour to the agency. The clerk works six hours prior to 31 January, but no cash will be paid until February.	▶ The company owes $90 for wages at month end. Under accrual accounting, expenses are recorded when incurred, not when paid. ▶ **Accrued wages [L]** is increased by $90, and **payroll expense [X]** is increased by $90. The accrued wage liability will be eliminated when the wages are paid.
12	▶ Mail out the first month's newsletter to customer. This subscription had been sold on 3 January.	▶ One month (or 1/12) of the $1,200 subscription has been satisfied, so $100 can be recognized as revenue. ▶ **Unearned fees [L]** is decreased by $100, and **fee revenue [R]** is increased by $100.
13	▶ Review of the investment portfolio shows that $100 of interest income was earned and the market value of the portfolio has increased by $2,000. The balance in the investment account is now $102,100. The securities are classified as "trading" securities.	▶ **Interest income [R]** is increased by $100, and the **investments** account **[A]** is increased by $100. ▶ The $2,000 increase in the value of the portfolio represents unrealized gains that are part of income for traded securities. The **investments** account **[A]** is increased by $2,000, and **unrealized gains [R]** is increased by $2,000.
3a	▶ In item 3, $3,000 was paid to the landlord for office/warehouse, including a $2,000 refundable deposit and $1,000 for the first month's rent. ▶ Now, the first month has ended, so this rent has become a cost of doing business.	▶ To reflect the full amount of the first month's rent as a cost of doing business, **prepaid rent [A]** is decreased by $1,000, and **rent expense [X]** is increased by $1,000.
4a	▶ In item 4, office equipment was purchased for $6,000 in cash. The equipment has an estimated life of two years with no salvage value. ▶ Now, one month (or 1/24) of the useful life of the equipment has ended, so a portion of the equipment cost has become a cost of doing business.	▶ A portion (1/24) of the total $6,000 cost of the office equipment is allocated to the current period's cost of doing business. ▶ **Depreciation expense [X]** is increased by $250, and **accumulated depreciation [A]** (a contra asset account) is increased by $250. ▶ Accumulated depreciation is a contra asset account to office equipment.
8a	▶ The company borrowed $12,000 from a bank on 15 January, with interest payable annually at 10 percent and the principal due in two years. ▶ Now, one-half of one month has passed since the borrowing.	▶ One-half of one month of interest expense has become a cost of doing business. $12,000 × 10% = $1,200 of annual interest, equivalent to $100 per month or $50 for one-half month. ▶ **Interest expense [X]** is increased by $50, and **interest payable [L]** is increased by $50.

Accounting elements: Assets (A), Liabilities (L), Equity (E), Revenue (R), and Expenses (X).
Notes: Items 11–13 are repeated from Exhibit 5. Items 3a, 4a, and 8a reflect adjustments relating to items 3, 4, and 8 from Exhibit 5.

EXHIBIT 8   Accounting System for Investment Advisers, Ltd.

#	Assets = Cash	Other Assets	Account	Liabilities Amount	Account	Owners' Equity Contributed Capital	Beginning Retained Earnings	Revenue	Expense (Enter as Negative)	Dividends (Enter as Negative)
Beg. Bal	0	0		0		0	0	0	0	0
1 Capitalize	150,000					150,000				
2 Investments	(100,000)	100,000	Investments							
3 Pay landlord	(3,000)	1,000	Prepaid rent							
		2,000	Rent deposit							
4 Buy equipment	(6,000)	6,000	Office equipment							
5 Sell subscript.	1,200			1,200	Unearned fees					
6 Buy books		10,000	Inventory	10,000	Accounts payable					
7 Advertise	(600)								(600)	
8 Borrow	12,000			12,000	Bank debt					
9 Sell books on account		(100)	Inventory					125	(100)	
		125	Accounts receivable							
10 Cash sale	250	(200)	Inventory					250	(200)	
11 Accrue wages				90	Accrued wages				(90)	
12 Earn subscription fees				(100)	Unearned fees			100		
13 Investment income		100	Investments					100		
		2,000	Investments					2,000		
3a Rent expense		(1,000)	Prepaid rent						(1,000)	
4a Depreciate equipment		(250)	Accumulated depreciation (equipment)						(250)	
8a Accrue interest				50	Interest payable				(50)	
Subtotal	**53,850**	**119,675**		**23,240**		**150,000**		**2,575**	**(2,290)**	

A final income statement and balance sheet can now be prepared reflecting all transactions and adjustments.

Investment Advisers, Ltd.
Income Statement
For the Period 1 January through 31 January 2006

Revenues	
Fee revenue	$ 100
Book sales	375
Investment income	2,100
Total revenues	$ 2,575
Expenses	
Cost of goods sold	$ 300
Advertising	600
Wage	90
Rent	1,000
Depreciation	250
Interest	50
Total expenses	2,290
Net income (loss)	$ 285

Investment Advisers, Ltd.
Balance Sheet
As of 31 January 2006

Assets	
Cash	$ 53,850
Accounts receivable	125
Investments	102,100
Inventory	9,700
Prepaid rent	0
Office equipment, net	5,750
Deposits	2,000
Total assets	$173,525
Liabilities and owners' equity	
Liabilities	
Accounts payable	$ 10,000
Accrued wages	90
Interest payable	50
Unearned fees	1,100
Bank debt	12,000

(Continued on next page . . .)

(continued)

Total liabilities	23,240
Equity	
Contributed capital	150,000
Retained earnings	285
Total equity	150,285
Total liabilities and owners' equity	$173,525

From the income statement, we can determine that the business was profitable for the month. The business earned $285 after expenses. The balance sheet presents the financial position. The company has assets of $173,525, and claims against those assets included liabilities of $23,240 and an owners' claim of $150,285. The owners' claim reflects their initial investment plus reinvested earnings. These statements are explored further in the next section.

4.3 Financial Statements

The spreadsheet in Exhibit 8 is an organized presentation of the company's transactions and can help in preparing the income statement and balance sheet presented above. Exhibit 9 presents all financial statements and demonstrates their relationships. Note that the data for the income statement come from the revenue and expense columns of the spreadsheet (which include gains and losses). The net income of $285 (revenue of $2,575 minus expenses of $2,290) was retained in the business rather than distributed to the owners as dividends. The net income, therefore, becomes part of ending retained earnings on the balance sheet. The detail of retained earnings is shown in the statement of owners' equity.

The balance sheet presents the financial position of the company using the assets, liabilities, and equity accounts from the accounting system spreadsheet. The statement of cash flows summarizes the data from the cash column of the accounting system spreadsheet to enable the owners and others to assess the sources and uses of cash. These sources and uses of cash are categorized according to group of business activity: operating, investing, or financing. The format of the statement of cash flows presented here is known as the **direct format**, which refers to the operating cash section appearing simply as operating cash receipts less operating cash disbursements. An alternative format for the operating cash section, which begins with net income and shows adjustments to derive operating cash flow, is known as the **indirect format**. The alternative formats and detailed rules are discussed in the reading on understanding the statement of cash flows.

EXHIBIT 9	Investment Advisers, Ltd., Financial Statements

Investment Advisers, Ltd.
Balance Sheet
As of

	12/31/2005	1/31/2006
Assets		
Cash	150,000	53,850
Accounts receivable	0	125
Investments	0	102,100
Inventory		9,700
Office equipment, net		5,750
Deposits		2,000
Total assets	150,000	173,525
Liabilities		
Accounts payable	0	10,000
Accrued expenses		140
Unearned fees		1,100
Bank debt		12,000
Total liabilities		23,240
Owners' equity		
Contributed capital	150,000	150,000
Retained earnings	0	285
Total equity	150,000	150,285
Total liabilities and equity	150,000	173,525

Investment Advisers, Ltd.
Income Statement
For the Month Ended 1/31/2006

Fee revenue	100
Book sales revenue	375
Investment income	2,100
Total revenue	2,575
Cost of goods sold	300
Other expense	1,990
Total expense	2,290
Net income (loss)	285

Investment Advisers, Ltd.
Statement of Cash Flows
For the Month Ended 1/31/2006

Cash received from customers	1,450
Cash paid to landlord	(3,000)
Cash paid for advertising	(600)
Investments in trading securities	(100,000)
Operating cash flows	(102,150)
Capital expenditures	(6,000)
Investing cash flows	(6,000)
Borrowing	12,000
Financing cash flows	12,000
Net decrease in cash	(96,150)
Cash at 12/31/05	150,000
Cash at 1/31/06	53,850

Investment Advisers, Ltd.
Statement of Owners' Equity
31 January 2006

	Contributed Capital	Retained Earnings	Total
Balance at 12/31/05	150,000	0	150,000
Issuance of stock			
Net income (loss)		285	285
Distributions			
Balance at 1/31/06	150,000	285	150,285

Financial statements use the financial data reported in the accounting system and present this data in a more meaningful manner. Each statement reports on critical areas. Specifically, a review of the financial statements for the IAL illustration provides the following information:

► **Balance Sheet**. This statement provides information about a company's financial position at a point in time. It shows an entity's assets, liabilities, and owners' equity at a particular date. Two years are usually presented so that comparisons can be made. Less significant accounts can be grouped into a single line item. One observation from the IAL illustration is that although total assets have increased significantly (about 16 percent), equity has increased less than 0.2 percent—most of the increase in total assets is due to the increase in liabilities.

► **Income Statement**. This statement provides information about a company's profitability over a period of time. It shows the amount of revenue, expense, and resulting net income or loss for a company during a period of time. Again, less significant accounts can be grouped into a single line item—in this illustration, expenses other than cost of goods sold are grouped into a single line item. The statement shows that IAL has three sources of revenue and made a small profit in its first month of operations. Significantly, most of the revenue came from investments rather than subscriptions or book sales.

► **Statement of Cash Flows**. This statement provides information about a company's cash flows over a period of time. It shows a company's cash inflows (receipts) and outflows (payments) during the period. These flows are categorized according to the three groups of business activities: operating, financing, and investing. In the illustration, IAL reported a large negative cash flow from operations ($102,150), primarily because its trading activities involved the purchase of a portfolio of securities but no sales were made from the portfolio. (Note that the purchase of investments for IAL appears in its operating section because the company is in the business of trading securities. In contrast, for a nontrading company, investment activity would be shown as investing cash flows rather than operating cash flows.) IAL's negative operating and investing cash flows were funded by $12,000 bank borrowing and a $96,150 reduction in the cash balance.

► **Statement of Owners' Equity**. This statement provides information about the composition and changes in owners' equity during a period of time. In this illustration, the only change in equity resulted from the net income of $285. A **Statement of Retained Earnings** (not shown) would report the changes in a company's retained earnings during a period of time.

These statements again illustrate the interrelationships among financial statements. On the balance sheet, we see beginning and ending amounts for assets, liabilities, and owners' equity. Owners' equity increased from $150,000 to $150,285. The statement of owners' equity presents a breakdown of this $285 change. The arrow from the statement of owners' equity to the owners' equity section of the balance sheet explains that section of the balance sheet. In the

IAL illustration, the entire $285 change resulted from an increase in retained earnings. In turn, the increase in retained earnings resulted from $285 net income. The income statement presents a breakdown of the revenues and expenses resulting in this $285. The arrow from the income statement to the net income figure in the owners' equity section explains how reported net income came about.

Also on the balance sheet, we see that cash decreased from $150,000 at the beginning of the month to $53,850 at the end of the month. The statement of cash flows provides information on the increases and decreases in cash by group of business activity. The arrow from the statement of cash flows to the ending cash figure shows that the statement of cash flows explains in detail the ending cash amount.

In summary, the balance sheet provides information at a point in time (financial position), whereas the other statements provide useful information regarding the activity during a period of time (profitability, cash flow, and changes in owners' equity).

ACCRUALS AND VALUATION ADJUSTMENTS   5

In a simple business model such as the investment company discussed in the illustration above, many transactions are handled in cash and settled in a relatively short time frame. Furthermore, assets and liabilities have a fixed and determinable value. Translating business transactions into the accounting system is fairly easy. Difficulty usually arises when a cash receipt or disbursement occurs in a different period than the related revenue or expense, or when the reportable values of assets vary. This section will address the accounting treatment for these situations—namely, accruals and valuation adjustments.

5.1 Accruals

Accrual accounting requires that revenue be recorded when earned and that expenses be recorded when incurred, irrespective of when the related cash movements occur. The purpose of accrual entries is to report revenue and expense in the proper accounting period. Because accrual entries occur due to timing differences between cash movements and accounting recognition of revenue or expense, it follows that there are only a few possibilities. First, cash movement and accounting recognition can occur at the same time, in which case there is no need for accruals. Second, cash movement may occur before or after accounting recognition, in which case accruals are required. The possible situations requiring accrual entries are summarized into four types of accrual entries shown in Exhibit 10 and discussed below. Each type of accrual involves an originating entry and at least one adjusting entry at a later date or dates.

EXHIBIT 10	Accruals

	Cash Movement prior to Accounting Recognition	**Cash Movement in the Same Period as Accounting Recognition**	**Cash Movement after Accounting Recognition**
Revenue	**UNEARNED (DEFERRED) REVENUE** ▶ **Originating entry**–record cash receipt and establish a liability (such as unearned revenue) ▶ **Adjusting entry**–reduce the liability while recording revenue	Settled transaction –no accrual entry needed	**UNBILLED (ACCRUED) REVENUE** ▶ **Originating entry**–record revenue and establish an asset (such as unbilled revenue) ▶ **Adjusting entry**–When billing occurs, reduce unbilled revenue and increase accounts receivable. When cash is collected, eliminate the receivable.
Expense	**PREPAID EXPENSE** ▶ **Originating entry**–record cash payment and establish an asset (such as prepaid expense) ▶ **Adjusting entry**–reduce the asset while recording expense		**ACCRUED EXPENSES** ▶ **Originating entry**–establish a liability (such as accrued expenses) and record an expense ▶ **Adjusting entry**–reduce the liability as cash is paid

Unearned (or **deferred**) **revenue** arises when a company receives cash prior to earning the revenue. In the IAL illustration, in Transaction 5, the company received $1,200 for a 12-month subscription to a monthly newsletter. At the time the cash was received, the company had an obligation to deliver 12 newsletters and thus had not yet earned the revenue. Each month, as a newsletter is delivered, this obligation will decrease by 1/12th (i.e., $100). And at the same time, $100 of revenue will be earned. The accounting treatment involves an originating entry (the initial recording of the cash received and the corresponding liability to deliver newsletters) and, subsequently, 12 future adjusting entries, the first one of which was illustrated as Transaction 12. Each adjusting entry reduces the liability and records revenue.

In practice, a large amount of unearned revenue may cause some concern about a company's ability to deliver on this future commitment. Conversely, a positive aspect is that increases in unearned revenue are an indicator of future revenues. For example, a large liability on the balance sheet of an airline relates to cash received for future airline travel. Revenue will be recognized as the travel occurs, so an increase in this liability is an indicator of future increases in revenue.

Unbilled (or **accrued**) **revenue** arises when a company earns revenue prior to receiving cash but has not yet recognized the revenue at the end of an accounting period. In such cases, the accounting treatment involves an originating entry to record the revenue earned through the end of the accounting period and a related receivable reflecting amounts due from customers. When the company receives payment (or if goods are returned), an adjusting entry eliminates the receivable.

Accrued revenue specifically relates to end-of-period accruals; however, the concept is similar to any sale involving deferred receipt of cash. In the IAL illustration, in Transaction 9, the company sold books on account, so the revenue was recognized prior to cash receipt. The accounting treatment involved an entry to record the revenue and the associated receivable. In the future, when the company receives payment, an adjusting entry (not shown) would eliminate the receivable. In practice, it is important to understand the quality of a company's receivables (i.e., the likelihood of collection).

Prepaid expense arises when a company makes a cash payment prior to recognizing an expense. In the illustration, in Transaction 3, the company prepaid one month's rent. The accounting treatment involves an originating entry to record the payment of cash and the prepaid asset reflecting future benefits, and a subsequent adjusting entry to record the expense and eliminate the prepaid asset. (See the boxes showing the accounting treatment of Transaction 3, which refers to the originating entry, and Transaction 3a, which refers to the adjusting entry.) In other words, prepaid expenses are assets that will be subsequently expensed. In practice, particularly in a valuation, one consideration is that prepaid assets typically have future value only as future operations transpire, unless they are refundable.

Accrued expenses arise when a company incurs expenses that have not yet been paid as of the end of an accounting period. Accrued expenses result in liabilities that usually require future cash payments. In the IAL illustration, the company had incurred wage expenses at month end, but the payment would not be made until after the end of the month (Transaction 11). To reflect the company's position at the end of the month, the accounting treatment involved an originating entry to record wage expense and the corresponding liability for wages payable, and a future adjusting entry to eliminate the liability when cash is paid (not shown because wages will be paid only in February). Similarly, the IAL illustration included interest accrual on the company's bank borrowing. (See the boxes showing the accounting treatment of Transaction 8, where Transaction 8 refers to the originating entry, and Transaction 8a, which refers to the adjusting entry.)

As with accrued revenues, accrued expenses specifically relate to end-of-period accruals. Accounts payable are similar to accrued expenses in that they involve a transaction that occurs now but the cash payment is made later. Accounts payable is also a liability but often relates to the receipt of inventory (or perhaps services) as opposed to recording an immediate expense. Accounts payable should be listed separately from other accrued expenses on the balance sheet because of their different nature.

Overall, in practice, complex businesses require additional accruals that are theoretically similar to the four categories of accruals discussed above but which require considerably more judgment. For example, there may be significant lags between a transaction and cash settlement. In such cases, accruals can span many accounting periods (even 10–20 years!), and it is not always clear when revenue has been earned or an expense has been incurred. Considerable judgment is required to determine how to allocate/distribute amounts across periods. An example of such a complex accrual would be the estimated annual revenue for a contractor on a long-term construction project, such as building a nuclear power plant. In general, however, accruals fall under the four general types and follow essentially the same pattern of originating and adjusting entries as the basic accruals described.

5.2 Valuation Adjustments

In contrast to accrual entries that allocate revenue and expenses into the appropriate accounting periods, valuation adjustments are made to a company's assets or liabilities—only where required by accounting standards—so that the accounting records reflect the current market value rather than the historical cost. In this discussion, we focus on valuation adjustments to assets. For example, in the IAL illustration, Transaction 13 adjusted the value of the company's investment portfolio to its current market value. The income statement reflects the $2,100 increase (including interest), and the ending balance sheets report the investment portfolio at its current market value of $102,100. In contrast, the equipment in the IAL illustration was not reported at its current market value and no valuation adjustment was required.

As this illustration demonstrates, accounting regulations do not require all types of assets to be reported at their current market value. Some assets (e.g., trading securities) are shown on the balance sheet at their current market value, and changes in that market value are reported in the income statement. Some assets are shown at their historical cost (e.g., specific classes of investment securities being held to maturity). Other assets (e.g., a particular class of investment securities) are shown on the balance sheet at their current market value, but changes in market value bypass the income statement and are recorded directly into shareholders' equity under a component referred to as "other comprehensive income." This topic will be discussed in more detail in later readings.

In summary, where valuation adjustment entries are required for assets, the basic pattern is the following for increases in assets: An asset is increased with the other side of the equation being a gain on the income statement or an increase to other comprehensive income. Conversely for decreases: An asset is decreased with the other side of the equation being a loss on the income statement or a decrease to other comprehensive income.

6   ACCOUNTING SYSTEMS

The accounting system set forth for the IAL illustration involved a very simple business, a single month of activity, and a small number of transactions. In practice, most businesses are more complicated and have many more transactions. Accordingly, actual accounting systems, although using essentially the same logic as discussed in the illustration, are both more efficient than a spreadsheet and more complex.

6.1 Flow of Information in an Accounting System

Accounting texts typically discuss accounting systems in detail because accountants need to understand each step in the process. While analysts do not need to know the same details, they should be familiar with the flow of information through a financial reporting system. This flow and the key related documents are described in Exhibit 11.

| **EXHIBIT 11** | **Accounting System Flow and Related Documents** |

Journal entries and adjusting entries

A journal is a document or computer file in which business transactions are recorded in the order in which they occur (chronological order). The general journal is the collection of all business transactions in an accounting system sorted by date. All accounting systems have a general journal to record all transactions. Some accounting systems also include special journals. For example, there may be one journal for recording sales transactions and another for recording inventory purchases.

Journal entries—recorded in journals—are dated, show the accounts affected, and the amounts. If necessary, the entry will include an explanation of the transaction and documented authorization to record the entry. As the initial step in converting business transactions into financial information, the journal entry is useful for obtaining detailed information regarding a particular transaction.

Adjusting journal entries, a subset of journal entries, are typically made at the end of an accounting period to record items such as accruals that are not yet reflected in the accounting system.

General ledger and T-accounts

A ledger is a document or computer file that shows all business transactions by account. Note that the general ledger, the core of every accounting system, contains all of the same entries as that posted to the general journal—the only difference is that the data are sorted by date in a journal and by account in the ledger. The general ledger is useful for reviewing all of the activity related to a single account. T-accounts, explained in Appendix 30, are representations of ledger accounts and are frequently used to describe or analyze accounting transactions.

Trial balance and adjusted trial balance

A trial balance is a document that lists account balances at a particular point in time. Trial balances are typically prepared at the end of an accounting period as a first step in producing financial statements. A key difference between a trial balance and a ledger is that the trial balance shows only total ending balances. An initial trial balance assists in the identification of any adjusting entries that may be required. Once these adjusting entries are made, an adjusted trial balance can be prepared.

Financial statements

The financial statements, a final product of the accounting system, are prepared based on the account totals from an adjusted trial balance.

6.2 Debits and Credits

Reviewing the example of IAL, it is clear that the accounting treatment of every transaction involved at least two accounts and the transaction either increased or decreased the value of any affected account. Traditionally, accounting systems have used the terms **debit** and **credit** to describe changes in an account resulting from the accounting processing of a transaction. The correct usage of "debit" and "credit" in an accounting context differs from how these terms are used in everyday language.[8] The accounting definitions of debit and credit ensure that, in processing a transaction, the sum of the debits equals the sum of the credits, which is consistent with the accounting equation always remaining in balance.

Although mastering the usage of the terms "debit" and "credit" is essential for an accountant, an analyst can still understand financial reporting mechanics without speaking in terms of debits and credits. In general, this text avoids the use of debit/credit presentation; however, for reference, Appendix 30 presents the IAL illustration in a debit and credit system.

The following section broadly describes some considerations for using financial statements in security analysis.

7   USING FINANCIAL STATEMENTS IN SECURITY ANALYSIS

Financial statements serve as a foundation for credit and equity analysis, including security valuation. Analysts may need to make adjustments to reflect items not reported in the statements (certain assets/liabilities and future earnings). Analysts may also need to assess the reasonableness of management judgment (e.g., in accruals and valuations). Because analysts typically will not have access to the accounting system or individual entries, they will need to infer what transactions were recorded by examining the financial statements.

7.1 The Use of Judgment in Accounts and Entries

Quite apart from deliberate misrepresentations, even efforts to faithfully represent the economic performance and position of a company require judgments and estimates. Financial reporting systems need to accommodate complex business models by recording accruals and changes in valuations of balance sheet accounts. Accruals and valuation entries require considerable judgment and thus create many of the limitations of the accounting model. Judgments could prove wrong or, worse, be used for deliberate earnings manipulation. An important first step in analyzing financial statements is identifying the types of accruals and valuation entries in an entity's financial statements. Most of these items will be noted in the critical accounting policies/estimates section of management's discussion and analysis (MD&A) and in the significant accounting policies footnote, both found in the annual report. Analysts should use this disclosure to identify the key accruals and valuations for a company. The analyst needs to be aware, as Example 4 shows, that the manipulation of earnings and assets can take place within the context of satisfying the mechanical rules governing the recording of transactions.

---

[8] In accounting, debits record increases of asset and expense accounts or decreases in liability and owners' equity accounts. Credits record increases in liability, owners' equity, and revenue accounts or decreases in asset accounts. Appendix 30 provides more details.

EXAMPLE 4

The Manipulation of Accounting Earnings

As discussed in this reading, the accounting equation can be expressed as Assets = Liabilities + Contributed capital + Ending retained earnings (Equation 5a). Although the equation must remain in balance with each transaction, management can improperly record a transaction to achieve a desired result. For example, when a company spends cash and records an expense, assets are reduced on the left side of the equation and expenses are recorded, which lowers retained earnings on the right side. The balance is maintained. If, however, a company spent cash but did not want to record an expense in order to achieve higher net income, the company could manipulate the system by reducing cash and increasing another asset. The equation would remain in balance and the right-hand side of the equation would not be affected at all. This was one of the techniques used by managers at WorldCom to manipulate financial reports, as summarized in a U.S. Securities and Exchange Commission complaint against the company (emphasis added):

> In general, WorldCom manipulated its financial results in two ways. First, WorldCom reduced its operating expenses by improperly releasing certain reserves held against operating expenses. Second, **WorldCom improperly reduced its operating expenses by recharacterizing certain expenses as capital assets.** Neither practice was in conformity with generally accepted accounting principles ("GAAP"). Neither practice was disclosed to WorldCom's investors, despite the fact that both practices constituted changes from WorldCom's previous accounting practices. Both practices falsely reduced WorldCom's expenses and, accordingly, had the effect of artificially inflating the income WorldCom reported to the public in its financial statements from 1999 through the first quarter of 2002.[9]

In 2005, the former CEO of WorldCom was sentenced to 25 years in prison for his role in the fraud.[10] The analyst should be aware of the possibility of manipulation of earnings and be on the lookout for large increases in existing assets, new unusual assets, and unexplained changes in financial ratios.

7.2 Misrepresentations

It is rare in this age of computers that the mechanics of an accounting system do not work. Most computer accounting systems will not allow a company to make one-sided entries. It is important to note, however, that just because the mechanics work does not necessarily mean that the judgments underlying the financial statements are correct. An unscrupulous accountant could structure entries to achieve a desired result. For example, if a manager wanted to record fictitious

---

[9] SEC vs. WorldCom, 5 November 2002: www.sec.gov/litigation/complaints/comp17829.htm.

[10] "Ebbers Is Sentenced to 25 Years For $11 Billion WorldCom Fraud," *Wall Street Journal*, 14 July 2005, A1.

revenue, a fictitious asset (a receivable) could be created to keep the accounting equation in balance. If the manager paid for something but did not want to record an expense, the transaction could be recorded in a prepaid asset account. If cash is received but the manager does not want to record revenue, a liability could be created. Understanding that there has to be another side to every entry is key in detecting inappropriate accounting because—usually in the course of "fixing" one account—there will be another account with a balance that does not make sense. In the case of recording fictitious revenue, there is likely to be a growing receivable whose collectibility is in doubt. Ratio analysis, which is discussed further in later readings, can assist in detecting suspect amounts in these accounts. Furthermore, the accounting equation can be used to detect likely accounts where aggressive or even fraudulent accounting may have occurred.

SUMMARY

The accounting process is a key component of financial reporting. The mechanics of this process convert business transactions into records necessary to create periodic reports on a company. An understanding of these mechanics is useful in evaluating financial statements for credit and equity analysis purposes and in forecasting future financial statements. Key concepts are as follows:

▶ Business activities can be classified into three groups: operating activities, investing activities, and financing activities.

▶ Companies classify transactions into common accounts that are components of the five financial statement elements: assets, liabilities, equity, revenue, and expense.

▶ The core of the accounting process is the basic accounting equation: Assets = Liabilities + Owners' equity.

▶ The expanded accounting equation is Assets = Liabilities + Contributed capital + Beginning retained earnings + Revenue − Expenses − Dividends.

▶ Business transactions are recorded in an accounting system that is based on the basic and expanded accounting equations.

▶ The accounting system tracks and summarizes data used to create financial statements: the balance sheet, income statement, statement of cash flows, and statement of owners' equity. The statement of retained earnings is a component of the statement of owners' equity.

▶ Accruals are a necessary part of the accounting process and are designed to allocate activity to the proper period for financial reporting purposes.

▶ The results of the accounting process are financial reports that are used by managers, investors, creditors, analysts, and others in making business decisions.

▶ An analyst uses the financial statements to make judgments on the financial health of a company.

▶ Company management can manipulate financial statements, and a perceptive analyst can use his or her understanding of financial statements to detect misrepresentations.

APPENDIX 30

A DEBIT/CREDIT ACCOUNTING SYSTEM

The main section of this reading presented a basic accounting system represented as a spreadsheet. An alternative system that underlies most manual and electronic accounting systems uses debits and credits. Both a spreadsheet and a debit/credit system are based on the basic accounting equation:

Assets = Liabilities + Owners' equity

Early generations of accountants desired a system for recording transactions that maintained the balance of the accounting equation and avoided the use of negative numbers (which could lead to errors in recording). The system can be illustrated with T-accounts for every account involved in recording transactions. The T-account is so named for its shape:

T-Account

Debit	Credit

The left-hand side of the T-account is called a "debit," and the right-hand side is termed a "credit." The names should not be construed as denoting value. A debit is not better than a credit and vice versa. Debit simply means the left side of the T-account, and credit simply means the right side. Traditionally, debit is abbreviated as "DR," whereas credit is abbreviated "CR." The T-account is also related to the balance sheet and accounting equation as follows:

Balance Sheet

Assets	Liabilities Owners' Equity

Assets are referred to as the left side of the balance sheet (and accounting equation) and hence are on the left side of the T-account. Assets are, therefore, recorded with a debit balance. In other words, to record an increase in an asset, an entry is made to the left-hand side of a T-account. A decrease to an asset is recorded on the right side of a T-account. Liabilities and owners' equity are referred to as the right side of the balance sheet (and accounting equation). Increases to liabilities and owners' equity are recorded on the right side of a T-account; decreases to liabilities and owners' equity are recorded on the left side.

At any point in time, the balance in an account is determined by summing all the amounts on the left side of the account, summing all the amounts on the right side of the account, and calculating the difference. If the sum of amounts on the left side of the account is greater than the sum of amounts on the right side of the account, the account has a debit balance equal to the difference. If the sum of amounts on the right side of the account is greater than the sum of amounts on the left side of the account, the account has a credit balance.

EXHIBIT 1	Balance Sheet T-Accounts for Investment Advisers, Ltd.

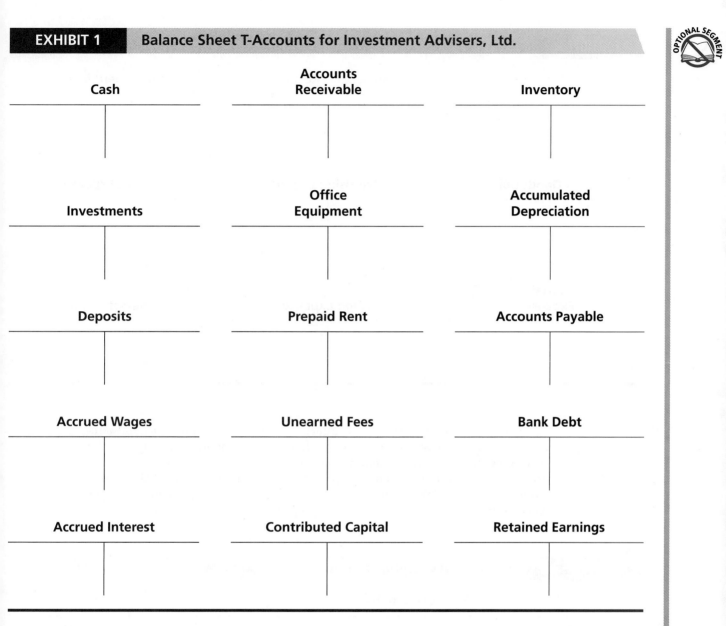

A T-account is created for each asset account, liability account, and owners' equity account. The collection of these T-accounts at the beginning of the year for a fictitious company, Investment Advisers, Ltd. (IAL), is presented in Exhibit 1. Each balance sheet T-account is termed a "permanent" or "real" account because the balance in the account carries over from year-to-year.

T-accounts are also set up for each income statement account. These T-accounts are referred to as "temporary" or "nominal" accounts because they are transferred at the end of each fiscal year by transferring any net income or loss to the balance sheet account, Retained Earnings. Income statement T-accounts for IAL are presented in Exhibit 2.

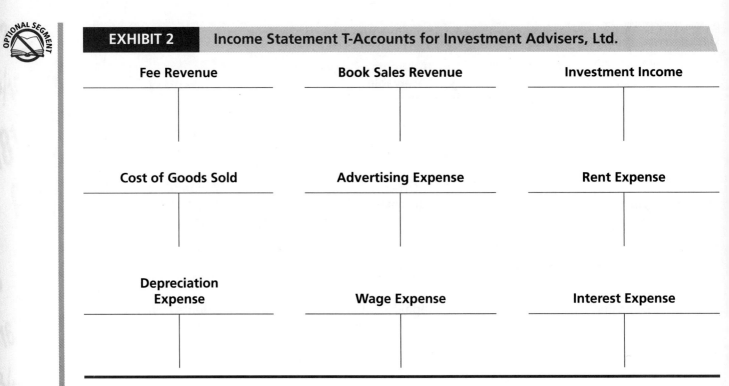

| EXHIBIT 2 | Income Statement T-Accounts for Investment Advisers, Ltd. |

The collection of all business transactions sorted by account, real and temporary, for a company comprise the general ledger. The general ledger is the core of every accounting system, where all transactions are ultimately entered. To illustrate the use of T-accounts, we will use the transactions for IAL summarized in Exhibit 3. We will first enter each transaction into the general ledger T-accounts, then use the information to prepare financial statements.

| EXHIBIT 3 | Business Transactions for Investment Advisers, Ltd. |

#	Date	Business Activity
1	31 December 2005	► File documents with regulatory authorities to establish a separate legal entity. Initially capitalize the company through deposit of $150,000 from the three owners.
2	2 January 2006	► Set up a $100,000 investment account and purchase a portfolio of equities and fixed-income securities.
3	2 January 2006	► Pay $3,000 to landlord for office/warehouse. $2,000 represents a refundable deposit, and $1,000 represents the first month's rent.
4	3 January 2006	► Purchase office equipment for $6,000. The equipment has an estimated life of two years with no salvage value.
5	3 January 2006	► Receive $1,200 cash for a one-year subscription to the monthly newsletter.

(Exhibit continued on next page . . .)

EXHIBIT 3   (continued)

6	10 January 2006	▶ Purchase and receive 500 books at a cost of $20 per book for a total of $10,000. Invoice terms are that payment from IAL is due in 30 days. No cash changes hands. These books are intended for resale.
7	10 January 2006	▶ Spend $600 on newspaper and trade magazine advertising for the month.
8	15 January 2006	▶ Borrow $12,000 from a bank for working capital. Interest is payable annually at 10 percent. The principal is due in two years.
9	15 January 2006	▶ Ship first order to a customer consisting of five books at $25 per book. Invoice terms are that payment is due in 30 days. No cash changes hands.
10	15 January 2006	▶ Sell for cash 10 books at $25 per book at an investment conference.
11	30 January 2006	▶ Hire a part-time clerk. The clerk is hired through an agency that also handles all payroll taxes. The company is to pay $15 per hour to the agency. The clerk works six hours prior to 31 January, but no cash will be paid until February.
12	31 January 2006	▶ Mail out the first month's newsletter to customer. This subscription had been sold on 3 January. See item 5.
13	31 January 2006	▶ Review of the investment portfolio shows that $100 of interest income was earned and the market value of the portfolio has increased by $2,000. The balance in the investment account is now $102,100. Securities are classified as "trading" securities.

Because this is a new business, the company's general ledger T-accounts initially have a zero balance.

31 December 2005 (excerpt from Exhibit 3)

#	Business Activity	Accounting Treatment
1	▶ File documents with regulatory authorities to establish a separate legal entity. Initially capitalize the company through deposit of $150,000 from the three owners.	▶ **Cash [A]** is increased by $150,000, and **contributed capital [E]**[1] is increased by $150,000.

Accounting elements: Assets (A), Liabilities (L), Equity (E), Revenue (R), and Expenses (X).

[1] The account title will vary depending upon the type of entity (incorporated or not) and jurisdiction. Alternative account titles are "common shares," "common stock," "members' capital," "partners' capital," etc.

This transaction affects two accounts: cash and contributed capital. (Cash is an asset, and contributed capital is part of equity.) The transaction is entered into the T-accounts as shown below. The number in parenthesis references the transaction number.

Cash		Contributed Capital	
150,000 (1)			150,000 (1)

Cash is an asset account, and assets are on the left-hand side of the balance sheet (and basic accounting equation); therefore, cash is increased by recording the $150,000 on the debit (left) side of the T-account. Contributed capital is an equity account, and equity accounts are on the right-hand side of the balance sheet; therefore, contributed capital is increased by recording $150,000 on the credit (right) side of the T-account. Note that the sum of the debits for this transaction equals the sum of the credits:

DR = $150,000

CR = $150,000

DR = CR

Each transaction must always maintain this equality. This ensures that the accounting system (and accounting equation) is kept in balance. At this point in time, the company has assets (resources) of $150,000, and the owners' claim on the resources equals $150,000 (their contributed capital) because there are no liabilities at this point.

Transactions are recorded in a journal, which is then "posted to" (recorded in) the general ledger. When a transaction is recorded in a journal, it takes the form:

Date	Account	DR	CR
13 Dec 2005	Cash	150,000	
	Contributed Capital		150,000

This kind of entry is referred to as a "journal entry," and it is a summary of the information that will be posted in the general ledger T-accounts.

2 January 2006 (excerpt from Exhibit 3)

#	Business Activity	Accounting Treatment
2	▶ Set up a $100,000 investment account and purchase a portfolio of equities and fixed-income securities.	▶ **Investments [A]** were increased by $100,000, and **cash [A]** was decreased by $100,000.

Accounting elements: Assets (A), Liabilities (L), Equity (E), Revenue (R), and Expenses (X).

This transaction affects two accounts but only one side of the accounting equation. Cash is reduced when the investments are purchased. Another type of asset, investments, increases. The T-account entries are shown below:

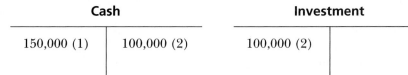

Cash		Investment	
150,000 (1)	100,000 (2)	100,000 (2)	

The cash account started with a $150,000 debit balance from the previous transaction. Assets are reduced by credit entries, so the reduction in cash is recorded by entering the $100,000 on the credit (right) side of the cash T-account. The investment account is also an asset, and the increase in investments is recorded by entering $100,000 on the debit side of the investments T-account. Transaction 2 balances because Transaction 2 debits equal Transaction 2 credits.

Going forward, we will use the traditional accounting terms of debit (debiting, debited) to indicate the action of entering a number in the debit side of an account, and credit (crediting, credited) to indicate the action of entering an amount on the credit side of an account.

2 January 2006 (excerpt from Exhibit 3)

#	Business Activity	Accounting Treatment
3	▶ Pay $3,000 to landlord for office/warehouse. $2,000 represents a refundable deposit, and $1,000 represents the first month's rent.	▶ **Cash [A]** was decreased by $3,000, **deposits [A]** were increased by $2,000, and **prepaid rent [A]** was increased by $1,000.

Accounting elements: Assets (A), Liabilities (L), Equity (E), Revenue (R), and Expenses (X).

Cash is reduced once again by crediting the account by $3,000. On the other side of the transaction, two asset accounts increase. Deposits are increased by debiting the account for $2,000, while prepaid rent is increased by debiting that account for $1,000:

Cash		Deposits		Prepaid Rent	
150,000 (1)	100,000 (2)	2,000 (3)		1,000 (3)	
	3,000 (3)				

The sum of the debits for Transaction 3 equals the sum of the credits (i.e., $3,000).

3 January 2006 (excerpt from Exhibit 3)

#	Business Activity	Accounting Treatment
4	► Purchase office equipment for $6,000 in cash. The equipment has an estimated life of two years with no salvage value.	► **Cash [A]** was decreased by $6,000, and **office equipment [A]** was increased by $6,000.

Accounting elements: Assets (A), Liabilities (L), Equity (E), Revenue (R), and Expenses (X).

Cash is credited for $6,000, while office equipment is debited for $6,000. Both are asset accounts, so these entries reflect a reduction in cash and an increase in office equipment.

Cash		Office Equipment	
150,000 (1)	100,000 (2)	6,000 (4)	
	3,000 (3)		
	6,000 (4)		

3 January 2006 (excerpt from Exhibit 3)

#	Business Activity	Accounting Treatment
5	► Receive $1,200 cash for a one-year subscription to the monthly newsletter.	► **Cash [A]** was increased by $1,200, and **unearned fees [L]** was increased by $1,200.

Accounting elements: Assets (A), Liabilities (L), Equity (E), Revenue (R), and Expenses (X).

In this transaction, the company has received cash related to the sale of subscriptions. However, the company has not yet actually earned the subscription fees because it has an obligation to deliver newsletters in the future. So, this amount is recorded as a liability called "unearned fees" (or "unearned revenue"). In the future, as the company delivers the newsletters and thus fulfills its obligation, this amount will be transferred to revenue. If they fail to deliver the newsletters, the fees will need to be returned to the customer. To record the transaction, cash is debited (increased), while a liability account, unearned fees, is credited. Liabilities are on the right-hand side of the balance sheet and are, therefore, increased by crediting the T-account.

Cash			Unearned Fees	
150,000 (1)	100,000 (2)			1,200 (5)
1,200 (5)	3,000 (3)			
	6,000 (4)			

The sum of Transaction 5 debits and credits each equal $1,200.

10 January 2006 (excerpt from Exhibit 3)

#	Business Activity	Accounting Treatment
6	▶ Purchase and receive 500 books at a cost of $20 per book for a total of $10,000. Invoice terms are that payment from IAL is due in 30 days. No cash changes hands. These books are intended for resale.	▶ **Inventory [A]** is increased by $10,000, and **accounts payable [L]** is increased by $10,000.

Accounting elements: Assets (A), Liabilities (L), Equity (E), Revenue (R), and Expenses (X).

The company has obtained an asset, inventory, which can be sold to customers at a later date. Rather than paying cash to the supplier currently, the company has an obligation to do so in 30 days. This represents a liability ("accounts payable") to the supplier. Inventory is debited for $10,000, while the liability, accounts payable, is credited for $10,000. Note that there is no impact on the cash account.

Inventory			Accounts Payable	
10,000 (6)				10,000 (6)

10 January 2006 (excerpt from Exhibit 3)

#	Business Activity	Accounting Treatment
7	▶ Spend $600 on newspaper and trade magazine advertising for the month.	▶ **Cash [A]** was decreased by $600, and **advertising expense [X]** was increased by $600.

Accounting elements: Assets (A), Liabilities (L), Equity (E), Revenue (R), and Expenses (X).

Unlike the previous expenditures, advertising is not an asset. Its future economic benefits are unclear, unlike equipment, which is expected to be useful over multiple periods. Expenditures such as advertising are recorded as an expense when they are incurred. To record the advertising expense, cash is credited for $600, and advertising expense is debited for $600. Expenses reduce net income, and thus reduce retained earnings. Decreases in retained earnings, as with any equity account, are recorded as debits. The entries with respect to retained earnings will be presented later in this section after the income statement.

Cash		Advertising Expense	
150,000 (1)	100,000 (2)	600 (7)	
1,200 (5)	3,000 (3)		
	6,000 (4)		
	600 (7)		

15 January 2006 (excerpt from Exhibit 3)

#	Business Activity	Accounting Treatment
8	▶ Borrow $12,000 from a bank for working capital. Interest is payable annually at 10 percent. The principal is due in two years.	▶ **Cash [A]** is increased by $12,000, and **Bank debt [L]** is increased by $12,000.

Accounting elements: Assets (A), Liabilities (L), Equity (E), Revenue (R), and Expenses (X).

Cash is debited, and a corresponding liability is credited. Initially, no entry is made for interest that is expected to be paid on the loan. Interest will be recorded in the future as time passes and interest accrues (accumulates) on the loan.

Cash		Bank Debt	
150,000 (1)	100,000 (2)		12,000 (8)
1,200 (5)	3,000 (3)		
12,000 (8)	6,000 (4)		
	600 (7)		

The debits and credits of Transaction 8 each total $12,000.

15 January 2006 (excerpt from Exhibit 3)

#	Business Activity	Accounting Treatment
9	▶ Ship first order to a customer consisting of five books at $25 per book. Invoice terms are that payment is due in 30 days. No cash changes hands.	▶ **Accounts receivable [A]** increased by $125, and **book sales revenue [R]** increased by $125. Additionally, **inventory [A]** decreased by $100, and **cost of goods sold [X]** increased by $100.

Accounting elements: Assets (A), Liabilities (L), Equity (E), Revenue (R), and Expenses (X).

The company has now made a sale. Sale transaction records have two parts. One part records the $125 revenue to be received from the customer, and the other part records the $100 cost of the goods that have been sold. For the first part, accounts receivable is debited (increased) for $125, and a revenue account is credited for $125.

Accounts Receivable		Book Sales Revenue	
125 (9)			125 (9)

For the second part, inventory is credited (reduced) for $100, and an expense, cost of goods sold, is debited (increased) to reflect the cost of inventory sold.

Inventory		Cost of Goods Sold	
10,000 (6)	100 (9)	100 (9)	

Note that the sum of debits and the sum of credits for Transaction 9 both equal $225. The $225 is not meaningful by itself. What is important is that the debits and credits balance.

15 January 2006 (excerpt from Exhibit 3)

#	Business Activity	Accounting Treatment
10	▶ Sell for cash 10 books at $25 per book at an investment conference.	▶ **Cash [A]** is increased by $250, and **book sales revenue [R]** is increased by $250. Additionally, **inventory [A]** is decreased by $200, and **cost of goods sold [X]** is increased by $200.

Accounting elements: Assets (A), Liabilities (L), Equity (E), Revenue (R), and Expenses (X).

Similar to the previous transaction, both the sales proceeds and cost of the goods sold must be recorded. In this case, however, the sales proceeds are received in cash. To record the sale proceeds, the entries include a debit to cash for $250 and a corresponding credit to book sales revenue for $250. To record cost of goods sold, the entries include a debit to cost of goods sold and a credit to inventory.

Cash		Book Sales Revenue	
150,000 (1)	100,000 (2)		125 (9)
1,200 (5)	3,000 (3)		250 (10)
12,000 (8)	6,000 (4)		
250 (10)	600 (7)		

Inventory		Cost of Goods Sold	
10,000 (6)	100 (9)	100 (9)	
	200 (10)	200 (10)	

Transaction 10's debits and credits are equal, maintaining the accounting system's balance.

30 January 2006 (excerpt from Exhibit 3)

#	Business Activity	Accounting Treatment
11	▶ Hire a part-time clerk. The clerk is hired through an agency that also handles all payroll taxes. The company is to pay $15 per hour to the agency. The clerk works six hours prior to 31 January, but no cash will be paid until February.	▶ The company owes $90 for wages at month-end. Under accrual accounting, expenses are recorded when incurred, not when paid. ▶ **Accrued wages [L]** is increased by $90, and **wage expense [X]** is increased by $90. The accrued wage liability will be eliminated when the wages are paid.

Accounting elements: Assets (A), Liabilities (L), Equity (E), Revenue (R), and Expenses (X).

Accrued wages is a liability that is increased by crediting that account, whereas payroll is an expense account that is increased with a debit.

Accrued Wages		Wage Expense	
	90 (11)	90 (11)	

31 January 2006 (excerpt from Exhibit 3)

#	Business Activity	Accounting Treatment
12	▶ Mail out the first month's newsletter to customer. This subscription had been sold on 3 January.	▶ One month (or 1/12) of the $1,200 subscription has been satisfied, and thus $100 can be recognized as revenue. ▶ **Unearned fees [L]** is decreased by $100, and **fee revenue [R]** is increased by $100.

Accounting elements: Assets (A), Liabilities (L), Equity (E), Revenue (R), and Expenses (X).

To record the recognition of one month of the subscription fee, the account fee revenue is credited (increased) by $100, and the related liability is debited (decreased) by $100.

Fee Revenue		Unearned Fees	
	100 (12)	100 (12)	1,200 (5)

31 January 2006 (excerpt from Exhibit 3)

#	Business Activity	Accounting Treatment
13	▶ Review of the investment portfolio shows that $100 of interest income was earned and the market value of the portfolio has increased by $2,000. The balance in the investment account is now $102,100. The securities are classified as "trading" securities.	▶ **Investment income [R]** is increased by $100, and the **investments** account **[A]** is increased by $100. ▶ The $2,000 increase in the value of the portfolio represents unrealized gains that are part of income for traded securities. The **investments** account **[A]** is increased by $2,000, and **investment income [R]** is increased by $2,000.

Accounting elements: Assets (A), Liabilities (L), Equity (E), Revenue (R), and Expenses (X).

The investments account is an asset account that is debited (increased) for $2,100, and investment income is a revenue account that is credited (increased) by $2,100.

Investments		Investment Income	
100,000 (2)			2,100 (13)
2,100 (13)			

These entries complete the recording of the first 13 transactions. In this illustration, there are three adjustments. An adjustment must be made related to Transaction 3 to account for the fact that a month has passed and rent expense has been incurred. We refer to this as Transaction 3a. Adjustments must also be made for an estimate of the depreciation of the office equipment (Transaction 4a) and for interest that has accrued on the loan (Transaction 8a).

31 January 2006

#	Business Activity	Accounting Treatment
3a	► In item 3, $3,000 was paid to the landlord for office/warehouse, including a $2,000 refundable deposit and $1,000 for the first month's rent. ► Now, the first month has ended, so this rent has become a cost of doing business.	► To reflect the full amount of the first month's rent as a cost of doing business, **prepaid rent [A]** is decreased by $1,000, and **rent expense [X]** is increased by $1,000.

Accounting elements: Assets (A), Liabilities (L), Equity (E), Revenue (R), and Expenses (X).

Prepaid rent (an asset) is credited for $1,000 to reduce the balance, and rent expense is debited for the same amount to record the fact that the expense has now been incurred. After this entry, the balance of the prepaid rent asset account is $0.

Prepaid Rent		Rent Expense	
1,000 (3)	1,000 (3a)	1,000 (3a)	

31 January 2006

#	Business Activity	Accounting Treatment
4a	► In item 4, office equipment was purchased for $6,000 in cash. The equipment has an estimated life of two years with no salvage value. ► Now, one month (or 1/24) of the useful life of the equipment has ended so a portion of the equipment cost has become a cost of doing business.	► A portion (1/24) of the total $6,000 cost of the office equipment is allocated to the current period's cost of doing business. ► **Depreciation expense [X]** is increased by $250, and **accumulated depreciation** is increased by $250. ► Accumulated depreciation is a contra asset account to office equipment.

Accounting elements: Assets (A), Liabilities (L), Equity (E), Revenue (R), and Expenses (X).

Because some time has passed, accounting principles require that the estimated depreciation of the equipment be recorded. In this case, one could directly credit office equipment for $250; however, a preferred method is to credit an account called "accumulated depreciation," which is associated with the office equipment account. This accumulated depreciation account "holds" the cumulative amount of the depreciation related to the office equipment. When financial reports are prepared, a user is able to see both the original cost of the equipment as well as the accumulated depreciation. The user, therefore, has insight into the age of the asset, and perhaps how much time remains before it is likely to be replaced. Accumulated depreciation is termed a "contra" asset account and is credited for $250, while depreciation expense is debited (increased) for $250.

Accumulated Depreciation		Depreciation Expense	
	250 (4a)	250 (4a)	

31 January 2006

#	Business Activity	Accounting Treatment
8a	▶ The company borrowed $12,000 from a bank on 15 January, with interest payable annually at 10 percent and the principal due in two years. ▶ Now, one-half of one month has passed since the borrowing.	▶ One-half of one month of interest expense has become a cost of doing business. $12,000 times 10% equals $1,200 of annual interest, equivalent to $100 per month and $50 for one-half month. ▶ **Interest expense [X]** is increased by $50, and **accrued interest [L]** is increased by $50.

Accounting elements: Assets (A), Liabilities (L), Equity (E), Revenue (R), and Expenses (X).

Accrued interest is a liability that is credited (increased) for $50, and interest expense is debited (increased) for $50. Accrued interest is also sometimes referred to as "interest payable."

Accrued Interest		Interest Expense	
	50 (8a)	50 (8a)	

Exhibit 4 summarizes the general ledger T-accounts for IAL at this point in time. For accounts with multiple entries, a line is drawn and the debit and credit columns are summed and netted to determine the current balance in the account. The balance is entered below the line. These individual account totals are then summarized in a trial balance as depicted in Exhibit 5. A trial balance is a summary of the account balances at a point in time. An accountant can prepare a trial balance at any time to ensure that the system is in balance and to review current amounts in the accounts. Note that the debit and credit columns each total $176,065, confirming that the system is in balance. Any difference in the column totals would indicate an error had been made. The trial balance totals have no particular significance and are not used in preparing financial statements. These totals are simply the sum of debits and credits in the accounting system at that point in time.

EXHIBIT 4	General Ledger T-Accounts for Investment Advisers, Ltd.

Cash

150,000	(1)	100,000	(2)
1,200	(5)	3,000	(3)
12,000	(8)	6,000	(4)
250	(10)	600	(7)
53,850			

Accounts Receivable

125	(9)	

Inventory

10,000	(6)	100	(9)
		200	(10)
9,700			

Investments

100,000	(2)	
2,100	(13)	
102,100		

Office Equipment

6,000	(4)	

Accumulated Depreciation

	250	(4a)

Deposits

2,000	(3)	

Prepaid Rent

1,000	(3)	1,000	(3a)
0			

Accounts Payable

	10,000	(6)

Accrued Wages

	90	(11)

Unearned Fees

100	(12)	1,200	(5)
		1,100	

Bank Debt

	12,000	(8)

Accrued Interest

	50	(8a)

Contributed Capital

	150,000	(1)

Retained Earnings

Fee Revenue

	100	(12)

Book Sales Revenue

	125	(9)
	250	(10)
	375	

Investment Income

	2,100	(13)

Cost of Goods Sold

100	(9)	
200	(10)	
300		

Advertising Expense

600	(7)	

Rent Expense

1,000	(3a)	

Depreciation Expense

250	(4a)	

Wage Expense

90	(11)	

Interest Expense

50	(8a)	

EXHIBIT 5	Investment Advisers, Ltd., Trial Balance		
		DR	CR
Cash		53,850	
Accounts receivable		125	
Inventory		9,700	
Investments		102,100	
Office equipment		6,000	
Accumulated depreciation			250
Deposits		2,000	
Prepaid rent		0	
Accounts payable			10,000
Accrued wages			90
Unearned fees			1,100
Bank debt			12,000
Accrued interest			50
Contributed capital			150,000
Retained earnings			
Fee revenue			100
Book sales revenue			375
Investment income			2,100
Cost of goods sold		300	
Advertising expense		600	
Rent expense		1,000	
Depreciation expense		250	
Wage expense		90	
Interest expense		50	
Total		**176,065**	**176,065**

After ensuring that the balances in the trial balance are correct (if there are errors, they are corrected and an adjusted trial balance is prepared), we prepare the financial statements. The trial balance provides the information necessary to prepare the balance sheet and the income statement. The detail in the general ledger must be reviewed to prepare the statement of cash flows and statement of owners' equity. After the income statement is prepared, the temporary accounts are closed out (i.e., taken to a zero balance) by transferring each of their balances to retained earnings. This typically occurs at year-end and is termed the "closing process." Exhibits 6 and 7 show the post-closing general ledger and trial balance, respectively.

| EXHIBIT 6 | Post-Closing General Ledger T-Accounts for Investment Advisers, Ltd. |

Cash

150,000 (1)	100,000 (2)
1,200 (5)	3,000 (3)
12,000 (8)	6,000 (4)
250 (10)	600 (7)
53,850	

Accounts Receivable

125 (9)	

Inventory

10,000 (6)	100 (9)
	200 (10)
9,700	

Investments

100,000 (2)	
2,100 (13)	
102,100	

Office Equipment

6,000 (4)	

Accumulated Depreciation

	250 (4a)

Deposits

2,000 (3)	

Prepaid Rent

1,000 (3)	1,000 (3a)
0	

Accounts Payable

	10,000 (6)

Accrued Wages

	90 (11)

Unearned Fees

100 (12)	1,200 (5)
	1,100

Bank Debt

	12,000 (8)

Accrued Interest

	50 (8a)

Contributed Capital

	150,000 (1)

Retained Earnings

	285

Fee Revenue

	0

Book Sales Revenue

	0

Investment Income

	0

Cost of Goods Sold

0	

Advertising Expense

0	

Rent Expense

0	

Depreciation Expense

0	

Wage Expense

0	

Interest Expense

0	

EXHIBIT 7	Investment Advisers, Ltd., Post-Closing Trial Balance		
		DR	**CR**
Cash		53,850	
Accounts receivable		125	
Inventory		9,700	
Investments		102,100	
Office equipment		6,000	
Accumulated depreciation			250
Deposits		2,000	
Prepaid rent		0	
Accounts payable			10,000
Accrued wages			90
Unearned fees			1,100
Bank debt			12,000
Accrued interest			50
Contributed capital			150,000
Retained earnings			285
Fee revenue			0
Book sales revenue			0
Investment income			0
Cost of goods sold		0	
Advertising expense		0	
Rent expense		0	
Depreciation expense		0	
Wage expense		0	
Interest expense		0	
Total		**173,775**	**173,775**

Financial statements are identical whether using a spreadsheet approach or a debit/credit approach. Accordingly, the financial statements for IAL that would be prepared using the trial balances are identical to those presented in the main body of the reading as Exhibit 9.

OPTIONAL SEGMENT

ENDS

PRACTICE PROBLEMS FOR READING 30

1. Which of the following items would most likely be classified as an operating activity?

   A. Issuance of debt.

   B. Acquisition of a competitor.

   C. Sale of automobiles by an automobile dealer.

2. Which of the following items would most likely be classified as a financing activity?

   A. Issuance of debt.

   B. Payment of income taxes.

   C. Investments in the stock of a supplier.

3. Which of the following elements represents an economic resource?

   A. Asset.

   B. Liability.

   C. Owners' equity.

4. Which of the following elements represents a residual claim?

   A. Asset.

   B. Liability.

   C. Owners' equity.

5. An analyst has projected that a company will have assets of €2,000 at year-end and liabilities of €1,200. The analyst's projection of total owners' equity should be *closest* to:

   A. €800.

   B. €2,000.

   C. €3,200.

6. An analyst has collected the following information regarding a company in advance of its year-end earnings announcement (in millions):

Estimated net income	$ 200
Beginning retained earnings	$1,400
Estimated distributions to owners	$ 100

   The analyst's estimate of ending retained earnings (in millions) should be *closest* to:

   A. $1,300.

   B. $1,500.

   C. $1,700.

7. An analyst has compiled the following information regarding Rubsam, Inc.

Liabilities at year-end	€1,000
Contributed capital at year-end	€500
Beginning retained earnings	€600
Revenue during the year	€5,000
Expenses during the year	€4,300

There have been no distributions to owners. The analyst's *most likely* estimate of total assets at year-end should be *closest* to:

A. €2,100.

B. €2,300.

C. €2,800.

8. A group of individuals formed a new company with an investment of $500,000. The *most likely* effect of this transaction on the company's accounting equation at the time of the formation is an increase in cash and:

A. an increase in revenue.

B. an increase in liabilities.

C. an increase in contributed capital.

9. HVG, LLC paid $12,000 of cash to a real estate company upon signing a lease on 31 December 2005. The payment represents a $4,000 security deposit and $4,000 of rent for each of January 2006 and February 2006. Assuming that the correct accounting is to reflect both January and February rent as prepaid, the *most likely* effect on HVG's accounting equation in December 2005 is:

A. no net change in assets.

B. a decrease in assets of $8,000.

C. a decrease in assets of $12,000.

10. TRR Enterprises sold products to customers on 30 June 2006 for a total price of €10,000. The terms of the sale are that payment is due in 30 days. The cost of the products was €8,000. The *most likely* net change in TRR's total assets on 30 June 2006 related to this transaction is:

A. €0.

B. €2,000.

C. €10,000.

11. On 30 April 2006, Pinto Products received a cash payment of $30,000 as a deposit on production of a custom machine to be delivered in August 2006. This transaction would *most likely* result in which of the following on 30 April 2006?

A. No effect on liabilities.

B. A decrease in assets of $30,000.

C. An increase in liabilities of $30,000.

12. Squires & Johnson, Ltd., recorded €250,000 of depreciation expense in December 2005. The *most likely* effect on the company's accounting equation is:

A. no effect on assets.

B. a decrease in assets of €250,000.

C. an increase in liabilities of €250,000.

13. An analyst who is interested in assessing a company's financial position is *most likely* to focus on which financial statement?

   A. Balance sheet.

   B. Income statement.

   C. Statement of cash flows.

14. The statement of cash flows presents the flows into which three groups of business activities?

   A. Operating, Nonoperating, and Financing.

   B. Operating, Investing, and Financing.

   C. Operating, Nonoperating, and Investing.

15. Which of the following statements about cash received prior to the recognition of revenue in the financial statements is *most* accurate? The cash is recorded as:

   A. deferred revenue, an asset.

   B. accrued revenue, a liability.

   C. deferred revenue, a liability.

16. When, at the end of an accounting period, a revenue has been recognized in the financial statements but no billing has occurred and no cash has been received, the accrual is to:

   A. unbilled (accrued) revenue, an asset.

   B. deferred revenue, an asset.

   C. unbilled (accrued) revenue, a liability.

17. When, at the end of an accounting period, cash has been paid with respect to an expense incurred but not yet recognized in the financial statements, the business should then record:

   A. an accrued expense, an asset.

   B. a prepaid expense, an asset.

   C. an accrued expense, a liability.

18. When, at the end of an accounting period, cash has not been paid with respect to an expense that has been incurred, the business should then record:

   A. an accrued expense, an asset.

   B. a prepaid expense, an asset.

   C. an accrued expense, a liability.

19. The collection of all business transactions sorted by account in an accounting system is referred to as:

   A. a trial balance.

   B. a general ledger.

   C. a general journal.

20. If a company reported fictitious revenue, it could try to cover up its fraud by:

   A. decreasing assets.

   B. increasing liabilities.

   C. creating a fictitious asset.

SOLUTIONS FOR READING 30

1. C is correct. Sales of products, a primary business activity, are classified as an operating activity. Issuance of debt would be a financing activity. Acquisition of a competitor and the sale of surplus equipment would both be classified as investing activities.

2. A is correct. Issuance of debt would be classified as a financing activity. B is incorrect because payment of income taxes would be classified as an operating activity. C is incorrect because the investments in common stock would be generally classified as investing activities.

3. A is correct. An asset is an economic resource of an entity that will either be converted into cash or consumed.

4. C is correct. Owners' equity is a residual claim on the resources of a business.

5. A is correct. Assets must equal liabilities plus owners' equity and, therefore, €2,000 = €1,200 + Owners' equity. Owners' equity must be €800.

6. B is correct.

Beginning retained earnings	$1,400
+ Net income	200
− Distributions to owners	(100)
= Ending retained earnings	$1,500

7. C is correct.

Assets = Liabilities + Contributed capital + Beginning retained earnings − Distributions to owners + Revenues − Expenses

Liabilities	$1,000
+ Contributed capital	500
+ Beginning retained earnings	600
− Distributions to owners	(0)
+ Revenues	5,000
− Expenses	(4,300)
= Assets	$2,800

8. C is correct. This is a contribution of capital by the owners. Assets would increase by $500,000 and contributed capital would increase by $500,000, maintaining the balance of the accounting equation.

9. A is correct. The payment of January rent represents prepaid rent (an asset), which will be adjusted at the end of January to record rent expense. Cash (an asset) decreases by $12,000. Deposits (an asset) increase by $4,000. Prepaid rent (an asset) increases by $8,000. There is no net change in assets.

10. B is correct. The sale of products without receipt of cash results in an increase in accounts receivable (an asset) of €10,000. The balance in inventory (an asset) decreases by €8,000. The net increase in assets is €2,000. This would be balanced by an increase in revenue of €10,000 and an increase in expenses (costs of goods sold) of €8,000.

11. C is correct. The receipt of cash in advance of delivering goods or services results in unearned revenue, which is a liability. The company has an obligation to deliver $30,000 in goods in the future. This balances the increase in cash (an asset) of $30,000.

12. B is correct. Depreciation is an expense and increases accumulated depreciation. Accumulated depreciation is a contra account which reduces property, plant, and equipment (an asset) by €250,000. Assets decrease by €250,000, and expenses increase by €250,000.

13. A is correct. The balance sheet shows the financial position of a company at a particular point in time. The balance sheet is also known as a "statement of financial position."

14. B is correct. The three sections of the statement of cash flows are operating, investing, and financing activities.

15. C is correct. Cash received prior to revenue recognition increases cash and deferred or unearned revenue. This is a liability until the company provides the promised goods or services.

16. A is correct. When cash is to be received after revenue has been recognized but no billing has actually occurred, an unbilled (accrued) revenue is recorded. Such accruals would usually occur when an accounting period ends prior to a company billing its customer. This type of accrual can be contrasted with a simple credit sale, which is reflected as an increase in revenue and an increase in accounts receivable. No accrual is necessary.

17. B is correct. Payment of expenses in advance is called a prepaid expense, which is classified as an asset.

18. C is correct. When an expense is incurred and no cash has been paid, expenses are increased and a liability ("accrued expense") is established for the same amount.

19. B is correct. The general ledger is the collection of all business transactions sorted by account in an accounting system. The general journal is the collection of all business activities sorted by date.

20. C is correct. In order to balance the accounting equation, the company would either need to increase assets or decrease liabilities. Creating a fictitious asset would be one way of attempting to cover up the fraud.

FINANCIAL REPORTING STANDARDS

by Thomas R. Robinson, CFA, Jan Hendrik van Greuning, CFA,
Karen O'Connor Rubsam, CFA, Elaine Henry, CFA, and
Michael A. Broihahn, CFA

LEARNING OUTCOMES

The candidate should be able to:	Mastery
a. explain the objective of financial statements and the importance of reporting standards in security analysis and valuation;	☐
b. explain the role of standard-setting bodies, such as the International Accounting Standards Board and the U.S. Financial Accounting Standards Board, and regulatory authorities such as the International Organization of Securities Commissions, the U.K. Financial Services Authority, and the U.S. Securities and Exchange Commission in establishing and enforcing financial reporting standards;	☐
c. discuss the ongoing barriers to developing one universally accepted set of financial reporting standards;	☐
d. describe the International Financial Reporting Standards (IFRS) framework, including the qualitative characteristics of financial statements, the required reporting elements, and the constraints and assumptions in preparing financial statements;	☐
e. explain the general requirements for financial statements;	☐
f. compare and contrast key concepts of financial reporting standards under IFRS and alternative reporting systems, and discuss the implications for financial analysis of differing financial reporting systems;	☐
g. identify the characteristics of a coherent financial reporting framework and barriers to creating a coherent financial reporting network;	☐
h. discuss the importance of monitoring developments in financial reporting standards and of evaluating company disclosures of significant accounting policies.	☐

Note:
New rulings and/or pronouncements issued after the publication of the readings on financial reporting and analysis may cause some of the information in these readings to become dated. Candidates are expected to be familiar with the overall analytical framework contained in the study session readings, as well as the implications of alternative accounting methods for financial analysis and valuation, as provided in the assigned readings. Candidates are not responsible for changes that occur after the material was written.

95

## 1

INTRODUCTION

Financial reporting standards determine the types and amounts of information that must be provided to investors and creditors so that they may make informed decisions. This reading focuses on the broad framework within which these standards are created. An understanding of the underlying framework of financial reporting standards, which is broader than knowledge of specific accounting rules, will allow an analyst to assess the valuation implications of *any* financial statement element or transaction—including newly developed transactions that are not specifically addressed by the standards.

Section 2 of this reading discusses the objective of financial statements and the importance of financial standards in security analysis and valuation. Section 3 describes the financial reporting standard-setting bodies and regulatory authorities that establish financial reporting standards. Section 4 examines the trend toward convergence of global financial reporting standards. The International Financial Reporting Standards (IFRS) framework is presented in Section 5, and Section 6 compares IFRS with alternative reporting systems.[1] Section 7 discusses the characteristics of an effective financial reporting framework. Section 8 discusses the importance of monitoring developments in financial reporting standards. A summary of the key points and practice problems in the CFA Institute multiple-choice format conclude the reading.

## 2

THE OBJECTIVE OF FINANCIAL REPORTING

Financial reporting begins with a simple enough premise. The International Accounting Standards Board (IASB), which is the international accounting standard-setting body, expresses it as follows in its *Framework for the Preparation and Presentation of Financial Statements*:

> The objective of financial statements is to provide information about the financial position, performance, and changes in financial position of an entity; this information should be useful to a wide range of users for the purpose of making economic decisions.[2]

Until recently, financial reporting standards were developed mostly independently by each country's standard-setting body. This has created a wide range

---

[1] The body of standards issued by the IASB is referred to as "International Financial Reporting Standards," which include previously issued International Accounting Standards (IAS). "Financial reporting" is a broad term including reporting on accounting, financial statements, and other information found in company financial reports.

[2] *Framework for the Preparation and Presentation of Financial Statements*, International Accounting Standards Committee, 1989, adopted by IASB 2001, paragraph 12.

of standards, some of which are quite comprehensive and complex, and others more general. Recent accounting scandals have raised awareness of the need for more uniform global financial reporting standards and provided the impetus for stronger coordination among the major standard-setting bodies. Such coordination is also a natural outgrowth of the increased globalization of capital markets.

Developing financial reporting standards is complicated because the underlying economic reality is complicated. The financial transactions and organizations that financial statements purport to represent are complicated. There is often uncertainty about transactions, resulting in the need for accruals and estimates. These accruals and estimates necessitate judgment. Judgment varies from one preparer to the next. Accordingly, standards are needed to achieve some type of consistency in these judgments. Even with such standards there will be no one right answer. Nevertheless, financial reporting standards try to limit the range of acceptable answers to ensure some measure of consistency in financial statements.

EXAMPLE 1

Estimates in Financial Reporting

In order to make comparisons across companies (cross-sectional analysis) and over time for a single company (time-series analysis), it is important that accounting methods are comparable and consistently applied. However, accounting standards must be flexible enough to recognize that there are differences in the underlying economics between businesses.

Suppose two companies buy the same model of machinery to be used in their respective businesses. The machine is expected to last for several years. Financial reporting standards should require that both companies account for this equipment by initially recording the cost of the machinery as an asset. Without such a standard, the companies could report the purchase of the equipment differently. For example, one company might record the purchase as an asset and the other might record the purchase as an expense. An accounting standard ensures that both companies would be required to record the transaction in a similar manner.

Accounting standards typically would require the cost of the machine to be apportioned over the estimated useful life of an asset as an expense called depreciation. Because the two companies may be operating the machinery differently, financial reporting standards must retain some flexibility. One company might operate the machinery only a few days per week, whereas the other company operates the equipment continuously throughout the week. Given the difference in usage, it would not be appropriate for the two companies to report an identical amount of depreciation expense each period. Financial reporting standards must allow for some discretion such that management can match their financial reporting choices to the underlying economics of their business while ensuring that similar transactions are recorded in a similar manner between companies.

The IASB and the U.S. Financial Accounting Standards Board (FASB) have developed similar financial reporting frameworks, both of which specify the overall objective and qualities of information to be provided. Financial reports are intended to provide information to many users, including investors, creditors, employees, customers, and others. As a result of this multipurpose nature, financial reports are *not* designed with only asset valuation in mind. However, financial reports provide important inputs into the process of valuing a company or the securities a company issues. Understanding the financial reporting framework—including how and when judgments and estimates can affect the numbers reported—enables an analyst to evaluate the information reported and to use the information appropriately when assessing a company's financial performance. Clearly, such an understanding is also important in assessing the financial impact of business decisions and in making comparisons across entities.

3 FINANCIAL REPORTING STANDARD-SETTING BODIES AND REGULATORY AUTHORITIES

A distinction needs to be made between standard-setting bodies and regulatory authorities. Standard-setting bodies, such as the IASB and FASB, are typically private sector organizations consisting of experienced accountants, auditors, users of financial statements, and academics. Regulatory authorities, such as the SEC in the United States and the FSA in the United Kingdom, are governmental entities that have the legal authority to enforce financial reporting requirements and exert other controls over entities that participate in the capital markets within their jurisdiction.

In other words, *generally*, standard-setting bodies make the rules and regulatory authorities enforce the rules. Note, however, that regulators often retain the legal authority to establish financial reporting standards in their jurisdiction and can overrule the private sector standard-setting bodies.

EXAMPLE 2

Industry-Specific Regulation

In certain cases, there exist multiple regulatory bodies that affect a company's financial reporting requirements. For example, in almost all jurisdictions around the world, banking-specific regulatory bodies establish requirements related to risk-based capital measurement, minimum capital adequacy, provisions for doubtful loans, and minimum monetary reserves. An awareness of such regulations provides an analyst with the context to understand a bank's business, including the objectives and scope of allowed activities.

In the United States, the Office of the Comptroller of the Currency charters and regulates all national banks. In the United Kingdom, the FSA regulates the financial services industry. In some countries, a single entity serves both as the central bank and as the regulatory body for the country's financial institutions.

This section provides a brief overview of the most important international standard-setting body, the IASB, followed by a description of the International Organization of Securities Commissions (IOSCO), capital markets regulation in the European Union (EU), and an overview of the U.S. Securities and Exchange Commission (SEC).

3.1 International Accounting Standards Board

The IASB is the standard-setting body responsible for developing international financial reporting and accounting standards. The four goals of the IASB are:

(a) to develop, in the public interest, a single set of high quality, understandable and enforceable global accounting standards that require high quality, transparent and comparable information in financial statements and other financial reporting to help participants in the world's capital markets and other users make economic decisions;

(b) to promote the use and rigorous application of those standards;

(c) in fulfilling the objectives associated with (a) and (b), to take account of, as appropriate, the special needs of small and medium-sized entities and emerging economies; and

(d) to bring about convergence of national accounting standards and International Accounting Standards and International Financial Reporting Standards to high quality solutions.[3]

The predecessor of the IASB, the International Accounting Standards Committee (IASC), was founded in June 1973 as a result of an agreement by accountancy bodies in Australia, Canada, France, Germany, Japan, Mexico, the Netherlands, the United Kingdom and Ireland, and the United States. By 1998, the IASC had expanded membership to 140 accountancy bodies in 101 countries. In 2001, the IASC was reconstituted into the IASB. The IASB has 14 full-time board members who deliberate new financial reporting standards.[4]

The IASB is overseen by the International Accounting Standards Committee Foundation, which has 19 trustees who appoint the members of the IASB, establish the budget, and monitor the IASB's progress. The IASB is advised by the Standards Advisory Council, which is composed of about 50 members representing organizations and individuals with an interest in international financial reporting.

3.2 International Organization of Securities Commissions

The IOSCO, formed in 1983 as the successor organization of an inter-American regional association (created in 1974), has 181 members that regulate more than 90 percent of the world's financial capital markets.

---

[3] *International Accounting Standards Committee Foundation Constitution*, IASCF, July 2005, part A, paragraph 2.

[4] Although the name of the IASB incorporates "Accounting Standards" and early standards were titled International Accounting Standards (IAS), the term "International Financial Reporting Standards" is being used for new standards. The use of the words "financial reporting" recognizes the importance of disclosures outside of the core financial statements, such as management discussion of the business, risks, and future plans.

In 1998, IOSCO adopted a comprehensive set of *Objectives and Principles of Securities Regulation,* which is recognized as international benchmarks for all markets. IOSCO sets out three core objectives of securities regulation:

▶ protecting investors;

▶ ensuring that markets are fair, efficient, and transparent; and

▶ reducing systematic risk.

Standards related to financial reporting, including accounting and auditing standards, are key components in achieving these objectives. The IOSCO's *Objectives and Principles of Securities Regulation* states:

> Full disclosure of information material to investors' decisions is the most important means for ensuring investor protection. Investors are, thereby, better able to assess the potential risks and rewards of their investments and, thus, to protect their own interests. As key components of disclosure requirements, accounting and auditing standards should be in place and they should be of a high and internationally acceptable quality.[5]

Historically, regulation and related financial reporting standards were developed within individual countries and were often based on the cultural, economic, and political norms of each country. As financial markets have become more global, it has become desirable to establish comparable financial reporting standards internationally. Ultimately, laws and regulations are established by individual jurisdictions, so this also requires cooperation among regulators. In order to ensure adherence to international financial standards, it is important to have uniform regulation across national boundaries. The IOSCO aims to assist in attaining this goal of uniform regulation.

3.3 Capital Markets Regulation in Europe

Each individual member state of the EU regulates capital markets in its jurisdiction. There are, however, certain regulations that have been adopted at the EU level. These include standards and directives related to enforcement of IFRS, a proposed directive to adopt International Standards on Auditing, and proposed directives concerning the board of directors' responsibility for a company's financial statements. The EU, under its Accounting Regulation, will likely serve a role similar to the SEC in the United States as it must endorse each international standard for use in Europe.

In 2001, the European Commission established two committees related to securities regulation: the European Securities Committee (ESC) and the Committee of European Securities Regulators (CESR). The ESC consists of high-level representatives of member states and advises the European Commission on securities policy issues. The CESR is an independent advisory body composed of representatives of regulatory authorities of the member states.

As noted earlier, regulation still rests with the individual member states and, therefore, requirements for registering shares and filing periodic financial reports vary from country to country. Over time, this process is expected to become more uniform in the EU.

---

[5] *Objectives and Principles of Securities Regulation,* IOSCO, May 2003, section 4.2.1.

3.4 Capital Markets Regulation in the United States

Any company issuing securities within the United States, or otherwise involved in U.S. capital markets, is subject to the rules and regulations of the U.S. SEC. The SEC, one of the oldest and most developed regulatory authorities, originated as a result of reform efforts made after the great stock market crash of 1929, sometimes referred to as simply the "Great Crash."

3.4.1 Significant Securities-Related Legislation

There are numerous SEC rules and regulations affecting reporting companies, broker/dealers, and other market participants. From a financial reporting and analysis perspective, the most significant of these acts are the Securities Acts of 1933 and 1934 and the Sarbanes–Oxley Act of 2002.

▶ **Securities Act of 1933 (The 1933 Act)**—This act specifies the financial and other significant information that investors must receive when securities are sold, prohibits misrepresentations, and requires initial registration of all public issuances of securities.

▶ **Securities Exchange Act of 1934 (The 1934 Act)**—This act created the SEC, gave the SEC authority over all aspects of the securities industry, and empowered the SEC to require periodic reporting by companies with publicly traded securities.

▶ **Sarbanes–Oxley Act of 2002**—The Sarbanes–Oxley Act of 2002 created the Public Company Accounting Oversight Board (PCAOB) to oversee auditors. The SEC is responsible for carrying out the requirements of the act and overseeing the PCAOB. The act addresses auditor independence; for example, it prohibits auditors from providing certain nonaudit services to the companies they audit. The act strengthens corporate responsibility for financial reports; for example, it requires the chief executive officer and the chief financial officer to certify that the company's financial reports fairly present the company's condition. Furthermore, Section 404 of the Sarbanes–Oxley Act requires management to report on the effectiveness of the company's internal control over financial reporting and to obtain a report from its external auditor attesting to management's assertion about the effectiveness of the company's internal control.

3.4.2 SEC Filings: Key Sources of Information for Analysts

Companies satisfy compliance with these acts principally through the completion and submission (i.e., filing) of standardized forms issued by the SEC. There are more than 50 different types of SEC forms that are used to satisfy reporting requirements; the discussion herein will be limited to those forms most relevant for financial analysts.

In 1993, the SEC began to mandate electronic filings of the required forms through its Electronic Data Gathering, Analysis, and Retrieval (EDGAR) system. As of 2005, most SEC filings are required to be made electronically. EDGAR has made corporate and financial information more readily available to investors and the financial community. Most of the SEC filings that an analyst would be interested in can be retrieved from the internet from one of many websites, including the SEC's own website. Some filings are required upon the initial offering of securities, whereas others are required on a periodic basis thereafter. The following are some of the more common information sources used by analysts.

▶ **Securities Offerings Registration Statement**—The 1933 Act requires companies offering securities to file a registration statement. New issuers as well as previously registered companies that are issuing new securities are required to file these statements. Required information and the precise form vary depending upon the size and nature of the offering. Typically, required information includes: 1) disclosures about the securities being offered for sale, 2) the relationship of these new securities to the issuer's other capital securities, 3) the information typically provided in the annual filings, 4) recent audited financial statements, and 5) risk factors involved in the business.

EXAMPLE 3

Initial Registration Statement

In 2004, Google filed a Form S-1 registration statement with the U.S. SEC to register its initial public offering of securities (Class A Common Stock). In addition to copious amounts of financial and business information, the registration statement provided a 20-page discussion of risks related to Google's business and industry. This type of qualitative information is helpful, if not essential, in making an assessment of a company's credit or investment risk.

▶ **Forms 10-K, 20-F, and 40-F**—These are forms that companies are required to file *annually*. Form 10-K is for U.S. registrants, Form 40-F is for certain Canadian registrants, and Form 20-F is for all other non-U.S. registrants. These forms require a comprehensive overview, including information concerning a company's business, financial disclosures, legal proceedings, and information related to management. The financial disclosures include a historical summary of financial data (usually 10 years), management's discussion and analysis (MD&A) of the company's financial condition and results of operations, and audited financial statements.[6]

▶ **Annual Report**—In addition to the SEC's annual filings (e.g., form 10-K), most companies prepare an annual report to shareholders. This is not a requirement of the SEC. The annual report is usually viewed as one of the most significant opportunities for a company to present itself to shareholders and other external parties; accordingly, it is often a highly polished marketing document with photographs, an opening letter from the chief executive officer, financial data, market segment information, research and development activities, and future corporate goals. In contrast, the Form 10-K is a more legal type of document with minimal marketing emphasis. Although the perspectives vary, there is considerable overlap between a company's annual report and its Form 10-K. Some companies elect to prepare just the Form 10-K or a document that integrates both the 10-K and annual report.

---

[6] In 2008, the Securities and Exchange Commission adopted rules to accept from foreign private issuers financial statements prepared in accordance with IFRS as issued by the IASB. These financial statements no longer need to be reconciled to U.S. GAAP.

▶ **Proxy Statement/Form DEF-14A**—The SEC requires that shareholders of a company receive a proxy statement prior to a shareholder meeting. A proxy is an authorization from the shareholder giving another party the right to cast its vote. Shareholder meetings are held at least once a year, but any special meetings also require a proxy statement. Proxies, especially annual meeting proxies, contain information that is often useful to financial analysts. Such information typically includes proposals that require a shareholder vote, details of security ownership by management and principal owners, biographical information on directors, and disclosure of executive compensation. Proxy statement information is filed with the SEC as Form DEF-14A.

▶ **Forms 10-Q and 6-K**—These are forms that companies are required to submit for interim periods (quarterly for U.S. companies on Form 10-Q, semiannually for many non-U.S. companies on Form 6-K). The filing requires certain financial information, including unaudited financial statements and an MD&A for the interim period covered by the report. Additionally, if certain types of nonrecurring events—such as the adoption of a significant accounting policy, commencement of significant litigation, or a material limitation on the rights of any holders of any class of registered securities— take place during the period covered by the report, these events must be included in the Form 10-Q report. Companies may provide the 10-Q report to shareholders or may prepare a separate, abbreviated, quarterly report to shareholders.

3.4.3 Other Filings

There are other SEC filings that a company or its officers make—either periodically, or, if significant events or transactions have occurred, in between the periodic reports noted above. By their nature, these forms sometimes contain the most interesting and timely information and may have significant valuation implications.

▶ **Form 8-K**—In addition to filing annual and interim reports, SEC registrants must report material corporate events on a more current basis. Form 8-K (6-K for non-U.S. registrants) is the "current report" companies must file with the SEC to announce such major events as acquisitions or disposals of corporate assets, changes in securities and trading markets, matters related to accountants and financial statements, corporate governance and management changes, and Regulation FD disclosures.[7]

▶ **Form 144**—This form must be filed with the SEC as notice of the proposed sale of restricted securities or securities held by an affiliate of the issuer in reliance on Rule 144. Rule 144 permits limited sales of restricted securities without registration.

▶ **Forms 3, 4, and 5**—These forms are required to report beneficial ownership of securities. These filings are required for any director or officer of a registered company as well as beneficial owners of greater than 10 percent of a class of registered equity securities. Form 3 is the initial statement, Form 4 reports changes, and Form 5 is the annual report. These forms, along with Form 144, can be used to examine purchases and sales of securities by officers, directors, and other affiliates of the company.

---

[7] Regulation FD provides that when an issuer discloses material nonpublic information to certain individuals or entities—generally, securities market professionals such as stock analysts or holders of the issuer's securities who may trade on the basis of the information—the issuer must make public disclosure of that information. In this way, the rule aims to promote full and fair disclosure.

▶ **Form 11-K**—This is the annual report of employee stock purchase, savings, and similar plans. It might be of interest to analysts for companies with significant employee benefit plans because it contains more information than that disclosed in the company's financial statements.

4 CONVERGENCE OF GLOBAL FINANCIAL REPORTING STANDARDS

Recent activities have moved the goal of one set of universally accepted financial reporting standards out of the theoretical sphere into the realm of reality.

In 2002, the IASB and FASB each acknowledged their commitment to the development of high-quality, compatible accounting standards that could be used for both domestic and cross-border financial reporting (in an agreement referred to as "The Norwalk Agreement"). Both the IASB and FASB pledged to use their best efforts to 1) make their existing financial reporting standards fully compatible as soon as practicable, and 2) to coordinate their future work programs to ensure that, once achieved, compatibility is maintained. The Norwalk Agreement was certainly an important milestone, and both bodies are working toward convergence through an ongoing short-term convergence project, a convergence research project, and joint projects such as revenue recognition and business combinations.

In 2004, the IASB and FASB agreed that, in principle, any significant accounting standard would be developed cooperatively. It is likely to take considerable time to work out differences on existing IFRS and U.S. generally accepted accounting principles (GAAP) because of other pressing priorities and honest differences in principles. Development of one universally accepted financial reporting framework is a major undertaking and is expected to take a number of years. Exhibit 1 provides a summary of the worldwide adoption status of IFRS.

In some ways, the move toward one global set of financial reporting standards has made the barriers to full convergence more apparent. Standard-setting bodies and regulators can have differing views. In addition, they may be influenced by strong industry lobbying groups and others that will be subject to these reporting standards. For example, the FASB faced strong opposition when it first attempted to adopt standards requiring companies to expense employee stock compensation plans.[8] The IASB has experienced similar political pressures. The issue of political pressure is compounded when international standards are involved, simply because there are many more interested parties and many more divergent views and objectives. The integrity of the financial reporting framework depends on the standard setter's ability to balance various points of view.

5 THE INTERNATIONAL FINANCIAL REPORTING STANDARDS FRAMEWORK

The IFRS *Framework for the Preparation and Presentation of Financial Statements* (referred to here as the "Framework") sets forth the concepts that underlie the preparation and presentation of financial statements for external uses. The *Framework* is designed to assist the IASB in developing standards and to instruct preparers of financial statements on the principles of financial statement

---

[8] The second attempt was successful and FASB Statement 123R required the expensing of stock options. The content of SFAS 123R is now contained in FASB ASC Topic 718 [Compensation–Stock Compensation].

EXHIBIT 1	**International Adoption Status of IFRS as of December 2006**
Europe	▶ The EU requires companies listed in EU countries to adopt IFRS for the 2005 financial statements.
	▶ The IASB decides in late 2006 that it will not require the application of new IFRS or major amendments to existing standards before 1 January 2009.
	▶ Switzerland requires that multinational main board companies must choose either U.S. GAAP or IFRS.
United States	▶ The SEC accepts IFRS for non-U.S. registrants but currently requires a reconciliation to U.S. GAAP. It has indicated that it will revisit this requirement after the filing of 2005 financial statements.
	▶ The FASB is engaged in numerous projects with the IASB to achieve convergence of U.S. GAAP to IFRS. Full convergence, however, is not expected to be completed in the foreseeable future.
Canada	▶ In 2006, Canada's Accounting Standards Board decided to converge Canadian GAAP with IFRS.
Central and South America	▶ Guatemala, Costa Rica, Ecuador, Nicaragua, Panama, Peru, and Honduras require IFRS for all domestic listed companies.
	▶ Venezuela required adoption of IFRS beginning in 2006 for listed companies and 2007 for others.
	▶ El Salvador permits IFRS for domestic listed companies.
Caribbean	▶ Bahamas, Barbados, Jamaica, Trinidad and Tobago, Dominican Republic, and Haiti require IFRS for all domestic listed companies.
Asia Pacific countries	▶ Bangladesh requires the use of IFRS, and Australia and New Zealand have adopted IFRS "equivalent" standards for the 2005 and 2007, respectively, financial statements.
	▶ Japan has launched a joint project with the IASB to reduce differences between Japanese accounting standards and IFRS.
	▶ China requires IFRS for some domestic listed companies.
	▶ Hong Kong and Philippines have adopted national standards that are equivalent to IFRS except for some effective dates and transition.
	▶ Singapore has adopted many IFRS.
	▶ Myanmar and Sri Lanka permit the use of IFRS for domestic listed companies.
Africa and the Middle East	▶ South Africa, Tanzania, Kenya, Egypt, and Malawi require IFRS for all domestic listed companies.
Russian Federation and former Soviet Union	▶ The Russian Federation requires IFRS for banks and has proposed phasing in requiring all domestic listed companies to use IFRS beginning in 2006.

Sources: Based on data from www.iasb.org and www.iasplus.com.

construction. Importantly, the *Framework* is also designed to assist users of financial statements—including financial analysts—in interpreting the information contained therein.

The *Framework* is diagrammed in Exhibit 2. The top part shows how the objective of financial statements determines the characteristics that the reporting elements (relating to performance and financial position) should embody. In practice, decisions in financial statement preparation must satisfy a number of constraints, such as cost–benefit trade-offs. Finally, underlying financial statement preparation, and, therefore, placed at the bottom of the exhibit, are certain important assumptions.

EXHIBIT 2   **IFRS Framework for the Preparation and Presentation of Financial Statements**

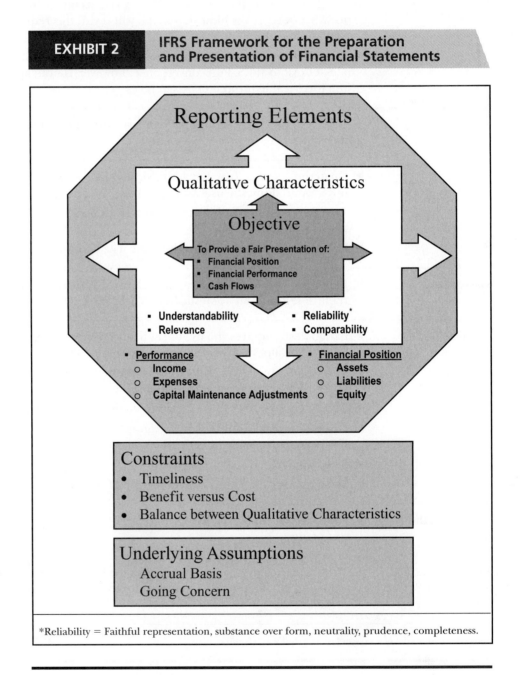

Reporting Elements

Qualitative Characteristics

Objective

To Provide a Fair Presentation of:
- Financial Position
- Financial Performance
- Cash Flows

- Understandability
- Relevance
- Reliability*
- Comparability

- Performance
  - Income
  - Expenses
  - Capital Maintenance Adjustments
- Financial Position
  - Assets
  - Liabilities
  - Equity

Constraints
- Timeliness
- Benefit versus Cost
- Balance between Qualitative Characteristics

Underlying Assumptions
Accrual Basis
Going Concern

*Reliability = Faithful representation, substance over form, neutrality, prudence, completeness.

In the following, we discuss the *Framework* starting at the center: the objective of financial statements.

5.1 Objective of Financial Statements

At the center of the *Framework* is the objective: fair presentation of the company's financial position, its financial performance, and its cash flows. All other aspects of the *Framework* flow from that central objective.

Fair presentation to whom? And for what purpose? The introduction to the *Framework* states that the objective of financial statements is:

> . . . to provide information about the financial position, performance, and changes in financial position of an entity; this information should be useful to a wide range of users for the purpose of making economic decisions.[9]

The range of users includes investors, employees, lenders, suppliers, other creditors, customers, government agencies, the public, and analysts. The purpose of all this information is to be useful in making economic decisions. The types of economic decisions differ by users, so the specific information needed differs as well. However, although these users may have unique information needs, there are some information needs that are common across all users. One common need is for information about the company's financial position: its resources and its financial obligations. Information about a company's financial performance explains how and why the company's financial position changed in the past and can be useful in evaluating potential changes in the future. The third common information need reflected in the *Framework* diagram is the need for information about a company's cash. How did the company obtain cash? By selling its products and services, borrowing, other? How did the company use cash? Paying expenses, investing in new equipment, paying dividends, other?

5.2 Qualitative Characteristics of Financial Statements

Flowing from the central objective of providing a *fair presentation* of information that is *useful* to decision makers, the *Framework* elaborates on what constitutes usefulness. The *Framework* identifies four principal qualitative characteristics that make financial information useful: understandability, relevance, reliability, and comparability.[10]

1. *Understandability.* Understandability of information is defined in terms of who should be able to understand it. The *Framework* specifies that the information should be readily understandable by users who have a basic knowledge of business, economic activities, and accounting, and who have a willingness to study the information with reasonable diligence.

2. *Relevance.* Relevance of information is defined in terms of whether the information influences economic decisions of users, helping them to evaluate past, present, and future events, or to confirm or correct their past evaluations. Relevant information is typically timely, rather than dated. Relevant information is detailed enough to help users assess the risks and opportunities of a company (e.g., information on business segments or

---

[9] *Framework for the Preparation and Presentation of Financial Statements*, IASC, 1989, adopted by IASB 2001, paragraph 12.

[10] Ibid., paragraphs 24–42.

geographical segments). In choosing the level of detail to present, a criterion of materiality is applied. **Materiality** means that omission or misstatement of the information could make a difference to users' decisions.

3. *Reliability.* Reliable information is free from material error and bias. It is information that a user can depend upon to represent a company's financial situation faithfully and completely (within the bounds of materiality and cost). Reliable information also reflects economic reality, not just the legal form of a transaction or event. The following factors contribute to reliability:

   ▶ *Faithful representation.* Information must represent faithfully the transactions and other events it either purports to represent or could reasonably be expected to represent.

   ▶ *Substance over form.* It is necessary that transactions and other events be accounted for and represented in accordance with their substance and economic reality and not merely their legal form.

   ▶ *Neutrality.* Information contained in the financial statements must be neutral—that is, free from bias.

   ▶ *Prudence.* Prudence is the inclusion of a degree of caution in making the estimates required under conditions of uncertainty. It does not, however, allow the deliberate misstatement of elements in the financial statements in an attempt to be conservative by providing for hidden reserves or excessive provisions.

   ▶ *Completeness.* Financial statements must be complete within the bounds of materiality and cost.

4. *Comparability.* Information should be presented in a consistent manner over time and in a consistent manner between entities to enable users to make significant comparisons.

Financial information exhibiting these principal qualitative characteristics normally results in fair presentation (sometimes termed a "true and fair view").

5.3 Constraints on Financial Statements

Although it would be ideal for financial statements to exhibit all of these qualitative characteristics and thus to achieve maximal usefulness, there are several constraints in achieving this goal.[11]

One constraint is the necessity for trade-offs across the desirable characteristics. For example, to be relevant, information must be timely; however, it may take considerable time to ensure the information is error-free (i.e., reliable). The aim is a balance between relevance and reliability.

Another constraint on useful financial information is the cost of providing this information. Optimally, benefits derived from information should exceed the cost of providing it. Again, the aim is a balance between costs and benefits.

A further constraint involves what financial statements omit. Financial statements, by necessity, omit information that is nonquantifiable. For example, the creativity, innovation, and competence of a company's work force are not directly captured in the financial statements. Similarly, customer loyalty, a positive corporate culture, environmental respectfulness, and many other nonquantifiable aspects about a company are not directly reflected in the financial

---

[11] Ibid., paragraphs 43–45.

statements. Of course, to the extent that these nonquantifiable items result in superior financial performance, a company's financial reports will reflect the results.

EXAMPLE 4

Balancing Qualitative Characteristics of Useful Information

A trade-off between qualitative characteristics often occurs. For example, when a company records sales revenue, it is required to simultaneously estimate and record an expense for potential bad debts (uncollectible accounts). This is considered to provide relevant information about the net profits for the accounting period. However, because bad debts may not be known with certainty until a later period, there is a sacrifice of reliability. The bad debt expense is simply an estimate. It is apparent that it is not always possible to simultaneously fulfill all qualitative characteristics.

5.4 The Elements of Financial Statements

Financial statements portray the financial effects of transactions and other events by grouping them into broad classes (elements) according to their economic characteristics.

Three elements of financial statements are directly related to the measurement of the financial position: assets, liabilities, and equity.[12]

► **Assets**. Resources controlled by the enterprise as a result of past events and from which future economic benefits are expected to flow to the enterprise. Assets are what a company owns (e.g., inventory and equipment).

► **Liabilities**. Present obligations of an enterprise arising from past events, the settlement of which is expected to result in an outflow of resources embodying economic benefits. Liabilities are what a company owes (e.g., bank borrowings).

► **Equity** (commonly known as "shareholders' equity"). Assets less liabilities. Equity is the residual interest in the assets after subtracting the liabilities.

The elements of financial statements directly related to the measurement of performance are income and expenses.[13]

► **Income**. Increases in economic benefits in the form of inflows or enhancements of assets, or decreases of liabilities that result in an increase in equity (other than increases resulting from contributions by owners). Income includes both revenues and gains. Revenues represent income from the ordinary activities of the enterprise (e.g., the sale of products). Gains may result from ordinary activities or other activities (the sale of surplus equipment).

---

[12] Ibid., paragraph 49.

[13] Ibid., paragraph 70.

▶ **Expenses**. Decreases in economic benefits in the form of outflows or depletions of assets, or increases in liabilities that result in decreases in equity (other than decreases because of distributions to owners). Expenses include losses, as well as those items normally thought of as expenses, such as the cost of goods sold or wages.

5.4.1 Underlying Assumptions in Financial Statements

At the base of the *Framework*, two important assumptions underlying financial statements are shown: accrual basis and going concern. These assumptions determine how financial statement elements are recognized and measured.[14]

"Accrual basis" refers to the underlying assumption that financial statements aim to reflect transactions when they actually occur, not necessarily when cash movements occur. For example, accrual accounting specifies that a company reports revenues *when they are earned*, regardless of whether the company received cash before delivering the product, after delivering the product, or at the time of delivery.

"Going concern" refers to the assumption that the company will continue in business for the foreseeable future. To illustrate, consider the value of a company's inventory if it is assumed that the inventory can be sold over a normal period of time versus the value of that same inventory if it is assumed that the inventory must all be sold in a day (or a week). Companies with the intent to liquidate or materially curtail operations would require different information for a fair presentation.

EXAMPLE 5

Going Concern

In reporting the financial position of a company that is assumed to be a going concern, it may be appropriate to list assets at some measure of a current value based upon normal market conditions. However, if a company is expected to cease operations and be liquidated, it may be more appropriate to list such assets at an appropriate liquidation value, namely, a value that would be obtained in a forced sale.

5.4.2 Recognition of Financial Statement Elements

Recognition is the process of incorporating in the balance sheet or income statement an item that meets the definition of an element and satisfies the criteria for recognition. A financial statement element (assets, liabilities, equity, income, and expenses) should be recognized in the financial statements if:[15]

▶ it is *probable* that any future economic benefit associated with the item will flow to or from the enterprise, and

▶ the item has a cost or value that can be *measured with reliability*.

---

[14] Ibid., paragraphs 22 and 23.

[15] Ibid., paragraph 83.

5.4.3 Measurement of Financial Statement Elements

Measurement is the process of determining the monetary amounts at which the elements of the financial statements are to be recognized and carried in the balance sheet and income statement. The following alternative bases of measurement are used to different degrees and in varying combinations to measure assets and liabilities:

▶ **Historical cost.** Historical cost is simply the amount of cash or cash equivalents paid to purchase an asset, including any costs of acquisition and/or preparation. If the asset was not bought for cash, historical cost is the fair value of whatever was given in order to buy the asset. When referring to liabilities, the historical cost basis of measurement means the amount of proceeds received in exchange for the obligation.

▶ **Current cost.** In reference to assets, current cost is the amount of cash or cash equivalents that would have to be paid to buy the same or an equivalent asset today. In reference to liabilities, the current cost basis of measurement means the undiscounted amount of cash or cash equivalents that would be required to settle the obligation today.

▶ **Realizable (settlement) value.** In reference to assets, realizable value is the amount of cash or cash equivalents that could currently be obtained by selling the asset in an orderly disposal. For liabilities, the equivalent to realizable value is called "settlement value"—that is, settlement value is the undiscounted amount of cash or cash equivalents expected to be paid to satisfy the liabilities in the normal course of business.

▶ **Present value.** For assets, present value is the present discounted value of the future net cash inflows that the asset is expected to generate in the normal course of business. For liabilities, present value is the present discounted value of the future net cash outflows that are expected to be required to settle the liabilities in the normal course of business.

▶ **Fair value.** Fair value is the amount at which an asset could be exchanged, or a liability settled, between knowledgeable, willing parties in an arm's-length transaction, which may involve either market measures or present value measures.

5.5 General Requirements for Financial Statements

The *Framework* provides a basis for establishing standards and the elements of financial statements, but it does not address the contents of the financial statements. Having discussed the *Framework*, we now need to address the general requirements for financial statements.

The required financial statements, the fundamental principles underlying their presentation, and the principles of presentation are provided by International Accounting Standard (IAS) No. 1, *Presentation of Financial Statements*. These general requirements are illustrated in Exhibit 3 and described in the following subsections.

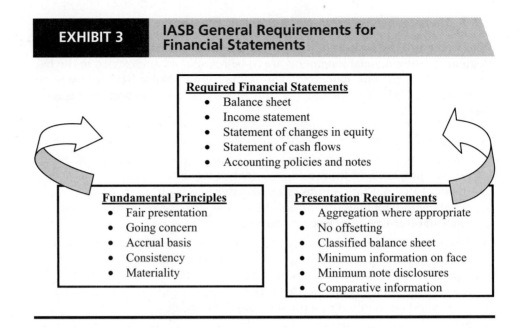

EXHIBIT 3   **IASB General Requirements for Financial Statements**

Required Financial Statements
- Balance sheet
- Income statement
- Statement of changes in equity
- Statement of cash flows
- Accounting policies and notes

Fundamental Principles
- Fair presentation
- Going concern
- Accrual basis
- Consistency
- Materiality

Presentation Requirements
- Aggregation where appropriate
- No offsetting
- Classified balance sheet
- Minimum information on face
- Minimum note disclosures
- Comparative information

In the following, we discuss required financial statements, the fundamental principles underlying the preparation of financial statements, and the principles of presentation in greater detail.

5.5.1 Required Financial Statements

Under IAS No. 1, a complete set of financial statements includes:[16]

► a statement of financial position (balance sheet);

► a statement of comprehensive income;[17]

► a statement of changes in equity showing either:

   ► all changes in equity, or

   ► changes in equity other than those arising from transactions with equityholders acting in their capacity as equityholders;[18]

► a statement of cash flows; and

► notes comprising a summary of significant accounting policies and other explanatory notes.

Entities are encouraged to furnish other related financial and nonfinancial information in addition to the financial statements. Financial statements need to present fairly the financial position, financial performance, and cash flows of an entity.

---

[16] IAS No. 1, *Presentation of Financial Statements*, paragraph 10.

[17] IAS 1 allows an entity to present all items of income and expense recognised in a period in either a single statement of comprehensive income or in two statements: an income statement and a statement of comprehensive income.

[18] Examples of transactions with equityholders acting in their capacity as equityholders include sale of equity securities to investors, distributions of earnings to investors, and repurchases of equity securities from investors.

5.5.2 Fundamental Principles Underlying the Preparation of Financial Statements

A company that applies the IFRS states explicitly in the notes to its financial statements that it is in compliance with the standards. Except in extremely rare circumstances, such a statement is only made when a company is in compliance with *all* requirements of IFRS.

IAS No. 1 specifies a number of fundamental principles underlying the preparation of financial statements. These principles clearly reflect the *Framework*.

▶ *Fair presentation.* The application of IFRS is presumed to result in financial statements that achieve a fair presentation. The IAS describes fair presentation as follows:

> Fair presentation requires faithful representation of the effects of transactions, events and conditions in accordance with the definitions and recognition criteria for assets, liabilities, income and expenses set out in the Framework.[19]

▶ *Going concern.* Financial statements are prepared on a going concern basis unless management either intends to liquidate the entity or to cease trading, or has no realistic alternative but to do so. If not presented on a going concern basis, the fact and rationale should be disclosed.

▶ *Accrual basis.* Financial statements (except for cash flow information) are to be prepared using the accrual basis of accounting.

▶ *Consistency.* The presentation and classification of items in the financial statements are usually retained from one period to the next. Comparative information of prior periods is disclosed for all amounts reported in the financial statements, unless an IFRS requires or permits otherwise.

▶ *Materiality.* Omissions or misstatements of items are material if they could, individually or collectively, influence the economic decisions of users taken on the basis of the financial statements. Any material item shall be presented separately.

5.5.3 Presentation Requirements

IAS No. 1 also specifies a number of principles that guide the presentation of financial statements. These principles include the following:

▶ *Aggregation.* Each material class of similar items is presented separately. Dissimilar items are presented separately unless they are immaterial.

▶ *No offsetting.* Assets and liabilities, and income and expenses, are not offset unless required or permitted by an IFRS.

▶ *Classified balance sheet.* The balance sheet should distinguish between current and noncurrent assets, and between current and noncurrent liabilities unless a presentation based on liquidity provides more relevant and reliable information (e.g., in the case of a bank or similar financial institution).

▶ *Minimum information on the face of the financial statements.* IAS No. 1 specifies the minimum line item disclosures on the face of, or in the notes to, the balance sheet, the income statement, and the statement of changes in equity. For example, companies are specifically required to disclose the amount of their plant, property, and equipment as a line item on the face of the balance sheet. The specific requirements are listed in Exhibit 4.

---

[19] IAS No. 1, *Presentation of Financial Statements*, paragraph 15.

▶ *Minimum information in the notes* (or on face of financial statements). IAS No. 1 specifies disclosures about information to be presented in the financial statements. This information must be provided in a systematic manner and cross-referenced from the face of the financial statements to the notes. The required information is summarized in Exhibit 5.

▶ *Comparative information.* For all amounts reported in a financial statement, comparative information should be provided for the previous period unless another standard requires or permits otherwise. Such comparative information allows users to better understand reported amounts.

EXHIBIT 4	IAS No. 1: Minimum Required Line Items in Financial Statements

On the face of the statement of financial position (balance sheet)

▶ Plant, property, and equipment
▶ Investment property
▶ Intangible assets
▶ Financial assets (not listed in other line items)
▶ Investments accounted for using the equity method
▶ Biological assets
▶ Inventories
▶ Trade and other receivables
▶ Cash and cash equivalents
▶ Total of assets classified as held for sale
▶ Trade and other payables
▶ Provisions
▶ Financial liabilities (not listed in other line items)
▶ Liabilities and assets for current tax
▶ Deferred tax liabilities and deferred tax assets
▶ Liabilities included in disposal groups classified as held for sale
▶ Non-controlling interests, presented within equity
▶ Issued capital and reserves attributable to owners of the parent

On the face of the comprehensive income statement[20]

▶ Revenue
▶ Finance costs
▶ Share of the profit or loss of associates and joint ventures accounted for using the equity method
▶ Tax expense
▶ Total after-tax profit or loss related to discontinued operations
▶ Profit or loss
▶ Each component of other comprehensive income classified by nature

(Exhibit continued on next page . . .)

---

[20] IAS 1 allows an entity to present all items of income and expense recognised in a period in either a single statement of comprehensive income or in two statements: an income statement and a statement of comprehensive income. With a single statement of comprehensive income, all items listed would appear in the single statement. With two statements, the item's revenue through profit or loss would appear in the income statement. The statement of comprehensive income begins with profit or loss and then displays components of other comprehensive income and total comprehensive income.

EXHIBIT 4	(continued)

	▶ Share of the other comprehensive income of associates and joint ventures accounted for using the equity method
	▶ Total comprehensive income
	▶ Profit or loss attributable to non-controlling interests and to owners of the parent
	▶ Total comprehensive income attributable to non-controlling interests and owners of the parent
On the face of the statement of changes in equity	▶ Total comprehensive income for the period attributable to non-controlling interests, and to owners of the parent
	▶ For each component of equity, the effects of changes in accounting policies and corrections of errors
	▶ For each component of equity, a reconciliation between the beginning and ending carrying amounts, separately disclosing changes resulting from profit or loss, each item of other comprehensive income, and transactions with owners in their capacity as owners

EXHIBIT 5	Summary of IFRS Required Disclosures in the Notes to the Financial Statements

Disclosure of accounting policies	▶ Measurement bases used in preparing financial statements
	▶ The other accounting policies used that are relevant to an understanding of the financial statements
	▶ Judgments made in applying accounting policies that have the most significant effect on the amounts recognized in the financial statements
Estimation uncertainty	▶ Key assumptions about the future and other key sources of estimation uncertainty that have a significant risk of causing material adjustment to the carrying amount of assets and liabilities within the next year
Other disclosures	▶ Description of the entity, including its domicile, legal form, country of incorporation, and registered office or business address
	▶ Nature of operations and its principal activities
	▶ Name of parent and ultimate parent

COMPARISON OF IFRS WITH ALTERNATIVE REPORTING SYSTEMS

6

The recent adoption of IFRS as the required financial reporting standard by the EU and other countries has advanced the goal of global convergence. Nevertheless, there are still significant differences in financial reporting in the global capital markets. Arguably, the most critical are the differences that exist between IFRS and U.S. GAAP. After the EU adoption of IFRS in 2005, these two reporting standards account for a significant number of the world's listed companies.

This section will discuss the differences between IFRS and U.S. GAAP that affect the framework and general financial reporting requirements. The readings on individual financial statements will review in more detail the differences in these financial reporting standards as they apply to specific financial statements. The reading on the convergence of international standards also makes relevant points.

6.1 U.S. GAAP

The FASB or its predecessor organizations have been issuing financial reporting standards in the United States since the 1930s. Currently, the FASB is the primary body setting these standards. There are, however, several other organizations that have issued guidance in the past. These include the American Institute of Certified Public Accountants' (AICPA) Accounting Standards Executive Committee (AcSEC), the Emerging Issues Task Force (EITF), and the FASB staff. Since the introduction of the Sarbanes–Oxley Act, changes have been made that essentially limit these other bodies from providing any new guidance unless it is directly under the direction of the FASB. The EITF has come under the more formal oversight of the FASB, and the AICPA AcSEC will no longer issue new standards applicable to public companies.

6.1.1 U.S. GAAP Authoritative Guidance

Together, the standards and interpretations issued by these bodies comprise U.S. GAAP. A "GAAP hierarchy" was established to provide guidance as to the order of authority of the various sources of accounting pronouncements. In other words, the GAAP hierarchy defines the sources of accounting principles and a framework for selecting the right principle. This hierarchy is especially important for new transactions and those policies where there is no explicit authoritative guidance. The GAAP hierarchy was originally established in the auditing area rather than the accounting area, but it is currently being re-examined by the FASB. The FASB is also working on a project to bring all authoritative guidance from these various sources into one set of authoritative literature called the "Codification." In 2009, the Financial Accounting Standards Board (FASB) released the FASB Accounting Standards Codification™. The Codification is the single source of authoritative nongovernmental U.S. generally accepted accounting principles (U.S. GAAP) effective for periods ending after 15 September 2009. The Codification supersedes all previous U.S. GAAP standards. We have attempted to update the readings to reference or cross-reference the Codification as appropriate.

As the previous standards had been developed over many years and by many bodies, they were more a patchwork than a cohesive framework. The Codification structure is different than that of previous accounting standards. This represents a change from a standards-based model to a topically based model.

6.1.2 Role of the SEC in U.S. GAAP

U.S. GAAP, as established by the standard-setting bodies noted above, is officially recognized as authoritative by the SEC (Financial Reporting Release No. 1, Section 101, and reaffirmed in the April 2003 Policy Statement). However, the SEC retains the authority to establish standards. Although it has rarely overruled the FASB, the SEC does issue Staff Accounting Bulletins (SABs). SABs reflect the SEC's views regarding accounting-related disclosure practices and can be found on the SEC website. The FASB Accounting Standards Codification includes relevant portions of authoritative content issued by the SEC and selected staff interpretations and administrative guidance. However, the Codification does not replace or affect guidance issued by the SEC or its staff for public companies in their filings with the SEC.

6.1.3 Convergence of the U.S. GAAP and IASB Framework

A joint IASB–FASB project was begun in October 2004 to develop a common conceptual framework. The project, which currently has a five-year timetable, is divided into seven phases. The initial focus is on achieving the convergence of the frameworks and improving particular aspects of the framework dealing with objectives, qualitative characteristics, elements recognition, and measurement. A December 2004 discussion paper presented the broad differences between the two frameworks. These differences are summarized in Exhibit 6. Additionally, under U.S. GAAP, there is not a single standard like IAS No. 1 that specifies the presentation of financial statements; instead, standards for presentation of financial statements are dispersed in many different FASB pronouncements and SEC regulations.[21]

EXHIBIT 6	Summary of Differences between IFRS and U.S. GAAP Frameworks
	U.S. GAAP (FASB) Framework
Purpose of the framework	The FASB framework is similar to the IASB framework in its purpose to assist in developing and revising standards, but it resides at a lower level in the hierarchy—a very important difference. Under IFRS, management is expressly required to consider the framework if there is no standard or interpretation for that issue. The FASB framework does not have a similar provision.
Objectives of financial statements	There is general agreement on the objectives of financial statements: Both frameworks have a broad focus to provide relevant information to a wide range of users. The principal difference is that the U.S. GAAP framework provides separate objectives for business entities versus nonbusiness entities rather than one objective as in the IASB framework.
Underlying assumptions	Although the U.S. GAAP framework recognizes the importance of the accrual and going concern assumptions, these are not given as much prominence as in the IASB framework. In particular, the going concern assumption is not well developed in the FASB framework.
Qualitative characteristics	The U.S. GAAP framework identifies the same qualitative characteristics but also establishes a hierarchy of those characteristics. Relevance and reliability are considered primary qualities, whereas comparability is deemed to be a secondary quality under the FASB framework. The fourth qualitative characteristic, understandability, is treated as a user-specific quality in the U.S. GAAP framework and is seen as a link between the characteristics of individual users and decision-specific qualities of information. The FASB framework indicates that it cannot base its decisions on the specific circumstances of individual users.
Constraints	There is similar discussion of the constraints in both frameworks.

(Exhibit continued on next page . . .)

---

[21] FASB ASC Topics 205 to 280 cover presentation of financial statements. These range from FASB ASC Topic 205 [Presentation of Financial Statements] to FASB ASC Topic 280 [Segment Reporting].

| EXHIBIT 6 | (continued) |

Financial statement elements (definition, recognition, and measurement)

▶ *Performance elements.* The FASB framework includes three elements relating to financial performance in addition to revenue and expenses: gains, losses, and comprehensive income. Comprehensive income is a more encompassing concept than net income, as it includes all changes in equity during a period except those resulting from investments by and distributions to owners.

▶ *Financial position elements.* The FASB framework defines an asset as "a future economic benefit" rather than the "resource" from which future economic benefits are expected to flow to the entity as in the IASB framework. It also includes the term "probable" to define the assets and liabilities elements. As discussed below, the term "probable" is part of the IASB framework recognition criteria. Additionally, the frameworks have different meanings of probable.

▶ *Recognition of elements.* The FASB framework does not discuss the term "probable" in its recognition criteria, whereas the IASB framework requires that it is probable that any future economic benefit flow to/from the entity. The FASB framework also has a separate recognition criterion of relevance.

▶ *Measurement of elements.* Measurement attributes (historical cost, current cost, settlement value, current market value, and present value) are broadly consistent, and both frameworks lack fully developed measurement concepts. Furthermore, the FASB framework prohibits revaluations except for certain categories of financial instruments, which have to be carried at fair value.

6.2 Implications of Other Reporting Systems

As more countries adopt IFRS, the need to examine other financial reporting systems will be minimized. Additionally, the IASB and FASB are considering frameworks from other jurisdictions in developing their joint framework. Nevertheless, analysts are likely to encounter financial statements that are prepared on a basis other than IFRS. Although the number and relevance of different local GAAP reporting systems are likely to decline, industry-specific financial reports—such as those required for banking or insurance companies—will continue to exist.

6.3 Reconciliation of Financials Prepared According to Different Standards

When analyzing financial statements created under different frameworks, reconciliation schedules and disclosures regarding the significant differences between the reporting bases are usually available. In 2008, the Securities and Exchange Commission eliminated the U.S. GAAP reconciliation requirement for foreign private issuers that prepare their financial statements in accordance with IFRS as issued by the IASB. The EU is currently considering requiring reconciliations for companies trading on European markets that do not prepare financial statements using IFRS. Such reconciliations can reveal additional information related to the more judgmental components of the financial statements and can have important implications for security valuation.

A first look at the disclosure related to any such differences can sometimes be daunting, particularly if the reconciliation is lengthy. For example, Syngenta's 2005 U.S. SEC Form 20-F filing discusses these differences in Note 33, "Significant Differences between IFRS and United States Generally Accepted Accounting Principles." This note is longer than 15 pages!

Given the length of reconciliation disclosure, a systematic method to quickly digest the information can be helpful. A good starting point is the chart that provides the numerical reconciliation of net income and shareholders' equity (see Exhibit 7). These reconciliations can be reviewed to identify the significant items; large amounts should be examined in more detail. The Syngenta disclosure indicates that the company's 2005 net income based on U.S. GAAP was $556 million, compared with the $622 million of net income reported under IFRS. The reconciliation indicates that most significant differences relate to accounting for acquisitions (purchase accounting adjustments include a $7 million decrease and an $80 million decrease), accounting for pension provisions ($15 million), and accounting for various tax-related items. In some instances, further analysis would be undertaken to determine the implications of each significant difference based on disclosures in the indicated notes.

EXHIBIT 7	Reconciliation of GAAP Income—Syngenta (US$ in Millions)		
	2005	**2004**	**2003 (adjusted)**
Net income (loss) reported under IFRS attributable to Syngenta AG shareholders	622	460	248
U.S. GAAP adjustments:			
Purchase accounting: Zaneca agrochemicals business	(7)	62	43
Purchase accounting: other acquisitions	(80)	(62)	(67)
Restructuring charges	(9)	47	32
Pension provisions (including post-retirement benefits)	(15)	43	2
Deferred taxes on stock-based compensation	3	(3)	2
Deferred taxes on unrealized profit in inventory	(33)	(61)	36
Impairment losses	(7)	(1)	
Other items	28	(17)	(4)
Valuation allowance against deferred tax assets	26	(34)	–
Tax on undistributed earnings of subsidiaries	1	(27)	–
Deferred tax effect of U.S. GAAP adjustments	27	(55)	(42)
Net income/(loss) reported under U.S. GAAP	556	352	250

Source: 2005 U.S. SEC Form 20-F.

7   EFFECTIVE FINANCIAL REPORTING

A discussion of the characteristics of an effective framework and the barriers to the creation of such a framework offer additional perspective on the financial reporting frameworks reviewed above.

7.1 Characteristics of an Effective Financial Reporting Framework

Any effective financial reporting system needs to be a coherent one (i.e., a framework in which all the pieces fit together according to an underlying logic). Such frameworks have several characteristics:

► *Transparency.* A framework should enhance the transparency of a company's financial statements. Transparency means that users should be able to see the underlying economics of the business reflected clearly in the company's financial statements. Full disclosure and fair presentation create transparency.

► *Comprehensiveness.* To be comprehensive, a framework should encompass the full spectrum of transactions that have financial consequences. This spectrum includes not only transactions currently occurring but also new types of transactions as they are developed. So, an effective financial reporting framework is based on principles that are universal enough to provide guidance for recording both existing and newly developed transactions.

► *Consistency.* An effective framework should ensure reasonable consistency across companies and time periods. In other words, similar transactions should be measured and presented in a similar manner regardless of industry, company size, geography, or other characteristics. Balanced against this need for consistency, however, is the need for sufficient flexibility to allow companies sufficient discretion to report results in accordance with underlying economic activity.

7.2 Barriers to a Single Coherent Framework

Although effective frameworks all share the characteristics of transparency, comprehensiveness, and consistency, there are some conflicts that create inherent limitations in any financial reporting standards framework. Specifically, it is difficult to completely satisfy all these characteristics concurrently, so any framework represents an attempt to balance the relative importance of these characteristics. Three areas of conflict include valuation, standard-setting approach, and measurement.

► *Valuation.* As discussed, various bases for measuring the value of assets and liabilities exist, such as historical cost, current cost, realizable value, and present value. Historical cost valuation, under which an asset's value is its initial cost, requires minimal judgment. In contrast, other valuation approaches require considerable judgment. Over time, both the IASB and FASB have recognized that it may be more appropriate to measure certain elements of financial statements using some fair value method in spite of the judgment required.[22] Fair value is the amount at which an asset could

---

[22] In 2006, the FASB issued SFAS 157 Fair Value Measurement. Effective after 15 November 2007, the standard provided a single definition of fair value, a framework for measuring fair value, and requires expanded disclosures about fair value. The content of this standard and any updates are now contained in FASB ASC Topic 820 [Fair Value Measurement and Disclosure].

be exchanged, or a liability settled, between knowledgeable willing parties in an arm's-length transaction; clearly, in many cases, determining fair value requires considerable judgment. Fair value may be more relevant, whereas historical cost may be more reliable.

▶ *Standard-setting approach.* Financial reporting standards can be established based on 1) principles, 2) rules, or 3) a combination of principles and rules (sometimes referred to as "objectives oriented"). A principles-based approach provides a broad financial reporting framework with little specific guidance on how to report a particular element or transaction. Such principles-based approaches require the preparers of financial reports and auditors to exercise considerable judgment in financial reporting. In contrast, a rules-based approach establishes specific rules for each element or transaction. Rules-based approaches are characterized by a list of yes-or-no rules, specific numerical tests for classifying certain transactions (known as "bright-line tests"), exceptions, and alternative treatments. The third alternative, an objectives-oriented approach, combines the other two approaches by including both a framework of principles and appropriate levels of implementation guidance.

IFRS has been referred to as a "principles-based approach." The FASB, which has been criticized for having a rules-based approach in the past, has explicitly stated that it is moving to adopt a more objectives-oriented approach to standard setting. There is a joint project underway to develop a common conceptual framework, and this is likely to be more objectives oriented.

▶ *Measurement.* The balance sheet presents elements at a point in time, whereas the income statement reflects changes during a period of time. Because these statements are related, standards regarding one of the statements have an effect on the other statement. Financial reporting standards can be established taking an "asset/liability" approach, which gives preference to proper valuation of the balance sheet, or a "revenue/expense" approach that focuses more on the income statement. This conflict can result in one statement being reported in a theoretically sound manner, but the other statement reflecting less relevant information. In recent years, standard setters have predominantly used an asset/liability approach.

EXAMPLE 6

Conflicts between Measurement Approaches

Prime Retailers (PR), a U.S.-based distributor of men's shirts, has a policy of marking its merchandise up by $5 per unit. At the beginning of 2006, PR had 10,000 units of inventory on hand, which cost $15 per unit. During 2006, PR purchased 100,000 units of inventory at a cost of $22 per unit. Also during 2006, PR sold 100,000 units of inventory at $27 per unit. How shall PR reflect the cost of the inventory sold: $15 or $22?

In order to match current costs with current revenues, PR (which does not operate in an IFRS jurisdiction) may decide that it is appropriate to use a method of inventory costing that assumes that the most recently purchased inventory is sold first. So, the assumption is that the

100,000 units of sales had a cost of $22. A partial income statement for PR would be:

Sales	$2,700,000
Cost of sales	$2,200,000
Gross profit	$500,000

The **gross profit** reflected in this manner reflects the current cost of goods matched with the current level of revenues.

But PR still has 10,000 units of inventory on hand. The assumption must be that the 10,000 remaining units had a cost of $15 per unit. Therefore, the value of the inventory reflected on the balance sheet would be $150,000.

Although the income statement reflects current costs, the remaining inventory on the balance sheet does not reflect current information. The inventory is reflected at the older cost of $15 per unit. An analyst would likely find this older cost less relevant than the current cost of that inventory.

8 MONITORING DEVELOPMENTS IN FINANCIAL REPORTING STANDARDS

In studying financial reporting and financial statement analysis in general, the analyst needs to be aware that reporting standards are evolving rapidly. Analysts need to monitor ongoing developments in financial reporting and assess their implications for security analysis and valuation. The need to monitor developments in financial reporting standards does not mean that analysts should be accountants. An accountant monitors these developments from a preparer's perspective; an analyst needs to monitor from a user's perspective. More specifically, analysts need to know how these developments will affect financial reports.

Analysts can remain aware of developments in financial reporting standards by monitoring three areas: new products or transactions, actions of standard setters and other groups representing users of financial statements (such as CFA Institute), and company disclosures regarding critical accounting policies and estimates.

8.1 New Products or Types of Transactions

New products and new types of transactions can have unusual or unique elements to them such that no explicit guidance in the financial reporting standards exists. New products or transactions typically arise from economic events, such as new businesses (e.g., the internet), or from a newly developed financial instrument or financial structure. Financial instruments, exchange traded or not, are typically designed to enhance a company's business or to mitigate inherent risks. However, at times, financial instruments or structured transactions have been developed primarily for purposes of financial report "window dressing."

Although companies might discuss new products and transactions in their financial reports, the analyst can also monitor business journals and the capital markets to identify such items. Additionally, when one company in an industry develops a new product or transaction, other companies in the industry often do the same. Once new products, financial instruments, or structured transactions are identified, it is helpful to gain an understanding of the business purpose. If necessary, an analyst can obtain further information from a company's management, which should be able to describe the economic purpose, the financial statement reporting, significant estimates, judgments applied in determining the reporting, and future cash flow implications for these items. The financial reporting framework presented here is useful in evaluating the potential effect on financial statements even though a standard may not have been issued as to how to report a particular transaction.

8.2 Evolving Standards and the Role of CFA Institute

Although the actions of standard setters and regulators are unlikely to be helpful in identifying new products and transactions given the lag between new product development and regulatory action, monitoring the actions of these authorities is, nonetheless, important for another reason: Changes in regulations can affect companies' financial reports and, thus, valuations. This is particularly true if the financial reporting standards change to require more explicit identification of matters affecting asset/liability valuation or financial performance. For example, a recent regulatory change requires companies to report the value of employee stock options as an expense in the income statement. Prior to the required expensing, an analyst could assess the impact of stock options on a company's performance and the dilutive effect to shareholders by reviewing information disclosed in the notes to the financial statements. To the extent that some market participants do not examine financial statement details and thus ignore this expense when valuing a company's securities, more explicit identification could affect the value of the company's securities.

The IASB and FASB have numerous major projects underway that will most likely result in new standards. It is important to keep up to date on these evolving standards. The IASB (www.iasb.org) and FASB (www.fasb.org) provide a great deal of information on their websites regarding new standards and proposals for future changes in standards. In addition, the IASB and FASB seek input from the financial analyst community—those who regularly use financial statements in making investment and credit decisions. When a new standard is proposed, an exposure draft is made available and users of financial statements can draft comment letters and position papers for submission to the IASB and FASB in order to evaluate the proposal.

CFA Institute is active through its CFA Centre for Financial Market Integrity in advocating improvements to financial reporting. Volunteer members of CFA Institute serve on several liaison committees that meet regularly to make recommendations to the IASB and FASB on proposed standards and to draft comment letters and position papers. You can view the CFA Centre's positions on financial reporting issues at www.cfainstitute.org/cfacentre/.

In October 2005, the CFA Centre issued a position paper titled *A Comprehensive Business Reporting Model: Financial Reporting for Investors*, which provides a suggested model for significantly improving financial reporting. The position paper states:

> Corporate financial statements and their related disclosures are critical to sound investment decision making. The well being of the world's financial markets, and of the millions of investors who entrust their financial present and future to those markets, depends directly on the quality of the information financial statements and disclosures provide. Consequently, the quality of the information drives global financial markets. The quality, in turn, depends directly on the quality of the

principles and standards by which managers recognize and measure the economic activities and events affecting their companies' operations. To succeed, a partnership is needed among standard setters, common shareowners, and other investors to bring full transparency and the highest integrity to the standards and the processes by which those standards are developed. CFA Institute and the CFA Centre for Financial Market Integrity are committed to join in a partnership to improve financial market integrity in the 21st century.[23]

Among other principles, the proposed model stresses the importance of information regarding the current fair value of assets and liabilities, of neutrality in financial reporting, and of providing detailed information on cash flows to investors through the choice of the so-called direct format for the statement of cash flows.[24]

In summary, analysts can improve their investment decision making by keeping current on financial reporting standards, and various web-based sources provide the means to do so. In addition, analysts can contribute to improving financial reporting by sharing their users' perspective with standard-setting bodies, which typically invite comments concerning proposed changes.

8.3 Company Disclosures

A good source for obtaining information regarding the effect of financial reporting standards on a company's financial statements is typically the company itself. This information is provided in the footnotes to the financial statements and accompanying discussion.

8.3.1 Disclosures Relating to Critical and Significant Accounting Policies

As noted earlier, financial reporting standards need to restrict alternatives but retain flexibility in allowing enterprises to match their accounting methods with underlying economics. As a result, companies choose among alternative accounting policies (e.g., depreciation methods) and use estimates (e.g., depreciable lives of assets). Under both IFRS and U.S. GAAP, companies are required to disclose their accounting policies and estimates in the footnotes to the financial statements. Public companies must discuss their accounting policies and estimates in management's discussion and analysis (MD&A). This disclosure indicates the policies that management deems most important. Although many of the policies are discussed in both the MD&A and the footnotes to the financial statements, there is typically a distinction between the two discussions. The MD&A disclosure relates to those policies that require significant judgments and estimates, whereas the footnote discusses all accounting policies, irrespective of whether judgment was required. Each disclosure has value.

In analyzing financial reporting disclosures, the following questions should be addressed:

► What policies have been discussed?

► Do these policies appear to cover all of the significant balances on the financial statements?

---

[23] *A Comprehensive Business Reporting Model: Financial Reporting for Investors*, CFA Institute Centre for Financial Market Integrity, 24 October 2005, p. 3.

[24] See the reading on the statement of cash flows for further information on the direct format.

▶ Which policies are identified as requiring significant estimates?

▶ Have there been any changes in these disclosures from one year to the next?

Example 7 summarizes the accounting policies discussed in Disney's 2004 annual report MD&A and Note 2, "Summary of Significant Accounting Policy."

Two items usually requiring significant judgment include revenue recognition and timing of reporting the related expenses. As a result, the types of judgments and estimates in revenue recognition and expense reporting are usually discussed in both the MD&A and in the footnotes.

8.3.2 Disclosures Regarding the Impact of Recently Issued Accounting Standards

Internationally, public companies face disclosure requirements related to recently issued accounting standards. In the United States, the SEC (in its SABs) also requires public companies to provide information regarding the likely future impact of recently issued accounting standards. Under IFRS, IAS No. 8

EXAMPLE 7

List of Significant Accounting Policy Disclosures: Disney MD&A Notes

▶ Film and television revenue and costs

▶ Revenue recognition

▶ Pension and post-retirement benefit plan actuarial assumptions

▶ Goodwill, intangible assets, long-lived assets, and investments

▶ Contingencies and litigation

▶ Income tax audit

▶ Principles of consolidation

▶ Accounting changes

▶ Use of estimates

▶ Advertising expenses

▶ Cash and cash equivalents

▶ Investments

▶ Translation policy

▶ Inventories

▶ Film and television costs

▶ Capitalized software costs

▶ Parks, resorts, and other property

▶ Goodwill and other intangible assets

▶ Risk management contracts

▶ Earnings per share

▶ Stock options

▶ Reclassifications

---

similarly requires discussion about pending implementations of new standards and the known or estimable information relevant to assessing the impact of the new standards. These disclosures can alert an analyst to significant changes in reported financial statement amounts that could affect security valuation. Although each discussion will be different, the conclusions that a company can reach about a new standard include:

1. the standard does not apply;
2. the standard will have no material impact;
3. management is still evaluating the impact; or
4. the impact of adoption is discussed.

Exhibit 8 provides some of the disclosures provided by Syngenta in its 2004 Form 20-F relating to recently issued accounting standards. In the exhibit, "IFRIC" refers to the International Financial Reporting Interpretations Committee—formerly known as the "Standing Interpretations Committee" or "SIC"—which is responsible for interpreting IAS and IFRS.

Clearly, disclosures indicating the expected impact provide the most meaningful information. In addition, disclosures indicating that the standard does not apply or will not have a material effect are also helpful. However, disclosures indicating that management is still evaluating the impact of a new standard create some uncertainty about whether the change might materially affect the company.

EXHIBIT 8	Impact of Recently Issued Accounting Standards: Syngenta
Standard does not apply	IFRIC amendment to SIC-12, "Special Purpose Entities," was published in October 2004 and requires employee share trusts and similar entities established under share participation plans to be consolidated with effect from 1 January 2005. *Syngenta operates its employee share participation plans without using entities of this type, and the amendment will have no effect on the consolidated financial statements.*
No material impact	Amendment to IAS No. 39, "Transition and Initial Recognition of Financial Assets and Financial Liabilities," was issued in December 2004. It will be effective from Syngenta as from 1 January 2005. The amendment changes the transitional requirements on adoption of IAS No. 39 (revised December 2003). *Syngenta does not expect the amendment to have a material effect on its consolidated financial statements.*
Evaluating the impact	IFRIC 4, "Determining Whether an Arrangement Contains a Lease," was issued in December 2004 and requires contracts for the supply of goods or services that depend upon the use of a specific asset to be treated in certain circumstances as containing a lease of that asset in addition to a supply contract. IFRIC 4 will be mandatory for Syngenta with effect from 1 January 2006. *During 2005, Syngenta will assess the impact on its consolidated financial statements from adopting IFRIC 4.*
Impact described	As stated in Note 2 above, Syngenta will apply IFRS 3, "Business Combinations," and the related revisions to IAS No. 36 and IAS No. 38, to all previous business combinations with effect from 1 January 2005. *Goodwill amortization expense will no longer be recorded. Goodwill amortization expense on these acquisitions in 2004 was US$56 million. The related tax credit was US$2 million because in most cases the amortization is not tax deductible. Syngenta will test goodwill for impairment annually.*

Note: Emphasis added.

SUMMARY

An awareness of the reporting framework underlying financial reports can assist in security valuation and other financial analysis. The framework describes the objectives of financial reporting, desirable characteristics for financial reports, the elements of financial reports, and the underlying assumptions and constraints of financial reporting. An understanding of the framework, broader than knowledge of a particular set of rules, offers an analyst a basis from which to infer the proper financial reporting, and thus security valuation implications, of *any* financial statement element or transaction.

We have discussed how financial reporting systems are developed, the conceptual objectives of financial reporting standards, the parties involved in standard-setting processes, and how financial reporting standards are converging into one global set of standards. A summary of the key points for each section is noted below:

- ▶ *The objective of financial reporting*:
    - ▶ The objective of financial statements is to provide information about the financial position, performance, and changes in financial position of an entity; this information should be useful to a wide range of users for the purpose of making economic decisions.[25]
    - ▶ Financial reporting requires policy choices and estimates. These choices and estimates require judgment, which can vary from one preparer to the next. Accordingly, standards are needed to attempt to ensure some type of consistency in these judgments.
- ▶ *Financial reporting standard-setting bodies and regulatory authorities.* Private sector standard-setting bodies and regulatory authorities play significant but different roles in the standard-setting process. In general, standard-setting bodies make the rules, and regulatory authorities enforce the rules. However, regulators typically retain legal authority to establish financial reporting standards in their jurisdiction.
- ▶ *Convergence of global financial reporting standards.* The IASB and FASB, along with other standard setters, are working to achieve convergence of financial reporting standards. Listed companies in many countries are adopting IFRS. Barriers to full convergence still exist.
- ▶ *The IFRS Framework.* The IFRS *Framework* sets forth the concepts that underlie the preparation and presentation of financial statements for external users, provides further guidance on the elements from which financial statements are constructed, and discusses concepts of capital and capital maintenance.
    - ▶ The objective of fair presentation of useful information is the center of the *Framework*. The qualitative characteristics of useful information include understandability, relevance, reliability, and comparability.
    - ▶ The IFRS *Framework* identifies the following elements of financial statements: assets, liabilities, equity, income, expense, and capital maintenance adjustments.

---

[25] *Framework for the Preparation and Presentation of Financial Statements*, IASC, 1989, adopted by IASB 2001, paragraph 12.

▶ The *Framework* is constructed based on the underlying assumptions of accrual basis and going concern but acknowledges three inherent constraints: timeliness, benefit versus cost, and balance between qualitative characteristics.

▶ *IFRS financial statements.* IAS No. 1 prescribes that a complete set of financial statements includes a balance sheet, an income statement, a statement of changes in equity, a statement of cash flows, and notes. The notes include a summary of significant accounting policies and other explanatory information.

  ▶ Financial statements need to adhere to the fundamental principles of fair presentation, going concern, accrual basis, consistency, and materiality.

  ▶ Financial statements must also satisfy the presentation requirements of appropriate aggregation, no offsetting, and a classified balance sheet. Statements must provide the required minimum information on the face of the financial statements and note disclosures.

▶ *Comparison of IFRS with alternative reporting systems.* A significant number of the world's listed companies report under either IFRS or U.S. GAAP. Although these standards are moving toward convergence, there are still significant differences in the framework and individual standards. Frequently, companies provide reconciliations and disclosures regarding the significant differences between reporting bases. These reconciliations can be reviewed to identify significant items that could affect security valuation.

▶ *Characteristics of a coherent financial reporting framework.* Effective frameworks share three characteristics: transparency, comprehensiveness, and consistency. Effective standards can, however, have conflicting approaches on valuation, the bases for standard setting (principle or rules based), and resolution of conflicts between balance sheet and income statement focus.

▶ *Monitoring developments.* Analysts can remain aware of ongoing developments in financial reporting by monitoring three areas: new products or transactions, standard setters' and regulators' actions, and company disclosures regarding critical accounting policies and estimates.

PRACTICE PROBLEMS FOR READING 31

1. Which of the following is *not* an objective of financial statements as expressed by the International Accounting Standards Board?

   A. To provide information about the performance of an entity.

   B. To provide information about the financial position of an entity.

   C. To provide information about the users of an entity's financial statements.

2. International accounting standards are currently developed by which entity?

   A. The Financial Services Authority.

   B. The International Accounting Standards Board.

   C. The International Accounting Standards Committee.

3. U.S. Financial Accounting Standards are currently developed by which entity?

   A. The United States Congress.

   B. The Financial Services Authority.

   C. The Financial Accounting Standards Board.

4. The SEC requires which of the following be issued to shareholders before a shareholder meeting?

   A. Form 10-K.

   B. Statement of cash flow.

   C. Proxy statement.

5. According to the *Framework for the Preparation and Presentation of Financial Statements*, which of the following is a qualitative characteristic of information in financial statements?

   A. Accuracy.

   B. Timeliness.

   C. Comparability.

6. Which of the following is *not* a constraint on the financial statements according to the IFRS *Framework*?

   A. Timeliness.

   B. Understandability.

   C. Benefit versus cost.

7. The assumption that an entity will continue to operate for the foreseeable future is called:

   A. accrual basis.

   B. comparability.

   C. going concern.

8. The assumption that the effects of transactions and other events are recognized when they occur, not necessarily when cash movements occur, is called:

   A. accrual basis.

   B. going concern.

   C. relevance.

9. Neutrality of information in the financial statements *most closely* contributes to which qualitative characteristic?

   A. Relevance.

   B. Reliability

   C. Comparability.

10. Does fair presentation entail full disclosure and transparency?

	Full Disclosure	Transparency
A.	No	Yes
B.	Yes	No
C.	Yes	Yes

11. Valuing assets at the amount of cash or equivalents paid or the fair value of the consideration given to acquire them at the time of acquisition *most closely* describes which measurement of financial statement elements?

    A. Current cost.

    B. Realizable cost.

    C. Historical cost.

12. The valuation technique under which assets are recorded at the amount that would be received in an orderly disposal is:

    A. current cost.

    B. present value.

    C. realizable value.

13. Which of the following is *not* a required financial statement according to IAS No. 1?

    A. Income statement.

    B. Statement of changes in equity.

    C. Statement of changes in income.

14. Which of the following elements of financial statements is *most closely* related to measurement of performance?

    A. Assets.

    B. Expenses.

    C. Liabilities.

15. Which of the following elements of financial statements is *most closely* related to measurement of financial position?

    A. Equity.

    B. Income.

    C. Expenses.

16. Which of the following is *not* a characteristic of a coherent financial reporting framework?

   A. Timeliness.

   B. Consistency.

   C. Transparency.

17. In the past, the Financial Accounting Standards Board has been criticized as having:

   A. a rules-based approach to standards.

   B. a principles-based approach to standards.

   C. an objectives-oriented approach to standards.

18. Which of the following types of discussions regarding new accounting standards in management's discussion would provide the *most* meaningful information to an analyst?

   A. The standard does not apply.

   B. The impact of adoption is discussed.

   C. The standard will have no material impact.

SOLUTIONS FOR READING 31

1. **C is correct.** Providing information about users is not an objective of financial statements. The objectives are to provide information about the entity's financial position, performance, and changes in financial position.

2. **B is correct.** The IASB is currently charged with developing International Accounting Standards. The IASC was the predecessor organization to the IASB.

3. **C is correct.** U.S. Financial Accounting Standards are developed by the FASB.

4. **C is correct.** The SEC requires that shareholders of a company receive a proxy statement prior to a shareholder meeting. Such meetings are held at least once a year, but any special meetings would also require a proxy.

5. **C is correct.** The qualitative characteristics of financial statements according to the IFRS *Framework* are understandability, relevance, reliability, and comparability.

6. **B is correct.** The *Framework* recognizes the following constraints on providing relevant, reliable information: timeliness, benefit versus cost, and balancing of the qualitative characteristics.

7. **C is correct.** The IFRS *Framework* identifies two important underlying assumptions of financial statements: accrual basis and going concern. Going concern is the assumption that the entity will continue to operate for the foreseeable future. Enterprises with the intent to liquidate or materially curtail operations would require different information for a fair presentation.

8. **A is correct.** The IFRS *Framework* identifies two important underlying assumptions of financial statements: accrual basis and going concern. Accrual basis reflects the effects of transactions and other events being recognized when they occur, not necessarily when cash movements occur. These effects are recorded and reported in the financial statements of the periods to which they relate.

9. **B is correct.** The qualitative characteristic of reliability is contributed to by faithful representation, substance over form, neutrality, prudence, and completeness.

10. **C is correct.** Fair presentation involves both full disclosure and transparency.

11. **C is correct.** Historical cost is the consideration paid to acquire an asset.

12. **C is correct.** The amount that would be received in an orderly disposal is realizable value.

13. **C is correct.** Under IAS No. 1, a complete set of financial statements includes: a balance sheet, an income statement, a statement of changes in equity, a statement of cash flows, and notes comprising a summary of significant accounting policies and other explanatory notes.

14. **B is correct.** The elements of financial statements related to the measure of performance are income and expenses.

15. **A is correct.** The elements of financial statements related to the measurement of financial position are assets, liabilities, and equity.

16. A is correct. Timeliness is not a characteristic of a coherent financial reporting framework. Consistency, transparency, and comprehensiveness are characteristics of a coherent financial reporting framework.

17. A is correct. The FASB has been criticized in the past as having a rules-based approach; however, it has indicated that it is moving toward an objectives-oriented approach.

18. B is correct. A discussion of the impact would be the most meaningful, although A and C would also be useful.

STUDY SESSION 8
FINANCIAL REPORTING AND ANALYSIS:
The Income Statement, Balance Sheet, and Cash Flow Statement

Each reading in this study session focuses on one of the three major financial statements: the balance sheet, the income statement, and the statement of cash flows. For each financial statement, the chapter details its purpose, construction, pertinent ratios, and common-size analysis. Understanding these concepts allows a financial analyst to evaluate trends in performance for several measurement periods and to compare the performance of different companies during the same period(s). Additional analyst tools, such as the earnings per share calculation, are also described.

READING ASSIGNMENTS

Reading 32 Understanding the Income Statement
International Financial Statement Analysis, by Thomas R. Robinson, CFA, Jan Hendrik van Greuning, CFA, Elaine Henry, CFA, and Michael A. Broihahn, CFA

Reading 33 Understanding the Balance Sheet
International Financial Statement Analysis, by Thomas R. Robinson, CFA, Jan Hendrik van Greuning, CFA, Elaine Henry, CFA, and Michael A. Broihahn, CFA

Reading 34 Understanding the Cash Flow Statement
International Financial Statement Analysis, by Thomas R. Robinson, CFA, Jan Hendrik van Greuning, CFA, Elaine Henry, CFA, and Michael A. Broihahn, CFA

Reading 35 Financial Analysis Techniques
International Financial Statement Analysis, by Thomas R. Robinson, CFA, Jan Hendrik van Greuning, CFA, Elaine Henry, CFA, and Michael A. Broihahn, CFA

Note:
New rulings and/or pronouncements issued after the publication of the readings on financial reporting and analysis may cause some of the information in these readings to become dated. Candidates are expected to be familiar with the overall analytical framework contained in the study session readings, as well as the implications of alternative accounting methods for financial analysis and valuation, as provided in the assigned readings. Candidates are not responsible for changes that occur after the material was written.

UNDERSTANDING THE INCOME STATEMENT

by Thomas R. Robinson, CFA, Jan Hendrik van Greuning, CFA, Elaine Henry, CFA, and Michael A. Broihahn, CFA

LEARNING OUTCOMES

The candidate should be able to:	Mastery
a. describe the components of the income statement, and construct an income statement using the alternative presentation formats of that statement;	☐
b. explain the general principles of revenue recognition and accrual accounting, demonstrate specific revenue recognition applications (including accounting for long-term contracts, installment sales, barter transactions, and gross and net reporting of revenue), and discuss the implications of revenue recognition principles for financial analysis;	☐
c. discuss the general principles of expense recognition, such as the matching principle, specific expense recognition applications (including depreciation of long-term assets and inventory methods), and the implications of expense recognition principles for financial analysis;	☐
d. demonstrate the appropriate method of depreciating long-term assets, accounting for inventory, or amortizing intangibles, based on facts that might influence the decision;	☐
e. distinguish between the operating and nonoperating components of the income statement;	☐
f. discuss the financial reporting treatment and analysis of nonrecurring items (including discontinued operations, extraordinary items, and unusual or infrequent items) and changes in accounting standards;	☐
g. describe the components of earnings per share and calculate a company's earnings per share (both basic and diluted earnings per share) for both a simple and complex capital structure;	☐
h. differentiate between dilutive and antidilutive securities, and discuss the implications of each for the earnings per share calculation;	☐

Note:
New rulings and/or pronouncements issued after the publication of the readings on financial reporting and analysis may cause some of the information in these readings to become dated. Candidates are expected to be familiar with the overall analytical framework contained in the study session readings, as well as the implications of alternative accounting methods for financial analysis and valuation, as provided in the assigned readings. Candidates are not responsible for changes that occur after the material was written.

International Financial Statement Analysis, by Thomas R. Robinson, CFA, Jan Hendrik van Greuning, CFA, Elaine Henry, CFA, and Michael A. Broihahn, CFA. Copyright © 2007 by CFA Institute. Reprinted with permission.

i. describe and calculate comprehensive income;   ☐

j. state the accounting classification for items that are excluded from the income statement but affect owners' equity, and list the major types of items receiving that treatment.   ☐

1   INTRODUCTION

The income statement presents information on the financial results of a company's business activities over a period of time. The income statement communicates how much revenue the company generated during a period and what costs it incurred in connection with generating that revenue. The basic equation underlying the income statement is Revenue minus Expense equals Net income. The income statement is also called the "statement of operations" or "statement of earnings," or, sometimes, in business jargon, it is called the "P&L" for profit and loss.

Investment analysts intensely scrutinize companies' income statements. Equity analysts are interested in them because equity markets often reward relatively high- or low-earnings growth companies with above-average or below-average valuations, respectively. Fixed-income analysts examine the components of income statements, past and projected, for information on companies' abilities to make promised payments on their debt over the course of the business cycle. Corporate financial announcements frequently emphasize income statements more than the other financial statements.

This reading is organized as follows. Section 2 describes the components of the income statement and its format. Section 3 describes basic principles and selected applications related to the recognition of revenue, and Section 4 describes basic principles and selected applications related to the recognition of expenses. Section 5 covers nonrecurring items and nonoperating items. Section 6 explains the calculation of earnings per share. Section 7 introduces income statement analysis. Section 8 explains comprehensive income and its reporting. A summary of the key points and practice problems in the CFA Institute multiple-choice format complete the reading.

COMPONENTS AND FORMAT OF THE INCOME STATEMENT

## 2

On the top line of the income statement, companies typically report revenue. **Revenue** refers to amounts charged for the delivery of goods or services in the ordinary activities of a business. The term **net revenue** means that the revenue number is shown after adjustments (e.g., for estimated returns or for amounts unlikely to be collected). "Revenue" is often used synonymously with "sales."[1] Exhibits 1 and 2 show the income statements for Groupe Danone, a French food manufacturer, and Kraft Foods, a U.S. food manufacturer. For the year ended 31 December 2004, Danone reports €13.7 billion of net sales, whereas Kraft reports $32.2 billion of net revenues.[2]

EXHIBIT 1	Groupe Danone Consolidated Statements of Income (in Millions of Euros)		
	Year Ended 31 December		
	2002	**2003**	**2004**
Net sales	13,555	13,131	13,700
Cost of goods sold	(6,442)	(5,983)	(6,369)
Selling expenses	(4,170)	(4,176)	(4,294)
General and administrative expenses	(964)	(977)	(997)
Research and development expenses	(133)	(130)	(131)
Other (expense) income	(256)	(261)	(204)
Operating income	1,590	1,604	1,705
Nonrecurring items	458	(60)	(105)
Interest expense, net	(110)	(70)	(73)
Income before provision for income taxes and minority interests	1,938	1,474	1,527
Provision for income taxes	(490)	(488)	(457)
Income before minority interests	1,448	986	1,070
Minority interests	(182)	(184)	(189)
Share in net income of affiliates	17	37	(564)
Net income	1,283	839	317

---

[1] **Sales** is sometimes understood to refer to the sale of goods, whereas "revenue" can include the sale of goods or services; however, the terms are often used interchangeably. In some countries, turnover is used in place of "revenue."

[2] Following net income, the income statement will also present **earnings per share**, the amount of earnings per common share of the company. Earnings per share will be discussed in detail later in this reading, and the per-share display has been omitted from these exhibits to focus on the core income statement.

EXHIBIT 2	Kraft Foods and Subsidiaries Consolidated Statements of Earnings (in Millions of Dollars, except Per-Share Data)		

	Year Ended 31 December		
	2004	**2003**	**2002**
Net revenues	$32,168	$30,498	$29,248
Cost of sales	20,281	18,531	17,463
Gross profit	11,887	11,967	11,785
Marketing, administration, and research costs	6,658	6,136	5,644
Integration costs and a loss on sale of a food factory		(13)	111
Asset impairment and exit costs	603	6	142
Losses (gains) on sales of businesses	3	(31)	(80)
Amortization of intangibles	11	9	7
Operating income	4,612	5,860	5,961
Interest and other debt expense, net	666	665	847
Earnings from continuing operations before income taxes and minority interest	3,946	5,195	5,114
Provision for income taxes	1,274	1,812	1,813
Earnings from continuing operations before minority interest	2,672	3,383	3,301
Minority interest in earnings from continuing operations, net	3	4	4
Earnings from continuing operations	2,669	3,379	3,297
(Loss) earnings from discontinued operations, net of income taxes	(4)	97	97
Net earnings	$2,665	$3,476	$3,394

Note that Groupe Danone lists the years in increasing order from left to right with the most recent year in the last column, whereas Kraft lists the years in decreasing order with the most recent year listed in the first column. These alternative formats are common. There are also differences in presentations of items, such as expenses. Groupe Danone shows expenses such as cost of goods sold in parenthesis to explicitly show that these are subtracted from revenue. Kraft, on the other hand, does not place cost of sales in parenthesis. Rather, it is implicitly understood that this is an expense and is subtracted in arriving at subtotals and totals. The analyst should always verify the order of years and presentation of negative items before analysis is begun because there is flexibility in how companies may present the income statement.

At the bottom of the income statement, companies report net income (or, essentially synonymously, net earnings or profit). For 2004, Danone reports €317 million of net income and Kraft reports $2,665 million of net earnings. Net income is often referred to as "the bottom line." The basis for this expression is that net income is the final—or bottom—line in an income statement. Because net income is often viewed as the single most relevant number to describe a company's performance over a period of time, the term "bottom line" sometimes is used in general business jargon to mean any final or most relevant result.

Net income also includes **gains** and **losses**, which are asset inflows and outflows, respectively, not directly related to the ordinary activities of the business. For example, if a company sells products, these are reported as revenue and the costs are listed separately. However, if a company sells surplus land that is not needed, the cost of the land is subtracted from the sales price and the net result is reported as a gain or a loss.

In addition to presenting the net income, income statements also present subtotals that are significant to users of financial statements. Some of the subtotals are specified by international financial reporting standards (IFRS), particularly nonrecurring items, but other subtotals are not specified.[3] International Accounting Standard (IAS) No. 1, *Presentation of Financial Statements*, requires that certain items, such as revenue, finance costs, and tax expense, be separately stated on the face of the income statement. IAS No. 1 also requires that headings and subtotals should also5 "be presented on the face of the income statement when such presentation is relevant to an understanding of the entity's financial performance."[4] IAS No. 1 states that expenses may be grouped together either by their nature or function. For example, grouping together expenses such as depreciation on manufacturing equipment and depreciation on administrative facilities into a single line item called "depreciation" represents a **grouping by nature** of the expense. An example of **grouping by function** would be grouping together expenses into a category such as cost of goods sold, which would include some salaries (e.g., salespeople's), material costs, depreciation, and other direct sales-related expenses.

One subtotal often shown in an income statement is **gross profit** (or, synonymously, **gross margin**). When an income statement shows a gross profit subtotal, it is said to use a **multi-step format** rather than a **single-step format**. The Kraft Foods income statement is an example of the multi-step format, whereas the Danone income statement is a single step. For manufacturing and merchandising companies, for whom gross profit is most relevant, gross profit is calculated as revenue minus the cost of the goods that were sold.[5] For service companies, gross profit is calculated as revenue minus the cost of services that were provided. In summary, gross profit is the amount of revenue available after subtracting the costs of delivering goods or services such as material and labor. Other expenses related to running the business are subtracted after gross profit.

Another important subtotal shown on the income statement is **operating profit** (or, synonymously, operating income). Operating profit further deducts

---

[3] The body of standards issued by the International Accounting Standards Board is now referred to as International Financial Reporting Standards, which include previously issued International Accounting Standards. "Financial reporting" is a broad term including reporting on accounting, financial statements, and other information found in company financial reports.

[4] IAS No. 1, *Presentation of Financial Statements*, paragraph 85.

[5] Later readings will provide additional information about alternative methods to calculate cost of goods sold.

operating expenses such as selling, general, administrative, and research and development expenses. Operating profit reflects a company's profits on its usual business activities before deducting taxes. For financial firms, interest expense would be included in operating expenses and subtracted in arriving at operating profit. For nonfinancial companies, interest expense would not be included in operating expenses and would be subtracted after operating profit because it relates to nonoperating activities for such companies. For some companies composed of a number of separate business segments, operating profit can be useful in evaluating the performance of the individual businesses, reflecting the reality that interest and tax expenses are more relevant at the level of the overall company rather than an individual segment level. For example, in its Investor Relations information, DaimlerChrysler notes, "Especially on the pre-tax level, Operating Profit is the principal earnings indicator for the Segments, Divisions and Business Units."[6] The specific calculations of gross margin and operating profit may vary by company, and a reader of financial statements can consult the notes to the statements to identify significant variations across companies.

Note that both Groupe Danone and Kraft Foods include a line item on their income statements referring to minority interest. Danone and Kraft both consolidate subsidiaries over which they have control. Consolidation means that they include all of the revenues and expenses of those subsidiaries even if they own less than 100 percent. Minority interest represents the portion of income that belongs to minority shareholders of these consolidated subsidiaries, as opposed to the parent company.

Exhibit 3 shows the income statement for CRA International (then known as Charles River Associates), a company providing management consulting services. These examples illustrate basic points about the income statement, including variations across the statements—some of which depend on the industry, whereas others reflect differences in accounting policies and practices of a particular company. In addition, some differences within an industry are primarily differences in terminology, whereas others are more fundamental accounting differences. Footnotes to the financial statements are helpful in identifying such differences.

Having introduced the components and format of an income statement, the next objective is to understand the actual reported numbers in it. To accurately interpret reported numbers, the analyst needs to be familiar with the principles of revenue and expense recognition—that is, how revenue and expenses are measured and attributed to a given accounting reporting period. Revenue and expense recognition are our next topics.

---

[6] DaimlerChrysler/Investor Relations/Basic Information/Controlling systems at www.daimlerchrysler.com.

| EXHIBIT 3 | Charles River Associates Incorporated Consolidated Statements of Income (in Thousands, except Per-Share Data) |

	Year Ended		
	27 Nov. 2004 (52 weeks)	29 Nov. 2003 (52 weeks)	30 Nov. 2002 (53 weeks)
Revenues	$216,735	$163,458	$130,690
Cost of services	127,716	100,168	80,659
Gross profit	89,019	63,290	50,031
Selling, general, and administrative expenses	57,286	43,055	36,600
Income from operations	31,733	20,235	13,431
Interest income	904	429	486
Interest expense	(1,751)	(38)	(120)
Other expense	(260)	(306)	(29)
Income before provision for income taxes and minority interest	30,626	20,320	13,768
Provision for income taxes	(13,947)	(8,737)	(5,879)
Income before minority interest	16,679	11,583	7,889
Minority interest	(335)	(154)	547
Net income	$16,344	$11,429	$8,436

REVENUE RECOGNITION   3

Revenue is the top line in an income statement, so we begin the discussion with revenue recognition. A first task is to explain some relevant accounting terminology.

The terms "revenue," "sales," "gains," "losses," and "net income" ("profit," "net earnings") have been previously briefly defined. The IFRS *Framework for the Preparation and Presentation of Financial Statements* (referred to here as "the Framework" for short) provides further relevant details. The *Framework* provides that profit is a frequently used measure of performance that is composed of income and expenses.[7] It defines **income** as follows:

> Income is increases in economic benefits during the accounting period in the form of inflows or enhancements of assets or decreases of liabilities that result in increases in equity, other than those relating to contributions from equity participants.[8]

International Financial Reporting Standards use the term "income" to include revenue and gains. Gains are similar to revenue; however, they arise from secondary or peripheral activities rather than from a company's primary business activities. For example, for a restaurant, the sale of surplus restaurant equipment for more than its cost is referred to as a gain rather than as revenue. Similarly, a

---

[7] IASB, *International Framework for the Preparation and Presentation of Financial Statements*, paragraph 69.
[8] Ibid., paragraph 70.

loss is like an expense but arises from secondary activities. Gains and losses may be considered part of operating activities (e.g., a loss due to a decline in the value of inventory) or may be considered part of nonoperating activities (e.g., the sale of nontrading investments).

In a simple hypothetical scenario, revenue recognition would not be an issue. For instance, a company sells goods to a buyer for cash with no returns allowed: When should the company recognize revenue? In this instance, it is clear that revenue should be recognized when the exchange of goods for cash takes place. In practice, however, determining when revenue should be recognized can be somewhat more complex for a number of reasons discussed in the following sections.

3.1 General Principles

An important concept concerning revenue recognition is that it can occur independently of cash movements. For example, assume a company sells goods to a buyer on credit and so does not actually receive cash until some later time. A fundamental principle of accrual accounting is that revenue is recognized when it is earned, so the company's financial records reflect the sale when it is made and a related accounts receivable is created. Later, when cash changes hands, the company's financial records simply reflect that cash has been received to settle an account receivable. Similarly, there are situations when a company receives cash up front and actually delivers the product or service later, perhaps over a period of time. In this case, the company would record **unearned revenue**, which is then recognized as being earned over time. (One example would be a subscription payment received up front for a publication that is to be delivered periodically over time, the accounting for which was illustrated earlier.)

The basic revenue recognition principles promulgated by accounting regulators deal with the definition of "earned." The International Accounting Standards Board (IASB) provides that revenue for the sale of goods is to be recognized (reported on the income statement) when the following conditions are satisfied:[9]

▶ the entity has transferred to the buyer the significant risks and rewards of ownership of the goods;

▶ the entity retains neither continuing managerial involvement to the degree usually associated with ownership nor effective control over the goods sold;

▶ the amount of revenue can be measured reliably;

▶ it is probable that the economic benefits associated with the transaction will flow to the entity; and

▶ the costs incurred or to be incurred in respect of the transaction can be measured reliably.

The IASB notes that the transfer of the risks and rewards of ownership normally occurs when goods are delivered to the buyer or when legal title to goods transfers. However, as noted by the above remaining conditions, transfer of goods will not always result in the recognition of revenue. For example, if goods are delivered to a retail store to be sold on consignment and title is not transferred, the revenue would not yet be recognized.[10]

---

[9] IASB, IAS No. 18, *Revenue*, paragraph 14.

[10] IAS No. 18 describes a "consignment sale" as one in which the recipient undertakes to sell the goods on behalf of the shipper (seller). Revenue is recognized by the shipper when the recipient sells the goods to a third party. IAS No. 18, Appendix, paragraph 2.

The Financial Accounting Standards Board (FASB)[11] specifies that revenue should be recognized when it is "realized or realizable and earned." The U.S. Securities and Exchange Commission (SEC),[12] motivated in part because of the frequency with which overstating revenue occurs in connection with fraud and/or misstatements, provides guidance on how to apply the accounting principles. This guidance names four criteria to determine when revenue is realized or realizable and earned:

1. There is evidence of an arrangement between buyer and seller. For instance, this would disallow the practice of recognizing revenue in a period by delivering the product just before the end of an accounting period and then completing a sales contract *after* the period end.

2. The product has been delivered, or the service has been rendered. For instance, this would preclude revenue recognition when the product has been shipped but the *risks and rewards of ownership have not actually passed* to the buyer.

3. The price is determined, or determinable. For instance, this would preclude a company from recognizing revenue that is based on some *contingency*.

4. The seller is reasonably sure of collecting money. For instance, this would preclude a company from recognizing revenue when the customer is *unlikely to pay*.

The IASB standards separately deal with the recognition of revenue for services:[13]

► When the outcome of a transaction involving the rendering of services can be estimated reliably, revenue associated with the transaction shall be recognized by reference to the stage of completion of the transaction at the balance sheet date.

► The outcome of a transaction can be estimated reliably when all the following conditions are satisfied:

   ► the amount of revenue can be measured reliably;

   ► it is probable that the economic benefits associated with the transaction will flow to the entity;

   ► the stage of completion of the transaction at the balance sheet date can be measured reliably; and

   ► the costs incurred for the transaction and the costs to complete the transaction can be measured reliably.

Companies must disclose their revenue recognition policies in the footnotes to their financial statements. Analysts should review these policies carefully to understand how and when a company recognizes revenue, which may differ depending upon the types of product sold and services rendered. Exhibit 4 presents a portion of the revenue recognition footnote for DaimlerChrysler from its 2005 annual report prepared under IFRS.

---

[11] See FASB ASC Section 605-10-25 [Revenue Recognition–Overall–Recognition].

[12] The content of SEC Staff Accounting Bulletin 101 is contained in FASB ASC Section 605-10-599 [Revenue Recognition–Overall–SEC Materials].

[13] IASB, IAS No. 18, paragraph 20.

EXHIBIT 4	Partial Revenue Recognition Footnote for DaimlerChrysler

Revenue for sales of vehicles, service parts and other related products is recognized when persuasive evidence of an arrangement exists, delivery has occurred or services have been rendered, the price of the transaction is fixed and determinable, and collectibility is reasonably assured.

Revenues are recognized net of discounts, cash sales incentives, customer bonuses and rebates granted. Non-cash sales incentives that do not reduce the transaction price to the customer are classified within cost of sales. Shipping and handling costs are recorded as cost of sales in the period incurred.

DaimlerChrysler uses price discounts to adjust market pricing in response to a number of market and product factors, including: pricing actions and incentives offered by competitors, economic conditions, the amount of excess industry production capacity, the intensity of market competition, and consumer demand for the product. The Group may offer a variety of sales incentive programs at any point in time, including: cash offers to dealers and consumers, lease subsidies which reduce the consumer's monthly lease payment, or reduced financing rate programs offered to consumers.

The Group records as a reduction to revenue at the time of sale to the dealer the estimated impact of sales incentives programs offered to dealers and consumers. This estimated impact represents the incentive programs offered to dealers and consumers as well as the expected modifications to these programs in order for the dealers to sell their inventory.

The topic of revenue recognition remains important, and new challenges have evolved, particularly in areas of e-commerce and services such as software development. Standard setters continue to evaluate current revenue recognition standards and issue new guidance periodically to deal with new types of transactions. Additionally, there are occasional special cases for revenue recognition, as discussed in the next section.

3.2 Revenue Recognition in Special Cases

The general principles discussed above are helpful for dealing with most revenue recognition issues. There are some areas where revenue recognition is more difficult to determine. For example, in limited circumstances, revenue may be recognized before or after goods are delivered or services are rendered, as summarized in Exhibit 5.

The following sections discuss revenue recognition in the case of long-term contracts, installment sales, and barter.

3.2.1 Long-Term Contracts

A **long-term contract** is one that spans a number of accounting periods. Such contracts raise issues in determining when the earnings process has been completed. How should a company apportion the revenue earned under a long-term

EXHIBIT 5	Revenue Recognition in Special Cases	
Before **Goods Are Delivered or Services Rendered**	**At the Time** **Goods Are Delivered or Services Rendered**	**After** **Goods Are Delivered or Services Rendered**
For example, with long-term contracts where the outcome can be reliably measured, the percentage-of-completion method is used.	Recognize revenues using normal revenue recognition criteria (IAS, FAS, SEC).	For example, with real estate sales where there is doubt about the buyer's ability to complete payments, the installment method and cost recovery method are appropriate.

contract to each accounting period? If, for example, the contract is a service contract or a licensing arrangement, the company may recognize the revenue ratably over the period of time of the contract rather than at the end of the contract term. As stated in IAS No. 18 regarding the rendering of services:

> The recognition of revenue by reference to the stage of completion of a transaction is often referred to as the percentage-of-completion method. Under this method, revenue is recognized in the accounting periods in which the services are rendered. The recognition of revenue on this basis provides useful information on the extent of service activity and performance during a period. IAS 11 *Construction Contracts* also requires the recognition of revenue on this basis. The requirements of that Standard are generally applicable to the recognition of revenue and the associated expenses for a transaction involving the rendering of services.[14]

As noted in IAS No. 18, construction contracts are another example of contracts that may span a number of accounting periods. IAS No. 11 provides that when the outcome of a construction contract can be measured reliably, revenue and expenses should be recognized in reference to the stage of completion. U.S. generally accepted accounting principles (U.S. GAAP) have a similar requirement. In both cases, the percentage-of-completion method of accounting is used. Under the **percentage-of-completion** method, in each accounting period, the company estimates what percentage of the contract is complete and then reports that percentage of the total contract revenue in its income statement. Contract costs for the period are expensed against the revenue. Therefore, net income or profit is reported each year as work is performed.

Under IAS No. 11, if the outcome of the contract cannot be measured reliably, then revenue is only reported to the extent of contract costs incurred (if it is probable the costs will be recovered). Costs are expensed in the period incurred. Under this method, no profit would be reported until completion of the contract. Under U.S. GAAP, a different method is used when the outcome cannot be measured reliably, termed the "completed contract method." Under the **completed contract** method, the company does not report any revenue until the contract is finished. Under U.S. GAAP, the completed contract method is also appropriate when the contract is not a long-term contract. Note, however, that when a contract is started and completed in the same period, there is no difference between the percentage-of-completion and completed contract methods.

---

[14] IAS No. 18, paragraph 21.

Examples 1, 2, and 3 provide illustrations of these revenue recognition methods. As shown, the percentage-of-completion method results in revenue recognition sooner than the completed contract method and thus may be considered a less conservative approach. In addition, the percentage-of-completion method relies on management estimates and is thus not as objective as the completed contract method. However, an advantage of the percentage-of-completion method is that it results in better matching of revenue recognition with the accounting period in which it was earned. Because of better matching with the periods in which work is performed, the percentage-of-completion method is the preferred method of revenue recognition for long-term contracts and is required when the outcome can be measured reliably under both IFRS and U.S. GAAP. Under both IFRS and U.S. GAAP, if a loss is expected on the contract, the loss is reported immediately, not upon completion of the contract, regardless of the method used (e.g., percentage-of-completion or completed contract).

EXAMPLE 1

Revenue Recognition for Long-Term Contracts: Recognizing Revenue Ratably

New Era Network Associates has a five-year license to provide networking support services to a customer. The total amount of the license fee to be received by New Era is $1 million. New Era recognizes license revenue ratably regardless of the time at which cash is received. How much revenue will New Era recognize for this license?

Solution: For this license, New Era Network Associates will recognize $200,000 each year for five years (calculated as $1 million divided by 5).

EXAMPLE 2

Revenue Recognition for Long-Term Contracts: Percentage-of-Completion Method

Stelle Technology has a contract to build a network for a customer for a total sales price of $10 million. The network will take an estimated three years to build, and total building costs are estimated to be $6 million. Stelle recognizes long-term contract revenue using the percentage-of-completion method and estimates percentage complete based on expenditure incurred as a percentage of total estimated expenditures.

1. At the end of Year 1, the company has spent $3 million. Total costs to complete are estimated to be another $3 million. How much revenue will Stelle recognize in Year 1?

2. At the end of Year 2, the company has spent $5.4 million. Total costs to complete are estimated to be another $0.6 million. How much revenue will Stelle recognize in Year 2?

3. At the end of Year 3, the contract is complete. The company spent a total of $6 million. How much revenue will Stelle recognize in Year 3?

Solution to 1: Stelle has spent 50 percent of the total project costs ($3 million divided by $6 million), so in Year 1, the company will recognize 50 percent of the total contract revenue (i.e., $5 million).

Solution to 2: Because Stelle has spent 90 percent of the total project costs ($5.4 million divided by $6 million), by the end of Year 2, it will need to have recognized 90 percent of the total contract revenue (i.e., $9 million). Stelle has already recognized $5 million of revenue in Year 1, so in Year 2, the company will recognize $4 million revenue ($9 million minus $5 million).

Solution to 3: Because Stelle has spent 100 percent of the total project costs, by the end of Year 3, it will need to have recognized 100 percent of the total contract revenue (i.e., $10 million). Stelle had already recognized $9 million of revenue by the end of Year 2, so in Year 3, the company will recognize $1 million revenue ($10 million minus $9 million).

	Year 1	Year 2	Year 3	Total
Revenue	$5 million	$4 million	$1 million	$10 million

EXAMPLE 3

Revenue Recognition for Long-Term Contracts: Completed Contract Method

Kolenda Technology Group has a contract to build a network for a customer for a total sales price of $10 million. This network will take an estimated three years to build, but considerable uncertainty surrounds total building costs because new technologies are involved. Kolenda recognizes contract revenue using the completed contract method.

1. At the end of Year 1, Kolenda has spent $3 million. How much revenue will the company recognize in Year 1?

2. At the end of Year 2, Kolenda has spent $5.4 million. How much revenue will the company recognize in Year 2?

3. At the end of Year 3, the contract is complete. Kolenda spent a total of $6 million. How much revenue will the company recognize in Year 3?

Solution to 1: No revenue will be recognized until the contract is complete. In Year 1, Kolenda will recognize $0.

Solution to 2: No revenue will be recognized until the contract is complete. In Year 2, Kolenda will recognize $0.

> **Solution to 3:** Because the contract is complete, Kolenda will recognize the total contract revenue (i.e., $10 million).
>
> | | Year 1 | Year 2 | Year 3 | Total |
> |---|---|---|---|---|
> | Revenue | $0 million | $0 million | $10 million | $10 million |

3.2.2 Installment Sales

As noted above, revenue is normally reported when goods are delivered or services are rendered, independent of the period in which cash payments for those goods or services are received. This principle applies even to **installment** sales—sales in which proceeds are to be paid in installments over an extended period. Under limited circumstances, recognition of revenue or profit may be required to be deferred for some installment sales.

An example of such deferral arises for certain sales of real estate on an installment basis. Revenue recognition for sales of real estate[15] varies depending on specific aspects of the sale transaction. Under normal conditions, sales of real estate are reported at the time of sale using the normal revenue recognition conditions. International standards note that in the case of real estate sales, the time at which legal title transfers may differ from the time at which the buyer acquires a vested interest. Continuing involvement in the real estate by the seller may also indicate that risks and rewards of ownership of the property have not been transferred. There may also be significant doubt of the ability of the buyer to complete payment for a real estate sales contract. IAS No. 18 provides that in the case of real estate where the down payment and payments received do not provide sufficient evidence of the commitment of the buyer, revenue should only be reported to the extent cash is received. This is a conservative treatment because the reporting of revenue is deferred. Similar provisions exist under U.S. GAAP except that under U.S. GAAP the full revenue is shown in the year of sale but some of the profit is deferred.

Two methods may be appropriate in these limited circumstances and relate to the amount of profit to be recognized each year from the transaction: the **installment method** and the **cost recovery method**. Under the installment method, the portion of the total profit of the sale that is recognized in each period is determined by the percentage of the total sales price for which the seller has received cash. Exhibit 6 presents an example of a disclosure of an installment sale of real estate under U.S. GAAP where a portion of the profit was recognized and the remainder was deferred.

---

[15] IAS No. 18, Appendix, paragraph 9, and FASB ASC Section 360-20-55 [Property, Plant, and Equipment–Real Estate Sales–Implementation Guidance and Illustrations].

EXHIBIT 6	Installment Sale Disclosure for First Bancshares

On June 22, 2004, an agreement was entered into to sell the property and equipment of South Central Missouri Title Company, Inc., for $252,000. In addition, South Central entered into a covenant not to compete agreement with the purchaser. Expense related to the sale totaled $61,512. As of the date of the sale, the assets sold had a net book value of $100,166. The majority of the sales price was in the form of a promissory note to South Central with a five year maturity. The transaction closed on July 16, 2004. As a result of this sale, the subsidiary will no longer offer sales of title insurance or real estate closing services. The company accounted for this sale on the installment method because the initial investment by the buyer was not substantial enough to warrant full recognition of the gain. However, the recovery of the cost of the property is reasonably assured if the buyer defaults. The following schedule summarizes certain information for the transaction:

Revenue	$252,000
Cost of sale	161,678
Deferred gain	90,322
Deferred gain recognized during FY 2005	8,026
Deferred gain at June 30, 2005	$82,296

Source: First Bancshares Form 10K, filed 11/1/2005.

The cost recovery method of revenue recognition is an appropriate alternative for many of the same situations as the installment method. Under the cost recovery method, the seller does not report any profit until the cash amounts paid by the buyer—including principal and interest on any financing from the seller—are greater than all the seller's costs of the property. Example 4 below provides an example of the differences between the installment method and the cost recovery method.

Installment sales and cost recovery treatment of revenue recognition are rare for financial reporting purposes, especially for assets other than real estate. IAS No. 18 provides that installment sales other than real estate generally require revenue to be recognized at the time of sale; however, it further provides that the guidance found in IAS No. 18 must be considered in light of local laws regarding the sale of goods in a particular country.

EXAMPLE 4

The Installment and Cost Recovery Methods of Revenue Recognition

Assume the total sales price and cost of a property are $2,000,000 and $1,100,000, respectively, so that the total profit to be recognized is $900,000. The amount of cash received by the seller as a down payment is $300,000, with the remainder of the sales price to be received over a 10-year period. It has been determined that there is significant doubt about the ability and commitment of the buyer to complete all payments. How much profit will be recognized attributable to the down payment if:

1. The installment method is used?
2. The cost recovery method is used?

Solution to 1: The installment method apportions the cash receipt between cost recovered and profit using the ratio of profit to sales value; here, this ratio equals $900,000/$2,000,000 = 0.45 or 45 percent. Therefore, the seller will recognize the following profit attributable to the down payment: 45 percent of $300,000 = $135,000.

Solution to 2: Under the cost recovery method of revenue recognition, the company would not recognize any profit attributable to the down payment because the cash amounts paid by the buyer still do not exceed the cost of $1,100,000.

3.2.3 Barter

Revenue recognition issues related to barter transactions became particularly important as e-commerce developed. As an example, if Company A exchanges advertising space for computer equipment from Company B but no cash changes hands, can Company A and B both report revenue? Such an exchange is referred to as a "barter transaction."

An even more challenging revenue recognition issue evolved from barter transactions—round-trip transactions. As an example, if Company A sells advertising services (or energy contracts, or commodities) to Company B and almost simultaneously buys an almost identical product from Company B, can Company A report revenue at the fair value of the product sold? Because the company's revenue would be approximately equal to its expense, the net effect of the transaction would have no impact on net income or cash flow. However, the amount of revenue reported would be higher, and the amount of revenue can be important to a company's valuation. In the earlier stages of e-commerce, for example, some equity valuations were based on sales (because many early internet companies reported no net income).

Under IFRS, revenue from barter transactions must be measured based on the fair value of revenue from similar nonbarter transactions with unrelated parties (parties other than the barter partner).[16] Similarly, the FASB states that revenue can be recognized at fair value only if a company has historically received cash payments for such services and can thus use this historical experience as a basis for determining fair value.[17]

3.2.4 Gross versus Net Reporting

Another revenue recognition issue that became particularly important with the emergence of e-commerce is the issue of gross versus net reporting. Merchandising companies typically sell products that they purchased from a supplier. In

---

[16] IASB, SIC Interpretation 31, Revenue—Barter Transactions Involving Advertising Services, paragraph 5.

[17] See FASB ASC paragraph 606-20-25-14 [Revenue Recognition–Services–Recognition–Advertising Barter Services].

accounting for their sales, the company records the amount of the sale proceeds as sales revenue and their cost of the products as the cost of goods sold. As internet-based merchandising companies developed, many sold products that they had never held in inventory; they simply arranged for the supplier to ship the products directly to the end customer. In effect, many such companies were agents of the supplier company, and the net difference between their sales proceeds and their costs was equivalent to a sales commission. What amount should these companies record as their revenues—the gross amount of sales proceeds received from their customers, or the net difference between sales proceeds and their cost?

U.S. GAAP indicates that the approach should be based on the specific situation and provides guidance for determining when revenue should be reported gross versus net.[18] To report gross revenues, the following criteria are relevant: The company is the primary obligor under the contract, bears inventory risk and credit risk, can choose its supplier, and has reasonable latitude to establish price. If these criteria are not met, the company should report revenues net. Example 5 provides an illustration.

EXAMPLE 5

Gross versus Net Reporting of Revenues

Flyalot has agreements with several major airlines to obtain airline tickets at reduced rates. The company pays only for tickets it sells to customers. In the most recent period, Flyalot sold airline tickets to customers over the internet for a total of $1.1 million. The cost of these tickets to Flyalot was $1 million. The company's direct selling costs were $2,000. Once the customers receive their ticket, the airline is responsible for providing all services associated with the customers' flight.

1. Demonstrate the reporting of revenues under:
   A. gross reporting.
   B. net reporting.
2. Determine and justify the appropriate method for reporting revenues.

Solution to 1: The table below shows how reporting would appear on a gross and a net basis.

	A. Gross Reporting	B. Net Reporting
Revenues	$1,100,000	$100,000
Cost of sales	1,002,000	2,000
Gross margin	$98,000	$98,000

---

[18] See FASB ASC Section 605-45-45 [Revenue Recognition–Principle Agent Considerations–Other Presentation Matters].

> **Solution to 2:** Flyalot should report revenue on a net basis. Flyalot pays only for tickets it sells to customers and thus did not bear inventory risk. In addition, the airline—not Flyalot—is the primary obligor under the contract. Revenues should be reported as $100,000.

3.3 Implications for Financial Analysis

As we have seen, companies use a variety of revenue recognition methods. Furthermore, a single company may use different revenue recognition policies for different businesses. Companies disclose their revenue recognition policies in the footnotes to their financial statement, often in the first note.

The following aspects of a company's revenue recognition policy are particularly relevant to financial analysis: whether a policy results in recognition of revenue sooner rather than later (sooner is less conservative), and to what extent a policy requires the company to make estimates. In order to analyze a company's financial statements, and particularly to compare one company's financial statements with those of another company, it is helpful to understand any differences in their revenue recognition policies. Although it may not be possible to calculate the monetary effect of differences between particular companies' revenue recognition policies and estimates, it is generally possible to characterize the relative conservatism of a company's policies and to qualitatively assess how differences in policies might affect financial ratios.

With familiarity of the basic principles of revenue recognition in hand, the next section begins a discussion of expense recognition.

EXAMPLE 6

Revenue Recognition Policy for Motorola

As disclosed in the footnotes to the financial statements shown below (emphasis added), Motorola (NYSE:MOT) uses different revenue recognition policies depending on the type of revenue-producing activity, including product sales, long-term contracts, contracts involving unproven technology, revenue for services, and revenue for licensing agreements.

> **Revenue Recognition:** The Company recognizes revenue for *product sales* when title transfers, the risks and rewards of ownership have been transferred to the customer, the fee is fixed and determinable, and collection of the related receivable is probable, which is generally at the time of shipment. Accruals are established, with the related reduction to revenue, for allowances for discounts and price protection, product returns and incentive programs for distributors and end customers related to these sales based on actual historical exposure at the time the related revenues are recognized. For *long-term contracts*, the Company uses the percentage-of-completion method to recognize revenues and costs based on the percentage of costs incurred to date compared to the total estimated contract costs. For *contracts involving new unproven technologies*, revenues and profits are deferred until technological feasibility is established, customer acceptance is obtained and other contract-specific terms have been completed. Provisions for losses are

recognized during the period in which the loss first becomes apparent. *Revenue for services* is recognized ratably over the contract term or as services are being performed. *Revenue related to licensing agreements* is recognized over the licensing period or at the time the Company has fulfilled its obligations and the fee to be received is fixed and determinable.

Source: Motorola 10-K financial statement footnotes for the year ended 31 December 2004, as filed with the SEC. Emphasis added.

EXAMPLE 7

Revenue Recognition of i2 Technologies

On 9 June 2004, the SEC announced it had settled a securities fraud case against i2 Technologies (NASDAQ: ITWO) involving the misstatement of approximately $1 billion in revenues. The SEC announcement explains that the company recognized revenue up front on its software licenses, which was inappropriate because some of the software lacked complete functionality either for general use or for use by a particular customer.

Source: SEC Accounting and Auditing Enforcement Release No. 2034.

EXPENSE RECOGNITION   4

Expenses are deducted against revenue to arrive at a company's net profit or loss. Under the IASB *Framework*, **expenses** are "decreases in economic benefits during the accounting period in the form of outflows or depletions of assets or incurrences of liabilities that result in decreases in equity, other than those relating to distributions to equity participants."[19]

The IASB *Framework* also states:

The definition of expenses encompasses losses as well as those expenses that arise in the course of the ordinary activities of the enterprise. Expenses that arise in the course of the ordinary activities of the enterprise include, for example, cost of sales, wages and depreciation. They usually take the form of an outflow or depletion of assets such as cash and cash equivalents, inventory, property, plant and equipment.

Losses represent other items that meet the definition of expenses and may, or may not, arise in the course of the ordinary activities of the enterprise. Losses represent decreases in economic benefits and as such they are no different in nature from other expenses. Hence, they are not regarded as a separate element in this Framework.

Losses include, for example, those resulting from disasters such as fire and flood.[20]

---

[19] IASB *Framework for the Preparation and Presentation of Financial Statements*, paragraph 70.
[20] Ibid., paragraphs 78–80.

Similar to the issues with revenue recognition, in a simple hypothetical scenario, expense recognition would not be an issue. For instance, assume a company purchased inventory for cash and sold the entire inventory in the same period. When the company paid for the inventory, absent indications to the contrary, it is clear that the inventory cost has been incurred and should be recognized as an expense (cost of goods sold) in the financial records. Assume also that the company paid all operating and administrative expenses in cash within each accounting period. In such a simple hypothetical scenario, no issues of expense recognition would arise. In practice, however, as with revenue recognition, determining when expenses should be recognized can be somewhat more complex.

4.1 General Principles

In general, a company recognizes expenses in the period that it consumes (i.e., uses up) the economic benefits associated with the expenditure, or loses some previously recognized economic benefit.[21]

A general principle of expense recognition is the **matching principle**, also known as the "matching of costs with revenues."[22] Under the matching principle, a company directly matches some expenses (e.g., cost of goods sold) with associated revenues. Unlike the simple scenario in which a company purchases inventory and sells all of the inventory within the same accounting period, in practice, it is more likely that some of the current period's sales are made from inventory purchased in a previous period. It is also more likely that some of the inventory purchased in the current period will remain unsold at the end of the current period and so will be sold in the following period. The matching principle requires that the company match the cost of goods sold with the revenues of the period.

Period costs, expenditures that less directly match the timing of revenues, are reflected in the period when a company makes the expenditure or incurs the liability to pay. Administrative expenses are an example of period costs. Other expenditures that also less directly match the timing of revenues relate more directly to future expected benefits; in this case, the expenditures are allocated systematically with the passage of time. An example is depreciation expense (discussed below).

Examples 8 and 9 demonstrate the matching principle applied to inventory and cost of goods sold.

---

[21] Ibid., paragraph 94.

[22] Ibid., paragraph 95.

EXAMPLE 8

The Matching of Inventory Costs with Revenues

Kahn Distribution Limited (KDL) purchases inventory items for resale. During 2006, Kahn had the following transactions:

Quarter Inventory Purchases

First quarter	2,000 units at $40 per unit
Second quarter	1,500 units at $41 per unit
Third quarter	2,200 units at $43 per unit
Fourth quarter	1,900 units at $45 per unit
Total	7,600 units at a total cost of $321,600

Inventory sales during the year were 5,600 units at $50 per unit. KDL determines that there were 2,000 remaining units of inventory and specifically identifies that 1,900 were those purchased in the fourth quarter and 100 were purchased in the third quarter. What are the revenue and expense associated with these transactions during 2006?

Solution: The revenue for 2006 would be $280,000 (5,600 units × $50 per unit). Initially, the total cost of the goods purchased would be recorded as inventory (an asset) in the amount of $321,600. During 2006, the cost of the 5,600 units sold would be expensed (matched against the revenue) while the cost of the 2,000 remaining unsold units would remain in inventory as follows:

Cost of Goods Sold

From the first quarter	2,000 units at $40 per unit =	$ 80,000
From the second quarter	1,500 units at $41 per unit =	$ 61,500
From the third quarter	2,100 units at $43 per unit =	$ 90,300
Total cost of goods sold		$231,800

Cost of Goods Remaining in Inventory

From the third quarter	100 units at $43 per unit =	$ 4,300
From the fourth quarter	1,900 units at $45 per unit =	$85,500
Total remaining (or ending) inventory cost		$89,800

To confirm that total costs are accounted for:
$231,800 + $89,800 = $321,600
The cost of the goods sold would be expensed against the revenue of $280,000 as follows:

Revenue	$280,000
Cost of goods sold	231,800
Gross profit	$ 48,200

The remaining inventory amount of $89,800 will be matched against revenue in a future year when the inventory items are sold.

EXAMPLE 9

Alternative Inventory Costing Methods

In Example 8, KDL was able to specifically identify which inventory items were sold and which remained in inventory to be carried over to later periods. That method is called the **specific identification method**. It is not always possible to specifically identify which items were sold, so the accounting standards permit the assignment of inventory costs to costs of goods sold and to ending inventory using cost flow assumptions. Under both IFRS and U.S. GAAP, companies may use either of two methods to assign costs: the First In, First Out (FIFO) method, or the weighted average cost method. Under the **FIFO method**, it is simply assumed that the earliest items purchased were sold first. Ending inventory would, therefore, include only the latest purchases. It turns out that those items specifically identified as sold in Example 8 were also the first items purchased, so in this example, under FIFO, the cost of goods sold would also be $231,800, calculated as above. The **weighted average cost method** simply averages the total available costs over the total available units.

For KDL, the weighted average cost would be
$321,600/7,600 units = $42.3158 per unit
Cost of goods sold using the weighted average cost method would be
5,600 units at $42.3158 = $236,968
Ending inventory using the weighted average cost method would be
2,000 units at $42.3158 = $ 84,632

Another method is available under U.S. GAAP but is not permitted under IFRS. This method is the Last In, First Out (LIFO) method. Under the **LIFO method**, it is assumed that the most recent items purchased were sold first. Although this may seem contrary to common sense, it is logical in certain circumstances. For example, lumber in a lumberyard may be stacked up with the oldest lumber on the bottom. As lumber is sold, it is sold from the top of the stack, so the last lumber in is the first lumber out. Theoretically, a company should choose this method under U.S. GAAP if the physical inventory flows in this manner.[23] Under the LIFO method, in the KDL example, it would be assumed that the 2,000 units remaining in ending inventory would have come from the first quarter's purchases:[24]

Ending inventory 2,000 units at $40 per unit = $80,000

The remaining costs would be allocated to cost of goods sold under LIFO:
Total costs of $321,600 less $80,000 remaining
in ending inventory = $241,600

---

[23] Practically, the reason some companies choose to use LIFO in the United States is to reduce taxes. When prices and inventory quantities are rising, LIFO will normally result in lower income and hence lower taxes. U.S. tax regulations require that if LIFO is used on a company's tax return, it must also be used on the company's GAAP financial statements.

[24] If data on the precise timing of quarterly sales were available, the answer would differ because the cost of goods sold would be determined during the quarter rather than at the end of the quarter.

Alternatively, the cost of the last 5,600 units purchased is allocated to cost of goods sold under LIFO:
1,900 units at $45 per unit + 2,200 units at $43 per unit + 1,500 units at $41 per unit = $241,600

Exhibit 7 summarizes and compares inventory costing methods.

EXHIBIT 7	Summary Table on Inventory Costing Methods		
Method	**Description**	**Cost of Goods Sold When Prices Are Rising, Relative to Other Two Methods**	**Ending Inventory When Prices Are Rising, Relative to Other Two Methods**
FIFO (first in, first out)	Assumes that earliest items purchased were sold first	Lowest	Highest
LIFO (last in, first out)	Assumes most recent items purchased were sold first	Highest[a]	Lowest[a]
Weighted average cost	Averages total costs over total units available	Middle	Middle

[a]Assumes no LIFO layer liquidation. **LIFO layer liquidation** occurs when the volume of sales rises above the volume of recent purchases so that some sales are made from existing, relatively low-priced inventory rather than from more recent purchases.

4.2 Issues in Expense Recognition

The following sections cover applications of the principles of expense recognition to certain common situations.

4.2.1 Doubtful Accounts

When a company sells its products or services on credit, it is likely that some customers will ultimately default on their obligations (i.e., fail to pay). At the time of the sale, it is not known which customer will default. (If it were known that a particular customer would ultimately default, presumably a company would not sell on credit to that customer.) One possible approach to recognizing credit losses on customer receivables would be for the company to wait until such time as a customer defaulted and only then recognize the loss (**direct write-off method**). Such an approach would usually not be consistent with generally accepted accounting principles.

Under the matching principle, at the time revenue is recognized on a sale, a company is required to record an estimate of how much of the revenue will ultimately be uncollectible. Companies make such estimates based on previous experience with uncollectible accounts. Such estimates may be expressed as a proportion of the overall amount of sales, the overall amount of receivables, or the amount of receivables overdue by a specific amount of time. The company records its estimate of uncollectible amounts as an expense on the income statement, not as a direct reduction of revenues.

4.2.2 Warranties

At times, companies offer warranties on the products they sell. If the product proves deficient in some respect that is covered under the terms of the warranty, the company will incur an expense to repair or replace the product. At the time of sale, the company does not know the amount of future expenses it will incur in connection with its warranties. One possible approach would be for a company to wait until actual expenses are incurred under the warranty and to reflect the expense at that time. However, this would not result in a matching of the expense with the associated revenue.

Under the matching principle, a company is required to estimate the amount of future expenses resulting from its warranties, to recognize an estimated warranty expense in the period of the sale, and to update the expense as indicated by experience over the life of the warranty.

4.2.3 Depreciation and Amortization

Companies commonly incur costs to obtain long-lived assets. **Long-lived assets** are assets expected to provide economic benefits over a future period of time greater than one year. Examples are land (property), plant, equipment, and **intangible assets** (assets lacking physical substance) such as trademarks. The costs of most long-lived assets are allocated over the period of time during which they provide economic benefits. The two main types of long-lived assets whose costs are *not* allocated over time are land and those intangible assets with indefinite useful lives.

Depreciation is the process of systematically allocating costs of long-lived assets over the period during which the assets are expected to provide economic benefits. "Depreciation" is the term commonly applied to this process for physical long-lived assets such as plant and equipment (land is not depreciated), and **amortization** is the term commonly applied to this process for intangible long-lived assets with a finite useful life.[25] Examples of intangible long-lived assets with a finite useful life include an acquired mailing list, an acquired patent with a set expiration date, and an acquired copyright with a set legal life. The term "amortization" is also commonly applied to the systematic allocation of a premium or discount relative to the face value of a fixed-income security over the life of the security.

IAS No. 16, *Property, Plant, and Equipment*, requires that the depreciable amount (cost less residual value) be allocated on a systematic basis over the remaining useful life of the asset. The method used to compute depreciation must reflect the pattern over which the economic benefits of the asset are expected to be consumed. IAS No. 16 does not prescribe a particular method for computing depreciation but notes that several methods are commonly used, such as the straight-line method, diminishing balance method (accelerated depreciation), and the units of production method (depreciation varies depending upon production or usage).

The **straight-line method** allocates evenly the cost of long-lived assets less estimated residual value over the estimated useful life of an asset. (The term

---

[25] Under FASB ASC paragraph 350-30-35-6 [Intangibles–Goodwill and other–General Intangibles other than Goodwill–Subsequent Measurement–Intangible Assets Subject to Amortization], intangible assets with indefinite life are not amortized. Instead, they are tested at least annually for impairment (i.e., if the current value of an intangible asset is materially lower than its value in the company's books, the value of the asset is considered to be impaired and its value must be decreased).

"straight line" derives from the fact that the annual depreciation expense, if represented as a line graph over time, would be a straight line. In addition, a plot of the cost of the asset minus the cumulative amount of annual depreciation expense, if represented as a line graph over time, would be a straight line with a negative downward slope.) Calculating depreciation and amortization requires two significant estimates: the estimated useful life of an asset and the estimated residual value (also known as "salvage value") of an asset. Under IAS No. 16, the residual value is the amount that the company expects to receive upon sale of the asset at the end of its useful life. Example 10 assumes that an item of equipment is depreciated using the straight-line method and illustrates how the annual depreciation expense varies under different estimates of the useful life and estimated residual value of an asset. As shown, annual depreciation expense is sensitive to both the estimated useful life and to the estimated residual value.

EXAMPLE 10

Sensitivity of Annual Depreciation Expense to Varying Estimates of Useful Life and Residual Value

Using the straight-line method of depreciation, annual depreciation expense is calculated as

$$\frac{\text{Cost} - \text{Residual value}}{\text{Estimated useful life}}$$

Assume the cost of an asset is \$10,000. If, for example, the residual value of the asset is estimated to be \$0 and its useful life is estimated to be 5 years, the annual depreciation expense under the straight-line method would be (\$10,000 − \$0)/5 years = \$2,000. In contrast, holding the estimated useful life of the asset constant at 5 years but increasing the estimated residual value of the asset to \$4,000 would result in annual depreciation expense of only \$1,200 [calculated as (\$10,000 − \$4,000)/5 years]. Alternatively, holding the estimated residual value at \$0 but increasing the estimated useful life of the asset to 10 years would result in annual depreciation expense of only \$1,000 [calculated as (\$10,000 − \$0)/10 years]. Exhibit 8 shows annual depreciation expense for various combinations of estimated useful life and residual value.

EXHIBIT 8   Annual Depreciation Expense (in Dollars)

Estimated Useful Life (Years)	Estimated Residual Value					
	0	1,000	2,000	3,000	4,000	5,000
2	5,000	4,500	4,000	3,500	3,000	2,500
4	2,500	2,250	2,000	1,750	1,500	1,250
5	2,000	1,800	1,600	1,400	1,200	1,000
8	1,250	1,125	1,000	875	750	625
10	1,000	900	800	700	600	500

Generally, alternatives to the straight-line method of depreciation are called **accelerated methods of depreciation** because they accelerate (i.e., speed up) the timing of depreciation. Accelerated depreciation methods allocate a greater proportion of the cost to the early years of an asset's useful life. These methods are appropriate if the plant or equipment is expected to be used up faster in the early years (e.g., an automobile). A commonly used accelerated method is the **diminishing balance method**, as mentioned in IAS No. 16 (also known as the declining balance method). The diminishing balance method is demonstrated in Example 11.

EXAMPLE 11

An Illustration of Diminishing Balance Depreciation

Assume the cost of computer equipment was $11,000, the estimated residual value is $1,000, and the estimated useful life is five years. Under the diminishing or declining balance method, the first step is to determine the straight-line rate, the rate at which the asset would be depreciated under the straight-line method. This rate is measured as 100 percent divided by the useful life or 20 percent for a five-year useful life. Under the straight-line method, 1/5 or 20 percent of the depreciable cost of the asset (here, $11,000 − $1,000 = $10,000) would be expensed each year for five years: The depreciation expense would be $2,000 per year.

The next step is to determine an acceleration factor that approximates the pattern of the asset's wear. Common acceleration factors are 150 percent and 200 percent. The latter is known as **double declining balance depreciation** because it depreciates the asset at double the straight-line rate. Using the 200 percent acceleration factor, the diminishing balance rate would be 40 percent (20 percent × 2.0). This rate is then applied to the remaining undepreciated balance of the asset each period (known as the **net book value**).

At the beginning of the first year, the net book value is $11,000. Depreciation expense for the first full year of use of the asset would be 40 percent of $11,000, or $4,400. Under this method, the residual value, if any, is generally not used in the computation of the depreciation each period (the 40 percent is applied to $11,000 rather than to $11,000 minus residual value). However, the company will stop taking depreciation when the salvage value is reached.

At the beginning of Year 2, the net book value is measured as

Asset cost	$11,000
Less: Accumulated depreciation	(4,400)
Net book value	$ 6,600

For the second full year, depreciation expense would be $6,600 × 40 percent, or $2,640. At the end of the second year (i.e., beginning of the third year), a total of $7,040 ($4,400 + $2,640) of depreciation would have been recorded. So, the remaining net book value at the beginning of the third year would be

Asset cost	$11,000
Less: Accumulated depreciation	(7,040)
Net book value	$ 3,960

For the third full year, depreciation would be $3,960 × 40 percent, or $1,584. At the end of the third year, a total of $8,624 ($4,400 + $2,640 + $1,584) of depreciation would have been recorded. So, the remaining net book value at the beginning of the fourth year would be

Asset cost	$11,000
Less: Accumulated depreciation	(8,624)
Net book value	$ 2,376

For the fourth full year, depreciation would be $2,376 × 40 percent, or $950. At the end of the fourth year, a total of $9,574 ($4,400 + $2,640 + $1,584 + $950) of depreciation would have been recorded. So, the remaining net book value at the beginning of the fifth year would be

Asset cost	$11,000
Less: Accumulated depreciation	(9,574)
Net book value	$ 1,426

For the fifth year, if deprecation were determined as in previous years, it would amount to $570 ($1,426 × 40 percent). However, this would result in a remaining net book value of the asset below its estimated residual value of $1,000. So, instead, only $426 would be depreciated, leaving a $1,000 net book value at the end of the fifth year.

Asset cost	$11,000
Less: Accumulated depreciation	(10,000)
Net book value	$ 1,000

Companies often use a zero or small residual value, which creates problems for diminishing balance depreciation because the asset never fully depreciates. In order to fully depreciate the asset over the initially estimated useful life when a zero or small residual value is assumed, companies often adopt a depreciation policy that combines the diminishing balance and straight-line methods. An example would be a depreciation policy of using double-declining balance depreciation and switching to the straight-line method halfway through the useful life.

Under accelerated depreciation methods, there is a higher depreciation expense in early years relative to the straight-line method. This results in higher expenses and lower net income in the early depreciation years. In later years, there is a reversal with accelerated depreciation expense lower than straight-line depreciation. Accelerated depreciation is sometimes referred to as a "conservative" accounting choice because it results in lower net income in the early years of asset use.

For those intangible assets that must be amortized (those with an identifiable useful life), the process is the same as for depreciation; only the name of the expense is different. IAS No. 38, *Intangible Assets*, states that if a pattern cannot be determined over the useful life, then the straight-line method should be used. In most cases under international accounting standards and U.S. GAAP, amortizable intangible assets are amortized using the straight-line method with no residual value. **Goodwill**[26] and intangible assets with indefinite life are not amortized. Instead, they are tested at least annually for impairment (i.e., if the current value of an intangible asset or goodwill is materially lower than its value in the company's books, the value of the asset is considered to be impaired and its value in the company's books must be decreased).

In summary, to calculate depreciation and amortization, a company must choose a method, estimate the asset's useful life, and estimate residual value. Clearly, different choices have a differing effect on depreciation or amortization expense and, therefore, on reported net income.

4.3 Implications for Financial Analysis

A company's estimates for doubtful accounts and/or for warranty expenses can affect its reported net income. Similarly, a company's choice of depreciation or amortization method, estimates of assets' useful lives, and estimates of assets' residual values can affect reported net income. These are only a few of the choices and estimates that affect a company's reported net income.

As with revenue recognition policies, a company's choice of expense recognition can be characterized by its relative conservatism. A policy that results in recognition of expenses later rather than sooner is considered less conservative. In addition, many items of expense require the company to make estimates that can significantly affect net income. Analysis of a company's financial statements, and particularly comparison of one company's financial statements with those of another, requires an understanding of differences in these estimates and their potential impact.

If, for example, a company shows a significant year-to-year change in its estimates of uncollectible accounts as a percentage of sales, warranty expenses as percentage of sales, or estimated useful lives of assets, the analyst should seek to understand the underlying reasons. Do the changes reflect a change in business operations (e.g., lower estimated warranty expenses reflecting recent experience of fewer warranty claims because of improved product quality)? Or are the changes seemingly unrelated to changes in business operations and thus possibly a signal that a company is manipulating estimates in order to achieve a particular effect on its reported net income?

As another example, if two companies in the same industry have dramatically different estimates for uncollectible accounts as a percentage of their sales, warranty expenses as a percentage of sales, or estimated useful lives as a percentage of assets, it is important to understand the underlying reasons. Are the differences consistent with differences in the two companies' business operations (e.g., lower uncollectible accounts for one company reflecting a different, more creditworthy customer base or possibly stricter credit policies)? Another difference consistent with differences in business operations would be a difference in estimated useful lives of assets if one of the companies employs newer equipment. Or, alternatively, are the differences seemingly inconsistent with differences in the two companies' business operations, possibly signaling that a company is manipulating estimates?

Information about a company's accounting policies and significant estimates are described in the footnotes to the financial statements and in the management discussion and analysis section of a company's annual report.

---

[26] Goodwill is recorded in acquisitions and is the amount by which the price to purchase an entity exceeds the amount of net identifiable assets acquired (the total amount of identifiable assets acquired less liabilities assumed).

When possible, the monetary effect of differences in expense recognition policies and estimates can facilitate more meaningful comparisons with a single company's historical performance or across a number of companies. An analyst can use the monetary effect to adjust the reported expenses so that they are on a comparable basis.

Even when the monetary effects of differences in policies and estimates cannot be calculated, it is generally possible to characterize the relative conservatism of the policies and estimates and, therefore, to qualitatively assess how such differences might affect reported expenses and thus financial ratios.

NONRECURRING ITEMS AND NONOPERATING ITEMS

5

From a company's income statements, we can see its earnings from last year and in the previous year. Looking forward, the question is: What will the company earn next year and in the years after?

To assess a company's future earnings, it is helpful to separate those prior years' items of income and expense that are likely to continue in the future from those items that are less likely to continue.[27] Some items from prior years are clearly not expected to continue in the future periods and are separately disclosed on a company's income statement. Two such items are 1) discontinued operations, and 2) extraordinary items (the latter category is no longer permitted under IFRS). These two items, if applicable, must be reported separately from continuing operations.[28]

For other items on a company's income statement, such as unusual items, accounting changes, and nonoperating income, the likelihood of their continuing in the future is somewhat less clear and requires the analyst to make some judgments.

5.1 Discontinued Operations

When a company disposes of or establishes a plan to dispose of one of its component operations and will have no further involvement in the operation, the income statement reports separately the effect of this disposal as a "discontinued" operation under both IFRS and U.S. GAAP. Financial standards provide various criteria for reporting the effect separately, which are generally that the discontinued component must be separable both physically and operationally.[29]

Because the discontinued operation will no longer provide earnings (or cash flow) to the company, an analyst can eliminate discontinued operations in formulating expectations about a company's future financial performance.

In Exhibit 2, Kraft reported a loss from discontinued operations of $4 million in 2004 and earnings of $97 million in both 2003 and 2002. In Footnote 5 of its financial statements, Kraft explains that it sold substantially all of its sugar confectionary business (including brands such as Life Savers and Altoids). The $4 million loss and $97 million earnings refer to the amount of loss (earnings) of the sugar confectionary business in each of those years.

---

[27] In business writing, items expected to continue in the future are often described as "persistent" or "permanent," whereas those not expected to continue are described as "transitory."

[28] These requirements apply to material amounts.

[29] IFRS No. 5, *Non-Current Assets Held for Sale and Discontinued Operations*, paragraphs 31–33.

5.2 Extraordinary Items

IAS No. 1 prohibits classification of any income or expense items as being "extraordinary."[30] Under U.S. GAAP, an extraordinary item is one that is both unusual in nature and infrequent in occurrence. Extraordinary items are presented separately on the income statement and allow a reader of the statements to see that these items are not part of a company's operating activities and are not expected to occur on an ongoing basis. Extraordinary items are shown net of tax and appear on the income statement below discontinued operations. An example of an extraordinary item is provided in Example 12.

EXAMPLE 12

Extraordinary Gain: Purchase of a Business for Less than the Fair Value of the Identifiable Net Assets

Vicon Industries in its annual report made the following disclosure:

> On October 1, 2004, the Company entered into an agreement to purchase all of the operating assets of Videotronic Infosystems GmbH ("Videotronic"), a Germany based video system supplier which was operating under insolvency protection, for 700,000 Eurodollars [sic] (approximately $868,000)... During the year ended September 30, 2005, the Company recognized a $211,000 extraordinary gain on the recovery of Videotronic net assets in excess of their allocated purchase price. Such gain includes adjustments to assigned values of accounts receivable, inventories, trade payables and severance liabilities.

Source: Vicon Industries 10-K Report for fiscal year ended 30 September 2005, filed 29 December 2005: Note 15.

Companies apply judgment to determine whether an item is extraordinary based on guidance from accounting standards (FASB ASC Section 225-20-45 [Income Statement–Extraordinary and Unusual Items–Other Presentation Matters]). Judgment on whether an item is unusual in nature requires consideration of the company's environment, including its industry and geography. Determining whether an item is infrequent in occurrence is based on expectations of whether it will occur again in the near future. Standard setters offer specific guidance in some cases. For example, following Hurricanes Katrina and Rita in 2005, the American Institute of Certified Public Accountants issued Technical Practice Aid 5400.05, which states (the material in square brackets has been added): "A natural disaster [such as a hurricane, tornado, fire, or earthquake] of a type that is reasonably expected to re-occur would not meet both conditions [for classification as an extraordinary item]."

Given the requirements for classification of an item as extraordinary—unusual and infrequent—an analyst can generally eliminate extraordinary items from expectations about a company's future financial performance unless there is some indication that such an extraordinary item may reoccur.

---

[30] IAS No. 1, *Presentation of Financial Statements*, paragraph 87, effective 2005. In prior years, classification of items as extraordinary was permitted.

5.3 Unusual or Infrequent Items

Items that do not meet the definition of extraordinary are shown as part of a company's continuing operations. Items that are unusual or infrequent—but not both—cannot be shown as extraordinary. For example, restructuring charges, such as costs to close plants and employee termination costs, are considered part of a company's ordinary activities. As another example, gains and losses arising when a company sells an asset or part of a business for more or less than its carrying value are also disclosed separately on the income statement but are not considered extraordinary because such sales are considered ordinary business activities.[31]

Highlighting the unusual or infrequent nature of these items assists an analyst in judging the likelihood that such items will reoccur.

In Exhibit 2, Kraft's income statement showed several such infrequent but not unusual items, all of which are included as part of operating income. The company reported a $111 million loss in 2002 from "integration costs and a loss on sale of a food factory," followed by a $13 million reduction of these costs in 2003. In Note 14 of its financial statements, the company explains that these costs arose from consolidating production lines in North America. Also, the company reported $142 million, $6 million, and $603 million in 2002, 2003, and 2004, respectively, for "asset impairment and exit costs" and explains in the footnotes that the large costs in 2004 are related to its restructuring program and reflect asset disposals, severance, and other implementation aspects.

Finally, Kraft reported an $80 million gain on the sale of businesses in 2002 and a $31 million gain in 2003, followed by a $3 million loss on the sale of businesses in 2004. In Note 14 of its financial statements, Kraft explains that the $80 million gain in 2002 arose from the sale of its Latin American bakery ingredient business and several small food businesses; the $31 million gain in 2003 arose from the sale of a European rice business and an Italian fresh cheese business; and the $3 million loss in 2004 arose from the sale of a Brazilian snack nuts business and Norwegian candy business trademarks. An analyst would seek to understand how these disposals fit with the company's strategy and what effect, if material, these disposals would have on the company's future operations.

Generally, in forecasting future operations, an analyst would assess whether the items reported are likely to reoccur and also possible implications for future earnings. It is generally not advisable simply to ignore all unusual items.

5.4 Changes in Accounting Standards

At times, standard setters issue new pronouncements that require companies to change accounting principles. In other cases, changes in accounting principles (e.g., from one acceptable inventory costing method to another) are made for other reasons, such as providing a better reflection of the company's performance. Changes in accounting principles are reported through retrospective application,[32] unless it is impractical to do so. *Retrospective application* means that the financial statements for all fiscal years shown in a company's financial report are presented as if the newly adopted accounting principle had been used

---

[31] In its financial statement footnotes, Groupe Danone provides a reconciliation between operating income under French GAAP, which excludes certain exceptional items (such as gains and losses on disposals), and U.S. GAAP.

[32] IAS No. 8, *Accounting Policies, Changes in Accounting Estimates and Errors*, and FASB ASC Topic 250 [Accounting Changes and Error Corrections].

throughout the entire period. Footnotes to the financial statements describe the change and explain the justification for the change.

Because changes in accounting principles are retrospectively applied, the financial statements that appear within a financial report are comparable. So, if a company's annual report for 2006 includes its financial statements for fiscal years 2004, 2005, and 2006, all of these statements will be comparable.

In years prior to 2005, under both IFRS and U.S. GAAP, the cumulative effect of changes in accounting policies was typically shown at the bottom of the income statement in the year of change instead of using retrospective application. It is possible that future accounting standards may occasionally require a company to report the change differently than retrospective application. Footnote disclosures are required to explain how the transition from the old standard to the new one was handled. During the period when companies make the transition from the old standard to the new, an analyst would examine disclosures to ensure comparability across companies.

In contrast to changes in accounting policies (such as whether to expense the cost of employee stock options), companies sometimes make *changes in accounting estimates* (such as the useful life of a depreciable asset). Changes in accounting estimates are handled prospectively, with the change affecting the financial statements for the period of change and future periods.[33] No adjustments are made to prior statements, and the adjustment is not shown on the face of the income statement. Significant changes should be disclosed in the footnotes.

Another possible adjustment is a *correction of an error for a prior period* (e.g., in financial statements issued for an earlier year). This cannot be handled by simply adjusting the current period income statement. Correction of an error for a prior period is handled by restating the financial statements (including the balance sheet, statement of owners' equity, and statement of cash flows) for the prior periods presented in the current financial statements.[34] Footnote disclosures are required regarding the error. These disclosures should be examined carefully because they may reveal weaknesses in the company's accounting systems and financial controls.

5.5 Nonoperating Items: Investing and Financing Activities

Nonoperating items are reported separately from operating income. For example, if a nonfinancial service company invests in equity or debt securities issued by another company, any interest, dividends, or profits from sales of these securities will be shown as nonoperating income. In general, for nonfinancial services companies,[35] nonoperating income that is disclosed separately on the income statement (or in the notes) includes amounts earned through investing activities.

Among nonoperating items on the income statement (or accompanying notes), nonfinancial service companies also disclose the interest expense on their debt securities, including amortization of any discount or premium. The amount of interest expense is related to the amount of a company's borrowings and is generally described in the financial footnotes. For financial service companies, interest income and expense are likely components of operating activities.

---

[33] Ibid.

[34] Ibid.

[35] Examples of financial services firms are insurance companies, banks, brokers, dealers, and investment companies.

In practice, investing and financing activities may be disclosed on a net basis, with the components disclosed separately in the footnotes. In its income statement for 2004, Kraft, for example, disclosed net interest and other debt expense of $666 million. The financial statement footnotes (not shown) further disclose that Kraft's total interest expense was $679 million and interest income was $13 million, thus the net $666 million. Groupe Danone's footnotes provide similar disclosures.

For purposes of assessing a company's future performance, the amount of financing expense will depend on the company's financing policy (target capital structure) and borrowing costs. The amount of investing income will depend on the purpose and success of investing activities. For a nonfinancial company, a significant amount of financial income would typically warrant further exploration. What are the reasons underlying the company's investments in the securities of other companies? Is the company simply investing excess cash in short-term securities to generate income higher than cash deposits, or is the company purchasing securities issued by other companies for strategic reasons, such as access to raw material supply or research?

EARNINGS PER SHARE   6

One metric of particular importance to an equity investor is earnings per share (EPS). EPS is an input into ratios such as the price/earnings ratio. Additionally, each shareholder in a company owns a different number of shares. A presentation of EPS, therefore, enables each shareholder to compute his or her share of the company's earnings. Under IFRS, IAS No. 33, *Earnings Per Share*, requires the presentation of EPS on the face of the income statement for net profit or loss (net income) and profit or loss (income) from continuing operations. Similar presentation is required under U.S. GAAP by FASB ASC Topic 260 [Earnings Per Share]. This section outlines the calculations for EPS and explains how the calculation differs for a simple versus complex capital structure.

6.1 Simple versus Complex Capital Structure

A company's capital is composed of its equity and debt. Some types of equity have preference over others, and some debt (and other instruments) may be converted into equity. Under IFRS, the type of equity for which EPS is presented are ordinary shares. **Ordinary shares** are those equity shares that are subordinate to all other types of equity. This is the basic ownership of the company—the equityholders who are paid last in a liquidation of the company and who benefit the most when the company does well. Under U.S. GAAP, this equity is referred to as **common stock** or **common shares**, reflecting U.S. language usage. The terms "ordinary shares," "common stock," and "common shares" are used equivalently in the remaining discussion.

When a company has any securities that are potentially convertible into common stock, it is said to have a complex capital structure. Specific examples of securities that are potentially convertible into common stock include convertible bonds, convertible preferred stock, employee stock options, and warrants.[36] If a

---

[36] A warrant is a call option typically attached to securities issued by a company, such as bonds. A warrant gives the holder the right to acquire the company's stock from the company at a specified price within a specified time period. IFRS and U.S. GAAP standards regarding earnings per share apply equally to call options, warrants, and equivalent instruments.

company's capital structure does not include securities that are potentially convertible into common stock, it is said to have a simple capital structure.

The distinction between simple versus complex capital structure is relevant to the calculation of EPS because any securities that are potentially convertible into common stock could, as a result of conversion, potentially dilute (i.e., decrease) EPS. Information about such a potential dilution is valuable to a company's current and potential shareholders; therefore, accounting standards require companies to disclose what their EPS would be if all dilutive securities were converted into common stock. The EPS that would result if all dilutive securities were converted is called **diluted EPS**. In contrast, **basic EPS** is calculated using the actual earnings available to common stock and the weighted average number of shares outstanding.

Companies are required to report both their basic EPS and their diluted EPS. Kraft reported basic EPS of $1.56 and diluted EPS of $1.55 for 2004, lower than EPS (from continuing operations) of $1.95 for 2003. Danone reported basic EPS of 1.26 and diluted EPS of 1.25 for 2004, much lower than 2003. An analyst would try to determine the causes underlying the changes in EPS, a topic we will address following an explanation of the calculations of both basic and diluted EPS.

6.2 Basic EPS

Basic EPS is the amount of income available to common shareholders divided by the weighted average number of common shares outstanding over a period. The amount of income available to common shareholders is the amount of net income remaining after preferred dividends (if any) have been paid. Thus, the formula to calculate basic EPS is:

$$\text{Basic EPS} = \frac{\text{Net income} - \text{Preferred dividends}}{\text{Weighted average number of shares outstanding}} \qquad \textbf{(1)}$$

The weighted average number of shares outstanding is a time weighting of common shares outstanding, and the methodology applies to calculating diluted EPS. As an example, assume a company began the year with 2,000,000 shares outstanding and repurchased 100,000 shares on 1 July. The weighted average number of shares outstanding would be the sum of 2,000,000 shares $\times$ 1/2 year + 1,900,000 shares $\times$ 1/2 year, or 1,950,000 shares. So, the company would use 1,950,000 shares in calculating its basic EPS.

If the number of shares of common stock increases as a result of a stock dividend, stock bonus, or a stock split (all three represent the receipt of additional shares by existing shareholders), the EPS calculation reflects the change retroactively to the beginning of the period.

Examples of a basic EPS computation are presented in Examples 13, 14, and 15.

EXAMPLE 13

A Basic EPS Calculation (1)

For the year ended 31 December 2006, Shopalot Company had net income of $1,950,000. The company had an average of 1,500,000 shares of common stock outstanding, no preferred stock, and no convertible securities. What was Shopalot's basic EPS?

Solution: Shopalot's basic EPS was $1.30, calculated as $1,950,000 divided by 1,500,000 shares.

EXAMPLE 14

A Basic EPS Calculation (2)

For the year ended 31 December 2006, Angler Products had net income of $2,500,000. The company declared and paid $200,000 of dividends on preferred stock. The company also had the following common stock share information:

Shares outstanding on 1 January 2006	1,000,000
Shares issued on 1 April 2006	200,000
Shares repurchased (treasury shares) on 1 October 2006	(100,000)
Shares outstanding on 31 December 2006	1,100,000

1. What is the company's weighted average number of shares outstanding?
2. What is the company's basic EPS?

Solution to 1: The weighted average number of shares outstanding is determined by the length of time each quantity of shares was outstanding:

$1,000,000 \times$ (3 months/12 months) =	250,000
$1,200,000 \times$ (6 months/12 months) =	600,000
$1,100,000 \times$ (3 months/12 months) =	275,000
Weighted average number of shares outstanding	1,125,000

Solution to 2: Basic EPS is (Net income − Preferred dividends)/ Weighted average number of shares = ($2,500,000 − $200,000)/ 1,125,000 = $2.04

EXAMPLE 15

A Basic EPS Calculation (3)

Assume the same facts as in Example 14 except that on 1 December 2006, the company institutes a 2 for 1 stock split. Each shareholder receives two shares in exchange for each current share that he or she owns. What is the company's basic EPS?

Solution: For EPS calculation purposes, a stock split is treated as if it occurred at the beginning of the period. The weighted average number of shares would, therefore, be 2,250,000, and the basic EPS would be $1.02.

6.3 Diluted EPS

If a company has a simple capital structure (i.e., one with no potentially dilutive securities), then its basic EPS is equal to its diluted EPS. If, however, a company has dilutive securities, its diluted EPS is lower than its basic EPS. The sections below describe the effects of three types of potentially dilutive securities: convertible preferred, convertible debt, and employee stock options.

6.3.1 Diluted EPS when a Company Has Convertible Preferred Stock Outstanding

When a company has convertible preferred stock outstanding, diluted EPS is calculated using the **if-converted method** (i.e., what EPS would have been *if* the convertible preferred securities had been converted at the beginning of the period). What would have been the effect if the securities had been converted? If the convertible preferred securities had been converted, these securities would no longer be outstanding; instead, additional common stock would be outstanding. Therefore, if such a conversion had been taken place, the company would not have paid preferred dividends and would have had more shares of common stock.

The diluted EPS using the if-converted method for convertible preferred stock is equal to the amount of net income divided by the weighted average number of shares outstanding plus the new shares of common stock that would be issued upon conversion of the preferred. Thus, the formula to calculate diluted EPS using the if-converted method for preferred stock is:

$$\text{Diluted EPS} = \frac{(\text{Net income})}{\left(\begin{array}{c}\text{Weighted average number of shares} \\ \text{outstanding} + \text{New common shares that} \\ \text{would have been issued at conversion}\end{array}\right)} \qquad \textbf{(2)}$$

A diluted EPS calculation using the if-converted method for preferred stock is provided in Example 16.

EXAMPLE 16

A Diluted EPS Calculation Using the If-Converted Method for Preferred Stock

For the year ended 31 December 2006, Bright-Warm Utility Company had net income of $1,750,000. The company had an average of 500,000 shares of common stock outstanding, 20,000 shares of convertible preferred, and no other potentially dilutive securities. Each share of preferred pays a dividend of $10 per share, and each is convertible into five shares of the company's common stock. Calculate the company's basic and diluted EPS.

Solution: If the 20,000 shares of convertible preferred had each converted into 5 shares of the company's common stock, the company would have had an additional 100,000 shares of common stock (5 shares of common for each of the 20,000 shares of preferred). If the conversion had taken place, the company would not have paid preferred dividends of $200,000 ($10 per share for each of the 20,000 shares of preferred). As shown in Exhibit 9, the company's basic EPS was $3.10 and its diluted EPS was $2.92.

EXHIBIT 9	Calculation of Diluted EPS for Bright-Warm Utility Company Using the If-Converted Method: Case of Preferred Stock

	Basic EPS	Diluted EPS Using If-Converted Method
Net income	$1,750,000	$1,750,000
Preferred dividend	−200,000	0
Numerator	$1,550,000	$1,750,000
Weighted average number of shares outstanding	500,000	500,000
If converted	0	100,000
Denominator	500,000	600,000
EPS	**$3.10**	**$2.92**

6.3.2 Diluted EPS when a Company Has Convertible Debt Outstanding

When a company has convertible debt outstanding, the diluted EPS calculation is similar to the calculation for convertible preferred: Diluted EPS is calculated using the if-converted method (i.e., what EPS would have been *if* the convertible debt had been converted at the beginning of the period). If the convertible debt had been converted, the debt securities would no longer be outstanding; instead, additional common stock would be outstanding. Therefore, if such a conversion had taken place, the company would not have paid interest on the convertible debt and would have had more shares of common stock.

To calculate diluted EPS using the if-converted method for convertible debt, the amount of net income available to common shareholders must be increased by the amount of after-tax interest related to the convertible debt. In addition, the weighted average number of shares in the denominator increases by the number of new shares of common stock that would be issued upon conversion of the convertible debt. Thus, the formula to calculate diluted EPS using the if-converted method for convertible debt is:

$$\text{Diluted EPS} = \frac{\begin{array}{c}\text{(Net income + After-tax interest on}\\\text{convertible debt − Preferred dividends)}\end{array}}{\begin{array}{c}\text{(Weighted average number of shares}\\\text{outstanding + New common shares that}\\\text{could have been issued at conversion)}\end{array}} \quad (3)$$

A diluted EPS calculation using the if-converted method for convertible debt is provided in Example 17.

EXAMPLE 17

A Diluted EPS Calculation Using the If-Converted Method for Convertible Debt

Oppnox Company reported net income of $750,000 for the year ended 31 December 2005. The company had an average of 690,000 shares of common stock outstanding. In addition, the company has only one potentially dilutive security: $50,000 of 6 percent convertible bonds, convertible into a total of 10,000 shares. Assuming a tax rate of 30 percent, calculate Oppnox's basic and diluted EPS.

Solution: If the convertible debt had been converted, the debt securities would no longer be outstanding; instead, an additional 10,000 shares of common stock would be outstanding. Also, if such a conversion had taken place, the company would not have paid interest on the convertible debt of $3,000, equivalent to $3,000(1 − 0.30) = $2,100 on an after-tax basis. To calculate diluted EPS using the if-converted method for convertible debt, the amount of net income available to common shareholders is increased by $2,100. Also, the weighted average number of shares in the denominator increases by 10,000 shares.

EXHIBIT 10	Calculation of Diluted EPS for Oppnox Company Using the If-Converted Method: Case of a Convertible Bond	
	Basic EPS	**Diluted EPS Using If-Converted Method**
Net income	$750,000	$750,000
After-tax cost of interest		2,100
Numerator	$750,000	$752,100
Weighted average number of shares outstanding	690,000	690,000
If converted	0	10,000
Denominator	690,000	700,000
EPS	**$1.09**	**$1.07**

6.3.3 Diluted EPS when a Company Has Stock Options, Warrants, or Their Equivalents Outstanding

Under U.S. GAAP, when a company has stock options, warrants, or their equivalents[37] outstanding, the diluted EPS is calculated using the **treasury stock method** (i.e., what EPS would have been *if* the options had been exercised and the company had used the proceeds to repurchase common stock). If the options had been exercised, the company would have received cash for the amount of the option exercise price. The options would no longer be outstanding; instead, additional common stock would be outstanding. Under the treasury stock method, a further calculation is made to adjust the number of shares outstanding by the number of shares that could have been purchased with the cash received upon exercise of the options.

To calculate diluted EPS using the treasury stock method for options, the weighted average number of shares in the denominator increases by the number of new shares of common stock that would be issued upon exercise of the options minus the number of shares that could have been purchased with the cash received upon exercise of the options. No change is made to the numerator. Thus, the formula to calculate diluted EPS using the treasury stock method for options is

$$\text{Diluted EPS} = \frac{(\text{Net income} - \text{Preferred dividends})}{\begin{array}{c}(\text{Weighted average number of shares} \\ \text{outstanding} + \text{New shares that could} \\ \text{have been issued at option exercise} - \\ \text{Shares that could have been purchased} \\ \text{with cash received upon exercise})\end{array}} \quad \textbf{(4)}$$

---

[37] Hereafter, options, warrants, and their equivalents will be referred to simply as "options" because the accounting treatment is interchangeable for these instruments under IFRS and U.S. GAAP.

A diluted EPS calculation using the treasury stock method for options is provided in Example 18.

EXAMPLE 18

A Diluted EPS Calculation Using the Treasury Stock Method for Options

Hihotech Company reported net income of $2.3 million for the year ended 30 June 2005 and had an average of 800,000 common shares outstanding. The company has outstanding 30,000 options with an exercise price of $35 and no other potentially dilutive securities. Over the year, the company's market price has averaged $55 per share. Calculate the company's basic and diluted EPS.

Solution: Using the treasury stock method, we first calculate that the company would have received $1,050,000 ($35 for each of the 30,000 options exercised) if all the options had been exercised. The options would no longer be outstanding; instead, 30,000 new shares of common stock would be outstanding. Under the treasury stock method, we reduce the number of new shares by the number of shares that could have been purchased with the cash received upon exercise of the options. At an average market price of $55 per share, the $1,050,000 proceeds from option exercise could have purchased 19,091 shares of treasury stock. Therefore, the net new shares issued would have been 10,909 (calculated as 30,000 minus 19,091). No change is made to the numerator. As shown in Exhibit 11, the company's basic EPS was $2.88 and the diluted EPS was $2.84.

EXHIBIT 11	Calculation of Diluted EPS for Hihotech Company Using the Treasury Stock Method: Case of Stock Options

	Basic EPS	Diluted EPS Using Treasury Stock Method
Net income	$2,300,000	$2,300,000
Numerator	$2,300,000	$2,300,000
Weighted average number of shares outstanding	800,000	800,000
If converted	0	10,909
Denominator	800,000	810,909
EPS	**$2.88**	**$2.84**

Under IFRS, IAS No. 33 requires a similar computation but does not refer to it as the "treasury stock method." The company is required to consider that any assumed proceeds are received from the issuance of new shares at the average market price for the period. These new "inferred" shares would be disregarded in the computation of diluted EPS, but the excess of the new shares issued under options contracts over the new "inferred" shares would be added into the weighted average number of shares outstanding. The results are similar to the treasury stock method, as shown in Example 19.

EXAMPLE 19

Diluted EPS for Options under IFRS

Assuming the same facts as in Example 18, calculate the weighted average number of shares outstanding for diluted EPS under IFRS.

Solution: If the options had been converted, the company would have received $1,050,000. If this amount had been received from the issuance of new shares at the average market price of $55 per share, the company would have sold 19,091 shares. The excess of the shares issued under options (30,000) over the shares the company could have sold at market prices (19,091) is 10,909. This amount is added to the weighted average number of shares outstanding of 800,000 to get diluted shares of 810,909. Note that this is the same result as that obtained under U.S. GAAP; it is just derived in a different manner.

6.3.4 Other Issues with Diluted EPS

It is possible that some potentially convertible securities could be **antidilutive** (i.e., their inclusion in the computation would result in an EPS higher than the company's basic EPS). Under accounting standards, antidilutive securities are not included in the calculation of diluted EPS. In general, diluted EPS reflects maximum potential dilution. Example 20 provides an illustration of an antidilutive security.

EXAMPLE 20

An Antidilutive Security

For the year ended 31 December 2006, Dim-Cool Utility Company had net income of $1,750,000. The company had an average of 500,000 shares of common stock outstanding, 20,000 shares of convertible preferred, and no other potentially dilutive securities. Each share of preferred pays a dividend of $10 per share, and each is convertible into three shares of the company's common stock. What was the company's basic and diluted EPS?

Solution: If the 20,000 shares of convertible preferred had each converted into 3 shares of the company's common stock, the company would have had an additional 60,000 shares of common stock (3 shares of common for each of the 20,000 shares of preferred). If the conversion had taken place, the company would not have paid preferred dividends of $200,000 ($10 per share for each of the 20,000 shares of preferred). The effect of using the if-converted method would be EPS of $3.13, as shown in Exhibit 12. Because this is greater than the company's basic EPS of $3.10, the securities are said to be antidilutive and the effect of their conversion would not be included in diluted EPS. Diluted EPS would be the same as basic EPS (i.e., $3.10).

EXHIBIT 12	**Calculation for an Antidilutive Security**	
	Basic EPS	**Diluted EPS Using If-Converted Method**
Net income	$1,750,000	$1,750,000
Preferred dividend	−200,000	0
Numerator	$1,550,000	$1,750,000
Weighted average number of shares outstanding	500,000	500,000
If converted	0	60,000
Denominator	500,000	560,000
EPS	**$3.10**	**$3.13**[a]

[a]Exceeds basic EPS; security is antidilutive and, therefore, not included.

7   ANALYSIS OF THE INCOME STATEMENT

In this section, we apply two analytical tools to analyze the income statement: common-size analysis and income statement ratios. In analyzing the income statement, the objective is to assess a company's performance over a period of time—compared with its own historical performance or to the performance of another company.

7.1 Common-Size Analysis of the Income Statement

Common-size analysis of the income statement can be performed by stating each line item on the income statement as a percentage of revenue.[38] Common-size statements facilitate comparison across time periods (time-series analysis) and across companies of different sizes (cross-sectional analysis).

To illustrate, Panel A of Exhibit 13 presents an income statement for three hypothetical companies. Company A and Company B, each with $10 million in sales, are larger (as measured by sales) than Company C, which has only $2 million in sales. In addition, Companies A and B both have higher operating profit: $2 million and $1.5 million, respectively, compared with Company C's operating profit of only $400,000.

EXHIBIT 13

Panel A: Income Statements for Companies A, B, and C ($)

	A	B	C
Sales	$10,000,000	$10,000,000	$2,000,000
Cost of sales	3,000,000	7,500,000	600,000
Gross profit	7,000,000	2,500,000	1,400,000
Selling, general, and administrative expenses	1,000,000	1,000,000	200,000
Research and development	2,000,000	–	400,000
Advertising	2,000,000	–	400,000
Operating profit	2,000,000	1,500,000	400,000

Panel B: Common-Size Income Statements for Companies A, B, and C (%)

	A	B	C
Sales	100%	100%	100%
Cost of sales	30	75	30
Gross profit	70	25	70
Selling, general, and administrative expenses	10	10	10
Research and development	20	0	20
Advertising	20	0	20
Operating profit	20	15	20

Note: Each line item is expressed as a percentage of the company's sales.

---

[38] This format can be distinguished as "vertical common-size analysis." As the reading on financial statement analysis discusses, there is another type of common-size analysis, known as "horizontal common-size analysis," that states items in relation to a selected base year value. Unless otherwise indicated, text references to "common-size analysis" refer to vertical analysis.

How can an analyst meaningfully compare the performance of these companies? By preparing a common-size income statement, as illustrated in Panel B, an analyst can readily see that the percentages of Company C's expenses and profit relative to its sales are exactly the same as for Company A. Furthermore, although Company C's operating profit is lower than Company B's in absolute dollars, it is higher in percentage terms (20 percent for Company C compared with only 15 percent for Company B). For each $100 of sales, Company C generates $5 more operating profit than Company B. In other words, Company C is more profitable than Company B based on this measure.

The common-size income statement also highlights differences in companies' strategies. Comparing the two larger companies, Company A reports significantly higher gross profit as a percentage of sales than does Company B (70 percent compared with 25 percent). Given that both companies operate in the same industry, why can Company A generate so much higher gross profit? One possible explanation is found by comparing the operating expenses of the two companies. Company A spends significantly more on research and development and on advertising than Company B. Expenditures on research and development likely result in products with superior technology. Expenditures on advertising likely result in greater brand awareness. So, based on these differences, it is likely that Company A is selling technologically superior products with a better brand image. Company B may be selling its products more cheaply (with a lower gross profit as a percentage of sales) but saving money by not investing in research and development or advertising. In practice, differences across companies are more subtle, but the concept is similar. An analyst, noting significant differences, would seek to understand the underlying reasons for the differences and their implications for the future performance of the companies.

For most expenses, comparison to the amount of sales is appropriate. However, in the case of taxes, it is more meaningful to compare the amount of taxes with the amount of pretax income. Using financial footnote disclosure, an analyst can then examine the causes for differences in effective tax rates. To project the companies' future net income, an analyst would project the companies' pretax income and apply an estimated effective tax rate determined in part by the historical tax rates.

Vertical common-size analysis of the income statement is particularly useful in cross-sectional analysis—comparing companies with each other for a particular time period or comparing a company with industry or sector data. The analyst could select individual peer companies for comparison, use industry data from published sources, or compile data from databases based on a selection of peer companies or broader industry data. For example, Exhibit 14 presents common-size income statement data compiled for the components of the Standard & Poor's 500 classified into the 10 S&P/MSCI Global Industrial Classification System (GICS) sectors using 2005 data. Note that when compiling aggregate data such as this, some level of aggregation is necessary and less detail may be available than from peer company financial statements. The performance of an individual company can be compared with industry or peer company data to evaluate its relative performance.

EXHIBIT 14 Common-Size Income Statement Statistics for the S&P 500 Classified by S&P/MSCI GICS Sector Data for 2005

Panel A: Median Data

	Energy	Materials	Industrials	Consumer Discretionary	Consumer Staples	Health Care	Financials	Information Technology	Telecom. Services	Utilities
No. observations	29	30	49	85	36	52	87	73	9	31
Operating margin	17.24	11.85	11.94	11.15	12.53	16.73	34.62	12.59	22.85	13.52
Pretax margin	19.17	10.95	10.55	10.17	10.76	14.03	23.28	13.60	18.18	9.27
Taxes	5.63	2.87	2.94	3.59	3.26	4.69	6.51	4.06	4.27	3.12
Profit margin	13.97	7.68	7.28	6.87	6.74	9.35	16.09	11.60	10.91	6.93
Cost of goods sold	66.52	68.35	69.02	63.29	56.24	45.29	42.29	47.17	41.76	76.79
Selling, general, and administrative expenses	3.82	10.20	15.88	22.46	25.07	31.77	28.98	31.81	22.40	4.91

Panel B: Mean Data

	Energy	Materials	Industrials	Consumer Discretionary	Consumer Staples	Health Care	Financials	Information Technology	Telecom. Services	Utilities
No. observations	29	30	49	85	36	52	87	73	9	31
Operating margin	23.13	14.12	13.16	12.69	14.51	17.84	35.45	15.13	20.66	14.60
Pretax margin	23.96	12.58	11.09	10.38	12.03	15.83	23.42	15.25	15.19	8.00
Taxes	7.72	3.38	3.33	3.94	3.81	4.94	6.65	4.98	5.14	2.48
Profit margin	16.02	8.58	7.69	6.32	8.15	10.80	16.37	10.26	9.52	5.68
Cost of goods sold	62.36	67.87	68.92	62.41	56.62	49.20	51.47	46.65	40.61	76.51
Selling, general, and administrative expenses	5.44	13.05	17.45	22.82	25.88	30.48	27.68	33.06	22.81	4.91
Average tax rate computed on mean	32.22	26.89	30.04	37.98	31.65	31.21	28.40	32.66	33.82	30.99

Source: Based on data from Compustat.

7.2 Income Statement Ratios

One aspect of financial performance is profitability. One indicator of profitability is **net profit margin**, also known as **profit margin** and **return on sales**, which is calculated as net income divided by revenue (or sales).[39]

$$\text{Net profit margin} = \frac{\text{Net income}}{\text{Revenue}}$$

Net profit margin measures the amount of income that a company was able to generate for each dollar of revenue. A higher level of net profit margin indicates higher profitability and is thus more desirable. Net profit margin can also be found directly on the common-size income statements.

For Kraft Foods, net profit margin for 2004 was 8.3 percent (calculated as earnings from continuing operations of $2,669 million, divided by net revenues of $32,168 million). To judge this ratio, some comparison is needed. Kraft's profitability can be compared with that of another company or with its own previous performance. Compared with previous years, Kraft's profitability has declined. In 2003, net profit margin was 11.1 percent, and in 2002, it was 11.3 percent.

Another measure of profitability is the gross profit margin. Gross profit is calculated as revenue minus cost of goods sold, and the **gross profit margin** is calculated as the gross profit divided by revenue.

$$\text{Gross profit margin} = \frac{\text{Gross profit}}{\text{Revenue}}$$

The gross profit margin measures the amount of gross profit that a company generated for each dollar of revenue. A higher level of gross profit margin indicates higher profitability and thus is generally more desirable, although differences in gross profit margins across companies reflect differences in companies' strategies. For example, consider a company pursuing a strategy of selling a differentiated product (e.g., a product differentiated based on brand name, quality, superior technology, or patent protection). The company would likely be able to sell the differentiated product at a higher price than a similar, but undifferentiated, product and, therefore, would likely show a higher gross profit margin than a company selling an undifferentiated product. Although a company selling a differentiated product would likely show a higher gross profit margin, this may take time. In the initial stage of the strategy, the company would likely incur costs to create a differentiated product, such as advertising or research and development, which would not be reflected in the gross margin calculation.

Kraft's gross profit (shown in Exhibit 2) was $11,785 in 2002 and $11,887 in 2004. In other words, in absolute terms, Kraft's gross profit increased. However, expressing gross profit as a percentage of net revenues,[40] it is apparent that Kraft's gross profit margin declined, as Exhibit 15 illustrates. From over 40 percent in 2002, Kraft's profit margin declined to 36.95 percent in 2004.

---

[39] In the definition of margin ratios of this type, "sales" is often used interchangeably with "revenue." "Return on sales" has also been used to refer to a class of profitability ratios having revenue in the denominator.

[40] Some items disclosed separately in Kraft's actual income statement have been summarized as "other operating costs (income)" for this display.

EXHIBIT 15	Kraft's Gross Profit Margin					
	2004		**2003**		**2002**	
	$ Millions	**%**	**$ Millions**	**%**	**$ Millions**	**%**
Net revenues	32,168	100.00	30,498	100.00	29,248	100.00
Cost of sales	20,281	63.05	18,531	60.76	17,463	59.71
Gross profit	11,887	**36.95**	11,967	**39.24**	11,785	**40.29**

The net profit margin and gross profit margin are just two of the many subtotals that can be generated from common-size income statements. Other "margins" used by analysts include the **operating margin** (operating income divided by revenue) and **pretax margin** (earnings before taxes divided by revenue).

COMPREHENSIVE INCOME   8

The general expression for net income is revenue minus expenses. There are, however, certain items of revenue and expense that, by accounting convention, are excluded from the net income calculation. To understand how reported shareholders' equity of one period links with reported shareholders' equity of the next period, we must understand these excluded items, known as **other comprehensive income**.

Comprehensive income is defined as "the change in equity [net assets] of a business enterprise during a period from transactions and other events and circumstances from nonowner sources. It includes all changes in equity during a period except those resulting from investments by owners and distributions to owners."[41] So, comprehensive income includes *both* net income and other revenue and expense items that are excluded from the net income calculation (other comprehensive income). Assume, for example, a company's beginning shareholders' equity is €110 million, its net income for the year is €10 million, its cash dividends for the year are €2 million, and there was no issuance or repurchase of common stock. If the company's actual ending shareholders' equity is €123 million, then €5 million [€123 − (€110 + €10 − €2)] has bypassed the net income calculation by being classified as other comprehensive income. (If the company had no other comprehensive income, its ending shareholders' equity would have been €118 million [€110 + €10 − €2].)

In U.S. financial statements, according to U.S. GAAP, four types of items are treated as other comprehensive income.

► Foreign currency translation adjustments. In consolidating the financial statements of foreign subsidiaries, the effects of translating the subsidiaries' balance sheet assets and liabilities at current exchange rates are included as other comprehensive income.

---

[41] See FASB ASC Section 220-10-05 [Comprehensive Income–Overall–Overview and Background].

▶ Unrealized gains or losses on derivatives contracts accounted for as hedges. Changes in the fair value of derivatives are recorded each period, but these changes in value for certain derivatives (those considered hedges) are treated as other comprehensive income and thus bypass the income statement.

▶ Unrealized holding gains and losses on a certain category of investment securities, namely, available-for-sale securities.

▶ Changes in the funded status of a company's defined benefit post-retirement plans.

The third type of item is perhaps the simplest to illustrate. Holding gains on securities arise when a company owns securities over an accounting period, during which time the securities' value increases. Similarly, holding losses on securities arise when a company owns securities over a period during which time the securities' value decreases. If the company has not sold the securities (i.e., realized the gain or loss), its holding gain or loss is said to be unrealized. The question is: Should the company reflect these unrealized holding gains and losses in its income statement?

According to accounting standards, the answer depends on how the company has categorized the securities. Categorization depends on what the company intends to do with the securities. If the company intends to actively trade the securities, the answer is yes; the company should categorize the securities as **trading securities** and reflect unrealized holding gains and losses in its income statement. However, if the company does not intend to actively trade the securities, the securities may be categorized as available-for-sale securities. For available-for-sale securities, the company does not reflect unrealized holding gains and losses in its income statement. Instead, unrealized holding gains and losses on available-for-sale securities bypass the income statement and go directly to shareholders' equity.

Even though unrealized holding gains and losses on available-for-sale securities are excluded from a company's net income, they are *included* in a company's comprehensive income.

The fourth item, concerning defined benefit post-retirement plans, recently changed. Until recently, so-called minimum pension liability adjustments were treated as other comprehensive income; however, a new standard (SFAS No. 158, which is effective for public companies as of the end of fiscal years after 15 December 2006), will eliminate the need for minimum pension liability adjustments. The need for those adjustments resulted from pension accounting which often created a divergence between a pension plan's funded status and the amount reported on the balance sheet. Under the new standard, companies are required to recognize the overfunded or underfunded status of a defined benefit post-retirement plan as an asset or liability on their balance sheet.[42]

FASB[43] allows companies to report comprehensive income at the bottom of the income statement, on a separate statement of comprehensive income, or as a column in the statement of shareholders' equity; however, presentation alternatives are currently being reviewed by both U.S. and non-U.S. standard setters.

Particularly in comparing financial statements of two companies, it is relevant to examine significant differences in comprehensive income.

---

[42] A defined benefit plan is said to be overfunded if the amount of assets in a trust fund for that plan exceeds that plan's obligations. If the amount of assets in a trust fund for that plan is less than the plan's obligations, it is underfunded.

[43] FASB ASC Section 220-10-55 [Comprehensive Income–Overall–Implementation Guidance and Illustrations].

EXAMPLE 21

Other Comprehensive Income

Assume a company's beginning shareholders' equity is €200 million, its net income for the year is €20 million, its cash dividends for the year are €3 million, and there was no issuance or repurchase of common stock. The company's actual ending shareholders' equity is €227 million.

1. What amount has bypassed the net income calculation by being classified as other comprehensive income?
    A. €0.
    B. €7 million.
    C. €10 million.
    D. €30 million.

2. Which of the following statements best describes other comprehensive income?
    A. Income earned from diverse geographic and segment activities.
    B. Income earned from activities that are not part of the company's ordinary business activities.
    C. Income related to the sale of goods and delivery of services.
    D. Income that increases stockholders' equity but is not reflected as part of net income.

Solution to 1: C is correct. If the company's actual ending shareholders' equity is €227 million, then €10 million [€227− (€200 + €20 − €3)] has bypassed the net income calculation by being classified as other comprehensive income.

Solution to 2: D is correct. Answers A and B are not correct because they do not specify whether such income is reported as part of net income and shown in the income statement. Answer C is not correct because such activities would typically be reported as part of net income on the income statement.

EXAMPLE 22

Other Comprehensive Income in Analysis

An analyst is looking at two comparable companies. Company A has a lower price/earnings (P/E) ratio than Company B, and the conclusion that has been suggested is that Company A is undervalued. As part of examining this conclusion, the analyst decides to explore the question: What would the company's P/E look like if total comprehensive income per share—rather than net income per share—were used as the relevant metric?

	Company A	Company B
Price	$35	$30
EPS	$1.60	$0.90
P/E ratio	21.9×	33.3×
Other comprehensive income (loss) $ million	$(16.272)	$(1.757)
Shares (millions)	22.6	25.1

Solution: As shown by the following table, part of the explanation for Company A's lower P/E ratio may be that its significant losses—accounted for as other comprehensive income (OCI)—are not included in the P/E ratio.

	Company A	Company B
Price	$35	$30
EPS	$1.60	$0.90
OCI (loss) $ million	($16.272)	$(1.757)
Shares (millions)	22.6	25.1
OCI (loss) per share	$(0.72)	$(0.07)
Comprehensive EPS = EPS + OCI per share	$0.88	$0.83
Price/Comprehensive EPS ratio	39.8×	36.1×

SUMMARY

This reading has presented the elements of income statement analysis. The income statement presents information on the financial results of a company's business activities over a period of time; it communicates how much revenue the company generated during a period and what costs it incurred in connection with generating that revenue. A company's net income and its components (e.g., gross margin, operating earnings, and pretax earnings) are critical inputs into both the equity and credit analysis processes. Equity analysts are interested in earnings because equity markets often reward relatively high- or low-earnings growth companies with above-average or below-average valuations, respectively. Fixed-income analysts examine the components of income statements, past and projected, for information on companies' abilities to make promised payments on their debt over the course of the business cycle. Corporate financial announcements frequently emphasize income statements more than the other financial statements. Key points to this reading include the following:

► The income statement presents revenue, expenses, and net income.

► The components of the income statement include: revenue; cost of sales; sales, general, and administrative expenses; other operating expenses; nonoperating income and expenses; gains and losses; nonrecurring items; net income; and EPS.

► An income statement that presents a subtotal for gross profit (revenue minus cost of goods sold) is said to be presented in a multi-step format. One that does not present this subtotal is said to be presented in a single-step format.

► Revenue is recognized in the period it is earned, which may or may not be in the same period as the related cash collection. Recognition of revenue when earned is a fundamental principle of accrual accounting.

► In limited circumstances, specific revenue recognition methods may be applicable, including percentage of completion, completed contract, installment sales, and cost recovery.

► An analyst should identify differences in companies' revenue recognition methods and adjust reported revenue where possible to facilitate comparability. Where the available information does not permit adjustment, an analyst can characterize the revenue recognition as more or less conservative and thus qualitatively assess how differences in policies might affect financial ratios and judgments about profitability.

► The general principles of expense recognition include the matching principle. Expenses are matched either to revenue or to the time period in which the expenditure occurs (period costs) or to the time period of expected benefits of the expenditures (e.g., depreciation).

► In expense recognition, choice of method (i.e., depreciation method and inventory cost method), as well as estimates (i.e., uncollectible accounts, warranty expenses, assets' useful life, and salvage value) affect a company's reported income. An analyst should identify differences in companies' expense recognition methods and adjust reported financial statements where possible to facilitate comparability. Where the available information does not permit adjustment, an analyst can characterize the policies and estimates as more or less conservative and thus qualitatively assess how differences in policies might affect financial ratios and judgments about companies' performance.

► To assess a company's future earnings, it is helpful to separate those prior years' items of income and expense that are likely to continue in the future from those items that are less likely to continue.

► Some items from prior years clearly are not expected to continue in future periods and are separately disclosed on a company's income statement. Two such items are 1) discontinued operations and 2) extraordinary items. Both of these items are required to be reported separately from continuing operations.

► For other items on a company's income statement, such as unusual items and accounting changes, the likelihood of their continuing in the future is somewhat less clear and requires the analyst to make some judgments.

► Nonoperating items are reported separately from operating items. For example, if a nonfinancial service company invests in equity or debt securities issued by another company, any interest, dividends, or profits from sales of these securities will be shown as nonoperating income.

► Basic EPS is the amount of income available to common shareholders divided by the weighted average number of common shares outstanding over a period. The amount of income available to common shareholders is the amount of net income remaining after preferred dividends (if any) have been paid.

► If a company has a simple capital structure (i.e., one with no potentially dilutive securities), then its basic EPS is equal to its diluted EPS. If, however, a company has dilutive securities, its diluted EPS is lower than its basic EPS.

► Diluted EPS is calculated using the if-converted method for convertible securities and the treasury stock method for options.

► Common-size analysis of the income statement involves stating each line item on the income statement as a percentage of sales. Common-size statements facilitate comparison across time periods and across companies of different sizes.

► Two income-statement-based indicators of profitability are net profit margin and gross profit margin.

► Comprehensive income includes *both* net income and other revenue and expense items that are excluded from the net income calculation.

PRACTICE PROBLEMS FOR READING 32

1. Expenses on the income statement may be grouped by:

   A. nature, but not by function.

   B. function, but not by nature.

   C. either function or nature.

2. An example of an expense classification by function is:

   A. tax expense.

   B. interest expense.

   C. cost of goods sold.

3. Denali Limited, a manufacturing company, had the following income statement information:

Revenue	$4,000,000
Cost of goods sold	$3,000,000
Other operating expenses	$ 500,000
Interest expense	$ 100,000
Tax expense	$ 120,000

Denali's gross profit is equal to:

   A. $280,000.

   B. $500,000.

   C. $1,000,000.

4. Under IFRS, income includes increases in economic benefits from:

   A. increases in owners' equity related to owners' contributions.

   B. increases in liabilities not related to owners' contributions.

   C. enhancements of assets not related to owners' contributions.

5. Fairplay had the following information related to the sale of its products during 2006, which was its first year of business:

Revenue	$1,000,000
Returns of goods sold	$ 100,000
Cash collected	$ 800,000
Cost of goods sold	$ 700,000

Under the accrual basis of accounting, how much net revenue would be reported on Fairplay's 2006 income statement?

   A. $200,000.

   B. $800,000.

   C. $900,000.

6. If the outcome of a long-term contract can be measured reliably, the preferred accounting method under both IFRS and U.S. GAAP is:

   A. the installment method.

   B. the completed contract method.

   C. the percentage-of-completion method.

7. At the beginning of 2006, Florida Road Construction entered into a contract to build a road for the government. Construction will take four years. The following information as of 31 December 2006 is available for the contract:

Total revenue according to contract	$10,000,000
Total expected cost	$ 8,000,000
Cost incurred during 2006	$ 1,200,000

Under the completed contract method, how much revenue will be reported in 2006?

A. None.

B. $300,000.

C. $1,500,000.

8. During 2006, Argo Company sold 10 acres of prime commercial zoned land to a builder for $5,000,000. The builder gave Argo a $1,000,000 down payment and will pay the remaining balance of $4,000,000 to Argo in 2007. Argo purchased the land in 1999 for $2,000,000. Using the installment method, how much profit will Argo report for 2006?

A. None.

B. $600,000.

C. $1,000,000.

9. Using the same information as in Question 8, how much profit will Argo report for 2006 by using the cost recovery method?

A. None.

B. $1,000,000.

C. $3,000,000.

10. Under IFRS, revenue from barter transactions should be measured based on the fair value of revenue from:

A. similar barter transactions with related parties.

B. similar barter transactions with unrelated parties.

C. similar nonbarter transactions with unrelated parties.

11. Apex Consignment sells items over the internet for individuals on a consignment basis. Apex receives the items from the owner, lists them for sale on the internet, and receives a 25 percent commission for any items sold. Apex collects the full amount from the buyer and pays the net amount after commission to the owner. Unsold items are returned to the owner after 90 days. During 2006, Apex had the following information:

▶ Total sales price of items sold during 2006 on consignment was €2,000,000.

▶ Total commissions retained by Apex during 2006 for these items was €500,000.

How much revenue should Apex report on its 2006 income statement?

A. €500,000.

B. €2,000,000.

C. €1,500,000.

12. During 2007, Accent Toys Plc., which began business in October of that year, purchased 10,000 units of its most popular toy at a cost of £10 per unit in October. In anticipation of heavy December sales, Accent purchased 5,000 additional units in November at a cost of £11 per unit. During 2007, Accent sold 12,000 units at a price of £15 per unit. Under the First In, First Out (FIFO) method, what is Accent's cost of goods sold for 2007?

    A. £105,000.

    B. £120,000.

    C. £122,000.

13. Using the same information as in Question 12, what would Accent's cost of goods sold be under the weighted average cost method?

    A. £120,000.

    B. £122,000.

    C. £124,000.

14. Which inventory method is least likely to be used under IFRS?

    A. First In, First Out (FIFO).

    B. Last In, First Out (LIFO).

    C. Weighted average.

15. At the beginning of 2007, Glass Manufacturing purchased a new machine for its assembly line at a cost of $600,000. The machine has an estimated useful life of 10 years and estimated residual value of $50,000. Under the straight-line method, how much depreciation would Glass take in 2008 for financial reporting purposes?

    A. None.

    B. $55,000.

    C. $60,000.

16. Using the same information as in Question 15, how much depreciation would Glass take in 2007 for financial reporting purposes under the double-declining balance method?

    A. $60,000.

    B. $110,000.

    C. $120,000.

17. Which combination of depreciation methods and useful lives is most conservative in the year a depreciable asset is acquired?

    A. Straight-line depreciation with a long useful life.

    B. Straight-line depreciation with a short useful life.

    C. Declining balance depreciation with a short useful life.

18. Under IFRS, a loss from the destruction of property in a fire would most likely be classified as:

    A. continuing operations.

    B. an extraordinary item.

    C. discontinued operations.

19. For 2007, Flamingo Products had net income of $1,000,000. At 1 January 2007, there were 1,000,000 shares outstanding. On 1 July 2007, the company issued 100,000 new shares for $20 per share. The company paid $200,000 in dividends to common shareholders. What is Flamingo's basic earnings per share for 2007?

  A. $0.73.

  B. $0.91.

  C. $0.95.

20. Cell Services (CSI) had 1,000,000 average shares outstanding during all of 2007. During 2007, CSI also had 10,000 options outstanding with exercise prices of $10 each. The average stock price of CSI during 2007 was $15. For purposes of computing diluted earnings per share, how many shares would be used in the denominator?

  A. 1,000,000.

  B. 1,003,333.

  C. 1,010,000.

SOLUTIONS FOR READING 32

1. C is correct. IAS No. 1 states that expenses may be categorized by either nature or function.

2. C is correct. Cost of goods sold is a classification by function. The other two expenses represent classifications by nature.

3. C is correct. Gross margin is revenue minus cost of goods sold. A represents net income and B represents operating income.

4. C is correct. Under IFRS, income includes increases in economic benefits from increases in assets, enhancement of assets, and decreases in liabilities.

5. C is correct. Net revenue is revenue for goods sold during the period less any returns and allowances, or $1,000,000 minus $100,000 = $900,000. A is incorrect; this represents gross profit. B is incorrect; this is the cash collected that is not used under the accrual basis.

6. C is correct. The preferred method is the percentage-of-completion method. The completed contract method should be used only when the outcome cannot be measured reliably.

7. A is correct. Under the completed contract method, no revenue would be reported until the project is completed. B is incorrect. This is the profit under the percentage-of-completion method. C is incorrect. This is the revenue under the percentage-of-completion method.

8. B is correct. The installment method apportions the cash receipt between cost recovered and profit using the ratio of profit to sales value (i.e., $3,000,000 ÷ $5,000,000 = 60 percent). Argo will, therefore, recognize $600,000 in profit for 2006 ($1,000,000 cash received × 60 percent). A uses the cost recovery method. C is the cash received.

9. A is correct. Under the cost recovery method, the company would not recognize any profit until the cash amounts paid by the buyer exceeded Argo's cost of $2,000,000.

10. C is correct. Revenue for barter transactions should be measured based on the fair value of revenue from similar nonbarter transactions with unrelated parties.

11. A is correct. Apex is not the owner of the goods and should only report its net commission as revenue. C is the amount paid to the owners. B is the total amount collected on behalf of the owners.

12. C is correct. Under the First In, First Out (FIFO) method, the first 10,000 units sold came from the October purchases at $10, and the next 2,000 units sold came from the November purchases at $11. A is incorrect; this is cost of goods sold under the Last In, First Out (LIFO) method. B is incorrect because it places a cost of $10 on all units.

13. C is correct. Under the weighted average cost method:

October purchases	10,000 units	£100,000
November purchases	5,000 units	£55,000
Total	15,000 units	£155,000

£155,000/15,000 units = £10.3333 × 12,000 units = £124,000.

14. B is correct. The Last In, First Out (LIFO) method is not permitted under IFRS. The other methods are permitted.

15. B is correct. Straight-line depreciation would be ($600,000 − $50,000)/10, or $55,000. A assumes the machine was totally expensed in 2007. C ignores the $50,000 residual value.

16. C is correct. Double-declining balance depreciation would be $600,000 × 20 percent (twice the straight-line rate). A uses 10 percent instead of 20 percent. B applies the depreciation percentage after the residual value has been subtracted from the initial book value.

17. C is correct. This would result in the highest amount of depreciation in the first year and hence the lowest amount of net income relative to the other choices.

18. A is correct. A fire may be infrequent, but it would still be part of continuing operations. IFRS does not permit classification of an item as extraordinary. Discontinued operations relate to a decision to dispose of an operating division.

19. C is correct. The weighted average number of shares outstanding for 2007 is 1,050,000. Basic earnings per share would be $1,000,000 divided by 1,050,000, or $0.95. A subtracts the common dividends from net income and uses 1,100,000 shares. B uses the proper net income but 1,100,000 shares.

20. B is correct. With stock options, the treasury stock method must be used. Under that method, the company would receive $100,000 (10,000 × $10) and would repurchase 6,667 shares ($100,000/$15). The shares for the denominator would be:

Shares outstanding	1,000,000
Options exercised	10,000
Treasury shares purchased	(6,667)
Denominator	1,003,333

UNDERSTANDING THE BALANCE SHEET

by Thomas R. Robinson, CFA, Jan Hendrik van Greuning, CFA, Elaine Henry, CFA, and Michael A. Broihahn, CFA

LEARNING OUTCOMES

The candidate should be able to:	Mastery
a. illustrate and interpret the components of the balance sheet and discuss the uses of the balance sheet in financial analysis;	☐
b. describe the various formats of balance sheet presentation;	☐
c. explain how assets and liabilities arise from the accrual process;	☐
d. compare and contrast current and noncurrent assets and liabilities;	☐
e. explain the measurement bases (e.g., historical cost and fair value) of assets and liabilities, including current assets, current liabilities, tangible assets, and intangible assets;	☐
f. demonstrate the appropriate classifications and related accounting treatments for marketable and nonmarketable financial instruments held as assets or owed by the company as liabilities;	☐
g. list and explain the components of owners' equity;	☐
h. interpret balance sheets and statements of changes in equity.	☐

Note:
New rulings and/or pronouncements issued after the publication of the readings on financial reporting and analysis may cause some of the information in these readings to become dated. Candidates are expected to be familiar with the overall analytical framework contained in the study session readings, as well as the implications of alternative accounting methods for financial analysis and valuation, as provided in the assigned readings. Candidates are not responsible for changes that occur after the material was written.

INTRODUCTION

1

The starting place for analyzing a company's financial position is typically the balance sheet. Creditors, investors, and analysts recognize the value of the balance sheet and also its limitations. The balance sheet provides such users with information on a company's resources (assets) and its sources of capital (its equity and liabilities/debt). It normally also provides information about the future earnings capacity of a company's assets as well as an indication of cash flows that may come from receivables and inventories.

International Financial Statement Analysis, by Thomas R. Robinson, CFA, Jan Hendrik van Greuning, CFA, Elaine Henry, CFA, and Michael A. Broihahn, CFA. Copyright © 2007 by CFA Institute. Reprinted with permission.

However, the balance sheet does have limitations, especially relating to how assets and liabilities are measured. Liabilities and, sometimes, assets may not be recognized in a timely manner. Furthermore, the use of historical costs rather than fair values to measure some items on the balance sheet means that the financial analyst may need to make adjustments to determine the real (economic) net worth of the company. By understanding how a balance sheet is constructed and how it may be analyzed, the reader should be able to make appropriate use of it.

This reading is organized as follows. In Section 2, we describe and illustrate the format, structure, and components of the balance sheet. Section 3 discusses the measurement bases for assets and liabilities. Section 4 describes the components of equity and illustrates the statement of changes in shareholders' equity. Section 5 introduces balance sheet analysis. A summary of the key points and practice problems in the CFA Institute multiple-choice format conclude the reading.

2   COMPONENTS AND FORMAT OF THE BALANCE SHEET

The **balance sheet** discloses what an entity owns and what it owes at a specific point in time; thus, it is also referred to as the **statement of financial position**.[1]

The financial position of an entity is described in terms of its assets, liabilities, and equity:

▶ **Assets (A)** are resources controlled by the company as a result of past events and from which future economic benefits are expected to flow to the entity.

▶ **Liabilities (L)** represent obligations of a company arising from past events, the settlement of which is expected to result in an outflow of economic benefits from the entity.

▶ **Equity (E)** Commonly known as shareholders' equity or **owners' equity**, equity is determined by subtracting the liabilities from the assets of a company, giving rise to the accounting equation: $A = L + E$ or $A - L = E$. Equity can be viewed as a residual or balancing amount, taking assets and liabilities into account.

Assets and liabilities arise as a result of business transactions (e.g., the purchase of a building or issuing a bond). The accounting equation is useful in assessing the impact of transactions on the balance sheet. For example, if a company borrows money in exchange for a note payable, assets and liabilities increase by the same amount. Assets and liabilities also arise from the accrual process. As noted in earlier readings, the income statement reflects revenue and expenses reported on an accrual basis regardless of the period in which cash is

---

[1] The balance sheet is also known as the *statement of financial condition*.

received and paid. Differences between accrued revenue and expenses and cash flows will result in assets and liabilities. Specifically:

► revenue reported on the income statement before cash is received; this results in accrued revenue or accounts receivable, which is an asset. This is ultimately reflected on the balance sheet as an increase in accounts receivable and an increase in retained earnings.

► cash received before revenue is to be reported on the income statement; this results in a deferred revenue or unearned revenue, which is a liability. For example, if a company pays in advance for delivery of custom equipment, the balance sheet reflects an increase in cash and an increase in liabilities.

► expense reported on the income statement before cash is paid; this results in an accrued expense, which is a liability. This is reflected on the balance sheet as an increase in liabilities and a decrease in retained earnings.

► cash paid before an expense is to be reported on the income statement; this results in a deferred expense, also known as a "prepaid expense," which is an asset. On the balance sheet, cash is reduced and prepaid assets are increased.

Exhibit 1 illustrates what an unformatted balance sheet might look like, providing examples of a selection of assets and liabilities. The account "trade creditors" (also known as "accounts payable") arises when goods are purchased on credit and received into inventory before their purchase price is paid in cash. Because an expense is recognized before cash is paid, it is an example of the type of accrual described in the third bullet point.

EXHIBIT 1	Listing of Assets, Liabilities, and Owners' Equity Funds			
Element	**20X9**	**20X8**	**Financial Statement Element**	**Equation**
Inventory	€20,000	€16,000	Asset	**+ A**
Property, plant, and equipment	53,000	27,000	Asset	
Subtotal	**73,000**	**43,000**		
Trade creditors	(14,000)	(7,000)	Liability	**– L**
Bond repayable in 5 years' time	(37,000)	(16,000)	Liability	
Owners' equity	**€22,000**	**€20,000**	**Equity** (balancing amount)	**= E**

2.1 Structure and Components of the Balance Sheet

As noted above, the balance sheet presents the financial position of a company. The financial position shows the relative amounts of assets, liabilities, and equity held by the enterprise at a particular point in time.

2.1.1 Assets

Assets are generated either through purchase (investing activities), or generated through business activities (operating activities), or financing activities, such as issuance of debt.

Through the analysis of the liabilities and equity of an entity, the analyst is able to determine *how* assets are acquired or funded. Funding for the purchase may come from shareholders (financing activities) or from creditors (either through direct financing activities, or indirectly through the surplus generated through operating activities that may be funded by current liabilities/trade finance).

The reading on financial reporting standards defined **assets** as "resources controlled by the enterprise as a result of past events and from which future economic benefits are expected to flow to the enterprise." This formal definition of an asset tells us that its essence lies in its capability to generate future benefits, which, therefore, alerts the reader of the financial statements about the future earnings capability of the entity's assets. A simpler definition of an asset is that it is a store of wealth (such as cash, marketable securities, and property).

Turning back to the official definition of assets, we note that financial statement elements (such as assets) should only be recognized in the financial statements if:

▶ it is probable that any future economic benefit associated with the item will flow to the entity, and

▶ the item has a cost or value that can be *measured* with reliability (this aspect will be discussed more fully in Section 3 of this reading).

Values that are typically included in assets will include amounts that have been spent but which have not been recorded as an expense on the income statement (as in the case of inventories) because of the matching principle, or amounts that have been reported as earned on an income statement but which have not been received (as in the case of accounts receivable).

Exhibit 1 included inventories as well as property, plant, and equipment as examples of assets. Exhibit 2 provides a more complete list of assets that may be found on the face of the balance sheet.

EXHIBIT 2   Typical Assets Disclosed on the Balance Sheet

Cash and cash equivalents

Inventories

Trade and other receivables

Prepaid expenses

Financial assets

Deferred tax assets

Property, plant, and equipment

Investment property

Intangible assets

Investments accounted for using the equity method

Natural resource assets

Assets held for sale

2.1.2 *Liabilities*

Liabilities (and equity capital) represent the ways in which the funds were raised to acquire the assets. **Liabilities** are technically defined as probable future sacrifices of economic benefits arising from present obligations of an entity to transfer assets or provide services to other entities in the future as a result of past transactions or events. Alternatively, a liability can be described as:

▶ Amounts received but which have not been reported as revenues or income on an income statement and/or will have to be repaid (e.g., notes payable).

▶ Amounts that have been reported as expenses on an income statement but which have not been paid (e.g., accounts payable, accruals, and taxes payable).

Exhibit 1 included trade creditors as well as a long-term bond payable as examples of liabilities. Exhibit 3 provides a more complete list of liabilities that may be found on the face of the balance sheet.

EXHIBIT 3	Typical Liabilities Disclosed on the Balance Sheet

Bank borrowings/notes payable

Trade and other payables

Provisions

Unearned revenues

Financial liabilities

Accrued liabilities

Deferred tax liabilities

2.1.3 *Equity*

Equity represents the portion belonging to the owners or shareholders of a business. **Equity** is the residual interest in the assets of an entity after deducting its liabilities, also referred to as net asset value:

$$\text{Equity} = \text{Assets} - \text{Liabilities}$$

Equity is increased by contributions by the owners or by profits (including gains) made during the year and is decreased by losses or withdrawals in the form of dividends.

Almost every aspect of a company is either directly or indirectly influenced by the availability and/or the cost of equity capital. The adequacy of equity capital is one of the key factors to be considered when the safety or soundness of a particular company is assessed. An adequate equity base serves as a safety net for a variety of risks to which any entity is exposed in the course of its business. Equity capital provides a cushion to absorb possible losses and thus provides a basis for maintaining creditor confidence in a company. Equity capital also is the ultimate determinant of a company's borrowing capacity. In practice, a company's balance sheet cannot be expanded beyond a level determined by its equity capital without increasing the risk of financial distress to an unacceptable level; the availability of equity capital consequently determines the maximum level of assets.

The cost and amount of capital affect a company's competitive position. Because shareholders expect a return on their equity, the obligation to earn such a return impacts the pricing of company products. There is also another important aspect to the level of capital, namely, the perspective of the market. The issuance of debt requires public confidence in a company, which, in turn, can best be established and maintained by an equity capital buffer. If a company faces a shortage of equity capital or if the cost of capital is high, a company stands to lose business to its competitors.

The key purposes of equity capital are to provide stability and to absorb losses, thereby providing a measure of protection to creditors in the event of liquidation. As such, the capital of a company should have three important characteristics:

▶ It should be permanent.

▶ It should not impose mandatory fixed charges against earnings (in the case of banks).

▶ It should allow for legal subordination to the rights of creditors.

Exhibit 4 provides a list of equity information that is disclosed on the balance sheet.

EXHIBIT 4	Typical Equity Information Disclosed on the Balance Sheet

Minority interest, presented within equity

Issued capital and paid-in capital attributable to equityholders of the parent

Earnings retained in the company

Parent shareholders' equity

Information that is usually disclosed for each class of equity on the face of the balance sheet or in notes to the financial statements includes:

▶ Number of shares authorized

▶ Number of shares issued and fully paid

▶ Number of shares issued and not fully paid

▶ Par (or stated) value per share, or a statement that it has no par (stated) value

▶ Reconciliation of shares at beginning and end of reporting period

▶ Rights, preferences, and restrictions attached to that class

▶ Shares in the entity held by entity, subsidiaries, or associates

▶ Shares reserved for issue under options and sales contracts

The total amount of equity capital is of fundamental importance. Also important is the nature of the company ownership—the identity of those owners who can directly influence the company's strategic direction and risk management policies. This is particularly critical for financial institutions, such as banks. For example, a bank's ownership structure must ensure the integrity of its capital, and owners must be able to supply more capital if and when needed.

2.2 Format of the Balance Sheet

As the balance sheet provides information about the financial position of the company, it should distinguish between major categories and classifications of assets and liabilities.

Detail and formats of balance sheets vary from company to company. The basic information contained in balance sheets is the same though, regardless of the format. When using the **report format**, assets, liabilities, and equity are listed in a single column. The **account format** follows the pattern of the traditional general ledger accounts, with assets at the left and liabilities and equity at the right of a central dividing line. The report format is most commonly preferred and used by financial statement preparers.

If a company were to have many assets and liabilities, the balance sheet might become quite difficult to read. Grouping together the various classes of assets and liabilities, therefore, results in a balance sheet format described as a **classified balance sheet**.

"Classification," in this case, is the term used to describe the grouping of accounts into subcategories—it helps readers to gain a quick perspective of the company's financial position. Classification assists in drawing attention to specific amounts and also to groups of accounts.

Classifications most often distinguish between current and noncurrent assets/liabilities, or by financial and nonfinancial categories—all in order to provide information related to the liquidity of such assets or liabilities (albeit indirectly in many cases).

2.2.1 Current and Noncurrent Distinction

The balance sheet should distinguish between current and noncurrent assets and between current and noncurrent liabilities unless a presentation based on liquidity provides more relevant and reliable information (e.g., in the case of a bank or similar financial institution).

From Exhibit 5, it should be clear that in essence, the current/noncurrent distinction is also an attempt at incorporating liquidity expectations into the structure of the balance sheet. Assets expected to be liquidated or used up within one year or one operating cycle of the business, whichever is greater, are classified as current assets. A company's operating cycle is the amount of time that elapses between spending cash for inventory and supplies and collecting the cash from its sales to customers. Assets not expected to be liquidated or used up within one year or one operating cycle of the business, whichever is greater, are classified as noncurrent (long-term) assets.

The excess of current assets over current liabilities is called **working capital**. The level of working capital tells analysts about the ability of an entity to meet liabilities as they fall due. Yet, working capital should not be too large because funds could be tied up that could be used more productively elsewhere.

EXHIBIT 5	Balance Sheet: Current versus Noncurrent Distinction	
Apex Corporation	**20X9**	**20X8**
Assets		
Current assets	€20,000	€16,000
Noncurrent assets	53,000	27,000
Total assets	**€73,000**	**€43,000**
Liabilities and equity		
Current liabilities	14,000	7,000
Noncurrent liabilities	37,000	16,000
Total liabilities	**51,000**	**23,000**
Equity	**22,000**	**20,000**
Total liabilities and equity	**€73,000**	**€43,000**

Some **current assets** are allocated to expenses immediately (e.g., inventory) when sales or cash transactions take place, whereas noncurrent assets are allocated over the useful lives of such assets. Current assets are maintained for operating purposes and represent cash or items expected to be converted into cash or used up (e.g., prepaid expenses) in the current period. Current assets, therefore, tell us more about the operating activities and the operating capability of the entity.

Noncurrent assets represent the infrastructure from which the entity operates and are not consumed or disposed in the current period. Such assets represent potentially less-liquid investments made from a strategic or longer-term perspective (e.g., to secure trading advantages, supply lines, or other synergies, such as equity securities held, investments in associates, or investments in subsidiaries).

A **current liability** is a liability that satisfies any of the following criteria:

► It is expected to be settled in the entity's normal operating cycle.

► It is held primarily for the purpose of being traded.

► It is due to be settled within one year after the balance sheet date.

► The entity does not have an unconditional right to defer settlement of the liability for at least one year after the balance sheet date.

Financial liabilities are classified as current if they are due to be settled within one year after the balance sheet date, even if the original term was for a period longer than one year. All other liabilities are classified as **noncurrent**.

International Accounting Standard (IAS) No. 1 specifies that some current liabilities, such as trade payables and some accruals for employee and other operating costs, are part of the working capital used in the entity's normal operating cycle. Such operating items are classified as current liabilities even if they will be settled more than one year after the balance sheet date. When the entity's normal operating cycle is not clearly identifiable, its duration is assumed to be one year.

Noncurrent liabilities include financial liabilities that provide financing on a long-term basis, and they are, therefore, not part of the working capital used in the entity's normal operating cycle; neither are they due for settlement within one year after the balance sheet date.

2.2.2 Liquidity-Based Presentation

Paragraph 60 of IAS No. 1 requires the use of the current/noncurrent format of presentation for the balance sheet, except when a presentation based on liquidity provides information that is reliable and is more relevant. When that exception applies, all assets and liabilities shall be presented broadly in order of liquidity.

Entities such as banks are clearly candidates for such a liquidity-based presentation in their balance sheets. Exhibit 6 shows how the asset side of a bank's balance sheet could be ordered using a liquidity-based presentation.

EXHIBIT 6	Bank Balance Sheet: Asset Side Order Using a Liquidity-Based Presentation

Assets

1. Cash and balances with the central bank
2. Trading securities
3. Securities held for stable liquidity portfolio purposes
4. Placements with and loans to banks and credit institutions (net of specific provisions)
5. Loans and advances to other customers
6. Investments—long-term interests in other entities
7. Property, plant, and equipment
8. Other assets (prepayments, etc.)

Total Assets

2.2.3 IFRS and U.S. GAAP Balance Sheet Illustrations

This section illustrates actual corporate balance sheets prepared under international financial reporting standards (IFRS) and generally accepted accounting principles (GAAP) via examples from Roche Group and Sony Corporation, respectively.

Roche is a leading international healthcare company based in Switzerland and prepares its financial statements in accordance with IFRS. Exhibit 7 presents the comparative balance sheets from the company's annual report for the fiscal years ended 31 December 2005 and 2004.

Roche prepares its balance sheets using the report format. The balance sheet also gives noncurrent assets before current assets and long-term liabilities before current liabilities, following common practice under IFRS. Note also that Roche shows the minority interest for its consolidated subsidiary companies in the shareholders' equity section as required under IFRS. **Minority interest** represents the portion of consolidated subsidiaries owned by others. For example, if a company owns 85 percent of a subsidiary, 100 percent of the subsidiary's assets and liabilities are included in the consolidated balance sheet. Minority interest represents the 15 percent of the net assets of the subsidiary not owned by the parent company.

EXHIBIT 7	Roche Group Consolidated Balance Sheets (CHF Millions)	
	31 December	
	2005	**2004**
Noncurrent assets		
Property, plant, and equipment	15,097	12,408
Goodwill	6,132	5,532
Intangible assets	6,256	6,340
Investments in associated companies	58	55
Financial long-term assets	2,190	1,227
Other long-term assets	660	484
Deferred income tax assets	1,724	1,144
Post-employment benefit assets	1,622	1,577
Total noncurrent assets	**33,739**	**28,767**
Current assets		
Inventories	5,041	4,614
Accounts receivables	7,698	7,014
Current income tax assets	299	159
Other current assets	1,703	2,007
Receivable from Bayer Group collected on 1 January 2005	—	2,886
Marketable securities	16,657	10,394
Cash and cash equivalents	4,228	2,605
Total current assets	**35,626**	**29,679**
Total assets	**69,365**	**58,446**
Noncurrent liabilities		
Long-term debt	(9,322)	(7,077)
Deferred income tax liabilities	(3,518)	(3,564)
Post-employment benefit liabilities	(2,937)	(2,744)
Provisions	(1,547)	(683)
Other noncurrent liabilities	(806)	(961)
Total noncurrent liabilities	**(18,130)**	**(15,029)**
Current liabilities		
Short-term debt	(348)	(2,013)
Current income tax liabilities	(811)	(947)
Provisions	(833)	(1,223)
Accounts payable	(2,373)	(1,844)
Accrued and other current liabilities	(5,127)	(4,107)
Total current liabilities	**(9,492)**	**(10,134)**
Total liabilities	**(27,622)**	**(25,163)**
Total net assets	**41,743**	**33,283**

(Exhibit continued on next page . . .)

EXHIBIT 7 **(continued)**

	31 December	
	2005	**2004**
Equity		
Capital and reserves attributable to Roche shareholders	34,922	27,998
Equity attributable to minority interests	6,821	5,285
Total equity	**41,743**	**33,283**

Sony Corporation and its consolidated subsidiaries are engaged in the development, design, manufacture, and sale of various kinds of electronic equipment, instruments, and devices for consumer and industrial markets. Sony is also engaged in the development, production, and distribution of recorded music and image-based software. Sony Corporation has prepared a set of consolidated financial statements in accordance with U.S. GAAP. Exhibit 8 presents the comparative balance sheets from the company's U.S. GAAP annual report for the fiscal years ended 31 March 2005 and 2004.

Sony prepares its balance sheets using the report format. Under U.S. GAAP, current assets are presented before long-term assets, and current liabilities are presented before long-term liabilities. The current/long-term presentation rule is applicable for all manufacturing, merchandising, and service companies, although there are some regulated industry exceptions (e.g., utility companies) where the presentation is reversed (similar to the common IFRS practice of presenting long-term assets before current assets and long-term liabilities before current liabilities). Note also that Sony shows the minority interest for its consolidated subsidiary companies in an "in-between" or "mezzanine" section between the liabilities and shareholders' equity sections. This mezzanine presentation for minority interest was common under U.S. GAAP. However, effective 15 December 2008, U.S. GAAP (FASB ASC 810-10-50 [Consolidation–Overall–Disclosure]) require that minority interests be presented on the consolidated balance sheet as a separate component of stockholders' equity. The minority interest must be clearly identified and labeled. Any entity with minority interests in more than one subsidiary may present those interests in aggregate in the consolidated financial statements. By contrast, under IFRS, a minority interest is presented in the shareholders' equity section. The Financial Accounting Standards Board (FASB) is considering a change to U.S. GAAP to conform their standards to IFRS.

EXHIBIT 8   **Sony Corporation Consolidated Balance Sheets (¥ Millions)**

	31 March	
	2005	**2004**
Assets		
Current assets:		
Cash and cash equivalents	779,103	849,211
Time deposits	1,492	4,662

(Exhibit continued on next page . . .)

| EXHIBIT 8 | (continued) | | |

| | **31 March** | |
	2005	**2004**
Marketable securities	460,202	274,748
Notes and accounts receivable, trade	1,113,071	1,123,863
Allowance for doubtful accounts and sales returns	(87,709)	(112,674)
Inventories	631,349	666,507
Deferred income taxes	141,154	125,532
Prepaid expenses and other current assets	517,509	431,506
Total current assets	3,556,171	3,363,355
Film costs	278,961	256,740
Investments and advances:		
Affiliated companies	252,905	86,253
Securities investments and other	2,492,784	2,426,697
	2,745,689	2,512,950
Property, plant, and equipment:		
Land	182,900	189,785
Buildings	925,796	930,983
Machinery and equipment	2,192,038	2,053,085
Construction in progress	92,611	98,480
Less—Accumulated depreciation	(2,020,946)	(1,907,289)
	1,372,399	1,365,044
Other assets:		
Intangibles, net	187,024	248,010
Goodwill	283,923	277,870
Deferred insurance acquisition costs	374,805	349,194
Deferred income taxes	240,396	203,203
Other	459,732	514,296
	1,545,880	1,592,573
Total assets	9,499,100	9,090,662
Liabilities and Stockholders' Equity		
Current liabilities:		
Short-term borrowings	63,396	91,260
Current portion of long-term debt	166,870	383,757
Notes and accounts payable, trade	806,044	778,773
Accounts payable, other and accrued expenses	746,466	812,175
Accrued income and other taxes	55,651	57,913
Deposits from customers in the banking business	546,718	378,851
Other	424,223	479,486
Total current liabilities	2,809,368	2,982,215

(Exhibit continued on next page . . .)

EXHIBIT 8	**(continued)**		
		31 March	
		2005	**2004**
Long-term liabilities:			
Long-term debt		678,992	777,649
Accrued pension and severance costs		352,402	368,382
Deferred income taxes		72,227	96,193
Future insurance policy benefits and other		2,464,295	2,178,626
Other		227,631	286,737
		3,795,547	3,707,587
Minority interest in consolidated subsidiaries		23,847	22,858
Stockholders' equity:			
Subsidiary tracking stock, no par value—			
Authorized 100,000,000 shares, outstanding 3,072,000 shares		3,917	3,917
Common stock, no par value—			
2004—Authorized 3,500,000,000 shares,			
outstanding 926,418,280 shares			476,350
2005—Authorized 3,500,000,000 shares,			
outstanding 997,211,213 shares		617,792	
Additional paid-in capital		1,134,222	992,817
Retained earnings		1,506,082	1,367,060
Accumulated other comprehensive income—			
Unrealized gains on securities		62,669	69,950
Unrealized losses on derivative investments		(2,490)	(600)
Minimum pension liability adjustments		(90,030)	(89,261)
Foreign currency translation adjustments		(355,824)	(430,048)
		(385,675)	(449,959)
Treasury stock, at cost			
Subsidiary tracking stock (2004—0 shares, 2005—32 shares)		(0)	(0)
Common stock (2004—2,468,258 shares, 2005—1,118,984 shares)		(6,000)	(12,183)
		2,870,338	2,378,002
Total liabilities and stockholders' equity		9,499,100	9,090,662

MEASUREMENT BASES OF ASSETS AND LIABILITIES

3

In portraying an asset or liability on the balance sheet, the question arises as to how it should be measured. For example, an asset may have been acquired many years ago at a cost of $1,000,000 but may have a current value of $5,000,000. Should this asset be listed at its historic cost or its current value? On the one hand, historical cost provides a reliable and objectively determined measurement base—there would be no dispute regarding what the asset cost. On the other hand, users of financial statements (e.g., creditors) may prefer to know what the asset could be sold for currently if the company needed to raise cash. Some assets and liabilities can be more objectively valued in the marketplace than others (e.g., when an established market exists in which the asset or liability trades regularly, such as an investment in another publicly traded company). As a result, the balance sheet under current standards is a mixed model: Some assets and liabilities are reported based on historical cost, sometimes with adjustments, whereas other assets and liabilities are measured based upon a current value intended to represent the asset's fair value. Fair value and historical value can be defined as follows.

▶ **Fair value**. Fair value is the amount at which an asset could be exchanged, or a liability settled, between knowledgeable willing parties in an arm's length transaction. When the asset or liability trades regularly, its fair value is usually readily determinable from its market price (sometimes referred to as **fair market value**).

▶ **Historical cost**. The historical cost of an asset or liability is its cost or fair value at acquisition, including any costs of acquisition and/or preparation.

In limited circumstances other measurement bases are sometimes used, such as **current cost** (the cost to replace an asset) or **present value** (the present discounted value of future cash flows). The key question for analysts is how the reported measures of assets and liabilities on the balance sheet relate to economic reality and to each other. To answer this question, the analyst needs to understand the accounting policies applied in preparing the balance sheet and the measurement bases used. Analysts may need to make adjustments to balance sheet measures of assets and liabilities in assessing the investment potential or credit-worthiness of a company. For example, land is generally reported at historical cost on the balance sheet because this measure is objective and any measure of current value (other than an actual sale) would be very subjective. Through diligent research, an analyst may find companies that own valuable land that is not adequately reflected on the balance sheet.[2]

For all of these reasons, the balance sheet value of total assets should not be accepted as an accurate measure of the total value of a company. The value of a company is a function of many factors, including future cash flows expected to be generated by the company and current market conditions. The balance sheet provides important information about the value of some assets and information about future cash flows but does not represent the value of the company as a whole.

Once individual assets and liabilities are measured, additional decisions may be necessary as to how these measures are reflected on the balance sheet. Accounting standards generally prohibit the offsetting of assets and liabilities other than in limited circumstances. For example, if a building is purchased for $10,000,000 subject to a mortgage of $8,000,000, the building is reported as an asset for $10,000,000 while the mortgage is shown separately as a liability ($8,000,000). It is important that these assets and liabilities be reported separately. Offsetting in the balance sheet, except when offsetting reflects the substance of the transaction or other event, detracts from the ability of users to understand the transactions, events, and conditions that have occurred and to assess the entity's future cash flows. However, disclosing or measuring assets net of valuation allowances (e.g., obsolescence allowances on inventories and doubtful accounts allowances on receivables) is not considered to be offsetting. Offsetting is also permitted in limited circumstances where there are restrictions on the availability of assets (such as with pension plans).

---

[2] See, for example, "Beyond the Balance-Sheet: Land-Ho," *Forbes*, 4 September 2006, pp. 84–85, which examines a handful of stocks with valuable land holdings not reflected on the balance sheet.

According to IFRS, fair presentation requires the faithful representation on the balance sheet of the effects of transactions, other events, and conditions in accordance with the definitions and recognition criteria for assets, liabilities, income, and expenses set out in the IFRS *Framework*, as presented in the reading on financial reporting standards. The application of IFRS is presumed to result in fair presentation.

The financial statements should disclose the following information related to the measures used for assets and liabilities shown on the balance sheet:

► accounting policies, including the cost formulas used;

► total carrying amount of inventories and amount per category;

► amount of inventories carried at fair value less costs to sell;

► amount of any write-downs and reversals of any write-down;

► circumstances or events that led to the reversal of a write-down;

► inventories pledged as security for liabilities; and

► amount of inventories recognized as an expense.

The notes to financial statements and management's discussion and analysis are integral parts of the U.S. GAAP and IFRS financial reporting processes. They provide important required detailed disclosures, as well as other information provided voluntarily by management. This information can be invaluable when determining whether the measurement of assets is comparable to other entities being analyzed. The notes include information on such topics as the following:

► specific accounting policies that were used in compiling the financial statements;

► terms of debt agreements;

► lease information;

► off-balance sheet financing;

► breakdowns of operations by important segments;

► contingent assets and liabilities; and

► detailed pension plan disclosure.

The notes would also provide information in respect of:

Disclosure of accounting policies	► Measurement bases used in preparing financial statements.
	► Each accounting policy used.
	► Judgments made in applying accounting policies that have the most significant effect on the amounts recognized in the financial statements.
Estimation uncertainty	► Key assumptions about the future and other key sources of estimation uncertainty that have a significant risk of causing material adjustment to the carrying amount of assets and liabilities within the next year.
Other disclosures	► Description of the entity, including its domicile, legal form, country of incorporation, and registered office or business address.
	► Nature of operations or principal activities, or both.
	► Name of parent and ultimate parent.

Analysis of Off-Balance Sheet Disclosures

Hewitt Associates (NYSE: HEW) posted the following table on page 43 of its SEC Form 10K for the fiscal year ending 30 September 2005. The table was included in the Management Discussion and Analysis.

Contractual Obligations
(in Millions)

		Payments Due in Fiscal Year			
	Total	2006	2007–08	2009–10	Thereafter
Operating leases (1)	737	89	149	123	376
Capital leases:					
Principal	80	4	9	11	56
Interest	41	6	11	9	15
Total leases:	121	10	20	20	71
Debt:					
Principal	259	36	50	30	143
Interest	50	12	18	13	7
Total debt:	309	48	68	43	150
Purchase commitments	73	34	37	2	—
Other long-term liabilities	72	8	16	9	39
Total contractual obligations	$1,312	$189	$290	$197	$636

On pages 56–57 of the 10K, Hewitt posted the following balance sheet (abbreviated on the following pages). Of the obligations listed above, only the capital leases and other long-term liabilities are included explicitly on the balance sheet.

Hewitt Associates, Inc.
Consolidated Balance Sheets
(Dollars in Thousands except Share and Per-Share Amounts)

	30 September	
	2005	**2004**
Assets		
Current assets:		
Cash and cash equivalents	$ 163,928	$ 129,481
Short-term investments	53,693	183,205
Client receivables and unbilled work in process	595,691	522,882
Refundable income taxes	23,100	—
Prepaid expenses and other current assets	60,662	50,546
Funds held for clients	97,907	14,693
Deferred income taxes, net	5,902	246
Total current assets	1,000,883	901,053
Noncurrent assets:		
Deferred contract costs	253,505	162,602
Property and equipment, net	302,875	236,099
Capitalized software, net	110,997	85,350
Other intangible assets, net	261,999	107,322
Goodwill	694,370	285,743
Other assets, net	32,711	29,805
Total noncurrent assets	1,656,457	906,921
Total assets	2,657,340	1,807,974
Liabilities		
Current liabilities:		
Accounts payable	57,412	20,909
Accrued expenses	156,575	83,226
Funds held for clients	97,907	14,693
Advanced billings to clients	156,257	106,934
Accrued compensation and benefits	141,350	181,812
Short-term debt and current portion of long-term debt	35,915	13,445
Current portion of capital lease obligations	3,989	5,373
Employee deferred compensation and accrued profit sharing	30,136	49,450
Total current liabilities	679,541	475,842
Long-term liabilities:		
Deferred contract revenues	140,474	118,025
Debt, less current portion	222,692	121,253
Capital lease obligations, less current portion	76,477	79,982

	30 September	
	2005	**2004**
Other long-term liabilities	127,376	83,063
Deferred income taxes, net	99,423	70,456
Total long-term liabilities	666,442	472,779
Total liabilities	1,345,983	948,621
Commitments and contingencies (Notes 12 and 17)		
Stockholders' Equity		
Total stockholders' equity	1,311,357	859,353
Total liabilities and stockholders' equity	$2,657,340	$1,807,974

Operating leases represent assets used by the company but for which accounting standards do not currently require the assets or related obligations to be reported on the company's balance sheet. Analysts, however, frequently prefer to adjust the balance sheet to determine how it would look if the assets had been purchased and financed. Credit analysts, such as Standard & Poor's, also make this adjustment to better reflect the credit-worthiness of the company. Ideally, the analyst would like to know the implied interest rate in the lease agreements and use this to determine the present value of the asset and related liability, because each lease payment effectively has an interest and a principal component. For this initial example, we will use a shortcut method. Assuming operating leases can be segregated into principal and interest components at approximately the same rate as the capital leases, they represent a liability worth nearly $500 million that is not recorded on the balance sheet. The analyst would adjust the balance sheet by adding that amount to fixed assets and liabilities to examine the current economic position. This information would not have been uncovered based solely upon a review of the balance sheet. Important disclosures about assets and liabilities can be found in the footnotes to the financial statements and in management's discussion of the financial statements.

3.1 Current Assets

Current assets are assets expected to be realized or intended for sale or consumption in the entity's normal operating cycle. Typical current assets that appear on the face of the balance sheet include:

▶ Assets held primarily for trading.

▶ Assets expected to be realized within 12 months after the balance sheet date.

▶ Cash or cash equivalents, unless restricted in use for at least 12 months.

▶ Marketable securities—Debt or equity securities that are owned by a business, traded in a public market, and whose value can be determined from price information in a public market. Examples of marketable securities include treasury bills, notes, bonds, and equity securities, such as common stocks and mutual fund shares.

▶ Trade receivables—Amounts owed to a business by its customers for products and services already delivered are included as trade receivables. Allowance has to be made for bad debt expenses, reducing the gross receivables amount.

▶ Inventories—Physical products on hand such as goods that will eventually be sold to an entity's customers, either in their current form (finished goods) or as inputs into a process to manufacture a final product (raw materials and work-in-process).

▶ Other current assets—Short-term items not easily classifiable into the above categories (e.g., prepaid expenses).

Exhibit 9 illustrates how the current asset amounts of €20,000 (20X9) and €16,000 (20X8) have been expanded from the one amount shown in Exhibit 5. In the sections below, some of the issues surrounding the measurement principles for inventories and prepaid expenses are discussed.

EXHIBIT 9	Apex Current Assets	
	20X9	20X8
Current assets	**€20,000**	**€16,000**
Cash and cash equivalents	3,000	2,000
Marketable securities	3,000	4,000
Trade receivables	5,000	3,000
Inventories	7,000	6,000
Other current assets—prepaid expenses	2,000	1,000

3.1.1 Inventories

Inventories should be measured at the lower of cost or net realizable value. The cost of inventories comprises all costs of purchase, costs of conversion, and other costs incurred in bringing the inventories to their present location and condition. The following amounts should be excluded in the determination of inventory costs:

▶ abnormal amounts of wasted materials, labor, and overheads;

▶ storage costs, unless they are necessary prior to a further production process;

▶ administrative overheads; and

▶ selling costs.

The net realizable value (NRV) is the estimated selling price less the estimated costs of completion and costs necessary to make the sale.

Accounting standards allow different valuation methods. For example, IAS No. 2 allows only the first-in, first-out (FIFO), weighted average cost (WAC), and specific identification methods. Some accounting standard setters (such as U.S. GAAP) also allow LIFO (last-in, first-out) as an additional inventory valuation method, whereas LIFO is not allowed under IFRS.

The following techniques can be used to measure the cost of inventories if the resulting valuation amount approximates cost:

▶ **Standard cost**, which should take into account the normal levels of materials, labor, and actual capacity. The standard cost should be reviewed regularly in order to ensure that it approximates actual costs.

▶ The **retail method** in which the sales value is reduced by the gross margin to calculate cost. An average gross margin percentage should be used for each homogeneous group of items. In addition, the impact of marked-down prices should be taken into consideration.

EXAMPLE 2

Analysis of Inventory

Cisco Systems is the world's leading provider of networking equipment. In its third quarter 2001 Form 10-Q filed with the U.S. Securities and Exchange Commission (U.S. SEC) on 1 June 2001, the company made the following disclosure:

> We recorded a provision for inventory, including purchase commitments, totaling $2.36 billion in the third quarter of fiscal 2001, of which $2.25 billion related to an additional excess inventory charge. Inventory purchases and commitments are based upon future sales forecasts. To mitigate the component supply constraints that have existed in the past, we built inventory levels for certain components with long lead times and entered into certain longer-term commitments for certain components. Due to the sudden and significant decrease in demand for our products, inventory levels exceeded our requirements based on current 12-month sales forecasts. This additional excess inventory charge was calculated based on the inventory levels in excess of 12-month demand for each specific product. We do not currently anticipate that the excess inventory subject to this provision will be used at a later date based on our current 12-month demand forecast.

Even after the inventory charge, Cisco held approximately $2 billion of inventory on the balance sheet, suggesting that the write-off amounted to half its inventory. In addition to the obvious concerns raised as to management's poor performance anticipating how much they would need, many analysts were concerned about how the write-off would affect Cisco's future reported earnings. When this inventory is sold in a future period, a "gain" could be reported based on a lower cost basis for the inventory. In this case, management indicated that the intent was to scrap the inventory. When the company subsequently released its annual earnings, the press release stated:[3]

> Net sales for fiscal 2001 were $22.29 billion, compared with $18.93 billion for fiscal 2000, an increase of 18%. Pro forma net income, which excludes the effects of acquisition charges, payroll tax on stock option exercises, restructuring costs and other special charges, excess inventory charge (benefit), and net gains realized on minority investments, was $3.09 billion or $0.41 per share for fiscal 2001, compared with pro forma net income of $3.91 billion or $0.53 per share for fiscal 2000, decreases of 21% and 23%, respectively.

---

[3] Cisco Press Release dated 7 August 2001 from www.cisco.com.

> Actual net loss for fiscal 2001 was $1.01 billion or $0.14 per share, compared with actual net income of $2.67 billion or $0.36 per share for fiscal 2000.
>
> Note that the company focused on "pro forma earnings" initially, which excluded the impact of many items, including the inventory write-off. The company only gave a brief mention of actual (U.S. GAAP) results.

3.1.2 Prepaid Expenses

Prepaid expenses are normal operating expenses that have been paid in advance. The advance payment creates an asset out of a transaction that would normally have resulted in an expense. Examples might include prepaid rent or prepaid insurance. Prepaid expenses will be expensed in future periods as they are used up. Generally, expenses are reported in the period in which they are incurred as opposed to when they are paid. If a company pays its insurance premium for the next calendar year on 31 December, the expense is not incurred at that date; the expense is incurred as time passes (in this example, 1/12 in each following month).

3.2 Current Liabilities

Current liabilities are those liabilities that are expected to be settled in the entity's normal operating cycle, held primarily for trading and due to be settled within 12 months after the balance sheet date.

Exhibit 10 illustrates how the current liabilities amounts of €14,000 (20X9) and €7,000 (20X8) have been expanded from the one amount shown in Exhibit 5. In the sections below, some of the issues surrounding the measurement principles for payables, accrued liabilities, and unearned revenue are discussed.

Noncurrent interest-bearing liabilities to be settled within 12 months after the balance sheet date can be classified as noncurrent liabilities if:

▶ the original term of the liability is greater than 12 months;
▶ it is the intention to refinance or reschedule the obligation; or
▶ the agreement to refinance or reschedule the obligation is completed on or before the balance sheet date.

EXHIBIT 10	Apex Current Liabilities	
	20X9	**20X8**
Current liabilities	**€14,000**	**€7,000**
Trade and other payables	5,000	2,000
Notes payable	3,000	1,000
Current portion of noncurrent borrowings	2,000	1,000
Current tax payable	2,000	2,000
Accrued liabilities	1,000	500
Unearned revenue	1,000	500

3.2.1 Trade and Other Payables (Accounts Payable)

Accounts payable are amounts that a business owes its vendors for goods and services that were purchased from them but which have not yet been paid.

3.2.2 Notes Payable

Notes payable are amounts owed by a business to creditors as a result of borrowings that are evidenced by a (short-term) loan agreement. Examples of notes payable include bank loans and other current borrowings other than those arising from trade credit. Notes payable may also appear in the long-term liability section of the balance sheet if they are due after one year or the operating cycle, whichever is longer.

3.2.3 Current Portion of Noncurrent Borrowings

By convention, liabilities expected to be repaid or liquidated within one year or one operating cycle of the business, whichever is greater, are classified as current liabilities. Other liabilities are classified as noncurrent. For example, Exhibit 10 shows that €2,000 of Apex's noncurrent borrowings will come due within a year; therefore, the €2,000 constitutes a current liability.

3.2.4 Current Tax Payable

Current taxes payable are tax expenses that have been determined and recorded on a company's income statement but which have not yet been paid.

3.2.5 Accrued Liabilities

Accrued liabilities (also known as **accrued expenses**) are expenses that have been reported on a company's income statement but which have not yet been paid because there is no legal obligation to pay them as of the balance sheet date. Common examples of accrued liabilities are accrued interest payable and accrued wages payable.

3.2.6 Unearned Revenue

Unearned revenue (also known as **deferred revenue**) is the collection of money in advance of delivery of the goods and services associated with the revenue. Examples include rental income received in advance, advance fees for servicing office equipment, and advance payments for magazine subscriptions received from customers.

3.3 Tangible Assets

Tangible assets are long-term assets with physical substance that are used in company operations. These noncurrent assets are carried at their historical cost less any accumulated depreciation or accumulated depletion. Historical cost generally consists of vendor invoice cost, freight cost, and any other additional costs incurred to

EXAMPLE 3

Analysis of Unearned Revenue

Germany's SAP AG is one of the world's leading providers of business software solutions and one of the world's three largest independent software companies based on market capitalization. At year-end 2005, SAP reported the following assets and liabilities on its balance sheet (in € thousands):[4]

	2005	2004
Assets		
Goodwill	€626,546	€456,707
Other intangible assets	139,697	68,186
Property, plant, and equipment	1,094,965	999,083
Financial assets	534,155	100,382
Fixed assets	2,395,363	1,624,358
Inventories	19,376	11,692
Accounts receivable, net	2,251,027	1,929,100
Other assets	635,554	537,645
Accounts receivable and other assets	2,886,581	2,466,745
Marketable securities	209,565	10,164
Liquid assets	3,213,572	3,196,542
Nonfixed assets	6,329,094	5,685,143
Deferred taxes	250,698	205,601
Prepaid expenses and deferred charges	87,587	70,370
Total assets	€9,062,742	€7,585,472
thereof total current assets	6,241,125	4,849,537
Shareholders' equity and liabilities		
Subscribed capital	316,458	316,004
Treasury stock	(775,318)	(569,166)
Additional paid-in capital	372,767	322,660
Retained earnings	5,986,186	4,830,156
Accumulated other comprehensive loss	(117,855)	(305,401)
Shareholders' equity	5,782,238	4,594,253
Minority interests	7,615	21,971
Pension liabilities and similar obligations	183,619	139,690
Other reserves and accrued liabilities	1,839,140	1,768,723
Reserves and accrued liabilities	2,022,759	1,908,413
Bonds	6,927	7,277
Other liabilities	838,778	728,838

---

[4] In its annual report, SAP AG chose to provide the subtotal of current assets and current liabilities at the bottom of the respective portions of the balance sheet rather than within the balance sheet to distinguish how much of its nonfixed assets are current. According to Footnote 1 of SAP AG's 2005 annual report: "Non-fixed assets are comprised of Inventories, Accounts receivable, Other assets, Marketable securities, and Liquid assets including amounts to be realized in excess of one year."

	2005	2004
Other liabilities	845,705	736,115
Deferred income	404,425	324,720
Total shareholders' equity and liabilities	€9,062,742	€7,585,472
thereof current liabilities	2,781,685	2,591,872

The final line shows that deferred income rose nearly 25 percent to end 2005 with a value of €404.4 million. SAP describes the line as follows:

> Deferred income consists mainly of prepayments for maintenance and deferred software license revenues. Such amounts will be recognized as software, maintenance, or service revenue, depending upon the reasons for the deferral when the basic criteria in SOP 97-2 have been met (see Note 3).

Although investors prefer to see many liabilities minimized, deferred revenue represents money the company has already been paid for services that will be delivered in the future. Because it will then be recognized as revenue, many investors monitor the deferred income line (when significant) as an indicator of future revenue growth.

make the asset operable. Examples of tangible assets include land, buildings, equipment, machinery, furniture, and natural resources owned by the company, such as copper mines, oil and gas properties, and timberlands. If any of these assets are not used in company operations, they must be classified as investment assets.

3.4 Intangible Assets

Intangible assets are amounts paid by a company to acquire certain rights that are not represented by the possession of physical assets. A distinction can be made between identifiable intangibles and unidentifiable intangibles. An **identifiable intangible** can be acquired singly and is typically linked to specific rights or privileges having finite benefit periods. Examples include patents and trademarks. An **unidentifiable intangible** cannot be acquired singly and typically possesses an indefinite benefit period. An example is accounting goodwill, discussed further in Section 3.4.2.

A company should assess whether the useful life of an intangible asset is finite or infinite and, if finite, the length of its life, or number of production or similar units constituting its useful life. Amortization and impairment principles apply as follows:

▶ An intangible asset with a finite useful life is amortized on a systematic basis over the best estimate of its useful life.

▶ An intangible asset with an infinite useful life should be tested for impairment annually but not amortized.

The balance sheet and notes should disclose the gross carrying amount (book value) less accumulated amortization for each class of asset at the beginning and the end of the period.

Companies may also have intangible assets that are not recorded on their balance sheets. These intangible assets might include management skill, valuable trademarks and name recognition, a good reputation, proprietary products, and so forth. Such assets are valuable and would fetch their worth if a company were to be sold.

Financial analysts have traditionally viewed the values assigned to intangible assets, particularly unidentifiable intangibles, with caution. Consequently, in assessing financial statements, they often exclude the book value assigned to intangibles, particularly unidentifiable intangibles, reducing net equity by an equal amount and increasing pretax income by any amortization expense or impairment associated with the intangibles. An arbitrary assignment of zero value to intangibles is not advisable. The analyst should examine each listed intangible and assess whether an adjustment should be made.

3.4.1 Specifically Identifiable Intangibles

Under IFRS, specifically identifiable intangible assets are nonfinancial assets without physical substance but which can be identified. Such assets are recognized on the balance sheet if it is probable that future economic benefits will flow to the company and the cost of the asset can be measured reliably. Examples of identifiable intangible assets include patents, trademarks, copyrights, franchises, and other rights. Identifiable intangible assets may have been created or purchased by a company. Determining the cost of internally created intangible assets can be difficult and subjective. For these reasons, internally created identifiable intangibles are less likely to be reported on the balance sheet under IFRS or U.S. GAAP. IAS No. 38 applies to all intangible assets that are not specifically dealt with in other international accounting standards. This standard determines that the intangible assets reported on a balance sheet are only those intangibles that have been *purchased* or *created* (in strictly limited instances).

IAS No. 38 provides that for internally created intangible assets, the company must identify the research phase and the development phase. The research phase includes activities that seek new knowledge or products. The development phase occurs after the research phase and includes design or testing of prototypes and models. IAS No. 38 prohibits the capitalization of costs as intangible assets during the research phase. Instead, these costs must be expensed on the income statement. Costs incurred in the development stage can be capitalized as intangible assets if certain criteria are met, including technological feasibility, the ability to use or sell the resulting asset, and the ability to complete the project.

All other expenses related to the following categories are **expensed**. They include:

▶ internally *generated* brands, mastheads, publishing titles, customer lists, etc.;

▶ start-up costs;

▶ training costs;

▶ administrative and other general overhead costs;

▶ advertising and promotion;

▶ relocation and reorganization expenses;

▶ redundancy and other termination costs.

U.S. GAAP prohibits the capitalization as an asset of almost all research and development costs. All such costs usually must be expensed. Generally, under U.S. GAAP, acquired intangible assets are reported as separately identifiable intangibles (as opposed to goodwill) if they arise from contractual rights (such as a licensing agreement), other legal rights (such as patents), or have the ability to be separated and sold (such as a customer list).

EXAMPLE 4

Measuring Intangible Assets

Alpha, Inc., a motor vehicle manufacturer, has a research division that worked on the following projects during the year:

Project 1: Research aimed at finding a steering mechanism that does not operate like a conventional steering wheel but reacts to the impulses from a driver's fingers.

Project 2: The design of a prototype welding apparatus that is controlled electronically rather than mechanically, which has been determined to be technologically feasible.

The following is a summary of the expenses of the particular department (in thousands of euros):

	General	Project 1	Project 2
Material and services	€128	€935	€620
Labor			
Direct labor	—	620	320
Administrative personnel	720	—	—
Overhead			
Direct	—	340	410
Indirect	270	110	60

Five percent of administrative personnel costs can be attributed to each of Projects 1 and 2. Explain the capitalization of Alpha's development costs for Projects 1 and 2 under IFRS.

Solution: Under IFRS, the capitalization of development costs for Projects 1 and 2 would be as follows:

Project 1: Classified as research so all costs are recognized as expenses.	NIL
Project 2: (620 + 320 + 410 + 60)	€1,410

Note that Project 2 is in the development stage and costs related to the project should be capitalized under IFRS. However, under IAS No. 38, administrative personnel costs should be expensed.

3.4.2 Goodwill

In a purchase acquisition, the excess of the cost of acquisition over the acquirer's interest in the fair value of the identifiable assets and liabilities acquired is described as goodwill and is recognized as an asset.

The subject of recognizing goodwill in financial statements has found both proponents and opponents among professionals. The proponents of goodwill recognition assert that goodwill is the "present value of excess returns that a company is able to earn." This group claims that determining the present value of these excess returns is analogous to determining the present value of future cash flows associated with other assets and projects. Opponents of goodwill recognition claim that the prices paid for acquisitions often turn out to be based on unrealistic expectations, thereby leading to future write-offs of goodwill.

Analysts should distinguish between accounting goodwill and economic goodwill. Economic goodwill is based on the economic performance of the entity, whereas accounting goodwill is based on accounting standards and only reported for past acquisitions. Economic goodwill is what should concern analysts and investors, and it is often not reflected on the balance sheet. This economic goodwill should be reflected in the stock price. Many analysts believe that goodwill should not be listed on the balance sheet, as it cannot be sold separately from the entity. These analysts believe that only assets that can be separately identified and sold be reflected on the balance sheet. Other financial statement users may desire to analyze goodwill and any subsequent impairment charges to assess management's performance on prior acquisitions.

Under IFRS and U.S. GAAP, goodwill should be capitalized and tested for impairment annually. Goodwill is not amortized. Impairment of goodwill is a noncash expense. If goodwill is deemed to be impaired, it is charged against income in the current period. This charge reduces current earnings. Assets are also reduced, so some performance measures, such as return on assets (net income divided by average total assets), may actually increase in future periods.

Under IFRS No. 3, the acquisition method of accounting can be summarized by the following steps:

▶ The cost of acquisition is determined.

▶ The fair value of the acquiree's assets is determined.

▶ The fair value of the acquiree's liabilities and contingent liabilities is determined.

▶ Calculate the goodwill arising from the purchase as follows:
  ▶ The book value of the acquirer's assets and liabilities should be combined with the fair value adjustments of the acquiree's assets, liabilities, and contingent liabilities.
  ▶ Any goodwill should be recognized as an asset in the combined entity's balance sheet.

Despite the clear guidance incorporated in IFRS No. 3, many analysts believe that the determination of fair values involves considerable management discretion. Values for intangible assets, such as computer software, might not be easily validated when analyzing purchase acquisitions.

Management judgment can be particularly apparent in the allocation of the excess purchase price (after all other allocations to assets and liabilities). If, for example, the remaining excess purchase price is allocated to goodwill, there will be no impact on the company's net income because goodwill is not amortized (but is tested for impairment). If the excess were to be allocated to fixed assets, depreciation would rise, thus reducing net income and producing incorrect financial statements. (**Depreciation** is the allocation of the costs of a long-term [tangible] asset over its useful life.)

Goodwill can significantly affect the comparability of financial statements between companies using different accounting methods. As such, an analyst should remove any distortion that the recognition, amortization, and impairment of goodwill might create by adjusting the company's financial statements. Adjustments should be made by:

► computing financial ratios using balance sheet data that exclude goodwill;

► reviewing operating trends using data that exclude the amortization of goodwill or impairment to goodwill charges; and

► evaluating future business acquisitions by taking into account the purchase price paid relative to the net assets and earnings prospects of the acquired company.

IFRS No. 3 requires disclosure of the factors that contributed to goodwill and a description of each intangible asset that was not recognized separately from goodwill.

EXAMPLE 5

Goodwill Impairment

Vodafone Group, PLC, is a leading international provider of mobile communications services. It entered many of its international markets by acquiring local carriers. On 27 February 2006, Vodafone issued a press release that included the following information:

> Reflecting the increasingly competitive environment in the industry, Vodafone has incorporated into its latest ten year plan a lower view of growth prospects for a number of key operating companies, particularly in the medium to long term, than those it has used previously.

> The result of these factors is that Vodafone expects to report:
> ► An impairment of the Group's goodwill in the range of GBP 23 billion to GBP 28 billion in respect of reductions in the aggregate goodwill for Vodafone Germany, Vodafone Italy and, potentially, Vodafone Japan. It is expected that most of the total will be attributable to Vodafone Germany.
> ► No impairment for any other subsidiary, joint venture or investment in associated undertakings.
> ► No impairment in respect of finite lived assets.

A summary of the Group's goodwill in respect of subsidiary undertakings and joint ventures as of 30 September 2005 follows.

GBP Billion	
Germany	35.5
Italy	19.7
Japan	9.0
Spain	10.3
U.K.	0.7
Other subsidiaries and joint ventures	6.3
	81.5

How significant is this goodwill impairment and, with reference to acquisition prices, what might it indicate?

Solution: Given that the goodwill impairment was approximately equal to one-third the total value of goodwill recorded, it would appear to be significant. According to the press release, the impairment has arisen due to a competitive environment and lower expected growth rates. The operations involved appear now to be worth less than the price that was paid for their acquisition.

3.5 Financial Instruments: Financial Assets and Financial Liabilities

International accounting standards define a financial instrument as a contract that gives rise to a financial asset of one entity, and a financial liability or equity instrument of another entity. Financial instruments, both assets and liabilities, come in a variety of forms. Financial assets include investments in stocks and bonds and similar instruments. Financial liabilities include bonds, notes payable, and similar instruments. Some financial instruments may be classified as either an asset or a liability depending upon the contractual terms and current market conditions. One example of such a complex financial instrument is a derivative. A **derivative** is a financial instrument for which the value is derived based on some underlying factor (interest rate, exchange rate, commodity price, security price, or credit rating) and for which little or no initial investment is required. Derivatives may be used to hedge business transactions or for speculation.

Mark-to-market (fair value adjustments to financial assets and liabilities) is the process whereby the value of most trading assets (e.g., those held for trading and that are available for sale) and trading liabilities are adjusted to reflect current fair value. Such adjustments are often made on a daily basis, and cumulative balances are reversed on the subsequent day, prior to recalculating a fresh cumulative mark-to-market adjustment.

All financial assets and financial liabilities (including derivatives) should be recognized when the entity becomes a party to the contractual provisions of an instrument. For the purchase or sale of financial assets where market convention determines a fixed period between trade and settlement dates, the trade or settlement date can be used for recognition. Interest is not normally accrued between trade and settlement dates, but mark-to-market adjustments are made regardless of whether the entity uses trade date or settlement date accounting. Although IAS No. 39 allows the use of either date, trade date accounting is preferred by most treasury accountants.

Exhibit 11 provides a summary of how various financial assets and liabilities are classified and measured.

From Exhibit 11, marketable securities such as stocks and bonds may be classified as trading, available for sale, and held to maturity. To illustrate the different accounting treatments of the gains and losses on marketable securities, consider an entity that invests €100,000,000 in a 5 percent coupon fixed-income security portfolio. After six months, the company receives the first coupon payment of €2,500,000. Additionally, interest rates have declined and the value of the fixed-income securities has increased by €2,000,000. Exhibit 12 illustrates how this situation will be portrayed in the balance sheet assets and equity, as well as the income statement of the entity concerned, under each of the following three accounting policies for marketable securities: assets held for trading purposes, assets available for sale, and held-to-maturity assets.

EXHIBIT 11   Measurement of Financial Assets and Liabilities

Measured at Fair Value	Measured at Cost or Amortized Cost
Financial Assets	**Financial Assets**
Financial assets held for trading (e.g., stocks and bonds)	Unlisted instruments (investments where the fair value is not reliably measurable)
Available-for-sale financial assets (e.g., stocks and bonds)	Held-to-maturity investments (bonds intended to be held to maturity)
Derivatives whether stand-alone or embedded in nonderivative instruments	Loans and receivables
Nonderivative instruments (including financial assets) with fair value exposures *hedged* by derivatives	
Financial Liabilities	**Financial Liabilities**
Derivatives	All other liabilities (such as bonds payable or notes payable)
Financial liabilities held for trading	
Nonderivative instruments (including financial liabilities) with fair value exposures *hedged* by derivatives	

EXHIBIT 12	Accounting for Gains and Losses on Marketable Securities		

Balance Sheet As of 30 June 200X	Trading Portfolio	Available-for- Sale Portfolio	Held to Maturity
Assets			
Deposits	2,500,000	2,500,000	2,500,000
Cost of securities	100,000,000	100,000,000	100,000,000
Unrealized gains (losses) on securities	2,000,000	2,000,000	—
	104,500,000	104,500,000	102,500,000
Liabilities			
Equity			
Paid-in capital	100,000,000	100,000,000	100,000,000
Retained earnings	4,500,000	2,500,000	2,500,000
Other comprehensive income (losses)	—	2,000,000	—
	104,500,000	104,500,000	102,500,000

Income Statement
For Period 1 January–30 June 200X

Interest income	2,500,000	2,500,000	2,500,000
Unrealized gains (losses)	2,000,000	—	—
	4,500,000	2,500,000	2,500,000

In the case of marketable securities classified as either trading or available for sale, the investments are listed under assets at fair market value. For exposition purposes, Exhibit 12 shows the unrealized gain on a separate line. Practically, the investments would be listed at their fair value of €102,000,000 on one line within assets. In the case of trading securities, the unrealized gain is included on the income statement and thus reflected in retained earnings. In the case of available-for-sale securities, the unrealized gain is not included on the income statement; rather, it is deferred as part of other comprehensive income within owners' equity. As noted in the reading on the income statement, other comprehensive income includes gains and losses that have not yet been reported on the income statement due to particular accounting standards. In the case of held-to-maturity securities, the unrealized gain is not reflected on either the balance sheet or income statement.

In the case of liabilities such as bonds issued by a company, these are normally reported at amortized cost on the balance sheet, as noted in Exhibit 11. For example, if a company issues bonds with a total par value of $10,000,000 at a price of $9,750,000 (issued at a discount), the bonds are reported as a liability of $9,750,000 (cost). As time passes, the discount of $250,000 is amortized such that the bond will be listed as a liability of $10,000,000 at maturity. Similarly, any bond premium would be amortized for bonds issued at a premium.

EQUITY

Equity is the residual claim on a company's assets after subtracting liabilities. It represents the claim of the owner against the company. Equity includes funds directly invested in the company by the owners, as well as earnings that have been reinvested over time. Equity can also include items of gain or loss that are not yet recognized on the company's income statement.

4.1 Components of Equity

IFRS and U.S. GAAP both define equity (or net assets) as the residual interest in the assets of an entity that remain after deducting its liabilities. There are five potential components that comprise the owners' equity section of the balance sheet:

1. *Capital contributed by owners.* Capital ownership in a corporation is evidenced through the issuance of common stock, although preferred stock (a hybrid security with some characteristics of debt) may be issued by some companies in addition to common stock. Preferred shares have rights that take precedence over the rights of common shareholders—rights that generally pertain to receipt of dividends (not always cumulative if omitted by the board of directors) and receipt of assets if the company is liquidated. Common and preferred shares may have a par value (or stated value) or may be issued as no par shares (depending on governmental requirements at the time of incorporation). Where par or stated value requirements exist, it must be disclosed in the stockholders' equity section of the balance sheet. In addition, the number of shares authorized, issued, and outstanding must be disclosed for each class of stock issued by the company. The number of authorized shares is the number of shares that may be sold by the company under its articles of incorporation. The number of issued shares is those shares that have been sold to investors while the number of outstanding shares consists of the issued shares less those shares repurchased (treasury stock) by the company.

2. *Minority interest (or noncontrolling interest).* The equity interests of minority shareholders in the subsidiary companies that have been consolidated by the parent (controlling) company but that are not wholly owned by the parent company.

3. *Retained earnings (or retained deficit).* Amounts that have been recognized as cumulatively earned in the company's income statements but which have not been paid to the owners of the company through dividends.

4. *Treasury stock (or own shares repurchased).* The repurchase of company shares may occur when management considers the shares undervalued or when it wants to limit the effects of dilution from various employee stock compensation plans. Treasury stock is a reduction of shareholders' equity and a reduction of total shares outstanding. Treasury shares are nonvoting and do not receive dividends if declared by the company.

5. *Accumulated comprehensive income (or other reserves).* Amounts that may either increase or decrease total shareholders' equity but are not derived from the income statement or through any company transactions in its own equity shares.

In June 1997, the FASB released Statement of Financial Accounting Standard (SFAS) No. 130, *Reporting of Comprehensive Income.*[5] This statement established certain standards for reporting and presenting comprehensive income in the general-purpose financial statements. SFAS No. 130 was issued in response to users' concerns that certain changes in assets and liabilities were bypassing the income statement and appearing in the statement of changes in stockholders' equity. The purpose of SFAS No. 130 was to report all items that met the definition of "comprehensive income" in a prominent financial statement for the same period in which they were recognized. In accordance with the definition provided by Statement of Financial Accounting Concepts No. 6, **comprehensive income** was to include all changes in owners' equity that resulted from transactions of the business entity with non-owners. Comprehensive income can be defined as:

$$\text{Comprehensive income} = \text{Net income} + \text{Other comprehensive income}$$

According to SFAS No. 130, **other comprehensive income** (OCI) is part of total comprehensive income but generally excluded from net income. Prior to SFAS No. 130, these three items—foreign currency translation adjustments, minimum pension liability adjustments, and unrealized gains or losses on available-for-sale investments—were disclosed as separate components of stockholders' equity on the balance sheet. Under SFAS No. 130, they are to be reported as OCI. Furthermore, they must be reported separately, as the FASB decided that information about each component is more important than information about the aggregate. Later, under SFAS No. 133,[6] net unrealized losses on derivatives were also included in the definition of OCI. The intent of SFAS No. 130 was that "if used with related disclosures and other information in financial statements, the information provided by reporting comprehensive income would assist investors, creditors, and other financial statement users in assessing an enterprise's economic activities and its timing and magnitude of future cash flows."

Although the FASB required that "an enterprise shall display total comprehensive income and its components in a financial statement that is displayed with the same prominence as other financial statements that constitute a full set of financial statements," it did not specify which format was required, except that net income should be shown as a component of comprehensive income in that financial statement. According to SFAS No. 130, three alternative formats are allowed for presenting OCI and total comprehensive income:

▶ below the line for net income in a traditional income statement (as a combined statement of net income and comprehensive income);

▶ in a separate statement of comprehensive income that begins with the amount of net income for the year; or

▶ in a statement of changes in stockholders' equity.

Under IFRS, the component changes are also reported in the statement of equity; however, it is not presently required that a comprehensive income amount be reported.

Exhibit 13 illustrates how the equity amounts of €22,000 (20X9) and €20,000 (20X8) have been expanded from the one amount shown in Exhibit 5.

---

[5] FASB ASC Topic 220 [Comprehensive Income].

[6] FASB ASC Topic 220 [Comprehensive Income].

EXHIBIT 13	Apex Stockholders' Equity		
		20X9	20X8
Equity		**€22,000**	**€20,000**
Share capital		10,000	10,000
Preferred shares		2,000	2,000
Share premium (paid-in capital)		—	—
Other reserves (unrealized gains and losses)		1,000	—
Retained earnings		9,000	8,000
Own shares repurchased (treasury shares)		—	—

4.2 Statement of Changes in Shareholders' Equity

The **statement of changes in shareholders' equity** reflects information about the increases or decreases to a company's net assets or wealth. With respect to comprehensive income, the following items, if present, must be disclosed:

► unrealized gains or losses on available-for-sale investments;

► gains or losses from derivatives that qualify as net investment hedges or cash flow hedges;

► minimum pension liability adjustments from underfunded defined-benefit plans; and

► foreign currency translation adjustments on foreign subsidiary companies.

Other information in the changes in equity statement or in notes includes the following:

► capital transactions with owners and distributions to owners;

► reconciliation of the balance of accumulated profit or loss (retained earnings) at the beginning and end of the year; and

► reconciliation of the carrying amount of each class of equity capital, share premium (paid-in capital), and accumulated comprehensive income (reserve) at the beginning and end of the period.

Exhibit 14 presents Sony Corporation's Consolidated Statement of Changes in Stockholders' Equity for the fiscal years ended 31 March 2004 and 2005. In this statement, Sony complies with the reconciliation and disclosure requirements that were discussed above.

EXHIBIT 14 — Sony Corporation and Consolidated Subsidiaries Consolidated Statement of Changes in Stockholders' Equity (¥ Millions)

	Subsidiary Tracking Stock	Common Stock	Additional Paid-In Capital	Retained Earnings	Accumulated Other Comprehensive Income	Treasury Stock, at Cost	Total
Balance at 31 March 2003	3,917	472,361	984,196	1,301,740	(471,978)	(9,341)	2,280,895
Conversion of convertible bonds		3,989	3,988				7,977
Stock issued under exchange offering			5,409				5,409
Comprehensive income:							
Net income				88,511			88,511
Other comprehensive income, net of tax							
Unrealized gains on securities:							
Unrealized holding gains or losses arising during period					57,971		57,971
Less: Reclassification adjustment for gains or losses included in net income					(5,679)		(5,679)
Unrealized losses on derivative instruments:							
Unrealized holding gains or losses arising during period					7,537		7,537
Less: Reclassification adjustment for gains or losses included in net income					(3,344)		(3,344)
Minimum pension liability adjustment					93,415		93,415
Foreign currency translation adjustments:							
Translation adjustments arising during period					(129,113)		(129,113)
Less: Reclassification adjustment for losses included in net income					1,232		1,232
Total comprehensive income							110,530
Stock issue costs, net of tax				(53)			(53)
Dividends declared				(23,138)			(23,138)
Purchase of treasury stock						(8,523)	(8,523)
Reissuance of treasury stock			(776)			5,681	4,905
Balance at 31 March 2004	3,917	476,350	992,817	1,367,060	(449,959)	(12,183)	2,378,022

(Exhibit continued on next page . . .)

EXHIBIT 14 (continued)

	Subsidiary Tracking Stock	Common Stock	Additional Paid-In Capital	Retained Earnings	Accumulated Other Comprehensive Income	Treasury Stock, at Cost	Total
Balance at 31 March 2004	3,917	476,350	992,817	1,367,060	(449,959)	(12,183)	2,378,022
Exercise of stock acquisition rights		52	53				105
Conversion of convertible bonds		141,390	141,354				282,744
Stock-based compensation			340				340
Comprehensive income:							
Net income				163,838			163,838
Other comprehensive income, net of tax							
Unrealized gains on securities:							
Unrealized holding gains or losses arising during period					5,643		5,643
Less: Reclassification adjustment for gains or losses included in net income					(12,924)		(12,924)
Unrealized losses on derivative instruments:							
Unrealized holding gains or losses arising during period					(209)		(209)
Less: Reclassification adjustment for gains or losses included in net income					(1,681)		(1,681)
Minimum pension liability adjustment					(769)		(769)
Foreign currency translation adjustments:							
Translation adjustments arising during period					74,224		74,224
Total comprehensive income							228,122
Stock issue costs, net of tax				(541)			(541)
Dividends declared				(24,030)			(24,030)
Purchase of treasury stock						(416)	(416)
Reissuance of treasury stock			(342)	(245)		6,599	6,012
Balance at 31 March 2005	**3,917**	**617,792**	**1,134,222**	**1,506,082**	**(385,675)**	**(6,000)**	**2,870,338**

USES AND ANALYSIS OF THE BALANCE SHEET   5

The classified sections of Apex Corporation's balance sheets have been discussed and illustrated throughout this reading. Exhibit 15 now presents the complete detailed balance sheets for Apex, which we will use as the basis for a discussion of how to analyze a balance sheet.

EXHIBIT 15	Apex Detailed Balance Sheets	

Balance Sheet (000)	20X9	20X8
Assets		
Current assets	**€20,000**	**€16,000**
Cash and cash equivalents	3,000	2,000
Marketable securities: 3 types	3,000	4,000
Trade receivables	5,000	3,000
Inventories	7,000	6,000
Other current assets	2,000	1,000
Noncurrent assets	**53,000**	**27,000**
Property, plant, and equipment	35,000	20,000
Goodwill	5,000	1,000
Other intangible assets	3,000	1,000
Noncurrent investments (subsidiaries, associates, joint ventures)	10,000	5,000
Total assets	**€73,000**	**€43,000**
Liabilities and Equity		
Current liabilities	**14,000**	**7,000**
Trade and other payables	5,000	2,000
Current borrowings	3,000	1,000
Current portion of noncurrent borrowings	2,000	1,000
Current tax payable	2,000	2,000
Accrued liabilities	1,000	500
Unearned revenue	1,000	500
Noncurrent liabilities	**37,000**	**16,000**
Noncurrent borrowings	30,000	10,000
Deferred tax	6,000	5,000
Noncurrent provisions	1,000	1,000
Total liabilities	**51,000**	**23,000**
Equity	**22,000**	**20,000**
Share capital	10,000	10,000
Preference shares	2,000	2,000
Share premium (paid-in capital)	—	—
Other reserves (unrealized gains and losses)	1,000	—
Retained earnings	9,000	8,000
Own shares repurchased (treasury shares)	—	—
Total liabilities and shareholders' equity	**€73,000**	**€43,000**

If a company is growing or shrinking, comparing balance sheet amounts from year to year may not clearly show trends. Additionally, comparing companies is difficult unless adjustments are made for size. Two techniques used to analyze balance sheets adjusted for differences or changes are common-size analysis and ratio analysis.

5.1 Common-Size Analysis of the Balance Sheet

The first technique, common-size analysis, involves stating all balance sheet items as a percentage of total assets.[7] Vertical common-size statements are useful in comparing a company's current balance sheet with prior-year balance sheets or to other companies in the same industry. Horizontal common-size analysis provides a format to accomplish the former but not the latter. Exhibit 16 illustrates vertical common-size balance sheets for Apex Corporation. Horizontal common-size analysis is demonstrated in a later reading.

EXHIBIT 16	Apex Common-Size Balance Sheets		
Balance Sheet (Percent of Total Assets)		**20X9**	**20X8**
Assets			
Current assets		**27.4**	**37.2**
Cash and cash equivalents		4.1	4.7
Marketable securities: 3 types		4.1	9.3
Trade receivables		6.8	7.0
Inventories		9.6	14.0
Other current assets		2.7	2.3
Noncurrent assets		**72.6**	**62.8**
Property, plant, and equipment		47.9	46.5
Goodwill		6.8	2.3
Other intangible assets		4.1	2.3
Noncurrent investments (subsidiaries, associates, joint ventures)		13.7	11.6
Total assets		**100.0**	**100.0**

(Exhibit continued on next page . . .)

---

[7] This format can be distinguished as "vertical common-size analysis." As the reading on financial statement analysis will discuss, another type of common-size analysis, known as "horizontal common-size analysis," states quantities in terms of a selected base-year value. Unless otherwise indicated, text references to "common-size analysis" refer to vertical analysis.

EXHIBIT 16   **(continued)**

Balance Sheet (Percent of Total Assets)	20X9	20X8
Liabilities and Equity		
Current liabilities	**19.2**	**16.3**
Trade and other payables	6.8	4.7
Current borrowings	4.1	2.3
Current portion of noncurrent borrowings	2.7	2.3
Current tax payable	2.7	4.7
Accrued liabilities	1.4	1.2
Unearned revenue	1.4	1.2
Noncurrent liabilities	**50.7**	**37.2**
Noncurrent borrowings	41.1	23.3
Deferred tax	8.2	11.6
Noncurrent provisions	1.4	2.3
Total liabilities	**69.9**	**53.5**
Shareholders' equity	**30.1**	**46.5**
Share capital	13.7	23.3
Preference shares	2.7	4.7
Share premium (paid-in capital)	—	—
Other reserves (unrealized gains and losses)	1.4	—
Retained earnings	12.3	18.6
Own shares repurchased (treasury shares)	—	—
Total liabilities and shareholders' equity	**100.0**	**100.0**

The common-size analysis for Apex clearly shows that for 20X9, the company is less liquid and is more leveraged than it was in 20X8. Regarding liquidity, current assets have decreased and current liabilities have increased when compared with the prior year. With respect to leverage, both noncurrent and total liabilities have increased when compared with the prior year.

EXAMPLE 6

Common-Size Analysis

Applying common-size analysis to the Roche Group balance sheets presented in Exhibit 7, which one of the following line items increased in 2005 relative to 2004?

A. Goodwill.
B. Inventories.
C. Long-term debt.
D. Accounts receivables.

Solution: C is correct. Long-term debt increased as a percentage of total assets from 12.1 percent of total assets in 2004 (CHF7,077 ÷ CHF58,446) to 13.4 percent in 2005 (CHF9,322 ÷ CHF69,365).

Although goodwill, inventories, and accounts receivables all increased in absolute Swiss franc amounts during 2005, they declined as a percentage of total assets when compared with the previous year.

Vertical common-size analysis of the balance sheet is particularly useful in cross-sectional analysis—comparing companies to each other for a particular time period or comparing a company with industry or sector data. The analyst could select individual peer companies for comparison, use industry data from published sources, or compile data from databases. Some common sources of published data are:

▶ *Annual Statement Studies*, published by the Risk Management Association (RMA). This volume provides abbreviated common-size (and ratio) data by industry. The source of data includes both public and nonpublic company data collected by financial institutions and may reflect non-GAAP, unaudited data.

▶ *Almanac of Business and Industrial Financial Ratios*, by Leo Troy. This is an annually revised publication, currently published by CCH.

When analyzing a company, many analysts prefer to select the peer companies for comparison or to compile their own industry statistics. For example, Exhibit 17 presents common-size balance sheet data compiled for the 10 sectors of Standard & Poor's 500 using 2005 data. The sector classification follows the S&P/MSCI Global Industrial Classification System (GICS). The exhibit presents mean and median common-size balance sheet data for those companies in the S&P 500 for which 2005 data was available in the Compustat database.[8]

---

[8] An entry of zero for an item (e.g., current assets) was excluded from the data, except in the case of preferred stock. Note that most financial institutions did not provide current asset or current liability data, so these are reported as not available in the database.

EXHIBIT 17 Common-Size Balance Sheet Statistics for the S&P 500 Grouped by S&P/MSCI GICS Sector (in Percent except No. of Observations; Data for 2005)

Panel A. Median Data

	Energy	Materials	Industrials	Consumer Discretionary	Consumer Staples	Health Care	Financials	Information Technology	Telecom Services	Utilities
No. observations	29	30	49	85	36	52	87	73	9	31
Cash	7.55	6.07	4.89	7.60	4.50	18.50	5.32	28.35	2.05	1.61
Receivables	11.16	13.56	16.50	9.60	9.92	11.91	28.95	10.64	4.71	5.49
Inventories	3.98	10.21	10.38	15.43	14.67	7.49	1.37	5.52	0.95	2.13
Other current	1.64	2.51	3.59	3.33	2.75	3.85	0.98	4.00	1.49	4.59
Current assets	27.29	35.65	36.58	43.92	33.18	41.61	NA	56.05	10.06	16.89
PPE	54.70	37.21	15.79	20.99	27.53	13.70	1.06	9.80	42.57	55.04
Accts payable	7.50	7.01	6.91	6.99	8.54	4.54	34.73	4.14	2.49	3.89
Current liabilities	17.94	20.18	24.48	27.13	29.55	23.87	NA	22.90	13.70	17.13
LT debt	14.77	19.86	17.43	17.81	21.39	11.43	11.98	8.01	23.13	29.35
Total liabilities	50.72	63.82	62.29	56.73	65.36	47.87	89.81	37.10	58.39	75.28
Preferred stock	0.00	0.00	0.00	0.00	0.00	0.00	0.00	0.00	0.00	0.28
Common equity	49.28	36.18	37.71	43.27	34.64	52.13	10.19	62.90	41.61	22.89
Total equity	49.28	36.18	37.71	43.27	34.64	52.13	10.19	62.90	41.61	24.72

LT = long term, PPE = property, plant, and equipment.

(Exhibit continued on next page . . .)

EXHIBIT 17 (continued)

Panel B. Mean Data

	Energy	Materials	Industrials	Consumer Discretionary	Consumer Staples	Health Care	Financials	Information Technology	Telecom Services	Utilities
No. observations	29	30	49	85	36	52	87	73	9	31
Cash	7.56	9.16	7.91	10.19	7.45	19.55	10.49	33.43	3.32	2.85
Receivables	11.83	14.30	17.92	12.46	9.92	12.96	34.02	12.78	5.16	6.78
Inventories	5.32	10.82	10.21	19.36	15.54	9.23	6.88	6.51	0.94	2.62
Other current	2.98	2.73	4.07	3.74	3.09	4.08	1.09	4.60	2.49	6.44
Current assets	27.14	36.82	36.41	40.18	36.35	44.62	NA	56.71	11.59	18.60
PPE	54.84	35.70	24.83	25.38	30.77	16.76	1.92	13.05	48.53	57.48
Accts payable	9.07	8.80	7.12	10.46	9.82	8.75	35.09	7.03	2.76	4.53
Current liabilities	19.00	21.02	25.48	27.71	28.66	25.50	NA	23.99	13.56	18.92
LT debt	17.84	20.18	18.78	19.05	23.51	14.83	18.16	10.60	31.00	31.94
Total liabilities	53.16	61.72	61.10	57.64	64.67	48.88	80.50	40.05	65.74	76.83
Preferred stock	0.50	0.76	0.14	0.11	0.01	0.18	0.93	0.06	0.04	0.60
Common equity	46.33	37.52	38.76	42.25	35.32	50.94	18.60	59.89	34.22	22.57
Total equity	46.84	38.28	38.90	42.36	35.33	51.12	19.50	59.95	34.26	23.17

LT = long term, PPE = property, plant, and equipment.

Source: Based on data from Compustat.

Some interesting general observations can be made from these data:

▶ Energy and utility companies have the largest amounts of property, plant, and equipment. Utilities also have the highest level of long-term debt and use some preferred stock.

▶ Financial companies have the greatest percentage of liabilities.

▶ Telecommunications services and utility companies have the lowest level of receivables.

▶ Inventory levels are highest for consumer discretionary and consumer staples companies.

▶ Information technology companies use the least amount of leverage as evidenced by the entries for long-term debt and total liabilities.

Example 7 shows an analyst using cross-sectional common-size balance sheet data.

EXAMPLE 7

Cross-Sectional Common-Size Analysis

Jason Lu is examining four companies in the computer industry to evaluate their relative financial position as reflected on their balance sheet. He has compiled the following vertical common-size data for Dell, Hewlett-Packard Co., Gateway, and Apple Computer.

Cross-Sectional Analysis

Consolidated Balance Sheets
(in Percent of Total Assets)

Company Fiscal Year	DELL 3 Feb 2006	HPQ 31 Oct 2005	GTW 31 Dec 2005	AAPL 30 Sep 2005
Assets				
Current assets:				
Cash and cash equivalents	30.47	17.99	21.99	30.22
Short-term investments	8.72	0.02	8.50	41.30
Accounts receivable, net	17.69	16.11	17.97	7.75
Financing receivables, net	5.90	n/a	n/a	n/a
Inventories	2.49	8.89	11.42	1.43
Other current assets	11.34	13.03	22.06	8.48
Total current assets	76.62	56.05	81.94	89.17
Property, plant, and equipment, net	8.68	8.34	4.33	7.07
Investments	11.64	9.70	0.00	0.00
Long-term financing receivables, net	1.41	n/a	n/a	n/a
Other assets	1.65	25.91	13.73	3.76
Total Assets	100.00	100.00	100.00	100.00

Company Fiscal Year	DELL 3 Feb 2006	HPQ 31 Oct 2005	GTW 31 Dec 2005	AAPL 30 Sep 2005
Liabilities and Stockholders' Equity				
Current liabilities:				
Accounts payable	42.58	13.22	39.66	15.40
Short-term debt	0.00	2.37	2.60	0.00
Accrued and other	26.34	25.10	23.60	14.76
Total current liabilities	68.92	40.69	65.86	30.16
Long-term debt	2.18	4.39	15.62	0.00
Other liabilities	11.03	6.84	2.98	5.20
Commitments and contingent liabilities	0.00	0.00	0.00	0.00
Total liabilities	82.13	51.92	84.46	35.36
Stockholders' equity				
Total stockholders' equity	17.87	48.08	15.54	64.64

HPQ = Hewlett-Packard Co., GTW = Gateway, AAPL = Apple Computer, n/a = not available.
Source: Based on data from Bloomberg.

From this data, Lu learns the following:

▶ All four companies have a high level of cash, consistent with the information technology sector. Dell and Apple have a much higher than normal balance in cash and investments combined. This may reflect their business models, which have generated large operating cash flows in recent years.

▶ Apple has the lowest level of accounts receivable. Further research is necessary to learn if this is related to Apple's cash sales through retail stores or if the company has been selling/factoring receivables to a greater degree than the other companies.

▶ Dell and Apple both have an extraordinarily low level of inventory. Both utilize a just-in-time inventory system and rely on suppliers to hold inventory until needed. Additional scrutiny of the footnotes accompanying their annual reports reveals that Dell includes some "in-transit" inventory in other current assets and that Apple regularly makes purchase commitments that are not currently recorded as inventory and uses contract manufacturers to assemble and test some finished products. Dell has a smaller relative amount of purchase commitments. Hewlett-Packard has similar purchase commitments to Apple, and all of the companies make some use of contract manufacturers, but no mention is made of them about the extent that inventory may be "understated" through such use. Overall, it appears that the inventory levels may be understated somewhat for Dell and Apple but that, all things considered, they have been more efficient at managing inventory than Hewlett-Packard or Gateway.

▶ All four companies have a level of property, plant, and equipment below that of the sector, with Gateway having the lowest level.

> ▶ Hewlett-Packard has a large amount of "other assets." Further analysis reveals that this represents purchased intangibles, particularly goodwill from acquisitions.
>
> ▶ Dell and Gateway have a large amount of accounts payable. Due to Dell's high level of cash and investments, this is likely not a problem for Dell; however, it could indicate that Gateway could have difficulty in paying suppliers. An analysis of Gateway's cash flows would be warranted.
>
> ▶ Consistent with the industry, Dell, Hewlett-Packard, and Apple have very low levels of long-term debt. Gateway has a high level relative to the industry, which warrants further examination to assess the company's financial risk.

5.2 Balance Sheet Ratios

The second technique permitting comparison across time (time-series analysis) and across companies (cross-sectional analysis) is ratio analysis. In ratio analysis, the analyst may examine the level and trend of a ratio in relation to past values of the ratio for the company, thereby providing information on changes in the financial position of a company over time. The analyst may also compare a ratio against the values of the ratio for comparable companies, thereby providing information on the financial position of a company in relation to that of its peer group. So-called **balance sheet ratios** are those involving balance sheet items only. Balance sheet ratios fall under the heading of **liquidity ratios** (measuring the company's ability to meet its short-term obligations) or **solvency ratios** (measuring the company's ability to meet long-term and other obligations). The use of these ratios along with other balance sheet ratios and ratios combining balance sheet data with other financial statement data are discussed in a later reading. Exhibit 18 summarizes the calculation and interpretation of selected balance sheet ratios.

EXHIBIT 18	Balance Sheet Ratios	
Liquidity Ratios	**Calculation**	**Measurement**
Current	Current assets ÷ Current liabilities	Ability to meet current liabilities
Quick (acid test)	(Cash + Marketable securities + Receivables) ÷ Current liabilities	Ability to meet current liabilities
Cash	(Cash + Marketable securities) ÷ Current liabilities	Ability to meet current liabilities
Solvency Ratios		
Long-term debt to equity	Total long-term debt ÷ Total equity	Financial risk and financial leverage
Debt to equity	Total debt ÷ Total equity	Financial risk and financial leverage
Total debt	Total debt ÷ Total assets	Financial risk and financial leverage
Financial leverage	Total assets ÷ Total equity	Financial risk and financial leverage

Some have questioned the usefulness of financial statement analysis in a world where capital markets are said to be efficient. After all, they say, an efficient market is forward looking, whereas the analysis of financial statements is a look at the past. However, the value of financial analysis is that it enables the analyst to gain insights that can assist in making forward-looking projections required by an efficient market. Financial ratios serve the following purposes:

▶ They provide insights into the microeconomic relationships within a company that help analysts project earnings and free cash flow (which is necessary to determine entity value and credit-worthiness).

▶ They provide insights into a company's financial flexibility, which is its ability to obtain the cash required to meet financial obligations or to make asset acquisitions, even if unexpected circumstances should develop. Financial flexibility requires a company to possess financial strength (a level and trend of financial ratios that meet or exceed industry norms), lines of credit, or assets that can be easily used as a means of obtaining cash, either by their outright sale or by using them as collateral.

▶ They provide a means of evaluating management's ability. Key performance ratios can serve as quantitative measures for ranking management's ability relative to a peer group.

EXAMPLE 8

Ratio Analysis

For the following ratio questions, refer to the balance sheet information for Roche Group presented in Exhibit 7.

1. The **current ratio** for Roche Group at 31 December 2005 is closest to:

    A. 1.29.
    B. 1.86.
    C. 1.97.
    D. 3.75.

2. Using the balance sheet information presented in Exhibit 7 for Roche Group, which one of the following ratios increased in 2005 relative to 2004?

    A. Current ratio.
    B. Total debt ratio.
    C. Debt-to-equity ratio.
    D. Financial leverage ratio.

Solution to 1: D is correct. The current ratio (current assets ÷ current liabilities) is 3.75 (CHF35,626 ÷ CHF9,492).

Solution to 2: A is correct. The current ratio (current assets ÷ current liabilities) increased from 2.93 (CHF29,679 ÷ CHF10,134) in 2004 to 3.75 (CHF35,626 ÷ CHF9,492) in 2005. The total debt ratio declined from 43.1 percent in 2004 to 39.8 percent in 2005; the **debt-to-equity ratio** declined from 75.6 percent in 2004 to 66.2 percent in 2005; and the **financial leverage ratio** declined from 1.756 in 2004 to 1.662 in 2005.

Financial ratio analysis is limited by:

- ▶ The use of alternative accounting methods. Accounting methods play an important role in the interpretation of financial ratios. It should be remembered that ratios are usually based on data taken from financial statements. Such data are generated via accounting procedures that might not be comparable among companies because companies have latitude in the choice of accounting methods. This lack of consistency across companies makes comparability difficult to analyze and limits the usefulness of ratio analysis. Some accounting alternatives currently found include the following:
    - ▶ first-in-first-out (FIFO) or last-in-first-out (LIFO) inventory valuation methods;
    - ▶ cost or equity methods of accounting for unconsolidated associates;
    - ▶ straight-line or accelerated consumption pattern methods of depreciation; and
    - ▶ capitalized or operating lease treatment.
- ▶ The homogeneity of a company's operating activities. Many companies are diversified with divisions operating in different industries. This makes it difficult to find comparable industry ratios to use for comparison purposes. It is better to examine industry-specific ratios by lines of business.
- ▶ The need to determine whether the results of the ratio analysis are mutually consistent. One set of ratios might show a problem and another set might indicate that this problem is short term in nature.
- ▶ The need to use judgment. The analyst must use judgment when performing ratio analysis. A key issue is whether a ratio for a company is within a reasonable range for an industry, with this range being determined by the analyst. Although financial ratios are used to help assess the growth potential and risk of a business, they cannot be used alone to directly value a company or determine its credit-worthiness. The entire operation of the business must be examined, and the external economic and industry setting in which it is operating must be considered when interpreting financial ratios.

SUMMARY

The starting place for analyzing a company is typically the balance sheet. It provides users such as creditors or investors with information regarding the sources of finance available for projects and infrastructure. At the same time, it normally provides information about the future earnings capacity of a company's assets as well as an indication of cash flows implicit in the receivables and inventories.

The balance sheet has many limitations, especially relating to the measurement of assets and liabilities. The lack of timely recognition of liabilities and, sometimes, assets, coupled with historical costs as opposed to fair value accounting for all items on the balance sheet, implies that the financial analyst must make numerous adjustments to determine the economic net worth of the company.

The balance sheet discloses what an entity owns (assets) and what it owes (liabilities) at a specific point in time, which is why it is also referred to as the statement of financial position. Equity represents the portion belonging to the owners or shareholders of a business. Equity is the residual interest in the assets of an entity after deducting its liabilities. The value of equity is increased by any generation of new assets by the business itself or by profits made during the year and is decreased by losses or withdrawals in the form of dividends.

The analyst must understand the structure and format of the balance sheet in order to evaluate the liquidity, solvency, and overall financial position of a company. Key points are:

▶ The "report format" of the balance sheet lists assets, liabilities, and equity in a single column. The "account format" follows the pattern of the traditional general ledger accounts, with assets at the left and liabilities and equity at the right of a central dividing line.

▶ The balance sheet should distinguish between current and noncurrent assets and between current and noncurrent liabilities unless a presentation based on liquidity provides more relevant and reliable information.

▶ Assets expected to be liquidated or used up within one year or one operating cycle of the business, whichever is greater, are classified as current assets. Assets not expected to be liquidated or used up within one year or one operating cycle of the business, whichever is greater, are classified as noncurrent assets.

▶ Liabilities expected to be settled or paid within one year or one operating cycle of the business, whichever is greater, are classified as current liabilities. Liabilities not expected to be settled or paid within one year or one operating cycle of the business, whichever is greater, are classified as noncurrent liabilities.

▶ Asset and liability values reported on a balance sheet may be measured on the basis of fair value or historical cost. Historical cost values may be quite different from economic values. Balance sheets must be evaluated critically in light of accounting policies applied in order to answer the question of how the values relate to economic reality and to each other.

▶ The notes to financial statements are an integral part of the U.S. GAAP and IFRS financial reporting processes. They provide important required detailed disclosures, as well as other information provided voluntarily by management. This information can be invaluable when determining whether the measurement of assets is comparable to other entities being analyzed.

▶ Tangible assets are long-term assets with physical substance that are used in company operations.

▶ Intangible assets are amounts paid by a company to acquire certain rights that are not represented by the possession of physical assets. A company should assess whether the useful life of an intangible asset is finite or infinite and, if finite, the length of its life.

▶ Under IFRS and U.S. GAAP, goodwill should be capitalized and tested for impairment annually. Goodwill is not amortized.

▶ Financial instruments are contracts that give rise to both a financial asset of one entity and a financial liability of another entity. Financial instruments come in a variety of instruments, including derivatives, hedges, and marketable securities.

▶ There are five potential components that comprise the owners' equity section of the balance sheet: contributed capital, minority interest, retained earnings, treasury stock, and accumulated comprehensive income.

▶ The statement of changes in equity reflects information about the increases or decreases to a company's net assets or wealth.

▶ Ratio analysis is used by analysts and managers to assess company performance and status. Another valuable analytical technique is common-size (relative) analysis, which is achieved through the conversion of all balance sheet items to a percentage of total assets.

1. Resources controlled by a company as a result of past events are:
   A. equity.
   B. assets.
   C. liabilities.

2. Equity equals:
   A. Assets – Liabilities.
   B. Liabilities – Assets.
   C. Assets + Liabilities.

3. Distinguishing between current and noncurrent items on the balance sheet and presenting a subtotal for current assets and liabilities is referred to as:
   A. the report format.
   B. the account format.
   C. a classified balance sheet.

4. All of the following are current assets *except*:
   A. cash.
   B. goodwill.
   C. inventories.

5. Debt due within one year is considered:
   A. current.
   B. preferred.
   C. long term.

6. Money received from customers for products to be delivered in the future is recorded as:
   A. revenue and an asset.
   B. an asset and a liability.
   C. revenue and a liability.

7. The carrying value of inventories reflects:
   A. their original cost.
   B. their current value.
   C. the lower of original cost or net realizable value.

8. When a company pays its rent in advance, its balance sheet will reflect a reduction in:
   A. assets and liabilities.
   B. liabilities and shareholders' equity.
   C. one category of assets and an increase in another.

9. Accrued liabilities are:
   A. balanced against an asset.
   B. expenses that have been paid.
   C. expenses that have been reported on the income statement.

10. The initial measurement of goodwill is:

    A. not subject to management discretion.

    B. based on an acquisition's purchase price.

    C. based on the acquired company's book value.

11. Defining total asset turnover as revenue divided by average total assets, all else equal, impairment write-downs of long-lived assets owned by a company will most likely result in an increase for that company in:

    A. the debt-to-equity ratio but not the total asset turnover.

    B. the total asset turnover but not the debt-to-equity ratio.

    C. both the debt-to-equity ratio and the total asset turnover.

12. For financial assets classified as trading securities, how are unrealized gains and losses reflected in shareholders' equity?

    A. They are not recognized.

    B. As an adjustment to paid-in capital.

    C. They flow through income into retained earnings.

13. For financial assets classified as available for sale, how are unrealized gains and losses reflected in shareholders' equity?

    A. They are not recognized.

    B. They flow through retained earnings.

    C. As a separate line item (other comprehensive income).

14. For financial assets classified as held to maturity, how are unrealized gains and losses reflected in shareholders' equity?

    A. They are not recognized.

    B. They flow through retained earnings.

    C. As a separate line item (valuation gains/losses).

15. Under IFRS, the minority interest in consolidated subsidiaries is presented on the balance sheet:

    A. as a long-term liability.

    B. separately, but as a part of shareholders' equity.

    C. as a mezzanine item between liabilities and shareholders' equity.

16. Retained earnings are a component of:

    A. liabilities.

    B. minority interest.

    C. owners' equity.

17. When a company buys shares of its own stock to be held in treasury, it records a reduction in:

    A. both assets and liabilities.

    B. both assets and shareholders' equity.

    C. assets and an increase in shareholders' equity.

18. A common-size analysis of the balance sheet is *most likely* to signal investors that the company:

    A. has increased sales.

    B. is using assets efficiently.

    C. is becoming more leveraged.

19. An investor concerned whether a company can meet its near-term obligations is *most likely* to calculate the:

    A. current ratio.

    B. debt-to-equity ratio.

    C. return on total capital.

20. The *most* stringent test of a company's liquidity is its:

    A. cash ratio.

    B. quick ratio.

    C. current ratio.

21. An investor worried that a company may go bankrupt would *most likely* examine its:

    A. current ratio.

    B. return on equity.

    C. debt-to-equity ratio.

22. Using the information presented in Exhibit 8, the quick ratio for Sony Corp. at 31 March 2005 is *closest* to:

    A. 0.44.

    B. 0.81.

    C. 0.84.

23. Applying common-size analysis to the Sony Corp. balance sheets presented in Exhibit 8, which one of the following line items increased in 2005 relative to 2004?

    A. Goodwill.

    B. Securities investments and other.

    C. Deferred insurance acquisition costs.

24. Using the information presented in Exhibit 8, the financial leverage ratio for Sony Corp. at 31 March 2005 is *closest* to:

    A. 2.30.

    B. 2.81.

    C. 3.31.

SOLUTIONS FOR READING 33

1. B is correct. Assets are resources controlled by a company as a result of past events.

2. A is correct. Assets = Liabilities + Equity and, therefore, Assets − Liabilities = Equity.

3. C is correct. A classified balance sheet is one that classifies assets and liabilities as current or noncurrent and provides a subtotal for current assets and current liabilities.

4. B is correct. Goodwill is a long-term asset, and the others are all current assets.

5. A is correct. Current liabilities are those liabilities, including debt, due within one year. Long-term liabilities are not due within the current year.

6. B is correct. The cash received from customers represents an asset. The obligation to provide a product in the future is a liability called "unearned income" or "unearned revenue." Once the product is delivered, the liability will be converted into revenue.

7. C is correct. Inventories are carried at historical cost, unless the current replacement cost of the inventory is less.

8. C is correct. Paying rent in advance will reduce cash and increase prepaid expenses, both of which are assets.

9. C is correct. Accrued liabilities are expenses that have been reported on a company's income statement but have not yet been paid.

10. B is correct. Initially, goodwill is measured as the difference between the purchase price paid for an acquisition and the fair value of the acquired company's net assets.

11. C is correct. Impairment write-downs reduce equity in the denominator of the debt-to-equity ratio but do not affect debt, so the debt-to-equity ratio is expected to increase. Impairment write-downs reduce total assets but do not affect revenue. Thus, total asset turnover is expected to increase.

12. C is correct. For financial assets classified as trading securities, unrealized gains and losses are reported on the income statement and flow to shareholders' equity as part of retained earnings.

13. C is correct. For financial assets classified as available for sale, unrealized gains and losses are not recorded on the income statement but do appear on the balance sheet. Shareholders' equity is adjusted through a separate line item for valuation gains and losses termed "other comprehensive income."

14. A is correct. When financial assets are classified as held to maturity, gains and losses are recognized only when realized.

15. B is correct. IFRS requires that minority interest in consolidated subsidiaries be classified as shareholders' equity.

16. C is correct. Retained earnings are a component of owners' equity.

17. B is correct. Share repurchases reduce the company's cash (an asset). Shareholders' equity is reduced because there are fewer shares outstanding and treasury stock is an offset to owners' equity.

18. C is correct. Common-size analysis (as presented in the reading) tells investors how the composition of assets is changing over time. As a result, it can signal when the company is becoming more leveraged.

19. A is correct. The current ratio compares assets that can quickly be turned into cash to liabilities that need to be paid within one year. The other ratios are more suited to longer-term concerns.

20. A is correct. The cash ratio determines how much of a company's near-term obligations can be settled with existing cash balances.

21. C is correct. The debt-to-equity ratio tells how much financial risk a company is exposed to.

22. B is correct. The quick ratio ([Cash + Marketable securities + Receivables] ÷ Current liabilities) is 0.81 ([¥779,103 + ¥1,492 + ¥460,202 + ¥1,113,071 − ¥87,709] ÷ ¥2,809,368).

23. C is correct. Deferred insurance acquisition costs increased as a percentage of total assets from 3.84 percent in 2004 (¥349,194 ÷ ¥9,090,662) to 3.95 percent in 2005 (¥374,805 ÷ ¥9,499,100). Although the accounts given in choices A and B increased in absolute Japanese yen terms during 2005, these accounts declined as a percentage of total assets in 2005.

24. C is correct. The financial leverage ratio (Total assets ÷ Total equity) is 3.31 (¥9,499,100 ÷ ¥2,870,338).

UNDERSTANDING THE CASH FLOW STATEMENT

by Thomas R. Robinson, CFA, Jan Hendrik van Greuning, CFA, Elaine Henry, CFA, and Michael A. Broihahn, CFA

LEARNING OUTCOMES

The candidate should be able to:	Mastery
a. compare and contrast cash flows from operating, investing, and financing activities and classify cash flow items as relating to one of these three categories, given a description of the items;	☐
b. describe how noncash investing and financing activities are reported;	☐
c. compare and contrast the key differences in cash flow statements prepared under international financial reporting standards and U.S. generally accepted accounting principles;	☐
d. demonstrate the difference between the direct and indirect methods of presenting cash from operating activities and explain the arguments in favor of each;	☐
e. demonstrate the steps in the preparation of direct and indirect cash flow statements, including how cash flows can be computed using income statement and balance sheet data;	☐
f. describe the process of converting a cash flow statement from the indirect to the direct method of presentation;	☐
g. analyze and interpret a cash flow statement;	☐
h. explain and calculate free cash flow to the firm, free cash flow to equity, and other cash flow ratios.	☐

READING

34

Note:
New rulings and/or pronouncements issued after the publication of the readings on financial reporting and analysis may cause some of the information in these readings to become dated. Candidates are expected to be familiar with the overall analytical framework contained in the study session readings, as well as the implications of alternative accounting methods for financial analysis and valuation, as provided in the assigned readings. Candidates are not responsible for changes that occur after the material was written.

INTRODUCTION — 1

The cash flow statement provides information about a company's *cash receipts* and *cash payments* during an accounting period, showing how these cash flows link the ending cash balance to the beginning balance shown on the company's balance sheet. The cash-based information provided by the cash flow statement contrasts with the accrual-based information from the income statement. For

International Financial Statement Analysis, by Thomas R. Robinson, CFA, Jan Hendrik van Greuning, CFA, Elaine Henry, CFA, and Michael A. Broihahn, CFA. Copyright © 2007 by CFA Institute. Reprinted with permission.

249

example, the income statement reflects revenues when earned rather than when cash is collected; in contrast, the cash flow statement reflects cash receipts when collected as opposed to when the revenue was earned. A reconciliation between reported income and cash flows from operating activities provides useful information about when, whether, and how a company is able to generate cash from its operating activities. Although income is an important measure of the results of a company's activities, cash flow is also essential. As an extreme illustration, a hypothetical company that makes all sales on account, without regard to whether it will ever collect its accounts receivable, would report healthy sales on its income statement and might well report significant income; however, with zero cash inflow, the company would not survive. The cash flow statement also provides a reconciliation of the beginning and ending cash on the balance sheet.

In addition to information about cash generated (or, alternatively, cash used) in operating activities, the cash flow statement provides information about cash provided (or used) in a company's investing and financing activities. This information allows the analyst to answer such questions as:

▶ Does the company generate enough cash from its operations to pay for its new investments, or is the company relying on new debt issuance to finance them?
▶ Does the company pay its dividends to common stockholders using cash generated from operations, from selling assets, or from issuing debt?

Answers to these questions are important because, in theory, generating cash from operations can continue indefinitely, but generating cash from selling assets, for example, is possible only as long as there are assets to sell. Similarly, generating cash from debt financing is possible only as long as lenders are willing to lend, and the lending decision depends on expectations that the company will ultimately have adequate cash to repay its obligations. In summary, information about the sources and uses of cash helps creditors, investors, and other statement users evaluate the company's liquidity, solvency, and financial flexibility.

This reading explains how cash flow activities are reflected in a company's cash flow statement. The reading is organized as follows. Section 2 describes the components and format of the cash flow statement, including the classification of cash flows under international financial reporting standards (IFRS) and U.S. generally accepted accounting principles (GAAP) and the direct and indirect formats for presenting the cash flow statement. Section 3 discusses the linkages of the cash flow statement with the income statement and balance sheet and the steps in the preparation of the cash flow statement. Section 4 demonstrates the analysis of cash flow statements, including the conversion of an indirect cash flow statement to the direct method and how to use common-size cash flow analysis, free cash flow measures, and cash flow ratios used in security analysis. A summary of the key points and practice problems in CFA Institute multiple-choice format conclude the reading.

COMPONENTS AND FORMAT OF THE CASH FLOW STATEMENT

2

The analyst needs to be able to extract and interpret information on cash flows from financial statements prepared according to any allowable format. The basic components and allowable formats of the cash flow statement are well established.

▶ The cash flow statement has subsections relating specific items to the operating, investing, and financing activities of the company.

▶ Two presentation formats are available: the direct and the indirect.

The following discussion presents these topics in greater detail.

2.1 Classification of Cash Flows and Noncash Activities

All companies engage in operating, investing, and financing activities. These activities are the classifications used in the cash flow statement under both IFRS and U.S. GAAP. Under IFRS, International Accounting Standard No. 7, (IAS No. 7), *Cash Flow Statements*, provides that cash flows are categorized as follows:[1]

▶ **Operating activities** include the company's day-to-day activities that create revenues, such as selling inventory and providing services. Cash inflows result from cash sales and from collection of accounts receivable. Examples include cash receipts from the provision of services and royalties, commissions, and other revenue. To generate revenue, companies undertake activities such as manufacturing inventory, purchasing inventory from suppliers, and paying employees. Cash outflows result from cash payments for inventory, salaries, taxes, and other operating-related expenses and from paying accounts payable. Additionally, operating activities include cash receipts and payments related to securities held for dealing or trading purposes (as opposed to being held for investment, as discussed below).

▶ **Investing activities** include purchasing and selling investments. Investments include property, plant, and equipment; intangible assets; other long-term assets; and both long-term and short-term investments in the equity and debt (bonds and loans) issued by other companies. For this purpose, investments in equity and debt securities exclude: a) any securities considered cash equivalents (very short-term, highly liquid securities) and b) **dealing** or **trading securities** (held for trading), the purchase and sale of which are considered operating activities even for companies where this is not a primary business activity. Cash inflows in the investing category

---

[1] IAS No. 7 became effective on 1 January 1994.

include cash receipts from the sale of nontrading securities (available-for-sale, held-to-maturity); property, plant, and equipment; intangibles; or other long-term assets. Cash outflows include cash payments for the purchase of these assets.

► **Financing activities** include obtaining or repaying capital, such as equity and long-term debt. The two primary sources of capital are shareholders and creditors. Cash inflows in this category include cash receipts from issuing stock (common or preferred) or bonds and cash receipts from borrowing. Cash outflows include cash payments to repurchase stock (e.g., treasury stock), to pay dividends, and to repay bonds and other borrowings. Note that indirect borrowing using accounts payable is not considered a financing activity—such borrowing would be classified as an operating activity.

EXAMPLE 1

Net Cash Flow from Investing Activities

A company recorded the following in Year 1:

Proceeds from issuance of long-term debt	$300,000
Purchase of equipment	$200,000
Loss on sale of equipment	$ 70,000
Proceeds from sale of equipment	$120,000
Equity in earnings of affiliate	$ 10,000

On the Year 1 cash flow statement, the company would report net cash flow from investing activities *closest* to:

A. −$150,000.
B. −$80,000.
C. $200,000.
D. $300,000.

Solution: The only two items that would affect the investing section are the purchase of equipment and the proceeds from sale of equipment. The loss on sale of equipment and the equity in earnings of affiliate affect net income but are not investing cash flows. The issuance of debt is a financing cash flow. B is correct: ($200,000) + $120,000 = ($80,000).

Under IFRS, there is some flexibility in reporting some items of cash flow, particularly interest and dividends. IAS No. 7 notes that while for a financial institution interest paid and received would normally be classified as operating activities, for other entities, alternative classifications may be appropriate. For this reason, under IFRS, interest received may be classified either as an operating activity or as an investing activity. Under IFRS, interest paid may be classified as either an operating activity or as a financing activity. Furthermore, under IFRS, dividends received may be classified as either an operating activity or an investing activity. On the other hand, dividends paid may be classified as either an operating activity or a financing activity. Companies must use a consistent classification from year to year and disclose where the amounts are reported.

Under U.S. GAAP, this discretion is not permitted: Interest received and paid is reported as operating activities for all companies.[2] Under U.S. GAAP, dividends received are always reported as operating activities and dividends paid are always reported as financing activities.

EXAMPLE 2

Operating versus Financing Cash Flows

On 31 December 2006, a company issued a $30,000, 90-day note at 8 percent to pay for inventory purchased that day and issued $110,000 long-term debt at 11 percent annually to pay for new equipment purchased that day. Which of the following *most* accurately reflects the combined effect of both transactions on the company's cash flows for the year ended 31 December 2006 under U.S. GAAP? Cash flow from:

A. operations increases $30,000.
B. financing increases $110,000.
C. operations decreases $30,000.
D. financing decreases $110,000.

Solution: C is correct. The increase in inventories would decrease cash flow from operations. The issuance of both short-term and long-term debt is part of financing activities. Equipment purchased is an investing activity. Note that because no interest was paid or received in this example, the answer would be the same under IFRS.

Companies may also engage in noncash investing and financing transactions. A noncash transaction is any transaction that does not involve an inflow or outflow of cash. For example, if a company exchanges one nonmonetary asset for another nonmonetary asset, no cash is involved. Similarly, no cash is involved when a company issues common stock either for dividends or in connection with conversion of a convertible bond or convertible preferred stock. Because no cash is involved in noncash transactions (by definition), these transactions are not incorporated in the cash flow statement. However, any significant noncash transaction is required to be disclosed, either in a separate note or a supplementary schedule to the cash flow statement.

---

[2] See Financial Accounting Standard No. 95, *Statement of Cash Flows*. This was originally issued in 1987 and modified somewhat in recent years. The content of SFAS No. 95 is contained in FASB ASC Topic 230 [Statement of Cash Flows].

2.2 A Summary of Differences between IFRS and U.S. GAAP

As highlighted in the previous section, there are some differences in cash flow statements prepared under IFRS and U.S. GAAP that the analyst should be aware of when comparing the cash flow statements of companies using U.S. GAAP or IFRS. The key differences are summarized in Exhibit 1. In short, the IASB allows more flexibility in the reporting of items such as interest paid or received and dividends paid or received, and in how income tax expense is classified.

U.S. GAAP classifies interest and dividends received from investments as operating activities, whereas IFRS allows companies to classify those items as either operating or investing cash flows. Likewise, U.S. GAAP classifies interest expense as an operating activity, even though the principal amount of the debt issued is classified as a financing activity. IFRS allows companies to classify interest expense as either an operating activity or a financing activity. U.S. GAAP classifies dividends paid to stockholders as a financing activity, whereas IFRS allows companies to classify dividends paid as either an operating activity or a financing activity.

EXHIBIT 1	Cash Flow Statements: Differences between IFRS and U.S. GAAP	
Topic	**IFRS**	**U.S. GAAP**
Classification of cash flows:		
Interest received	Operating or investing	Operating
Interest paid	Operating or financing	Operating
Dividends received	Operating or investing	Operating
Dividends paid	Operating or financing	Financing
Bank overdrafts	Considered part of cash equivalents	Not considered part of cash and cash equivalents and classified as financing
Taxes paid	Generally operating, but a portion can be allocated to investing or financing if it can be specifically identified with these categories	Operating
Format of statement	Direct or indirect; direct is encouraged	Direct or indirect; direct is encouraged. If direct is used, a reconciliation of net income and operating cash flow must also be provided
Disclosures	Tax cash flows must be separately disclosed in the cash flow statement	Interest and taxes paid must be disclosed in footnotes if not presented on the cash flow statement

Sources: IAS No. 7, FAS No. 95, and "Similarities and Differences: A Comparison of IFRS and U.S. GAAP," PricewaterhouseCoopers, October 2004, available at www.pwc.com.

U.S. GAAP classifies all income tax expenses as an operating activity. IFRS also classifies income tax expense as an operating activity, unless the tax expense can be specifically identified with an investing or financing activity (e.g., the tax effect of the sale of a discontinued operation could be classified under investing activities). Under either of the two sets of standards, companies currently have a choice of formats for presenting cash flow statements, as discussed in the next section.

2.3 Direct and Indirect Cash Flow Formats for Reporting Operating Cash Flow

There are two acceptable formats for reporting **cash flow from operations** (also known as **cash flow from operating activities** or **operating cash flow**), defined as the net amount of cash provided from operating activities: the direct and the indirect methods. The *amount* of operating cash flow is identical under both methods; only the *presentation format* of the operating cash flow section differs. The presentation format of the cash flows from investing and financing is exactly the same, regardless of which method is used to present operating cash flows.

The **direct method** shows the specific cash inflows and outflows that result in reported cash flow from operating activities. It shows each cash inflow and outflow related to a company's cash receipts and disbursements, adjusting income statement items to remove the effect of accruals. In other words, the direct method eliminates any impact of accruals and shows only cash receipts and cash payments. The primary argument in favor of the direct method is that it provides information on the specific sources of operating cash receipts and payments in contrast to the indirect method, which shows only the net result of these receipts and payments. Just as information on the specific sources of revenues and expenses is more useful than knowing only the net result—net income—the analyst gets additional information from a direct-format cash flow statement. The additional information is useful in understanding historical performance and in predicting future operating cash flows.

The **indirect method** shows how cash flow from operations can be obtained from reported net income as the result of a series of adjustments. The indirect format begins with net income. To reconcile net income with operating cash flow, adjustments are made for noncash items, for nonoperating items, and for the net changes in operating accruals. The main argument for the indirect approach is that it shows the reasons for differences between net income and operating cash flows. (It may be noted, however, that the differences between net income and operating cash flows are equally visible on an indirect-format cash flow statement and in the supplementary reconciliation required if the company uses the direct method.) Another argument for the indirect method is that it mirrors a forecasting approach that begins by forecasting future income and then derives cash flows by adjusting for changes in balance sheet accounts that occur due to the timing differences between accrual and cash accounting.

Under IFRS, IAS No. 7 encourages the use of the direct method but permits either. Similarly, under U.S. GAAP, the Financial Accounting Standards Board (FASB) in Financial Accounting Standard No. 95 encourages the use of the direct method but allows companies to use the indirect method.[3] Under FAS No. 95, if the direct method is presented, footnote disclosure must also be provided of the indirect method. If the indirect method is chosen, no direct-format

---

[3] FASB ASC Section 230-10-55 [Statement of Cash Flows–Overall–Implementation Guidance and Illustrations].

disclosures are required. As a result, few U.S. companies present the direct format for operating cash flows.

Many users of financial statements prefer the direct format, particularly analysts and commercial lenders, because of the importance of information about operating receipts and payments to assessing a company's financing needs and capacity to repay existing obligations. In 1987, at the time the FASB was adopting FAS No. 95, some companies argued that it is less costly to adjust net income to operating cash flow, as in the indirect format, than it is to report gross operating cash receipts and payments, as in the direct format. With subsequent progress in accounting systems and technology, it is not clear that this argument remains valid. CFA Institute has advocated that standard setters require the use of the direct format for the main presentation of the cash flow statement, with indirect cash flows as supplementary disclosure.[4]

2.3.1 An Indirect-Format Cash Flow Statement Prepared under IFRS

Exhibit 2 presents cash flow statements prepared under IFRS from Roche Group's annual report for the fiscal years ended 31 December 2005 and 2004, which show the use of the indirect method. Roche is a leading international healthcare company based in Switzerland.[5]

In the cash flows from operating activities section of Roche's cash flow statement, the company reconciles its net income to net cash provided by operating activities. Under IFRS, payments for interest and taxes are disclosed in the body of the cash flow statement. Note that Roche discloses the income taxes paid (CHF 1,997 million in 2005) as a separate item in the cash flows from operating activities section. Separate disclosure of this is not useful if an analyst is trying to assess the impact on cash flow of changes in tax rates (income tax expense provided on the income statement does not reflect the flow of cash due to prepaid and deferred items). Roche reports its interest paid in the cash flows from financing activities section, showing a total of CHF 1,983 million in interest and dividends paid in 2005. As noted earlier under U.S. GAAP, interest paid—or the reconciliation adjustment for the net change in interest payable—must be reported in the operating section of the cash flow statement. Furthermore, U.S. GAAP does not require that interest and taxes paid be disclosed as separate line items on the cash flow statement; however, it does require that these amounts be provided in a supplemental note.

---

[4] *A Comprehensive Business Reporting Model: Financial Reporting for Investors*, CFA Institute Centre for Financial Market Integrity, October 2005, p. 27.

[5] The cash flow statement presented here includes a reconciliation of net income to cash generated from operations, which Roche Group reported in the footnotes to the financial statement rather than on the statement itself.

EXHIBIT 2	Roche Group Consolidated Cash Flow Statements (Millions of CHF)		
Fiscal Years Ended 31 December		**2005**	**2004**
Cash flows from operating activities:			
Net income		6,730	7,063
Add back nonoperating (income) expense:			
Income from associated companies		(1)	43
Financial income		(678)	(369)
Financing costs		382	602
Exceptional income from bond conversion and redemption		–	(872)
Income taxes		2,224	1,865
Discontinued businesses		12	(2,337)
Operating profit		8,669	5,995
Depreciation of property, plant, and equipment		1,302	1,242
Amortization of goodwill		–	572
Amortization of intangible assets		1,011	1,000
Impairment of long-term assets		66	39
Changes in group organization		–	199
Major legal cases		356	–
Expenses for defined-benefit postemployment plans		313	532
Expenses for equity-settled equity compensation plans		364	169
Other adjustments		455	(335)
Cash generated from continuing operations		12,526	9,413
Operating cash flows generated from discontinued businesses		(5)	335
Cash generated from operations		12,521	9,748
(Increase) decrease in working capital		488	227
Vitamin case payments		(82)	(66)
Major legal cases		(98)	(65)
Payments made for defined-benefit postemployment plans		(303)	(653)
Utilization of restructuring provisions		(119)	(163)
Utilization of other provisions		(310)	(128)
Other operating cash flows		(125)	(75)
Income taxes paid		(1,997)	(1,490)
Total cash flows from operating activities		9,975	7,335
Cash flows from investing activities:			
Purchase of property, plant, and equipment		(3,319)	(2,344)
Purchase of intangible assets		(349)	(191)
Disposal of property, plant, and equipment		353	196
Disposal of intangible assets		2	12
Disposal of products		56	431

(Exhibit continued on next page . . .)

EXHIBIT 2 (continued)		

Fiscal Years Ended 31 December	2005	2004
Acquisitions of subsidiaries and associated companies	(233)	(1,822)
Divestments of discontinued businesses and associated companies	2,913	696
Interest and dividends received	383	255
Sales of marketable securities	9,859	4,965
Purchases of marketable securities	(15,190)	(4,281)
Other investing cash flows	(161)	64
Total cash flows from investing activities	(5,686)	(2,019)
Cash flows from financing activities:		
Proceeds from issue of long-term debt instruments	2,565	–
Repayment of long-term debt instruments	(1,178)	(3,039)
Increase (decrease) in other long-term debt	(1,083)	(1,156)
Transactions in own equity instruments	779	237
Increase (decrease) in short-term borrowings	(422)	(939)
Interest and dividends paid	(1,983)	(1,971)
Exercises of equity-settled equity compensation plans	1,090	643
Genentech and Chugai share repurchases	(2,511)	(1,699)
Other financing cash flows	(38)	61
Total cash flows from financing activities	(2,781)	(7,863)
Net effect of currency translation on cash and cash equivalents	115	(124)
Increase (decrease) in cash and cash equivalents	1,623	(2,671)
Cash and cash equivalents at 1 January	2,605	5,276
Cash and cash equivalents at 31 December	4,228	2,605

Roche reports its dividends and interest received (CHF 383 million in 2005) in the cash flows from investing activities section. Under U.S. GAAP, investment income received (or the reconciliation adjustment for the net change in investment income receivable) must be reported in the operating section of the cash flow statement.

2.3.2 A Direct-Format Cash Flow Statement Prepared under IFRS

Exhibit 3 presents a direct-method format cash flow statement prepared under IFRS for Telefónica Group, a diversified telecommunications company based in Madrid.[6] Note that in this format of the cash flow statement, the cash received from customers, as well as other operating items, is clearly shown. The analyst can then contrast the change in revenues from the income statement with the change in cash received from customers. An increase in revenues coupled with a decrease in cash received from customers could signal collection problems. However, in the case of Telefónica Group, cash received from customers has increased.

EXHIBIT 3	Telefónica Group Consolidated Cash Flow Statements (Millions of Euros)	
Fiscal Years Ended 31 December	**2005**	**2004**
Cash flows from operating activities		
Cash received from customers	44,353.14	36,367.10
Cash paid to suppliers and employees	(30,531.54)	(24,674.10)
Dividends received	70.58	71.24
Net interest and other financial expenses paid	(1,520.00)	(1,307.11)
Taxes paid	(1,233.04)	(326.00)
Net cash from operating activities	11,139.14	10,131.13
Cash flows from investing activities		
Proceeds on disposals of property, plant, and equipment and intangible assets	113.20	241.27
Payments on investments in property, plant, and equipment and intangible assets	(4,423.22)	(3,488.15)
Proceeds on disposals of companies, net of cash, and cash equivalents disposed	501.59	531.98
Payments on investments in companies, net of cash, and cash equivalents acquired	(6,571.40)	(4,201.57)
Proceeds on financial investments not included under cash equivalents	147.61	31.64
Payments made on financial investments not included under cash equivalents	(17.65)	(76.35)
Interest received on short-term investments not included under cash equivalents	625.18	1,139.51
Capital grants received	32.67	13.51
Net cash used in investing activities	(9,592.02)	(5,808.16)

(Exhibit continued on next page . . .)

---

[6] Excludes supplemental cash flow reconciliation provided at the bottom of the original cash flow statement by the company.

EXHIBIT 3 (continued)		
Fiscal Years Ended 31 December	**2005**	**2004**
Cash flows from financing activities		
Dividends paid	(2,768.60)	(2,865.81)
Proceeds from issue of stock	(2,054.12)	(1,938.56)
Proceeds on issue of debentures and bonds	875.15	572.99
Proceeds on loans, credits, and promissory notes	16,533.96	10,135.11
Cancellation of debentures and bonds	(3,696.52)	(1,790.57)
Repayments of loans, credits, and promissory notes	(9,324.54)	(8,049.77)
Net cash from financing activities	(434.67)	(3,936.61)
Effect of foreign exchange rate changes on collections and payments	165.73	74.18
Effect of changes in consolidation methods and other nonmonetary effects	9.62	(36.76)
Net increase (decrease) in cash and cash equivalents during the year	1,287.80	423.78
Cash and cash equivalents at beginning of year	914.35	490.57
Cash and cash equivalents at end of year	2,202.15	914.35

2.3.3 Illustrations of Cash Flow Statements Prepared under U.S. GAAP

Previously, we presented a cash flow statement prepared under IFRS. In this section, we illustrate cash flow statements prepared under U.S. GAAP. This section presents the cash flow statements of two companies, Tech Data Corporation and Wal-Mart. Tech Data reports its operating activities using the direct method, whereas Wal-Mart reports its operating activities using the more common indirect method.

Tech Data Corporation is a leading distributor of information technology products. Exhibit 4 presents comparative cash flow statements from the company's annual report for the fiscal years ended 31 January 2005 and 2004.[7]

Tech Data Corporation prepares its cash flow statements under the direct method. In the cash flows from operating activities section of Tech Data's cash flow statements, the company identifies the amount of cash it received from customers, $19.7 billion for 2005, and the amount of cash that it paid to suppliers and employees, $19.6 billion for 2005. Net cash provided by operating activities of $106.9 million was adequate to cover the company's investing activities, primarily purchases of property and equipment ($25.9 million) and software development ($17.9 million). In 2005, the company issued $32.7 million of common stock, providing net cash from financing activities of $12.2 million after its debt repayments. Overall, the company's cash increased by $86.3 million, from $108.8 million at the beginning of the year to $195.1 million at the end of the year.

---

[7] Under U.S. GAAP, companies present three years of the cash flow statement. For purposes of presentation and comparison with the IFRS statements presented above, only two years are presented here.

EXHIBIT 4	Tech Data Corporation and Subsidiaries Consolidated Cash Flow Statements (in Thousands)	

Fiscal Years Ended 31 January	2005	2004
Cash flows from operating activities:		
Cash received from customers	$19,745,283	$17,390,674
Cash paid to suppliers and employees	(19,571,824)	(17,027,162)
Interest paid	(18,837)	(17,045)
Income taxes paid	(47,677)	(43,233)
Net cash provided by operating activities	106,945	303,234
Cash flows from investing activities:		
Acquisition of businesses, net of cash acquired	–	(203,010)
Proceeds from sale of property and equipment	5,130	4,484
Expenditures for property and equipment	(25,876)	(31,278)
Software development costs	(17,899)	(21,714)
Net cash used in investing activities	(38,645)	(251,518)
Cash flows from financing activities:		
Proceeds from the issuance of common stock	32,733	28,823
Net repayments on revolving credit loans	(11,319)	(138,039)
Principal payments on long-term debt	(9,214)	(1,492)
Net cash provided by (used in) financing activities	12,200	(110,708)
Effect of exchange rate changes on cash	5,755	10,602
Net increase (decrease) in cash and cash equivalents	86,255	(48,390)
Cash and cash equivalents at beginning of year	108,801	157,191
Cash and cash equivalents at end of year	$ 195,056	$ 108,801
Reconciliation of net income to net cash provided by operating activities:		
Net income	$ 162,460	$ 104,147
Adjustments to reconcile net income to net cash provided by operating activities:		
Depreciation and amortization	55,472	55,084
Provision for losses on accounts receivable	13,268	29,214
Deferred income taxes	(3,616)	7,369
Changes in operating assets and liabilities, net of acquisitions:		
Accounts receivable	(44,305)	(15,699)
Inventories	(119,999)	(140,203)
Prepaid and other assets	(32,193)	14,713
Accounts payable	55,849	300,350
Accrued expenses and other liabilities	20,009	(51,741)
Total adjustments	(55,515)	199,087
Net cash provided by operating activities	$ 106,945	$ 303,234

Whenever the direct method is used, FAS No. 95 mandates a disclosure note and schedule that reconciles net income with the net cash flow from operating activities. Tech Data shows this reconciliation at the bottom of its consolidated cash flow statements. The disclosure note and reconciliation schedule are exactly the information that would have been presented in the body of the cash flow statement if the company had elected instead to use the indirect method.

Wal-Mart is a global retailer that conducts business under the names of Wal-Mart and Sam's Club. Exhibit 5 presents the comparative cash flow statements from the company's annual report for the fiscal years ended 31 January 2005 and 2004.[8]

EXHIBIT 5	Wal-Mart Cash Flow Statements (in Millions)		
Fiscal Years Ended 31 January		**2005**	**2004**
Cash flows from operating activities:			
Income from continuing operations		$10,267	$ 8,861
Adjustments to reconcile net income to net cash provided by operating activities:			
Depreciation and amortization		4,405	3,852
Deferred income taxes		263	177
Other operating activities		378	173
Changes in certain assets and liabilities, net of effects of acquisitions:			
Decrease (increase) in accounts receivable		(304)	373
Increase in inventories		(2,635)	(1,973)
Increase in accounts payable		1,694	2,587
Increase in accrued liabilities		976	1,896
Net cash provided by operating activities of continuing operations		15,044	15,946
Net cash provided by operating activities of discontinued operations		–	50
Net cash provided by operating activities		15,044	15,996
Cash flows from investing activities:			
Payments for property and equipment		(12,893)	(10,308)
Investment in international operations		(315)	(38)
Proceeds from the disposal of fixed assets		953	481
Proceeds from the sale of McLane		–	1,500
Other investing activities		(96)	78
Net cash used in investing activities of continuing operations		(12,351)	(8,287)
Net cash used in investing activities of discontinued operations		–	(25)
Net cash used in investing activities		(12,351)	(8,312)

(Exhibit continued on next page . . .)

---

[8] Under U.S. GAAP, companies present three years of the cash flow statement. For purposes of presentation and comparison with the IFRS statements presented above, only two years are presented here.

EXHIBIT 5	(continued)		

Cash flows from financing activities:

Increase in commercial paper		544	688
Proceeds from issuance of long-term debt		5,832	4,099
Purchase of company stock		(4,549)	(5,046)
Dividends paid		(2,214)	(1,569)
Payment of long-term debt		(2,131)	(3,541)
Payment of capital lease obligations		(204)	(305)
Other financing activities		113	111
Net cash used in financing activities		(2,609)	(5,563)
Effect of exchange rate changes on cash		205	320
Net increase in cash and cash equivalents		289	2,441
Cash and cash equivalents at beginning of year		5,119	2,758
Cash and cash equivalents at end of year		$ 5,488	$ 5,199
Income tax paid		$ 5,593	$ 4,358
Interest paid		1,163	1,024
Capital lease obligations incurred		377	252

Wal-Mart prepares its cash flow statements under the indirect method. In the cash flows from operating activities section of Wal-Mart's cash flow statement, the company reconciles its net income of $10.3 billion to net cash provided by operating activities of $15 billion. Whenever the indirect method is used, U.S. GAAP mandates a supplemental note that discloses how much cash was paid for interest and income taxes. Wal-Mart discloses the amount of cash paid for income tax ($5.6 billion), interest ($1.2 billion), and capital lease obligations (i.e., the interest expense component of the capital lease payments) at the bottom of its cash flow statements.

THE CASH FLOW STATEMENT: LINKAGES AND PREPARATION

3

The indirect format of the cash flow statement demonstrates that changes in balance sheet accounts are an important factor in determining cash flows. The next section addresses the linkages between the cash flow statement and other financial statements.

3.1 Linkages of the Cash Flow Statement with the Income Statement and Balance Sheet

Recall the accounting equation that summarizes the balance sheet:

Assets = Liabilities + Owners' equity

Cash is an asset. The cash flow statement ultimately shows the change in cash during an accounting period. The beginning and ending balances of cash are shown on the company's balance sheets for the previous and current years, and the bottom of the cash flow statement reconciles beginning cash with ending cash. For example, the Roche Group's cash flow statement for 2005, presented in Exhibit 2, shows that operating, investing, and financing activities during the year imply a CHF 1,623 increase in cash and cash equivalents, which is the amount by which end-of-year cash and cash equivalents (CHF 4,228) exceeds beginning-of-year cash and cash equivalents (CHF 2,605). The relationship, stated in general terms, is as shown below.

Beginning Balance Sheet At 31 December 20X6	Cash Flow Statement For Year Ended 31 December 20X7		Ending Balance Sheet At 31 December 20X7
Beginning cash	Plus: Cash receipts (from operating, investing, and financing activities)	Less: Cash payments (for operating, investing, and financing activities)	Ending cash

In the case of cash held in foreign currencies, there would also be an impact from changes in exchange rates. The body of the cash flow statement shows why the change in cash occurred; in other words, it shows the company's operating, investing, and financing activities (as well as the impact of foreign currency translation). The beginning and ending balance sheet values of cash and cash equivalents are linked through the cash flow statement. The linkage is similar to the one that relates net income and dividends as shown in the income statement to the beginning and ending values of retained earnings in the owners' equity section of the balance sheet, as shown below.

Beginning Balance Sheet At 31 December 20X6	Statement of Owners' Equity For Year Ended 31 December 20X7		Ending Balance Sheet At 31 December 20X7
Beginning retained earnings	Plus: Net income or minus net loss from the income statement for year ended 31 December 20X7	Minus: Dividends	Ending retained earnings

A company's operating activities are reported on an accrual basis in the income statement, and any differences between the accrual basis and the cash basis of accounting for an operating transaction result in an increase or decrease in some (usually) short-term asset or liability on the balance sheet. For example, if revenue reported using accrual accounting is higher than the cash actually collected, the result will be an increase in accounts receivable. If expenses reported using accrual accounting are lower than cash actually paid, the result will be a decrease in accounts payable.

A company's investing activities typically relate to the long-term asset section of the balance sheet, and its financing activities typically relate to the equity and long-term debt sections of the balance sheet. Each item on the balance sheet is also related to the income statement and/or cash flow statement through the change in the beginning and ending balance. Consider, for example, accounts receivable:

Beginning Balance Sheet At 31 December 20X6	Income Statement For Year Ended 31 December 20X7	Cash Flow Statement For Year Ended 31 December 20X7	Ending Balance Sheet At 31 December 20X7
Beginning accounts receivable	Plus: Revenues	Minus: Cash collected from customers	Ending accounts receivable

Knowing any three of these four items makes it easy to compute the fourth. For example, if you know beginning accounts receivable, revenues, and cash collected from customers, you can easily compute ending accounts receivable. Understanding these interrelationships between the balance sheet, income statement, and cash flow statement is useful in not only understanding the company's financial health but also in detecting accounting irregularities. The next section demonstrates the preparation of cash flow information based upon income statement and balance sheet information.

3.2 Steps in Preparing the Cash Flow Statement

The preparation of the cash flow statement uses data from both the income statement and the comparative balance sheets.

As noted earlier, companies often only disclose indirect operating cash flow information, whereas analysts prefer direct-format information. Understanding how cash flow information is put together will enable you to take an indirect statement apart and reconfigure it in a more useful manner. The following demonstration of how a cash flow statement is prepared uses the income statement and the comparative balance sheets for Acme Corporation (a fictitious retail company) shown in Exhibits 6 and 7.

EXHIBIT 6	Acme Corporation Income Statement Year Ended 31 December 2006 (in Thousands)	
Revenue		$23,598
Cost of goods sold		11,456
Gross profit		12,142
Salary and wage expense	4,123	
Depreciation expense	1,052	
Other operating expenses	3,577	
Total operating expenses		8,752
Operating profit		3,390

(Exhibit continued on next page . . .)

EXHIBIT 6	(continued)

Other revenues (expenses):		
Gain on sale of equipment	205	
Interest expense	(246)	(41)
Income before tax		3,349
Income tax expense		1,139
Net income		$ 2,210

EXHIBIT 7	Acme Corporation Comparative Balance Sheets 31 December 2006 and 2005 (in Thousands)

	2006	2005	Net Change
Cash	$ 1,011	$ 1,163	$ (152)
Accounts receivable	1,012	957	55
Inventory	3,984	3,277	707
Prepaid expenses	155	178	(23)
Total current assets	6,162	5,575	587
Land	510	510	–
Buildings	3,680	3,680	–
Equipment[a]	8,798	8,555	243
Less: accumulated depreciation	(3,443)	(2,891)	(552)
Total long-term assets	9,545	9,854	(309)
Total assets	$15,707	$15,429	278
Accounts payable	$ 3,588	$ 3,325	$ 263
Salary and wage payable	85	75	10
Interest payable	62	74	(12)
Income tax payable	55	50	5
Other accrued liabilities	1,126	1,104	22
Total current liabilities	4,916	4,628	288
Long-term debt	3,075	3,575	(500)
Common stock	3,750	4,350	(600)
Retained earnings	3,966	2,876	1,090
Total liabilities and equity	$15,707	$15,429	278

[a] During 2006, Acme purchased new equipment for a total cost of $1,300. No items impacted retained earnings other than net income and dividends.

The first step in preparing the cash flow statement is to determine the total cash flows from operating activities. The direct method of presenting cash from operating activities will be illustrated first, followed by the indirect method. Cash flows from investing activities and from financing activities are identical under either method.

3.2.1 Operating Activities: Direct Method

We first determine how much cash Acme received from its customers, followed by how much cash was paid to suppliers and to employees as well as how much cash was paid for other operating expenses, interest, and income taxes.

3.2.1.1 Cash Received from Customers The income statement for Acme reported revenue of $23,598 (in thousands) for the year ended 31 December 2006. To determine the cash receipts from its customers, it is necessary to adjust this revenue amount by the net change in accounts receivable for the year. If accounts receivable increase during the year, revenue on an accrual basis is higher than cash receipts from customers, and vice versa. For Acme Corporation, accounts receivable increased by $55, so cash received from customers was $23,543, as follows:

Revenue	$23,598
Less: Increase in accounts receivable	(55)
Cash received from customers	**$23,543**

Cash received from customers affects the accounts receivable account as follows:

Beginning accounts receivable	$ 957
Plus revenue	23,598
Minus cash collected from customers	**(23,543)**
Ending accounts receivable	$ 1,012

The accounts receivable account information can also be presented as follows:

Beginning accounts receivable	$ 957
Plus revenue	23,598
Minus ending accounts receivable	(1,012)
Cash collected from customers	**$23,543**

EXAMPLE 3

Computing Cash Received from Customers

Blue Bayou, an advertising company, reported revenues of $50 million, total expenses of $35 million, and net income of $15 million in the most recent year. If accounts receivable decreased by $12 million, how much cash did the company receive from customers?

A. $62 million.
B. $50 million.
C. $38 million.
D. $15 million.

Solution: A is correct. Revenues of $50 million plus the decrease in accounts receivable of $12 million equals $62 million in cash received from customers. The decrease in accounts receivable means that the company received more in cash than the amount of revenue it reported.

"Cash received from customers" is sometimes referred to as "cash collections from customers" or "cash collections."

3.2.1.2 Cash Paid to Suppliers　For Acme, the cash paid to suppliers was $11,900, determined as follows:

Cost of goods sold	$11,456
Plus: Increase in inventory	707
Equals purchases from suppliers	$12,163
Less: Increase in accounts payable	(263)
Cash paid to suppliers	**$11,900**

There are two pieces to this calculation: the amount of inventory purchased and the amount paid for it. To determine purchases from suppliers, cost of goods sold is adjusted for the change in inventory. If inventory increased during the year, then purchases during the year exceeded cost of goods sold, and vice versa. Acme reported cost of goods sold of $11,456 for the year ended 31 December 2006. For Acme Corporation, inventory increased by $707, so purchases from suppliers was $12,163. Purchases from suppliers affects the inventory account, as shown below:

Beginning inventory	3,277
Plus purchases	12,163
Minus cost of goods sold	(11,456)
Ending inventory	3,984

Acme purchased $12,163 of inventory from suppliers this year, but is this the amount of cash that Acme paid to its suppliers during the year? Not necessarily. Acme may not have yet paid for all of these purchases and may yet owe for some of the purchases made this year. In other words, Acme may have paid less cash to its suppliers than the amount of this year's purchases, in which case Acme's liability (accounts payable) will have increased by the difference. Alternatively, Acme may have paid even more to its suppliers than the amount of this year's purchases, in which case Acme's accounts payable will have decreased.

Therefore, once purchases have been determined, cash paid to suppliers can be calculated by adjusting purchases for the change in accounts payable. If the company made all purchases for cash, then accounts payable would not change and cash outflows would equal purchases. If accounts payable increased during the year, then purchases on an accrual basis are higher than they are on a cash basis, and vice versa. In this example, Acme made more purchases than it paid in cash, so the balance in accounts payable has increased. For Acme, the cash paid to suppliers was $11,900, determined as follows:

Purchases from suppliers	$12,163
Less: Increase in accounts payable	(263)
Cash paid to suppliers	**$11,900**

The amount of cash paid to suppliers is reflected in the accounts payable account, as shown below:

Beginning accounts payable	$ 3,325
Plus purchases	12,163
Minus cash paid to suppliers	**(11,900)**
Ending accounts payable	$ 3,588

EXAMPLE 4

Computing Cash Paid to Suppliers

Orange Beverages Plc., a manufacturer of tropical drinks, reported cost of goods sold for the year of $100 million. Total assets increased by $55 million, but inventory declined by $6 million. Total liabilities increased by $45 million, but accounts payable decreased by $2 million. How much cash did the company pay to its suppliers during the year?

A. $110 million.
B. $108 million.
C. $104 million.
D. $96 million.

Solution: D is correct. Cost of goods sold of $100 million less the decrease in inventory of $6 million equals purchases from suppliers of $94 million. The decrease in accounts payable of $2 million means that the company paid $96 million in cash ($94 million plus $2 million).

3.2.1.3 Cash Paid to Employees To determine the cash paid to employees, it is necessary to adjust salary and wage expense by the net change in salary and wage payable for the year. If salary and wage payable increased during the year, then salary and wage expense on an accrual basis is higher than the amount of cash paid for this expense, and vice versa. For Acme, salary and wage payable increased by $10, so cash paid for salary and wages was $4,113, as follows:

Salary and wage expense	$4,123
Less: Increase in salary and wage payable	(10)
Cash paid to employees	**$4,113**

The amount of cash paid to employees is reflected in the salary and wage payable account, as shown below:

Beginning salary and wages payable	$ 75
Plus salary and wage expense	4,123
Minus cash paid to employees	**(4,113)**
Ending salary and wages payable	$ 85

3.2.1.4 Cash Paid for Other Operating Expenses   To determine the cash paid for other operating expenses, it is necessary to adjust the other operating expenses amount on the income statement by the net changes in prepaid expenses and accrued expense liabilities for the year. If prepaid expenses increased during the year, other operating expenses on a cash basis were higher than on an accrual basis, and vice versa. Likewise, if accrued expense liabilities increased during the year, other operating expenses on a cash basis were lower than on an accrual basis, and vice versa. For Acme Corporation, the amount of cash paid for operating expenses in 2006 was $3,532, as follows:

Other operating expenses	$3,577
Less: Decrease in prepaid expenses	23
Less: Increase in other accrued liabilities	22
Cash paid for other operating expenses	**$3,532**

EXAMPLE 5

Computing Cash Paid for Other Operating Expenses

Black Ice, a sportswear manufacturer, reported other operating expenses of $30 million. Prepaid insurance expense increased by $4 million, and accrued utilities payable decreased by $7 million. Insurance and utilities are the only two components of other operating expenses. How much cash did the company pay in other operating expenses?

A. $41 million.
B. $33 million.
C. $27 million.
D. $19 million.

Solution: A is correct. Other operating expenses of $30 million plus the increase in prepaid insurance expense of $4 million plus the decrease in accrued utilities payable of $7 million equals $41 million.

3.2.1.5 Cash Paid for Interest The company is either subject to U.S. GAAP, which requires that interest expense be included in operating cash flows, or it is subject to IFRS, which gives companies the option to treat interest expense in this manner. To determine the cash paid for interest, it is necessary to adjust interest expense by the net change in interest payable for the year. If interest payable increases during the year, then interest expense on an accrual basis is higher than the amount of cash paid for interest, and vice versa. For Acme Corporation, interest payable decreased by $12 and cash paid for interest was $258, as follows:

Interest expense	$246
Plus: Decrease in interest payable	12
Cash paid for interest	**$258**

Alternatively, cash paid for interest may also be determined by an analysis of the interest payable account, as shown below:

Beginning interest payable	$ 74
Plus interest expense	246
Minus cash paid for interest	**(258)**
Ending interest payable	$ 62

3.2.1.6 Cash Paid for Income Taxes To determine the cash paid for income taxes, it is necessary to adjust the income tax expense amount on the income statement by the net changes in taxes receivable, taxes payable, and deferred income taxes for the year. If taxes receivable or deferred tax assets increase during the year, income taxes on a cash basis will be higher than on an accrual basis, and vice versa. Likewise, if taxes payable or deferred tax liabilities increase during the year, income tax expense on a cash basis will be lower than on an accrual basis, and vice versa. For Acme Corporation, the amount of cash paid for income taxes in 2006 was $1,134, as follows:

Income tax expense	$1,139
Less: Increase in income tax payable	(5)
Cash paid for income taxes	**$1,134**

3.2.2 Investing Activities: Direct Method

The second and third steps in preparing the cash flow statement are to determine the total cash flows from investing activities and from financing activities. The presentation of this information is identical, regardless of whether the direct or indirect method is used for operating cash flows. Investing cash flows are always presented using the direct method.

Purchases and sales of equipment were the only investing activities undertaken by Acme in 2006, as evidenced by the fact that the amounts reported for land and buildings were unchanged during the year. An informational note in Exhibit 7 tells us that Acme *purchased* new equipment in 2006 for a total cost of $1,300. However, the amount of equipment shown on Acme's balance sheet increased by only $243 (ending balance of $8,798 minus beginning balance of $8,555); therefore, Acme must have also *sold* some equipment during the year. To determine the cash inflow from the sale of equipment, we analyze the equipment and accumulated depreciation accounts as well as the gain on the sale of equipment from Exhibits 6 and 7.

The historical cost of the equipment sold was $1,057. This amount is determined as follows:

Beginning balance equipment (from balance sheet)	$8,555
Plus equipment purchased (from informational note)	1,300
Minus ending balance equipment (from balance sheet)	(8,798)
Equals historical cost of equipment sold	$1,057

The accumulated depreciation on the equipment sold was $500, determined as follows:

Beginning balance accumulated depreciation (from balance sheet)	$2,891
Plus depreciation expense (from income statement)	1,052
Minus ending balance accumulated depreciation (from balance sheet)	(3,443)
Equals accumulated depreciation on equipment sold	$500

The historical cost information, accumulated depreciation information, and information from the income statement about the gain on the sale of equipment can be used to determine the cash received from the sale.

Historical cost of equipment sold (calculated above)	$1,057
Less accumulated depreciation on equipment sold (calculated above)	(500)
Equals: Book value of equipment sold	557
Plus: Gain on sale of equipment (from the income statement)	205
Equals: Cash received from sale of equipment	$762

EXAMPLE 6

Computing Cash Received from the Sale of Equipment

Copper, Inc., a brewery and restaurant chain, reported a gain on the sale of equipment of $12 million. In addition, the company's income statement shows depreciation expense of $8 million, and the cash flow statement shows capital expenditure of $15 million, all of which was for the purchase of new equipment.

Balance Sheet Item	12/31/2005	12/31/2006	Change
Equipment	$100 million	$109 million	$9 million
Accumulated depreciation —equipment	$30 million	$36 million	$6 million

Using the information from the comparative balance sheets, how much cash did the company receive from the equipment sale?

A. $16 million.
B. $9 million.
C. $6 million.
D. $3 million.

Solution: A is correct. Selling price (cash inflow) minus book value equals gain or loss on sale; therefore, gain or loss on sale plus book value equals selling price (cash inflow). The amount of gain is given, $12 million. To calculate the book value of the equipment sold, find the historical cost of the equipment and the accumulated depreciation on the equipment.

► Beginning balance of equipment of $100 million plus equipment purchased of $15 million minus ending balance of equipment of $109 million equals historical cost of equipment sold, or $6 million.

► Beginning accumulated depreciation on equipment of $30 million plus depreciation expense for the year of $8 million minus ending balance of accumulated depreciation of $36 million equals accumulated depreciation on the equipment sold, or $2 million.

► Therefore, the book value of the equipment sold was $6 million minus $2 million, or $4 million.

► Because the gain on the sale of equipment was $12 million, the amount of cash received must have been $16 million.

3.2.3 Financing Activities: Direct Method

As with investing activities, financing activities are always presented using the direct method.

3.2.3.1 Long-Term Debt and Common Stock   The change in long-term debt, based on the beginning and ending balance sheets in Exhibit 7, was a decrease of $500. Absent other information, this indicates that Acme retired $500 of long-term debt. Retiring long-term debt is a cash outflow relating to financing activities.

Similarly, the change in common stock during 2006 was a decrease of $600. Absent other information, this indicates that Acme repurchased $600 of its common stock. Repurchase of common stock is also a cash outflow related to financing activity.

3.2.3.2 Dividends   Recall the following relationship:

Beginning retained earnings + Net income − Dividends
    = Ending retained earnings

Based on this relationship, the amount of cash dividends paid in 2006 can be determined from an analysis of retained earnings, as follows:

Beginning balance of retained earnings (from the balance sheet)	$2,876
Plus net income (from the income statement)	2,210
Minus ending balance of retained earnings (from the balance sheet)	(3,966)
Equals dividends paid	**$1,120**

3.2.4 Overall Cash Flow Statement: Direct Method

Exhibit 8 summarizes the information about Acme's operating, investing, and financing cash flows in the cash flow statement. At the bottom of the statement, the total net change in cash is shown to be a decrease of $152 (from $1,163 to $1,011). This can also be seen on the comparative balance sheet in Exhibit 7. The cash provided by operating activities of $2,606 was adequate to cover the net cash used in investing activities of $538; however, the company's debt repayments, cash payments for dividends, and repurchase of common stock (i.e., its financing activities) of $2,220 resulted in an overall decrease of $152.

EXHIBIT 8	Acme Corporation Cash Flow Statement (Direct Method) for Year Ended 31 December 2006 (in Thousands)

Cash flow from operating activities:	
Cash received from customers	$23,543
Cash paid to suppliers	(11,900)
Cash paid to employees	(4,113)
Cash paid for other operating expenses	(3,532)
Cash paid for interest	(258)
Cash paid for income tax	(1,134)
Net cash provided by operating activities	2,606
Cash flow from investing activities:	
Cash received from sale of equipment	762
Cash paid for purchase of equipment	(1,300)
Net cash used for investing activities	(538)
Cash flow from financing activities:	
Cash paid to retire long-term debt	(500)
Cash paid to retire common stock	(600)
Cash paid for dividends	(1,120)
Net cash used for financing activities	(2,220)
Net decrease in cash	(152)
Cash balance, 31 December 2005	1,163
Cash balance, 31 December 2006	$ 1,011

3.2.5 Overall Cash Flow Statement: Indirect Method

Using the alternative approach to reporting cash from operating activities, the indirect method, we will present the same amount of cash provided by operating activities. Under this approach, we reconcile Acme's net income of $2,210 to its operating cash flow of $2,606.

To perform this reconciliation, net income is adjusted for the following: a) any nonoperating activities; b) any noncash expenses; and c) changes in operating working capital items.

The only nonoperating activity in Acme's income statement, the sale of equipment, resulted in a gain of $205. This amount is removed from the operating cash flow section; the cash effects of the sale are shown in the investing section.

Acme's only noncash expense was depreciation expense of $1,052. Under the indirect method, depreciation expense must be added back to net income because it was a noncash deduction in the calculation of net income.

Changes in working capital accounts include increases and decreases in the current operating asset and liability accounts. The changes in these accounts arise from applying accrual accounting; that is, recognizing revenues when they are earned and expenses when they are incurred instead of when the cash is received or paid. To make the working capital adjustments under the indirect method, any increase in a current operating asset account is subtracted from net income while a net decrease is added to net income. As described above, the increase in accounts receivable, for example, resulted from Acme recording income statement revenue higher than the amount of cash received from customers; therefore, to reconcile back to operating cash flow, that increase in accounts receivable must be deducted from net income. For current operating liabilities, a net increase is added to net income while a net decrease is subtracted from net income. As described above, the increase in wages payable, for example, resulted from Acme recording income statement expenses higher than the amount of cash paid to employees.

Exhibit 9 presents a tabulation of the most common types of adjustments that are made to net income when using the indirect method to determine net cash flow from operating activities.

EXHIBIT 9	Adjustments to Net Income Using the Indirect Method

Additions   Noncash items

      Depreciation expense of tangible assets

      Amortization expense of intangible assets

      Depletion expense of natural resources

      Amortization of bond discount

    Nonoperating losses

      Loss on sale or write-down of assets

      Loss on retirement of debt

      Loss on investments accounted for under the equity method

    Increase in deferred income tax liability

    Changes in working capital resulting from accruing higher expenses than cash payments, or lower revenues than cash receipts

(Exhibit continued on next page . . .)

EXHIBIT 9	(continued)

Increase in current operating liabilities (e.g., accounts payable and accrued expense liabilities)

Decrease in current operating assets (e.g., accounts receivable, inventory, and prepaid expenses)

Subtractions	Noncash items (e.g., amortization of bond premium)

Nonoperating items

   Gain on sale of assets

   Gain on retirement of debt

   Income on investments accounted for under the equity method

Decrease in deferred income tax liability

Changes in working capital resulting from accruing lower expenses than cash payments, or higher revenues than cash receipts

   Decrease in current operating liabilities (e.g., accounts payable and accrued expense liabilities)

   Increase in current operating assets (e.g., accounts receivable, inventory, and prepaid expenses)

Accordingly, for Acme Corporation, the $55 increase in accounts receivable and the $707 increase in inventory are subtracted from net income while the $23 decrease in prepaid expenses is added to net income. For Acme's current liabilities, the increases in accounts payable, salary and wage payable, income tax payable, and other accrued liabilities ($263, $10, $5, and $22, respectively) are added to net income while the $12 decrease in interest payable is subtracted from net income. Exhibit 10 presents the cash flow statement for Acme Corporation under the indirect method by using the information that we have determined from our analysis of the income statement and the comparative balance sheets. Note that the investing and financing sections are identical to the cash flow statement prepared using the direct method.

EXHIBIT 10	Acme Corporation Cash Flow Statement (Indirect Method) Year Ended 31 December 2006 (in Thousands)

Cash flow from operating activities:

Net income	$2,210
Depreciation expense	1,052
Gain on sale of equipment	(205)
Increase in accounts receivable	(55)
Increase in inventory	(707)

(Exhibit continued on next page . . .)

EXHIBIT 10	**(continued)**	
Decrease in prepaid expenses		23
Increase in accounts payable		263
Increase in salary and wage payable		10
Decrease in interest payable		(12)
Increase in income tax payable		5
Increase in other accrued liabilities		22
Net cash provided by operating activities		2,606
Cash flow from investing activities:		
Cash received from sale of equipment		762
Cash paid for purchase of equipment		(1,300)
Net cash used for investing activities		(538)
Cash flow from financing activities:		
Cash paid to retire long-term debt		(500)
Cash paid to retire common stock		(600)
Cash paid for dividends		(1,120)
Net cash used for financing activities		(2,220)
Net decrease in cash		(152)
Cash balance, 31 December 2005		1,163
Cash balance, 31 December 2006		$ 1,011

EXAMPLE 7

Adjusting Net Income to Compute Operating Cash Flow

Based on the following information for Pinkerly Inc., what are the total adjustments that the company would make to net income in order to derive operating cash flow?

	Year Ended		
Income statement item		12/31/2006	
Net income		$30 million	
Depreciation		$7 million	
Balance sheet item	12/31/2005	12/31/2006	Change
Accounts receivable	$15 million	$30 million	$15 million
Inventory	$16 million	$13 million	($3 million)
Accounts payable	$10 million	$20 million	$10 million

> **A.** Add $5 million.
> **B.** Add $29 million.
> **C.** Subtract $5 million.
> **D.** Subtract $29 million.
>
> **Solution:** A is correct. To derive operating cash flow, the company would make the following adjustments to net income: add depreciation (a noncash expense) of $7 million; add the decrease in inventory of $3 million; add the increase in accounts payable of $10 million; and subtract the increase in accounts receivable of $15 million. Total additions would be $20 million, and total subtractions would be $15 million for net additions of $5 million.

3.3 Conversion of Cash Flows from the Indirect to the Direct Method

An analyst may desire to review direct-format operating cash flow to review trends in cash receipts and payments (such as cash received from customers or cash paid to suppliers). If a direct-format statement is not available, cash flows from operating activities reported under the indirect method can be converted to the direct method. Accuracy of conversion depends on adjustments using data available in published financial reports. The method described here is sufficiently accurate for most analytical purposes.

The three-step conversion process is demonstrated for Acme Corporation in Exhibit 11. Referring again to Exhibits 6 and 7 for Acme Corporation's income statement and balance sheet information, begin by disaggregating net income of $2,210 into total revenues and total expenses (Step 1). Next, remove any nonoperating and noncash items (Step 2). For Acme, we therefore remove the nonoperating gain on the sale of equipment of $205 and the noncash depreciation expense of $1,052. Then, convert accrual amounts of revenues and expenses to cash flow amounts of receipts and payments by adjusting for changes in working capital accounts (Step 3). The results of these adjustments are the items of information for the direct format of operating cash flows. These line items are shown as the results of Step 3.

EXHIBIT 11	Conversion from the Indirect to the Direct Method	
Step 1	Total revenues	$23,803
Aggregate all revenue and all expenses	Total expenses	21,593
	Net income	$ 2,210

Step 2	Total revenue less noncash item revenues:	
Remove all noncash items from aggregated revenues and expenses and break out remaining items into relevant cash flow items	($23,803 − $205) =	$23,598
	Revenue	$23,598
	Total expenses less noncash item expenses:	
	($21,593 − $1,052) =	$20,541

(Exhibit continued on next page . . .)

EXHIBIT 11	(continued)	
	Cost of goods sold	$11,456
	Salary and wage expenses	4,123
	Other operating expenses	3,577
	Interest expense	246
	Income tax expense	1,139
	Total	$20,541

Step 3	Cash received from customers[a]	$23,543
Convert accrual amounts to cash flow	Cash paid to suppliers[b]	11,900
amounts by adjusting for working	Cash paid to employees[c]	4,113
capital changes	Cash paid for other operating expenses[d]	3,532
	Cash paid for interest[e]	258
	Cash paid for income tax[f]	1,134

Calculations for Step 3

[a] Revenue of $23,598 less increase in accounts receivable of $55.

[b] Cost of goods sold of $11,456 plus increase in inventory of $707 less increase in accounts payable of $263.

[c] Salary and wage expense of $4,123 less increase in salary and wage payable of $10.

[d] Other operating expenses of $3,577 less decrease in prepaid expenses of $23 less increase in other accrued liabilities of $22.

[e] Interest expense of $246 plus decrease in interest payable of $12.

[f] Income tax expense of $1,139 less increase in income tax payable of $5.

CASH FLOW STATEMENT ANALYSIS   4

The analysis of a company's cash flows can provide useful information for understanding a company's business and earnings and for predicting its future cash flows. This section describes tools and techniques for analyzing the cash flow statement, including the analysis of major sources and uses of cash, cash flow, common-size analysis, conversion of the cash flow statement from the indirect method to the direct method, and computation of free cash flow and cash flow ratios.

4.1 Evaluation of the Sources and Uses of Cash

Evaluation of the cash flow statement should involve an overall assessment of the sources and uses of cash between the three main categories as well as an assessment of the main drivers of cash flow within each category, as follows:

1. Evaluate where the major sources and uses of cash flow are between operating, investing, and financing activities.

2. Evaluate the primary determinants of operating cash flow.

3. Evaluate the primary determinants of investing cash flow.

4. Evaluate the primary determinants of financing cash flow.

Step 1 The major sources of cash for a company can vary with its stage of growth. For a mature company, it is desirable to have the primary source of cash be operating activities. Over the long term, a company must generate cash from its operating activities. If operating cash flow were consistently negative, a company would need to borrow money or issue stock (financing activities) to fund the shortfall. Eventually, these providers of capital need to be repaid from operations or they will no longer be willing to provide capital. Cash generated from operating activities can either be used in investing or financing activities. If the company has good opportunities to grow the business or other investment opportunities, it is desirable to use the cash in investing activities. If the company does not have profitable investment opportunities, the cash should be returned to capital providers, a financing activity. For a new or growth stage company, operating cash flow may be negative for some period of time as it invests in inventory and receivables (extending credit to new customers) in order to grow the business. This cannot sustain itself over the long term, so eventually the cash must start to come primarily from operating activities so that capital can be returned to the providers of capital. Lastly, it is desirable that operating cash flows are sufficient to cover capital expenditures (in other words, the company has free cash flow as discussed further below). In summary, major points to consider at this step are:

► What are the major sources and uses of cash flow?

► Is operating cash flow positive and sufficient to cover capital expenditures?

Step 2 Turning to the operating section, the analysts should examine the most significant determinates of operating cash flow. Some companies need to raise cash for use in operations (to hold receivables, inventory, etc.), while occasionally a company's business model generates cash flow (e.g., when cash is received from customers before it needs to be paid out to suppliers). Under the indirect method, the increases and decreases in receivables, inventory, payables, and so on can be examined to determine whether the company is using or generating cash in operations and why. It is also useful to compare operating cash flow with net income. For a mature company, because net income includes noncash expenses (depreciation and amortization), it is desirable that operating cash flow exceeds net income. The relationship between net income and operating cash flow is also an indicator of earnings quality. If a company has large net income but poor operating cash flow, it may be a sign of poor earnings quality. The company may be making aggressive accounting choices to increase net income but not be generating cash for its business. You should also examine the variability of both earnings and cash flow and consider the impact of this variability on the company's risk as well as the ability to forecast future cash flows for valuation purposes. In summary:

► What are the major determinants of operating cash flow?

► Is operating cash flow higher or lower than net income? Why?

► How consistent are operating cash flows?

Step 3 Within the investing section, you should evaluate each line item. Each line item represents either a source or use of cash. This enables you to understand where the cash is being spent (or received). This section will tell you how much cash is being invested for the future in property, plant, and equipment; how much is used to acquire entire companies; and how much is put aside in liquid investments, such as stocks and bonds. It will also tell you how much cash is being raised by selling these types of assets. If the company is making major capital investments, you should consider where the cash is coming from to cover these investments (e.g., is the cash coming from excess operating cash flow or from the financing activities described in Step 4?).

Step 4 Within the financing section, you should examine each line item to understand whether the company is raising capital or repaying capital and what the nature of its capital sources are. If the company is borrowing each year, you should consider when repayment may be required. This section will also present dividend payments and repurchases of stock that are alternative means of returning capital to owners.

Example 8 provides an example of a cash flow statement evaluation.

EXAMPLE 8

Analysis of the Cash Flow Statement

Derek Yee, CFA, is preparing to forecast cash flow for Groupe Danone as an input into his valuation model. He has asked you to evaluate the historical cash flow statement of Groupe Danone, which is presented in Exhibit 12. Groupe Danone prepares its financial statements in conformity with International Financial Reporting Standards as adopted by the European Union.

EXHIBIT 12	Groupe Danone Consolidated Financial Statements Consolidated Statements of Cash Flows (Millions of Euros)		
Fiscal Years Ended 31 December		**2004**	**2005**
Net income		449	1,464
Minority interests in net income of consolidated subsidiaries		189	207
Net income from discontinued operations		(47)	(504)
Net income (loss) of affiliates		550	(44)
Depreciation and amortization		481	478
Dividends received from affiliates		45	45
Other flows		(93)	70
Cash flows provided by operations		1,574	1,716
(Increase) decrease in inventories		(70)	(17)
(Increase) decrease in trade accounts receivable		(27)	(87)
Increase (decrease) in trade accounts payable		143	123
Changes in other working capital items		74	112
Net change in current working capital		120	131
Cash flows provided by operating activities		1,694	1,847
Capital expenditures		(520)	(607)
Purchase of businesses and other investments net of cash and cash equivalent acquired		(98)	(636)

(Exhibit continued on next page . . .)

EXHIBIT 12	(continued)		
Proceeds from the sale of businesses and other investments net of cash and cash equivalent disposed of		650	1,659
(Increase) decrease in long-term loans and other long-term assets		130	(134)
Changes in cash and cash equivalents of discontinued operations		52	30
Cash flows provided by investing activities		214	312
Increase in capital and additional paid-in capital		38	61
Purchases of treasury stock (net of disposals)		(213)	(558)
Dividends		(456)	(489)
Increase (decrease) in noncurrent financial liabilities		(290)	(715)
Increase (decrease) in current financial liabilities		(536)	(191)
(Increase) decrease in marketable securities		(415)	(210)
Cash flows used in financing activities		(1,872)	(2,102)
Effect of exchange rate changes on cash and cash equivalents		(21)	53
Increase (decrease) in cash and cash equivalents		15	110
Cash and cash equivalents at beginning of period		451	466
Cash and cash equivalents at end of period		466	576
Supplemental disclosures:			
Cash paid during the year:			
Interest		152	172
Income tax		439	424

Yee would like answers to the following questions:

▶ What are the major sources of cash for Groupe Danone?

▶ What are the major uses of cash for Groupe Danone?

▶ What is the relationship between net income and cash flow from operating activities?

▶ Is cash flow from operating activities sufficient to cover capital expenditures?

▶ Other than capital expenditures, is cash being used or generated in investing activities?

▶ What types of financing cash flows does Groupe Danone have?

Solution: The major categories of cash flows can be summarized as follows (in millions of euros):

	2004	**2005**
Cash flows from operating activities	1,694	1,847
Cash flows from investing activities	214	312
Cash flows from financing activities	(1,872)	(2,102)
Exchange rate effects on cash	(21)	53
Increase in cash	15	110

The primary source of cash for Groupe Danone is operating activities. The secondary source of cash is investing activities. Most of this cash flow is being spent in financing activities. The fact that the primary source of cash is from operations is a good sign. Additionally, operating cash flow exceeds net income in both years—a good sign. Operating cash flows are much higher than capital expenditures, indicating that the company can easily fund capital expenditures from operations. The company has generated investing cash flows by selling business and investments in the two years presented. In the financing category, Groupe Danone is spending cash by repurchasing its own stock, paying dividends, and paying down debt. This could be an indicator that the company lacks investment opportunities and is, therefore, returning cash to the providers of capital.

4.2 Common-Size Analysis of the Cash Flow Statement

In common-size analysis of a company's income statement, each income and expense line item is expressed as a percentage of net revenues (net sales). For the common-size balance sheet, each asset, liability, and equity line item is expressed as a percentage of total assets. For the common-size cash flow statement, there are two alternative approaches. The first approach is to express each line item of cash inflow (outflow) as a percentage of total inflows (outflows) of cash, and the second approach is to express each line item as a percentage of net revenue.

Exhibit 13 demonstrates the total cash inflows/total outflows method for Acme Corporation. Under this approach, each of the cash inflows is expressed as a percentage of the total cash inflows, whereas each of the cash outflows is expressed as a percentage of the total cash outflows. In Panel A, Acme's common-size statement is based on a cash flow statement using the direct method of presenting operating cash flows. Operating cash inflows and outflows are separately presented on the cash flow statement and, therefore, the common-size cash flow statement shows each of these operating inflows (outflows) as a percentage of total inflows (outflows). In Panel B, Acme's common-size statement is based on a cash flow statement using the indirect method of presenting operating cash flows. When a cash flow statement has been presented using the indirect method, operating cash inflows and outflows are not separately presented; therefore, the common-size cash flow statement shows only the net operating cash flows as a percentage of total inflows or outflows, depending on whether the net amount was an in- or out-cash flow. Because Acme's net operating cash flow is positive, it is shown as a percentage of total inflows.

EXHIBIT 13	Acme Corporation Common-Size Cash Flow Statement: Year Ended 31 December 2006

Panel A. Direct Format for Operating Cash Flow

Inflows		Percentage of Total Inflows
Receipts from customers	$23,543	96.86%
Sale of equipment	762	3.14
Total	$24,305	100.00%

Outflows		Percentage of Total Outflows
Payments to suppliers	$11,900	48.66%
Payments to employees	4,113	16.82
Payments for other operating expenses	3,532	14.44
Payments for interest	258	1.05
Payments for income tax	1,134	4.64
Purchase of equipment	1,300	5.32
Retirement of long-term debt	500	2.04
Retirement of common stock	600	2.45
Dividend payments	1,120	4.58
Total	$24,457	100.00%

Panel B. Indirect Format for Operating Cash Flow

Inflows		Percentage of Total Inflows
Operations	$ 2,606	77.38%
Sale of equipment	762	22.62
Total	$ 3,368	100.00%

Outflows		Percentage of Total Outflows
Purchase of equipment	1,300	36.93%
Retirement of long-term debt	500	14.20
Retirement of common stock	600	17.05
Dividend payments	1,120	31.82
Total	$ 3,520	100.00%

Exhibit 14 demonstrates the net revenue common-size cash flow statement for Acme Corporation. Under the net revenue approach, each line item in the cash flow statement is shown as a percentage of net revenue. The common-size statement in this exhibit has been developed based on Acme's cash flow statement using the indirect method for operating cash flows. Each line item of the reconciliation between net income and net operating cash flows is expressed as a percentage of net revenue. The common-size format makes it easier to see trends in cash flow rather than just looking at the total amount. This method is also useful to the analyst in forecasting future cash flows because individual items in the common-size statement (e.g., depreciation, fixed capital expenditures, debt borrowing, and repayment) are expressed as a percentage of net revenue. Thus, once the analyst has forecast revenue, the common-size statement provides a basis for forecasting cash flows.

EXHIBIT 14	Acme Corporation Common-Size Cash Flow Statement: Indirect Format Year Ended 31 December 2006	
		Percentage of Net Revenue
Cash flow from operating activities:		
Net income	$2,210	9.37
Depreciation expense	1,052	4.46
Gain on sale of equipment	(205)	(0.87)
Increase in accounts receivable	(55)	(0.23)
Increase in inventory	(707)	(3.00)
Decrease in prepaid expenses	23	0.10
Increase in accounts payable	263	1.11
Increase in salary and wage payable	10	0.04
Decrease in interest payable	(12)	(0.05)
Increase in income tax payable	5	0.02
Increase in other accrued liabilities	22	0.09
Net cash provided by operating activities	2,606	11.04
Cash flow from investing activities:		
Cash received from sale of equipment	762	3.23
Cash paid for purchase of equipment	(1,300)	(5.51)
Net cash used for investing activities	(538)	(2.28)
Cash flow from financing activities:		
Cash paid to retire long-term debt	(500)	(2.12)
Cash paid to retire common stock	(600)	(2.54)
Cash paid for dividends	(1,120)	(4.75)
Net cash used for financing activities	(2,220)	(9.41)
Net decrease in cash	$ (152)	(0.64)

EXAMPLE 9

Analysis of a Common-Size Cash Flow Statement

Andrew Potter is examining an abbreviated common-size cash flow statement based on net revenues for Dell, which is reproduced below:

	Period Ending				
	3 Feb 2006	28 Jan 2005	30 Jan 2004	31 Jan 2003	1 Feb 2002
Net income	6.39%	6.18%	6.38%	5.99%	4.00%
Cash flows—operating activities					
Depreciation	0.70	0.68	0.63	0.60	0.77
Net income adjustments	0.93	−0.56	−0.92	−0.61	4.57
Changes in operating activities					
Accounts receivable	−1.84	0.00	−1.96	0.54	0.71
Inventory	−0.21	0.00	−0.13	−0.06	0.36
Other operating activities	−0.54	4.49	−0.34	−0.50	−0.20
Liabilities	3.22	0.00	5.19	4.04	1.98
Net cash flow—operating	8.66%	10.79%	8.86%	9.99%	12.18%
Cash flows—investing activities					
Capital expenditures	−1.30	−1.07	−0.79	−0.86	−0.97
Investments	8.24	−3.64	−4.88	−3.04	−6.28
Other investing activities	0.00	0.00	−1.12	0.00	0.00
Net cash flows—investing	6.94%	−4.71%	−6.79%	−3.90%	−7.25%
Cash flows—financing activities					
Sale and purchase of stock	−11.14	−6.36	−3.34	−5.72	−8.68
Other financing activities	0.00	0.00	0.00	0.00	0.01
Net cash flows—financing	−11.14%	−6.36%	−3.34%	−5.72%	−8.67%
Effect of exchange rate	−0.35	1.15	1.48	1.30	−0.33
Net cash flow	4.10%	0.87%	0.21%	1.67%	−4.07%

Based on the information in the above exhibit, address the following:

1. Characterize the importance of:
   A. depreciation.
   B. capital expenditures.
2. Contrast Dell's operating cash flow as a percentage of revenue with Dell's net profit margin (on a cash basis).
3. Identify Dell's major use of its positive operating cash flow.

> **Solution to 1:**
>
> **A.** Dell has very little depreciation expense (less than 1 percent), which is added back to determine operating cash flow.
>
> **B.** Dell's level of capital expenditures is relatively small, less than 1 percent of revenues in most years, but this increased in the most recent year. This is consistent with Dell's low amount of depreciation.
>
> **Solution to 2:** Dell's operating cash flow as a percentage of revenue is consistently much higher than net profit margin. Dell's business model appears to generate cash flow instead of requiring working capital, as many companies do. Dell collects cash flow from customers, on average, sooner than cash is paid out to suppliers.
>
> **Solution to 3:** Most of Dell's operating cash flow has been used to repurchase large amounts of its own stock (financing activities).

4.3 Free Cash Flow to the Firm and Free Cash Flow to Equity

In the initial evaluation of the cash flow statement above, it was mentioned that it is desirable that operating cash flows are sufficient to cover capital expenditures. The excess of operating cash flow over capital expenditures is known generically as **free cash flow**. For purposes of valuing a company or its equity securities, an analyst may want to determine a more precise free cash flow measure, such as free cash flow to the firm (FCFF) or free cash flow to equity (FCFE).

FCFF is the cash flow available to the company's suppliers of debt and equity capital after all operating expenses (including income taxes) have been paid and necessary investments in working capital and fixed capital have been made. FCFF can be computed starting with net income as[9]

$$FCFF = NI + NCC + Int(1-Tax\ rate) - FCInv - WCInv$$

where

NI	= Net income
NCC	= Noncash charges (such as depreciation and amortization)
Int	= Interest expense
FCInv	= Capital expenditures (fixed capital, such as equipment)
WCInv	= Working capital expenditures

The reason for adding back interest is that FCFF is the cash flow available to the suppliers of debt capital as well as equity capital. Conveniently, FCFF can also be computed from cash flow from operating activities as

$$FCFF = CFO + Int(1-Tax\ rate) - FCInv$$

---

[9] See Stowe, Robinson, Pinto, and McLeavey (2002) for a detailed discussion of free cash flow computations.

CFO represents cash flow from operating activities under U.S. GAAP or under IFRS where the company has chosen to place interest expense in operating activities. Under IFRS, if the company has placed interest and dividends received in investing activities, these should be added back to CFO to determine FCFF. Additionally, if dividends paid were subtracted in the operating section, these should be added back in to compute FCFF.

The computation of FCFF for Acme Corporation (based on the data from Exhibits 6, 7, and 8) is as follows:

CFO	$2,606
Plus: Interest paid times $(1 - \text{income tax rate})$	
$\{\$258\,[1 - (\$1,139 \div \$3,349)]\}$	170
Less: Net investments in fixed capital	
$(\$1,300 - \$762)$	(538)
FCFF	$2,238

FCFE is the cash flow available to the company's common stockholders after all operating expenses and borrowing costs (principal and interest) have been paid and necessary investments in working capital and fixed capital have been made. FCFE can be computed as

$$\text{FCFE} = \text{CFO} - \text{FCInv} + \text{Net borrowing} - \text{Net debt repayment}$$

The computation of FCFE for Acme Corporation (based on the data from Exhibits 6, 7, and 8) is as follows:

CFO	$2,606
Less: Net investments in fixed capital $[\$1,300 - \$762]$	538
Less: Debt repayment	500
FCFE	$1,568

Positive FCFE means that the company has an excess of operating cash flow over amounts needed for investments for the future and repayment of debt. This cash would be available for distribution to owners.

4.4 Cash Flow Ratios

The cash flow statement provides information that can be analyzed over time to obtain a better understanding of the past performance of a company and its future prospects. This information can also be effectively used to compare the performance and prospects of different companies in an industry and of different industries. There are several ratios based on cash flow from operating activities that are useful in this analysis. These ratios generally fall into cash flow performance (profitability) ratios and cash flow coverage (solvency) ratios. Exhibit 15 summarizes the calculation and interpretation of some of these ratios.

EXHIBIT 15	Cash Flow Ratios	
Performance Ratios	**Calculation**	**What It Measures**
Cash flow to revenue	CFO ÷ Net revenue	Cash generated per dollar of revenue
Cash return on assets	CFO ÷ Average total assets	Cash generated from all resources
Cash return on equity	CFO ÷ Average shareholders' equity	Cash generated from owner resources
Cash to income	CFO ÷ Operating income	Cash-generating ability of operations
Cash flow per share	(CFO − Preferred dividends) ÷ Number of common shares outstanding	Operating cash flow on a per-share basis
Coverage Ratios	**Calculation**	**What It Measures**
Debt coverage	CFO ÷ Total debt	Financial risk and financial leverage
Interest coverage	(CFO + Interest paid + Taxes paid) ÷ Interest paid	Ability to meet interest obligations
Reinvestment	CFO ÷ Cash paid for long-term assets	Ability to acquire assets with operating cash flows
Debt payment	CFO ÷ Cash paid for long-term debt repayment	Ability to pay debts with operating cash flows
Dividend payment	CFO ÷ Dividends paid	Ability to pay dividends with operating cash flows
Investing and financing	CFO ÷ Cash outflows for investing and financing activities	Ability to acquire assets, pay debts, and make distributions to owners

EXAMPLE 10

A Cash Flow Analysis of Comparables

Andrew Potter is comparing the cash-flow-generating ability of Dell with that of several other computer manufacturers: Hewlett Packard, Gateway, and Apple. He collects the following information:

	Operating Cash Flow		
Revenue	**2005 (%)**	**2004 (%)**	**2003 (%)**
DELL	8.66	10.79	8.86
HPQ	9.26	6.37	8.29
GTW	−0.65	−11.89	2.15
AAPL	18.20	11.28	4.66

(continued on next page . . .)

(continued)

Average Total Assets	2005 (%)	2004 (%)	2003 (%)
DELL	20.89	24.97	21.10
HPQ	10.46	6.75	8.33
GTW	−1.35	−22.84	3.22
AAPL	25.87	12.57	4.41

AAPL = Apple, GTW = Gateway, HPQ = Hewlett Packard.

What is Potter likely to conclude about the relative cash-flow-generating ability of these companies?

Solution: Dell has consistently generated operating cash flow relative to both revenue and assets. Hewlett Packard also has a good level of operating cash flow relative to revenue, but its operating cash flow is not as strong as Dell relative to assets. This is likely due to Dell's lean business model and lack of a need for large amounts of property, plant, and equipment. Gateway has poor operating cash flow on both measures. Apple has dramatically improved its operating cash flow over the three years and in 2005 had the strongest operating cash flow of the group.

SUMMARY

The cash flow statement provides important information about a company's cash receipts and cash payments during an accounting period as well as information about a company's operating, investing, and financing activities. Although the income statement provides a measure of a company's success, cash and cash flow are also vital to a company's long-term success. Information on the sources and uses of cash helps creditors, investors, and other statement users evaluate the company's liquidity, solvency, and financial flexibility. Key concepts are as follows:

▶ Cash flow activities are classified into three categories: operating activities, investing activities, and financing activities. Significant noncash transaction activities (if present) are reported by using a supplemental disclosure note to the cash flow statement.

▶ The cash flow statement under IFRS is similar to U.S. GAAP; however, IFRS permits greater discretion in classifying some cash flow items as operating, investing, or financing activities.

▶ Companies can use either the direct or the indirect method for reporting their operating cash flow:

  ▶ The direct method discloses operating cash inflows by source (e.g., cash received from customers, cash received from investment income) and operating cash outflows by use (e.g., cash paid to suppliers, cash paid for interest) in the operating activities section of the cash flow statement.

  ▶ The indirect method reconciles net income to net cash flow from operating activities by adjusting net income for all noncash items and the net changes in the operating working capital accounts.

▶ The cash flow statement is linked to a company's income statement and comparative balance sheets and is constructed from the data on those statements.

▶ Although the indirect method is most commonly used by companies, the analyst can generally convert it to the direct format by following a simple three-step process.

▶ The analyst can use common-size statement analysis for the cash flow statement. Two prescribed approaches are the total cash inflows/total cash outflows method and the percentage of net revenues method.

▶ The cash flow statement can be used to determine FCFF and FCFE.

▶ The cash flow statement may also be used in financial ratios measuring a company's profitability, performance, and financial strength.

PRACTICE PROBLEMS FOR READING 34

1. The three major classifications of activities in a cash flow statement are:
   A. inflows, outflows, and balances.
   B. beginning balance, ending balance, and change.
   C. operating, investing, and financing.

2. The sale of a building for cash would be classified as what type of activity on the cash flow statement?
   A. Operating.
   B. Investing.
   C. Financing.

3. Which of the following is an example of a financing activity on the cash flow statement under U.S. GAAP?
   A. Payment of dividends.
   B. Receipt of dividends.
   C. Payment of interest.

4. A conversion of a face value $1,000,000 convertible bond for $1,000,000 of common stock would *most likely* be:
   A. reported as a $1,000,000 financing cash outflow and inflow.
   B. reported as supplementary information to the cash flow statement.
   C. reported as a $1,000,000 financing cash outflow and a $1,000,000 investing cash inflow.

5. Interest expense may be classified as an operating cash flow:
   A. under U.S. GAAP, but may be classified as either operating or investing cash flows under IFRS.
   B. under IFRS, but may be classified as either operating or investing cash flows under U.S. GAAP.
   C. under U.S. GAAP, but may be classified as either operating or financing cash flows under IFRS.

6. Tax cash flows:
   A. must be separately disclosed in the cash flow statement under IFRS only.
   B. must be separately disclosed in the cash flow statement under U.S. GAAP only.
   C. are not separately disclosed in the cash flow statement under IFRS or U.S. GAAP.

7. Which of the following components of the cash flow statement may be prepared under the indirect method under both IFRS and U.S. GAAP?
   A. Operating.
   B. Investing.
   C. Financing.

8. Which of the following is *most likely* to appear in the operating section of a cash flow statement under the indirect method under U.S. GAAP?

    A. Net income.

    B. Cash paid for interest.

    C. Cash paid to suppliers.

9. Red Road Company, a consulting company, reported total revenues of $100 million, total expenses of $80 million, and net income of $20 million in the most recent year. If accounts receivable increased by $10 million, how much cash did the company receive from customers?

    A. $110 million.

    B. $90 million.

    C. $30 million.

10. Green Glory Corp., a garden supply wholesaler, reported cost of goods sold for the year of $80 million. Total assets increased by $55 million, including an increase of $5 million in inventory. Total liabilities increased by $45 million, including an increase of $2 million in accounts payable. How much cash did the company pay to its suppliers during the year?

    A. $90 million.

    B. $83 million.

    C. $77 million.

11. Purple Fleur S.A., a retailer of floral products, reported cost of goods sold for the year of $75 million. Total assets increased by $55 million, but inventory declined by $6 million. Total liabilities increased by $45 million, and accounts payable increased by $2 million. How much cash did the company pay to its suppliers during the year?

    A. $85 million.

    B. $79 million.

    C. $67 million.

12. White Flag, a women's clothing manufacturer, reported wage expense of $20 million. The beginning balance of wages payable was $3 million, and the ending balance of wages payable was $1 million. How much cash did the company pay in wages?

    A. $24 million.

    B. $23 million.

    C. $22 million.

13. An analyst gathered the following information from a company's 2004 financial statements ($ millions):

Year Ended 31 December	2003	2004
Net sales	245.8	254.6
Cost of goods sold	168.3	175.9
Accounts receivable	73.2	68.3
Inventory	39.0	47.8
Accounts payable	20.3	22.9

Based only on the information above, the company's 2004 cash flow statement prepared using the direct method would include amounts ($ millions) for cash received from customers and cash paid to suppliers, respectively, that are *closest* to:

	cash received from customers	cash paid to suppliers
A.	249.7	182.1
B.	259.5	169.7
C.	259.5	182.1

14. Golden Cumulus Corp., a commodities trading company, reported interest expense of $19 million and taxes of $6 million. Interest payable increased by $3 million, and taxes payable decreased by $4 million. How much cash did the company pay for interest and taxes?

A. $22 million for interest and $2 million for taxes.

B. $16 million for interest and $2 million for taxes.

C. $16 million for interest and $10 million for taxes.

15. An analyst gathered the following information from a company's 2005 financial statements prepared under U.S. GAAP ($ millions):

Balances as of Year Ended 31 December	2004	2005
Retained earnings	120	145
Accounts receivable	38	43
Inventory	45	48
Accounts payable	36	29

The company declared and paid cash dividends of $10 million in 2005 and recorded depreciation expense in the amount of $25 million for 2005. The company's 2005 cash flow from operations ($ millions) was *closest* to:

A. 25.

B. 35.

C. 45.

16. Silverago Incorporated, an international metals company, reported a loss on the sale of equipment of $2 million. In addition, the company's income statement shows depreciation expense of $8 million and the cash flow statement shows capital expenditure of $10 million, all of which was for the purchase of new equipment. Using the following information from the comparative balance sheets, how much cash did the company receive from the equipment sale?

Balance Sheet Item	12/31/2005	12/31/2006	Change
Equipment	$100 million	$105 million	$5 million
Accumulated depreciation—equipment	$40 million	$46 million	$6 million

   A. $6 million.
   B. $5 million.
   C. $1 million.

17. Jaderong Plinkett Stores reported net income of $25 million, which equals the company's comprehensive income. The company has no outstanding debt. Using the following information from the comparative balance sheets (in millions), what should the company report in the financing section of the cash flow statement?

Balance Sheet Item	12/31/2005	12/31/2006	Change
Common stock	$100	$102	$2
Additional paid-in capital common stock	$100	$140	$40
Retained earnings	$100	$115	$15
Total stockholders' equity	$300	$357	$57

   A. Issuance of common stock $42 million; dividends paid of $10 million.
   B. Issuance of common stock $38 million; dividends paid of $10 million.
   C. Issuance of common stock $42 million; dividends paid of $40 million.

18. Based on the following information for Pinkerly Inc., what are the total net adjustments that the company would make to net income in order to derive operating cash flow?

Income Statement Item		Year Ended 12/31/2006	
Net income		$20 million	
Depreciation		$2 million	

Balance Sheet Item	12/31/2005	12/31/2006	Change
Accounts receivable	$25 million	$22 million	($3 million)
Inventory	$10 million	$14 million	$4 million
Accounts payable	$8 million	$13 million	$5 million

  A. Add $6 million.

  B. Add $8 million.

  C. Subtract $6 million.

19. The first step in evaluating the cash flow statement should be to examine:

  A. individual investing cash flow items.

  B. individual financing cash flow items.

  C. the major sources and uses of cash.

20. Which of the following would be valid conclusions from an analysis of the cash flow statement for Telefónica Group presented in Exhibit 3?

  A. The company does not pay dividends.

  B. The primary use of cash is financing activities.

  C. The primary source of cash is operating activities.

21. Which is an appropriate method of preparing a common-size cash flow statement?

  A. Begin with net income and show the items that reconcile net income and operating cash flows.

  B. Show each line item on the cash flow statement as a percentage of net revenue.

  C. Show each line item on the cash flow statement as a percentage of total cash outflows.

22. Which of the following is an appropriate method of computing free cash flow to the firm?

   A. Add operating cash flows plus capital expenditures and deduct after-tax interest payments.

   B. Add operating cash flows plus after-tax interest payments and deduct capital expenditures.

   C. Deduct both after-tax interest payments and capital expenditures from operating cash flows.

23. An analyst has calculated a ratio using as the numerator the sum of operating cash flow, interest, and taxes, and as the denominator the amount of interest. What is this ratio, what does it measure, and what does it indicate?

   A. This ratio is an interest coverage ratio, measuring a company's ability to meet its interest obligations and indicating a company's solvency.

   B. This ratio is an effective tax ratio, measuring the amount of a company's operating cash flow used for taxes, and indicating a company's efficiency in tax management.

   C. This ratio is an operating profitability ratio, measuring the operating cash flow generated accounting for taxes and interest and indicating a company's liquidity.

SOLUTIONS FOR READING 34

1. C is correct. Answers A and B are incorrect: these are items of information involved in making calculations for the statement of cash flows.

2. B is correct. Purchases and sales of long-term assets are considered investing activities. Note: Absent information to the contrary, it is assumed that the sale of a building involves cash. If, for example, the transaction had involved the exchange of a building for common stock or the exchange of a building for a long-term note payable, it would have been considered a significant noncash activity.

3. A is correct. Answers B and C are items that are included in operating cash flows. Note: International accounting standards allow companies to include receipt of interest and dividends as either operating or investing cash flows, and international accounting standards allow companies to include payment of interest and dividends as either operating or financing cash flows.

4. B is correct. Noncash transactions, if significant, are reported as supplementary information, not in the investing or financing sections of the cash flow statement.

5. C is correct. Interest expense is always classified as an operating cash flow under U.S. GAAP but may be classified as either an operating or financing cash flow under IFRS.

6. A is correct. Taxes are only required to be separately disclosed on the cash flow statement under IFRS.

7. A is correct. The operating section may be prepared under the indirect method. The other sections are always prepared under the direct method.

8. A is correct. Under the indirect method, the operating section would begin with net income and adjust it to arrive at operating cash flow. The other items would appear under the direct method as a cash flow statement prepared under U.S. GAAP. Note that cash paid for interest may appear on an indirect cash flow statement under IFRS if classified as a financing activity.

9. B is correct. Revenues of $100 million minus the increase in accounts receivable of $10 million equal $90 million cash received from customers. The increase in accounts receivable means that the company received less in cash than it reported as revenue.

10. B is correct. Cost of goods sold of $80 million plus the increase in inventory of $5 million equals purchases from suppliers of $85 million. The increase in accounts payable of $2 million means that the company paid $83 million in cash ($85 million minus $2 million) to its suppliers.

11. C is correct. Cost of goods sold of $75 million less the decrease in inventory of $6 million equals purchases from suppliers of $69 million. The increase in accounts payable of $2 million means that the company paid $67 million in cash ($69 million minus $2 million).

12. C is correct. Beginning wages payable of $3 million plus wage expense of $20 million, minus ending wages payable of $1 million equals $22 million. The expense of $20 million plus the $2 million decrease in wages payable equals $22 million.

13. C is correct. Cash received from customers = Sales + Decrease in accounts receivable = 254.6 + 4.9 = 259.5. Cash paid to suppliers = Cost of goods sold + Increase in inventory − Increase in accounts payable = 175.9 + 8.8 − 2.6 = 182.1

14. C is correct. Interest expense of $19 million less the increase in interest payable of $3 million equals $16 million. Tax expense of $6 million plus the decrease in taxes payable of $4 million equals $10 million.

15. C is correct. Net income (NI) for 2005 can be computed as the change in retained earnings, $25, plus the dividends paid in 2005, $10. NI can also be calculated from the formula: Beginning retained earnings + NI − Dividends paid = Ending retained earnings. Depreciation of $25 would be added back to net income while the increases in accounts receivable, $5, and in inventory, $3, would be subtracted from net income because they are uses of cash. The decrease in accounts payable is also a use of cash and, therefore, a subtraction from net income. Thus, cash flow from operations for 2005 is $25 + $10 + $25 − $5 − $3 − $7 = $45 ($ millions).

16. C is correct. Selling price (cash inflow) minus book value equals gain or loss on sale; therefore, gain or loss on sale plus book value equals selling price (cash inflow). The amount of loss is given, $2 million. To calculate the book value of the equipment sold, find the historical cost of the equipment and the accumulated depreciation on the equipment.

   ▶ Beginning balance of equipment of $100 million plus equipment purchased of $10 million minus ending balance of equipment of $105 million equals the historical cost of equipment sold, or $5 million.

   ▶ Beginning accumulated depreciation of $40 million plus depreciation expense for the year of $8 million minus ending balance of accumulated depreciation of $46 million equals accumulated depreciation on the equipment sold, or $2 million.

   ▶ Therefore, the book value of the equipment sold was $5 million minus $2 million, or $3 million.

   ▶ Because the loss on the sale of equipment was $2 million, the amount of cash received must have been $1 million.

17. A is correct. The increase of $42 million in common stock and additional paid-in capital indicates that the company issued stock during the year. The increase in retained earnings of $15 million indicates that the company paid $10 million in cash dividends during the year, determined as beginning retained earnings of $100 million plus net income of $25 million, minus ending retained earnings of $115, which equals $10 million in cash dividends.

18. A is correct. To derive operating cash flow, the company would make the following adjustments to net income: add depreciation (a noncash expense) of $2 million; add the decrease in accounts receivable of $3 million; add the increase in accounts payable of $5 million; and subtract the increase in inventory of $4 million. Total additions would be $10 million, and total subtractions would be $4 million for net additions of $6 million.

19. C is correct. Before examining individual cash flows, the major sources and uses of cash should be evaluated.

20. C is correct. The primary source of cash is operating activities. An examination of the financing section indicates that the company pays dividends. The primary use of cash is investing activities. Interest received for Telefónica is classified as an investing activity.

21. B is correct. Dividing each line item on the cash flow statement by net revenue is one of two acceptable approaches for preparing a common-size cash flow statement. The other acceptable approach involves expressing each line item of cash inflow (outflow) as a percentage of total inflows (outflows) of cash. Answer A is a description of the indirect method of determining cash flow from operations. Answer C is incorrect because in describing an alternative way to prepare a common-size cash flow statement it fails to distinguish between the divisor appropriate for cash outflows and cash inflows.

22. B is correct. Free cash flow to the firm can be computed as operating cash flows plus after-tax interest expense less capital expenditures.

23. A is correct. This is the interest coverage ratio using operating cash flow rather than earnings before interest, tax, depreciation, and amortization (EBITDA).

FINANCIAL ANALYSIS TECHNIQUES

by Thomas R. Robinson, CFA, Jan Hendrik van Greuning, CFA,
Elaine Henry, CFA, and Michael A. Broihahn, CFA

LEARNING OUTCOMES

The candidate should be able to:	Mastery
a. evaluate and compare companies using ratio analysis, common-size financial statements, and charts in financial analysis;	☐
b. describe the limitations of ratio analysis;	☐
c. describe the various techniques of common-size analysis and interpret the results of such analysis;	☐
d. calculate, classify, and interpret activity, liquidity, solvency, profitability, and valuation ratios;	☐
e. demonstrate how ratios are related and how to evaluate a company using a combination of different ratios;	☐
f. demonstrate the application of and interpret changes in the component parts of the DuPont analysis (the decomposition of return on equity);	☐
g. calculate and interpret the ratios used in equity analysis, credit analysis, and segment analysis;	☐
h. describe how ratio analysis and other techniques can be used to model and forecast earnings.	☐

Note:
New rulings and/or pronouncements issued after the publication of the readings on financial reporting and analysis may cause some of the information in these readings to become dated. Candidates are expected to be familiar with the overall analytical framework contained in the study session readings, as well as the implications of alternative accounting methods for financial analysis and valuation, as provided in the assigned readings. Candidates are not responsible for changes that occur after the material was written.

INTRODUCTION 1

Financial analysis applies analytical tools to financial data to assess a company's performance and trends in that performance. In essence, an analyst converts data into financial metrics that assist in decision making. Analysts seek to answer such questions as: How successfully has the company performed, relative to its own past performance and relative to its competitors? How is the company likely

International Financial Statement Analysis, by Thomas R. Robinson, CFA, Jan Hendrik van Greuning, CFA, Elaine Henry, CFA, and Michael A. Broihahn, CFA. Copyright © 2007 by CFA Institute. Reprinted with permission.

to perform in the future? Based on expectations about future performance, what is the value of this company or the securities it issues?

A primary source of data is a company's financial reports, including the financial statements, footnotes, and management's discussion and analysis. This reading focuses on data presented in financial reports prepared under international financial reporting standards (IFRS) and United States generally accepted accounting principles (U.S. GAAP). However, even financial reports prepared under these standards do not contain all the information needed to perform effective financial analysis. Although financial statements do contain data about the *past* performance of a company (its income and cash flows) as well as its *current* financial condition (assets, liabilities, and owners' equity), such statements may not provide some important nonfinancial information nor do they forecast *future* results. The financial analyst must be capable of using financial statements in conjunction with other information in order to reach valid conclusions and make projections. Accordingly, an analyst will most likely need to supplement the information found in a company's financial reports with industry and economic data.

The purpose of this reading is to describe various techniques used to analyze a company's financial statements. Financial analysis of a company may be performed for a variety of reasons, such as valuing equity securities, assessing credit risk, conducting due diligence related to an acquisition, or assessing a subsidiary's performance. This reading will describe the techniques common to any financial analysis and then discuss more specific aspects for the two most common categories: equity analysis and credit analysis.

Equity analysis incorporates an owner's perspective, either for valuation or performance evaluation. Credit analysis incorporates a creditor's (such as a banker or bondholder) perspective. In either case, there is a need to gather and analyze information to make a decision (ownership or credit); the focus of analysis varies due to the differing interest of owners and creditors. Both equity and credit analysis assess the entity's ability to generate and grow earnings and cash flow, as well as any associated risks. Equity analysis usually places a greater emphasis on growth, whereas credit analysis usually places a greater emphasis on risks. The difference in emphasis reflects the different fundamentals of these types of investments: The value of a company's equity generally increases as the company's earnings and cash flow increase, whereas the value of a company's debt has an upper limit.[1]

---

[1] The upper limit is equal to the undiscounted sum of the principal and remaining interest payments (i.e., the present value of these contractual payments at a zero percent discount rate).

The balance of this reading is organized as follows: Section 2 recaps the framework for financial statements and the place of financial analysis techniques within it. Section 3 provides a description of analytical tools and techniques. Section 4 explains how to compute, analyze, and interpret common financial ratios. Sections 4 through 8 explain the use of ratios and other analytical data in equity analysis, debt analysis, segment analysis, and forecasting, respectively. A summary of the key points and practice problems in the CFA Institute multiple-choice format conclude the reading.

THE FINANCIAL ANALYSIS PROCESS 2

In financial analysis, as in any business task, a clear understanding of the end goal and the steps required to get there is essential. In addition, the analyst needs to know the typical questions to address when interpreting financial data and how to communicate the analysis and conclusions.

2.1 The Objectives of the Financial Analysis Process

Due to the variety of reasons for performing financial analysis, the numerous available techniques, and the often substantial amount of data, it is important that the analytical approach be tailored to the specific situation. Prior to embarking on any financial analysis, the analyst should clarify purpose and context, and clearly understand the following:

► What is the purpose of the analysis? What questions will this analysis answer?

► What level of detail will be needed to accomplish this purpose?

► What data are available for the analysis?

► What are the factors or relationships that will influence the analysis?

► What are the analytical limitations, and will these limitations potentially impair the analysis?

Having clarified the purpose and context of the analysis, the analyst can select the techniques (e.g., ratios) that will best assist in making a decision. Although there is no single approach to structuring the analysis process, a general framework is set forth in Exhibit 1.[2] The steps in this process were discussed in more detail in the reading that introduced financial statement analysis. The primary focus of this reading is on Phases 3 and 4, processing and analyzing data.

---

[2] Components of this framework have been adapted from van Greuning and Bratanovic (2003, p. 300) and Benninga and Sarig (1997, pp. 134–156).

EXHIBIT 1	A Financial Statement Analysis Framework	
Phase	**Sources of Information**	**Output**
1. Articulate the purpose and context of the analysis	▶ The nature of the analyst's function, such as evaluating an equity or debt investment or issuing a credit rating. ▶ Communication with client or superior on needs and concerns. ▶ Institutional guidelines related to developing specific work product.	▶ Statement of the purpose or objective of analysis. ▶ A list (written or unwritten) of specific questions to be answered by the analysis. ▶ Nature and content of report to be provided. ▶ Timetable and budgeted resources for completion.
2. Collect input data	▶ Financial statements, other financial data, questionnaires, and industry/economic data. ▶ Discussions with management, suppliers, customers, and competitors. ▶ Company site visits (e.g., to production facilities or retail stores).	▶ Organized financial statements. ▶ Financial data tables. ▶ Completed questionnaires, if applicable.
3. Process data	▶ Data from the previous phase.	▶ Adjusted financial statements. ▶ Common-size statements. ▶ Ratios and graphs. ▶ Forecasts.
4. Analyze/interpret the processed data	▶ Input data as well as processed data.	▶ Analytical results.
5. Develop and communicate conclusions and recommendations (e.g., with an analysis report)	▶ Analytical results and previous reports. ▶ Institutional guidelines for published reports.	▶ Analytical report answering questions posed in Phase 1. ▶ Recommendation regarding the purpose of the analysis, such as whether to make an investment or grant credit.
6. Follow-up	▶ Information gathered by periodically repeating above steps as necessary to determine whether changes to holdings or recommendations are necessary.	▶ Updated reports and recommendations.

2.2 Distinguishing between Computations and Analysis

An effective analysis encompasses both computations and interpretations. A well-reasoned analysis differs from a mere compilation of various pieces of information, computations, tables, and graphs by integrating the data collected into a cohesive whole. Analysis of past performance, for example, should address not only what happened but also why it happened and whether it advanced the company's strategy. Some of the key questions to address include:

▶ What aspects of performance are critical for this company to successfully compete in this industry?

▶ How well did the company's performance meet these critical aspects? (This is established through computation and comparison with appropriate benchmarks, such as the company's own historical performance or competitors' performance.)

▶ What were the key causes of this performance, and how does this performance reflect the company's strategy? (This is established through analysis.)

If the analysis is forward looking, additional questions include:

▶ What is the likely impact of an event or trend? (Established through interpretation of analysis.)

▶ What is the likely response of management to this trend? (Established through evaluation of quality of management and corporate governance.)

▶ What is the likely impact of trends in the company, industry, and economy on future cash flows? (Established through assessment of corporate strategy and through forecasts.)

▶ What are the recommendations of the analyst? (Established through interpretation and forecasting of results of analysis.)

▶ What risks should be highlighted? (Established by an evaluation of major uncertainties in the forecast.)

Example 1 demonstrates how a company's financial data can be analyzed in the context of its business strategy and changes in that strategy. An analyst must be able to understand the "why" behind the numbers and ratios, not just what the numbers and ratios are.

EXAMPLE 1

Change in Strategy Reflected in Financial Performance

Motorola (NYSE:MOT) and Nokia (NYSE:NOK) engage in the design, manufacture, and sale of mobility products worldwide. Selected financial data for 2003 through 2005 for these two competitors are given below.

Selected Financial Data for Motorola (in $Millions)

Years ended 31 December	2005	2004	2003
Net sales	36,843	31,323	23,155
Operating earnings	4,696	3,132	1,273

Selected Financial Data for Nokia Corporation (in €Millions)

Years ended 31 December	2005	2004	2003
Net sales	34,191	29,371	29,533
Operating profit	4,639	4,326	4,960

Source: Motorola 10-K and Nokia 20-F, both filed 2 March 2006.

Although the raw numbers for Motorola and Nokia are not directly comparable because Motorola reports in U.S. dollars and Nokia in euros, the relative changes can be compared. Motorola reported a 35 percent increase in net sales from 2003 to 2004 and a further increase in 2005 of approximately 18 percent. Also, the company's operating earnings more than doubled from 2003 to 2004 and grew another 50 percent in 2005. Over the 2003 to 2004 time period, industry leader Nokia reported a decrease in both sales and operating profits, although sales growth was about 16 percent in 2005.

What caused Motorola's dramatic growth in sales and operating profits? One of the most important factors was the introduction of new products, such as the stylish RAZR cell phone in 2004. Motorola's 2005 10-K indicates that more than 23 million RAZRs had been sold since the product was launched. The handset segment represents 54 percent of the company's 2004 sales and nearly 58 percent of 2005 sales, so the impact on sales and profitability of the successful product introduction was significant. The introduction of branded, differentiated products not only increased demand but also increased the potential for higher pricing. The introduction of the new products was one result of the company's strategic shift to develop a consumer marketing orientation as a complement to its historically strong technological position.

Analysts often need to communicate the findings of their analysis in a written report. Their reports should, therefore, communicate how conclusions were reached and why recommendations were made. For example, a report might present the following:[3]

- ► the purpose of the report, unless it is readily apparent;
- ► relevant aspects of the business context:
  - ► economic environment (country, macro economy, sector);
  - ► financial and other infrastructure (accounting, auditing, rating agencies);
  - ► legal and regulatory environment (and any other material limitations on the company being analyzed);
- ► evaluation of corporate governance;
- ► assessment of financial and operational data;
- ► conclusions and recommendations (including risks and limitations to the analysis).

An effective storyline and well-supported conclusions and recommendations are normally enhanced by using 3–10 years of data, as well as analytic techniques appropriate to the purpose of the report.

---

[3] The nature and content of reports will vary depending upon the purpose of the analysis and the ultimate recipient of the report. For an example of the contents of an equity research report, see Stowe, Robinson, Pinto, and McLeavey (2002, pages 22–28).

ANALYSIS TOOLS AND TECHNIQUES

The tools and techniques presented in this section facilitate evaluations of company data. Evaluations require comparisons. It is difficult to say that a company's financial performance was "good" without clarifying the basis for comparison.

In assessing a company's ability to generate and grow earnings and cash flow, and the risks related to those earnings and cash flows, the analyst draws comparisons to other companies (cross-sectional analysis) and over time (trend or time-series analysis).

For example, an analyst may wish to compare the profitability in 2004 of Dell and Gateway. These companies differ significantly in size, so comparing net income in raw dollars is not useful. Instead, ratios (which express one number in relation to another) and common-size financial statements can remove size as a factor and enable a more relevant comparison.

The analyst may also want to examine Dell's performance relative to its own historic performance. Again, the raw dollar amounts of sales or net income may not highlight significant changes. However, using ratios (see Example 2), horizontal financial statements, and graphs can make such changes more apparent.

EXAMPLE 2

Ratio Analysis

Dell computer reported the following data for three recent fiscal years:

Fiscal Year Ended (FY)	Net Income (Millions of USD)
1/31/2003	2,122
1/30/2004	2,645
1/28/2005	3,043

Overall net income has grown steadily over the three-year period. Net income for FY2005 is 43 percent higher than net income in 2003, which is a good sign. However, has profitability also steadily increased? We can obtain some insight by looking at the **net profit margin** (net income divided by revenue) for each year.

Fiscal Year Ended	Net Profit Margin (%)
1/31/2003	5.99
1/30/2004	6.38
1/28/2005	6.18

The net profit margin indicates that profitability improved from FY2003 to FY2004 but deteriorated slightly from FY2004 to FY2005. Further analysis is needed to determine the cause of the profitability decline and assess whether this decline is likely to persist in future years.

The following paragraphs describe the tools and techniques of ratio analysis in more detail.

3.1 Ratios

There are many relationships between financial accounts and between expected relationships from one point in time to another. Ratios are a useful way of expressing these relationships. Ratios express one quantity in relation to another (usually as a quotient).

Notable academic research has examined the importance of ratios in predicting stock returns (Ou and Penman, 1989; Abarbanell and Bushee, 1998) or credit failure (Altman, 1968; Ohlson, 1980; Hopwood et al., 1994). This research has found that financial statement ratios are effective in selecting investments and in predicting financial distress. Practitioners routinely use ratios to communicate the value of companies and securities.

Several aspects of ratio analysis are important to understand. First, the computed ratio is not "the answer." The ratio is an *indicator* of some aspect of a company's performance, telling what happened but not why it happened. For example, an analyst might want to answer the question: Which of two companies was more profitable? The net profit margin, which expresses profit relative to revenue, can provide insight into this question. Net profit margin is calculated by dividing net income by revenue:[4]

$$\frac{\text{Net income}}{\text{Revenue}}$$

Assume Company A has €100,000 of net income and €2,000,000 of revenue, and thus a net profit margin of 5 percent. Company B has €200,000 of net income and €6,000,000 of revenue, and thus a net profit margin of 3.33 percent. Expressing net income as a percentage of revenue clarifies the relationship: For each €100 of revenue, Company A earns €5 in net income, while Company B earns only €3.33 for each €100 of revenue. So, we can now answer the question of which company was more profitable in percentage terms: Company A was more profitable, as indicated by its higher net profit margin of 5 percent. We also note that Company A was more profitable despite the fact that Company B reported higher absolute amounts of net income and revenue. However, this ratio by itself does not tell us *why* Company A has a higher profit margin. Further analysis is required to determine the reason (perhaps higher relative sales prices or better cost control).

Company size sometimes confers economies of scale, so the absolute amounts of net income and revenue are useful in financial analysis. However, ratios reduce the effect of size, which enhances comparisons between companies and over time.

A second important aspect of ratio analysis is that differences in accounting policies (across companies and across time) can distort ratios, and a meaningful comparison may, therefore, involve adjustments to the financial data. Third, not all ratios are necessarily relevant to a particular analysis. The ability to select a

---

[4] The term "sales" is often used interchangeably with the term "revenues." Other times it is used to refer to revenues derived from sales of products versus services. Furthermore, the income statement usually reflects "revenues" or "sales" after returns and allowances (e.g., returns of products or discounts offered after a sale to induce the customer to not return a product). Additionally, in some countries including the United Kingdom, the term "turnover" is used in the sense of "revenue."

relevant ratio or ratios to answer the research question is an analytical skill. Finally, as with financial analysis in general, ratio analysis does not stop with computation; interpretation of the result is essential. In practice, differences in ratios across time and across companies can be subtle, and interpretation is situation specific.

3.1.1 The Universe of Ratios

There are no authoritative bodies specifying exact formulas for computing ratios or providing a standard, comprehensive list of ratios. Formulas and even names of ratios often differ from analyst to analyst or from database to database. The number of different ratios that can be created is practically limitless. There are, however, widely accepted ratios that have been found to be useful. Section 4 of this reading will focus primarily on these broad classes and commonly accepted definitions of key ratios. However, the analyst should be aware that different ratios may be used in practice and that certain industries have unique ratios tailored to the characteristics of that industry. When faced with an unfamiliar ratio, the analyst can examine the underlying formula to gain insight into what the ratio is measuring. For example, consider the following ratio formula:

$$\frac{\text{Operating income}}{\text{Average total assets}}$$

Never having seen this ratio, an analyst might question whether a result of 12 percent is better than 8 percent. The answer can be found in the ratio itself. The numerator is operating income and the denominator is average total assets, so the ratio can be interpreted as the amount of operating income generated per unit of assets. For every €100 of average total assets, generating €12 of operating income is better than generating €8 of operating income. Furthermore, it is apparent that this particular ratio is an indicator of profitability (and, to a lesser extent, efficiency in use of assets in generating operating profits). When facing a ratio for the first time, the analyst should evaluate the numerator and denominator to assess what the ratio is attempting to measure and how it should be interpreted. This is demonstrated in Example 3.

EXAMPLE 3

Interpreting a Financial Ratio

An insurance company reports that its "combined ratio" is determined by dividing losses and expenses incurred by net premiums earned. It reports the following combined ratios:

	2005	2004	2003	2002	2001
Combined ratio	90.1%	104.0%	98.5%	104.1%	101.1%

Explain what this ratio is measuring and compare and contrast the results reported for each of the years shown in the chart. What other information might an analyst want to review before concluding on this information?

Solution: The combined ratio is a profitability measure. The ratio is explaining how much the costs (losses and expenses) were for every dollar of revenue (net premiums earned). The underlying formula indicates that a lower ratio is better. The 2005 ratio of 90.1 percent means that for every dollar of net premiums earned, the costs were $.901, yielding a gross profit of $.099. Ratios greater than 100 percent indicate an overall loss. A review of the data indicates that there does not seem to be a consistent trend in this ratio. Profits were achieved in 2005 and 2003. The results for 2004 and 2002 show the most significant losses at 104 percent.

   The analyst would want to discuss this data further with management and understand the characteristics of the underlying business. He or she would want to understand why the results are so volatile. The analyst would also want to determine what ratio should be used as a benchmark.

The Operating income/Average total assets ratio shown above is one of many versions of the **return on assets (ROA)** ratio. Note that there are other ways of specifying this formula based on how assets are defined. Some financial ratio databases compute ROA using the ending value of assets rather than average assets. In limited cases, one may also see beginning assets in the denominator. Which one is right? It depends upon what you are trying to measure and the underlying company trends. If the company has a stable level of assets, the answer will not differ greatly under the three measures of assets (beginning, average, and ending). If, however, the assets are growing (or shrinking), the results will differ. When assets are growing, operating income divided by ending assets may not make sense because some of the income would have been generated before some assets were purchased, and this would understate the company's performance. Similarly, if beginning assets are used, some of the operating income later in the year may have been generated only because of the addition of assets; therefore, the ratio would overstate the company's performance. Because operating income occurs throughout the period, it generally makes sense to use some average measure of assets. A good general rule is that when an income statement or statement of cash flows number is in the numerator of a ratio and a balance sheet number is in the denominator, then an average should be used for the denominator. It is generally not necessary to use averages when only balance sheet numbers are used in both the numerator and denominator because both are determined as of the same date. However, as we shall see later, there are occasions when even balance sheet data may be averages (e.g., in analyzing the components of **return on equity [ROE]**, which is defined as net income divided by average shareholders' equity).

   If an average is used, there is also judgment required as to what average should be used. For simplicity, most ratio databases use a simple average of the beginning and end-of-year balance sheet amounts. If the company's business is seasonable so that levels of assets vary by interim period (semiannual or quarterly), then it may be beneficial to take an average over all interim periods, if available (if the analyst is working within a company and has access to monthly data, this can also be used).

3.1.2 Value, Purposes, and Limitations of Ratio Analysis

The value of ratio analysis is that it enables the equity or credit analyst to evaluate past performance, assess the current financial position of the company, and gain insights useful for projecting future results. As noted previously, the ratio itself is not "the answer" but an indicator of some aspect of a company's performance. Financial ratios provide insights into:

- ► microeconomic relationships within a company that help analysts project earnings and free cash flow;
- ► a company's financial flexibility, or ability to obtain the cash required to grow and meet its obligations, even if unexpected circumstances develop; and
- ► management's ability.

There are also limitations to ratio analysis:

- ► *The homogeneity of a company's operating activities.* Companies may have divisions operating in many different industries. This can make it difficult to find comparable industry ratios to use for comparison purposes.
- ► *The need to determine whether the results of the ratio analysis are consistent.* One set of ratios may indicate a problem, whereas another set may prove that the potential problem is only short term in nature.
- ► *The need to use judgment.* A key issue is whether a ratio for a company is within a reasonable range. Although financial ratios are used to help assess the growth potential and risk of a company, they cannot be used alone to directly value a company or its securities, or to determine its credit-worthiness. The entire operation of the company must be examined, and the external economic and industry setting in which it is operating must be considered when interpreting financial ratios.
- ► *The use of alternative accounting methods.* Companies frequently have latitude when choosing certain accounting methods. Ratios taken from financial statements that employ different accounting choices may not be comparable unless adjustments are made. Some important accounting considerations include the following:
  - ► FIFO (first in, first out), LIFO (last in, first out), or average cost inventory valuation methods (IFRS no longer allow LIFO);
  - ► Cost or equity methods of accounting for unconsolidated affiliates;
  - ► Straight line or accelerated methods of depreciation; and
  - ► Capital or operating lease treatment.

  The expanding use of IFRS and the planned convergence between U.S. GAAP and IFRS seek to make the financial statements of different companies comparable and so overcome some of these difficulties. Nonetheless, there will remain accounting choices that the analyst must consider.

3.1.3 Sources of Ratios

Ratios may be computed using data directly from companies' financial statements or from a database such as Bloomberg, Baseline, FactSet, or Thomson Reuters. These databases are popular because they provide easy access to many years of historical data so that trends over time can be examined. They also allow for ratio calculations based on periods other than the company's fiscal year, such as for the trailing 12 months (TTM) or most recent quarter (MRQ).

Analysts should be aware that the underlying formulas may differ by vendor. The formula used should be obtained from the vendor, and the analyst should determine whether any adjustments are necessary. Furthermore, database providers often exercise judgment when classifying items. For example, operating income may not appear directly on a company's income statement, and the vendor may use judgment to classify income statement items as "operating" or "nonoperating." Variation in such judgments would affect any computation involving operating income. It is, therefore, a good practice to use the same source for data when comparing different companies or when evaluating the historical record of a single given company. Analysts should verify the consistency of formulas and data classifications of the data source. Analysts should also be mindful of the judgments made by a vendor in data classifications and refer back to the source financial statements until they are comfortable that the classifications are appropriate.

Systems are under development that collect financial data from regulatory filings and can automatically compute ratios. The eXtensible Business Reporting Language (XBRL) is a mechanism that attaches "smart tags" to financial information (e.g., total assets), so that software can automatically collect the data and perform desired computations. The organization developing XBRL (www.xbrl.org) is a worldwide nonprofit consortium of organizations, including the International Accounting Standards Board.

Analysts can compare a subject company to similar (peer) companies in these databases or use aggregate industry data. For nonpublic companies, aggregate industry data can be obtained from such sources as Annual Statement Studies by the Risk Management Association or Dun & Bradstreet. These publications provide industry data with companies sorted into quartiles. Twenty-five percent of companies' ratios fall within the lowest quartile, 25 percent have ratios between the lower quartile and median value, and so on. Analysts can then determine a company's relative standing in the industry.

3.2 Common-Size Analysis

Common-size analysis involves expressing financial data, including entire financial statements, in relation to a single financial statement item, or base. Items used most frequently as the bases are total assets or revenue. In essence, common-size analysis creates a ratio between every financial statement item and the base item.

Common-size analysis was demonstrated in readings for the income statement, balance sheet, and statement of cash flows. In this section, we present common-size analysis of financial statements in greater detail and include further discussion of their interpretation.

3.2.1 Common-Size Analysis of the Balance Sheet

A vertical[5] common-size balance sheet, prepared by dividing each item on the balance sheet by the same period's total assets and expressing the results as percentages, highlights the composition of the balance sheet. What is the mix of assets being used? How is the company financing itself? How does one company's balance sheet composition compare with that of peer companies, and what is behind any differences?

A horizontal common-size balance sheet, prepared by computing the increase or decrease in percentage terms of each balance sheet item from the

---

[5] The term vertical analysis is used to denote a common-size analysis using only one reporting period or one base financial statement, whereas horizontal analysis can refer either to an analysis comparing a specific financial statement with prior or future time periods or to a cross-sectional analysis of one company with another.

prior year, highlights items that have changed unexpectedly or have unexpectedly remained unchanged.

For example, Exhibit 2 presents a vertical common-size (partial) balance sheet for a hypothetical company in two different time periods. In this example, receivables have increased from 35 percent to 57 percent of total assets. What are possible reasons for such an increase? The increase might indicate that the company is making more of its sales on a credit basis rather than a cash basis, perhaps in response to some action taken by a competitor. Alternatively, the increase in receivables as a percentage of assets may have occurred because of a change in another current asset category—for example, a decrease in the level of inventory; the analyst would then need to investigate why that asset category had changed. Another possible reason for the increase in receivables as a percentage of assets is that the company has lowered its credit standards, relaxed its collection procedures, or adopted more aggressive revenue recognition policies. The analyst can turn to other comparisons and ratios (e.g., comparing the rate of growth in accounts receivable with the rate of growth in sales to help determine which explanation is most likely).

EXHIBIT 2	Vertical Common-Size (Partial) Balance Sheet for a Hypothetical Company	
	Period 1 **% of Total Assets**	**Period 2** **% of Total Assets**
Cash	25	15
Receivables	35	57
Inventory	35	20
Fixed assets, net of depreciation	5	8
Total assets	100	100

3.2.2 Common-Size Analysis of the Income Statement

A vertical common-size income statement divides each income statement item by revenue, or sometimes by total assets (especially in the case of financial institutions). If there are multiple revenue sources, a decomposition of revenue in percentage terms is useful. For example, Exhibit 3 presents a hypothetical company's vertical common-size income statement in two different time periods. Revenue is separated into the company's four services, each shown as a percentage of total revenue. In this example, revenues from Service A have become a far greater percentage of the company's total revenue (45 percent in Period 2). What are possible reasons for and implications of this change in business mix? Did the company make a strategic decision to sell more of Service A, perhaps because it is more profitable? Apparently not, because the company's earnings before interest, taxes, depreciation, and amortization (EBITDA) declined from 53 percent of sales to 45 percent, so other possible explanations should be examined. In addition, we note from the composition of operating expenses that the main reason for this decline in profitability is that salaries and employee benefits have increased from 15 percent to 25 percent of total revenue. Are more highly compensated employees required for Service A? Were higher training costs incurred in order to increase Service A revenues? If the analyst wants to predict future performance, the causes of these changes must be understood.

In addition, Exhibit 3 shows that the company's income tax as a percentage of sales has declined dramatically (from 15 percent to 8 percent). Furthermore, as a percentage of earnings before tax (EBT) (usually the more relevant comparison), taxes have decreased from 36 percent to 23 percent. Is Service A provided in a jurisdiction with lower tax rates? If not, what is the explanation?

The observations based on Exhibit 3 summarize the issues that can be raised through analysis of the vertical common-size income statement.

EXHIBIT 3	Vertical Common-Size Income Statement for Hypothetical Company	
	Period 1 % of Total Revenue	**Period 2 % of Total Revenue**
Revenue source: Service A	30	45
Revenue source: Service B	23	20
Revenue source: Service C	30	30
Revenue source: Service D	17	5
Total revenue	**100**	**100**
Operating expenses (excluding depreciation)		
Salaries and employee benefits	15	25
Administrative expenses	22	20
Rent expense	10	10
EBITDA	**53**	**45**
Depreciation and amortization	4	4
EBIT	**49**	**41**
Interest paid	7	7
EBT	**42**	**34**
Income tax provision	15	8
Net income	**27**	**26**

Note: EBIT = earnings before interest and tax.

3.2.3 Cross-Sectional Analysis

As noted previously, ratios and common-size statements derive part of their meaning through comparison to some benchmark. **Cross-sectional analysis** (sometimes called "relative analysis") compares a specific metric for one company with the same metric for another company or group of companies, allowing comparisons even though the companies might be of significantly different sizes and/or operate in different currencies.

Exhibit 4 presents a vertical common-size (partial) balance sheet for two hypothetical companies at the same point in time. Company 1 is clearly more liquid (liquidity is a function of how quickly assets can be converted into cash) than Company 2, which has only 12 percent of assets available as cash, compared with the highly liquid Company 1, where cash is 38 percent of assets. Given that cash

EXHIBIT 4	Vertical Common-Size (Partial) Balance Sheet for Two Hypothetical Companies	
	Company 1 % of Total Assets	**Company 2 % of Total Assets**
Cash	38	12
Receivables	33	55
Inventory	27	24
Fixed assets net of depreciation	1	2
Investments	1	7
Total assets	**100**	**100**

is generally a relatively low-yielding asset and thus not a particularly efficient use of the balance sheet, why does Company 1 hold such a large percentage of total assets in cash? Perhaps the company is preparing for an acquisition, or maintains a large cash position as insulation from a particularly volatile operating environment. Another issue highlighted by the comparison in this example is the relatively high percentage of receivables in Company 2's assets, which (as discussed in Section 3.2.1) may indicate a greater proportion of credit sales, overall changes in asset composition, lower credit or collection standards, or aggressive accounting policies.

3.2.4 Trend Analysis[6]

When looking at financial statements and ratios, trends in the data, whether they are improving or deteriorating, are as important as the current absolute or relative levels. Trend analysis provides important information regarding historical performance and growth and, given a sufficiently long history of accurate seasonal information, can be of great assistance as a planning and forecasting tool for management and analysts.

Exhibit 5A presents a partial balance sheet for a hypothetical company over five periods. The last two columns of the table show the changes for Period 5 compared with Period 4, expressed both in absolute currency (in this case, dollars) and in percentages. A small percentage change could hide a significant currency change and vice versa, prompting the analyst to investigate the reasons despite one of the changes being relatively small. In this example, the largest percentage change was in investments, which decreased by 33.3 percent.[7] However, an examination of the absolute currency amount of changes shows that investments changed by only $2 million and the more significant change was the $12 million increase in receivables.

Another way to present data covering a period of time is to show each item in relation to the same item in a base year (i.e., a horizontal common-size balance

---

[6] In financial statement analysis, the term "trend analysis" usually refers to comparisons across time periods of 3–10 years not involving statistical tools. This differs from the use of the term in the quantitative methods portion of the CFA curriculum, where "trend analysis" refers to statistical methods of measuring patterns in time-series data.

[7] Percentage change is calculated as: (Ending value − Beginning value)/Beginning value, or equivalently, (Ending value/Beginning value) − 1.

sheet). Exhibit 5B presents the same partial balance sheet as in Exhibit 5A but with each item indexed relative to the same item in Period 1. For example, in Period 2, the company had $29 million cash, which is 75 percent of the amount of cash it had in Period 1, or expressed as an index relative to Period 1, 75 ($29/$39 = 0.75 × 100 = 75). Presenting data this way highlights significant changes. In this example, we see easily that the company has less than half the amount of cash in Period 1, four times the amount of investments, and eight times the amount of property, plant, and equipment.

An analysis of horizontal common-size balance sheets highlights structural changes that have occurred in a business. Past trends are obviously not necessarily an accurate predictor of the future, especially when the economic or competitive environment changes. An examination of past trends is more valuable when the macroeconomic and competitive environments are relatively stable and when the analyst is reviewing a stable or mature business. However, even in less stable contexts, historical analysis can serve as a basis for developing expecta-

| EXHIBIT 5A | Partial Balance Sheet for a Hypothetical Company over Five Periods |

| | Period | | | | | Change 4 to | Change 4 |
Assets ($ Millions)	1	2	3	4	5	5 ($ Million)	to 5 (%)
Cash	39	29	27	19	16	−3	−15.8
Investments	1	7	7	6	4	−2	−33.3
Receivables	44	41	37	67	79	12	17.9
Inventory	15	25	36	25	27	2	8
Fixed assets net of depreciation	1	2	6	9	8	−1	−11.1
Total assets	100	105	112	126	133	8	5.6

| EXHIBIT 5B | Horizontal Common-Size (Partial) Balance Sheet for a Hypothetical Company over Five Periods, with Each Item Expressed Relative to the Same Item in Period One |

| | Period | | | | |
Assets	1	2	3	4	5
Cash	1.00	0.75	0.69	0.48	0.41
Investments	1.00	7.35	6.74	6.29	4.00
Receivables	1.00	0.93	0.84	1.52	1.79
Inventory	1.00	1.68	2.40	1.68	1.78
Fixed assets net of depreciation	1.00	2.10	5.62	8.81	8.00
Total assets	1.00	1.05	1.12	1.26	1.33

tions. Understanding past trends is helpful in assessing whether these trends are likely to continue or if the trend is likely to change direction.

One measure of success is for a company to grow at a rate greater than the rate of the overall market in which it operates. Companies that grow slowly may find themselves unable to attract equity capital. Conversely, companies that grow too quickly may find that their administrative and management information systems cannot keep up with the rate of expansion.

3.2.5 Relationships among Financial Statements

Trend data generated by a horizontal common-size analysis can be compared across financial statements. For example, the growth rate of assets for the hypothetical company in Exhibit 5 can be compared with the company's growth in revenue over the same period of time. If revenue is growing more quickly than assets, the company may be increasing its efficiency (i.e., generating more revenue for every dollar invested in assets).

As another example, consider the following year-over-year percentage changes for a hypothetical company:

Revenue	+20%
Net income	+25%
Operating cash flow	−10%
Total assets	+30%

Net income is growing faster than revenue, which indicates increasing profitability. However, the analyst would need to determine whether the faster growth in net income resulted from continuing operations or from nonoperating, nonrecurring items. In addition, the 10 percent decline in operating cash flow despite increasing revenue and net income clearly warrants further investigation because it could indicate a problem with earnings quality (perhaps aggressive reporting of revenue). Lastly, the fact that assets have grown faster than revenue indicates the company's efficiency may be declining. The analyst should examine the composition of the increase in assets and the reasons for the changes. Example 4 provides a recent example of a company where comparisons of trend data from different financial statements can indicate aggressive accounting policies.

EXAMPLE 4

Use of Comparative Growth Information[8]

Sunbeam, a U.S. company, brought in new management to turn the company around during July 1996. For the following year, 1997, the following common-size trends were apparent:

Revenue	+19%
Inventory	+58%
Receivables	+38%

---

[8] Adapted from Robinson and Munter (2004, pp. 2–15).

It is generally more desirable to observe inventory and receivables growing at a slower (or similar) rate to revenue growth. Receivables growing faster than revenue can indicate operational issues, such as lower credit standards or aggressive accounting policies for revenue recognition. Similarly, inventory growing faster than revenue can indicate an operational problem with obsolescence or aggressive accounting policies, such as an improper overstatement of inventory to increase profits.

In this case, the explanation lay in aggressive accounting policies. Sunbeam was later charged by the U.S. SEC with improperly accelerating the recognition of revenue and engaging in other practices, such as billing customers for inventory prior to shipment.

3.3 The Use of Graphs as an Analytical Tool

Graphs facilitate comparison of performance and financial structure over time, highlighting changes in significant aspects of business operations. In addition, graphs provide the analyst (and management) with a visual overview of risk trends in a business. Graphs may also be used effectively to communicate the analyst's conclusions regarding financial condition and risk management aspects.

Exhibit 6 presents the information from Exhibit 5A in a stacked column format. The graph makes the significant decline in cash and growth in receivables (both in absolute terms and as a percentage of assets) readily apparent.

Choosing the appropriate graph to communicate the most significant conclusions of a financial analysis is a skill. In general, pie graphs are most useful to communicate the composition of a total value (e.g., assets over a limited amount of time, say one or two periods). Line graphs are useful when the focus is on the

| EXHIBIT 6 | Stacked Column Graph of Asset Composition of Hypothetical Company over Five Periods |

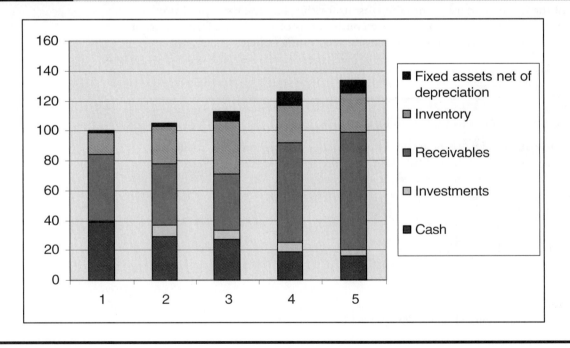

change in amount for a limited number of items over a relatively longer time period. When the composition and amounts, as well as their change over time, are all important, a stacked column graph can be useful.

When comparing Period 5 with Period 4, the growth in receivables appears to be within normal bounds, but when comparing Period 5 with earlier periods, the dramatic growth becomes apparent. In the same manner, a simple line graph will also illustrate the growth trends in key financial variables. Exhibit 7 presents the information from Exhibit 5 as a line graph, illustrating the growth of assets of a hypothetical company over five periods. The steady decline in cash, volatile movements of inventory, and dramatic growth of receivables is clearly illustrated.

EXHIBIT 7	Line Graph of Growth of Assets of Hypothetical Company over Five Periods

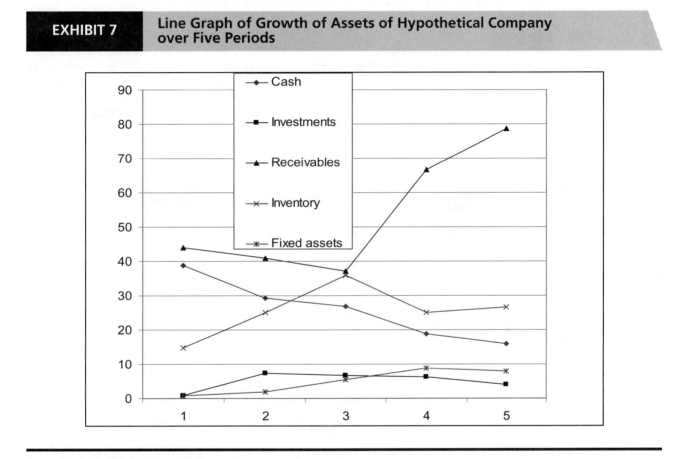

3.4 Regression Analysis

When analyzing the trend in a specific line item or ratio, frequently it is possible simply to visually evaluate the changes. For more complex situations, regression analysis can help identify relationships (or correlation) between variables. For example, a regression analysis could relate a company's sales to GDP over time, providing insight into whether the company is cyclical. In addition, the statistical relationship between sales and GDP could be used as a basis for forecasting sales.

Other examples of such relationships are the relation between a company's sales and inventory over time, or the relation between hotel occupancy and a company's hotel revenues. In addition to providing a basis for forecasting, regression analysis facilitates identification of items or ratios that are not behaving as expected, given historical statistical relationships.

4

COMMON RATIOS USED IN FINANCIAL ANALYSIS

In the previous section, we focused on ratios resulting from common-size analysis. In this section, we expand the discussion to include other commonly used financial ratios and the broad classes into which they are categorized. There is some overlap with common-size financial statement ratios. For example, a common indicator of profitability is the net profit margin, which is calculated as net income divided by sales. This ratio appears on a common-size vertical income statement. Other ratios involve information from multiple financial statements or even data from outside the financial statements.

Due to the large number of ratios, it is helpful to think about ratios in terms of broad categories based on what aspects of performance a ratio is intended to detect. Financial analysts and data vendors use a variety of categories to classify ratios. The category names and the ratios included in each category can differ. Common ratio categories include activity, liquidity, solvency, and profitability. These categories are summarized in Exhibit 8. Each category measures a different aspect of analysis, but all are useful in evaluating a company's overall ability to generate cash flows from operating its business and the associated risks.

EXHIBIT 8	Categories of Financial Ratios
Category	**Description**
Activity	**Activity ratios** measure how efficiently a company performs day-to-day tasks, such as the collection of receivables and management of inventory.
Liquidity	**Liquidity ratios** measure the company's ability to meet its short-term obligations.
Solvency	**Solvency ratios** measure a company's ability to meet long-term obligations. Subsets of these ratios are also known as "leverage" and "long-term debt" ratios.
Profitability	**Profitability ratios** measure the company's ability to generate profitable sales from its resources (assets).
Valuation	**Valuation ratios** measure the quantity of an asset or flow (e.g., earnings) associated with ownership of a specified claim (e.g., a share or ownership of the enterprise).

These categories are not mutually exclusive; some ratios are useful in measuring multiple aspects of the business. For example, an activity ratio measuring how quickly a company collects accounts receivable is also useful in assessing the company's liquidity because collection of revenues increases cash. Some profitability ratios also reflect the operating efficiency of the business. In summary, analysts appropriately use certain ratios to evaluate multiple aspects of the business. Analysts also need to be aware of variations in industry practice in the calculation of financial ratios. In the text that follows, alternative views on ratio calculations are often provided.

4.1 Interpretation and Context

Financial ratios can only be interpreted in the context of other information, including benchmarks. In general, the financial ratios of a company are compared with those of its major competitors (cross-sectional and trend analysis) and to the company's prior periods (trend analysis). The goal is to understand the underlying causes of divergence between a company's ratios and those of the industry. Even ratios that remain consistent require understanding because consistency can sometimes indicate accounting policies selected to smooth earnings. An analyst should evaluate financial ratios based on the following:

1. *Company goals and strategy.* Actual ratios can be compared with company objectives to determine whether objectives are being attained and whether the results are consistent with the company's strategy.

2. *Industry norms (cross-sectional analysis).* A company can be compared with others in its industry by relating its financial ratios to industry norms or to a subset of the companies in an industry. When industry norms are used to make judgments, care must be taken because:

    ▶ Many ratios are industry specific, and not all ratios are important to all industries.

    ▶ Companies may have several different lines of business. This will cause aggregate financial ratios to be distorted. It is better to examine industry-specific ratios by lines of business.

    ▶ Differences in accounting methods used by companies can distort financial ratios.

    ▶ Differences in corporate strategies can affect certain financial ratios.

3. *Economic conditions.* For cyclical companies, financial ratios tend to improve when the economy is strong and weaken during recessions. Therefore, financial ratios should be examined in light of the current phase of the business cycle.

The following sections discuss activity, liquidity, solvency, and profitability ratios in turn. Selected valuation ratios are presented later in the section on equity analysis.

4.2 Activity Ratios

Activity ratios are also known as **asset utilization ratios** or **operating efficiency ratios**. This category is intended to measure how well a company manages various activities, particularly how efficiently it manages its various assets. Activity ratios are analyzed as indicators of ongoing operational performance—how effectively assets are used by a company. These ratios reflect the efficient management of both working capital and longer-term assets. As noted, efficiency has a direct impact on liquidity (the ability of a company to meet its short-term obligations), so some activity ratios are also useful in assessing liquidity.

4.2.1 Calculation of Activity Ratios

Exhibit 9 presents the most commonly used activity ratios. The exhibit shows the numerator and denominator of each ratio.

EXHIBIT 9	Definitions of Commonly Used Activity Ratios	
Activity Ratios	**Numerator**	**Denominator**
Inventory turnover	Cost of goods sold	Average inventory
Days of inventory on hand (DOH)	Number of days in period	Inventory turnover
Receivables turnover	Revenue	Average receivables
Days of sales outstanding (DSO)	Number of days in period	Receivables turnover
Payables turnover	Purchases	Average trade payables
Number of days of payables	Number of days in period	Payables turnover
Working capital turnover	Revenue	Average working capital
Fixed asset turnover	Revenue	Average net fixed assets
Total asset turnover	Revenue	Average total assets

Activity ratios measure how efficiently the company utilizes assets. They generally combine information from the income statement in the numerator with balance sheet items in the denominator. Because the income statement measures what happened *during* a period whereas the balance sheet shows the condition only at the end of the period, average balance sheet data are normally used for consistency. For example, to measure inventory management efficiency, cost of goods sold (from the income statement) is divided by average inventory (from the balance sheet). Most databases, such as Bloomberg and Baseline, use this averaging convention when income statement and balance sheet data are combined. These databases typically average only two points: the beginning of the year and the end of the year. The examples that follow based on annual financial statements illustrate that practice. However, some analysts prefer to average more observations if they are available, especially if the business is seasonal. If a semiannual report is prepared, an average can be taken over three data points (beginning, middle, and end of year). If quarterly data are available, a five-point average can be computed (beginning of year and end of each quarterly period) or a four-point average using the end of each quarterly period. Note that if the company's year ends at a low or high point for inventory for the year, there can still be bias in using three or five data points, because the beginning and end of year occur at the same time of the year and are effectively double counted.

Because cost of goods sold measures the cost of inventory that has been sold, this ratio measures how many times per year the entire inventory was theoretically turned over, or sold. (We say that the entire inventory was "theoretically" sold because in practice companies do not generally sell out their entire inventory.) If, for example, a company's cost of goods sold for a recent year was €120,000 and its average inventory was €10,000, the inventory turnover ratio would be 12. The company theoretically turns over (i.e., sells) its entire inventory 12 times per year (i.e., once a month). (Again, we say "theoretically" because in practice the company likely carries some inventory from one month into another.) Turnover can then be converted to days of inventory on hand (DOH) by dividing inventory turnover into the number of days in the accounting period. In this example, the result is a DOH of 30.42 (365/12), meaning that, on average, the company's inventory was on hand for about 30 days, or, equivalently, the company kept on hand about 30 days' worth of inventory, on average, during the period.

Activity ratios can be computed for any annual or interim period, but care must be taken in the interpretation and comparison across periods. For example, if the same company had cost of goods sold for the first quarter (90 days) of the following year of €35,000 and average inventory of €11,000, the inventory turnover would be 3.18 times. However, this turnover rate is 3.18 times per quarter, which is not directly comparable to the 12 times per year in the preceding year. In this case, we can annualize the quarterly inventory turnover rate by multiplying the quarterly turnover by 4 (12 months/3 months; or by 4.06, using 365 days/90 days) for comparison to the annual turnover rate. So, the quarterly inventory turnover is equivalent to a 12.72 annual inventory turnover (or 12.91 if we annualize the ratio using a 90-day quarter and a 365-day year). To compute the DOH using quarterly data, we can use the quarterly turnover rate and the number of days in the quarter for the numerator—or, we can use the annualized turnover rate and 365 days; either results in DOH of around 28.3, with slight differences due to rounding (90/3.18 = 28.30 and 365/12.91 = 28.27). Another time-related computational detail is that for companies using a 52/53-week annual period and for leap years, the actual days in the year should be used rather than 365.

In some cases, an analyst may want to know how many days of inventory are on hand at the end of the year rather than the average for the year. In this case, it would be appropriate to use the year-end inventory balance in the computation rather than the average. If the company is growing rapidly or if costs are increasing rapidly, analysts should consider using cost of goods sold just for the fourth quarter in this computation because the cost of goods sold of earlier quarters may not be relevant. Example 5 further demonstrates computation of activity ratios using Hong Kong Exchange-listed Lenovo Group Limited.

EXAMPLE 5

Computation of Activity Ratios

Ya-Wen Yang would like to evaluate how efficient Lenovo Group Limited is at collecting its trade accounts receivable on average during the fiscal year ended 31 March 2005. Yang has gathered the following information from Lenovo's annual and interim reports:

	HK$ in Thousands
Trade receivables as of 31 March 2004	1,230,944
Trade receivables as of 31 March 2005	851,337
Revenue for year ended 31 March 2005	22,554,678

What is Lenovo's receivables turnover and number of days of sales outstanding (DSO) for the fiscal year ended 31 March 2005?

Solution:

$$\text{Receivables turnover} = \text{Revenue/Average receivables}$$
$$= 22{,}554{,}678/[(1{,}230{,}944 + 851{,}337)/2]$$
$$= 22{,}554{,}678/1{,}041{,}140.50$$
$$= 21.6634 \text{ times}$$

$$\text{DSO} = \text{Number of days in period/Receivables turnover}$$
$$= 365/21.6634$$
$$= 16.85 \text{ days}$$

On average, it took Lenovo 16.85 days to collect receivables during the fiscal year ended 31 March 2005.

4.2.2 Interpretation of Activity Ratios

In the following, we discuss the activity ratios that were defined in Exhibit 9.

Inventory Turnover and DOH Inventory turnover lies at the heart of operations for many entities. It indicates the resources (money) tied up in inventory (i.e., the carrying costs) and can, therefore, be used to indicate inventory management effectiveness. The higher the inventory turnover ratio, the shorter the period that inventory is held and so the lower DOH. In general, inventory turnover (and DOH) should be benchmarked against industry norms.

A high inventory turnover ratio relative to industry norms might indicate highly effective inventory management. Alternatively, a high inventory turnover ratio (and commensurately low DOH) could possibly indicate the company does not carry adequate inventory, so shortages could potentially hurt revenue. To assess which explanation is more likely, the analyst can compare the company's revenue growth with that of the industry. Slower growth combined with higher inventory turnover could indicate inadequate inventory levels. Revenue growth at or above the industry's growth supports the interpretation that the higher turnover reflects greater inventory management efficiency.

A low inventory turnover ratio (and commensurately high DOH) relative to the rest of the industry could be an indicator of slow-moving inventory, perhaps due to technological obsolescence or a change in fashion. Again, comparing the company's sales growth with the industry can offer insight.

Receivables Turnover and DSO The number of DSO represents the elapsed time between a sale and cash collection, reflecting how fast the company collects cash from customers it offers credit. Although limiting the numerator to sales made on credit would be more appropriate, credit sales information is not always available to analysts; therefore, revenue as reported in the income statement is generally used as an approximation.

A relatively high receivables turnover ratio (and commensurately low DSO) might indicate highly efficient credit and collection. Alternatively, a high receivables turnover ratio could indicate that the company's credit or collection policies are too stringent, suggesting the possibility of sales being lost to competitors offering more lenient terms. A relatively low receivables turnover ratio would typically raise questions about the efficiency of the company's credit and collections procedures. As with inventory management, comparison of the company's sales growth relative to the industry can help the analyst assess whether sales are being lost due to stringent credit policies. In addition, comparing the company's estimates of uncollectible accounts receivable and actual credit losses with past experience and with peer companies can help assess whether low turnover reflects credit management issues. Companies often provide details of receivables aging (how much receivables have been outstanding by age). This can be used along with DSO to understand trends in collection, as demonstrated in Example 6.

EXAMPLE 6

Evaluation of an Activity Ratio

Ya-Wen Yang has computed the average DSO for fiscal years ended 31 March 2004 and 2005:

	2005	2004
Days of sales outstanding	16.85	14.05

Yang would like to better understand why, on average, it took almost 17 days to collect receivables in 2005 versus 14 days in 2004. He collects accounts receivable aging information from Lenovo's annual reports and computes the percentage of accounts receivable by days outstanding. This information is presented below:

	31 March 2005		31 March 2004		31 March 2003	
	HK$000	**Percent**	**HK$000**	**Percent**	**HK$000**	**Percent**
0–30 days	588,389	69.11	944,212	76.71	490,851	88.68
31–60 days	56,966	6.69	84,481	6.86	27,213	4.92
61–90 days	40,702	4.78	20,862	1.69	10,680	1.93
Over 90 days	165,280	19.41	181,389	14.74	24,772	4.48
Total	851,337	100.00	1,230,944	100.00	553,516	100.00

From these data, it appears that over the past three years there has been a trend of fewer receivables due within 30 days and more due for periods of longer than 90 days. Lenovo's footnotes disclose that general trade customers are provided with 30-day credit terms but that systems integration customers (consulting jobs) are given 180 days. Furthermore, the footnotes reveal that consulting revenues increased dramatically over the 2003 to 2004 period. In the third quarter of fiscal year ending 31 March 2005, Lenovo spun off its systems integration business to another company, retaining a small percentage interest. Yang concludes that the higher DSO in fiscal year ending 31 March 2005 appears to be due to the higher revenue in systems integration, which has longer credit terms. Yang may further surmise that DSO should drop in the next fiscal year since this business has been spun off.

Payables Turnover and the Number of Days of Payables   The number of days of payables reflects the average number of days the company takes to pay its suppliers, and the payables turnover ratio measures how many times per year the company theoretically pays off all its creditors. For purposes of calculating these ratios, an implicit assumption is that the company makes all its purchases using credit. If the amount of purchases is not directly available, it can be computed as cost of goods sold plus ending inventory less beginning inventory. Alternatively, cost of goods sold is sometimes used as an approximation of purchases.

A payables turnover ratio that is high (low days payable) relative to the industry could indicate that the company is not making full use of available credit facilities; alternatively, it could result from a company taking advantage of early payment discounts. An excessively low turnover ratio (high days payable) could indicate trouble making payments on time, or alternatively, exploitation of lenient supplier terms. This is another example where it is useful to look simultaneously at other ratios. If liquidity ratios indicate that the company has sufficient cash and other short-term assets to pay obligations and yet the days payable ratio is relatively high, the analyst would favor the lenient supplier credit and collection policies as an explanation.

Working Capital Turnover   **Working capital** is defined as current (expected to be consumed or converted into cash within one year) assets minus current liabilities. Working capital turnover indicates how efficiently the company generates revenue with its working capital. For example, a working capital turnover ratio of 4.0 indicates that the company generates €4 of revenue for every €1 of working capital. A high working capital turnover ratio indicates greater efficiency (i.e., the company is generating a high level of revenues relative to working capital). For some companies, working capital can be near zero or negative, rendering this ratio incapable of being interpreted. The following two ratios are more useful in those circumstances.

Fixed Asset Turnover   This ratio measures how efficiently the company generates revenues from its investments in fixed assets. Generally, a higher fixed asset turnover ratio indicates more efficient use of fixed assets in generating revenue. A low ratio can indicate inefficiency, a capital-intensive business environment, or a new business not yet operating at full capacity—in which case the analyst will not be able to link the ratio directly to efficiency. In addition, asset turnover can be affected by factors other than a company's efficiency. The fixed asset turnover ratio would be lower for a company whose assets are newer (and, therefore, less depreciated and so reflected in the financial statements at a higher carrying value) than the ratio for a company with older assets (that are thus more depreciated and so reflected at a lower carrying value). The fixed asset ratio can be erratic because, although revenue may have a steady growth rate, increases in fixed assets may not follow a smooth pattern; so, every year-to-year change in the ratio does not necessarily indicate important changes in the company's efficiency.

Total Asset Turnover   The total asset turnover ratio measures the company's overall ability to generate revenues with a given level of assets. A ratio of 1.20 would indicate that the company is generating €1.20 of revenues for every €1 of average assets. A higher ratio indicates greater efficiency. Because this ratio includes both fixed and current assets, inefficient working capital management can distort overall interpretations. It is, therefore, helpful to analyze working capital and fixed asset turnover ratios separately.

A low asset turnover ratio can be an indicator of inefficiency or of relative capital intensity of the business. The ratio also reflects strategic decisions by management: for example, the decision whether to use a more labor-intensive (and less capital-intensive) approach to its business or a more capital-intensive (and less labor-intensive) approach.

When interpreting activity ratios, the analysts should examine not only the individual ratios but also the collection of relevant ratios to determine the overall efficiency of a company. Example 7 demonstrates the evaluation of activity ratios, both narrow (e.g., number of days inventory) and broad (total asset turnover) for a Taiwanese semiconductor manufacturer.

EXAMPLE 7

Evaluation of Activity Ratios

United Microelectronics Corp. (UMC) is a semiconductor foundry company based in Taiwan. As part of an analysis of management's operating efficiency, an analyst collects the following activity ratios from Bloomberg:

Ratio	2004	2003	2002	2001
DOH	35.68	40.70	40.47	48.51
DSO	45.07	58.28	51.27	76.98
Total asset turnover	0.35	0.28	0.23	0.22

These ratios indicate that the company has improved on all three measures of activity over the four-year period. The company has fewer DOH, is collecting receivables faster, and is generating a higher level of revenues relative to total assets. The overall trend is good, but thus far, the analyst has only determined *what* happened. A more important question is *why* the ratios improved, because understanding good changes as well as bad ones facilitates judgments about the company's future performance. To answer this question, the analyst examines company financial reports as well as external information about the industry and economy. In examining the annual report, the analyst notes that in the fourth quarter of 2004, the company experienced an "inventory correction" and that the company recorded an allowance for the decline in market value and obsolescence of inventory of TWD 1,786,493, or about 15 percent of year-end inventory value (compared with about a 5.9 percent allowance in the prior year). This reduction in the value of inventory accounts for a large portion of the decline in DOH from 40.7 in 2003 to 35.68 in 2004. Management claims that this inventory obsolescence is a short-term issue; analysts can watch DOH in future interim periods to confirm this assertion. In any event, all else being equal, the analyst would likely expect DOH to return to a level closer to 40 days going forward.

More positive interpretations can be drawn from the total asset turnover. The analyst finds that the company's revenues increased more than 35 percent while total assets only increased by about 6 percent. Based on external information about the industry and economy, the analyst attributes the increased revenues largely to the recovery of the semiconductor industry in 2004. However, management was able to achieve this growth in revenues with a comparatively modest increase in assets, leading to an improvement in total asset turnover. Note further that part of the reason for the modest increase in assets is lower DOH and DSO.

4.3 Liquidity Ratios

Liquidity analysis, which focuses on cash flows, measures a company's ability to meet its short-term obligations. Liquidity measures how quickly assets are converted into cash. Liquidity ratios also measure the ability to pay off short-term obligations. In day-to-day operations, liquidity management is typically achieved through efficient use of assets. In the medium term, liquidity in the nonfinancial sector is also addressed by managing the structure of liabilities. (See discussion on financial sector below.)

The level of liquidity needed differs from one industry to another. A particular company's liquidity position may also vary according to the anticipated need for funds at any given time. Judging whether a company has adequate liquidity requires analysis of its historical funding requirements, current liquidity position, anticipated future funding needs, and options for reducing funding needs or attracting additional funds (including actual and potential sources of such funding).

Larger companies are usually better able to control the level and composition of their liabilities than smaller companies. Therefore, they may have more potential funding sources, including public capital and money markets. Greater discretionary access to capital markets also reduces the size of the liquidity buffer needed relative to companies without such access.

Contingent liabilities, such as letters of credit or financial guarantees, can also be relevant when assessing liquidity. The importance of contingent liabilities varies for the nonbanking and banking sector. In the nonbanking sector, contingent liabilities (usually disclosed in the footnotes to the company's financial statements) represent potential cash outflows, and when appropriate, should be included in an assessment of a company's liquidity. In the banking sector, contingent liabilities represent potentially significant cash outflows that are not dependent on the bank's financial condition. Although outflows in normal market circumstances typically may be low, a general macroeconomic or market crisis can trigger a substantial increase in cash outflows related to contingent liabilities because of the increase in defaults and business bankruptcies that often accompany such events. In addition, such crises are usually characterized by diminished levels of overall liquidity, which can further exacerbate funding shortfalls. Therefore, for the banking sector, the effect of contingent liabilities on liquidity warrants particular attention.

4.3.1 Calculation of Liquidity Ratios

Common liquidity ratios are presented in Exhibit 10. These liquidity ratios reflect a company's position at a point in time and, therefore, typically use data from the ending balance sheet rather than averages. The current, quick, and cash ratios reflect three measures of a company's ability to pay current liabilities. Each uses a progressively stricter definition of liquid assets.

The defensive interval ratio measures how long a company can pay its daily cash expenditures using only its existing liquid assets, without additional cash flow coming in. This ratio is similar to the "burn rate" often computed for start-up internet companies in the late 1990s or for biotechnology companies. The numerator of this ratio includes the same liquid assets used in the quick ratio, and the denominator is an estimate of daily cash expenditures. To obtain daily cash expenditures, the total of cash expenditures for the period is divided by the number of days in the period. Total cash expenditures for a period can be approximated by summing all expenses on the income statement—such as cost

EXHIBIT 10	Definitions of Commonly Used Liquidity Ratios	
Liquidity Ratios	**Numerator**	**Denominator**
Current ratio	Current assets	Current liabilities
Quick ratio	Cash + Short-term marketable investments + Receivables	Current liabilities
Cash ratio	Cash + Short-term marketable investments	Current liabilities
Defensive interval ratio	Cash + Short-term marketable investments + Receivables	Daily cash expenditures
Additional Liquidity Measure		
Cash conversion cycle (net operating cycle)	DOH + DSO − Number of days of payables	

of goods sold; selling, general, and administrative expenses; and research and development expenses—and then subtracting any noncash expenses, such as depreciation and amortization. (Typically, taxes are not included.)

The **cash conversion cycle**, a financial metric not in ratio form, measures the length of time required for a company to go from cash (invested in its operations) to cash received (as a result of its operations). During this period of time, the company needs to finance its investment in operations through other sources (i.e., through debt or equity).

4.3.2 *Interpretation of Liquidity Ratios*

In the following, we discuss the interpretation of the five basic liquidity ratios presented in Exhibit 10.

Current Ratio This ratio expresses current assets (assets expected to be consumed or converted into cash within one year) in relation to current liabilities (liabilities falling due within one year). A higher ratio indicates a higher level of liquidity (i.e., a greater ability to meet short-term obligations). A current ratio of 1.0 would indicate that the book value of its current assets exactly equals the book value of its current liabilities.

A lower ratio indicates less liquidity, implying a greater reliance on operating cash flow and outside financing to meet short-term obligations. Liquidity affects the company's capacity to take on debt. The current ratio implicitly assumes that inventories and accounts receivable are indeed liquid (which is presumably not the case when related turnover ratios are low).

Quick Ratio The quick ratio is more conservative than the current ratio because it includes only the more liquid current assets (sometimes referred to as "quick assets") in relation to current liabilities. Like the current ratio, a higher quick ratio indicates greater liquidity.

The quick ratio reflects the fact that certain current assets—such as prepaid expenses, some taxes, and employee-related prepayments—represent costs of the current period that have been paid in advance and cannot usually be converted back into cash. This ratio also reflects the fact that inventory might not be easily and quickly converted into cash, and furthermore, that a company would probably not be able to sell all of its inventory for an amount equal to its carrying value, especially if it were required to sell the inventory quickly. In situations where inventories are illiquid (as indicated, for example, by low inventory turnover ratios), the quick ratio may be a better indicator of liquidity than the current ratio.

Cash Ratio   The cash ratio normally represents a reliable measure of an individual entity's liquidity in a crisis situation. Only highly marketable short-term investments and cash are included. In a general market crisis, the fair value of marketable securities could decrease significantly as a result of market factors, in which case even this ratio might not provide reliable information.

Defensive Interval Ratio   This ratio measures how long the company can continue to pay its expenses from its existing liquid assets without receiving any additional cash inflow. A defensive interval ratio of 50 would indicate that the company can continue to pay its operating expenses for 50 days before running out of quick assets, assuming no additional cash inflows. A higher defensive interval ratio indicates greater liquidity. If a company's defensive interval ratio is very low relative to peer companies or to the company's own history, the analyst would want to ascertain whether there is sufficient cash inflow expected to mitigate the low defensive interval ratio.

Cash Conversion Cycle (Net Operating Cycle)   This metric indicates the amount of time that elapses from the point when a company invests in working capital until the point at which the company collects cash. In the typical course of events, a merchandising company acquires inventory on credit, incurring accounts payable. The company then sells that inventory on credit, increasing accounts receivable. Afterwards, it pays out cash to settle its accounts payable, and it collects cash in settlement of its accounts receivable. The time between the outlay of cash and the collection of cash is called the "cash conversion cycle." A shorter cash conversion cycle indicates greater liquidity. The short cash conversion cycle implies that the company only needs to finance its inventory and accounts receivable for a short period of time. A longer cash conversion cycle indicates lower liquidity; it implies that the company must finance its inventory and accounts receivable for a longer period of time, possibly indicating a need for a higher level of capital to fund current assets. Example 8 demonstrates the advantages of a short cash conversion cycle as well as how a company's business strategies are reflected in financial ratios.

EXAMPLE 8

Evaluation of Liquidity Ratios

An analyst is evaluating the liquidity of Dell and finds that Dell provides a computation of the number of days of receivables, inventory, and accounts payable, as well as the overall cash conversion cycle, as follows:

Fiscal Year Ended	28 Jan 2005	30 Jan 2004	31 Jan 2003
DSO	32	31	28
DOH	4	3	3
Less: Number of days of payables	73	70	68
Equals: Cash conversion cycle	(37)	(36)	(37)

The minimal DOH indicates that Dell maintains lean inventories, which is attributable to key aspects of the company's business model—namely, the company does not build a computer until it is ordered. Furthermore, Dell has a sophisticated just-in-time manufacturing system. In isolation, the increase in number of days payable (from 68 days in 2003 to 73 days in 2005) might suggest an inability to pay suppliers; however, in Dell's case, the balance sheet indicates that the company has almost $10 billion of cash and short-term investments, which would be more than enough to pay suppliers sooner if Dell chose to do so. Instead, Dell takes advantage of the favorable credit terms granted by its suppliers. The overall effect is a negative cash cycle, a somewhat unusual result. Instead of requiring additional capital to fund working capital as is the case for most companies, Dell has excess cash to invest for about 37 days (reflected on the balance sheet as short-term investments) on which it is earning, rather than paying, interest.

For comparison, the analyst computes the cash conversion cycle for three of Dell's competitors:

Fiscal Year	2004	2003	2002
HP Compaq	27	37	61
Gateway	(7)	(9)	(3)
Apple	(40)	(41)	(40)

The analyst notes that of the group, only HP Compaq has to raise capital for working capital purposes. Dell is outperforming HP Compaq and Gateway on this metric, its negative cash conversion cycle of minus 37 days indicating stronger liquidity than either of those two competitors. Apple, however, is slightly more liquid than Dell, evidenced by its slightly more negative cash conversion cycle, and Apple also has a similarly stable negative cash conversion cycle.

4.4 Solvency Ratios

Solvency refers to a company's ability to fulfill its long-term debt obligations. Assessment of a company's ability to pay its long-term obligations (i.e., to make interest and principal payments) generally includes an in-depth analysis of the components of its financial structure. Solvency ratios provide information regarding the relative amount of debt in the company's capital structure and the adequacy of earnings and cash flow to cover interest expenses and other fixed charges (such as lease or rental payments) as they come due.

Analysts seek to understand a company's use of debt for several main reasons. One reason is that the amount of debt in a company's capital structure is important for assessing the company's risk and return characteristics, specifically its financial leverage. Leverage is a magnifying effect that results from the use of **fixed costs**—costs that stay the same within some range of activity—and can take two forms: **operating leverage** and **financial leverage**. Operating leverage results from the use of fixed costs in conducting the company's business. Operating leverage magnifies the effect of changes in sales on operating income. Profitable companies may use operating leverage because when revenues increase, with operating leverage, their operating income increases at a faster rate. The explanation is that, although **variable costs** will rise proportionally with revenue, fixed costs will not. When financing a firm (i.e., raising capital for it), the use of debt constitutes financial leverage because interest payments are essentially fixed financing costs. As a result of interest payments, a given percent change in EBIT results in a larger percent change in earnings before taxes (EBT). Thus, financial leverage tends to magnify the effect of changes in EBIT on returns flowing to equityholders. Assuming that a company can earn more on the funds than it pays in interest, the inclusion of some level of debt in a company's capital structure may lower a company's overall cost of capital and increase returns to equityholders. However, a higher level of debt in a company's capital structure increases the risk of default and results in higher borrowing costs for the company to compensate lenders for assuming greater credit risk. Starting with Modigliani and Miller (1958, 1963), a substantial amount of research has focused on a company's optimal capital structure, and the subject remains an important one in corporate finance. In analyzing financial statements, an analyst aims to understand levels and trends in a company's use of financial leverage in relation to past practices and the practices of peer companies. Analysts also need to be aware of the relationship between operating leverage and financial leverage. The greater a company's use of operating leverage, the greater the risk of the operating income stream available to cover debt payments; operating leverage can thus limit a company's capacity to use financial leverage.

A company's relative solvency is fundamental to valuation of its debt securities and its credit-worthiness. Finally, understanding a company's use of debt can provide analysts with insight into the company's future business prospects because management's decisions about financing often signal their beliefs about a company's future.

4.4.1 Calculation of Solvency Ratios

Solvency ratios are primarily of two types. Debt ratios, the first type, focus on the balance sheet and measure the amount of debt capital relative to equity capital. Coverage ratios, the second type, focus on the income statement and measure the ability of a company to cover its debt payments. All of these ratios are useful in assessing a company's solvency and, therefore, in evaluating the quality of a company's bonds and other debt obligations.

Exhibit 11 describes commonly used solvency ratios. The first three of the debt ratios presented use total debt in the numerator. The definition of total debt used in these ratios varies among informed analysts and financial data vendors, with some using the total of interest-bearing short-term and long-term debt, excluding liabilities such as accrued expenses and accounts payable. (For calculations in this reading, we use this definition.) Other analysts use defini-

EXHIBIT 11	Definitions of Commonly Used Solvency Ratios	
Solvency Ratios	**Numerator**	**Denominator**
Debt Ratios		
Debt-to-assets ratio[a]	Total debt[b]	Total assets
Debt-to-capital ratio	Total debt[b]	Total debt[b] + Total shareholders' equity
Debt-to-equity ratio	Total debt[b]	Total shareholders' equity
Financial leverage ratio	Average total assets	Average total equity
Coverage Ratios		
Interest coverage	EBIT	Interest payments
Fixed charge coverage	EBIT + Lease payments	Interest payments + Lease payments

[a] "Total debt ratio" is another name sometimes used for this ratio.

[b] In this reading, we take total debt in this context to be the sum of interest-bearing short-term and long-term debt.

tions that are more inclusive (e.g., all liabilities) or restrictive (e.g., long-term debt only, in which case the ratio is sometimes qualified as "long-term," as in "long-term debt-to-equity ratio"). If using different definitions of total debt materially changes conclusions about a company's solvency, the reasons for the discrepancies warrant further investigation.

4.4.2 Interpretation of Solvency Ratios

In the following, we discuss the interpretation of the basic solvency ratios presented in Exhibit 11.

Debt-to-Assets Ratio This ratio measures the percentage of total assets financed with debt. For example, a debt-to-assets ratio of 0.40 or 40 percent indicates that 40 percent of the company's assets are financed with debt. Generally, higher debt means higher financial risk and thus weaker solvency.

Debt-to-Capital Ratio The debt-to-capital ratio measures the percentage of a company's capital (debt plus equity) represented by debt. As with the previous ratio, a higher ratio generally means higher financial risk and thus indicates weaker solvency.

Debt-to-Equity Ratio The debt-to-equity ratio measures the amount of debt capital relative to equity capital. Interpretation is similar to the preceding two ratios (i.e., a higher ratio indicates weaker solvency). A ratio of 1.0 would indicate equal amounts of debt and equity, which is equivalent to a debt-to-capital ratio of 50 percent. Alternative definitions of this ratio use the market value of stockholders' equity rather than its book value (or use the market values of both stockholders' equity and debt).

Financial Leverage Ratio   This ratio (often called simply the "leverage ratio") measures the amount of total assets supported for each one money unit of equity. For example, a value of 3 for this ratio means that each €1 of equity supports €3 of total assets. The higher the financial leverage ratio, the more leveraged the company is in the sense of using debt and other liabilities to finance assets. This ratio is often defined in terms of average total assets and average total equity and plays an important role in the DuPont decomposition of return on equity that will be presented in Section 4.6.2.

Interest Coverage   This ratio measures the number of times a company's EBIT could cover its interest payments. A higher interest coverage ratio indicates stronger solvency, offering greater assurance that the company can service its debt (i.e., bank debt, bonds, notes) from operating earnings.

Fixed Charge Coverage   This ratio relates fixed charges, or obligations, to the cash flow generated by the company. It measures the number of times a company's earnings (before interest, taxes, and lease payments) can cover the company's interest and lease payments.[9] Similar to the interest coverage ratio, a higher fixed charge coverage ratio implies stronger solvency, offering greater assurance that the company can service its debt (i.e., bank debt, bonds, notes, and leases) from normal earnings. The ratio is sometimes used as an indication of the quality of the preferred dividend, with a higher ratio indicating a more secure preferred dividend.

Example 9 demonstrates the use of solvency ratios in evaluating the creditworthiness of a company.

EXAMPLE 9

Evaluation of Solvency Ratios

A credit analyst is evaluating the solvency of Alcatel (now known as Alcatel-Lucent) as of the beginning of 2005. The following data are gathered from the company's 2005 annual report (in € millions):

	2004	2003
Total equity	4,389	4,038
Accrued pension	1,144	1,010
Other reserves	2,278	3,049
Total financial debt	4,359	5,293
Other liabilities	6,867	7,742
Total assets	19,037	21,132

---

[9] For computing this ratio, an assumption sometimes made is that one-third of the lease payment amount represents interest on the lease obligation and that the rest is a repayment of principal on the obligation. For this variant of the fixed charge coverage ratio, the numerator is EBIT plus one-third of lease payments and the denominator is interest payments plus one-third of lease payments.

The analyst concludes that, as used by Alcatel in its 2005 annual report, "total financial debt" consists of noncurrent debt and the interest-bearing, borrowed portion of current liabilities.

1. **A.** Calculate the company's financial leverage ratio for 2004.

   B. Interpret the financial leverage ratio calculated in Part A.

2. **A.** What are the company's debt-to-assets, debt-to-capital, and debt-to-equity ratios for the two years?

   B. Is there any discernable trend over the two years?

Solution to 1:

A. Average total assets was $(19,037 + 21,132)/2 = 20,084.50$ and average total equity was $(4,389 + 4,038)/2 = 4,213.5$. Thus, financial leverage was $20,084.50/4,213.5 = 4.77$.

B. For 2004, every €1 in total equity supported €4.77 in total assets, on average.

Solution to 2:

A. Debt-to-assets for 2003 = $5,293/21,132 = 25.05\%$

   Debt-to-assets for 2004 = $4,359/19,037 = 22.90\%$

   Debt-to-capital for 2003 = $5,293/(5,293 + 4,038) = 56.72\%$

   Debt-to-capital for 2004 = $4,359/(4,359 + 4,389) = 49.83\%$

   Debt-to-equity for 2003 = $5,293/4,038 = 1.31$

   Debt-to-equity for 2004 = $4,359/4,389 = 0.99$

B. On all three metrics, the company's level of debt has declined. This decrease in debt as part of the company's capital structure indicates that the company's solvency has improved. From a creditor's perspective, higher solvency (lower debt) indicates lower risk of default on obligations.

4.5 Profitability Ratios

The ability to generate profit on capital invested is a key determinant of a company's overall value and the value of the securities it issues. Consequently, many equity analysts would consider profitability to be a key focus of their analytical efforts.

Profitability reflects a company's competitive position in the market, and by extension, the quality of its management. The income statement reveals the sources of earnings and the components of revenue and expenses. Earnings can be distributed to shareholders or reinvested in the company. Reinvested earnings enhance solvency and provide a cushion against short-term problems.

4.5.1 Calculation of Profitability Ratios

Profitability ratios measure the return earned by the company during a period. Exhibit 12 provides the definitions of a selection of commonly used profitability

EXHIBIT 12	Definitions of Commonly Used Profitability Ratios	
Profitability Ratios	**Numerator**	**Denominator**
Return on Sales[10]		
Gross profit margin	Gross profit	Revenue
Operating profit margin	Operating income[11]	Revenue
Pretax margin	EBT (earnings before tax but after interest)	Revenue
Net profit margin	Net income	Revenue
Return on Investment		
Operating ROA	Operating income	Average total assets
ROA	Net income	Average total assets
Return on total capital	EBIT	Short- and long-term debt and equity
ROE	Net income	Average total equity
Return on common equity	Net income − Preferred dividends	Average common equity

ratios. Return-on-sales profitability ratios express various subtotals on the income statement (e.g., gross profit, operating profit, net profit) as a percentage of revenue. Essentially, these ratios constitute part of a common-size income statement discussed earlier. Return on investment profitability ratios measure income relative to assets, equity, or total capital employed by the company. For operating ROA, returns are measured as operating income (i.e., prior to deducting interest on debt capital). For ROA and ROE, returns are measured as net income (i.e., after deducting interest paid on debt capital). For return on common equity, returns are measured as net income minus preferred dividends (because preferred dividends are a return to preferred equity).

4.5.2 Interpretation of Profitability Ratios

In the following, we discuss the interpretation of the profitability ratios presented in Exhibit 12. For each of the profitability ratios, a higher ratio indicates greater profitability.

Gross Profit Margin   Gross profit margin indicates the percentage of revenue available to cover operating and other expenditures. Higher gross profit margin indicates some combination of higher product pricing and lower product costs.

---

[10] "Sales" is being used as a synonym for "revenue."

[11] Some analysts use EBIT as a shortcut representation of operating income. Note that EBIT, strictly speaking, includes nonoperating items such as dividends received and gains and losses on investment securities. Of utmost importance is that the analyst compute ratios consistently whether comparing different companies or analyzing one company over time.

The ability to charge a higher price is constrained by competition, so gross profits are affected by (and usually inversely related to) competition. If a product has a competitive advantage (e.g., superior branding, better quality, or exclusive technology), the company is better able to charge more for it. On the cost side, higher gross profit margin can also indicate that a company has a competitive advantage in product costs.

Operating Profit Margin   Operating profit is calculated as gross margin minus operating costs. So, an operating margin increasing faster than the gross margin can indicate improvements in controlling operating costs, such as administrative overheads. In contrast, a declining operating profit margin could be an indicator of deteriorating control over operating costs.

Pretax Margin   Pretax income (also called "earnings before tax") is calculated as operating profit minus interest, so this ratio reflects the effects on profitability of leverage and other (nonoperating) income and expenses. If a company's pretax margin is rising primarily as a result of increasing nonoperating income, the analyst should evaluate whether this increase reflects a deliberate change in a company's business focus and, therefore, the likelihood that the increase will continue.

Net Profit Margin   Net profit, or net income, is calculated as revenue minus all expenses. Net income includes both recurring and nonrecurring components. Generally, the net profit margin adjusted for nonrecurring items offers a better view of a company's potential future profitability.

ROA   ROA measures the return earned by a company on its assets. The higher the ratio, the more income is generated by a given level of assets. Most databases compute this ratio as:

$$\frac{\text{Net income}}{\text{Average total assets}}$$

The problem with this computation is net income is the return to equityholders, whereas assets are financed by both equityholders and creditors. Interest expense (the return to creditors) has already been subtracted in the numerator. Some analysts, therefore, prefer to add back interest expense in the numerator. In such cases, interest must be adjusted for income taxes because net income is determined after taxes. With this adjustment, the ratio would be computed as:

$$\frac{\text{Net income} \ + \ \text{Interest expense} \ (1 \ - \ \text{Tax rate})}{\text{Average total assets}}$$

Alternatively, some analysts elect to compute ROA on a pre-interest and pretax basis as:

$$\frac{\text{Operating income or EBIT}}{\text{Average total assets}}$$

As noted, returns are measured prior to deducting interest on debt capital (i.e., as operating income or EBIT). This measure reflects the return on all assets invested in the company, whether financed with liabilities, debt, or equity. Whichever form of ROA that is chosen, the analyst must use it consistently in comparisons to other companies or time periods.

Return on Total Capital   Return on total capital measures the profits a company earns on all of the capital that it employs (short-term debt, long-term debt, and equity). As with ROA, returns are measured prior to deducting interest on debt capital (i.e., as operating income or EBIT).

ROE   ROE measures the return earned by a company on its equity capital, including minority equity, preferred equity, and common equity. As noted, return is measured as net income (i.e., interest on debt capital is not included in the return on equity capital). A variation of ROE is return on common equity, which measures the return earned by a company only on its common equity.

Both ROA and ROE are important measures of profitability and will be explored in more detail below. As with other ratios, profitability ratios should be evaluated individually and as a group to gain an understanding of what is driving profitability (operating versus nonoperating activities). Example 10 demonstrates the evaluation of profitability ratios and the use of management's discussion that accompanies financial statements to explain the trend in ratios.

EXAMPLE 10

Evaluation of Profitability Ratios

An analyst is evaluating the profitability of DaimlerChrysler (NYSE: DCX) over a recent three-year period and collects the following profitability ratios:

	2004 (%)	2003 (%)	2002 (%)
Gross profit margin	19.35	19.49	18.99
Operating profit margin	3.19	2.83	3.35
Pretax margin	2.49	0.44	4.06
Net profit margin	1.74	0.33	3.15

DCX's 2003 Annual Report indicates that revenue declined in 2003. Furthermore, management's discussion of results in that report notes the following:

> General administrative expenses of €5.4 billion remained virtually flat on the prior-year level. General administrative expenses as a percentage of revenues were 3.9 percent in 2003 and 3.6 percent in 2002, reflecting the limited variability of these expenses. Slightly higher personnel expenses, primarily caused by higher net periodic pension and post-retirement benefit costs, resulted in a moderate increase of general administrative expenses.

1. Contrast gross profit margins and operating profit margins over 2002 to 2004.
2. Explain the decline in operating profit margin in 2003.
3. Explain why the pretax margin might decrease to a greater extent than the operating profit margin in 2003.

4. Compare and contrast net profit margins and pretax margins over 2002 to 2004.

Solution to 1: Gross margin improved from 2002 to 2003 as a result of some combination of price increases and/or cost control. However, gross margin declined slightly in 2004. Operating profit margin, on the other hand, declined from 2002 to 2003, and then improved in 2004.

Solution to 2: The decline in operating profit from 3.35 percent in 2002 to 2.83 percent in 2003 appears to be the result of DCX's operating leverage, discussed in management's discussion. Revenue declined in 2003 but, according to management, general administrative expenses were virtually flat compared with 2002. These expenses thus increased as a proportion of revenue in 2003, lowering the operating profit margin. This is an example of the effects of fixed cost on profitability. In general, as revenues rise, to the extent that costs remain fixed, operating margins should increase. However, if revenue declines, the opposite occurs.

Solution to 3: Pretax margin was down substantially in 2003, indicating that the company may have had some nonoperating losses or high interest expense in that year. A review of the company's financial statement footnotes confirms that the cause was nonoperating losses: Specifically, the company had a significant impairment loss on investments in 2003.

Solution to 4: Net profit margin followed the same pattern as pretax margin, declining substantially in 2003, then improving in 2004 but not reaching 2002 levels. In the absence of major variation in the applicable tax rates, this would be the expected as net income is $EBT(1 - \text{tax rate})$.

4.6 Integrated Financial Ratio Analysis

In prior sections, the text presented separately activity, liquidity, solvency, and profitability ratios. In the following, we illustrate the importance of examining a portfolio of ratios, not a single ratio or category of ratios in isolation, to ascertain the overall position and performance of a company. Experience shows that the information from one ratio category can be helpful in answering questions raised by another category and that the most accurate overall picture comes from integrating information from all sources. Section 4.6.1 provides some introductory examples of such analysis and Section 4.6.2 shows how return on equity can be analyzed into components related to profit margin, asset utilization (activity), and financial leverage.

4.6.1 The Overall Ratio Picture: Examples

This section presents two simple illustrations to introduce the use of a portfolio of ratios to address an analytical task. Example 11 shows how the analysis of a pair of activity ratios resolves an issue concerning a company's liquidity. Example 12 shows that examining the overall ratios of multiple companies can assist an analyst in drawing conclusions about their relative performances.

EXAMPLE 11

A Portfolio of Ratios

An analyst is evaluating the liquidity of a Canadian manufacturing company and obtains the following liquidity ratios:

	2005	2004	2003
Current ratio	2.1	1.9	1.6
Quick ratio	0.8	0.9	1.0

The ratios present a contradictory picture of the company's liquidity. Based on the increase in its current ratio from 1.6 to 2.1, the company appears to have strong and improving liquidity; however, based on the decline of the quick ratio from 1.0 to 0.8, its liquidity appears to be deteriorating. Because both ratios have exactly the same denominator, current liabilities, the difference must be the result of changes in some asset that is included in the current ratio but not in the quick ratio (e.g., inventories). The analyst collects the following activity ratios:

DOH	55	45	30
DSO	24	28	30

The company's DOH has deteriorated from 30 days to 55 days, meaning that the company is holding increasingly greater amounts of inventory relative to sales. The decrease in DSO implies that the company is collecting receivables faster. If the proceeds from these collections were held as cash, there would be no effect on either the current ratio or the quick ratio. However, if the proceeds from the collections were used to purchase inventory, there would be no effect on the current ratio and a decline in the quick ratio (i.e., the pattern shown in this example). Collectively, the ratios suggest that liquidity is declining and that the company may have an inventory problem that needs to be addressed.

EXAMPLE 12

A Comparison of Two Companies (1)

An analyst collects the following information for two companies:

Anson Industries	2005	2004	2003	2002
Inventory turnover	76.69	89.09	147.82	187.64
DOH	4.76	4.10	2.47	1.95

Anson Industries	2005	2004	2003	2002
Receivables turnover	10.75	9.33	11.14	7.56
DSO	33.95	39.13	32.77	48.29
Accounts payable turnover	4.62	4.36	4.84	4.22
Days payable	78.97	83.77	75.49	86.56
Cash from operations/ Total liabilities	31.41%	11.15%	4.04%	8.81%
ROE	5.92%	1.66%	1.62%	−0.62%
ROA	3.70%	1.05%	1.05%	−0.39%
Net profit margin (Net income/Revenue)	3.33%	1.11%	1.13%	−0.47%
Total asset turnover (Revenue/Average assets)	1.11	0.95	0.93	0.84
Leverage (Average assets/ Average equity)	1.60	1.58	1.54	1.60

Clarence Corporation	2005	2004	2003	2002
Inventory turnover	9.19	9.08	7.52	14.84
DOH	39.73	40.20	48.51	24.59
Receivables turnover	8.35	7.01	6.09	5.16
DSO	43.73	52.03	59.92	70.79
Accounts payable turnover	6.47	6.61	7.66	6.52
Days payable	56.44	55.22	47.64	56.00
Cash from operations/ Total liabilities	13.19%	16.39%	15.80%	11.79%
ROE	9.28%	6.82%	−3.63%	−6.75%
ROA	4.64%	3.48%	−1.76%	3.23%
Net profit margin (Net income/Revenue)	4.38%	3.48%	−1.60%	−2.34%
Total asset turnover (Revenue/Average assets)	1.06	1.00	1.10	1.38
Leverage (Average assets/ Average equity)	2.00	1.96	2.06	2.09

Which of the following choices best describes reasonable conclusions an analyst might make about the companies' efficiency?

A. Over the past four years, Anson has shown greater improvement in efficiency than Clarence, as indicated by its total asset turnover ratio increasing from 0.84 to 1.11.

B. In 2005, Anson's DOH of only 4.76 indicated that it was less efficient at inventory management than Clarence, which had DOH of 39.73.

C. In 2005, Clarence's receivables turnover of 8.35 times indicated that it was more efficient at receivables management than Anson, which had receivables turnover of 10.75.

D. Over the past four years, Clarence has shown greater improvement in efficiency than Anson, as indicated by its net profit margin of 4.38 percent.

Solution: A is correct. Over the past four years, Anson has shown greater improvement in efficiency than Clarence, as indicated by its total asset turnover ratio increasing from 0.84 to 1.11. Over the same period of time, Clarence's total asset turnover ratio has declined from 1.38 to 1.06. Choice B is incorrect because it misinterprets DOH. Choice C is incorrect because it misinterprets receivables turnover. Choice D is incorrect because net profit margin is not an indicator of efficiency.

4.6.2 DuPont Analysis: The Decomposition of ROE

As noted earlier, ROE measures the return a company generates on its equity capital. To understand what drives a company's ROE, a useful technique is to decompose ROE into its component parts. (Decomposition of ROE is sometimes referred to as **DuPont analysis** because it was developed originally at that company.) Decomposing ROE involves expressing the basic ratio (i.e., net income divided by average shareholders' equity) as the product of component ratios. Because each of these component ratios is an indicator of a distinct aspect of a company's performance that affects ROE, the decomposition allows us to evaluate how these different aspects of performance affected the company's profitability as measured by ROE.[12]

Decomposing ROE is useful in determining the reasons for changes in ROE over time for a given company and for differences in ROE for different companies in a given time period. The information gained can also be used by management to determine which areas they should focus on to improve ROE. This decomposition will also show why a company's overall profitability, measured by ROE, is a function of its efficiency, operating profitability, taxes, and use of financial leverage. DuPont analysis shows the relationship between the various categories of ratios discussed in this reading and how they all influence the return to the investment of the owners.

Analysts have developed several different methods of decomposing ROE. The decomposition presented here is one of the most commonly used and the one found in popular research databases, such as Bloomberg. Return on equity is calculated as:

ROE = Net income/Average shareholders' equity

---

[12] For purposes of analyzing ROE, this method usually uses average balance sheet factors; however, the math will work out if beginning or ending balances are used throughout. For certain purposes, these alternative methods may be appropriate. See Stowe et al. (2002, pp. 85–88).

The decomposition of ROE makes use of simple algebra and illustrates the relationship between ROE and ROA. Expressing ROE as a product of only two of its components, we can write:

$$\text{ROE} = \frac{\text{Net income}}{\text{Average shareholders' equity}}$$

$$= \frac{\text{Net income}}{\text{Average total assets}} \times \frac{\text{Average total assets}}{\text{Average shareholders' equity}}$$

(1a)

which can be interpreted as:

$$\text{ROE} = \text{ROA} \times \text{Leverage}$$

In other words, ROE is a function of a company's ROA and its use of financial leverage ("leverage" for short, in this discussion). A company can improve its ROE by improving ROA or making more effective use of leverage. Consistent with the definition given earlier, leverage is measured as average total assets divided by average shareholders' equity. If a company had no leverage (no liabilities), its leverage ratio would equal 1.0 and ROE would exactly equal ROA. As a company takes on liabilities, its leverage increases. As long as a company is able to borrow at a rate lower than the marginal rate it can earn investing the borrowed money in its business, the company is making an effective use of leverage and ROE would increase as leverage increases. If a company's borrowing cost exceeds the marginal rate it can earn on investing, ROE would decline as leverage increased because the effect of borrowing would be to depress ROA.

Using the data from Example 12 for Anson Industries, an analyst can examine the trend in ROE and determine whether the increase from an ROE of −0.625 percent in 2002 to 5.925 percent in 2005 is a function of ROA or the use of leverage:

	ROE	=	ROA	×	Leverage
2005	5.92%		3.70%		1.60
2004	1.66%		1.05%		1.58
2003	1.62%		1.05%		1.54
2002	−0.62%		−0.39%		1.60

Over the four-year period, the company's leverage factor was relatively stable. The primary reason for the increase in ROE is the increase in profitability measured by ROA.

Just as ROE can be decomposed, the individual components such as ROA can be decomposed. Further decomposing ROA, we can express ROE as a product of three component ratios:

$$\frac{\text{Net income}}{\text{Average shareholders' equity}} = \frac{\text{Net income}}{\text{Revenue}} \times \frac{\text{Revenue}}{\text{Average total assets}}$$

$$\times \frac{\text{Average total assets}}{\text{Average shareholders' equity}}$$

(1b)

which can be interpreted as:

$$ROE = \text{Net profit margin} \times \text{Asset turnover} \times \text{Leverage}$$

The first term on the right-hand side of this equation is the net profit margin, an indicator of profitability: how much income a company derives per one money unit (e.g., euro or dollar) of sales. The second term on the right is the asset turnover ratio, an indicator of efficiency: how much revenue a company generates per one money unit of assets. Note that ROA is decomposed into these two components: net profit margin and asset turnover. A company's ROA is a function of profitability (net profit margin) and efficiency (asset turnover). The third term on the right-hand side of Equation 1b is a measure of financial leverage, an indicator of solvency: the total amount of a company's assets relative to its equity capital. This decomposition illustrates that a company's ROE is a function of its net profit margin, its efficiency, and its leverage. Again, using the data from Example 12 for Anson Industries, the analyst can evaluate in more detail the reasons behind the trend in ROE:[13]

	ROE	=	Net profit margin	×	Asset turnover	×	Leverage
2005	5.92%		3.33%		1.11		1.60
2004	1.66%		1.11%		0.95		1.58
2003	1.62%		1.13%		0.93		1.54
2002	−0.62%		−0.47%		0.84		1.60

This further decomposition confirms that increases in profitability (measured here as net profit margin) are indeed an important contributor to the increase in ROE over the four-year period. However, Anson's asset turnover has also increased steadily. The increase in ROE is, therefore, a function of improving profitability and improving efficiency. As noted above, ROE decomposition can also be used to compare the ROEs of peer companies, as demonstrated in Example 13.

EXAMPLE 13

A Comparison of Two Companies (2)

Referring to the data for Anson Industries and Clarence Corporation in Example 12, which of the following choices best describes reasonable conclusions an analyst might make about the companies' ROE?

A. Anson's inventory turnover of 76.69 indicates it is more profitable than Clarence.

B. The main drivers of Clarence's superior ROE in 2005 are its greater use of debt financing and higher net profit margin.

C. The main driver of Clarence's superior ROE in 2005 is its more efficient use of assets.

D. Anson's days payable of 78.97 indicates it is more profitable than Clarence.

---

[13] Please note that ratios are expressed in terms of two decimal places and are rounded. Therefore, ROE may not be the exact product of the three ratios.

> **Solution:** B is correct. The main driver of Clarence's superior ROE (9.29 percent compared with only 5.94 percent for Anson) in 2005 is its greater use of debt financing (leverage of 2.00 compared with Anson's leverage of 1.60) and higher net profit margin (4.38 percent compared with only 3.33 percent for Anson). A and D are incorrect because neither inventory turnover nor days payable is an indicator of profitability. C is incorrect because Clarence has less-efficient use of assets than Anson, indicated by turnover of 1.06 for Clarence compared with Anson's turnover of 1.11.

To separate the effects of taxes and interest, we can further decompose the net profit margin and write:

$$\frac{\text{Net income}}{\text{Average shareholders' equity}} = \frac{\text{Net income}}{\text{EBT}} \times \frac{\text{EBT}}{\text{EBIT}} \times \frac{\text{EBIT}}{\text{Revenue}}$$

$$\times \frac{\text{Revenue}}{\text{Average total assets}} \times \frac{\text{Average total assets}}{\text{Average shareholders' equity}} \qquad \textbf{(1c)}$$

which can be interpreted as:

ROE = Tax burden $\times$ Interest burden $\times$ EBIT margin
$\times$ Asset turnover $\times$ Leverage

This five-way decomposition is the one found in financial databases such as Bloomberg. The first term on the right-hand side of this equation measures the effect of taxes on ROE. Essentially, it reflects one minus the average tax rate, or how much of a company's pretax profits it gets to keep. This can be expressed in decimal or percentage form. So, a 30 percent tax rate would yield a factor of 0.70 or 70 percent. A higher value for the tax burden implies that the company can keep a higher percentage of its pretax profits, indicating a lower tax rate. A decrease in the tax burden ratio implies the opposite (i.e., a higher tax rate leaving the company with less of its pretax profits).

The second term on the right-hand side captures the effect of interest on ROE. Higher borrowing costs reduce ROE. Some analysts prefer to use operating income instead of EBIT for this factor and the following one (consistency is required!). In such a case, the second factor would measure both the effect of interest expense and nonoperating income.

The third term on the right-hand side captures the effect of operating margin (if operating income is used in the numerator) or EBIT margin (if EBIT is used) on ROE. In either case, this factor primarily measures the effect of operating profitability on ROE.

The fourth term on the right-hand side is again the asset turnover ratio, an indicator of the overall efficiency of the company (i.e., how much revenue it generates per unit of assets). The fifth term on the right-hand side is the financial leverage ratio described above—the total amount of a company's assets relative to its equity capital.

This decomposition expresses a company's ROE as a function of its tax rate, interest burden, operating profitability, efficiency, and leverage. An analyst can use this framework to determine what factors are driving a company's ROE. The decomposition of ROE can also be useful in forecasting ROE based upon expected efficiency, profitability, financing activities, and tax rates. The relationship of the individual factors, such as ROA to the overall ROE, can also be expressed in the form of an ROE tree to study the contribution of each of the five factors, as shown in Exhibit 13 for Anson Industries.[14]

Exhibit 13 shows that Anson's ROE of 5.92 percent in 2005 can be decomposed into ROA of 3.7 percent and leverage of 1.60. ROA can further be decomposed into a net profit margin of 3.33 percent and total asset turnover of 1.11. Net profit margin can be decomposed into a tax burden of 0.70 (an average tax rate of 30 percent), an interest burden of 0.90, and an EBIT margin of 5.29 percent. Overall ROE is decomposed into five components.

EXHIBIT 13	DuPont Analysis of Anson Industries' ROE: 2005

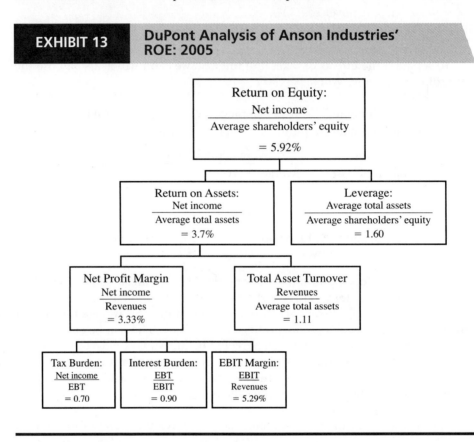

Example 14 demonstrates how the five-component decomposition can be used to determine reasons behind the trend in a company's ROE.

EXAMPLE 14

Five-Way Decomposition of ROE

An analyst examining BP PLC (BP) wishes to understand the factors driving the trend in ROE over a recent three-year period. The analyst obtains the following data from Bloomberg and ascertains that Bloomberg has included nonoperating income in the interest burden factor:

---

[14] Note that a breakdown of net profit margin was not provided in Example 12, but is added here.

	2004	2003	2002
ROE	20.62%	14.42%	10.17%
Tax burden	64.88%	62.52%	60.67%
Interest burden	130.54%	112.60%	130.50%
EBIT margin	6.51%	6.40%	4.84%
Asset turnover	1.55	1.38	1.19
Leverage	2.42	2.32	2.24

What might the analyst conclude?

Solution: Because the tax burden reflects the relation of after-tax profits to pretax profits, the increase from 60.67 percent to 64.88 percent indicates that taxes declined as a percentage of pretax profits. This decline in average tax rates could be due to lower tax rates from new legislation or revenue in a lower tax jurisdiction. An interest burden factor greater than 100 percent means that nonoperating income exceeded interest expense in all three years. Operating margin (EBIT margin) improved, particularly from 2002 to 2003, indicating the company's operations were more profitable. The company's efficiency (asset turnover) increased each year as did its leverage. Overall, the trend in ROE (doubling in three years) did not result from a single aspect of the company's performance, but instead was a function of lower average tax rates, increasing operating profits, greater efficiency, and increased use of leverage. Additional research on the causes of the various changes is required in order to develop expectations about the company's future performance.

The most detailed decomposition of ROE that we have presented is a five-way decomposition. Nevertheless, an analyst could further decompose individual components of a five-way analysis. For example, EBIT margin (EBIT/Revenue) could be further decomposed into a nonoperating component (EBIT/Operating income) and an operating component (Operating income/Revenues). The analyst can also examine which other factors contributed to these five components. For example, an improvement in efficiency (total asset turnover) may have resulted from better management of inventory (DOH) or better collection of receivables (DSO).

EQUITY ANALYSIS   5

One application of financial analysis is to select securities as part of the equity portfolio management process. Analysts are interested in valuing a security to assess its merits for inclusion or retention in a portfolio. The valuation process has several steps, including:[15]

---

[15] Stowe et al. (2002, p. 6).

1. understanding the business and the existing financial profile
2. forecasting company performance
3. selecting the appropriate valuation model
4. converting forecasts to a valuation
5. making the investment decision

Financial analysis assists in providing the core information to complete the first two steps of this valuation process: understanding the business and forecasting performance.

Fundamental equity analysis involves evaluating a company's performance and valuing its equity in order to assess its relative attractiveness as an investment. Analysts use a variety of methods to value a company's equity, including valuation ratios (e.g., the price-to-earnings or P/E ratio), discounted cash flow approaches, and residual income approaches (ROE compared with the cost of capital), among others. The following section addresses the first of these approaches—the use of valuation ratios.

5.1 Valuation Ratios

Valuation ratios have long been used in investment decision making. A well-known example is the P/E ratio—probably the most widely used indicator in discussing the value of equity securities—which relates share price to the earnings per share (EPS). Additionally, some analysts use other market multiples, such as price to book value (P/B) and price to cash flow (P/CF). The following sections explore valuation ratios and other quantities related to valuing equities.

5.1.1 Calculation of Valuation Ratios and Related Quantities

Exhibit 14 describes the calculation of some common valuation ratios and related quantities.

The P/E ratio expresses the relationship between the price per share and the amount of earnings attributable to a single share. In other words, the P/E ratio tells us how much an investor in common stock pays per dollar of current earnings.

Because P/E ratios are calculated using net income, the ratios can be sensitive to nonrecurring earnings or one-off earnings events. In addition, because net income is generally considered to be more susceptible to manipulation than are cash flows, analysts may use **price to cash flow** as an alternative measure—particularly in situations where earnings quality may be an issue. EBITDA per share, because it is calculated using income before interest, taxes, and depreciation, can be used to eliminate the effect of different levels of fixed asset investment across companies. It facilitates comparison between companies in the same sector but at different stages of infrastructure maturity. **Price to sales** is calculated in a similar manner and is sometimes used as a comparative price metric when a company does not have positive net income.

Another price-based ratio that facilitates useful comparisons of companies' stock prices is **price to book value**, or P/B, which is the ratio of price to book value per share. This ratio is often interpreted as an indicator of market judgment about the relationship between a company's required rate of return and its actual rate of return. Assuming that book values reflect the fair values of the assets, a price to book ratio of one can be interpreted as an indicator that the company's future returns are expected to be exactly equal to the returns required by the market. A

EXHIBIT 14	Definitions of Selected Valuation Ratios and Related Quantities	
	Numerator	**Denominator**
Valuation Ratios		
P/E	Price per share	Earnings per share
P/CF	Price per share	Cash flow per share
P/S	Price per share	Sales per share
P/BV	Price per share	Book value per share
Per-Share Quantities		
Basic EPS	Net income minus preferred dividends	Weighted average number of ordinary shares outstanding
Diluted EPS	Adjusted income available for ordinary shares, reflecting conversion of dilutive securities	Weighted average number of ordinary and potential ordinary shares outstanding
Cash flow per share	Cash flow from operations	Average number of shares outstanding
EBITDA per share	EBITDA	Average number of shares outstanding
Dividends per share	Common dividends declared	Weighted average number of ordinary shares outstanding
Dividend-Related Quantities		
Dividend payout ratio	Common share dividends	Net income attributable to common shares
Retention rate (b)	Net income attributable to common shares − Common share dividends	Net income attributable to common shares
Sustainable growth rate	$b \times$ ROE	

ratio greater than one would indicate that the future profitability of the company is expected to exceed the required rate of return, and values of this ratio less than one indicate that the company is not expected to earn excess returns.[16]

5.1.2 Interpretation of Earnings per Share

Exhibit 14 presented a number of per-share quantities that can be used in valuation ratios. In the following, we discuss the interpretation of one such critical quantity, EPS.

---

[16] For more detail on valuation ratios as used in equity analysis, see Stowe et al. (2002).

EPS is simply the amount of earnings attributable to each share of common stock. In isolation, EPS does not provide adequate information for comparison of one company with another. For example, assume that two companies have only common stock outstanding and no dilutive securities outstanding. In addition, assume the two companies have identical net income of $10 million, identical book equity of $100 million and, therefore, identical profitability (10 percent, using ending equity in this case for simplicity). Furthermore, assume that Company A has 100 million weighted average common shares outstanding, whereas Company B has 10 million weighted average common shares outstanding. So, Company A will report EPS of $0.10 per share, and Company B will report EPS of $1 per share. The difference in EPS does not reflect a difference in profitability—the companies have identical profits and profitability. The difference reflects only a different number of common shares outstanding.

Analysts should understand in detail the types of EPS information that companies report:

Basic EPS provides information regarding the earnings attributable to each share of common stock. International Accounting Standards (IAS) No. 33 contains the international principles for the determination and presentation of EPS. This standard applies to entities whose shares are publicly traded or in the process of being issued in public securities markets, and other entities that choose to disclose EPS. U.S. Financial Accounting Standards Board Statement No. 128 contains the standards for computing and presenting EPS.[17]

To calculate basic EPS, the weighted average number of shares outstanding during the period is first calculated. The weighted average number of shares consists of the number of ordinary shares outstanding at the beginning of the period, adjusted by those bought back or issued during the period, multiplied by a time-weighting factor.

Accounting standards generally require the disclosure of basic as well as diluted EPS (**diluted EPS** includes the effect of all the company's securities whose conversion or exercise would result in a reduction of basic EPS; dilutive securities include convertible debt, convertible preferred, warrants, and options). Basic EPS and diluted EPS must be shown with equal prominence on the face of the income statement for each class of ordinary share. Disclosure includes the amounts used as the numerators in calculating basic and diluted EPS, and a reconciliation of those amounts to the company's profit or loss for the period. Because both basic and diluted EPS are presented in a company's financial statements, an analyst does not need to calculate these measures for reported financial statements. Understanding the calculations is, however, helpful for situations requiring an analyst to calculate expected future EPS.

To calculate diluted EPS, earnings are adjusted for the after-tax effects assuming conversion, and the following adjustments are made to the weighted number of shares:

▶ The weighted average number of shares for basic EPS, *plus* those that would be issued on conversion of all dilutive potential ordinary shares. Potential ordinary shares are treated as dilutive when their conversion would decrease net profit per share from continuing ordinary operations.

▶ These shares are deemed to have been converted into ordinary shares at the beginning of the period or, if later, at the date of the issue of the shares.

▶ Options, warrants (and their equivalents), convertible instruments, contingently issuable shares, contracts that can be settled in ordinary shares or cash, purchased options, and written put options should be considered.

---

[17] FASB ASC Topic 260 [Earnings Per Share].

5.1.3 Dividend-Related Quantities

In the following, we discuss the interpretation of the dividend-related quantities presented in Exhibit 14. These quantities play a role in some present value models for valuing equities.

Dividend Payout Ratio   The dividend payout ratio measures the percentage of earnings that the company pays out as dividends to shareholders. The amount of dividends per share tends to be relatively fixed because any reduction in dividends has been shown to result in a disproportionately large reduction in share price. Because dividend amounts are relatively fixed, the dividend payout ratio tends to fluctuate with earnings. Therefore, conclusions about a company's dividend payout policies should be based on examination of payout over a number of periods. Optimal dividend policy, similar to optimal capital structure, has been examined in academic research and continues to be a topic of significant interest in corporate finance.

Retention Rate   The retention rate is the complement of the payout ratio (i.e., 1 − payout ratio). Whereas the payout ratio measures the percentage of earnings that a company pays out as dividends, the retention rate is the percentage of earnings that a company retains. It is simply one minus the payout ratio. (Note that both the dividend payout ratio and retention rate are both percentages of earnings. The difference in terminology—"ratio" versus "rate" versus "percentage"—reflects common usage rather than any substantive differences.)

Sustainable Growth Rate   A company's sustainable growth rate is viewed as a function of its profitability (measured as ROE) and its ability to finance itself from internally generated funds (measured as the retention rate). A higher ROE and a higher retention rate result in a higher sustainable growth rate. This calculation can be used to estimate a company's growth rate, a factor commonly used in equity valuation.

5.2 Industry-Specific Ratios

As stated earlier in this reading, a universally accepted definition and classification of ratios do not exist. The purpose of ratios is to serve as indicators of important aspects of a company's performance and value. Aspects of performance that are considered important in one industry may be irrelevant in another, and industry-specific ratios reflect these differences. For example, companies in the retail industry may report same-store sales changes because, in the retail industry, it is important to distinguish between growth that results from opening new stores and growth that results from generating more sales at existing stores. Industry-specific metrics can be especially important to the value of equity in early stage industries, where companies are not yet profitable.

In addition, regulated industries—especially in the financial sector—often are required to comply with specific regulatory ratios. For example, the banking sector's liquidity and cash reserve ratios provide an indication of banking liquidity and reflect monetary and political requirements. Banking capital adequacy requirements, although not perfect, do relate banks' solvency requirements directly to their specific levels of risk exposure.

Exhibit 15 presents some industry-specific and task-specific ratios.[18]

---

[18] These are provided for illustrative purposes only. There are many other industry-specific ratios that are outside the scope of this reading. Resources such as Standard and Poor's Industry Surveys present useful ratios for each industry.

EXHIBIT 15	Definitions of Some Common Industry and Task-Specific Ratios	

Ratios	Numerator	Denominator
Business Risk		
Coefficient of variation of operating income	Standard deviation of operating income	Average operating income
Coefficient of variation of net income	Standard deviation of net income	Average net income
Coefficient of variation of revenues	Standard deviation of revenue	Average revenue
Financial Sector Ratios		
Capital adequacy—banks	Various components of capital	Risk-weighted assets, market risk exposure, and level of operational risk assumed
Monetary reserve requirement	Reserves held at central bank	Specified deposit liabilities
Liquid asset requirement	Approved "readily marketable" securities	Specified deposit liabilities
Net interest margin	Net interest income	Total interest-earning assets
Retail Ratios		
Same (or comparable) store sales	Average revenue growth year over year for stores open in both periods	Not applicable
Sales per square foot (meter)	Revenue	Total retail space in feet or meters
Service Companies		
Revenue per employee	Revenue	Total number of employees
Net income per employee	Net income	Total number of employees
Hotel		
Average daily rate	Room revenue	Number of rooms sold
Occupancy rate	Number of rooms sold	Number of rooms available

5.3 Research on Ratios in Equity Analysis

Some ratios should be expected to be particularly useful in equity analysis. The end product of equity analysis is often a valuation and investment recommendation. Theoretical valuation models are useful in selecting ratios that would be useful in this process. For example, a company's P/B is theoretically linked to ROE, growth, and the required return. ROE is also a primary determinate of residual income in a residual income valuation model. In both cases, higher ROE relative to the required return denotes a higher valuation. Similarly, profit margin is related to justified price-to-sales (P/S) ratios. Another common valuation method involves forecasts of future cash flows that are discounted back to the present. Trends in ratios can be useful in forecasting future earnings and cash flows (e.g., trends in operating profit margin and collection of customer receivables). Future growth expectations are a key component of all of these valuation models. Trends may be useful in assessing growth prospects (when used in conjunction with overall economic and industry trends). The variability in ratios and common-size data can be useful in assessing risk, an important component of the required rate of return in valuation models. A great deal of academic research has focused on the use of these fundamental ratios in evaluating equity investments.

A classic study, Ou and Penman (1989a and 1989b), found that ratios and common-size metrics generated from accounting data were useful in forecasting earnings and stock returns. Ou and Penman examined a variety of 68 such metrics and found that these variables could be reduced to a more parsimonious list and combined in a statistical model that was particularly useful for selecting investments. These variables included:

▶ percentage change in current ratio;

▶ percentage change in quick ratio;

▶ percentage change in inventory turnover;

▶ inventory/total assets (a common-size measure) and the percentage change in this metric;

▶ percentage change in inventory;

▶ percentage change in sales;

▶ percentage change in depreciation;

▶ change in dividend per share;

▶ percentage change in depreciation to plant assets ratio;

▶ ROE;

▶ change in ROE;

▶ percentage change in capital expenditures to total assets ratio (contemporaneously and lagged);

▶ debt-to-equity ratio and the percentage change in this ratio;

▶ percentage change in total asset turnover;

▶ ROA;

▶ gross margin;

▶ pretax margin;

▶ sales to total cash;

▶ percentage change in total assets;

▶ cash flow to debt;

▶ working capital to total assets;

- ▶ operating ROA;
- ▶ repayment of long-term debt to total long-term debt;
- ▶ cash dividend to cash flows.

Subsequent studies have also demonstrated the use of ratios in evaluation of equity investments and valuation. Lev and Thiagarajan (1993) examined fundamental financial variables used by analysts to assess whether they are useful in security valuation. They found that fundamental variables add about 70 percent to the explanatory power of earnings alone in predicting excess returns (stock returns in excess of those expected). The fundamental variables they found useful included percentage changes in inventory and receivables relative to sales, gross margin, sales per employee, and the change in bad debts relative to the change in accounts receivable, among others. Abarbanell and Bushee (1997) found some of the same variables useful in predicting future accounting earnings. Abarbanell and Bushee (1998) devised an investment strategy using these same variables and found that they can generate excess returns under this strategy.

Piotroski (2000) used financial ratios to supplement a value investing strategy and found that he can generate significant excess returns. Variables used by Piotroski include ROA, cash flow ROA, change in ROA, change in leverage, change in liquidity, change in gross margin, and change in inventory turnover.

This research shows that in addition to being useful in evaluating the past performance of a company, ratios can be useful in predicting future earnings and equity returns.

6   CREDIT ANALYSIS

Credit risk is the risk of loss caused by a counterparty's or debtor's failure to make a promised payment. For example, credit risk with respect to a bond is the risk that the obligor (the issuer of the bond) is not able to pay interest and principal according to the terms of the bond indenture (contract). **Credit analysis** is the evaluation of credit risk.

Approaches to credit analysis vary and, as with all financial analysis, depend on the purpose of the analysis and the context in which it is done. Credit analysis for specific types of debt (e.g., acquisition financing and other highly leveraged financing) often involves projections of period-by-period cash flows similar to projections made by equity analysts. Whereas the equity analyst may discount projected cash flows to determine the value of the company's equity, a credit analyst would use the projected cash flows to assess the likelihood of a company complying with its financial covenants in each period and paying interest and principal as due.[19] The analysis would also include expectations about asset sales and refinancing options open to the company.

Credit analysis may relate to the borrower's credit risk in a particular transaction or to its overall credit-worthiness. In assessing overall credit-worthiness, one general approach is credit scoring, a statistical analysis of the determinants of credit default.

Another general approach to credit analysis is the credit rating process that is used, for example, by credit rating agencies to assess and communicate the proba-

---

[19] Financial covenants are clauses in bond indentures relating to the financial condition of the bond issuer.

bility of default by an issuer on its debt obligations (e.g., commercial paper, notes, and bonds). A credit rating can be either long term or short term and is an indication of the rating agency's opinion of the credit-worthiness of a debt issuer with respect to a specific debt security or other obligation. Where a company has no debt outstanding, a rating agency can also provide an issuer credit rating that expresses an opinion of the issuer's overall capacity and willingness to meet its financial obligations. The following sections review research on the use of ratios in credit analysis and the ratios commonly used in credit analysis.

6.1 The Credit Rating Process

The rating process involves both the analysis of a company's financial reports as well as a broad assessment of a company's operations. The credit rating process includes many of the following procedures:[20]

▶ Meeting with management, typically including the chief financial officer, to discuss, for example, industry outlook, overview of major business segments, financial policies and goals, distinctive accounting practices, capital spending plans, and financial contingency plans.

▶ Tours of major facilities, time permitting.

▶ Meeting of a ratings committee where the analyst's recommendations are voted on, after considering factors that include:

   ▶ Business risk, including the evaluation of:

      ▶ operating environment;

      ▶ industry characteristics (e.g., cyclicality and capital intensity);

      ▶ success factors and areas of vulnerability;

      ▶ company's competitive position, including size and diversification;

   ▶ Financial risk, including:

      ▶ the evaluation of capital structure, interest coverage, and profitability using ratio analysis;

      ▶ the examination of debt covenants;

   ▶ Evaluation of management.

▶ Monitoring of publicly distributed ratings—including reconsideration of ratings due to changing conditions.

In assigning credit ratings, rating agencies emphasize the importance of the relationship between a company's business risk profile and its financial risk. "The company's business risk profile determines the level of financial risk appropriate for any rating category."[21]

When analyzing financial ratios, rating agencies normally investigate deviations of ratios from the median ratios of the universe of companies for which such ratios have been calculated and also use the median ratings as an indicator for the ratings grade given to a specific debt issuer. This so-called universe of rated companies changes constantly, and any calculations are obviously affected by economic factors as well as by mergers and acquisitions. International ratings include the influence of country and economic risk factors. Exhibit 16 presents

---

[20] Based on Standard & Poor's Corporate Ratings Criteria (2006).

[21] Standard & Poor's Corporate Ratings Criteria (2006), p. 23.

EXHIBIT 16	Selected Credit Ratios Used by Standard & Poor's	
Credit Ratio	**Numerator[a]**	**Denominator[b]**
EBIT interest coverage	EBIT	Gross interest (prior to deductions for capitalized interest or interest income)
EBITDA interest coverage	EBITDA	Gross interest (prior to deductions for capitalized interest or interest income)
Funds from operations to total debt	FFO (net income adjusted for non-cash items)[c]	Total debt
Free operating cash flow to total debt	CFO (adjusted) less capital expenditures[d]	Total debt
Total debt to EBITDA	Total debt	EBITDA
Return on capital	EBIT	Capital = Average equity (common and preferred stock) and short-term portions of debt, noncurrent deferred taxes, minority interest
Total debt to total debt plus equity	Total debt	Total debt plus equity

[a] Emphasis is on earnings from *continuing* operations.

[b] Note that both the numerator and denominator definitions are adjusted from ratio to ratio and may not correspond to the definitions used in this reading.

[c] FFO = funds from operations.

[d] CFO = cash flow from operations.

Source: Based on data from Standard & Poor's Corporate Ratings Criteria 2006, p. 43.

key financial ratios used by Standard & Poor's in evaluating industrial companies. Note that before calculating ratios, rating agencies make certain adjustments to reported financials such as adjusting debt to include off-balance sheet debt in a company's total debt.

6.2 Research on Ratios in Credit Analysis

A great deal of academic and practitioner research has focused on determining which ratios are useful in assessing the credit risk of a company, including the risk of bankruptcy.

One of the earliest studies examined individual ratios to assess their ability to predict failure of a company up to five years in advance. Beaver (1967) found that six ratios could correctly predict company failure one year in advance 90 percent of the time and five years in advance at least 65 percent of the time. The ratios found effective by Beaver were cash flow to total debt, ROA, total debt to total assets, working capital to total assets, the current ratio, and the no-credit interval ratio (the length of time a company could go without borrowing).

Altman (1968) and Altman, Haldeman, and Narayanan (1977) found that financial ratios could be combined in an effective model for predicting bankruptcy. Altman's initial work involved creation of a Z-score that was able to correctly predict financial distress. The Z-score was computed as

$$Z = 1.2 \times (\text{Current assets} - \text{Current liabilities})/\text{Total assets}$$
$$+ 1.4 \times (\text{Retained earnings}/\text{Total assets})$$
$$+ 3.3 \times (\text{EBIT}/\text{Total assets})$$
$$+ 0.6 \times (\text{Market value of stock}/\text{Book value of liabilities})$$
$$+ 1.0 \times (\text{Sales}/\text{Total assets})$$

In his initial study, a Z-score of lower than 1.81 predicted failure, and the model was able to accurately classify 95 percent of companies studied into a failure group and a nonfailure group. The original model was designed for manufacturing companies. Subsequent refinements to the models allow for other company types and time periods. Generally, the variables found to be useful in prediction include profitability ratios, coverage ratios, liquidity ratios, capitalization ratios, and earnings variability (Altman 2000).

Similar research has been performed on the ability of ratios to predict bond ratings and bond yields. For example, Ederington, Yawtiz, and Roberts (1987) found that a small number of variables (total assets, interest coverage, leverage, variability of coverage, and subordination status) were effective in explaining bond yields. Similarly, Ederington (1986) found that nine variables in combination could correctly classify more than 70 percent of bond ratings. These variables included ROA, long-term debt to assets, interest coverage, cash flow to debt, variability of coverage and cash flow, total assets, and subordination status. These studies have shown that ratios are effective in evaluating credit risk, bond yields, and bond ratings.

BUSINESS AND GEOGRAPHIC SEGMENTS   7

Analysts often need to evaluate the performance underlying business segments (subsidiary companies, operating units, or simply operations in different geographic areas) to understand in detail the company as a whole. Unfortunately, companies are not required to provide full financial statements for segments for which all of the traditional ratios can be computed. Publicly traded companies are required to provide limited segment information under both IFRS and U.S. GAAP.

7.1 IAS 14 Requirements

Under IAS 14 (Segment Reporting), disclosures are required for reportable segments. U.S. GAAP requirements are similar to IFRS but less detailed. One noticeable omission under U.S. GAAP is the disclosure of segment liabilities.

A reportable segment is defined as a business or geographical segment where both of the following apply:

▶ the majority (greater than 50 percent) of its revenue is earned externally, and

▶ its income from sales, segment result, or assets is greater than or equal to 10 percent of the appropriate total amount of all segments.

A business segment is a distinguishable component of a company that is engaged in providing an individual product or service or a group of related products or services and that is subject to risks and returns that are different from those of other business segments. A geographical segment is a distinguishable component of a company that is engaged in providing products or services within a particular economic environment.

Different business and geographical segments should be identified. A company's business and geographical segments for external reporting purposes should be those organizational units for which information is reported to the board of directors and to the chief executive officer. If a company's internal organizational and management structure and its system of internal financial reporting to the board of directors and the chief executive officer are not based on individual products, services, groups of related products or services, or on geography, the directors and management of the company should choose either business segments or geographical segments as the company's primary segment reporting format, based on their assessment of which type of segment reflects the primary source of the company's risks and returns. Under this standard, most entities would identify their business and geographical segments as the organizational units for which information is reported to the nonexecutive board of directors and senior management.

If the total revenue from external customers for all reportable segments combined is less than 75 percent of the total company revenue, additional reportable segments should be identified until the 75 percent level is reached. Small segments might be combined as one if they share a substantial number of factors that define a business or geographical segment, or they might be combined with a similar significant reportable segment. If they are not separately reported or combined, they are included as an unallocated reconciling item.

The company must identify a primary segment reporting format (either business or geographical) with the other segment used for the secondary reporting format. The dominant source and nature of risks and returns govern whether a company's primary segment reporting format will be its business segments or its geographical segments. The company's internal organization and management structure, and its system of internal financial reporting to the board of directors and the chief executive officer, are normally the basis for identifying the predominant source and nature of risks and differing rates of return facing the company.

For each primary segment, the following should be disclosed:

► segment revenue, distinguishing between revenue to external customers and revenue from other segments;

► segment result (segment revenue minus segment expenses);

► carrying amount of segment assets;

► segment liabilities;

► cost of property, plant, and equipment, and intangible assets acquired;

► depreciation and amortization expense;

► other noncash expenses;

► share of the net profit or loss of an investment accounted for under the equity method; and

► reconciliation between the information of reportable segments and the consolidated financial statements in terms of segment revenue, result, assets, and liabilities.

For each secondary segment, the following should be disclosed:

► revenue from external customers;

► carrying amount of segment assets; and

► cost of property, plant, and equipment, and intangible assets acquired.

Other required disclosures are as follows:

► revenue of any segment whereby the external revenue of the segment is greater than or equal to 10 percent of company revenue but that is not a reportable segment (because a majority of its revenue is from internal transfers);

► basis of pricing intersegment transfers;

► changes in segment accounting policies;

► types of products and services in each business segment; and

► composition of each geographical segment.

7.2 Segment Ratios

Based on the limited segment information that companies are required to present, a variety of useful ratios can be computed, as shown in Exhibit 17.

EXHIBIT 17	Definitions of Segment Ratios	
Segment Ratios	**Numerator**	**Denominator**
Segment margin	Segment profit (loss)	Segment revenue
Segment turnover	Segment revenue	Segment assets
Segment ROA	Segment profit (loss)	Segment assets
Segment debt ratio	Segment liabilities	Segment assets

The segment margin measures the operating profitability of the segment relative to revenues, whereas the segment ROA measures the operating profitability relative to assets. Segment turnover measures the overall efficiency of the segment: how much revenue is generated per unit of assets. The segment debt ratio examines the level of liabilities (hence solvency) of the segment. Example 15 demonstrates the evaluation of segment ratios.

EXAMPLE 15

The Evaluation of Segment Ratios

The following information relates to the business segments of Nokia for 2004 in millions of euros. Evaluate the performance of the segments using the segment margin, segment ROA, and segment turnover.

	Revenue	Operating Profit	Segment Assets
Mobile phones	18,429	3,768	3,758
Multimedia	3,636	179	787
Enterprise solutions	806	−199	210
Networks	6,367	878	3,055

	Segment Margin (%)	Segment ROA (%)	Segment Turnover
Mobile phones	20.45	100.27	4.90
Multimedia	4.92	22.74	4.62
Enterprise solutions	−24.69	−94.76	3.84
Networks	13.79	28.74	2.08

Solution: Mobile phones is the best performing segment with the highest segment margin, segment ROA, and efficiency. Networks is the second highest in terms of profitability but lowest in efficiency (the ability to generate revenue from assets). Enterprise solutions is not profitable; however, it is the smallest segment and may still be in the development stage.

8   MODEL BUILDING AND FORECASTING

Analysts often need to forecast future financial performance. For example, EPS forecasts of analysts are widely followed by Wall Street. Analysts use data about the economy, industry, and company in arriving at a company's forecast. The results of an analyst's financial analysis, including common-size and ratio analysis, are integral to this process, along with the judgment of the analysts.

Based upon forecasts of growth and expected relationships among the financial statement data, the analyst can build a model (sometimes referred to as an "earnings model") to forecast future performance. In addition to budgets, pro forma financial statements are widely used in financial forecasting within companies, especially for use by senior executives and boards of directors. Last but not least, these budgets and forecasts are also used in presentations to credit analysts and others in obtaining external financing.

For example, based on a revenue forecast, an analyst may budget expenses based on expected common-size data. Forecasts of balance sheet and statement of cash flows can be derived from expected ratio data, such as DSO. Forecasts are not limited to a single point estimate but should involve a range of possibilities. This can involve several techniques:

▶ **Sensitivity analysis:** Also known as "what if" analysis, sensitivity analysis shows the range of possible outcomes as specific assumptions are changed; this could, in turn, influence financing needs or investment in fixed assets.

▶ **Scenario analysis**: Scenario analysis shows the changes in key financial quantities that result from given (economic) events, such as the loss of customers, the loss of a supply source, or a catastrophic event. If the list of events is mutually exclusive and exhaustive and the events can be assigned probabilities, the analyst can evaluate not only the range of outcomes but also standard statistical measures such as the mean and median value for various quantities of interest.

▶ **Simulation**: This is computer-generated sensitivity or scenario analysis based on probability models for the factors that drive outcomes. Each event or possible outcome is assigned a probability. Multiple scenarios are then run using the probability factors assigned to the possible values of a variable.

SUMMARY

Financial analysis techniques, including common-size and ratio analysis, are useful in summarizing financial reporting data and evaluating the performance and financial position of a company. The results of financial analysis techniques provide important inputs into security valuation. Key facets of financial analysis include the following:

▶ Common-size financial statements and financial ratios remove the effect of size, allowing comparisons of a company with peer companies (cross-sectional analysis) and comparison of a company's results over time (trend or time-series analysis).

▶ Activity ratios measure the efficiency of a company's operations, such as collection of receivables or management of inventory. Major activity ratios include inventory turnover, days of inventory on hand, receivables turnover, days of sales outstanding, payables turnover, number of days of payables, working capital turnover, fixed asset turnover, and total asset turnover.

▶ Liquidity ratios measure the ability of a company to meet short-term obligations. Major liquidity ratios include the current ratio, quick ratio, cash ratio, and defensive interval ratio.

▶ Solvency ratios measure the ability of a company to meet long-term obligations. Major solvency ratios include debt ratios (including the debt-to-assets ratio, debt-to-capital ratio, debt-to-equity ratio, and financial leverage ratio) and coverage ratios (including interest coverage and fixed charge coverage).

▶ Profitability ratios measure the ability of a company to generate profits from revenue and assets. Major profitability ratios include return on sales ratios (including gross profit margin, operating profit margin, pretax margin, and net profit margin) and return on investment ratios (including operating ROA, ROA, ROE, and return on common equity).

▶ Ratios can also be combined and evaluated as a group to better understand how they fit together and how efficiency and leverage are tied to profitability.

▶ ROE can be analyzed as the product of the net profit margin, asset turnover, and financial leverage.

▶ Ratio analysis is useful in the selection and valuation of debt and equity securities and is a part of the credit rating process.

▶ Ratios can also be computed for business segments to evaluate how units within a business are doing.

▶ The results of financial analysis provide valuable inputs into forecasts of future earnings and cash flow.

PRACTICE PROBLEMS FOR READING 35

1. Comparison of a company's financial results to other peer companies for the same time period is called:

   A. horizontal analysis.

   B. time-series analysis.

   C. cross-sectional analysis.

2. In order to assess a company's ability to fulfill its long-term obligations, an analyst would *most likely* examine:

   A. activity ratios.

   B. liquidity ratios.

   C. solvency ratios.

3. Which ratio would a company *most likely* use to measure its ability to meet short-term obligations?

   A. Current ratio.

   B. Payables turnover.

   C. Gross profit margin.

4. Which of the following ratios would be *most useful* in determining a company's ability to cover its debt payments?

   A. ROA.

   B. Total asset turnover.

   C. Fixed charge coverage.

5. John Chan is interested in assessing both the efficiency and liquidity of Spherion PLC. Chan has collected the following data for Spherion:

	2005	2004	2003
Days of inventory on hand	32	34	40
Days' sales outstanding	28	25	23
Number of days of payables	40	35	35

   Based on this data, what is Chan *least likely* to conclude?

   A. Inventory management has contributed to improved liquidity.

   B. Management of payables has contributed to improved liquidity.

   C. Management of receivables has contributed to improved liquidity.

6. Marcus Lee is examining the solvency of Apex Manufacturing and has collected the following data (in millions of euros):

	2005	2004	2003
Total debt	€2,000	€1,900	€1,750
Total equity	€4,000	€4,500	€5,000

Which of the following would be the *most appropriate* conclusion for Lee?

A. The company is becoming increasingly less solvent, as evidenced by the increase in its debt-to-equity ratio from 0.35 to 0.50 from 2003 to 2005.

B. The company is becoming less liquid, as evidenced by the increase in its debt-to-equity ratio from 0.35 to 0.50 from 2003 to 2005.

C. The company is becoming increasingly more liquid, as evidenced by the increase in its debt-to-equity ratio from 0.35 to 0.50 from 2003 to 2005.

7. With regard to the data in Problem 6, what would be a reasonable explanation of these financial results?

A. The decline in the company's equity results from a decline in the market value of this company's common shares.

B. The increase in the company's debt of €250 from 2003 to 2005 indicates that lenders are viewing the company as increasingly creditworthy.

C. The decline in the company's equity indicates that the company may be incurring losses on its operations, paying dividends greater than income, and/or repurchasing shares.

8. Linda Roper observes a decrease in a company's inventory turnover. Which of the following would explain this trend?

A. The company installed a new inventory management system, allowing more efficient inventory management.

B. Due to problems with obsolescent inventory last year, the company wrote off a large amount of its inventory at the beginning of the period.

C. The company installed a new inventory management system but experienced some operational difficulties resulting in duplicate orders being placed with suppliers.

9. Which of the following would best explain an increase in receivables turnover?

A. The company adopted new credit policies last year and began offering credit to customers with weak credit histories.

B. Due to problems with an error in its old credit scoring system, the company had accumulated a substantial amount of uncollectible accounts and wrote off a large amount of its receivables.

C. To match the terms offered by its closest competitor, the company adopted new payment terms now requiring net payment within 30 days rather than 15 days, which had been its previous requirement.

10. Brown Corporation had an average days sales outstanding of 19 days in 2005. Brown wants to decrease its collection period in 2006 to match the industry average of 15 days. Credit sales in 2005 were $300 million, and Brown expects credit sales to increase to $390 million in 2006. To achieve Brown's goal of decreasing the collection period, the change in the average accounts receivable balance from 2005 to 2006 that must occur is *closest* to:

   A. −$1.22 million.

   B. −$0.42 million.

   C. $0.42 million.

11. An analyst gathered the following data for a company:

	2003	**2004**	**2005**
ROE	19.8%	20.0%	22.0%
Return on total assets	8.1%	8.0%	7.9%
Total asset turnover	2.0	2.0	2.1

Based only on the information above, the *most* appropriate conclusion is that, over the period 2003 to 2005, the company's:

   A. net profit margin and financial leverage have decreased.

   B. net profit margin and financial leverage have increased.

   C. net profit margin has decreased but its financial leverage has increased.

12. A decomposition of ROE for Integra SA is as follows:

	2005	**2004**
ROE	18.90%	18.90%
Tax burden	0.70	0.75
Interest burden	0.90	0.90
EBIT margin	10.00%	10.00%
Asset turnover	1.50	1.40
Leverage	2.00	2.00

Which of the following choices *best* describes reasonable conclusions an analyst might make based on this ROE decomposition?

   A. Profitability and the liquidity position both improved in 2005.

   B. The higher average tax rate in 2005 offset the improvement in profitability, leaving ROE unchanged.

   C. The higher average tax rate in 2005 offset the improvement in efficiency, leaving ROE unchanged.

13. A decomposition of ROE for Company A and Company B is as follows:

	Company A		Company B	
	2005	**2004**	**2005**	**2004**
ROE	26.46%	18.90%	26.33%	18.90%
Tax burden	0.7	0.75	0.75	0.75
Interest burden	0.9	0.9	0.9	0.9
EBIT margin	7.00%	10.00%	13.00%	10.00%
Asset turnover	1.5	1.4	1.5	1.4
Leverage	4	2	2	2

Which of the following choices *best* describes reasonable conclusions an analyst might make based on this ROE decomposition?

A. Company A's ROE is higher than Company B's in 2005, but the difference between the two companies' ROE is very small and was mainly the result of Company A's increase in its financial leverage.

B. Company A's ROE is higher than Company B's in 2005, apparently reflecting a strategic shift by Company A to a product mix with higher profit margins.

C. Company A's ROE is higher than Company B's in 2005, which suggests that Company A may have purchased new, more efficient equipment.

14. Rent-A-Center reported the following information related to total debt and shareholders' equity in its 2003 annual report.

	As of 31 December				
($ in Thousands)	**2003**	**2002**	**2001**	**2000**	**1999**
Total debt	698,000	521,330	702,506	741,051	847,160
Stockholders' equity	794,830	842,400	405,378	309,371	206,690

What would an analyst's *most* appropriate conclusion be based on this data?

A. The company's solvency has improved from 1999 to 2002.

B. The company's solvency has improved from 2002 to 2003.

C. The data suggest the company increased debt in 2002.

15. Frank Collins observes the following data for two companies:

	Company A ($)	Company B ($)
Revenue	4,500	6,000
Net income	50	1,000
Current assets	40,000	60,000
Total assets	100,000	700,000
Current liabilities	10,000	50,000
Total debt	60,000	150,000
Shareholders' equity	30,000	500,000

Which of the following choices *best* describes reasonable conclusions that Collins might make about the two companies' ability to pay their current and long-term obligations?

A. Company A's current ratio of 4.0x indicates it is more liquid than Company B, whose current ratio is only 1.2x, but Company B is more solvent, as indicated by its lower debt-to-equity ratio.

B. Company A's current ratio of 25 percent indicates it is less liquid than Company B, whose current ratio is 83 percent, and Company A is also less solvent, as indicated by a debt-to-equity ratio of 200 percent compared with Company B's debt-to-equity ratio of only 30 percent.

C. Company A's current ratio of 4.0x indicates it is more liquid than Company B, whose current ratio is only 1.2x, and Company A is also more solvent, as indicated by a debt-to-equity ratio of 200 percent compared with Company B's debt-to-equity ratio of only 30 percent.

The following information relates to Questions 16–19

The data below appear in the five-year summary of a major international company. A business combination with another major manufacturer took place in 2003. The term "turnover" in this financial data is a synonym for revenue.

	2000	2001	2002	2003	2004
Financial statements	GBP m	GBP m	GBP m	GBP m	GBP m
Income statements					
Turnover (i.e., revenue)	4,390	3,624	3,717	8,167	11,366
Profit before interest and taxation (EBIT)	844	700	704	933	1,579
Net interest payable	−80	−54	−98	−163	−188
Taxation	−186	−195	−208	−349	−579
Minorities	−94	−99	−105	−125	−167
Profit for the year	484	352	293	296	645
Balance sheets					
Fixed assets	3,510	3,667	4,758	10,431	11,483
Current asset investments, cash at bank and in hand	316	218	290	561	682
Other current assets	558	514	643	1,258	1,634
Total assets	4,384	4,399	5,691	12,250	13,799
Interest bearing debt (long term)	−602	−1,053	−1,535	−3,523	−3,707
Other creditors and provisions (current)	−1,223	−1,054	−1,102	−2,377	−3,108
Total liabilities	−1,825	−2,107	−2,637	−5,900	−6,815
Net assets	2,559	2,292	3,054	6,350	6,984
Shareholders' funds	2,161	2,006	2,309	5,572	6,165
Equity minority interests	398	286	745	778	819
Capital employed	2,559	2,292	3,054	6,350	6,984
Cash flow					
Working capital movements	−53	5	71	85	107
Net cash inflow from operating activities	864	859	975	1,568	2,292

16. The company's total assets at year-end 1999 were GBP 3,500 million. Which of the following choices *best* describes reasonable conclusions an analyst might make about the company's efficiency?

    A. Comparing 2004 with 2000, the company's efficiency improved, as indicated by a total asset turnover ratio of 0.86 compared with 0.64.

    B. Comparing 2004 with 2000, the company's efficiency deteriorated, as indicated by its current ratio.

    C. Comparing 2004 with 2000, the company's efficiency deteriorated due to asset growth faster than turnover (i.e., revenue) growth.

17. Which of the following choices *best* describes reasonable conclusions an analyst might make about the company's solvency?

    A. Comparing 2004 with 2000, the company's solvency improved, as indicated by an increase in its debt-to-assets ratio from 0.14 to 0.27.

    B. Comparing 2004 with 2000, the company's solvency deteriorated, as indicated by a decrease in interest coverage from 10.6 to 8.4.

    C. Comparing 2004 with 2000, the company's solvency improved, as indicated by the growth in its profits to GBP 645 million.

18. Which of the following choices *best* describes reasonable conclusions an analyst might make about the company's liquidity?

    A. Comparing 2004 with 2000, the company's liquidity improved, as indicated by an increase in its debt-to-assets ratio from 0.14 to 0.27.

    B. Comparing 2004 with 2000, the company's liquidity deteriorated, as indicated by a decrease in interest coverage from 10.6 to 8.4.

    C. Comparing 2004 with 2000, the company's liquidity improved, as indicated by an increase in its current ratio from 0.71 to 0.75.

19. Which of the following choices *best* describes reasonable conclusions an analyst might make about the company's profitability?

    A. Comparing 2004 with 2000, the company's profitability improved, as indicated by an increase in its debt-to-assets ratio from 0.14 to 0.27.

    B. Comparing 2004 with 2000, the company's profitability deteriorated, as indicated by a decrease in its net profit margin from 11.0 percent to 5.7 percent.

    C. Comparing 2004 with 2000, the company's profitability improved, as indicated by the growth in its shareholders' equity to GBP 6,165 million.

20. In general, a creditor would consider a decrease in which of the following ratios to be positive news?

    A. Interest coverage (times interest earned).

    B. Debt to total assets.

    C. Return on assets.

21. Assuming no changes in other variables, which of the following would decrease ROA?

    A. A decrease in the effective tax rate.

    B. A decrease in interest expense.

    C. An increase in average assets.

22. What does the P/E ratio measure?

    A. The "multiple" that the stock market places on a company's EPS.

    B. The relationship between dividends and market prices.

    C. The earnings for one common share of stock.

SOLUTIONS FOR READING 35

1. C is correct. Cross-sectional analysis involved the comparison of companies with each other for the same time period. Time-series analysis is the comparison of financial data across different time periods.

2. C is correct. Solvency ratios are used to evaluate the ability of a company to meet its long-term obligations.

3. A is correct. The current ratio is a liquidity ratio. It compares the net amount of current assets expected to be converted into cash within the year, compared with liabilities falling due in the same period. A current ratio of 1.0 would indicate that the company would have just enough current assets to pay current liabilities.

4. C is correct. Solvency ratios measure the ability to cover debt payments. There are two main types of solvency ratios. Debt ratios focus on the balance sheet and measure the amount of capital raised by debt relative to equity. Coverage ratios focus on the income statement and measure the ability of a company to cover its debt payments. The fixed charge coverage ratio is a coverage ratio that relates known fixed obligations to the cash flow generated by the entity.

5. C is correct. Chan is very *unlikely* to reach the conclusion given in Statement C because days' sales outstanding increased from 23 days in 2003 to 25 days in 2004 to 28 days in 2005, indicating that the time required to collect receivables has increased over the period, which is a negative factor for Spherion's liquidity. By contrast, days of inventory on hand dropped over the period 2003 to 2005, a positive for liquidity. Thus Statement A is an appropriate conclusion. The company's increase in days' payable from 35 days' to 40 days shorted its cash collection cycle, thus contributing to improved liquidity; therefore, Statement B is also an appropriate conclusion.

6. A is correct. The company is becoming increasingly less solvent, as evidenced by its debt-to-equity ratio increasing from 0.35 to 0.50 from 2003 to 2005. B is incorrect because it incorrectly interprets the debt-to-equity ratio as a measure of liquidity. C is incorrect because it incorrectly interprets the direction of the trend and misinterprets the ratio as an indicator of liquidity.

Debt to equity:
  2005:   2,000/4,000 = 0.5000
  2004:   1,900/4,500 = 0.4222
  2003:   1,750/5,000 = 0.3500

7. C is correct. The decline in the company's equity indicates that the company may be incurring losses on its operations, paying dividends greater than income, or repurchasing shares. Recall that Beginning equity + New shares issuance − Shares repurchased + Net income − Dividends = Ending equity. A is incorrect because the book value of a company's equity is not affected by changes in the market value of its common stock. B is incorrect because an increased amount of lending does not necessarily indicate that lenders view a company as increasingly creditworthy. Credit-worthiness is not evaluated based on how much a company has increased its debt but rather on its willingness to pay its obligations and its ability to pay. (Its financial strength is indicated by its solvency, liquidity, profitability, efficiency, and other aspects of credit analysis.)

8. C is correct. The company's problems with its inventory management system causing duplicate orders would result in a higher amount of inventory than needed and would, therefore, likely result in a decrease in inventory turnover. A is incorrect because a more efficient inventory management system would likely be reflected in the inventory turnover ratio, an indicator of more efficient inventory management. B is incorrect because a write-off of inventory at the beginning of the period would decrease the average inventory for the period (the denominator of the inventory turnover ratio), thus increasing the ratio rather than decreasing it.

9. B is correct. A write-off of receivables would decrease the average amount of accounts receivable (the denominator of the receivables turnover ratio), thus increasing this ratio. A is incorrect because weaker credit customers are more likely to make payments more slowly or to pose collection difficulties, which would likely increase the average amount of accounts receivable and thus decrease receivables turnover. C is incorrect because a longer payment period would likely increase the average amount of accounts receivable and thus decrease receivables turnover.

10. C is correct because accounts receivable turnover can be calculated to determine the average DSO. Turnovers are equal to 365/19 (DSO) = 19.2 for 2005 and 365/15 = 24.3 in 2006. Sales/turnovers are equal to accounts receivable balances. For 2005, $300,000,000/19.2 = $15,625,000, and for 2006, $390,000,000/24.3 = $16,049,383. The difference is an increase in receivables of $424,383.

   A is incorrect because the accounts receivable balance must increase.

   B is incorrect because the accounts receivable balance must increase.

11. C is correct. ROE = Return on assets × Financial leverage. ROA can be decomposed into the product of net profit margin (net income divided by revenue) and total asset turnover (revenue divided by average total assets). Because ROA has been decreasing over 2003 to 2005 while total asset turnover has been increasing, it must be the case that the net profit margin has been declining. Furthermore, because ROE has increased despite the drop in ROA, financial leverage must have increased. Statement C is the only statement that correctly identifies the trends in net profit margin and financial leverage.

12. C is correct. The increase in the average tax rate in 2005, as indicated by the decrease in the value of the tax burden (the tax burden equals one minus the average tax rate), offset the improvement in efficiency indicated by higher asset turnover); as a result, ROE remained unchanged at 18.90 percent. Statement A is not correct because the EBIT margin, measuring profitability, was unchanged in 2005; furthermore, no information is given on liquidity. Statement B is not correct because profitability was unchanged in 2005.

13. A is correct. The difference between the two companies' ROE in 2005 is very small and is mainly the result of Company A's increase in its financial leverage, indicated by the increase in its assets/equity ratio from 2 to 4. B is incorrect because Company A has experienced a significant decline in its operating margin, from 10 percent to 7 percent which, all else equal, would not suggest that it is selling more of products with higher profit margin. C is incorrect because the impact of efficiency on ROE is identical for the two companies, as indicated by both companies' asset turnover ratios of 1.5. Furthermore, if Company A had purchased newer equipment to replace older, depreciated equipment, then the company's asset turnover ratio (computed as sales/assets) would have declined, assuming constant sales.

14. A is correct. The debt-to-equity ratio has improved from 1999 to 2002 from 410 percent to 88 percent (calculations below). The decrease in total debt implies that debt has been repaid, not borrowed. B is incorrect because the company's solvency has deteriorated from 2002 to 2003, as indicated by the higher debt-to-equity ratio. C is incorrect because lower total debt in 2002 suggests repayment of debt.

	2003	**2002**	**2001**	**2000**	**1999**
Total debt	698,000	521,330	702,506	741,051	847,160
Stockholders' equity	794,830	842,400	405,378	309,371	206,690
Total debt-to-equity ratio	88%	62%	173%	240%	410%

15. A is correct. Company A's current ratio of 4.0× ($40,000/$10,000 = 4.0) indicates it is more liquid than Company B, whose current ratio is only 1.2× ($60,000/$50,000 = 1.2). Company B is more solvent, as indicated by its lower debt-to-equity ratio of 30 percent ($150,000/$500,000 = 0.30) compared with Company A's debt-to-equity ratio of 200 percent ($60,000/$30,000 = 2.0). The other choices are incorrect either because the current ratio is incorrectly calculated or because the debt-to-equity ratio was incorrectly interpreted.

16. C is correct. The company's efficiency deteriorated, as indicated by the decline in its total asset turnover ratio from 1.11 (GBP 4,390/[(GBP 4,384 + 3,500)/2 = 1.11]) for the year 2000 to 0.87 (GBP 11,366/[(GBP 12,250 + GBP 13,799)/2] = 0.87) for the year 2004. The decline in the total asset turnover ratio resulted from an increase in average assets from GBP 3,942 (GBP 4,384 + 3,500)/2 = GBP 3,942 in 2000 to GBP 13,024.5 in 2004, an increase of 330 percent, compared with an increase in turnover (i.e., revenues) from GBP 4,390 in 2000 to GBP 11,366 in 2004, an increase of only 259 percent. A is incorrect because the asset turnover ratio is calculated incorrectly. B is incorrect because the current ratio is not an indicator of efficiency.

17. B is correct. Comparing 2004 with 2000, the company's solvency deteriorated, as indicated by a decrease in interest coverage from 10.6 (GBP 844/GBP 80 = 10.6) in 2000 to 8.4 (GBP 1,579/GBP 188 = 8.4). A is incorrect because it misinterprets the debt-to-asset ratio. C is incorrect because, in isolation, the amount of profits does not provide enough information to assess solvency.

18. C is correct. Comparing 2004 with 2000, the company's liquidity improved, as indicated by an increase in its current ratio from 0.71 ([GBP 316 + GBP 558]/GBP 1,223 = 0.71) in 2000 to 0.75 ([GBP 682 + GBP 1,634]/GBP 3,108 = 0.75) in 2004. Note, however, comparing only current investments with the level of current liabilities shows a decline in liquidity from 0.25 (316/1223 = 0.25) in 2000 to 0.22 (GBP 682/GBP 3,108 = 0.22) in 2004. A is incorrect because the debt-to-assets ratio is not an indicator of liquidity. B is incorrect because interest coverage is not an indicator of liquidity.

19. B is correct. Comparing 2004 with 2000, the company's profitability deteriorated, as indicated by a decrease in its net profit margin from 11 percent (484/4,390 = 0.11) to 5.7 percent (645/11,366 = 0.057). A is incorrect because the debt-to-assets ratio is not an indicator of profitability. C is incorrect because growth in shareholders' equity, in isolation, does not provide enough information to assess profitability.

20. B is correct. In general, a creditor would consider a decrease in debt to total assets as positive news. A higher level of debt in a company's capital structure increases the risk of default and will result in higher borrowing costs for the company to compensate lenders for assuming greater credit risk.

21. C is correct. Assuming no changes in other variables, an increase in average assets would decrease ROA.

22. A is correct. The P/E ratio measures the "multiple" that the stock market places on a company's EPS.

STUDY SESSION 9
FINANCIAL REPORTING ANALYSIS:
Inventories, Long-lived Assets, Income Taxes, and Non-current Liabilities

The readings in this study session examine specific categories of assets and liabilities that are particularly susceptible to the impact of alternative accounting policies and estimates. Analysts must understand the effects of alternative policies on financial statements and ratios and be able to execute appropriate adjustments to enhance comparability between companies. In addition, analysts must be alert to differences between a company's reported financial statements and economic reality.

The description and measurement of inventories require careful attention because the investment in inventories is frequently the largest current asset for merchandising and manufacturing companies. For these companies, the measurement of inventory cost (i.e., cost of goods sold) is a critical factor in determining gross profit and other measures of profitability. Long-lived operating assets are often the largest category of assets on a company's balance sheet. The analyst needs to scrutinize management's choices with respect to recognizing expenses associated with these operating assets because of the potentially large impact such choices can have on reported earnings and the opportunities for financial statement manipulation.

A company's accounting policies (such as depreciation choices) can cause differences in taxes reported in financial statements and taxes reported on tax returns. The reading "Income Taxes" discusses several issues that arise relating to deferred taxes.

Non-current liabilities affect a company's liquidity and solvency and have consequences for its long-term growth and viability. The notes of the financial statements must be carefully reviewed to ensure that all potential liabilities (e.g., leasing arrangements and other contractual commitments) are appropriately evaluated for their conformity to economic reality. Adjustments to the financial statements may be required to achieve comparability when evaluating several companies and may also be required to improve credit and investment decision-making.

Note:
New rulings and/or pronouncements issued after the publication of the readings on financial reporting and analysis may cause some of the information in these readings to become dated. Candidates are expected to be familiar with the overall analytical framework contained in the study session readings, as well as the implications of alternative accounting methods for financial analysis and valuation, as provided in the assigned readings. Candidates are not responsible for changes that occur after the material was written.

375

READING ASSIGNMENTS

INVENTORIES

by Michael A. Broihahn, CFA

LEARNING OUTCOMES

The candidate should be able to:	Mastery
a. distinguish between costs included in inventories and costs recognized as expenses in the period in which they are incurred;	☐
b. describe different inventory valuation methods (cost formulas);	☐
c. calculate cost of sales and ending inventory using different inventory valuation methods and explain the impact of the inventory valuation method choice on gross profit;	☐
d. calculate, compare, and contrast cost of sales, gross profit, and ending inventory using perpetual and periodic inventory systems;	☐
e. compare and contrast cost of sales, ending inventory, and gross profit using different inventory valuation methods;	☐
f. discuss the measurement of inventory at the lower of cost and net realisable value;	☐
g. describe the financial statement presentation of and disclosures relating to inventories;	☐
h. calculate and interpret ratios used to evaluate inventory management.	☐

INTRODUCTION 1

Merchandising and manufacturing companies generate revenues and profits through the sale of inventory. Further, inventory may represent a significant asset on these companies' balance sheets. Merchandisers (wholesalers and retailers) purchase inventory, ready for sale, from manufacturers and thus account for only one type of inventory—finished goods inventory. Manufacturers, however, purchase raw materials from suppliers and then add value by transforming the raw materials into finished goods. They typically classify

Note:
New rulings and/or pronouncements issued after the publication of the readings on financial reporting and analysis may cause some of the information in these readings to become dated. Candidates are expected to be familiar with the overall analytical framework contained in the study session readings, as well as the implications of alternative accounting methods for financial analysis and valuation, as provided in the assigned readings. Candidates are not responsible for changes that occur after the material was written.

inventory into three different categories:[1] raw materials, work in progress,[2] and finished goods. Work-in-progress inventories have started the conversion process from raw materials but are not yet finished goods ready for sale. Manufacturers may report either the separate carrying amounts of their raw materials, work-in-progress, and finished goods inventories on the balance sheet or simply the total inventory amount. If the latter approach is used, the company must then disclose the carrying amounts of its raw materials, work-in-progress, and finished goods inventories in a footnote to the financial statements.

An important consideration in calculating profits for merchandising and manufacturing companies is measuring the cost of sales (cost of goods sold).[3] The measurement process would be simple if inventory costs remained constant over time; however, that is not economic reality. Financial analysis would also be much easier if all companies used the same inventory valuation method. International Financial Reporting Standards (IFRS) and U.S. generally accepted accounting principles (U.S. GAAP), however, allow more than one inventory valuation method. Inventory valuation methods are referred to as cost formulas and cost flow assumptions under IFRS and U.S. GAAP, respectively. Differences in the choice of inventory valuation method can result in significantly different amounts being assigned to the cost of sales and inventory.

IFRS allow companies to choose from three cost formulas: specific identification; weighted average cost; and first-in, first-out (FIFO). U.S. GAAP allow the same three cost flow assumptions but also allow a fourth method: last-in, first-out (LIFO). Analysts must clearly understand the various inventory valuation methods and the related impact on financial statements and financial ratios in order to evaluate a company's performance over time and relative to industry peers. The company's financial statements and related notes provide important information that the analyst can use in assessing the impact of the choice of inventory valuation method on financial statements and financial ratios.

This reading is organized as follows: Section 2 discusses the costs that are included in inventory and the costs that are recognised as expenses in the period in which they are incurred. Section 3 discusses inventory valuation methods and the measurement of ending inventory and cost of sales under each method. Section 4 discusses the measurement and reporting of inventory when its value changes. Section 5 describes the presentation of inventories on the financial statements and their related disclosures. Section 6 focuses on the calculation and interpretation of inventory management ratios. A summary and practice problems conclude the reading.

---

[1] Other classifications are possible. Inventory classifications should be appropriate to the entity.

[2] This category is commonly referred to as *work in process* under U.S. GAAP.

[3] Typically, *cost of sales* is IFRS terminology and *cost of goods sold* is U.S. GAAP terminology.

COST OF INVENTORIES   2

Under IFRS, the costs to include in inventories are "all costs of purchase, costs of conversion, and other costs incurred in bringing the inventories to their present location and condition."[4] The costs of purchase include the purchase price, import and tax-related duties, transport, insurance during transport, handling, and other costs directly attributable to the acquisition of finished goods, materials, and services. Trade discounts, rebates, and similar items reduce the price paid and the costs of purchase. The costs of conversion include costs directly related to the units produced, such as direct labour, and fixed and variable overhead costs.[5] Including these product-related costs in inventory (i.e., as an asset) means that they will not be recognised as an expense (i.e., as cost of sales) on the income statement until the inventory is sold. U.S. GAAP provide a similar description of the costs to be included in inventory.[6]

Both IFRS and U.S. GAAP exclude the following costs from inventory: abnormal costs incurred as a result of waste of materials, labour or other production conversion inputs, any storage costs (unless required as part of the production process), and all administrative overhead and selling costs. These excluded costs are treated as expenses and recognised on the income statement in the period in which they are incurred. Including costs in inventory defers their recognition as an expense on the income statement until the inventory is sold. Therefore, including costs in inventory that should be expensed will overstate profitability on the income statement (because of the inappropriate deferral of cost recognition) and create an overstated inventory value on the balance sheet.

EXAMPLE 1

Treatment of Inventory-Related Costs

Acme Enterprises, a hypothetical company that prepares its financial statements in accordance with IFRS, manufactures tables. In 2009, the factory produced 900,000 finished tables and scrapped 1,000 tables. For the finished tables, raw material costs were €9 million, direct labour conversion costs were €18 million, and production overhead costs were €1.8 million. The 1,000 scrapped tables (attributable to abnormal waste) had a total production cost of €30,000 (€10,000 raw material costs and €20,000 conversion costs; these costs are not included in the €9 million raw material and €19.8 million total conversion costs of the finished tables). During the year, Acme spent €1 million for freight delivery charges on raw materials and €500,000 for storing finished goods inventory. Acme does not have any work-in-progress inventory at the end of the year.

1. What costs should be included in inventory in 2009?
2. What costs should be expensed in 2009?

---

[4] International Accounting Standard (IAS) 2 [Inventories].

[5] Fixed production overhead costs (depreciation, factory maintenance, and factory management and administration) represent indirect costs of production that remain relatively constant regardless of the volume of production. Variable production overhead costs are indirect production costs (indirect labour and materials) that vary with the volume of production.

[6] FASB Accounting Standards Codification™ (ASC) Topic 330 [Inventory].

Solution to 1: Total inventory costs for 2009 are as follows:

Raw materials	€9,000,000
Direct labour	18,000,000
Production overhead	1,800,000
Transportation for raw materials	1,000,000
Total inventory costs	€29,800,000

Solution to 2: Total costs that should be expensed (not included in inventory) are as follows:

Abnormal waste	€30,000
Storage of finished goods inventory	500,000
Total	€530,000

3   INVENTORY VALUATION METHODS

Generally, inventory purchase costs and manufacturing conversion costs change over time. As a result, the allocation of total inventory costs (i.e., cost of goods available for sale) between cost of sales on the income statement and inventory on the balance sheet will vary depending on the inventory valuation method used by the company. As mentioned in the introduction, inventory valuation methods are referred to as cost formulas and cost flow assumptions under IFRS and U.S. GAAP, respectively. If the choice of method results in more cost being allocated to cost of sales and less cost being allocated to inventory than would be the case with other methods, the chosen method will cause, in the current year, reported gross profit, net income, and inventory carrying amount to be lower than if alternative methods had been used. Accounting for inventory, and consequently the allocation of costs, thus has a direct impact on financial statements and their comparability.

Both IFRS and U.S. GAAP allow companies to use the following inventory valuation methods: specific identification; first-in, first-out (FIFO); and weighted average cost. U.S. GAAP allow companies to use an additional method: last-in, first-out (LIFO). A company must use the same inventory valuation method for all items that have a similar nature and use. For items with a different nature or use, a different inventory valuation method can be used.[7] When items are sold, the carrying amount of the inventory is recognised as an expense (cost of sales) according to the cost formula (cost flow assumption) in use.

Specific identification is used for inventory items that are not ordinarily interchangeable, whereas FIFO, weighted average cost, and LIFO are typically used when there are large numbers of interchangeable items in inventory. Specific identification matches the actual historical costs of the specific inventory items to their physical flow; the costs remain in inventory until the actual identifiable inventory is sold. FIFO, weighted average cost, and LIFO are based on cost flow assumptions. Under these methods, companies must make certain assumptions about which goods are sold and which goods remain in ending inventory. As a result, the allocation of costs to the units sold and to the units in ending inventory can be different from the physical movement of the items.

---

[7] For example, if a clothing manufacturer produces both a retail line and one-of-a-kind designer garments, the retail line might be valued using FIFO and the designer garments using specific identification.

The choice of inventory valuation method would be largely irrelevant if inventory costs remained constant or relatively constant over time. Given relatively constant prices, the allocation of costs between cost of goods sold and ending inventory would be very similar under each of the four methods. Given changing price levels, however, the choice of inventory valuation method can have a significant impact on the amount of reported cost of sales and inventory. And the reported cost of sales and inventory balances affect other items, such as gross profit, net income, current assets, and total assets.

3.1 Specific Identification

The specific identification method is used for inventory items that are not ordinarily interchangeable and for goods that have been produced and segregated for specific projects. This method is also commonly used for expensive goods that are uniquely identifiable, such as precious gemstones. Under this method, the cost of sales and the cost of ending inventory reflect the actual costs incurred to purchase (or manufacture) the items specifically identified as sold and the items specifically identified as remaining in inventory. Therefore, this method matches the physical flow of the specific items sold and remaining in inventory to their actual cost.

3.2 First-In, First-Out (FIFO)

FIFO assumes that the oldest goods purchased (or manufactured) are sold first and the newest goods purchased (or manufactured) remain in ending inventory. In other words, the first units included in inventory are assumed to be the first units sold from inventory. Therefore, cost of sales reflects the cost of goods in beginning inventory plus the cost of items purchased (or manufactured) earliest in the accounting period, and the value of ending inventory reflects the costs of goods purchased (or manufactured) more recently. In periods of rising prices, the costs assigned to the units in ending inventory are higher than the costs assigned to the units sold. Conversely, in periods of declining prices, the costs assigned to the units in ending inventory are lower than the costs assigned to the units sold.

3.3 Weighted Average Cost

Weighted average cost assigns the average cost of the goods available for sale (beginning inventory plus purchase, conversion, and other costs) during the accounting period to the units that are sold as well as to the units in ending inventory. In an accounting period, the weighted average cost per unit is calculated as the total cost of the units available for sale divided by the total number of units available for sale in the period (Total cost of goods available for sale/Total units available for sale).

3.4 Last-In, First-Out (LIFO)

LIFO is permitted only under U.S. GAAP. This method assumes that the newest goods purchased (or manufactured) are sold first and the oldest goods purchased (or manufactured), including beginning inventory, remain in ending inventory. In other words, the last units included in inventory are assumed to be the first units sold from inventory. Therefore, cost of sales reflects the cost of goods purchased (or manufactured) more recently, and the value of ending inventory reflects the cost of older goods. In periods of rising prices, the costs assigned to the units in ending inventory are lower than the costs assigned to the units sold. Conversely, in periods of declining prices, the costs assigned to the units in ending inventory are higher than the costs assigned to the units sold.

3.5 Calculation of Cost of Sales, Gross Profit, and Ending Inventory

In periods of changing prices, the allocation of total inventory costs (i.e., cost of goods available for sale) between cost of sales on the income statement and inventory on the balance sheet will vary depending on the inventory valuation method used by the company. The following example illustrates how cost of sales, gross profit, and ending inventory differ based on the choice of inventory valuation method.

EXAMPLE 2

Inventory Cost Flow Illustration for the Specific Identification, Weighted Average Cost, FIFO, and LIFO Methods

Global Sales, Inc. (GSI) is a hypothetical distributor of consumer products, including bars of violet essence soap. The soap is sold by the kilogram. GSI began operations in 2009, during which it purchased and received initially 100,000 kg of soap at 110 yuan/kg, then 200,000 kg of soap at 100 yuan/kg, and finally 300,000 kg of soap at 90 yuan/kg. GSI sold 520,000 kg of soap at 240 yuan/kg. GSI stores its soap in its warehouse so that soap from each shipment received is readily identifiable. During 2009, the entire 100,000 kg from the first shipment received, 180,000 kg of the second shipment received, and 240,000 kg of the final shipment received was sent to customers. Answers to the following questions should be rounded to the nearest 1,000 yuan.

1. What are the reported cost of sales, gross profit, and ending inventory balances for 2009 under the specific identification method?

2. What are the reported cost of sales, gross profit, and ending inventory balances for 2009 under the weighted average cost method?

3. What are the reported cost of sales, gross profit, and ending inventory balances for 2009 under the FIFO method?

4. What are the reported cost of sales, gross profit, and ending inventory balances for 2009 under the LIFO method?

Solution to 1: Under the specific identification method, the physical flow of the specific inventory items sold is matched to their actual cost.

$$\text{Sales} = 520{,}000 \times 240 = 124{,}800{,}000 \text{ yuan}$$
$$\text{Cost of sales} = (100{,}000 \times 110) + (180{,}000 \times 100)$$
$$+ (240{,}000 \times 90) = 50{,}600{,}000 \text{ yuan}$$

Gross profit = 124,800,000 − 50,600,000 = 74,200,000 yuan
Ending inventory = (20,000 × 100) + (60,000 × 90)
= 7,400,000 yuan

Note that in spite of the segregation of inventory within the warehouse, it would be inappropriate to use specific identification for this inventory of interchangeable items. The use of specific identification could potentially result in earnings manipulation through the shipment decision.

Solution to 2: Under the weighted average cost method, costs are allocated to cost of sales and ending inventory by using a weighted average mix of the actual costs incurred for all inventory items. The weighted average cost per unit is determined by dividing the total cost of goods available for sale by the number of units available for sale.

Weighted average cost = [(100,000 × 110) + (200,000 × 100)
+ (300,000 × 90)]/600,000
= 96.667 yuan/kg
Sales = 520,000 × 240 = 124,800,000 yuan
Cost of sales = 520,000 × 96.667 = 50,267,000 yuan
Gross profit = 124,800,000 − 50,267,000 = 74,533,000 yuan
Ending inventory = 80,000 × 96.667 = 7,733,000 yuan

Solution to 3: Under the FIFO method, the oldest inventory units acquired are assumed to be the first units sold. Ending inventory, therefore, is assumed to consist of those inventory units most recently acquired.

Sales = 520,000 × 240 = 124,800,000 yuan
Cost of sales = (100,000 × 110) + (200,000 × 100)
+ (220,000 × 90) = 50,800,000 yuan
Gross profit = 124,800,000 − 50,800,000 = 74,000,000 yuan
Ending inventory = 80,000 × 90 = 7,200,000 yuan

Solution to 4: Under the LIFO method, the newest inventory units acquired are assumed to be the first units sold. Ending inventory, therefore, is assumed to consist of the oldest inventory units.

Sales = 520,000 × 240 = 124,800,000 yuan
Cost of sales = (20,000 × 110) + (200,000 × 100) + (300,000 × 90)
= 49,200,000 yuan
Gross profit = 124,800,000 − 49,200,000 = 75,600,000 yuan
Ending inventory = 80,000 × 110 = 8,800,000 yuan

The following table (in thousands of yuan) summarizes the cost of sales, the ending inventory, and the cost of goods available for sale that were calculated for each of the four inventory valuation methods. Note that in the first year of operation, the total cost of goods available for sale is the same under all four methods. Subsequently, the cost of goods available for sale will typically differ because beginning inventories will differ. Also shown is the gross profit figure for each of the four methods. Because the cost of a kg of soap declined over the period, LIFO had the highest ending inventory amount, the lowest cost of sales, and the highest gross profit. FIFO had the lowest ending inventory amount, the highest cost of sales, and the lowest gross profit.

Inventory Valuation Method	Specific ID	Weighted Average Cost	FIFO	LIFO
Cost of sales	50,600	50,267	50,800	49,200
Ending inventory	7,400	7,733	7,200	8,800
Total cost of goods available for sale	58,000	58,000	58,000	58,000
Gross profit	74,200	74,533	74,000	75,600

3.6 Periodic versus Perpetual Inventory Systems

Companies typically record changes to inventory in one of two ways. Under a periodic inventory system, a company determines the quantity of inventory on hand periodically. Purchases are recorded in a purchases account. The total of purchases and beginning inventory is the amount of goods available for sale during the period. The ending inventory amount is subtracted from the goods available for sale to arrive at the cost of sales. The quantity of goods in ending inventory is usually obtained or verified through a physical count of the units in inventory. Under a perpetual inventory system, changes in the inventory account are continuously updated. Purchases and sales of goods are recorded directly in inventory as they occur.

The use of periodic versus perpetual inventory systems will arrive at the same values for cost of sales and ending inventory using the specific identification and FIFO methods of inventory valuation. The choice of system, however, will potentially affect the ending inventory and cost of sales when either the LIFO or weighted average cost method is used. Example 3 illustrates the impact of the choice of system under LIFO.

EXAMPLE 3

Perpetual versus Periodic Inventory Systems

If GSI (the company in Example 2) had used a perpetual inventory system, the timing of purchases and sales would affect the amounts of cost of sales and inventory. Below is a record of the purchases, sales, and quantity of inventory on hand after the transaction in 2009.

Date	Purchased	Sold	Inventory on Hand
5 January	100,000 kg at 110 yuan/kg		100,000 kg
1 February		80,000 kg at 240 yuan/kg	20,000 kg
8 March	200,000 kg at 100 yuan/kg		220,000 kg
6 April		100,000 kg at 240 yuan/kg	120,000 kg
23 May		60,000 kg at 240 yuan/kg	60,000 kg
7 July		40,000 kg at 240 yuan/kg	20,000 kg

(continued on next page . . .)

(*continued*)

Date	Purchased	Sold	Inventory on Hand
2 August	300,000 kg at 90 yuan/kg		320,000 kg
5 September		70,000 kg at 240 yuan/kg	250,000 kg
17 November		90,000 kg at 240 yuan/kg	160,000 kg
8 December		80,000 kg at 240 yuan/kg	80,000 kg
	Total goods available for sale = 58,000,000 yuan	Total sales = 124,800,000 yuan	

The amounts for total goods available for sale and sales are the same under either the perpetual or periodic system in this first year of operation. The carrying amount of the ending inventory, however, may differ because the perpetual system will apply LIFO continuously throughout the year. Under the periodic system, it was assumed that the ending inventory was composed of 80,000 units of the oldest inventory, which cost 110 yuan/kg.

What are the ending inventory, cost of sales, and gross profit amounts using the perpetual system and the LIFO method? How do these compare with the amounts using the periodic system and the LIFO method, as in Example 2?

Solution: The carrying amounts of the inventory at the different time points using the perpetual inventory system are as follows:

Date	Quantity on Hand	Quantities and Cost	Carrying Amount
5 January	100,000 kg	100,000 kg at 110 yuan/kg	11,000,000 yuan
1 February	20,000 kg	20,000 kg at 110 yuan/kg	2,200,000 yuan
8 March	220,000 kg	20,000 kg at 110 yuan/kg + 200,000 kg at 100 yuan/kg	22,200,000 yuan
6 April	120,000 kg	20,000 kg at 110 yuan/kg + 100,000 kg at 100 yuan/kg	12,200,000 yuan
23 May	60,000 kg	20,000 kg at 110 yuan/kg + 40,000 kg at 100 yuan/kg	6,200,000 yuan
7 July	20,000 kg	20,000 kg at 110 yuan/kg	2,200,000 yuan
2 August	320,000 kg	20,000 kg at 110 yuan/kg + 300,000 kg at 90 yuan/kg	29,200,000 yuan
5 September	250,000 kg	20,000 kg at 110 yuan/kg + 230,000 kg at 90 yuan/kg	22,900,000 yuan
17 November	160,000 kg	20,000 kg at 110 yuan/kg + 140,000 kg at 90 yuan/kg	14,800,000 yuan
8 December	80,000 kg	20,000 kg at 110 yuan/kg + 60,000 kg at 90 yuan/kg	7,600,000 yuan

Perpetual system

Sales = 520,000 × 240 = 124,800,000 yuan

Cost of sales = 58,000,000 − 7,600,000 = 50,400,000 yuan

Gross profit = 124,800,000 − 50,400,000 = 74,400,000 yuan

Ending inventory = 7,600,000 yuan

Periodic system from Example 2
> Sales = 520,000 × 240 = 124,800,000 yuan
> Cost of sales = (20,000 × 110) + (200,000 × 100)
> + (300,000 × 90) = 49,200,000 yuan
> Gross profit = 124,800,000 − 49,200,000 = 75,600,000 yuan
> Ending inventory = 80,000 × 110 = 8,800,000 yuan

In this example, the ending inventory amount is lower under the perpetual system because only 20,000 kg of the oldest inventory with the highest cost is assumed to remain in inventory. The cost of sales is higher and the gross profit is lower under the perpetual system compared to the periodic system.

3.7 Comparison of Inventory Valuation Methods

As shown in Example 2, the allocation of the total cost of goods available for sale to cost of sales on the income statement and to ending inventory on the balance sheet varies under the different inventory valuation methods. In an environment of declining inventory unit costs and constant or increasing inventory quantities, FIFO (in comparison with weighted average cost or LIFO) will allocate a higher amount of the total cost of goods available for sale to cost of sales on the income statement and a lower amount to ending inventory on the balance sheet. Accordingly, because cost of sales will be higher under FIFO, a company's gross profit, operating profit, and income before taxes will be lower.

Conversely, in an environment of rising inventory unit costs and constant or increasing inventory quantities, FIFO (in comparison with weighted average cost or LIFO) will allocate a lower amount of the total cost of goods available for sale to cost of sales on the income statement and a higher amount to ending inventory on the balance sheet. Accordingly, because cost of sales will be lower under FIFO, a company's gross profit, operating profit, and income before taxes will be higher.

The carrying amount of inventories under FIFO will more closely reflect current replacement values because inventories are assumed to consist of the most recently purchased items. The cost of sales under LIFO will more closely reflect current replacement value. LIFO ending inventory amounts are typically not reflective of current replacement value because the ending inventory is assumed to be the oldest inventory and costs are allocated accordingly.

4   MEASUREMENT OF INVENTORY VALUE

Significant financial risk can result from the holding of inventory. The cost of inventory may not be recoverable because of spoilage, obsolescence, or declines in selling prices. Under IFRS, "inventories shall be measured at the lower of cost and net realisable value."[8] **Net realisable value** is the estimated selling price in the ordinary course of business less the estimated costs necessary to get the inventory in condition for sale and to make the sale. The assessment of net real-

---

[8] IAS 2, paragraph 9.

isable value is typically done by item or by groups of similar or related items. In the event that the value of inventory declines below the carrying amount on the balance sheet, the inventory carrying amount must be written down to its net realisable value and the loss (reduction in value) recognised as an expense on the income statement. Rather than write down the inventory through the inventory account, a company may use an inventory valuation allowance (reserve) account. The inventory amount net of the valuation allowance equals the carrying amount of the inventory after write-downs.

In each subsequent period, a new assessment of net realisable value is made. Reversal (limited to the amount of the original write-down) is required for a subsequent increase in value of inventory previously written down. The amount of any reversal of any write-down of inventory arising from an increase in net realisable value is recognised as a reduction in cost of sales (a reduction in the amount of inventories recognised as an expense).

Under U.S. GAAP, inventory is measured at the lower of cost or market.[9] Market value is defined as current replacement cost subject to upper and lower limits. Market value cannot exceed net realisable value (selling price less reasonably estimated costs of completion and disposal). The lower limit of market value is net realisable value less a normal profit margin. Any write-down reduces the value of the inventory, and the loss in value (expense) is generally reflected in the income statement in cost of goods sold. U.S. GAAP prohibit the reversal of a write-down; this rule is different from the treatment under IFRS.

IAS 2 does not apply to the inventories of producers of agricultural and forest products, producers of minerals and mineral products, and commodity broker–traders whose inventories are measured at net realisable value (fair value less costs to sell and, if necessary, complete) according to well-established industry practices. If an active market exists for these products, the quoted market price in that market is the appropriate basis for determining the fair value of that asset. If an active market does not exist, a company may use market-determined prices or values (such as the most recent market transaction price) when available. Changes in the value of inventory (increases or decreases) are recognised in profit or loss in the period of the change. U.S. GAAP are similar to IFRS in the treatment of inventories of agricultural and forest products and mineral ores. Mark-to-market inventory accounting is allowed for refined bullion of precious metals.

EXAMPLE 4

Accounting for Declines and Recoveries of Inventory Value

Acme Enterprises, a hypothetical company, manufactures computers and prepares its financial statements in accordance with IFRS. In 2008, the cost of ending inventory was €5.2 million but its net realisable value was €4.9 million. The current replacement cost of the inventory is €4.7 million. This figure exceeds the net realisable value less a normal profit margin. In 2009, the net realisable value of Acme's inventory was €0.5 million greater than the carrying amount.

---

[9] ASC Section 330-10-35 [Inventory–Overall–Subsequent Measurement].

1. What was the effect of the write-down on Acme's 2008 financial statements? What was the effect of the recovery on Acme's 2009 financial statements?

2. Under U.S. GAAP, what would be the effects of the write-down on Acme's 2008 financial statements and of the recovery on Acme's 2009 financial statements?

3. What would be the effect of the recovery on Acme's 2009 financial statements if Acme's inventory were agricultural products instead of computers?

Solution to 1: For 2008, Acme would write its inventory down to €4.9 million and record the change in value of €0.3 million as an expense on the income statement. For 2009, Acme would increase the carrying amount of its inventory and reduce the cost of sales by €0.3 million (the recovery is limited to the amount of the original write-down).

Solution to 2: Under U.S. GAAP, for 2008, Acme would write its inventory down to €4.7 million and typically include the change in value of €0.5 million in cost of goods sold on the income statement. For 2009, Acme would not reverse the write-down.

Solution to 3: If Acme's inventory were agricultural products instead of computers, inventory would be measured at net realisable value and Acme would, therefore, increase inventory by and record a gain of €0.5 million for 2009.

5   PRESENTATION AND DISCLOSURE

IFRS require the following financial statement disclosures concerning inventory:

a. the accounting policies adopted in measuring inventories, including the cost formula (inventory valuation method) used;

b. the total carrying amount of inventories and the carrying amount in classifications (for example, merchandise, raw materials, production supplies, work in progress, and finished goods) appropriate to the entity;

c. the carrying amount of inventories carried at fair value less costs to sell;

d. the amount of inventories recognised as an expense during the period (cost of sales);

e. the amount of any write-down of inventories recognised as an expense in the period;

f. the amount of any reversal of any write-down that is recognised as a reduction in cost of sales in the period;

g. the circumstances or events that led to the reversal of a write-down of inventories; and

h. the carrying amount of inventories pledged as security for liabilities.

Inventory-related disclosures under U.S. GAAP are very similar to the disclosures above, except that requirements (f) and (g) are not relevant because U.S.

GAAP do not permit the reversal of prior-year inventory write-downs. U.S. GAAP also require disclosure of significant estimates applicable to inventories and of any material amount of income resulting from the liquidation of LIFO inventory.[10]

5.1 Changes in Inventory Valuation Method

In rare situations, a company may decide that it is appropriate to change its inventory valuation method (cost formula). Under IFRS,[11] a change in accounting policy (including a change in cost formula) is acceptable only if the change results in the financial statements providing reliable and more relevant information about the effects of transactions, other events, or conditions on the business entity's financial position, financial performance, or cash flows. Changes in accounting policy are accounted for retrospectively. If the change is justifiable, historical information is restated for all accounting periods (typically the previous one or two years) that are presented for comparability purposes with the current year in annual financial reports. Adjustments of financial statement information relating to accounting periods prior to those presented are reflected in the beginning balance of retained earnings for the earliest year presented for comparison purposes. This retrospective restatement requirement enhances the comparability of financial statements over time. An exemption to the retrospective restatement requirement applies when it is impracticable to determine either the period-specific effects or the cumulative effect of the change.

Under U.S. GAAP, a company making a change in inventory valuation method is required to explain why the newly adopted inventory valuation method is superior and preferable to the old method. In addition, U.S. tax regulations may also restrict changes in inventory valuation methods and require permission from the Internal Revenue Service (IRS) prior to implementation. If a company decides to change from LIFO to another inventory method, U.S. GAAP require a retrospective restatement of inventory and retained earnings. Historical financial statements are also restated for the effects of the change. If a company decides to change to the LIFO method, it must do so on a prospective basis. Retrospective adjustments are not made to the financial statements. Instead, the carrying value of inventory under the old method will become the initial LIFO layer in the year of LIFO adoption.

EVALUATION OF INVENTORY MANAGEMENT   6

The choice of inventory valuation method impacts the financial statements, as illustrated in Example 2. The financial statement items impacted include cost of sales, gross profit, net income, inventories, current assets, and total assets. Therefore, the choice of inventory valuation method also affects financial ratios that contain these items. Ratios such as current ratio, return on assets, gross profit margin, and inventory turnover are impacted. As a consequence, analysts must carefully consider inventory valuation method differences when evaluating a company's performance over time or when comparing its performance with the

---

[10] LIFO liquidation is a CFA Level II curriculum topic.

[11] IAS 8 [Accounting Policies, Changes in Accounting Estimates and Errors].

performance of the industry or industry competitors. Additionally, the financial statement items and ratios may be impacted by adjustments of inventory carrying amounts to net realisable value or current replacement cost.

6.1 Inventory Ratios

Three ratios often used to evaluate the efficiency and effectiveness of inventory management are **inventory turnover**, **days of inventory on hand**, and **gross profit margin**.[12] These ratios are directly impacted by a company's choice of inventory valuation method. Analysts should be aware, however, that many other ratios are also affected by the choice of inventory valuation method, although less directly. These include the current ratio, because inventory is a component of current assets; the return-on-assets ratio, because cost of sales is a key component in deriving net income and inventory is a component of total assets; and even the debt-to-equity ratio, because the cumulative measured net income from the inception of a business is an aggregate component of retained earnings.

The inventory turnover ratio measures the number of times during the year a company sells (i.e., turns over) its inventory. The higher the turnover ratio, the more times that inventory is sold during the year and the lower the relative investment of resources in inventory. Days of inventory on hand can be calculated as days in the period divided by inventory turnover. Thus, inventory turnover and days of inventory on hand are inversely related. It may be that inventory turnover, however, is calculated using average inventory in the year whereas days of inventory on hand is based on the ending inventory amount. In general, inventory turnover and the number of days of inventory on hand should be benchmarked against industry norms and compared across years.

A high inventory turnover ratio and a low number of days of inventory on hand might indicate highly effective inventory management. Alternatively, a high inventory ratio and a low number of days of inventory on hand could indicate that the company does not carry an adequate amount of inventory or that the company has written down inventory values. Inventory shortages could potentially result in lost sales or production problems in the case of the raw materials inventory of a manufacturer. To assess which explanation is more likely, analysts can compare the company's inventory turnover and sales growth rate with those of the industry and review financial statement disclosures. Slower growth combined with higher inventory turnover could indicate inadequate inventory levels. Write-downs of inventory could reflect poor inventory management. Minimal write-downs and sales growth rates at or above the industry's growth rates would support the interpretation that the higher turnover reflects greater efficiency in managing inventory.

A low inventory turnover ratio and a high number of days of inventory on hand relative to industry norms could be an indicator of slow-moving or obsolete inventory. Again, comparing the company's sales growth across years and with the industry and reviewing financial statement disclosures can provide additional insight.

The gross profit margin, the ratio of gross profit to sales, indicates the percentage of sales being contributed to net income as opposed to covering the cost of sales. Firms in highly competitive industries generally have lower gross profit margins than firms in industries with fewer competitors. A company's gross profit margin may be a function of its type of product. A company selling luxury products will generally have higher gross profit margins than a company selling

---

[12] *Days of inventory on hand* is also referred to as *days in inventory* and *average inventory days outstanding*.

staple products. The inventory turnover of the company selling luxury products, however, is likely to be much lower than the inventory turnover of the company selling staple products.

6.2 Financial Analysis Illustration

Selected excerpts from the consolidated financial statements and notes to consolidated financial statements for Alcatel-Lucent (NYSE: ALU) are presented in Exhibits 1, 2, and 3. Exhibit 1 contains excerpts from the consolidated income statements, and Exhibit 2 contains excerpts from the consolidated balance sheets. Exhibit 3 contains excerpts from three of the notes to consolidated financial statements.

Note 1 (i) discloses that ALU's finished goods inventories and work in progress are valued at the lower of cost or net realisable value. Note 2 (a) discloses that the impact of inventory and work in progress write-downs on ALU's income before tax was a net reduction of €285 million in 2008, a net reduction of €186 million in 2007, and a net reduction of €77 million in 2006.[13] The inventory impairment loss amounts steadily increased from 2006 to 2008 and are included as a component, (additions)/reversals, of ALU's change in valuation allowance as disclosed in Note 19 (b) from Exhibit 3. Observe also that ALU discloses its valuation allowance at 31 December 2008, 2007, and 2006 in Note 19 (b) and details on the allocation of the allowance are included in Note 19 (a). The €654 million valuation allowance is the total of a €629 million allowance for inventories and a €25 million allowance for work in progress on construction contracts. Finally, observe that the €2,196 million net value for inventories (excluding construction contracts) at 31 December 2008 in Note 19 (a) reconciles with the balance sheet amount for inventories and work in progress, net, on 31 December 2008, as presented in Exhibit 2.

The inventory valuation allowance represents the total amount of inventory write-downs taken for the inventory reported on the balance sheet (which is measured at the lower of cost or net realisable value). Therefore, an analyst can determine the historical cost of the company's inventory by adding the inventory valuation allowance to the reported inventory carrying amount on the balance sheet. The valuation allowance increased in magnitude and as a percentage of gross inventory values from 2006 to 2008.

EXHIBIT 1	Alcatel-Lucent Consolidated Income Statements (€ Millions)		
For Years Ended 31 December	**2008**	**2007**	**2006**
Revenues	16,984	17,792	12,282
Cost of sales	(11,190)	(12,083)	(8,214)
Gross profit	5,794	5,709	4,068
Administrative and selling expenses	(3,093)	(3,462)	(1,911)
Research and development costs	(2,757)	(2,954)	(1,470)
Income from operating activities before restructuring costs, impairment of assets, gain/(loss) on disposal of consolidated entities, and post-retirement benefit plan amendments	(56)	(707)	687

(Exhibit continued on next page . . .)

---

[13] This reduction is often referred to as a *charge*. An accounting charge is the recognition of a loss or expense. In this case, the charge is attributable to the impairment of assets.

EXHIBIT 1	(continued)			

For Years Ended 31 December	2008	2007	2006
Restructuring costs	(562)	(856)	(707)
Impairment of assets	(4,725)	(2,944)	(141)
Gain/(loss) on disposal of consolidated entities	(7)	—	15
Post-retirement benefit plan amendments	47	258	—
Income (loss) from operating activities	(5,303)	(4,249)	(146)
⋮	⋮	⋮	⋮
Income (loss) from continuing operations	(5,206)	(4,087)	(219)
Income (loss) from discontinued operations	33	610	158
Net income (loss)	(5,173)	(3,477)	(61)

EXHIBIT 2	Alcatel-Lucent Consolidated Balance Sheets (€ Millions)			

31 December	2008	2007	2006
Total non-current assets	12,742	20,135	25,665
Inventories and work in progress, net	2,196	2,235	2,259
Amounts due from customers on construction contracts	495	704	615
Trade receivables and related accounts, net	4,330	4,163	3,877
Advances and progress payments	99	110	87
⋮	⋮	⋮	⋮
Total current assets	14,569	13,695	16,225
Total assets	27,311	33,830	41,890
⋮	⋮	⋮	⋮
Retained earnings, fair value, and other reserves	(8,820)	(3,821)	(3,441)
⋮	⋮	⋮	⋮
Total shareholders' equity	5,224	11,702	16,323
Pensions, retirement indemnities, and other post-retirement benefits	4,807	4,447	5,449
Bonds and notes issued, long-term	3,931	4,517	4,901
Other long-term debt	67	48	147
Deferred tax liabilities	1,152	1,897	2,583
Other non-current liabilities	443	366	276
Total non-current liabilities	10,400	11,275	13,356
Provisions	2,424	2,566	2,366
Current portion of long-term debt	1,097	483	1,161
Customers' deposits and advances	929	847	778
Amounts due to customers on construction contracts	188	407	273

(Exhibit continued on next page . . .)

EXHIBIT 2	(continued)		

31 December	2008	2007	2006
Trade payables and related accounts	4,571	4,514	4,027
Liabilities related to disposal groups held for sale	—	—	1,606
Current income tax liabilities	185	70	66
Other current liabilities	2,293	1,966	1,934
Total current liabilities	11,687	10,853	12,211
Total liabilities and shareholders' equity	27,311	33,830	41,890

EXHIBIT 3	Alcatel-Lucent Selected Notes to Consolidated Financial Statements

Note 1. Summary of significant accounting policies

(i) Inventories and work in progress

Inventories and work in progress are valued at the lower of cost (including indirect production costs where applicable) or net realizable value.[14] Net realizable value is the estimated sales revenue for a normal period of activity less expected completion and selling costs.

Note 2. Principal uncertainties regarding the use of estimates

(a) Valuation allowance for inventories and work in progress

Inventories and work in progress are measured at the lower of cost or net realizable value. Valuation allowances for inventories and work in progress are calculated based on an analysis of foreseeable changes in demand, technology, or the market, in order to determine obsolete or excess inventories and work in progress.

The valuation allowances are accounted for in cost of sales or in restructuring costs, depending on the nature of the amounts concerned.

	31 December		
(€ millions)	2008	2007	2006
Valuation allowance for inventories and work in progress on construction contracts	(654)	(514)	(378)
Impact of inventory and work in progress write-downs on income (loss) before income tax related reduction of goodwill and discontinued operations	(285)	(186)	(77)

(Exhibit continued on next page . . .)

---

[14] *Cost* approximates cost on a first-in, first-out basis.

EXHIBIT 3	(continued)

Note 19. Inventories and work in progress

(a) Analysis of net value

(€ millions)	2008	2007	2006
Raw materials and goods	649	564	542
Work in progress excluding construction contracts	972	958	752
Finished goods	1,204	1,185	1,320
Gross value (excluding construction contracts)	2,825	2,707	2,614
Valuation allowance	(629)	(472)	(355)
Net value (excluding construction contracts)	2,196	2,235	2,259
Work in progress on construction contracts, gross*	219	272	347
Valuation allowance	(25)	(42)	(23)
Work in progress on construction contracts, net	194	230	324
Total, net	2,390	2,465	2,583

* Included in the amounts due from/to construction contracts

(b) Change in valuation allowance

(€ millions)	2008	2007	2006
At 1 January	(514)	(378)	(423)
(Additions)/reversals	(285)	(186)	(77)
Utilization	69	38	54
Changes in consolidation group	—	—	54
Net effect of exchange rate changes and other changes	75	12	14
At 31 December	(654)	(514)	(378)

Note: Rounding differences may result in totals that are different from the sum.

EXAMPLE 5

Financial Analysis Illustration

The consolidated income statements and consolidated balance sheets for Alcatel-Lucent are provided in Exhibits 1 and 2, respectively. Exhibit 3 includes selected financial note disclosures concerning ALU's inventory accounting policies.

1. Calculate ALU's inventory turnover, number of days of inventory on hand, gross profit margin, current ratio, debt-to-equity ratio, and return on total assets for 2008 and 2007 based on the numbers reported. Use an average for inventory and total asset amounts and year-end numbers for other ratio items. For debt, include only

bonds and notes issued, long-term; other long-term debt; and current portion of long-term debt.

2. Based on the answer to Question 1, comment on the changes from 2007 to 2008.

3. If ALU had used the weighted average cost method instead of the FIFO method during 2008, 2007, and 2006, what would be the effect on ALU's reported cost of sales and inventory carrying amounts? What would be the directional impact on the financial ratios that were calculated for ALU in Question 1, above?

Solution to 1: The financial ratios are as follows:

	2008	2007
Inventory turnover ratio	5.05	5.38
Number of days of inventory	72.3 days	67.8 days
Gross profit margin	34.1%	32.1%
Current ratio	1.25	1.26
Debt-to-equity ratio	0.98	0.43
Return on total assets	−16.9%	−9.2%

Inventory turnover ratio = Cost of sales ÷ Average inventory
2008 inventory turnover ratio = 5.05 = 11,190 ÷ [(2,196 + 2,235) ÷ 2]
2007 inventory turnover ratio = 5.38 = 12,083 ÷ [(2,235 + 2,259) ÷ 2]

Number of days of inventory = 365 days ÷ Inventory turnover ratio
2008 number of days of inventory = 72.3 days = 365 days ÷ 5.05
2007 number of days of inventory = 67.8 days = 365 days ÷ 5.38

Gross profit margin = Gross profit ÷ Total revenue
2008 gross profit margin = 34.1% = 5,794 ÷ 16,984
2007 gross profit margin = 32.1% = 5,709 ÷ 17,792

Current ratio = Current assets ÷ Current liabilities
2008 current ratio = 1.25 = 14,569 ÷ 11,687
2007 current ratio = 1.26 = 13,695 ÷ 10,853

Debt-to-equity ratio = Total debt ÷ Total shareholders' equity
2008 debt-to-equity ratio = 0.98 = (3,931 + 67 + 1,097) ÷ 5,224
2007 debt-to-equity ratio = 0.43 = (4,517 + 48 + 483) ÷ 11,702

Return on assets = Net income ÷ Average total assets
2008 return on assets = −16.9% = −5,173 ÷ [(27,311 + 33,830) ÷ 2]
2007 return on assets = −9.2% = −3,477 ÷ [(33,830 + 41,890) ÷ 2]

Solution to 2: From 2007 to 2008, the inventory turnover ratio declined and the number of days of inventory increased by 4.5 days. ALU appears to be managing inventory less efficiently. The gross profit margin improved by 2.0 percent, from 32.1 percent in 2007 to

34.1 percent in 2008. The current ratio is relatively unchanged from 2007 to 2008. The debt-to-equity ratio has risen significantly in 2008 compared to 2007. Although ALU's total debt has been relatively stable during this time period, the company's equity has been declining rapidly because of the cumulative effect of its net losses on retained earnings.

The return on assets is negative and got worse in 2008 compared to 2007. A larger net loss and lower total assets in 2008 resulted in a higher negative return on assets. The analyst should investigate the underlying reasons for the sharp decline in ALU's return on assets. From Exhibit 1, it is apparent that ALU's gross profit margins were insufficient to cover the administrative and selling expenses and research and development costs in 2007 and 2008. Large restructuring costs and asset impairment losses contributed to the loss from operating activities in both 2007 and 2008.

Solution to 3: If inventory replacement costs were increasing during 2006, 2007, and 2008 (and inventory quantity levels were stable or increasing), ALU's cost of sales would have been higher and its gross profit margin would have been lower under the weighted average cost inventory method than what was reported under the FIFO method (assuming no inventory write-downs that would otherwise neutralize the differences between the inventory valuation methods). FIFO allocates the oldest inventory costs to cost of sales; the reported cost of sales would be lower under FIFO given increasing inventory costs. Inventory carrying amounts would be higher under the FIFO method than under the weighted average cost method because the more recently purchased inventory items would be included in inventory at their higher costs (again assuming no inventory write-downs that would otherwise neutralize the differences between the inventory valuation methods). Consequently, ALU's reported gross profit, net income, and retained earnings would also be higher for those years under the FIFO method.

The effects on ratios are as follows:

▶ The inventory turnover ratios would all be higher under the weighted average cost method because the numerator (cost of sales) would be higher and the denominator (inventory) would be lower than what was reported by ALU under the FIFO method.

▶ The number of days of inventory would be lower under the weighted average cost method because the inventory turnover ratios would be higher.

▶ The gross profit margin ratios would all be lower under the weighted average cost method because cost of sales would be higher under the weighted average cost method than under the FIFO method.

▶ The current ratios would all be lower under the weighted average cost method because inventory carrying values would be lower than under the FIFO method (current liabilities would be the same under both methods).

▶ The return-on-assets ratios would all be lower under the weighted average cost method because the incremental profit added to the numerator (net income) has a greater impact than the incremental increase to the denominator (total assets). By way of example, assume that a company has €3 million in net income and €100 million in total assets using the weighted average cost method. If the company reports another €1 million in net income by using FIFO instead of weighted average cost, it would then also report an additional €1 million in total assets (after tax). Based on this example, the return on assets is 3.00 percent (€3/€100) under the weighted average cost method and 3.96 percent (€4/€101) under the FIFO method.

► The debt-to-equity ratios would all be higher under the weighted average cost method because retained earnings would be lower than under the FIFO method (again assuming no inventory write-downs that would otherwise neutralize the differences between the inventory valuation methods).

Conversely, if inventory replacement costs were decreasing during 2006, 2007, and 2008 (and inventory quantity levels were stable or increasing), ALU's cost of sales would have been lower and its gross profit and inventory would have been higher under the weighted average cost method than were reported under the FIFO method (assuming no inventory write-downs that would otherwise neutralize the differences between the inventory valuation methods). As a result, the ratio assessment that was performed above would result in directly opposite conclusions.

SUMMARY

The choice of inventory valuation method (cost formula or cost flow assumption) can have a potentially significant impact on inventory carrying amounts and cost of sales. These in turn impact other financial statement items, such as current assets, total assets, gross profit, and net income. The financial statements and accompanying notes provide important information about a company's inventory accounting policies that the analyst needs to correctly assess financial performance and compare it with that of other companies.

Key concepts in this reading are as follows:

▶ Inventories are a major factor in the analysis of merchandising and manufacturing companies. Such companies generate their sales and profits through inventory transactions on a regular basis. An important consideration in determining profits for these companies is measuring the cost of sales when inventories are sold.

▶ The total cost of inventories comprises all costs of purchase, costs of conversion, and other costs incurred in bringing the inventories to their present location and condition. Storage costs of finished inventory and abnormal costs due to waste are typically treated as expenses in the period in which they occurred.

▶ IFRS allow three inventory valuation methods (cost formulas): first-in, first-out (FIFO); weighted average cost; and specific identification. The specific identification method is used for inventories of items that are not ordinarily interchangeable and for goods or services produced and segregated for specific projects. U.S. GAAP allow the three methods above plus the last-in, first-out (LIFO) method.

▶ A company must use the same cost formula for all inventories having a similar nature and use to the entity.

▶ The inventory accounting system (perpetual or periodic) may result in different values for cost of sales and ending inventory when the weighted average cost or LIFO inventory valuation method is used.

▶ Under IFRS, inventories are measured at the lower of cost and net realisable value. Net realisable value is the estimated selling price in the ordinary course of business less the estimated costs necessary to make the sale. Under U.S. GAAP, inventories are measured at the lower of cost or market value. Market value is defined as current replacement cost subject to an upper limit of net realizable value and a lower limit of net realizable value less a normal profit margin. Reversals of previous write-downs are permissible under IFRS but not under U.S. GAAP.

▶ Consistency of inventory accounting policies is required under both U.S. GAAP and IFRS. If a company changes an inventory accounting policy, the change must be justifiable and all financial statements are accounted for retrospectively. The one exception is for a change to the LIFO method under U.S. GAAP; the change is accounted for prospectively, and there is no retrospective adjustment to the financial statements.

▶ The choice of inventory valuation method affects a number of items on the financial statements and any financial ratios that include inventory or cost of sales, whether directly or indirectly. As a consequence, the analyst must carefully consider differences in inventory valuation methods when evaluating a company's performance in comparison to industry performance or industry competitors' performance.

- The inventory turnover ratio, number of days of inventory ratio, and gross profit margin ratio are useful in evaluating the management of a company's inventory.

- Financial statement disclosures provide information regarding the accounting policies adopted in measuring inventories, the principal uncertainties regarding the use of estimates related to inventories, and details of the inventory carrying amounts and costs. This information can greatly assist analysts in their evaluation of a company's inventory management.

PRACTICE PROBLEMS FOR READING 36

1. Inventory cost is *least likely* to include:
   A. production-related storage costs.
   B. cost incurred as a result of normal waste of materials.
   C. transportation costs of shipping inventory to customers.

2. Mustard Seed PLC adheres to IFRS. It recently purchased inventory for €100 million and spent €5 million for storage prior to selling the goods. The amount it charged to inventory expense (€ millions) was *closest* to:
   A. €95.
   B. €100.
   C. €105.

3. Carrying inventory at a value above its historical cost would *most likely* be permitted if:
   A. the inventory was held by a producer of agricultural products.
   B. financial statements were prepared using U.S. GAAP.
   C. the change resulted from a reversal of a previous write-down.

4. Eric's Used Book Store prepares its financial statements in accordance with IFRS. Inventory was purchased for £1 million and later marked down to £550,000. One of the books, however, was later discovered to be a rare collectible item, and the inventory is now worth an estimated £3 million. The inventory is *most likely* reported on the balance sheet at:
   A. £550,000.
   B. £1,000,000.
   C. £3,000,000.

5. Fernando's Pasta purchased inventory and later wrote it down. The current net realisable value is higher than the value when written down. Fernando's inventory balance will *most likely* be:
   A. higher if it complies with IFRS.
   B. higher if it complies with U.S. GAAP.
   C. the same under U.S. GAAP and IFRS.

For Questions 6–17, assume the companies use a periodic inventory system.

6. Cinnamon Corp. started business in 2007 and uses the weighted average cost method. During 2007, it purchased 45,000 units of inventory at €10 each and sold 40,000 units for €20 each. In 2008, it purchased another 50,000 units at €11 each and sold 45,000 units for €22 each. Its 2008 cost of sales (€ thousands) was *closest* to:
   A. €490.
   B. €491.
   C. €495.

7. Zimt AG started business in 2007 and uses the FIFO method. During 2007, it purchased 45,000 units of inventory at €10 each and sold 40,000 units for €20 each. In 2008, it purchased another 50,000 units at €11 each and sold 45,000 units for €22 each. Its 2008 ending inventory balance (€ thousands) was *closest* to:

   A. €105.

   B. €109.

   C. €110.

8. Zimt AG uses the FIFO method, and Nutmeg Inc. uses the LIFO method. Compared to the cost of replacing the inventory, during periods of rising prices, the cost of sales reported by:

   A. Zimt is too low.

   B. Nutmeg is too low.

   C. Nutmeg is too high.

9. Zimt AG uses the FIFO method, and Nutmeg Inc. uses the LIFO method. Compared to the cost of replacing the inventory, during periods of rising prices the ending inventory balance reported by:

   A. Zimt is too high.

   B. Nutmeg is too low.

   C. Nutmeg is too high.

10. Like many technology companies, TechnoTools operates in an environment of declining prices. Its reported profits will tend to be *highest* if it accounts for inventory using the:

   A. FIFO method.

   B. LIFO method.

   C. weighted average cost method.

11. Compared to using the weighted average cost method to account for inventory, during a period in which prices are generally rising, the current ratio of a company using the FIFO method would *most likely* be:

   A. lower.

   B. higher.

   C. dependent upon the interaction with accounts payable.

12. Zimt AG wrote down the value of its inventory in 2007 and reversed the write-down in 2008. Compared to the ratios that would have been calculated if the write-down had never occurred, Zimt's reported 2007:

   A. current ratio was too high.

   B. gross margin was too high.

   C. inventory turnover was too high.

13. Zimt AG wrote down the value of its inventory in 2007 and reversed the write-down in 2008. Compared to the results the company would have reported if the write-down had never occurred, Zimt's reported 2008:

   A. profit was overstated.

   B. cash flow from operations was overstated.

   C. year-end inventory balance was overstated.

14. Compared to a company that uses the FIFO method, during periods of rising prices a company that uses the LIFO method will *most likely* appear more:

   A. liquid.

   B. efficient.

   C. profitable.

15. Nutmeg Inc. uses the LIFO method to account for inventory. During years in which inventory unit costs are generally rising and in which the company purchases more inventory than it sells to customers, its reported gross profit margin will *most likely* be:

   A. lower than it would be if the company used the FIFO method.

   B. higher than it would be if the company used the FIFO method.

   C. about the same as it would be if the company used the FIFO method.

16. Compared to using the FIFO method to account for inventory, during periods of rising prices, a company using the LIFO method is *most likely* to report higher:

   A. net income.

   B. cost of sales.

   C. income taxes.

17. Carey Company adheres to U.S. GAAP, whereas Jonathan Company adheres to IFRS. It is *least likely* that:

   A. Carey has reversed an inventory write-down.

   B. Jonathan has reversed an inventory write-down.

   C. Jonathan and Carey both use the FIFO inventory accounting method.

The following information relates to Questions 18–25[1]

Hans Annan, CFA, a food and beverage analyst, is reviewing Century Chocolate's inventory policies as part of his evaluation of the company. Century Chocolate, based in Switzerland, manufactures chocolate products and purchases and resells other confectionery products to complement its chocolate line. Annan visited Century Chocolate's manufacturing facility last year. He learned that cacao beans, imported from Brazil, represent the most significant raw material and that the work-in-progress inventory consists primarily of three items: roasted cacao beans, a thick paste produced from the beans (called chocolate liquor), and a sweetened mixture that needs to be "conched" to produce chocolate. On the tour, Annan learned that the conching process ranges from a few hours for lower-quality products to six days for the highest-quality chocolates. While there, Annan saw the facility's climate-controlled area where manufactured finished products (cocoa and chocolate) and purchased finished goods are stored prior to shipment to customers. After touring the facility, Annan had a discussion with Century Chocolate's CFO regarding the types of costs that were included in each inventory category.

Annan has asked his assistant, Joanna Kern, to gather some preliminary information regarding Century Chocolate's financial statements and inventories. He also asked Kern to calculate the inventory turnover ratios for

---

[1] Developed by Karen Rubsam, CFA (Fountain Hills, Arizona, USA).

Century Chocolate and another chocolate manufacturer for the most recent five years. Annan does not know Century Chocolate's most direct competitor, so he asks Kern to do some research and select the most appropriate company for the ratio comparison.

Kern reports back that Century Chocolate prepares its financial statements in accordance with IFRS. She tells Annan that the policy footnote states that raw materials and purchased finished goods are valued at purchase cost whereas work in progress and manufactured finished goods are valued at production cost. Raw material inventories and purchased finished goods are accounted for using the FIFO (first-in, first-out) method, and the weighted average cost method is used for other inventories. An allowance is established when the net realisable value of any inventory item is lower than the value calculated above.

Kern provides Annan with the selected financial statements and inventory data for Century Chocolate shown in Exhibits 1 through 5. The ratio exhibit Kern prepared compares Century Chocolate's inventory turnover ratios to those of Gordon's Goodies, a U.S.-based company. Annan returns the exhibit and tells Kern to select a different competitor that reports using IFRS rather than U.S. GAAP. During this initial review, Annan asks Kern why she has not indicated whether Century Chocolate uses a perpetual or a periodic inventory system. Kern replies that she learned that Century Chocolate uses a perpetual system but did not include this information in her report because inventory values would be the same under either a perpetual or periodic inventory system. Annan tells Kern she is wrong and directs her to research the matter.

While Kern is revising her analysis, Annan reviews the most recent month's Cocoa Market Review from the International Cocoa Organization. He is drawn to the statement that "the ICCO daily price, averaging prices in both futures markets, reached a 29-year high in US$ terms and a 23-year high in SDRs terms (the SDR unit comprises a basket of major currencies used in international trade: US$, euro, pound sterling and yen)." Annan makes a note that he will need to factor the potential continuation of this trend into his analysis.

EXHIBIT 1	Century Chocolate Income Statements (CHF Millions)	
For Years Ended 31 December	**2009**	**2008**
Sales	95,290	93,248
Cost of sales	−41,043	−39,047
Marketing, administration, and other expenses	−35,318	−42,481
Profit before taxes	**18,929**	**11,720**
Taxes	−3,283	−2,962
Profit for the period	**15,646**	**8,758**

EXHIBIT 2	Century Chocolate Balance Sheets (CHF Millions)	

31 December	2009	2008
Cash, cash equivalents, and short-term investments	6,190	8,252
Trade receivables and related accounts, net	11,654	12,910
Inventories, net	8,100	7,039
Other current assets	2,709	2,812
Total current assets	**28,653**	**31,013**
Property, plant, and equipment, net	18,291	19,130
Other non-current assets	45,144	49,875
Total assets	**92,088**	**100,018**
Trade and other payables	10,931	12,299
Other current liabilities	17,873	25,265
Total current liabilities	**28,804**	**37,564**
Non-current liabilities	15,672	14,963
Total liabilities	**44,476**	**52,527**
Equity		
Share capital	332	341
Retained earnings and other reserves	47,280	47,150
Total equity	**47,612**	**47,491**
Total liabilities and shareholders' equity	**92,088**	**100,018**

EXHIBIT 3	Century Chocolate Supplementary Footnote Disclosures: Inventories (CHF Millions)	

31 December	2009	2008
Raw Materials	2,154	1,585
Work in Progress	1,061	1,027
Finished Goods	5,116	4,665
Total inventories before allowance	8,331	7,277
Allowance for write-downs to net realisable value	−231	−238
Total inventories net of allowance	8,100	7,039

EXHIBIT 4	Century Chocolate Inventory Record for Purchased Lemon Drops		

Date		Cartons	Per Unit Amount (CHF)
	Beginning inventory	100	22
4 Feb 09	Purchase	40	25
3 Apr 09	Sale	50	32
23 Jul 09	Purchase	70	30
16 Aug 09	Sale	100	32
9 Sep 09	Sale	35	32
15 Nov 09	Purchase	100	28

EXHIBIT 5	Century Chocolate Net Realisable Value Information for Black Licorice Jelly Beans	

	2009	2008
FIFO cost of inventory at 31 December (CHF)	314,890	374,870
Ending inventory at 31 December (GBP)	77,750	92,560
Cost per unit (CHF)	4.05	4.05
Net Realisable Value (CHF per GBP)	4.20	3.95

18. The costs *least likely* to be included by the CFO as inventory are:

  A. storage costs for the chocolate liquor.

  B. excise taxes paid to the government of Brazil for the cacao beans.

  C. storage costs for chocolate and purchased finished goods awaiting shipment to customers.

19. What is the *most likely* justification for Century Chocolate's choice of inventory valuation method for its finished goods?

  A. It is the preferred method under IFRS.

  B. It allocates the same per unit cost to both cost of sales and inventory.

  C. Ending inventory reflects the cost of goods purchased most recently.

20. In Kern's comparative ratio analysis, the 2009 inventory turnover ratio for Century Chocolate is *closest* to:

  A. 5.07.

  B. 5.42.

  C. 5.55.

21. The *most accurate* statement regarding Annan's reasoning for requiring Kern to select a competitor that reports under IFRS for comparative purposes is that under U.S. GAAP:

    A. fair values are used to value inventory.

    B. the LIFO method is permitted to value inventory.

    C. the specific identification method is permitted to value inventory.

22. Annan's statement regarding the perpetual and periodic inventory systems is most significant when which of the following costing systems is used?

    A. LIFO.

    B. FIFO.

    C. Specific identification.

23. Using the inventory record for purchased lemon drops shown in Exhibit 4, the cost of sales for 2009 will be *closest* to:

    A. CHF 3,550.

    B. CHF 4,550.

    C. CHF 4,850.

24. Ignoring any tax effect, the 2009 net realisable value reassessment for the black licorice jelly beans will *most likely* result in:

    A. an increase in gross profit of CHF 9,256.

    B. an increase in gross profit of CHF 11,670.

    C. no impact on cost of sales because under IFRS, write-downs cannot be reversed.

25. If the trend noted in the ICCO report continues and Century Chocolate plans to maintain constant or increasing inventory quantities, the *most likely* impact on Century Chocolate's financial statements related to its raw materials inventory will be:

    A. a cost of sales that more closely reflects current replacement values.

    B. a higher allocation of the total cost of goods available for sale to cost of sales.

    C. a higher allocation of the total cost of goods available for sale to ending inventory.

SOLUTIONS FOR READING 36

1. C is correct. Transportation costs incurred to ship inventory to customers are an expense and may not be capitalized in inventory. (Transportation costs incurred to bring inventory to the business location can be capitalized in inventory.) Storage costs required as part of production, as well as costs incurred as a result of normal waste of materials, can be capitalized in inventory. (Costs incurred as a result of abnormal waste must be expensed.)

2. B is correct. Inventory expense includes costs of purchase, costs of conversion, and other costs incurred in bringing the inventories to their present location and condition. It does not include storage costs not required as part of production.

3. A is correct. IFRS allow the inventories of producers and dealers of agricultural and forest products, agricultural produce after harvest, and minerals and mineral products to be carried at net realisable value even if above historical cost. (U.S. GAAP treatment is similar.)

4. B is correct. Under IFRS, the reversal of write-downs is required if net realisable value increases. The inventory will be reported on the balance sheet at £1,000,000. The inventory is reported at the lower of cost or net realisable value. Under U.S. GAAP, inventory is carried at the lower of cost or market value. After a write-down, a new cost basis is determined and additional revisions may only reduce the value further. The reversal of write-downs is not permitted.

5. A is correct. IFRS require the reversal of inventory write-downs if net realisable values increase; U.S. GAAP do not permit the reversal of write-downs.

6. B is correct. Cinnamon uses the weighted average cost method, so in 2008, 5,000 units of inventory were 2007 units at €10 each and 50,000 were 2008 purchases at €11. The weighted average cost of inventory during 2008 was thus $(5{,}000 \times 10) + (50{,}000 \times 11) = 50{,}000 + 550{,}000 = $€600,000, and the weighted average cost was approximately €10.91 = €600,000/55,000. Cost of sales was €10.91 × 45,000, which is approximately €490,950.

7. C is correct. Zimt uses the FIFO method, and thus the first 5,000 units sold in 2008 depleted the 2007 inventory. Of the inventory purchased in 2008, 40,000 units were sold and 10,000 remain, valued at €11 each, for a total of €110,000.

8. A is correct. Zimt uses the FIFO method, so its cost of sales represents units purchased at a (no longer available) lower price. Nutmeg uses the LIFO method, so its cost of sales is approximately equal to the current replacement cost of inventory.

9. B is correct. Nutmeg uses the LIFO method, and thus some of the inventory on the balance sheet was purchased at a (no longer available) lower price. Zimt uses the FIFO method, so the carrying value on the balance sheet represents the most recently purchased units and thus approximates the current replacement cost.

10. B is correct. In a declining price environment, the newest inventory is the lowest-cost inventory. In such circumstances, using the LIFO method (selling the newer, cheaper inventory first) will result in lower cost of sales and higher profit.

11. B is correct. In a rising price environment, inventory balances will be higher for the company using the FIFO method. Accounts payable are based on amounts due to suppliers, not the amounts accrued based on inventory accounting.

12. C is correct. The write-down reduced the value of inventory and increased cost of sales in 2007. The higher numerator and lower denominator mean that the inventory turnover ratio as reported was too high. Gross margin and the current ratio were both too low.

13. A is correct. The reversal of the write-down shifted cost of sales from 2008 to 2007. The 2007 cost of sales was higher because of the write-down, and the 2008 cost of sales was lower because of the reversal of the write-down. As a result, the reported 2008 profits were overstated. Inventory balance in 2008 is the same because the write-down and reversal cancel each other out. Cash flow from operations is not affected by the non-cash write-down, but the higher profit in 2008 likely resulted in higher taxes and thus lower cash flow from operations.

14. B is correct. LIFO will result in lower inventory and higher cost of sales. Gross margin (a profitability ratio) will be lower, the current ratio (a liquidity ratio) will be lower, and inventory turnover (an efficiency ratio) will be higher.

15. A is correct. LIFO will result in lower inventory and higher cost of sales in periods of rising costs compared to FIFO. Consequently, LIFO results in a lower gross profit margin than FIFO.

16. B is correct. The LIFO method increases cost of sales, thus reducing profits and the taxes thereon.

17. A is correct. U.S. GAAP do not permit inventory write-downs to be reversed.

18. C is correct. The storage costs for inventory awaiting shipment to customers are not costs of purchase, costs of conversion, or other costs incurred in bringing the inventories to their present location and condition and are not included in inventory. The storage costs for the chocolate liquor occur during the production process and are thus part of the conversion costs. Excise taxes are part of the purchase cost.

19. C is correct. The carrying amount of inventories under FIFO will more closely reflect current replacement values because inventories are assumed to consist of the most recently purchased items. FIFO is an acceptable, but not preferred, method under IFRS. Weighted average cost, not FIFO, is the cost formula that allocates the same per unit cost to both cost of sales and inventory.

20. B is correct. Inventory turnover = Cost of sales/Average inventory = 41,043/7,569.5 = 5.42. Average inventory is (8,100 + 7,039)/2 = 7,569.5.

21. B is correct. For comparative purposes, the choice of a competitor that reports under IFRS is requested because LIFO is permitted under U.S. GAAP.

22. A is correct. The carrying amount of the ending inventory may differ because the perpetual system will apply LIFO continuously throughout the year, liquidating layers as sales are made. Under the periodic system, the sales will start from the last layer in the year. Under FIFO, the sales will occur from the same layers regardless of whether a perpetual or periodic system is used. Specific identification identifies the actual products sold and remaining in inventory and there will be no difference under a perpetual or periodic system.

23. B is correct. The cost of sales is closest to CHF 4,550. Under FIFO, the inventory acquired first is sold first. Using Exhibit 4, a total of 310 cartons were available for sale (100 + 40 + 70 + 100) and 185 cartons were sold (50 + 100 + 35), leaving 125 in ending inventory. The FIFO cost would be as follows:

> 100 (beginning inventory) × 22 = 2,200
> 40 (4 February 2009) × 25 = 1,000
> 45 (23 July 2009) × 30 = 1,350
> Cost of sales = 2,200 + 1,000 + 1,350 = CHF 4,550

24. A is correct. Gross profit will most likely increase by CHF 9,256. The net realisable value has increased and now exceeds the cost. The write-down from 2008 can be reversed. The write-down in 2008 was 9,256 [92,560 × (4.05 − 3.95)]. IFRS require the reversal of any write-downs for a subsequent increase in value of inventory previously written down. The reversal is limited to the lower of the subsequent increase or the original write-down. The amount of any reversal of a write-down is recognised as a reduction in cost of sales. This reduction results in an increase in gross profit.

25. C is correct. Using the FIFO method to value inventories when prices are rising will allocate more of the cost of goods available for sale to ending inventories (the most recent purchases, which are at higher costs, are assumed to remain in inventory) and less to cost of sales (the oldest purchases, which are at lower costs, are assumed to be sold first).

LONG-LIVED ASSETS
by Elaine Henry, CFA and Elizabeth A. Gordon

LEARNING OUTCOMES

The candidate should be able to:	Mastery
a. distinguish between costs that are capitalised and costs that are expensed in the period in which they are incurred;	☐
b. distinguish between intangible assets with finite and indefinite useful lives;	☐
c. discuss the different depreciation methods for property, plant, and equipment, and the effect of the choice of depreciation method on the financial statements, and the assumptions concerning useful life, and residual value on depreciation expense;	☐
d. calculate depreciation expense given the necessary information;	☐
e. discuss the different amortisation methods for intangible assets with finite lives, the effect of the choice of amortisation method, and the assumptions concerning useful life and residual value on amortisation expense;	☐
f. calculate amortisation expense given the necessary information;	☐
g. discuss the revaluation model;	☐
h. discuss the impairment of property, plant, and equipment, and intangible assets;	☐
i. discuss the derecognition of property, plant, and equipment, and intangible assets;	☐
j. discuss the financial statement presentation of and disclosures relating to property, plant, and equipment, and intangible assets.	☐

Note:
New rulings and/or pronouncements issued after the publication of the readings on financial reporting and analysis may cause some of the information in these readings to become dated. Candidates are expected to be familiar with the overall analytical framework contained in the study session readings, as well as the implications of alternative accounting methods for financial analysis and valuation, as provided in the assigned readings. Candidates are not responsible for changes that occur after the material was written.

1   INTRODUCTION

Long-lived assets, also referred to as non-current assets or long-term assets, are assets that are expected to provide economic benefits over a future period of time, typically greater than one year.[1] Long-lived assets may be tangible, intangible, or financial assets. Examples of long-lived tangible assets, typically referred to as **property, plant, and equipment** and sometimes as fixed assets, include land, buildings, furniture and fixtures, machinery and equipment, and vehicles; examples of long-lived **intangible assets** (assets lacking physical substance) include patents and trademarks; and examples of long-lived financial assets include investments in equity or debt securities issued by other companies. The scope of this reading is limited to long-lived tangible and intangible assets (hereafter, referred to for simplicity as long-lived assets).

The first issue in accounting for a long-lived asset is determining its cost at acquisition. The second issue is how to allocate the cost to expense over time. The costs of most long-lived assets are capitalised and then allocated as expenses in the profit or loss (income) statement over the period of time during which they are expected to provide economic benefits. The two main types of long-lived assets with costs that are typically *not* allocated over time are land, which is not depreciated, and those intangible assets with indefinite useful lives. Additional issues that arise are the treatment of subsequent costs incurred related to the asset, the use of the cost model versus the revaluation model, unexpected declines in the value of the asset, classification of the asset with respect to intent (for example, held for use or held for sale), and the derecognition of the asset.

This reading is organised as follows. Section 2 describes and illustrates accounting for the acquisition of long-lived assets. Section 3 describes the allocation of the costs of long-lived assets over their useful lives. Section 4 discusses the revaluation model that is based on changes in the fair value of an asset. Section 5 covers the concepts of impairment (unexpected decline in the value of an asset). Section 6 describes accounting for the derecognition of long-lived assets. Section 7 describes the financial statement presentation of and disclosures about long-lived assets. A summary is followed by practice problems in the CFA Institute multiple-choice format.

2   ACQUISITION OF LONG-LIVED ASSETS

Upon acquisition, property, plant, and equipment (tangible assets with an economic life of longer than one year and intended to be held for the company's own use) are recorded on the balance sheet at cost, which is typically the same as

---

[1] In some instances, industry practice is to include as current assets (inventory) some assets that will be held longer than one year (e.g., leaf tobacco, which is cured and aged over a period longer than one year, and whiskey, which is barrel aged for a period longer than one year).

their fair value.[2] Accounting for an intangible asset depends on how the asset is acquired. If several assets are acquired as part of a group, the purchase price is allocated to each asset on the basis of its fair value. An asset's cost potentially includes expenditures additional to the purchase price.

A key concept in accounting for expenditures related to long-lived assets is whether and when such expenditures are capitalised (i.e., included in the asset shown on the balance sheet) versus expensed (i.e., treated as an expense of the period on the income statement). Before turning to specific treatment of expenditures, we consider the general financial statement impact of capitalising versus expensing and two analytical issues related to the decision—namely, the effects on an individual company's trend analysis and on comparability across companies.

In the period of the expenditure, an expenditure that is capitalised increases the amount of assets on the balance sheet and appears as an investing cash outflow on the statement of cash flows. In subsequent periods, a company usually allocates the capitalised amount over the asset's useful life as depreciation or amortisation expense. This depreciation or amortisation expense reduces profit on the income statement and reduces the carrying amount of the asset on the balance sheet. Depreciation and amortisation are non-cash expenses and, therefore, apart from a potential effect on taxes payable (a reduction in taxes payable), have no impact on cash flows. When the indirect method is used to report cash flows from operating activities, depreciation and amortisation expenses appear on the statement of cash flows: In reconciling net income to operating cash flow as required by the indirect method, the company must adjust profit or loss by adding back depreciation and amortisation expenses.

When an expenditure does not meet asset recognition criteria, the expenditure is treated as an expense in the period it is made and reduces net income and operating cash flows by the entire after-tax amount of the expenditure. No asset is recorded on the balance sheet, and thus, no depreciation or amortisation expense is recognised in future periods. The lower amount of net income in the initial period is reflected in lower retained earnings on the ending balance sheet of the period. There is no additional effect on the financial statements of subsequent periods. Compared with a company that capitalises an expenditure, a company that expenses an expenditure will have lower net income in the period of expensing and higher net income thereafter.

In general, all else equal, accounting decisions that result in recognising expenses sooner will give the appearance of greater subsequent growth (i.e., a more positive earnings trend in periods following the recognition of the expense). In contrast, capitalising rather than expensing an expenditure results in a greater amount reported as cash from operations because the capitalised expenditure is shown as an investment cash outflow whereas the expense is an operating cash outflow. Cash from operations is an important consideration in valuation, so companies may aim to maximize reported cash from operations. WorldCom is an infamous example of a company violating accounting standards; in 2001, the company wrongly capitalised more than $3 billion in line costs (charges paid for access to telecommunication lines) that should have been expensed. This action resulted in higher reported cash from operations and net income. Of course, distinguishing between WorldCom's fraudulent financial reporting and allowable accounting discretion is important. Nonetheless, in

---

[2] Fair value is defined in International Financial Reporting Standards (IFRS) as "the amount for which an asset could be exchanged, or a liability settled, between knowledgeable, willing parties in an arm's length transaction" and under U.S. generally accepted accounting principles (U.S. GAAP) in the Financial Accounting Standards Board (FASB) Accounting Standards Codification (ASC) as "the price that would be received to sell an asset or paid to transfer a liability in an orderly transaction between market participants at the measurement date."

general, a capitalised expenditure increases investment cash outflows whereas an expenditure treated as an expense would reduce operating cash flows. In cross-company analysis, variations in companies' decisions about expensing or capitalising expenditures can impede comparability.

Assets can be acquired by methods other than purchase.[3] When an asset is exchanged for another asset, the asset acquired is recorded at fair value if reliable measures of fair value exist. Fair value is the fair value of the asset given up unless the fair value of the asset acquired is more clearly evident. If there is no reliable measure of fair value, the acquired asset is measured at the carrying amount of the asset given up. In this case, the carrying amount of the assets is unchanged, and no gain or loss is reported.

Typically, accounting for the exchange involves removing the carrying amount of the asset given up, adding a fair value for the asset acquired, and reporting any difference between the carrying amount and the fair value as a gain or loss. A gain would be reported when the fair value used for the newly acquired asset exceeds the carrying amount of the asset given up. A loss would be reported when the fair value used for the newly acquired asset is less than the carrying amount of the asset given up.

2.1 Property, Plant, and Equipment

This section discusses the accounting treatment for the acquisition of long-lived tangible assets (property, plant, and equipment) through purchase, with an emphasis on the capitalisation versus expensing of expenditures. At acquisition, the buyer records property, plant, and equipment at cost. In addition to the purchase price, the buyer also includes, as part of the cost of an asset, all the expenditures necessary to get the asset ready for its intended use. For example, freight costs borne by the purchaser to get the asset to the purchaser's place of business and special installation and testing costs required to make the asset usable are included in the total cost of the asset.

Subsequent expenditures related to long-lived assets are included as part of the recorded value of the assets on the balance sheet (i.e., capitalised) if they are expected to provide benefits beyond one year in the future and are expensed if they are not expected to provide benefits in future periods. Expenditures that extend the original life of the asset are typically capitalised. Example 1 illustrates the difference between costs that are capitalised and costs that are expensed in a period.

EXAMPLE 1

Capitalising versus Expensing

Assume a (hypothetical) company, Trofferini S.A., incurred the following expenditures to purchase a towel and tissue roll machine: €10,900 purchase price including taxes, €200 for delivery of the machine, €300 for installation and testing of the machine, and €100 to train staff on maintaining the machine. In addition, the company paid a construction

---

[3] IAS 16 *Property, Plant and Equipment*, paragraphs 24–26 [Measurement of Cost]; IAS 38 *Intangible Assets*, paragraphs 45–47 [Exchange of Assets]; and FASB ASC Section 845-10-30 [Nonmonetary Transactions–Overall–Initial Measurement].

team €350 to reinforce the factory floor and ceiling joists to accommodate the machine's weight. The company also paid €1,500 to repair the factory roof (a repair expected to extend the useful life of the factory by five years) and €1,000 to have the exterior of the factory and adjoining offices repainted for maintenance reasons. The repainting neither extends the life of factory and offices nor improves their usability.

1. Which of these expenditures will be capitalised and which will be expensed?
2. How will the treatment of these expenditures affect the company's financial statements?

Solution to 1: The company will capitalise as part of the cost of the machine all costs that are necessary to get the new machine ready for its intended use: €10,900 purchase price, €200 for delivery, €300 for installation and testing, and €350 to reinforce the factory floor and ceiling joists to accommodate the machine's weight (which was necessary to use the machine and does not increase the value of the factory). The €100 to train staff is not necessary to get the asset ready for its intended use and will be expensed.

The company will capitalise the expenditure of €1,500 to repair the factory roof because the repair is expected to extend the useful life of the factory. The company will expense the €1,000 to have the exterior of the factory and adjoining offices repainted because the painting does not extend the life or alter the productive capacity of the buildings.

Solution to 2: The costs related to the machine that are capitalised—€10,900 purchase price, €200 for delivery, €300 for installation and testing, and €350 to prepare the factory—will increase the carrying amount of the machine asset as shown on the balance sheet and will be included as investing cash outflows. The item related to the factory that is capitalised—the €1,500 roof repair—will increase the carrying amount of the factory asset as shown on the balance sheet and is an investing cash outflow. The expenditures of €100 to train staff and €1,000 to paint are expensed in the period and will reduce the amount of income reported on the company's income statement (and thus reduce retained earnings on the balance sheet) and the operating cash flow.

Example 1 describes capitalising versus expensing in the context of purchasing property, plant, and equipment. When a company constructs an asset (or acquires an asset that requires a long period of time to get ready for its intended use), borrowing costs incurred directly related to the construction are generally capitalised. Constructing a building, whether for sale (in which case, the building is classified as inventory) or for the company's own use (in which case, the building is classified as a long-lived asset), typically requires a substantial amount of time. To finance construction, any borrowing costs incurred prior to the asset being ready for its intended use are capitalised as part of the cost of the asset. The company determines the interest rate to use on the basis of its existing borrowings or, if applicable, on a borrowing specifically incurred for constructing the asset. If a company takes out a loan specifically to construct a building, the interest cost on that loan during the time of construction would be capitalised as part of the building's cost. Under IFRS, but not under U.S. GAAP, income earned on temporarily investing the borrowed monies decreases the amount of borrowing costs eligible for capitalisation.

Thus, a company's interest costs for a period are included either on the balance sheet (to the extent they are capitalised as part of an asset) or on the income statement (to the extent they are expensed). If the interest expenditure is incurred in connection with constructing an asset for the company's own use, the capitalised interest appears on the balance sheet as a part of the relevant long-lived asset (i.e., property, plant, and equipment). The capitalised interest is expensed over time as the property is depreciated and is thus part of subsequent years' depreciation expense rather than interest expense of the current period. If the interest expenditure is incurred in connection with constructing an asset to sell (for example, by a home builder), the capitalised interest appears on the company's balance sheet as part of inventory. The capitalised interest is expensed as part of the cost of goods sold when the asset is sold. Interest payments made prior to completion of construction that are capitalised are classified as an investing cash outflow. Expensed interest may be classified as an operating or financing cash outflow under IFRS and is classified as an operating cash outflow under U.S. GAAP.

EXAMPLE 2

Effect of Capitalised Borrowing Costs

BILDA S.A., a (hypothetical) company, borrows €1,000,000 at an interest rate of 10 percent per year on 1 January 2010 to finance the construction of a factory that will have a useful life of 40 years. Construction is completed after two years, during which time the company earns €20,000 by temporarily investing the loan proceeds.

1. What is the amount of interest that will be capitalised under IFRS, and how would that amount differ from the amount that would be capitalised under U.S. GAAP?

2. Where will the capitalised borrowing cost appear on the company's financial statements?

Solution to 1: The total amount of interest paid on the loan during construction is €200,000 (= €1,000,000 × 10% × 2 years). Under IFRS, the amount of borrowing cost eligible for capitalisation is reduced by the €20,000 interest income from temporarily investing the loan proceeds, so the amount to be capitalised is €180,000. Under U.S. GAAP, the amount to be capitalised is €200,000.

Solution to 2: The capitalised borrowing costs will appear on the company's balance sheet as a component of property, plant, and equipment. In the years prior to completion of construction, the interest paid will appear on the statement of cash flows as an investment activity. Over time, as the property is depreciated, the capitalised interest component is part of subsequent years' depreciation expense on the company's income statement.

The treatment of capitalised interest raises issues for consideration by an analyst. First, capitalised interest appears as part of investing cash outflows, whereas expensed interest reduces operating or financing cash flow under IFRS and operating cash flow under U.S. GAAP. An analyst may want to examine the impact on reported cash flows of interest expenditures when comparing companies. Second, interest coverage ratios are solvency indicators measuring the extent to which a company's earnings (or cash flow) in a period covered its interest costs. To provide a true picture of a company's interest coverage, the entire amount of interest, both the capitalised portion and the expensed portion, should be used in calculating interest coverage ratios. Generally, including capitalised interest in the calculation of interest coverage ratios provides a better assessment of a company's solvency. In assigning credit ratings, rating agencies include capitalised interest in coverage ratios. For example, Standard & Poor's calculates the earnings before interest and taxes (EBIT) interest coverage ratio as EBIT divided by gross interest (defined as interest prior to deductions for capitalised interest or interest income).

2.2 Intangible Assets

Intangible assets are assets lacking physical substance. Intangible assets include items that involve exclusive rights, such as patents, copyrights, trademarks, and franchises. Under IFRS, identifiable intangible assets must meet three definitional criteria. They must be 1) identifiable (either capable of being separated from the entity or arising from contractual or legal rights), 2) under the control of the company, and 3) expected to generate future economic benefits. In addition, two recognition criteria must be met: 1) It is probable that the expected future economic benefits of the asset will flow to the company, and 2) the cost of the asset can be reliably measured. Goodwill, which is not considered an identifiable intangible asset,[4] arises when one company purchases another and the acquisition price exceeds the fair value of the identifiable assets (both the tangible assets and the identifiable intangible assets) acquired.

Accounting for an intangible asset depends on how it is acquired. The following sections describe accounting for intangible assets obtained in three ways: purchased in situations other than business combinations, developed internally, and acquired in business combinations.

2.2.1 Intangible Assets Purchased in Situations Other than Business Combinations

Intangible assets purchased in situations other than business combinations, such as buying a patent, are treated at acquisition the same as long-lived tangible assets; they are recorded at their fair value when acquired, which is assumed to be equivalent to the purchase price. If several intangible assets are acquired as part of a group, the purchase price is allocated to each asset on the basis of its fair value.

In deciding how to treat individual intangible assets for analytical purposes, analysts are particularly aware that companies must use a substantial amount of judgment and numerous assumptions to determine the fair value of individual intangible assets. For analysis, therefore, understanding the types of intangible

---

[4] The IFRS definition of an intangible asset as an "identifiable non-monetary asset without physical substance" applies to intangible assets not specifically dealt with in standards other than IAS 38. The definition of intangible assets under U.S. GAAP—"assets (other than financial assets) that lack physical substance"—includes goodwill in the definition of an intangible asset.

assets acquired can often be more useful than focusing on the values assigned to the individual assets. In other words, an analyst would typically be more interested in understanding what assets a company acquired (for example, franchise rights and a mailing list) than in the precise portion of the purchase price a company allocated to each asset. Understanding the types of assets a company acquires can offer insights into the company's strategic direction and future operating potential.

2.2.2 *Intangible Assets Developed Internally*

In contrast with the treatment of construction costs of tangible assets, the costs to internally develop intangible assets are generally expensed when incurred. There are some situations, however, in which the costs incurred to internally develop an intangible asset are capitalised. The general analytical issues related to the capitalising-versus-expensing decision apply here—namely, comparability across companies and the effect on an individual company's trend analysis.

The general requirement that costs to internally develop intangible assets be expensed should be compared with capitalising the cost of acquiring intangible assets in situations other than business combinations. Because costs associated with internally developing intangible assets are usually expensed, a company that has internally developed such intangible assets as patents, copyrights, or brands through expenditures on R&D or advertising will recognise a lower amount of assets than a company that has obtained intangible assets through external purchase. In addition, on the statement of cash flows, costs of internally developing intangible assets are classified as operating cash outflows whereas costs of acquiring intangible assets are classified as investing cash outflows. Differences in strategy (developing versus acquiring intangible assets) can thus impact financial ratios.

IFRS require that expenditures on research (or during the research phase of an internal project) be expensed rather than capitalised as an intangible asset.[5] Research is defined as "original and planned investigation undertaken with the prospect of gaining new scientific or technical knowledge and understanding."[6] The "research phase of an internal project" refers to the period during which a company cannot demonstrate that an intangible asset is being created—for example, the search for alternative materials or systems to use in a production process. IFRS allow companies to recognise an intangible asset arising from development (or the development phase of an internal project) if certain criteria are met, including a demonstration of the technical feasibility of completing the intangible asset and the intent to use or sell the asset. Development is defined as "the application of research findings or other knowledge to a plan or design for the production of new or substantially improved materials, devices, products, processes, systems or services before the start of commercial production or use."[7]

Generally, U.S. GAAP require that both research and development costs be expensed as incurred but require capitalisation of certain costs related to software development.[8] Costs incurred to develop a software product for sale are

---

[5] IAS 38 *Intangible Assets*.

[6] IAS 38 *Intangible Assets*, paragraph 8 [Definitions].

[7] IAS 38 *Intangible Assets*, paragraph 8 [Definitions].

[8] FASB ASC Section 350-40-25 [Intangibles–Goodwill and Other–Internal-Use Software–Recognition] and FASB ASC Section 985-20-25 [Software–Costs of Software to be Sold, Leased, or Marketed–Recognition] specify U.S. GAAP accounting for software development costs for software for internal use and for software to be sold, respectively.

expensed until the product's technological feasibility is established and are capitalised thereafter. Similarly, companies expense costs related to the development of software for internal use until it is probable that the project will be completed and that the software will be used as intended. Thereafter, development costs are capitalised. The probability that the project will be completed is easier to demonstrate than is technological feasibility. The capitalised costs, related directly to developing software for sale or internal use, include the costs of employees who help build and test the software. The treatment of software development costs under U.S. GAAP is similar to the treatment of all costs of internally developed intangible assets under IFRS.

EXAMPLE 3

Software Development Costs

Assume JHH AG, a (hypothetical) company, incurs expenditures of €1,000 per month during the fiscal year ended 31 December 2009 to develop software for internal use. Under IFRS, the company must treat the expenditures as an expense until the software meets the criteria for recognition as an intangible asset, after which time the expenditures can be capitalised as an intangible asset.

1. What is the accounting impact of the company being able to demonstrate that the software met the criteria for recognition as an intangible asset on 1 February versus 1 December?

2. How would the treatment of expenditures differ if the company reported under U.S. GAAP and it had established in 2008 that the project was likely to be completed?

Solution to 1: If the company is able to demonstrate that the software met the criteria for recognition as an intangible asset on 1 February, the company would recognise €1,000 of expense (on the income statement) during the fiscal year ended 31 December 2009. The other €11,000 of expenditures would be recognised as an intangible asset (on the balance sheet). Alternatively, if the company is not able to demonstrate that the software met the criteria for recognition as an intangible asset until 1 December, the company would recognise €11,000 of expense during the fiscal year ended 31 December 2009, with the other €1,000 of expenditures recognised as an intangible asset.

Solution to 2: Under U.S. GAAP, the company would capitalise the entire €12,000 spent to develop software for internal use.

Even though standards require companies to capitalise software development costs after a product's feasibility is established, judgment in determining feasibility means that companies' capitalisation practices differ. For example, as illustrated in Exhibit 1, Microsoft judges product feasibility to be established very shortly before manufacturing begins and, therefore, effectively expenses—rather than capitalises—research and development costs.

| EXHIBIT 1 | Disclosure on Software Development Costs |

[Excerpt from Management's Discussion and Analysis (MD&A) of Microsoft Corporation (NASDAQGS: MSFT), Application of Critical Accounting Policies, Research and Development Costs]

SFAS No. 86 specifies that costs incurred internally in researching and developing a computer software product should be charged to expense until technological feasibility has been established for the product. Once technological feasibility is established, all software costs should be capitalized until the product is available for general release to customers. Judgment is required in determining when technological feasibility of a product is established. We have determined that technological feasibility for our software products is reached after all high-risk development issues have been resolved through coding and testing. Generally, this occurs shortly before the products are released to manufacturing. The amortization of these costs is included in cost of revenue over the estimated life of the products.

Source: Microsoft Corporation Annual Report 2009, p. 36.

Expensing rather than capitalising development costs results in lower net income in the current period. Expensing rather than capitalising will continue to result in lower net income so long as the amount of the current-period development expenses is higher than the amortisation expense that would have resulted from amortising prior periods' capitalised development costs—the typical situation when a company's development costs are increasing. On the statement of cash flows, expensing rather than capitalising development costs results in lower net operating cash flows and higher net investing cash flows. This is because the development costs are reflected as operating cash outflows rather than investing cash outflows.

2.2.3 Intangible Assets Acquired in a Business Combination

When one company acquires another company, the transaction is accounted for using the **acquisition method** of accounting.[9] Under the acquisition method, the company identified as the acquirer allocates the purchase price to each asset acquired (and each liability assumed) on the basis of its fair value. If the purchase price exceeds the sum of the amounts that can be allocated to individual identifiable assets and liabilities, the excess is recorded as goodwill. Goodwill cannot be identified separately from the business as a whole.

Under IFRS, the acquired individual assets include identifiable intangible assets that meet the definitional and recognition criteria.[10] Otherwise, if the item is acquired in a business combination and cannot be recognised as a tangible or

---

[9] Both IFRS and U.S. GAAP require the use of the acquisition method in accounting for business combinations (IFRS 3 and ASC 805).

[10] As previously described, the definitional criteria are identifiability, control by the company, and expected future benefits. The recognition criteria are probable flows of the expected economic benefits to the company and measurability.

identifiable intangible asset, it is recognised as goodwill. Under U.S. GAAP, there are two criteria to judge whether an intangible asset acquired in a business combination should be recognised separately from goodwill: The asset must be either an item arising from contractual or legal rights or an item that can be separated from the acquired company. Examples of intangible assets treated separately from goodwill include the intangible assets previously mentioned that involve exclusive rights (patents, copyrights, franchises, licenses), as well as such items as internet domain names and video and audiovisual materials.

Exhibit 2 describes how InBev allocated the €40.3 billion purchase price for its acquisition of Anheuser-Busch. The majority of the identifiable intangible asset valuation (€16.473 billion) relates to brands with indefinite life. Another €256 million or €0.256 billion was for the identifiable intangible assets with definite useful lives—distribution agreements and favorable contracts. These assets are being amortised over the life of the associated contracts. In addition, €24.7 billion of goodwill was recognised.

EXHIBIT 2	Acquisition of Intangible Assets through a Business Combination

[Excerpt from annual report of AB InBev (BRU: ABI)]

On 18 November, InBev has completed the acquisition of Anheuser-Busch, following approval from shareholders of both companies. . . . Effective the date of the closing, InBev has changed its name to AB InBev to reflect the heritage and traditions of Anheuser-Busch. Under the terms of the merger agreement, all shares of Anheuser-Busch were acquired for 70 US dollar per share in cash for an aggregate amount of approximately 52.5b US dollar or 40.3b euro.

The transaction resulted in 24.7b euro goodwill provisionally allocated primarily to the US business on the basis of expected synergies . . . The valuation of the property, plant and equipment, intangible assets, investment in associates, interest bearing loans and borrowings and employee benefits is based on the valuation performed by independent valuation specialist. The other assets and liabilities are based on the current best estimates of AB InBev's management.

The majority of the intangible asset valuation relates to brands with indefinite life. The valuation of the brands with indefinite life is based on a series of factors, including the brand history, the operating plan and the countries in which the brands are sold. The brands with indefinite life include the Budweiser family (including Bud and Bud Light), the Michelob brand family, the Busch brand family and the Natural brand family and have been fair valued for a total amount of 16,473m euro. Distribution agreements and favorable contracts have been fair valued for a total amount of 256m euro. These are being amortised over the term of the associated contracts ranging from 3 to 18 years.

Source: AB InBev 2008 Annual Report, pp. 74–75.

Having described the accounting for acquisition of long-lived assets, we now turn to the topic of measuring long-lived assets in subsequent periods.

## 3

DEPRECIATION AND AMORTISATION OF LONG-LIVED ASSETS

Under the cost model of reporting long-lived assets, which is permitted under IFRS and required under U.S. GAAP, the capitalised costs of long-lived tangible assets (other than land, which is not depreciated) and intangible assets with finite useful lives are allocated to subsequent periods as depreciation and amortisation expenses. Depreciation and amortisation are effectively the same concept, with the term depreciation referring to the process of allocating tangible assets' costs and the term amortisation referring to the process of allocating intangible assets' costs.[11] The alternative model of reporting long-lived assets is the **revaluation model**, which is permitted under IFRS but not under U.S. GAAP. Under the revaluation model, a company reports the long-lived asset at fair value rather than at acquisition cost (historical cost) less accumulated depreciation or amortisation, as in the cost model.

An asset's carrying amount is the amount at which the asset is reported on the balance sheet. Under the cost model, at any point in time, the carrying amount (also called carrying value or net book value) of a long-lived asset is equal to its historical cost minus the amount of depreciation or amortisation that has been accumulated since the asset's purchase (assuming that the asset has not been impaired, a topic which will be addressed in Section 5). Companies may present on the balance sheet the total net amount of property, plant, and equipment and the total net amount of intangible assets. However, more detail is disclosed in the notes to financial statements. The details disclosed typically include the acquisition costs, the depreciation and amortisation expenses, the accumulated depreciation and amortisation amounts, the depreciation and amortisation methods used, and information on the assumptions used to depreciate and amortise long-lived assets.

3.1 Depreciation Methods and Calculation of Depreciation Expense

Depreciation methods include the **straight-line method**, in which the cost of an asset is allocated to expense evenly over its useful life; **accelerated methods**, in which the allocation of cost is greater in earlier years; and the **units-of-production method**, in which the allocation of cost corresponds to the actual use of an asset in a particular period. The choice of depreciation method affects the amounts reported on the financial statements, including the amounts for reported assets and operating and net income. This, in turn, affects a variety of financial ratios, including fixed asset turnover, total asset turnover, operating profit margin, operating return on assets, and return on assets.

Using the straight-line method, depreciation expense is calculated as depreciable cost divided by estimated useful life and is the same for each period. Depreciable cost is the historical cost of the tangible asset minus the estimated residual (salvage) value.[12] A commonly used accelerated method is the declining balance method, in which the amount of depreciation expense for a period is calculated as some percentage of the carrying amount (i.e., cost net of accumulated depreciation at the beginning of the period). When an accelerated method is used,

---

[11] Depletion is the term applied to a similar concept for natural resources; costs associated with those resources are allocated to a period on the basis of the usage or extraction of those resources.

[12] The residual value is the estimated amount that an entity will obtain from disposal of the asset at the end of its useful life.

depreciable cost is not used to calculate the depreciation expense but the carrying amount should not be reduced below the estimated residual value. In the units-of-production method, the amount of depreciation expense for a period is based on the proportion of the asset's production during the period compared with the total estimated productive capacity of the asset over its useful life. The depreciation expense is calculated as depreciable cost times production in the period divided by estimated productive capacity. Equivalently, the company may estimate a depreciation cost per unit (depreciable cost divided by estimated productive capacity) and calculate depreciation expense as depreciation cost per unit times production in the period. Regardless of the depreciation method used, the carrying amount of the asset is not reduced below the estimated residual value. Example 4 provides an example of these depreciation methods.

EXAMPLE 4

Alternative Depreciation Methods

You are analyzing three hypothetical companies: EVEN-LI Co., SOONER Inc., and AZUSED Co. At the beginning of Year 1, each company buys an identical piece of box manufacturing equipment for $2,300 and has the same assumptions about useful life, estimated residual value, and productive capacity. The annual production of each company is the same, but each company uses a different method of depreciation. As disclosed in each company's notes to the financial statements, each company's depreciation method, assumptions, and production are as follows:

Depreciation method

▶ EVEN-LI Co.: straight-line method

▶ SOONER Inc.: double-declining balance method (the rate applied to the carrying amount is double the depreciation rate for the straight-line method)

▶ AZUSED Co.: units-of-production method

Assumptions and production

▶ Estimated residual value: $100

▶ Estimated useful life: 4 years

▶ Total estimated productive capacity: 800 boxes

▶ Production in each of the four years: 200 boxes in the first year, 300 in the second year, 200 in the third year, and 100 in the fourth year

1. Using the following template, record each company's beginning and ending net book value (carrying amount), end-of-year accumulated depreciation, and annual depreciation expense for the box manufacturing equipment.

Template:

	Beginning Net Book Value	Depreciation Expense	Accumulated Depreciation	Ending Net Book Value
Year 1				
Year 2				
Year 3				
Year 4				

2. Explain the significant differences in the timing of the recognition of the depreciation expense.

3. For each company, assume that sales, earnings before interest, taxes, and depreciation, and assets other than the box manufacturing equipment are as shown in the following table. Calculate the total asset turnover ratio, the operating profit margin, and the operating return on assets for each company for each of the four years. Discuss the ratios, comparing results within and across companies.

	Sales	Earnings before Interest, Taxes, and Depreciation	Carrying Amount of Total Assets, Excluding the Box Manufacturing Equipment, at Year End*
Year 1	$300,000	$36,000	$30,000
Year 2	320,000	38,400	32,000
Year 3	340,000	40,800	34,000
Year 4	360,000	43,200	36,000

*Assume that total assets at the beginning of Year 1, *including* the box manufacturing equipment, had a value of $30,300. Assume that depreciation expense on assets other than the box manufacturing equipment totaled $1,000 per year.

Solution to 1: For *each* company, the following information applies: Beginning net book value in Year 1 equals the purchase price of $2,300; accumulated year-end depreciation equals the balance from the previous year plus the current year's depreciation expense; ending net book value (carrying amount) equals original cost minus accumulated year-end depreciation (which is the same as beginning net book value minus depreciation expense); and beginning net book value in Years 2, 3, and 4 equals the ending net book value of the prior year. The following notes describe how depreciation *expense* is calculated for each company.

EVEN-LI Co. uses the straight-line method, so depreciation expense in each year equals $550, which is calculated as ($2,300 original cost − $100 residual value)/4 years. The net book value at the end of Year 4 is the estimated residual value of $100.

EVEN-LI Co.	Beginning Net Book Value	Depreciation Expense	Accumulated Year-End Depreciation	Ending Net Book Value
Year 1	$2,300	$550	$550	$1,750
Year 2	1,750	550	1,100	1,200
Year 3	1,200	550	1,650	650
Year 4	650	550	2,200	100

SOONER Inc. uses the double-declining balance method. The depreciation rate for the double declining balance method is double the depreciation rate for the straight-line method. The depreciation rate under the straight-line method is 25 percent (100 percent divided by 4 years). Thus, the depreciation rate for the double-declining balance method is 50 percent (2 times 25 percent). The depreciation expense for the first year is $1,150 (50 percent of $2,300). Note that under this method, the depreciation rate of 50 percent is applied to the carrying amount (net book value) of the asset, without adjustment for expected residual value. Because the carrying amount of the asset is not depreciated below its estimated residual value, however, the depreciation expense in the final year of depreciation decreases the ending net book value (carrying amount) to the estimated residual value.

SOONER Inc.	Beginning Net Book Value	Depreciation Expense	Accumulated Year-End Depreciation	Ending Net Book Value
Year 1	$2,300	$1,150	$1,150	$1,150
Year 2	1,150	575	1,725	575
Year 3	575	288	2,013	277
Year 4	277	177	2,200	100

Another common approach is to use an accelerated method, such as the double-declining method, for some period (a year or more) and then to change to the straight-line method for the remaining life of the asset. If SOONER had used the double-declining method for the first year and then switched to the straight-line method for Years 2, 3, and 4, the depreciation expense would be $350 [($1,150 − $100 estimated residual value)/3 years] a year for Years 2, 3, and 4. The results for SOONER under this alternative approach are shown below.

SOONER Inc.	Beginning Net Book Value	Depreciation Expense	Accumulated Year-End Depreciation	Ending Net Book Value
Year 1	$2,300	$1,150	$1,150	$1,150
Year 2	1,150	350	1,500	800
Year 3	575	350	1,850	450
Year 4	277	350	2,200	100

AZUSED Co. uses the units-of-production method. Dividing the equipment's total depreciable cost by its total productive capacity gives a cost per unit of $2.75, calculated as ($2,300 original cost − $100 residual value)/800. The depreciation expense recognised each year is the number of units produced times $2.75. For Year 1, the amount of depreciation expense is $550 (200 units times $2.75). For Year 2, the amount is $825 (300 units times $2.75). For Year 3, the amount is $550. For Year 4, the amount is $275.

AZUSED Co.	Beginning Net Book Value	Depreciation Expense	Accumulated Year-End Depreciation	Ending Net Book Value
Year 1	$2,300	$550	$550	$1,750
Year 2	1,750	825	1,375	925
Year 3	925	550	1,925	375
Year 4	375	275	2,200	100

Solution to 2: All three methods result in the same total amount of accumulated depreciation over the life of the equipment. The significant differences are simply in the timing of the recognition of the depreciation expense. The straight-line method recognises the expense evenly, the accelerated method recognises most of the expense in the first year, and the units-of-production method recognises the expense on the basis of production (or use of the asset). Under all three methods, the ending net book value is $100.

Solution to 3:
Total asset turnover ratio = Total revenue ÷ Average total assets
Operating profit margin = Earnings before interest and taxes ÷ Total revenue
Operating return on assets = Earnings before interest and taxes ÷ Average total assets

Ratios are shown in the table below, and details of the calculations for Years 1 and 2 are described after discussion of the ratios.

| | EVEN-LI Co. | | | SOONER Inc. | | | AZUSED Co. | | |
Ratio*	AT	PM (%)	ROA (%)	AT	PM (%)	ROA (%)	AT	PM (%)	ROA (%)
Year 1	9.67	11.48	111.04	9.76	11.28	110.17	9.67	11.48	111.04
Year 2	9.85	11.52	113.47	10.04	11.51	115.57	9.90	11.43	113.10
Year 3	10.02	11.54	115.70	10.17	11.62	118.21	10.10	11.54	116.64
Year 4	10.18	11.57	117.74	10.23	11.67	119.42	10.22	11.65	118.98

*AT = Total asset turnover ratio. PM = Operating profit margin. ROA = Operating return on assets.

For all companies, the asset turnover ratio increased over time because sales grew at a faster rate than that of the assets. SOONER had consistently higher asset turnover ratios than the other two companies, however, because higher depreciation expense in the earlier periods decreased its average total assets. In addition, the higher depreciation in earlier periods resulted in SOONER having lower operating profit margin and operating ROA in the first year and higher operating profit margin and operating ROA in the later periods. SOONER appears to be more efficiently run, on the basis of its higher asset turnover and greater increases in profit margin and ROA over time; however, these comparisons reflect differences in the companies' choice of depreciation method. In addition, an analyst might question the sustainability of the extremely high ROAs for all three companies because such high profitability levels would probably attract new competitors, which would likely put downward pressure on the ratios.

EVEN-LI Co.

Year 1:
Total asset turnover ratio = 300,000/[(30,300 + 30,000 + 1,750)/2] = 300,000/31,025 = 9.67
Operating profit margin = (36,000 − 1,000 − 550)/300,000 = 34,450/300,000 = 11.48%
Operating ROA = 34,450/31,025 = 111.04%

Year 2:
Total asset turnover ratio = 320,000/[(30,000 + 1,750 + 32,000 + 1,200)/2] = 320,000/32,475 = 9.85
Operating profit margin = (38,400 − 1,000 − 550)/320,000 = 36,850/320,000 = 11.52%
Operating ROA = 36,850/32,475 = 113.47%

SOONER Inc.

Year 1:

Total asset turnover ratio = $300,000/[(30,300 + 30,000 + 1,150)/2]$
$= 300,000/30,725 = 9.76$

Operating profit margin = $(36,000 - 1,000 - 1,150)/300,000$
$= 33,850/300,000 = 11.28\%$

Operating ROA = $33,850/30,725 = 110.17\%$

Year 2:

Total asset turnover ratio = $320,000/[(30,000 + 1,150 + 32,000 + 575)/2] = 320,000/31,862.50 = 10.04$

Operating profit margin = $(38,400 - 1,000 - 575)/320,000$
$= 36,825/320,000 = 11.51\%$

Operating ROA = $36,825/31,862.50 = 115.57\%$

AZUSED Co.

Year 1:

Total asset turnover ratio = $300,000/[(30,300 + 30,000 + 1,750)/2]$
$= 300,000/31,025 = 9.67$

Operating profit margin = $(36,000 - 1,000 - 550)/300,000$
$= 34,450/300,000 = 11.48\%$

Operating ROA = $34,450/31,025 = 111.04\%$

Year 2:

Total asset turnover ratio = $320,000/[(30,000 + 1,750 + 32,000 + 925)/2] = 320,000/32,337.50 = 9.90$

Operating profit margin = $(38,400 - 1,000 - 825)/320,000$
$= 36,575/320,000 = 11.43\%$

Operating ROA = $36,575/32,337.50 = 113.10\%$

In many countries, a company must use the same depreciation methods for both financial and tax reporting. In other countries, including the United States, a company need not use the same depreciation method for financial reporting and taxes. As a result of using different depreciation methods for financial and tax reporting, pre-tax income on the income statement and taxable income on the tax return may differ. Thus, the amount of tax expense computed on the basis of pre-tax income and the amount of taxes actually owed on the basis of taxable income may differ. Although these differences eventually reverse because the total depreciation is the same regardless of the timing of its recognition in financial statements versus on tax returns, during the period of the difference, the balance sheet will show what is known as deferred taxes. For instance, if a company uses straight-line depreciation for financial reporting and an accelerated depreciation method for tax purposes, the company's financial statements will report lower depreciation expense and higher pre-tax income in the first year, compared with the amount of depreciation expense and taxable income in its tax reporting. (Compare the depreciation expense in Year 1 for EVEN-LI Co. and SOONER Inc. in the previous example.) Tax expense calculated on the basis of the financial statements' pre-tax income will be higher than taxes payable on the basis of taxable income; the difference between the two amounts represents a deferred tax liability. The deferred tax liability will be reduced as the difference reverses (i.e., when depreciation for financial reporting is higher than the depreciation for tax purposes) and the income tax is paid.

Significant estimates required for calculating depreciation include the useful life of the asset (or its total lifetime productive capacity) and its expected residual value at the end of that useful life. A longer useful life and higher expected residual value decrease the amount of annual depreciation expense relative to a shorter useful life and lower expected residual value. Companies should review their estimates periodically to ensure they remain reasonable. IFRS requires companies to review estimates annually.

Although no significant differences exist between IFRS and U.S. GAAP with respect to the definition of depreciation and the acceptable depreciation methods, IFRS require companies to use a component method of depreciation.[13] Companies are required to separately depreciate the significant components of an asset (parts of an item with a cost that is significant in relation to the total cost and/or with different useful lives) and thus require additional estimates for the various components. For instance, it may be appropriate to depreciate separately the engine, frame, and interior furnishings of an aircraft. Under U.S. GAAP, the component method of depreciation is allowed but is seldom used in practice.[14] Example 5 illustrates depreciating components of an asset.

EXAMPLE 5

Illustration of Depreciating Components of an Asset

CUTITUP Co., a hypothetical company, purchases a milling machine, a type of machine used for shaping metal, at a total cost of $10,000. $2,000 was estimated to represent the cost of the rotating cutter, a significant component of the machine. The company expects the machine to have a useful life of eight years and a residual value of $3,000 and that the rotating cutter will need to be replaced every two years. Assume the entire residual value is attributable to the milling machine itself, and assume the company uses straight-line depreciation for all assets.

1. How much depreciation expense would the company report in Year 1 if it uses the component method of depreciation, and how much depreciation expense would the company report in Year 1 if it does not use the component method?

2. Assuming a new cutter with an estimated two-year useful life is purchased at the end of Year 2 for $2,000, what depreciation expenses would the company report in Year 3 if it uses the component method and if it does not use the component method?

3. Assuming replacement of the cutter every two years at a price of $2,000, what is the total depreciation expense over the eight years if the company uses the component method compared with the total depreciation expense if the company does not use the component method?

4. How many different items must the company estimate in the first year to compute depreciation expense for the milling machine if it uses the component method, and how does this compare with what would be required if it does not use the component method?

---

[13] IAS 16 *Property, Plant and Equipment*, paragraphs 43–47 [Depreciation].

[14] According to the Ernst & Young Academic Resource Center.

Solution to 1: Depreciation expense in Year 1 under the component method would be $1,625. For the portion of the machine excluding the cutter, the depreciable base is total cost minus the cost attributable to the cutter minus the estimated residual value = $10,000 − $2,000 − $3,000 = $5,000. Depreciation expense for the machine excluding the cutter in the first year equals $625 (depreciable cost divided by the useful life of the machine = $5,000/8 years). For the cutter, the depreciation expense equals $1,000 (depreciable cost divided by the useful life of the cutter = $2,000/2 years). Thus, the total depreciation expense for Year 1 under the component method is $1,625 (the sum of the depreciation expenses of the two components = $625 + $1,000). Depreciation expense in Year 2 would also be $1,625.

If the company does not use the component method, depreciation expense in Year 1 is $875 (the depreciable cost of the total milling machine divided by its useful life = [$10,000 − $3,000]/8 years). Depreciation expense in Year 2 would also be $875.

Solution to 2: Assuming that at the end of Year 2, the company purchases a new cutter for $2,000 with an estimated two-year life, under the component method, the depreciation expense in Year 3 will remain at $1,625. If the company does not use the component method and purchases a new cutter with an estimated two-year life for $2,000 at the end of Year 2, the depreciation expense in Year 3 will be $1,875 [$875 + ($2,000/2) = $875 + $1,000].

Solution to 3: Over the eight years, assuming replacement of the cutters every two years at a price of $2,000, the total depreciation expense will be $13,000 [$1,625 × 8 years] when the component method is used. When the component method is not used, the total depreciation expense will also be $13,000 [$875 × 2 years + $1,875 × 6 years]. This amount equals the total expenditures of $16,000 [$10,000 + 3 cutters × $2,000] less the residual value of $3,000.

Solution to 4: The following table summarizes the estimates required in the first year to compute depreciation expense if the company does or does not use the component method:

Estimate	Required Using Component Method?	Required if Not Using Component Method?
Useful life of milling machine	Yes	Yes
Residual value of milling machine	Yes	Yes
Portion of machine cost attributable to cutter	Yes	No
Portion of residual value attributable to cutter	Yes	No
Useful life of cutter	Yes	No

Total depreciation expense may be allocated between the cost of sales and other expenses. Within the income statement, depreciation expense of assets used in production is usually allocated to the cost of sales, and the depreciation expense of assets not used in production may be allocated to some other expense category. For instance, depreciation expense may be allocated to selling, general, and administrative expenses if depreciable assets are used in those functional areas. Notes to the financial statements sometimes disclose information regarding which income statement line items include depreciation expense, although the exact amount of detail disclosed by individual companies varies.

3.2 Amortisation Methods and Calculation of Amortisation Expense

Amortisation is similar in concept to depreciation. The term amortisation applies to intangible assets, and the term depreciation applies to tangible assets. Both terms refer to the process of allocating the cost of an asset over the asset's useful life. Only those intangible assets assumed to have finite useful lives are amortised over their useful lives, following the pattern in which the benefits are used up. Acceptable amortisation methods are the same as the methods acceptable for depreciation. Assets assumed to have an indefinite useful life (in other words, without a finite useful life) are not amortised. An intangible asset is considered to have an indefinite useful life when there is "no foreseeable limit to the period over which the asset is expected to generate net cash inflows" for the company.[15]

Intangible assets with finite useful lives include an acquired customer list expected to provide benefits to a direct-mail marketing company for two to three years, an acquired patent or copyright with a specific expiration date, an acquired license with a specific expiration date and no right to renew the license, and an acquired trademark for a product that a company plans to phase out over a specific number of years. Examples of intangible assets with indefinite useful lives include an acquired license that, although it has a specific expiration date, can be renewed at little or no cost and an acquired trademark that, although it has a specific expiration, can be renewed at a minimal cost and relates to a product that a company plans to continue selling for the foreseeable future.

As with depreciation for a tangible asset, the calculation of amortisation for an intangible asset requires the original amount at which the intangible asset is recognised and estimates of the length of its useful life and its residual value at the end of its useful life. Useful lives are estimated on the basis of the expected use of the asset, considering any factors that may limit the life of the asset, such as legal, regulatory, contractual, competitive, or economic factors.

EXAMPLE 6

Amortisation Expense

IAS 38 *Intangible Assets* provides illustrative examples regarding the accounting for intangible assets, including the following:

> A direct-mail marketing company acquires a customer list and expects that it will be able to derive benefit from the information on the list for at least one year, but no more than three years. The

---

[15] IAS 38 *Intangible Assets*, paragraph 88.

customer list would be amortised over management's best estimate of its useful life, say 18 months. Although the direct-mail marketing company may intend to add customer names and other information to the list in the future, the expected benefits of the acquired customer list relate only to the customers on that list at the date it was acquired.

In this example, in what ways would management's decisions and estimates affect the company's financial statements?

Solution: Because the acquired customer list is expected to generate future economic benefits for a period greater than one year, the cost of the list should be capitalised and not expensed. The acquired customer list is determined to not have an indefinite life and must be amortised. Management must estimate the useful life of the customer list and must select an amortisation method. In this example, the list appears to have no residual value. Both the amortisation method and the estimated useful life affect the amount of the amortisation expense in each period. A shorter estimated useful life, compared with a longer estimated useful life, results in a higher amortisation expense each year over a shorter period but the *total* accumulated amortisation expense over the life of the intangible asset is unaffected by the estimate of the useful life. Similarly, the total accumulated amortisation expense over the life of the intangible asset is unaffected by the choice of amortisation method. The amortisation expense per period depends on the amortisation method. If the straight-line method is used, the amortisation expense is the same for each year of useful life. If an accelerated method is used, the amortisation expense will be higher in earlier years.

THE REVALUATION MODEL

4

The revaluation model is an alternative to the cost model for the periodic valuation and reporting of long-lived assets. IFRS permit the use of either the revaluation model or the cost model, but the revaluation model is not allowed under U.S. GAAP. Revaluation changes the carrying amounts of classes of long-lived assets to fair value (the fair value must be measured reliably). Under the cost model, carrying amounts are historical costs less accumulated depreciation or amortisation. Under the revaluation model, carrying amounts are the fair values at the date of revaluation less any subsequent accumulated depreciation or amortisation.

IFRS allow companies to value long-lived assets either under a cost model at historical cost minus accumulated depreciation or amortisation, or under a revaluation model at fair value. In contrast, U.S. accounting standards require the cost model be used. A key difference between the two models is that the cost model allows only decreases in the values of long-lived assets compared with historical costs but the revaluation model may result in increases in the values of long-lived assets to amounts greater than historical costs.

IFRS allow a company to use the cost model for some classes of assets and the revaluation model for others, but the company must apply the same model to all assets within a particular class of assets and must revalue all items within a class to avoid selective revaluation. Examples of different classes of assets include land,

land and buildings, machinery, motor vehicles, furniture and fixtures, and office equipment. The revaluation model may be used for classes of intangible assets but only if an active market for the assets exists, because the revaluation model may only be used if the fair values of the assets can be measured reliably. For practical purposes, the revaluation model is rarely used for either tangible or intangible assets, but its use is especially rare for intangible assets.

Under the revaluation model, whether an asset revaluation affects earnings depends on whether the revaluation initially increases or decreases an asset class' carrying amount. If a revaluation initially decreases the carrying amount of the asset class, the decrease is recognised in profit or loss. Later, if the carrying amount of the asset class increases, the increase is recognised in profit or loss to the extent that it reverses a revaluation decrease of the same asset class previously recognised in profit or loss. Any increase in excess of the reversal amount will not be recognised in the income statement but will be recorded directly to equity in a revaluation surplus account. An upward revaluation is treated the same as the amount in excess of the reversal amount. In other words, if a revaluation initially increases the carrying amount of the asset class, the increase in the carrying amount of the asset class bypasses the income statement and goes directly to equity under the heading of revaluation surplus. Any subsequent decrease in the asset's value first decreases the revaluation surplus and then goes to income.

The next two examples illustrate revaluation of long-lived assets under IFRS.

EXAMPLE 7

Revaluation Resulting in an Increase in Carrying Amount Followed by Subsequent Revaluation Resulting in a Decrease in Carrying Amount

UPFIRST, a (hypothetical) manufacturing company, has elected to use the revaluation model for its machinery. Assume for simplicity that the company owns a single machine, which it purchased for €10,000 on the first day of its fiscal period, and that the measurement date occurs simultaneously with the company's fiscal period end.

1. At the end of the first fiscal period after acquisition, assume the fair value of the machine is determined to be €11,000. How will the company's financial statements reflect the asset?

2. At the end of the second fiscal period after acquisition, assume the fair value of the machine is determined to be €7,500. How will the company's financial statements reflect the asset?

Solution to 1: At the end of the first fiscal period, the company's balance sheet will show the asset at a value of €11,000. The €1,000 increase in the value of the asset will appear in other comprehensive income and be accumulated in equity under the heading of revaluation surplus.

Solution to 2: At the end of the second fiscal period, the company's balance sheet will show the asset at a value of €7,500. The total decrease in the carrying amount of the asset is €3,500 (€11,000 − €7,500). Of the €3,500 decrease, the first €1,000 will reduce the amount previously accumulated in equity under the heading of revaluation surplus. The other €2,500 will be shown as a loss on the income statement.

EXAMPLE 8

Revaluation Resulting in a Decrease in Asset's Carrying Amount Followed by Subsequent Revaluation Resulting in an Increase in Asset's Carrying Amount

DOWNFIRST, a (hypothetical) manufacturing company, has elected to use the revaluation model for its machinery. Assume for simplicity that the company owns a single machine, which it purchased for €10,000 on the first day of its fiscal period, and that the measurement date occurs simultaneously with the company's fiscal period end.

1. At the end of the first fiscal period after acquisition, assume the fair value of the machine is determined to be €7,500. How will the company's financial statements reflect the asset?

2. At the end of the second fiscal period after acquisition, assume the fair value of the machine is determined to be €11,000. How will the company's financial statements reflect the asset?

Solution to 1: At the end of the first fiscal period, the company's balance sheet will show the asset at a value of €7,500. The €2,500 decrease in the value of the asset will appear as a loss on the company's income statement.

Solution to 2: At the end of the second fiscal period, the company's balance sheet will show the asset at a value of €11,000. The total increase in the carrying amount of the asset is an increase of €3,500 (€11,000 − €7,500). Of the €3,500 increase, the first €2,500 reverses a previously reported loss and will be reported as a gain on the income statement. The other €1,000 will bypass profit or loss and be reported as other comprehensive income and be accumulated in equity under the heading of revaluation surplus.

Exhibit 3 provides an example of a company's disclosures concerning revaluation. The exhibit shows an excerpt from the 2006 annual report of KPN, a Dutch telecommunications and multimedia company. The excerpt is from the section of the annual report in which the company explains differences between its reporting under IFRS and its reporting under U.S. GAAP.[16] One of these differences, as previously noted, is that U.S. GAAP do not allow revaluation of fixed assets held for use. KPN elected to report a class of fixed assets (cables) at fair value and explained that under U.S. GAAP, using the cost model, the value of the class at the end of 2006 would have been €350 million lower.

EXHIBIT 3   Impact of Revaluation

[Excerpt from the Annual Report of Koninklijke KPN N.V. (NYSE: KPN) explaining certain differences between IFRS and U.S. GAAP regarding "Deemed cost fixed assets"]

> KPN elected the exemption to revalue certain of its fixed assets upon the transition to IFRS to fair value and to use this fair value as their deemed cost. KPN applied the depreciated replacement cost method to determine this fair value. The revalued assets pertain to certain cables, which form part of property, plant & equipment. Under U.S. GAAP, this revaluation is not allowed and therefore results in a reconciling item. As a result, the value of these assets as of December 31, 2006 under U.S. GAAP is EUR 350 million lower (2005: EUR 415 million; 2004: EUR 487 million) than under IFRS.

Source: KPN's Form 20-F, page 168, filed 1 March 2007.

Clearly, the use of the revaluation model as opposed to the cost model can have a significant impact on the financial statements of companies. This has potential consequences for comparing financial performance using financial ratios of companies that use different models.

5   IMPAIRMENT OF ASSETS

In contrast with depreciation and amortisation charges, which serve to allocate the depreciable cost of a long-lived asset over its useful life, impairment charges reflect an unanticipated decline in the value of an asset. Both IFRS and U.S. GAAP require companies to write down the carrying amount of impaired assets. Impairment reversals are permitted under IFRS but not under U.S. GAAP.

An asset is considered to be impaired when its carrying amount exceeds its recoverable amount ("the higher of fair value less cost to sell or value in use" according to IAS 36 Impairment of Assets) or under U.S. GAAP when its carrying amount exceeds its fair value. Under U.S. GAAP, however, impairment losses are only recognizable when the carrying amount of the impaired asset is determined

---

[16] On 15 November 2007, the SEC approved rule amendments under which financial statements from foreign private issuers in the United States will be accepted without reconciliation to U.S. GAAP if the financial statements are prepared in accordance with IFRS as issued by the IASB. The new rule is effective for the 2007 fiscal year. As a result, companies such as KPN no longer need to provide reconciliations to U.S. GAAP.

to be not recoverable. Therefore, in general, impairment losses are recognized when the asset's carrying amount is not recoverable. However, IFRS and U.S. GAAP define recoverability differently. The following paragraphs describe accounting for impairment for different categories of assets.

5.1 Impairment of Property, Plant, and Equipment

Accounting standards do not require that property, plant, and equipment be tested annually for impairment. Rather, at the end of each reporting period (generally, a fiscal year), a company assesses whether there are indications of asset impairment. If there is no indication of impairment, the asset is not tested for impairment. If there is an indication of impairment, such as evidence of obsolescence, decline in demand for products, or technological advancements, the recoverable amount of the asset should be measured in order to test for impairment. For property, plant, and equipment, impairment losses are recognised when the asset's carrying amount is not recoverable; the carrying amount is less than the recoverable amount. The amount of the impairment loss will reduce the carrying amount of the asset on the balance sheet and will reduce net income on the income statement. The impairment loss is a non-cash item and will not affect cash from operations.

IFRS and U.S. GAAP differ somewhat both in the guidelines for determining that impairment has occurred and in the measurement of an impairment loss. Under IAS 36, an impairment loss is measured as the excess of carrying amount over the recoverable amount of the asset. The recoverable amount of an asset is defined as "the higher of its fair value less costs to sell and its value in use." Value in use is a discounted measure of expected future cash flows. Under U.S. GAAP, assessing recoverability is separate from measuring the impairment loss. An asset's carrying amount is considered not recoverable when it exceeds the undiscounted expected future cash flows. If the asset's carrying amount is considered not recoverable, the impairment loss is measured as the difference between the asset's fair value and carrying amount.

EXAMPLE 9

Impairment of Property, Plant, and Equipment

Sussex, a (hypothetical) manufacturing company in the United Kingdom, has a machine it uses to produce a single product. The demand for the product has declined substantially since the introduction of a competing product. The company has assembled the following information with respect to the machine:

Carrying amount	£18,000
Undiscounted expected future cash flows	£19,000
Present value of expected future cash flows	£16,000
Fair value if sold	£17,000
Costs to sell	£2,000

1. Under IFRS, what would the company report for the machine?
2. Under U.S. GAAP, what would the company report for the machine?

> **Solution to 1:** Under IFRS, the company would compare the carrying amount (£18,000) with the higher of its fair value less costs to sell (£15,000) and its value in use (£16,000). The carrying amount exceeds the value in use, the higher of the two amounts, by £2,000. The machine would be written down to the recoverable amount of £16,000, and a loss of £2,000 would be reported in the income statement. The carrying amount of the machine is now £16,000. A new depreciation schedule based on the carrying amount of £16,000 would be developed.
>
> **Solution to 2:** Under U.S. GAAP, the carrying amount (£18,000) is compared with the undiscounted expected future cash flows (£19,000). The carrying amount is less than the undiscounted expected future cash flows, so the carrying amount is considered recoverable. The machine would continue to be carried at £18,000, and no loss would be reported.

5.2 Impairment of Intangible Assets with a Finite Life

Intangible assets with a finite life are amortised (carrying amount decreases over time) and may become impaired. As is the case with property, plant, and equipment, the assets are not tested annually for impairment. Instead, they are tested only when significant events suggest the need to test. The company assesses at the end of each reporting period whether a significant event suggesting the need to test for impairment has occurred. Examples of such events include a significant decrease in the market price or a significant adverse change in legal or economic factors. Impairment accounting for intangible assets with a finite life is essentially the same as for tangible assets; the amount of the impairment loss will reduce the carrying amount of the asset on the balance sheet and will reduce net income on the income statement.

5.3 Impairment of Intangibles with Indefinite Lives

Intangible assets with indefinite lives are not amortised. Instead, they are carried on the balance sheet at historical cost but are tested at least annually for impairment. Impairment exists when the carrying amount exceeds its fair value.

5.4 Impairment of Long-lived Assets Held for Sale

A long-lived (non-current) asset is reclassified as held for sale rather than held for use when it ceases to be used and management's intent is to sell it. For instance, if a building ceases to be used and management's intent is to sell it, the building is reclassified from property, plant, and equipment to non-current assets held for sale. At the time of reclassification, assets previously held for use are tested for impairment. If the carrying amount at the time of reclassification exceeds the fair value less costs to sell, an impairment loss is recognised and the asset is written down to fair value less costs to sell. Long-lived assets held for sale cease to be depreciated or amortised.

5.5 Reversals of Impairments of Long-lived Assets

After an asset has been deemed impaired and an impairment loss has been reported, the asset's recoverable amount could potentially increase. For instance, a lawsuit appeal may successfully challenge a patent infringement by another company, with the result that a patent previously written down has a higher recoverable amount. IFRS permit impairment losses to be reversed if the recoverable amount of an asset increases regardless of whether the asset is classified as held for use or held for sale. Note that IFRS permit the reversal of impairment losses only. IFRS do not permit the revaluation to the recoverable amount if the recoverable amount exceeds the previous carrying amount. Under U.S. GAAP, the accounting for reversals of impairments depends on whether the asset is classified as held for use or held for sale.[17] Under U.S. GAAP, once an impairment loss has been recognised for assets held for use, it cannot be reversed. In other words, once the value of an asset held for use has been decreased by an impairment charge, it cannot be increased. For assets held for sale, if the fair value increases after an impairment loss, the loss can be reversed.

DERECOGNITION   6

A company derecognises an asset (i.e., removes it from the financial statements) when the asset is disposed of or is expected to provide no future benefits from either use or disposal. A company may dispose of a long-lived operating asset by selling it, exchanging it, or abandoning it. As previously described, non-current assets that are no longer in use and are to be sold are reclassified as non-current assets held for sale.

6.1 Sale of Long-lived Assets

The gain or loss on the sale of long-lived assets is computed as the sales proceeds minus the carrying amount of the asset at the time of sale. An asset's carrying amount is typically the net book value (i.e., the historical cost minus accumulated depreciation), unless the asset's carrying amount has been changed to reflect impairment and/or revaluation, as previously discussed.

EXAMPLE 10

Calculation of Gain or Loss on the Sale of Long-lived Assets

Moussilauke Diners Inc. (hypothetical company), as a result of revamping its menus to focus on healthier food items, sells 450 used pizza ovens and reports a gain on the sale of $1.2 million. The ovens had a carrying amount of $1.9 million (original cost of $5.1 million less $3.2 million of accumulated depreciation). At what price did Moussilauke sell the ovens?

A. $0.7 million.
B. $3.1 million.
C. $6.3 million.

---

[17] FASB ASC Section 360-10-35 [Property, Plant, and Equipment–Overall–Subsequent Measurement].

> **Solution:** B is correct. The ovens had a carrying amount of $1.9 million, and Moussilauke recognised a gain of $1.2 million. Therefore, Moussilauke sold the ovens at a price of $3.1 million. The gain on the sale of $1.2 million is the selling price of $3.1 million minus the carrying amount of $1.9 million. Ignoring taxes, the cash flow from the sale is $3.1 million, which would appear as a cash inflow from investing.

A gain or loss on the sale of an asset is disclosed on the income statement, either as a component of other gains and losses or in a separate line item when the amount is material. A company typically discloses further detail about the sale in the management discussion and analysis and/or financial statement footnotes. In addition, a statement of cash flows prepared using the indirect method adjusts net income to remove any gain or loss on the sale from operating cash flow and to include the amount of proceeds from the sale in cash from investing activities. Recall that the indirect method of the statement of cash flows begins with net income and makes all adjustments to arrive at cash from operations, including removal of gains or losses from non-operating activities.

6.2 Long-lived Assets Disposed of Other than by a Sale

Long-lived assets to be disposed of other than by a sale (e.g., abandoned, exchanged for another asset, or distributed to owners in a spin-off) are classified as held for use until disposal.[18] Thus, the long-lived assets continue to be depreciated and tested for impairment, unless their carrying amount is zero, as required for other long-lived assets owned by the company.

When an asset is retired or abandoned, the accounting is similar to a sale, except that the company does not record cash proceeds. Assets are reduced by the carrying amount of the asset at the time of retirement or abandonment, and a loss equal to the asset's carrying amount is recorded.

When an asset is exchanged, accounting for the exchange typically involves removing the carrying amount of the asset given up, adding a fair value for the asset acquired, and reporting any difference between the carrying amount and the fair value as a gain or loss. The fair value used is the fair value of the asset given up unless the fair value of the asset acquired is more clearly evident. If no reliable measure of fair value exists, the acquired asset is measured at the carrying amount of the asset given up. A gain is reported when the fair value used for the newly acquired asset exceeds the carrying amount of the asset given up. A loss is reported when the fair value used for the newly acquired asset is less than the carrying amount of the asset given up. If the acquired asset is valued at the carrying amount of the asset given up because no reliable measure of fair value exists, no gain or loss is reported.

When a spin-off occurs, typically, an entire cash generating unit of a company with all its assets is spun off. As an illustration of a spin-off, Altria Group, Inc. effected a spin-off of Kraft Foods on 30 March 2007 by distributing about 89 percent of Kraft's shares to Altria's shareholders. The company prepared

---

[18] In a spin-off, shareholders of the parent company receive a proportional number of shares in a new, separate entity.

unaudited pro forma income statements and balance sheets (for illustrative purposes only) as if the spin-off had occurred at the beginning of the year. Exhibit 4 summarizes information from the asset portion of the company's pro forma balance sheets. The items in the column labeled "Spin-off of Kraft" reflect Kraft's assets being removed from Altria's balance sheet at the time of the spin-off. For example, Kraft's property, plant, and equipment (net of depreciation) totaled $9.7 billion.

EXHIBIT 4	Altria Group, Inc. and Subsidiaries Pro Forma Condensed Consolidated Balance Sheet [Partial] As of 31 December 2006 (Unaudited)			
Assets ($ Millions)	**Historical Altria**[a]	**Spin-Off of Kraft**[b]	**Adjustments**[c]	**Pro Forma Altria**
Cash and cash equivalents	$5,020	($239)	$369	$5,150
Receivables, net	6,070	(3,869)		2,201
Inventories	12,186	(3,506)		8,680
Other current assets	2,876	(640)		2,236
Total current assets	$26,152	($8,254)	$369	$18,267
Property, plant, and equipment, net	17,274	(9,693)		7,581
Goodwill	33,235	(25,553)	($1,485)	6,197
Other intangible assets, net	12,085	(10,177)		1,908
Other assets	8,734	(1,897)	$305	7,142
Total consumer products assets	$97,480	($55,574)	($811)	$41,095
Financial services assets	6,790	0		6,790
Total assets	$104,270	($55,574)	($811)	$47,885

[a] Historical consolidated balance sheet of Altria.

[b] Reflects the removal of Kraft's consolidated balance sheet from the Altria historical consolidated balance sheet.

[c] Represents adjustments, such as for pro forma cash payments by Kraft to Altria, arising from modifications to existing stock awards and tax contingencies, adjustments to goodwill, etc.

Source: Altria's Form 8-K filed with the SEC on 5 April 2007.

PRESENTATION AND DISCLOSURES   7

Under IFRS, for each class of property, plant, and equipment, a company must disclose the measurement bases, the depreciation method, the useful lives (or equivalently the depreciation rate) used, the gross carrying amount and the accumulated depreciation at the beginning and end of the period, and a reconciliation of the carrying amount at the beginning and end of the period.[19] In addition, disclosures of restrictions on title and pledges as security of property, plant, and equipment and contractual agreements to acquire property, plant,

---

[19] IAS 16 *Property, Plant and Equipment*, paragraphs 73–78 [Disclosure].

and equipment are required. If the revaluation model is used, the date of revaluation, details of how the fair value was obtained, the carrying amount under the cost model, and the revaluation surplus must be disclosed.

The disclosure requirements under U.S. GAAP are less exhaustive.[20] A company must disclose the depreciation expense for the period, the balances of major classes of depreciable assets, accumulated depreciation by major classes or in total, and a general description of the depreciation method(s) used in computing depreciation expense with respect to the major classes of depreciable assets.

Under IFRS, for each class of intangible assets, a company must disclose whether the useful lives are indefinite or finite. If finite, for each class of intangible asset, a company must disclose the useful lives (or equivalently the amortisation rate) used, the amortisation methods used, the gross carrying amount and the accumulated amortisation at the beginning and end of the period, where amortisation is included on the income statement, and a reconciliation of the carrying amount at the beginning and end of the period.[21] If an asset has an indefinite life, the company must disclose the carrying amount of the asset and why it is considered to have an indefinite life. Similar to property, plant, and equipment, disclosures of restrictions on title and pledges as security of intangible assets and contractual agreements to acquire intangible assets are required. If the revaluation model is used, the date of revaluation, details of how the fair value was obtained, the carrying amount under the cost model, and the revaluation surplus must be disclosed.

Under U.S. GAAP, companies are required to disclose the gross carrying amounts and accumulated amortisation in total and by major class of intangible assets, the aggregate amortisation expense for the period, and the estimated amortisation expense for the next five fiscal years.[22]

The disclosures related to impairment losses also differ under IFRS and U.S. GAAP. Under IFRS, a company must disclose for each class of assets the amounts of impairment losses and reversals of impairment losses recognised in the period and where those are recognised on the financial statements.[23] The company must also disclose in aggregate the main classes of assets affected by impairment losses and reversals of impairment losses and the main events and circumstances leading to recognition of these impairment losses and reversals of impairment losses. Under U.S. GAAP, there is no reversal of impairment losses. The company must disclose a description of the impaired asset, what led to the impairment, the method of determining fair value, the amount of the impairment loss, and where the loss is recognised on the financial statements.[24]

To illustrate financial statement presentation and disclosures, Example 11 provides excerpts relating to intangible assets and property, plant, and equipment from the annual report of Vodafone Group Plc for the year ended 31 March 2009.

---

[20] FASB ASC Section 360-10-50 [Property, Plant, and Equipment–Overall–Disclosure].

[21] IAS 38 *Intangible Assets*, paragraphs 118–128 [Disclosure].

[22] FASB ASC Section 350-30-50 [Intangibles–General–Disclosure].

[23] IAS 36 *Impairment of Assets*, paragraphs 126–131 [Disclosure].

[24] FASB ASC Section 360-10-50 [Property, Plant, and Equipment–Overall–Disclosure] and FASB ASC Section 350-30-50 [Intangibles–General–Disclosure].

EXAMPLE 11

Financial Statement Presentation and Disclosures for Long-Lived Assets

The following exhibits include excerpts from the annual report for the year ended 31 March 2009 of Vodafone Group Plc (London: VOD), a global mobile telecommunications company headquartered in the United Kingdom.

EXHIBIT 5	Vodafone Group Plc Excerpts from the Consolidated Financial Statements

Excerpt from the Consolidated Income Statement
For the Years Ended 31 March (Currency in £ Millions)

	Note	2009	2008
Revenue	3	41,017	35,478
⋮	⋮	⋮	⋮
Impairment losses	10*	(5,900)	—
⋮	⋮	⋮	⋮
Operating profit/(loss)	4	5,857	10,047
⋮	⋮	⋮	⋮
Profit/(loss) before taxation		4,189	9,001
Income tax expense	6	(1,109)	(2,245)
Profit/(loss) for the financial year from continuing operations		3,080	6,756
Loss for the year from discontinued operations	30	—	—
Profit/(loss) for the financial year		**3,080**	**6,756**
Attributable to:			
– Equity shareholders	23	3,078	6,660
– Minority interests		2	96
		3,080	**6,756**

*Notes relating to property, plant, and equipment and intangible assets are underlined.

(*Exhibit continued on next page . . .*)

EXHIBIT 5	(continued)

Excerpt from the Consolidated Statement of Recognised Income and Expense
For the Years Ended 31 March (Currency in £ Millions)

	Note	2009	2008
(Losses)/gains on revaluation of available-for-sale investments, net of tax	22	(2,383)	1,949
⋮	⋮	⋮	⋮
Revaluation gain	22	68	—
⋮	⋮	⋮	⋮
Net gain/(loss) recognised directly in equity		**9,854**	**6,909**
Profit/(loss) for the financial year		3,080	6,756
Total recognised income and expense relating to the year		**12,934**	**13,665**
Attributable to:			
– Equity shareholders		13,037	13,912
– Minority interests		(103)	(247)
		12,934	**13,665**

Excerpt from the Consolidated Balance Sheet
at 31 March (Currency in £ Millions)

	Note	2009	2008
Non-current assets			
Goodwill	9	53,958	51,336
Other intangible assets	9	20,980	18,995
Property, plant and equipment	11	19,250	16,735
⋮	⋮	⋮	⋮
		139,670	118,546
Current assets		13,029	8,724
Total Assets		**152,699**	**127,270**
Equity			
⋮	⋮	⋮	⋮
Accumulated other recognised income and expense	22	20,517	10,588
⋮	⋮	⋮	⋮
Total equity		84,777	76,471
Non-current liabilities		39,975	28,826
Current liabilities		27,947	21,973
Total equity and liabilities		**152,699**	**127,270**

| EXHIBIT 6 | Vodafone Group Plc
Excerpts from the Notes to the Consolidated Financial Statements |

Excerpt from Note 9, Intangible Assets
(Currency in £ Millions)

Intangible Assets	Goodwill	Licences and Spectrum	Computer Software	Other	Total
Cost:					
31 March 2008	91,762	22,040	5,800	1,188	120,790
Exchange movements	14,298	2,778	749	153	17,978
Arising on acquisition	613	199	69	130	1,011
Additions	—	1,138	1,144	—	2,282
Disposals	—	(1)	(403)	—	(404)
Transfer to investments in associated undertakings	(9)	(16)	—	—	(25)
31 March 2009	106,664	26,138	7,359	1,471	141,632
Accumulated impairment losses and amortisation:					
31 March 2008	40,426	5,132	4,160	741	50,459
Exchange movements	6,630	659	569	126	7,984
Amortisation charge for the year	—	1,522	885	346	2,753
Impairment losses	5,650	250	—	—	5,900
Disposals	—	—	(391)	—	(391)
Transfers to investments in associated undertakings	—	(11)	—	—	(11)
31 March 2009	52,706	7,552	5,223	1,213	66,694
Net book value:					
31 March 2008	51,336	16,908	1,640	447	70,331
31 March 2009	53,958	18,586	2,136	258	74,938

For licences and spectrum and other intangible assets, amortisation is included within the cost of sales line within the consolidated income statement. Licences and spectrum with a net book value of £2,765m (2008: £nil) have been pledged as security against borrowings.

(Exhibit continued on next page . . .)

EXHIBIT 6   (continued)

Excerpt from Note 10, Impairment
Impairment Losses

Impairment losses recognised in the consolidated income statement as a separate line item within operating profit, in respect of goodwill and licences and spectrum fees are as follows (£m):

Cash Generating Unit	Reportable Segment	2009	2008	2007
			—	—
⋮	⋮	⋮		
Turkey	Other Africa and Central Europe	2,250	—	—
			—	—
⋮	⋮	⋮		
[Total]		5,900	—	11,600

The impairment losses were based on value in use calculations. . . .

Turkey

At September 30 2008, the goodwill was impaired by £1,700 million . . . During the second half of the 2009 financial year, impairment losses of £300 million in relation to goodwill and £250 million in relation to licences and spectrum resulted from adverse changes in both the discount rate and a fall in the long term GDP growth rate. The cash flow projections . . . were substantially unchanged from those used at 30 September 2008. . . .

Sensitivity to changes in assumptions

The estimated recoverable amount of the Group's operations in Spain, Turkey and Ghana equaled their respective carrying value and, consequently, any adverse change in key assumption would, in isolation, cause a further impairment loss to be recognised. . . .

(*Exhibit continued on next page* . . .)

EXHIBIT 6   (continued)

The changes in the following table to assumptions used in the impairment review would, in isolation, lead to an (increase)/decrease to the aggregate impairment loss recognised in the year ended 31 March 2009:

			Spain		Turkey		Ghana		All Other	
				Increase by 2% £bn	Decrease by 2% £bn					
			:	:	:	:	:	:	:	:
Pre-tax adjusted discount rate	:	:	(0.4)	0.6	:	:	:	:		
Long term growth rate	:	:	0.3	(0.2)	:	:	:	:		
Budgeted EBITDA	:	:	0.1	(0.1)	:	:	:	:		
Budgeted capital expenditure	:	:	(0.1)	0.1	:	:	:	:		

Excerpt from Note 11, Property, Plant, and Equipment

The net book value of land and buildings and equipment, fixtures and fittings includes £106 million and £82 million, respectively (2008: £110 million and £51 million) in relation to assets held under finance leases. Included in the net book value of land and buildings and equipment, fixtures and fittings are assets in the course of construction, which are not depreciated, with a cost of £44 million and £1,186 million, respectively (2008: £28 million and £1,013 million). Property, plant and equipment with a net book value of £148 million (2008: £1,503 million) has been pledged as security against borrowings.

Excerpt from Note 22, Movements in Accumulated Other Recognised Income and Expense
(Currency in £ Millions)

	Translation Reserve	Pensions Reserve	Available-for-Sale Investments Reserve	Asset Revaluation Surplus	Other	Total
:	:	:	:	:	:	:
31 March 2008	5,974	(96)	4,531	112	37	10,558
Gains/(losses) arising in the year	:	:	:	68	:	10,023
Transfer to the income statement on disposal	:	:	:	:	:	(3)
Tax effect	:	:	:	:	:	(61)
31 March 2009	18,451	(259)	2,148	180	(3)	20,517

1. As of 31 March 2009, what percentage of other intangible assets and property, plant, and equipment is pledged as security against borrowings?

2. What caused the £250 million impairment losses in relation to licences and spectrum during the year ended 31 March 2009?

3. By what amount would impairment losses related to Turkey change if the pre-tax adjusted discount rate decreased by 2 percent?

4. Where are impairment losses reported on the financial statements? Where is amortisation included within the consolidated income statement?

5. What percentage of property, plant, and equipment, based on net book value, is held under finance leases rather than owned as of 31 March 2009?

6. The gains and losses arising in the year on asset revaluation are:

    A. reflected on the consolidated income statement.

    B. reported in the notes to the financial statements only.

    C. recognised directly in equity and shown on the consolidated statement of recognised income and expense.

Solution to 1: Assets that have been pledged as security against borrowings are licences and spectrum, with a net book value of £2,765 million (Note 9), and property, plant, and equipment, with a net book value of £148 million (Note 11). These assets represent 7.24 percent $[(2,765 + 148)/(20,980 + 19,250)]$ of the other intangible assets and property, plant, and equipment.

Solution to 2: The £250 million impairment losses in relation to licences and spectrum resulted from an increase in the pre-tax adjusted discount rate and a decrease in the long-term growth rate in Turkey (Note 10).

Solution to 3: A 2 percent decrease in the pre-tax adjusted discount rate related to Turkey would reduce impairment losses by £0.6 billion or £600 million (Note 10).

Solution to 4: Impairment losses are reported on the consolidated income statement (Exhibit 5). Impairment losses reduce the value of the assets impaired (Note 9) and are thus recognised within the consolidated balance sheet. Amortisation is included within the cost of sales line within the consolidated income statement (Note 9).

Solution to 5: The net book value of land and buildings and equipment, fixtures, and fittings includes £106 million and £82 million, respectively, in relation to assets held under finance leases (Note 22). The sum of these values represents 0.98 percent of the property, plant, and equipment $[(106 + 82)/19,250]$.

Solution to 6: C is correct. The gains and losses arising in the year on asset revaluation are recognised directly in equity and shown on the consolidated statement of recognised income and expense. They are also reported in the notes to the financial statements (Note 22).

Note that the exhibits in the previous example contain relatively brief excerpts from the company's disclosures. The complete text of the disclosures concerning the company's non-current assets spans seven different footnotes, most of which are several pages long. In addition to information about the discount rate and other assumptions used to calculate impairment charges, the disclosures provide information about the sensitivity of impairment charges to changes in the assumptions.

Overall, an analyst can use the disclosures to understand a company's investments in tangible and intangible assets, how those investments changed during a reporting period, how those changes affected current performance, and what those changes might indicate about future performance.

SUMMARY

Understanding the reporting of long-lived assets at inception requires distinguishing between expenditures that are capitalised (i.e., reported as long-lived assets) and those that are expensed. Once a long-lived asset is recognised, it is reported under the cost model at its historical cost less accumulated depreciation (amortisation) and less any impairment and under the revaluation model at its fair value. IFRS permit the use of either the cost model or the revaluation model, whereas U.S. GAAP require the use of the cost model. Most companies reporting under IFRS use the cost model. The choice of different methods to depreciate (amortise) long-lived assets can create challenges for analysts comparing companies.

Key points include the following:

▶ Expenditures related to long-lived assets are capitalised as part of the cost of assets if they are expected to provide future benefits, typically beyond one year. Otherwise, expenditures related to long-lived assets are expensed as incurred.

▶ Although capitalising expenditures, rather than expensing them, results in higher reported profitability in the initial year, it results in lower profitability in subsequent years; however, if a company continues to purchase similar or increasing amounts of assets each year, the profitability-enhancing effect of capitalisation continues.

▶ Capitalising an expenditure rather than expensing it results in a greater amount reported as cash from operations because capitalised expenditures are classified as an investing cash outflow rather than an operating cash outflow.

▶ Companies must capitalise interest costs associated with acquiring or constructing an asset that requires a long period of time to prepare for its intended use.

▶ Including capitalised interest in the calculation of interest coverage ratios provides a better assessment of a company's solvency.

▶ IFRS require research costs be expensed but allow all development costs (not only software development costs) to be capitalised under certain conditions. Generally, U.S. accounting standards require that research and development costs be expensed; however, certain costs related to software development are required to be capitalised.

▶ When one company acquires another company, the transaction is accounted for using the acquisition method of accounting in which the company identified as the acquirer allocates the purchase price to each asset acquired (and each liability assumed) on the basis of its fair value. Under acquisition accounting, if the purchase price of an acquisition exceeds the sum of the amounts that can be allocated to individual identifiable assets and liabilities, the excess is recorded as goodwill.

▶ The capitalised costs of long-lived tangible assets and of intangible assets with finite useful lives are allocated to expense in subsequent periods over their useful lives. For tangible assets, this process is referred to as depreciation, and for intangible assets, it is referred to as amortisation.

► Long-lived tangible assets and intangible assets with finite useful lives are reviewed for impairment whenever changes in events or circumstances indicate that the carrying amount of an asset may not be recoverable.

► Intangible assets with an indefinite useful life are not amortised but are reviewed for impairment annually.

► Methods of calculating depreciation or amortisation expense include the straight-line method, in which the cost of an asset is allocated to expense in equal amounts each year over its useful life; accelerated methods, in which the allocation of cost is greater in earlier years; and the units-of-production method, in which the allocation of cost corresponds to the actual use of an asset in a particular period.

► Estimates required for depreciation and amortisation calculations include the useful life of the equipment (or its total lifetime productive capacity) and its expected residual value at the end of that useful life. A longer useful life and higher expected residual value result in a smaller amount of annual depreciation relative to a shorter useful life and lower expected residual value.

► IFRS permit the use of either the cost model or the revaluation model, but the revaluation model is not allowed under U.S. GAAP.

► Under the revaluation model, carrying amounts are the fair values at the date of revaluation less any subsequent accumulated depreciation or amortisation.

► In contrast with depreciation and amortisation charges, which serve to allocate the cost of a long-lived asset over its useful life, impairment charges reflect an unexpected decline in the fair value of an asset to an amount lower than its carrying amount.

► IFRS permit impairment losses to be reversed, with the reversal reported in profit. U.S. GAAP do not permit the reversal of impairment losses.

► The gain or loss on the sale of long-lived assets is computed as the sales proceeds minus the carrying amount of the asset at the time of sale.

► Long-lived assets reclassified as held for sale cease to be depreciated or amortised. Long-lived assets to be disposed of other than by a sale (e.g., by abandonment, exchange for another asset, or distribution to owners in a spin-off) are classified as held for use until disposal. Thus, they continue to be depreciated and tested for impairment.

PRACTICE PROBLEMS FOR READING 37

1. JOOVI Inc. has recently purchased and installed a new machine for its manufacturing plant. The company incurred the following costs:

Purchase price	$12,980
Freight and insurance	$1,200
Installation	$700
Testing	$100
Maintenance staff training costs	$500

The total cost of the machine to be shown on JOOVI's balance sheet is *closest* to:

A. $14,180.

B. $14,980.

C. $15,480.

2. BAURU, S.A., a Brazilian corporation, borrows capital from a local bank to finance the construction of its manufacturing plant. The loan has the following conditions:

Borrowing date	1 January 2009
Amount borrowed	500 million Brazilian real (BRL)
Annual interest rate	14 percent
Term of the loan	3 years
Payment method	Annual payment of interest only. Principal amortisation is due at the end of the loan term.

The construction of the plant takes two years, during which time BAURU earned BRL 10 million by temporarily investing the loan proceeds. Which of the following is the amount of interest related to the plant construction (in BRL million) that can be capitalised in BAURU's balance sheet?

A. 130.

B. 140.

C. 210.

3. After reading the financial statements and footnotes of a company that follows IFRS, an analyst identified the following intangible assets:

▶ product patent expiring in 40 years;

▶ copyright with no expiration date; and

▶ goodwill acquired 2 years ago in a business combination.

Which of these assets is an intangible asset with finite useful life?

	Product Patent	Copyright	Goodwill
A.	Yes	Yes	No
B.	Yes	No	No
C.	No	Yes	Yes

4. Intangible assets with finite useful lives *mostly* differ from intangible assets with infinite useful lives with respect to accounting treatment of:

A. revaluation.

B. impairment.

C. amortisation.

5. A financial analyst is studying the income statement effect of two alternative depreciation methods for a recently acquired piece of equipment. She gathers the following information about the equipment's expected production life and use:

	Year 1	Year 2	Year 3	Year 4	Year 5	Total
Units of production	2,000	2,000	2,000	2,000	2,500	10,500

Compared with the units-of-production method of depreciation, if the company uses the straight-line method to depreciate the equipment, its net income in Year 1 will *most likely* be:

A. lower.

B. higher.

C. the same.

6. Juan Martinez, CFO of VIRMIN, S.A., is selecting the depreciation method to use for a new machine. The machine has an expected useful life of six years. Production is expected to be relatively low initially but to increase over time. The method chosen for tax reporting must be the same as the method used for financial reporting. If Martinez wants to minimize tax payments in the first year of the machine's life, which of the following depreciation methods is Martinez *most likely* to use?

A. Straight-line method.

B. Units-of-production method.

C. Double-declining balance method.

The following information relates to Questions 7–8

Miguel Rodriguez of MARIO S.A., an Uruguayan corporation, is computing the depreciation expense of a piece of manufacturing equipment for the fiscal year ended 31 December 2009. The equipment was acquired on 1 January 2009. Rodriguez gathers the following information (currency in Uruguayan pesos, UYP):

Cost of the equipment	UYP 1,200,000
Estimated residual value	UYP 200,000
Expected useful life	8 years
Total productive capacity	800,000 units
Production in FY 2009	135,000 units
Expected production for the next 7 years	95,000 units each year

7. If MARIO uses the straight-line method, the amount of depreciation expense on MARIO's income statement related to the manufacturing equipment is *closest* to:

   A. 125,000.

   B. 150,000.

   C. 168,750.

8. If MARIO uses the units-of-production method, the amount of depreciation expense (in UYP) on MARIO's income statement related to the manufacturing equipment is *closest* to:

   A. 118,750.

   B. 168,750.

   C. 202,500.

9. Which of the following amortisation methods is *most likely* to evenly distribute the cost of an intangible asset over its useful life?

   A. Straight-line method.

   B. Units-of-production method.

   C. Double-declining balance method.

10. Which of the following will cause a company to show a lower amount of amortisation of intangible assets in the first year after acquisition?

    A. A higher residual value.

    B. A higher amortisation rate.

    C. A shorter useful life.

11. An analyst in the finance department of BOOLDO S.A., a French corporation, is computing the amortisation of a customer list, an intangible asset, for the fiscal year ended 31 December 2009. She gathers the following information about the asset:

Acquisition cost	€2,300,000
Acquisition date	1 January 2008
Expected residual value at time of acquisition	€500,000

The customer list is expected to result in extra sales for three years after acquisition. The present value of these expected extra sales exceeds the cost of the list.

If the analyst uses the straight-line method, the amount of accumulated amortisation related to the customer list as of 31 December 2009 is *closest* to:

   A. €600,000.

   B. €1,200,000.

   C. €1,533,333.

12. A financial analyst is analyzing the amortisation of a product patent acquired by MAKETTI S.p.A., an Italian corporation. He gathers the following information about the patent:

Acquisition cost	€5,800,000
Acquisition date	1 January 2009
Patent expiration date	31 December 2015
Total plant capacity of patented product	40,000 units per year
Production of patented product in fiscal year ended 31 December 2009	20,000 units
Expected production of patented product during life of the patent	175,000 units

If the analyst uses the units-of-production method, the amortisation expense on the patent for fiscal year 2009 is *closest* to:

   A. €414,286.

   B. €662,857.

   C. €828,571.

13. MARU S.A. de C.V., a Mexican corporation that follows IFRS, has elected to use the revaluation model for its property, plant, and equipment. One of MARU's machines was purchased for 2,500,000 Mexican pesos (MXN) at the beginning of the fiscal year ended 31 March 2010. As of 31 March 2010, the machine has a fair value of MXN 3,000,000. Should MARU show a profit for the revaluation of the machine?

   A. Yes.

   B. No, because this revaluation is recorded directly in equity.

   C. No, because value increases resulting from revaluation can never be recognized as a profit.

14. An analyst is studying the impairment of the manufacturing equipment of PALL Corp., a U.K.-based corporation that follows IFRS. He gathers the following information about the equipment:

Fair value	£16,800,000
Costs to sell	£800,000
Value in use	£14,500,000
Net carrying amount	£19,100,000

The amount of the impairment loss on PALL Corp.'s income statement related to its manufacturing equipment is *closest* to:

A. £2,300,000.

B. £3,100,000.

C. £4,600,000.

15. A financial analyst at BETTO S.A. is analyzing the result of the sale of a vehicle for 85,000 Argentine pesos (ARP) on 31 December 2009. The analyst compiles the following information about the vehicle:

Acquisition cost of the vehicle	ARP 100,000
Acquisition date	1 January 2007
Estimated residual value at acquisition date	ARP 10,000
Expected useful life	9 years
Depreciation method	Straight-line

The result of the sale of the vehicle is *most likely*:

A. a loss of ARP 15,000.

B. a gain of ARP 15,000.

C. a gain of ARP 18,333.

16. CROCO S.p.A sells an intangible asset with a historical acquisition cost of €12 million and an accumulated depreciation of €2 million and reports a loss on the sale of €3.2 million. Which of the following amounts is *most likely* the sale price of the asset?

A. €6.8 million.

B. €8.8 million.

C. €13.2 million.

17. According to IFRS, all of the following pieces of information about property, plant, and equipment must be disclosed in a company's financial statements and footnotes *except*:

A. useful lives.

B. acquisition dates.

C. amount of disposals.

18. According to IFRS, all of the following pieces of information about intangible assets must be disclosed in a company's financial statements and footnotes *except*:

A. fair value.

B. impairment loss.

C. amortisation rate.

SOLUTIONS FOR READING 37

1. **B is correct.** Only costs necessary for the machine to be ready to use can be capitalised. Therefore, total capitalised costs = 12,980 + 1,200 + 700 + 100 = $14,980.

2. **A is correct.** Borrowing costs can be capitalised under IFRS until the tangible asset is ready for use. Also, under IFRS, income earned on temporarily investing the borrowed monies decreases the amount of borrowing costs eligible for capitalisation. Therefore, Total capitalised interest = (500 million × 14% × 2 years) − 10 million = 130 million.

3. **B is correct.** A product patent with a defined expiration date is an intangible asset with a finite useful life. A copyright with no expiration date is an intangible asset with an indefinite useful life. Goodwill is no longer considered an intangible asset under IFRS and is considered to have an indefinite useful life.

4. **C is correct.** An intangible asset with a finite useful life is amortised, whereas an intangible asset with an indefinite useful life is not.

5. **A is correct.** If the company uses the straight-line method, the depreciation expense will be one-fifth (20 percent) of the depreciable cost in Year 1. If it uses the units-of-production method, the depreciation expense will be 19 percent (2,000/10,500) of the depreciable cost in Year 1. Therefore, if the company uses the straight-line method, its depreciation expense will be higher and its net income will be lower.

6. **C is correct.** If Martinez wants to minimize tax payments in the first year of the machine's life, he should use an accelerated method, such as the double-declining balance method.

7. **A is correct.** Using the straight-line method, depreciation expense amounts to

   Depreciation expense = (1,200,000 − 200,000)/8 years = 125,000.

8. **B is correct.** Using the units-of-production method, depreciation expense amounts to

   Depreciation expense = (1,200,000 − 200,000) × (135,000/800,000) = 168,750.

9. **A is correct.** The straight-line method is the method that evenly distributes the cost of an asset over its useful life because amortisation is the same amount every year.

10. **A is correct.** A higher residual value results in a lower total depreciable cost and, therefore, a lower amount of amortisation in the first year after acquisition (and every year after that).

11. **B is correct.** Using the straight-line method, accumulated amortisation amounts to

    Accumulated amortisation = [(2,300,000 − 500,000)/3 years] × 2 years = 1,200,000.

12. **B is correct.** Using the units-of-production method, depreciation expense amounts to

    Depreciation expense = 5,800,000 × (20,000/175,000) = 662,857.

13. B is correct. In this case, the value increase brought about by the revaluation should be recorded directly in equity. The reason is that under IFRS, an increase in value brought about by a revaluation can only be recognised as a profit to the extent that it reverses a revaluation decrease of the same asset previously recognised in the income statement.

14. B is correct. The impairment loss equals

$$\text{Impairment loss} = \max(\text{Recoverable amount; Value in use}) \\ - \text{Net carrying amount}$$

$$\text{Impairment loss} = \max(16{,}800{,}000 - 800{,}000;\ 14{,}500{,}000) \\ - 19{,}100{,}000 = -3{,}100{,}000$$

15. B is correct. The result on the sale of the vehicle equals

Gain or loss on the sale = Sale proceeds − Carrying amount

= Sale proceeds − (Acquisition cost − Accumulated depreciation)

= 85,000 − {100,000 − [((100,000 − 10,000)/9 years) × 3 years]}

= 15,000.

16. A is correct. Gain or loss on the sale = Sale proceeds − Carrying amount. Rearranging this equation, Sale proceeds = Carrying amount + Gain or loss on sale. Thus, Sale price = (12 − 2) + (−3.2) = 6.8.

17. B is correct. IFRS do not require acquisition dates to be disclosed.

18. A is correct. IFRS do not require fair value of intangible assets to be disclosed.

INCOME TAXES

by Elbie Antonites, CFA and Michael A. Broihahn, CFA

LEARNING OUTCOMES

The candidate should be able to:	Mastery
a. explain the differences between accounting profit and taxable income, and define key terms, including deferred tax assets, deferred tax liabilities, valuation allowance, taxes payable, and income tax expense;	☐
b. explain how deferred tax liabilities and assets are created and the factors that determine how a company's deferred tax liabilities and assets should be treated for the purposes of financial analysis;	☐
c. determine the tax base of a company's assets and liabilities;	☐
d. calculate income tax expense, income taxes payable, deferred tax assets, and deferred tax liabilities, and calculate and interpret the adjustment to the financial statements related to a change in the income tax rate;	☐
e. evaluate the impact of tax rate changes on a company's financial statements and ratios;	☐
f. distinguish between temporary and permanent items in pre-tax financial income and taxable income;	☐
g. discuss the valuation allowance for deferred tax assets—when it is required and what impact it has on financial statements;	☐
h. compare and contrast a company's deferred tax items;	☐
i. analyze disclosures relating to deferred tax items and the effective tax rate reconciliation, and discuss how information included in these disclosures affects a company's financial statements and financial ratios;	☐
j. identify the key provisions of and differences between income tax accounting under IFRS and U.S. GAAP.	☐

Note:
New rulings and/or pronouncements issued after the publication of the readings on financial reporting and analysis may cause some of the information in these readings to become dated. Candidates are expected to be familiar with the overall analytical framework contained in the study session readings, as well as the implications of alternative accounting methods for financial analysis and valuation, as provided in the assigned readings. Candidates are not responsible for changes that occur after the material was written.

International Financial Statement Analysis, by Thomas R. Robinson, CFA, Jan Hendrik van Greuning, CFA, Elaine Henry, CFA, and Michael A. Broihahn, CFA. Copyright © 2008 by CFA Institute. Reprinted with permission.

1   INTRODUCTION

For those companies reporting under International Financial Reporting Standards (IFRS), IAS 12 covers accounting for a company's income taxes and the reporting of deferred taxes. For those companies reporting under United States generally accepted accounting principles (U.S. GAAP), SFAS No. 109[1] is the primary source for information on accounting for income taxes. Although IFRS and U.S. GAAP follow similar conventions on many income tax issues, there are some key differences that will be discussed in the reading.

Differences between how and when transactions are recognized for financial reporting purposes relative to tax reporting can give rise to differences in tax expense and related tax assets and liabilities. To reconcile these differences, companies that report under either IFRS or U.S. GAAP create a provision on the balance sheet called deferred tax assets or deferred tax liabilities, depending on the nature of the situation.

Deferred tax assets or liabilities usually arise when accounting standards and tax authorities recognize the timing of revenues and expenses at different times. Because timing differences such as these will eventually reverse over time, they are called "temporary differences." Deferred tax assets represent taxes that have been recognized for tax reporting purposes (or often the carrying forward of losses from previous periods) but have not yet been recognized on the income statement prepared for financial reporting purposes. Deferred tax liabilities represent tax expense that has appeared on the income statement for financial reporting purposes, but has not yet become payable under tax regulations.

This reading provides a primer on the basics of income tax accounting and reporting. The reading is organized as follows. Section 2 describes the differences between taxable income and accounting profit. Section 3 explains the determination of tax base, which relates to the valuation of assets and liabilities for tax purposes. Section 4 discusses several types of timing differences between the recognition of taxable and accounting profit. Section 5 examines unused tax losses and tax credits. Section 6 describes the recognition and measurement of current and deferred tax. Section 7 discusses the disclosure and presentation of income tax information on companies' financial statements and illustrates its practical implications for financial analysis. Section 8 provides an overview of the similarities and differences for income-tax reporting between IFRS and U.S. GAAP. A summary of the key points and practice problems in the CFA Institute multiple-choice format conclude the reading.

---

[1] FASB ASC Topic 740 [Income Taxes].

DIFFERENCES BETWEEN ACCOUNTING PROFIT AND TAXABLE INCOME

## 2

A company's **accounting profit** is reported on its income statement in accordance with prevailing accounting standards. Accounting profit (also referred to as income before taxes or pretax income) does not include a provision for income tax expense.[2] A company's **taxable income** is the portion of its income that is subject to income taxes under the tax laws of its jurisdiction. Because of different guidelines for how income is reported on a company's financial statements and how it is measured for income tax purposes, accounting profit and taxable income may differ.

A company's taxable income is the basis for its **income tax payable** (a liability) or recoverable (an asset), which is calculated on the basis of the company's tax rate and appears on its balance sheet. A company's **tax expense**, or tax benefit in the case of a recovery, appears on its income statement and is an aggregate of its income tax payable (or recoverable in the case of a tax benefit) and any changes in deferred tax assets and liabilities.

When a company's taxable income is greater than its accounting profit, then its income taxes payable will be higher than what would have otherwise been the case had the income taxes been determined based on accounting profit. **Deferred tax assets**, which appear on the balance sheet, arise when an excess amount is paid for income taxes (taxable income higher than accounting profit) and the company expects to recover the difference during the course of future operations. Actual income taxes payable will thus exceed the financial accounting income tax expense (which is reported on the income statement and is determined based on accounting profit). Related to deferred tax assets is a **valuation allowance**, which is a reserve created against deferred tax assets. The valuation allowance is based on the likelihood of realizing the deferred tax assets in future accounting periods. **Deferred tax liabilities**, which also appear on the balance sheet, arise when a deficit amount is paid for income taxes and the company expects to eliminate the deficit over the course of future operations. In this case, financial accounting income tax expense exceeds income taxes payable.

Income tax paid in a period is the actual amount paid for income taxes (not a provision, but the actual cash outflow). The income tax paid may be less than the income tax expense because of payments in prior periods or refunds received in the current period. Income tax paid reduces the income tax payable, which is carried on the balance sheet as a liability.

The **tax base** of an asset or liability is the amount at which the asset or liability is valued for tax purposes, whereas the **carrying amount** is the amount at which the asset or liability is valued according to accounting principles.[3] Differences between the tax base and the carrying amount also result in differences between accounting profit and taxable income. These differences can carry through to future periods. For example, a **tax loss carry forward** occurs when a company experiences a loss in the current period that may be used to reduce future taxable income. The company's tax expense on its income statement must not only reflect the taxes payable based on taxable income, but also the effect of these differences.

---

[2] As defined under IAS 12, paragraph 5.

[3] The terms "tax base" and "tax basis" are interchangeable. "Tax basis" is more commonly used in the United States. Similarly, "carrying amount" and "book value" refer to the same concept.

2.1 Current Tax Assets and Liabilities

A company's current tax liability is the amount payable in taxes and is based on current taxable income. If the company expects to receive a refund for some portion previously paid in taxes, the amount recoverable is referred to as a current tax asset. The current tax liability or asset may, however, differ from what the liability would have been if it was based on accounting profit rather than taxable income for the period. Differences in accounting profit and taxable income are the result of the application of different rules. Such differences between accounting profit and taxable income can occur in several ways, including:

▶ Revenues and expenses may be recognized in one period for accounting purposes and a different period for tax purposes;

▶ Specific revenues and expenses may be either recognized for accounting purposes and not for tax purposes; or not recognized for accounting purposes but recognized for tax purposes;

▶ The carrying amount and tax base of assets and/or liabilities may differ;

▶ The deductibility of gains and losses of assets and liabilities may vary for accounting and income tax purposes;

▶ Subject to tax rules, tax losses of prior years might be used to reduce taxable income in later years, resulting in differences in accounting and taxable income (tax loss carryforward); and

▶ Adjustments of reported financial data from prior years might not be recognized equally for accounting and tax purposes or might be recognized in different periods.

2.2 Deferred Tax Assets and Liabilities

Deferred tax assets represent taxes that have been paid (or often the carrying forward of losses from previous periods) but have not yet been recognized on the income statement. Deferred tax liabilities occur when financial accounting income tax expense is greater than regulatory income tax expense. Deferred tax assets and liabilities usually arise when accounting standards and tax authorities recognize the timing of taxes due at different times; for example, when a company uses accelerated depreciation when reporting to the tax authority (to increase expense and lower tax payments in the early years) but uses the straight-line method on the financial statements. Although not similar in treatment on a year-to-year basis (e.g., depreciation of 5 percent on a straight-line basis may be permitted for accounting purposes whereas 10 percent is allowed for tax purposes) over the life of the asset, both approaches allow for the total cost of the asset to be depreciated (or amortized). Because these timing differences will eventually reverse or self-correct over the course of the asset's depreciable life, they are called "temporary differences."

Under IFRS, deferred tax assets and liabilities are always classified as noncurrent. Under U.S. GAAP, however, deferred tax assets and liabilities are classified on the balance sheet as current and noncurrent based on the classification of the underlying asset or liability.

Any deferred tax asset or liability is based on temporary differences that result in an excess or a deficit amount paid for taxes, which the company expects to recover from future operations. Because taxes will be recoverable or payable at a future date, it is only a temporary difference and a deferred tax asset or liability is created. Changes in the deferred tax asset or liability on the balance sheet reflect the difference between the amounts recognized in the previous period and the current period. The changes in deferred tax assets and liabilities are added to income tax payable to determine the company's income tax expense (or credit) as it is reported on the income statement.

At the end of each fiscal year, deferred tax assets and liabilities are recalculated by comparing the tax bases and carrying amounts of the balance sheet items. Identified temporary differences should be assessed on whether the difference will result in future economic benefits. For example, Pinto Construction (a hypothetical company) depreciates equipment on a straight-line basis of 10 percent per year. The tax authorities allow depreciation of 15 percent per year. At the end of the fiscal year, the carrying amount of the equipment for accounting purposes would be greater than the tax base of the equipment thus resulting in a temporary difference. A deferred tax item may only be created if it is not doubtful that the company will realize economic benefits in the future. In our example, the equipment is used in the core business of Pinto Construction. If the company is a going concern and stable, there should be no doubt that future economic benefits will result from the equipment and it would be appropriate to create the deferred tax item.

Should it be doubtful that future economic benefits will be realized from a temporary difference (such as Pinto Construction being under liquidation), the temporary difference will not lead to the creation of a deferred tax asset or liability. If a deferred tax asset or liability resulted in the past, but the criteria of economic benefits is not met on the current balance sheet date, then, under IFRS, an existing deferred tax asset or liability related to the item will be reversed. Under U.S. GAAP, a valuation allowance is established. In assessing future economic benefits, much is left to the discretion of the auditor in assessing the temporary differences and the issue of future economic benefits.

EXAMPLE 1

The following information pertains to a fictitious company, Reston Partners:

Reston Partners
Consolidated Income Statement

Period Ending 31 March (£ Millions)	2006	2005	2004
Revenue	£40,000	£30,000	£25,000
Other net gains	2,000	0	0
Changes in inventories of finished goods and work in progress	400	180	200
Raw materials and consumables used	(5,700)	(4,000)	(8,000)
Depreciation expense	(2,000)	(2,000)	(2,000)
Other expenses	(6,000)	(5,900)	(4,500)
Interest expense	(2,000)	(3,000)	(6,000)
Profit before tax	£26,700	£15,280	£4,700

The financial performance and accounting profit of Reston Partners on this income statement is based on accounting principles appropriate for the jurisdiction in which Reston Partners operates. The principles used to calculate accounting profit (profit before tax in the example above) may differ from the principles applied for tax purposes (the calculation of taxable income). For illustrative purposes, however, assume that all income and expenses on the income statement are treated identically for tax and accounting purposes *except* depreciation.

The depreciation is related to equipment owned by Reston Partners. For simplicity, assume that the equipment was purchased at the beginning of the 2004 fiscal year. Depreciation should thus be calculated and expensed for the full year. Assume that accounting standards permit equipment to be depreciated on a straight-line basis over a 10-year period, whereas the tax standards in the jurisdiction specify that equipment should be depreciated on a straight-line basis over a 7-year period. For simplicity, assume a salvage value of £0 at the end of the equipment's useful life. Both methods will result in the full depreciation of the asset over the respective tax or accounting life.

The equipment was originally purchased for £20,000. In accordance with accounting standards, over the next 10 years the company will recognize annual depreciation of £2,000 (£20,000 ÷ 10) as an expense on its income statement and for the determination of accounting profit. For tax purposes, however, the company will recognize £2,857 (£20,000 ÷ 7) in depreciation each year. Each fiscal year the depreciation expense related to the use of the equipment will, therefore, differ for tax and accounting purposes (tax base vs. carrying amount), resulting in a difference between accounting profit and taxable income.

The previous income statement reflects accounting profit (depreciation at £2,000 per year). The following table shows the taxable income for each fiscal year.

Taxable Income (£ Millions)	2006	2005	2004
Revenue	£40,000	£30,000	£25,000
Other net gains	2,000	0	0
Changes in inventories of finished goods and work in progress	400	180	200
Raw materials and consumables used	(5,700)	(4,000)	(8,000)
Depreciation expense	(2,857)	(2,857)	(2,857)
Other expenses	(6,000)	(5,900)	(4,500)
Interest expense	(2,000)	(3,000)	(6,000)
Taxable income	£25,843	£14,423	£3,843

The carrying amount and tax base for the equipment is as follows:

(£ Millions)	2006	2005	2004
Equipment value for accounting purposes (*carrying amount*) (depreciation of £2,000/year)	£14,000	£16,000	£18,000
Equipment value for tax purposes (*tax base*) (depreciation of £2,857/year)	£11,429	£14,286	£17,143
Difference	£2,571	£1,714	£857

At each balance sheet date, the tax base and carrying amount of all assets and liabilities must be determined. The income tax payable by Reston Partners will be based on the taxable income of each fiscal year. If a tax rate of 30 percent is assumed, then the income taxes payable for 2004, 2005, and 2006 are £1,153 (30% × 3,843), £4,327 (30% × 14,423), and £7,753 (30% × 25,843).

Remember, though, that if the tax obligation is calculated based on accounting profits, it will differ because of the differences between the tax base and the carrying amount of equipment. The difference in each fiscal year is reflected in the table above. In each fiscal year the carrying amount of the equipment exceeds its tax base. For tax purposes, therefore, the asset tax base is less than its carrying value under financial accounting principles. The difference results in a deferred tax liability.

(£ Millions)	2006	2005	2004
Deferred tax liability	£771	£514	£257
(Difference between tax base and carrying amount)			

2004: £(18,000 − 17,143) × 30% = 257

2005: £(16,000 − 14,286) × 30% = 514

2006: £(14,000 − 11,429) × 30% = 771

The comparison of the tax base and carrying amount of equipment shows what the deferred tax liability should be on a particular balance sheet date. In each fiscal year, only the change in the deferred tax liability should be included in the calculation of the income tax expense reported on the income statement prepared for accounting purposes.

On the income statement, the company's income tax expense will be the sum of the deferred tax liability and income tax payable.

(£ Millions)	2006	2005	2004
Income tax payable (based on tax accounting)	£7,753	£4,327	£1,153
Deferred tax liability	257	257	257
Income tax (based on financial accounting)	£8,010	£4,584	£1,410

(Difference between tax base and carrying amount)

2004: £(18,000 − 17,143) × 30% = 257

2005: £(16,000 − 14,286) × 30% − 257 = 257

2006: £(14,000 − 11,429) × 30% − 514 = 257

Note that because the different treatment of depreciation is a temporary difference, the income tax on the income statement is 30 percent of the accounting profit, although only a part is income tax payable and the rest is a deferred tax liability.

The consolidated income statement of Reston Partners including income tax is presented as follows:

Reston Partners
Consolidated Income Statement

Period Ending 31 March (£ Millions)	2006	2005	2004
Revenue	£40,000	£30,000	£25,000
Other net gains	2,000	0	0
Changes in inventories of finished goods and work in progress	400	180	200
Raw materials and consumables used	(5,700)	(4,000)	(8,000)
Depreciation expense	(2,000)	(2,000)	(2,000)
Other expenses	(6,000)	(5,900)	(4,500)
Interest expense	(2,000)	(3,000)	(6,000)
Profit before tax	£26,700	£15,280	£4,700
Income tax	(8,010)	(4,584)	(1,410)
Profit after tax	£18,690	£10,696	£3,290

Any amount paid to the tax authorities will reduce the liability for income tax payable and be reflected on the statement of cash flows of the company.

DETERMINING THE TAX BASE OF ASSETS AND LIABILITIES

## 3

As mentioned in Section 2, temporary differences arise from a difference in the tax base and carrying amount of assets and liabilities. The tax base of an asset or liability is the amount attributed to the asset or liability for tax purposes, whereas the carrying amount is based on accounting principles. Such a difference is considered temporary if it is expected that the taxes will be recovered or payable at a future date.

3.1 Determining the Tax Base of an Asset

The tax base of an asset is the amount that will be deductible for tax purposes in future periods as the economic benefits become realized and the company recovers the carrying amount of the asset.

For example, our previously mentioned Reston Partners (from Example 1) depreciates equipment on a straight-line basis at a rate of 10 percent per year. The tax authorities allow depreciation of approximately 15 percent per year. At the end of the fiscal year, the carrying amount of equipment for accounting purposes is greater than the asset tax base thus resulting in a temporary difference.

EXAMPLE 2

Determining the Tax Base of an Asset

The following information pertains to Entiguan Sports, a hypothetical developer of products used to treat sports-related injuries. (The treatment of items for accounting and tax purposes is based on fictitious accounting and tax standards and is not specific to a particular jurisdiction.) Calculate the tax base and carrying amount for each item.

1. *Dividends receivable*: On its balance sheet, Entiguan Sports reports dividends of €1 million receivable from a subsidiary. Assume that dividends are not taxable.

2. *Development costs*: Entiguan Sports capitalized development costs of €3 million during the year. Entiguan amortized €500,000 of this amount during the year. For tax purposes amortization of 25 percent per year is allowed.

3. *Research costs*: Entiguan incurred €500,000 in research costs, which were all expensed in the current fiscal year for financial reporting purposes. Assume that applicable tax legislation requires research costs to be expensed over a four-year period rather than all in one year.

4. *Accounts receivable*: Included on the income statement of Entiguan Sports is a provision for doubtful debt of €125,000. The accounts receivable amount reflected on the balance sheet, after taking the provision into account, amounts to €1,500,000. The tax authorities allow a deduction of 25 percent of the gross amount for doubtful debt.

Solutions:

	Carrying Amount (€)	Tax Base (€)	Temporary Difference (€)
1. Dividends receivable	1,000,000	1,000,000	0
2. Development costs	2,500,000	2,250,000	250,000
3. Research costs	0	375,000	(375,000)
4. Accounts receivable	1,500,000	1,218,750	281,250

Comments:

1. *Dividends receivable*: Although the dividends received are economic benefits from the subsidiary, we are assuming that dividends are not taxable. Therefore, the carrying amount equals the tax base for dividends receivable.

2. *Development costs*: First, we assume that development costs will generate economic benefits for Entiguan Sports. Therefore, it may be included as an asset on the balance sheet for the purposes of this example. Second, the amortization allowed by the tax authorities exceeds the amortization accounted for based on accounting rules. Therefore, the carrying amount of the asset exceeds its tax base. The carrying amount is (€3,000,000 − €500,000) = €2,500,000 whereas the tax base is [€3,000,000 − (25% × €3,000,000)] = €2,250,000.

3. *Research costs*: We assume that research costs will result in future economic benefits for the company. If this were not the case, creation of a deferred tax asset or liability would not be allowed. The tax base of research costs exceeds their carrying amount. The carrying amount is €0 because the full amount has been expensed for financial reporting purposes in the year in which it was incurred. Therefore, there would not have been a balance sheet item "Research costs" for tax purposes, and only a proportion may be deducted in the current fiscal year. The tax base of the asset is (€500,000 − €500,000/4) = €375,000.

4. *Accounts receivable*: The economic benefits that should have been received from accounts receivable have already been included in revenues included in the calculation of the taxable income when the sales occurred. Because the receipt of a portion of the accounts receivable is doubtful, the provision is allowed. The provision, based on tax legislation, results in a greater amount allowed in the current fiscal year than would be the case under accounting principles. This results in the tax base of accounts receivable being lower than its carrying amount. Note that the example specifically states that the balance sheet amount for accounts receivable after the provision for accounting purposes amounts to €1,500,000. Therefore, accounts receivable before any provision was €1,500,000 + €125,000 = €1,625,000. The tax base is calculated as (€1,500,000 + €125,000) − [25% × (€1,500,000 + €125,000)] = €1,218,750.

3.2 Determining the Tax Base of a Liability

The tax base of a liability is the carrying amount of the liability less any amounts that will be deductible for tax purposes in the future. With respect to payments from customers received in advance of providing the goods and services, the tax base of such a liability is the carrying amount less any amount of the revenue that will not be taxable in future. Keep in mind the following fundamental principle: In general, a company will recognize a deferred tax asset or liability when recovery/settlement of the carrying amount will affect future tax payments by either increasing or reducing the taxable profit. Remember, an analyst is not only evaluating the difference between the carrying amount and the tax base, but the relevance of that difference on future profits and losses and thus by implication future taxes.

IFRS offers specific guidelines with regard to revenue received in advance: IAS 12 states that the tax base is the carrying amount less any amount of the revenue that will not be taxed at a future date. Under U.S. GAAP, an analysis of the tax base would result in a similar outcome. The tax legislation within the jurisdiction will determine the amount recognized on the income statement and whether the liability (revenue received in advance) will have a tax base greater than zero. This will depend on how tax legislation recognizes revenue received in advance.

EXAMPLE 3

Determining the Tax Base of a Liability

The following information pertains to Entiguan Sports for the 2006 year-end. The treatment of items for accounting and tax purposes is based on fictitious accounting and tax standards and is not specific to a particular jurisdiction. Calculate the tax base and carrying amount for each item.

1. *Donations*: Entiguan Sports made donations of €100,000 in the current fiscal year. The donations were expensed for financial reporting purposes, but are not tax deductible based on applicable tax legislation.

2. *Interest received in advance*: Entiguan Sports received in advance interest of €300,000. The interest is taxed because tax authorities recognize the interest to accrue to the company (part of taxable income) on the date of receipt.

3. *Rent received in advance*: Entiguan recognized €10 million for rent received in advance from a lessee for an unused warehouse building. Rent received in advance is deferred for accounting purposes but taxed on a cash basis.

4. *Loan*: Entiguan Sports secured a long-term loan for €550,000 in the current fiscal year. Interest is charged at 13.5 percent per annum and is payable at the end of each fiscal year.

Solutions:

	Carrying Amount (€)	Tax Base (€)	Temporary Difference (€)
1. Donations	0	0	0
2. Interest received in advance	300,000	0	(300,000)
3. Rent received in advance	10,000,000	0	(10,000,000)
4. Loan (capital)	550,000	550,000	0
Interest paid	0	0	0

Comments:

1. *Donations*: The amount of €100,000 was immediately expensed on Entiguan's income statement; therefore, the carrying amount is €0. Tax legislation does not allow donations to be deducted for tax purposes, so the tax base of the donations equals the carrying amount. Note that while the carrying amount and tax base are the same, the difference in the treatment of donations for accounting and tax purposes (expensed for accounting purposes, but not deductible for tax purposes) represents a permanent difference (a difference that will not be reversed in future). Permanent and temporary differences are elaborated on in Section 4 and it will refer to this particular case with an expanded explanation.

2. *Interest received in advance*: Based on the information provided, for tax purposes, interest is deemed to accrue to the company on the date of receipt. For tax purposes, it is thus irrelevant whether it is for the current or a future accounting period; it must be included in taxable income in the financial year received. Interest received in advance is, for accounting purposes though, included in the financial period in which it is deemed to have been earned. For this reason, the interest income received in advance is a balance sheet liability. It was not included on the income statement because the income relates to a future financial year. Because the full €300,000 is included in taxable income in the current fiscal year, the tax base is €300,000 − 300,000 = €0. Note that although interest received in advance and rent received in advance are both taxed, the timing depends on how the particular item is treated in tax legislation.

3. *Rent received in advance*: The result is similar to interest received in advance. The carrying amount of rent received in advance would be €10,000,000 while the tax base is €0.

4. *Loan*: Repayment of the loan has no tax implications. The repayment of the capital amount does not constitute an income or expense. The interest paid is included as an expense in the calculation of taxable income as well as accounting income. Therefore, the tax base and carrying amount is €0. For clarity, the interest paid that would be included on the income statement for the year amounts to 13.5% × €550,000 = €74,250 if the loan was acquired at the beginning of the current fiscal year.

3.3 Changes in Income Tax Rates

The measurement of deferred tax assets and liabilities is based on current tax law. But if there are subsequent changes in tax laws or new income tax rates, existing deferred tax assets and liabilities must be adjusted for the effects of these changes. The resulting effects of the changes are also included in determining accounting profit in the period of change.

When income tax rates change, the deferred tax assets and liabilities are adjusted to the new tax rate. If income tax rates increase, deferred taxes (that is, the deferred tax assets and liabilities) will also increase. Likewise, if income tax rates decrease, deferred taxes will decrease. A decrease in tax rates decreases deferred tax liabilities, which reduces future tax payments to the taxing authorities. A decrease in tax rates will also decrease deferred tax assets, which reduces their value toward the offset of future tax payments to the taxing authorities.

To illustrate the effect of a change in tax rate, consider Example 1 again. In that illustration, the timing difference that led to the recognition of a deferred tax liability for Reston Partners was attributable to differences in the method of depreciation and the related effects on the accounting carrying value and the asset tax base. The relevant information is restated below.

The carrying amount and tax base for the equipment is:

(£ Millions)	2006	2005	2004
Equipment value for accounting purposes (*carrying amount*) (depreciation of £2,000/year)	£14,000	£16,000	£18,000
Equipment value for tax purposes (*tax base*) (depreciation of £2,857/year)	£11,429	£14,286	£17,143
Difference	£2,571	£1,714	£857

At a 30 percent income tax rate, the deferred tax liability was then determined as follows:

(£ Millions)	2006	2005	2004
Deferred tax liability	£771	£514	£257
(Difference between tax base and carrying amount)			
2004: £(18,000 − 17,143) × 30% = £257			
2005: £(16,000 − 14,286) × 30% = £514			
2006: £(14,000 − 11,429) × 30% = £771			

For this illustration, assume that the taxing authority has changed the income tax rate to 25 percent for 2006. Although the difference between the carrying amount and the tax base of the depreciable asset are the same, the deferred tax liability for 2006 will be £643 (instead of £771 or a reduction of £128 in the liability). 2006: £(14,000 − 11,429) × 25% = £643.

Reston Partners' provision for income tax expense is also affected by the change in tax rates. Taxable income for 2006 will now be taxed at a rate of 25 percent. The benefit of the 2006 accelerated depreciation tax shield is now only £214 (£857 × 25%) instead of the previous £257 (a reduction of £43). In addition, the reduction in the beginning carrying value of the deferred tax liability for 2006 (the year of change) further reduces the income tax expense for 2006. The reduction in income tax expense attributable to the change in tax rate is £85. 2006: (30% − 25%) × £1,714 = £85. Note that these two components together account for the reduction in the deferred tax liability (£43 + £85 = £128).

As may be seen from this discussion, changes in the income tax rate have an effect on a company's deferred tax asset and liability carrying values as well as an effect on the measurement of income tax expense in the year of change. The analyst must thus note that proposed changes in tax law can have a quantifiable effect on these accounts (and any related financial ratios that are derived from them) if the proposed changes are subsequently enacted into law.

4 TEMPORARY AND PERMANENT DIFFERENCES BETWEEN TAXABLE AND ACCOUNTING PROFIT

Temporary differences arise from a difference between the tax base and the carrying amount of assets and liabilities. The creation of a deferred tax asset or liability from a temporary difference is only possible if the difference reverses itself at some future date and to such an extent that the balance sheet item is expected to create future economic benefits for the company. IFRS and U.S. GAAP both prescribe the balance sheet liability method for recognition of deferred tax. This balance sheet method focuses on the recognition of a deferred tax asset or liability should there be a temporary difference between the carrying amount and tax base of balance sheet items.[4]

Permanent differences are differences between tax and financial reporting of revenue (expenses) that *will not* be reversed at some future date. Because they will not be reversed at a future date, these differences do not give rise to deferred tax. These items typically include

- ▶ Income or expense items not allowed by tax legislation, and
- ▶ Tax credits for some expenditures that directly reduce taxes.

Because no deferred tax item is created for permanent differences, all permanent differences result in a difference between the company's effective tax rate and statutory tax rate. The effective tax rate is also influenced by different statutory taxes should an entity conduct business in more than one tax jurisdiction. The formula for the reported effective tax rate is thus equal to:

$$\text{Reported effective tax rate} = \text{Income tax expense} \div \text{Pretax income (accounting profit)}$$

---

[4] Previously, IAS 12 required recognition of deferred tax based on the deferred method (also known as the income statement method), which focused on timing differences. Timing differences are differences in the recognition of income and expenses for accounting and tax purposes that originate in one period and will reverse in a future period. Given the definition of timing differences, all timing differences are temporary differences, such as the different treatment of depreciation for tax and accounting purposes (although the timing is different with regard to the allowed depreciation for tax and accounting purposes, the asset will eventually be fully depreciated).

The net change in deferred tax during a reporting period is the difference between the balance of the deferred tax asset or liability for the current period and the balance of the previous period.

4.1 Taxable Temporary Differences

Temporary differences are further divided into two categories, namely taxable temporary differences and deductible temporary differences. **Taxable temporary differences** are temporary differences that result in a taxable amount in a future period when determining the taxable profit as the balance sheet item is recovered or settled. Taxable temporary differences result in a deferred tax liability when the carrying amount of an asset exceeds its tax base and, in the case of a liability, when the tax base of the liability exceeds its carrying amount.

Under U.S. GAAP, a deferred tax asset or liability is not recognized for unamortizable goodwill. Under IFRS, a deferred tax account is not recognized for goodwill arising in a business combination. Since goodwill is a residual, the recognition of a deferred tax liability would increase the carrying amount of goodwill. Discounting deferred tax assets or liabilities is generally not allowed for temporary differences related to business combinations as it is for other temporary differences.

IFRS provides an exemption (that is, deferred tax is not provided on the temporary difference) for the initial recognition of an asset or liability in a transaction that: a) is not a business combination (e.g., joint ventures, branches and unconsolidated investments); and b) affects neither accounting profit nor taxable profit at the time of the transaction. U.S. GAAP does not provide an exemption for these circumstances.

As a simple example of a temporary difference with no recognition of deferred tax liability, assume that a fictitious company, Corporate International, a holding company of various leisure related businesses and holiday resorts, buys an interest in a hotel in the current financial year. The goodwill related to the transaction will be recognized on the financial statements, but the related tax liability will not, as it relates to the initial recognition of goodwill.

4.2 Deductible Temporary Differences

Deductible temporary differences are temporary differences that result in a reduction or deduction of taxable income in a future period when the balance sheet item is recovered or settled. Deductible temporary differences result in a deferred tax asset when the tax base of an asset exceeds its carrying amount and, in the case of a liability, when the carrying amount of the liability exceeds its tax base. The recognition of a deferred tax asset is only allowed to the extent there is a reasonable expectation of future profits against which the asset or liability (that gave rise to the deferred tax asset) can be recovered or settled.

To determine the probability of sufficient future profits for utilization, one must consider the following: 1) Sufficient taxable temporary differences must exist that are related to the same tax authority and the same taxable entity; and 2) The taxable temporary differences that are expected to reverse in the same periods as expected for the reversal of the deductible temporary differences.

As with deferred tax liabilities, IFRS states that deferred tax assets should not be recognized in cases that would arise from the initial recognition of an asset or liability in transactions that are not a business combination and when, at the time of the transaction, there is no impact on either accounting or taxable profit.

Subsequent to initial recognition under IFRS and U.S. GAAP, any deferred tax assets that arise from investments in subsidiaries, branches, associates, and interests in joint ventures are recognized as a deferred tax asset.

IFRS and U.S. GAAP allow the creation of a deferred tax asset in the case of tax losses and tax credits. These two unique situations will be further elaborated on in Section 6. IAS 12 *does not* allow the creation of a deferred tax asset arising from negative goodwill. Negative goodwill arises when the amount that an entity pays for an interest in a business is less than the net fair market value of the portion of assets and liabilities of the acquired company, based on the interest of the entity.

4.3 Examples of Taxable and Deductible Temporary Differences

Exhibit 1 summarizes how differences between the tax bases and carrying amounts of assets and liabilities give rise to deferred tax assets or deferred tax liabilities.

EXHIBIT 1	Treatment of Temporary Differences	
Balance Sheet Item	**Carrying Amount vs. Tax Base**	**Results in Deferred Tax Asset/Liability**
Asset	Carrying amount > tax base	Deferred tax liability
Asset	Carrying amount < tax base	Deferred tax asset
Liability	Carrying amount > tax base	Deferred tax asset
Liability	Carrying amount < tax base	Deferred tax liability

EXAMPLE 4

Taxable and Deductible Temporary Differences

Examples 2 and 3 illustrated how to calculate the tax base of assets and liabilities, respectively. Based on the information provided in Examples 2 and 3, indicate whether the difference in the tax base and carrying amount of the assets and liabilities are temporary or permanent differences and whether a deferred tax asset or liability will be recognized based on the difference identified.

Solution to Example 2:

	Carrying Amount (€)	Tax Base (€)	Temporary Difference (€)	*Will Result in Deferred Tax Asset/Liability*
1. Dividends receivable	1,000,000	1,000,000	0	*N/A*
2. Development costs	2,500,000	2,250,000	250,000	*Deferred tax liability*
3. Research costs	0	375,000	(375,000)	*Deferred tax asset*
4. Accounts receivable	1,500,000	1,218,750	281,250	*Deferred tax liability*

Example 2 included comments on the calculation of the carrying amount and tax base of the assets.

1. *Dividends receivable*: As a result of non-taxability, the carrying amount equals the tax base of dividends receivable. This constitutes a permanent difference and will not result in the recognition of any deferred tax asset or liability. A temporary difference constitutes a difference that will, at some future date, be reversed. Although the timing of recognition is different for tax and accounting purposes, in the end the full carrying amount will be expensed/recognized as income. A permanent difference will never be reversed. Based on tax legislation, dividends from a subsidiary are not recognized as income. Therefore, no amount will be reflected as dividend income when calculating the taxable income, and the tax base of dividends receivable must be the total amount received, namely €1,000,000. The taxable income and accounting profit will permanently differ with the amount of dividends receivable, even on future financial statements as an effect on the retained earnings reflected on the balance sheet.

2. *Development costs*: The difference between the carrying amount and tax base is a temporary difference that, in the future, will reverse. In this fiscal year, it will result in a deferred tax liability.

3. *Research costs*: The difference between the carrying amount and tax base is a temporary difference that results in a deferred tax asset. Remember the explanation in Section 2 for deferred tax assets—a deferred tax asset arises because of an excess amount paid for taxes (when taxable income is greater than accounting profit), which is expected to be recovered from future operations. Based on accounting principles, the full amount was deducted resulting in a lower accounting profit, while the taxable income by implication, should be greater because of the lower amount expensed.

4. *Accounts receivable*: The difference between the carrying amount and tax base of the asset is a temporary difference that will result in a deferred tax liability.

Solution to Example 3:

	Carrying Amount (€)	Tax Base (€)	Temporary Difference (€)	*Will Result in Deferred Tax Asset/Liability*
1. Donations	0	0	0	*N/A*
2. Interest received in advance	300,000	0	(300,000)	*Deferred tax asset*
3. Rent received in advance	10,000,000	0	(10,000,000)	*Deferred tax asset*
4. Loan (capital)	550,000	550,000	0	*N/A*
Interest paid	0	0	0	*N/A*

Example 3 included extensive comments on the calculation of the carrying amount and tax base of the liabilities.

1. *Donations*: It was assumed that tax legislation does not allow donations to be deducted for tax purposes. No temporary difference results from donations, and thus a deferred tax asset or liability will not be recognized. This constitutes a permanent difference.

2. *Interest received in advance*: Interest received in advance results in a temporary difference that gives rise to a deferred tax asset. A deferred tax asset arises because of an excess amount paid for taxes (when taxable income is greater than accounting profit), which is expected to be recovered from future operations.

3. *Rent received in advance*: The difference between the carrying amount and tax base is a temporary difference that leads to the recognition of a deferred tax asset.

4. *Loan*: There are no temporary differences as a result of the loan or interest paid, and thus no deferred tax item is recognized.

4.4 Temporary Differences at Initial Recognition of Assets and Liabilities

In some situations the carrying amount and tax base of a balance sheet item may vary at initial recognition. For example, a company may deduct a government grant from the initial carrying amount of an asset or liability that appears on the balance sheet. For tax purposes, such grants may not be deducted when determining the tax base of the balance sheet item. In such circumstances, the carrying amount of the asset or liability will be lower than its tax base. Differences in the tax base of an asset or liability as a result of the circumstances described above may not be recognized as deferred tax assets or liabilities.

For example, a government may offer grants to Small, Medium, and Micro Enterprises (SMME) in an attempt to assist these entrepreneurs in their endeavors that contribute to the country's GDP and job creation. Assume that a particular grant is offered for infrastructure needs (office furniture, property, plant, and equipment, etc). In these circumstances, although the carrying amount will be lower than the tax base of the asset, the related deferred tax may not be recognized. As mentioned earlier, deferred tax assets and liabilities should not be recognized in cases that would arise from the initial recognition of an asset or liability in transactions that are not a business combination and when, at the time of the transaction, there is no impact on either accounting or taxable profit.

A deferred tax liability will also not be recognized at the initial recognition of goodwill. Although goodwill may be treated differently across tax jurisdictions, which may lead to differences in the carrying amount and tax base of goodwill, IAS 12 does not allow the recognition of such a deferred tax liability. Any impairment that an entity should, for accounting purposes, impose on goodwill will again result in a temporary difference between its carrying amount and tax base. Any impairment that an entity should, for accounting purposes, impose on goodwill and if part of the goodwill is related to the initial recognition, that part of the difference in tax base and carrying amount should not result in any deferred taxation because the initial deferred tax liability was not recognized. Any future differences between the carrying amount and tax base as a result of amortization and the deductibility of a portion of goodwill constitute a temporary difference for which provision should be made.

4.5 Business Combinations and Deferred Taxes

The fair value of assets and liabilities acquired in a business combination is determined on the acquisition date and may differ from the previous carrying amount. It is highly probable that the values of acquired intangible assets, including goodwill, would differ from their carrying amounts. This temporary difference will affect deferred taxes as well as the amount of goodwill recognized as a result of the acquisition.

4.6 Investments in Subsidiaries, Branches, Associates and Interests in Joint Ventures

Investments in subsidiaries, branches, associates and interests in joint ventures may lead to temporary differences on the consolidated versus the parent's financial statements. The related deferred tax liabilities as a result of temporary differences will be recognized unless both of the following criterion are satisfied:

▶ The parent is in a position to control the timing of the future reversal of the temporary difference, and

▶ It is probable that the temporary difference will not reverse in the future.

With respect to deferred tax assets related to subsidiaries, branches, and associates and interests, deferred tax assets will only be recognized if the following criteria are satisfied:

▶ The temporary difference will reverse in the future, and

▶ Sufficient taxable profits exist against which the temporary difference can be used.

UNUSED TAX LOSSES AND TAX CREDITS   5

IAS 12 allows the recognition of unused tax losses and tax credits only to the extent that it is probable that in the future there will be taxable income against which the unused tax losses and credits can be applied. Under U.S. GAAP, a deferred tax asset is recognized in full but is then reduced by a valuation allowance if it is more likely than not that some or all of the deferred tax asset will not be realized. The same requirements for creation of a deferred tax asset as a result of deductible temporary differences also apply to unused tax losses and tax credits. The existence of tax losses may indicate that the entity cannot reasonably be expected to generate sufficient future taxable income. All other things held constant, the greater the history of tax losses, the greater the concern regarding the company's ability to generate future taxable profits.

Should there be concerns about the company's future profitability, then the deferred tax asset may not be recognized until it is realized. When assessing the probability that sufficient taxable profit will be generated in the future, the following criteria can serve as a guide:

▶ If there is uncertainty as to the probability of future taxable profits, a deferred tax asset as a result of unused tax losses or tax credits is only recognized to the extent of the available taxable temporary differences;

▶ Assess the probability that the entity will in fact generate future taxable profits before the unused tax losses and/or credits expire pursuant to tax rules regarding the carry forward of the unused tax losses;

▶ Verify that the above is with the same tax authority and based on the same taxable entity;

▶ Determine whether the past tax losses were a result of specific circumstances that are unlikely to be repeated; and

▶ Discover if tax planning opportunities are available to the entity that will result in future profits. These may include changes in tax legislation that is phased in over more than one financial period to the benefit of the entity.

It is imperative that the timing of taxable and deductible temporary differences also be considered before creating a deferred tax asset based on unused tax credits.

6   RECOGNITION AND MEASUREMENT OF CURRENT AND DEFERRED TAX

Current taxes payable or recoverable from tax authorities are based on the applicable tax rates at the balance sheet date. Deferred taxes should be measured at the tax rate that is expected to apply when the asset is realized or the liability settled. With respect to the income tax for a current or prior period not yet paid, it is recognized as a tax liability until paid. Any amount paid in excess of any tax obligation is recognized as an asset. The income tax paid in excess or owed to tax authorities is separate from deferred taxes on the company's balance sheet.

When measuring deferred taxes in a jurisdiction, there are different forms of taxation such as income tax, capital gains tax (any capital gains made), or secondary tax on companies (tax payable on the dividends that a company declares) and possibly different tax bases for a balance sheet item (as in the case of government grants influencing the tax base of an asset such as property). In assessing which tax laws should apply, it is dependent on how the related asset or liability will be settled. It would be prudent to use the tax rate and tax base that is consistent with how it is expected the tax base will be recovered or settled.

Although deferred tax assets and liabilities are related to temporary differences expected to be recovered or settled at some future date, neither are discounted to present value in determining the amounts to be booked. Both must be adjusted for changes in tax rates.

Deferred taxes as well as income taxes should always be recognized on the income statement of an entity unless it pertains to:

► Taxes or deferred taxes charged directly to equity, or

► A possible provision for deferred taxes relates to a business combination.

The carrying amount of the deferred tax assets and liabilities should also be assessed. The carrying amounts may change even though there may have been no change in temporary differences during the period evaluated. This can result from:

► Changes in tax rates;

► Reassessments of the recoverability of deferred tax assets; or

► Changes in the expectations for how an asset will be recovered and what influences the deferred tax asset or liability.

All unrecognized deferred tax assets and liabilities must be reassessed at the balance sheet date and measured against the criteria of probable future economic benefits. If such a deferred asset is likely to be recovered, it may be appropriate to recognize the related deferred tax asset.

Different jurisdictions have different requirements for determining tax obligations that can range from different forms of taxation to different tax rates based on taxable income. When comparing financial statements of entities that conduct business in different jurisdictions subject to different tax legislation, the analyst should be cautious in reaching conclusions because of the potentially complex tax rules that may apply.

6.1 Recognition of a Valuation Allowance

Deferred tax assets must be assessed at each balance sheet date. If there is any doubt whether the deferral will be recovered, then the carrying amount should be reduced to the expected recoverable amount. Should circumstances subsequently change and suggest the future will lead to recovery of the deferral, the reduction may be reversed.

Under U.S. GAAP, deferred tax assets are reduced by creating a valuation allowance. Establishing a valuation allowance reduces the deferred tax asset and income in the period in which the allowance is established. Should circumstances change to such an extent that a deferred tax asset valuation allowance may be reduced, the reversal will increase the deferred tax asset and operating income. Because of the subjective judgment involved, an analyst should carefully scrutinize any such changes.

6.2 Recognition of Current and Deferred Tax Charged Directly to Equity

In general, IFRS and U.S. GAAP require that the recognition of deferred tax liabilities and current income tax should be treated similarly to the asset or liability that gave rise to the deferred tax liability or income tax based on accounting treatment. Should an item that gives rise to a deferred tax liability be taken directly to equity, the same should hold true for the resulting deferred tax.

The following are examples of such items:

▶ Revaluation of property, plant, and equipment (revaluations are not permissible under U.S. GAAP);

▶ Long-term investments at fair value;

▶ Changes in accounting policies;

▶ Errors corrected against the opening balance of retained earnings;

▶ Initial recognition of an equity component related to complex financial instruments; and

▶ Exchange rate differences arising from the currency translation procedures for foreign operations.

Whenever it is determined that a deferred tax liability will not be reversed, an adjustment should be made to the liability. The deferred tax liability will be reduced and the amount by which it is reduced should be taken directly to equity. Any deferred taxes related to a business combination must also be recognized in equity.

Depending on the items that gave rise to the deferred tax liabilities, an analyst should exercise judgment regarding whether the taxes should be included with deferred tax liabilities or whether it should be taken directly to equity. It may be more appropriate simply to ignore deferred taxes.

EXAMPLE 5

Taxes Charged Directly to Equity

The following information pertains to Anderson Company (a hypothetical company). A building owned by Anderson Company was originally purchased for €1,000,000 on 1 January 2004. For accounting purposes, buildings are depreciated at 5 percent a year on a straight-line basis, and depreciation for tax purposes is 10 percent a year on a straight-line basis. On the first day of the 2006, the building is revalued at €1,200,000. It is estimated that the remaining useful life of the building from the date of revaluation is 20 years. *Important*: For tax purposes the revaluation of the building is not recognized.

Based on the information provided, the following illustrates the difference in treatment of the building for accounting and tax purposes.

	Carrying Amount of Building	Tax Base of Building
Balance on 1 January 2004	€1,000,000	€1,000,000
Depreciation 2004	50,000	100,000
Balance on 31 December 2004	€950,000	€900,000
Depreciation 2005	50,000	100,000
Balance on 31 December 2005	€900,000	€800,000
Revaluation on 1 January 2006	300,000	n/a
Balance on 1 January 2006	€1,200,000	€800,000
Depreciation 2006	60,000	100,000
Balance on 31 December 2006	€1,140,000	€700,000
Accumulated depreciation		
Balance on 1 January 2004	€0	€0
Depreciation 2004	50,000	100,000
Balance on 31 December 2004	€50,000	€100,000
Depreciation 2005	50,000	100,000
Balance on 31 December 2005	€100,000	€200,000
Revaluation at 1 January 2006	(100,000)	n/a
Balance on 1 January 2006	€0	€200,000
Depreciation 2006	60,000	100,000
Balance on 30 November 2006	€60,000	€300,000

	Carrying Amount	Tax Base
On 31 December 2004	€950,000	€900,000
On 31 December 2005	€900,000	€800,000
On 31 December 2006	€1,140,000	€700,000

31 December 2004: On 31 December 2004, different treatments for depreciation expense result in a temporary difference that gives rise to a deferred tax liability. The difference in the tax base and carrying amount of the building was a result of different depreciation amounts for tax and accounting purposes. Depreciation appears on the income statement. For this reason the deferred tax liability will also be reflected on the income statement. If we assume that the applicable tax rate in 2004 was 40 percent, then the resulting deferred tax liability will be 40% × (€950,000 − €900,000) = €20,000.

31 December 2005: As of 31 December 2005, the carrying amount of the building remains greater than the tax base. The temporary difference again gives rise to a deferred tax liability. Again, assuming the applicable tax rate to be 40 percent, the deferred tax liability from the building is 40% × (€900,000 − €800,000) = €40,000.

31 December 2006: On 31 December 2006, the carrying amount of the building again exceeds the tax base. This is not the result of disposals or additions, but is a result of the revaluation at the beginning of the 2006 fiscal year and the different rates of depreciation. The deferred tax liability would seem to be 40% × (€1,140,000 − €700,000) = €176,000, *but* the treatment is different than it was for the 2004 and 2005. In 2006, revaluation of the building gave rise to a balance sheet liability, namely "Revaluation Surplus" in the amount of €300,000, which is not recognized for tax purposes.

The deferred tax liability would usually have been calculated as follows:

	2006	2005	2004
Deferred tax liability (closing balance at end of fiscal year)	€176,000	€40,000	€20,000

(Difference between tax base and carrying amount)

2004: €(950,000 − 900,000) × 40% = 20,000

2005: €(900,000 − 800,000) × 40% = 40,000

2006: €(1,140,000 − 700,000) × 40% = 176,000

The change in the deferred tax liability in 2004 is €20,000, in 2005: €20,000 (€40,000 − €20,000) and, it would seem, in 2006: €136,000 (€176,000 − €40,000). In 2006, although it would seem that the balance for deferred tax liability should be €176,000, the revaluation is not recognized for tax purposes. Only the portion of the difference between the tax base and carrying amount that is not a result of the revaluation is recognized as giving rise to a deferred tax liability.

The effect of the revaluation surplus and the associated tax effects are accounted for in a direct adjustment to equity. The revaluation surplus is reduced by the tax provision associated with the excess of the fair value over the carry value and it affects retained earnings (€300,000 × 40% = €120,000).

> The deferred tax liability that should be reflected on the balance sheet is thus not €176,000 but only €56,000 (€176,000 − €120,000). Given the balance of deferred tax liability at the beginning of the 2006 fiscal year in the amount of €40,000, the change in the deferred tax liability is only €56,000 − €40,000 = €16,000.
>
> In the future, at the end of each year, an amount equal to the depreciation as a result of the revaluation minus the deferred tax effect will be transferred from the revaluation reserve to retained earnings. In 2006 this will amount to a portion of depreciation resulting from the revaluation, €15,000 (€300,000 ÷ 20), minus the deferred tax effect of €6,000 (€15,000 × 40%), thus €9,000.

7   PRESENTATION AND DISCLOSURE

We will discuss the presentation and disclosure of income tax related information by way of example. The Consolidated Statements of Operations (Income Statements) and Consolidated Balance Sheets for Micron Technology (MU) are provided in Exhibits 2 and 3, respectively. Exhibit 4 provides the income tax note disclosures for MU for the 2004, 2005, and 2006 fiscal years.

MU's income tax provision (i.e., income tax expense) for fiscal year 2006 is $18 million (see Exhibit 2). The income tax note disclosure in Exhibit 4 reconciles how the income tax provision was determined beginning with MU's reported income before taxes (shown in Exhibit 2 as $433 million for fiscal year 2006). The note disclosure then denotes the income tax provision for 2006 that is current ($42 million), which is then offset by the deferred tax benefit for foreign taxes ($24 million), for a net income tax provision of $18 million. Exhibit 4 further shows a reconciliation of how the income tax provision was derived from the U.S. federal statutory rate. Many public companies comply with this required disclosure by displaying the information in percentage terms, but MU has elected to provide the disclosure in absolute dollar amounts. From this knowledge, we can see that the dollar amount shown for U.S. federal income tax provision at the statutory rate ($152 million) was determined by multiplying MU's income before taxes by the 35 percent U.S. federal statutory rate ($433 × 0.35 = $152). Furthermore, after considering tax credits and changes in the valuation allowance for deferred tax assets, MU's $18 million tax provision for 2006 is only 4.16 percent of its income before taxes ($18 ÷ $433 = 4.16%).

In addition, the note disclosure in Exhibit 4 provides detailed information about the derivation of the deferred tax assets ($26 million current and $49 million noncurrent) and deferred tax liabilities ($28 million noncurrent) that are shown on MU's consolidated balance sheet for fiscal year 2006 in Exhibit 3.

EXHIBIT 2	Micron Technology, Inc. Consolidated Statements of Operations (Amounts in Millions except Per Share)		
For the Year Ended	**31 Aug. 2006**	**1 Sept. 2005**	**2 Sept. 2004**
Net sales	$5,272	$4,880	$4,404
Cost of goods sold	4,072	3,734	3,090
Gross margin	1,200	1,146	1,314
Selling, general and administrative	460	348	332
Research and development	656	604	755
Restructure	—	(1)	(23)
Other operating (income) expense, net	(266)	(22)	—
Operating income	350	217	250
Interest income	101	32	15
Interest expense	(25)	(47)	(36)
Other non-operating income (expense), net	7	(3)	3
Income before taxes	433	199	232
Income tax (provision)	(18)	(11)	(75)
Noncontrolling interests in net income	(7)	—	—
Net income	$408	$188	$157
Earnings per share:			
Basic	$0.59	$0.29	$0.24
Diluted	$0.56	$0.27	$0.24
Number of shares used in per share calculations:			
Basic	692	648	641
Diluted	725	702	646

EXHIBIT 3	Micron Technology, Inc. Consolidated Balance Sheets (Dollars in Millions)	
As of	**31 Aug. 2006**	**1 Sept. 2005**
Assets		
Cash and equivalents	$1,431	$524
Short-term investments	1,648	766
Receivables	956	794
Inventories	963	771
Prepaid expenses	77	39
Deferred income taxes	26	32
Total current assets	5,101	2,926

(Exhibit continued on next page . . .)

EXHIBIT 3	(continued)

As of	31 Aug. 2006	1 Sept. 2005
Intangible assets, net	388	260
Property, plant and equipment, net	5,888	4,684
Deferred income taxes	49	30
Goodwill	502	16
Other assets	293	90
Total assets	$12,221	$8,006
Liabilities and shareholders' equity		
Accounts payable and accrued expenses	$1,319	$753
Deferred income	53	30
Equipment purchase contracts	123	49
Current portion of long-term debt	166	147
Total current liabilities	1,661	979
Long-term debt	405	1,020
Deferred income taxes	28	35
Other liabilities	445	125
Total liabilities	2,539	2,159
Commitments and contingencies	—	—
Noncontrolling interests in subsidiaries	1,568	—
Common stock of $0.10 par value, authorized 3 billion shares, issued and outstanding 749.4 million and 616.2 million shares	75	62
Additional capital	6,555	4,707
Retained earnings	1,486	1,078
Accumulated other comprehensive loss	(2)	—
Total shareholders' equity	8,114	5,847
Total liabilities and shareholders' equity	$12,221	$8,006

EXHIBIT 4	Micron Technology, Inc. Income Taxes Note to the Consolidated Financial Statements

Income (loss) before taxes and the income tax (provision) benefit consisted of the following:

(Millions)	2006	2005	2004
Income (loss) before taxes:			
U.S.	$351	$108	($19)
Foreign	82	91	251
	$433	$199	$232

(Exhibit continued on next page . . .)

EXHIBIT 4 (continued)			
(Millions)	**2006**	**2005**	**2004**
Income tax (provision) benefit:			
Current:			
U.S. federal	($12)	$—	$—
State	(1)	(3)	—
Foreign	(29)	(18)	(12)
	(42)	(21)	(12)
Deferred:			
U.S. federal	—	—	—
State	—	—	—
Foreign	24	10	(63)
	24	10	(63)
Income tax (provision)	($18)	($11)	($75)

The company's income tax (provision) computed using the U.S. federal statutory rate and the company's income tax (provision) benefit is reconciled as follows:

(Millions)	**2006**	**2005**	**2004**
U.S. federal income tax (provision) benefit at statutory rate	$(152)	$(70)	$(81)
State taxes, net of federal benefit	5	6	(9)
Foreign operations	3	9	(44)
Change in valuation allowance	103	(7)	(11)
Tax credits	7	28	7
Export sales benefit	13	16	16
Resolution of tax matters	—	—	37
Other	3	7	10
	$(18)	$(11)	$(75)

State taxes reflect investment tax credits of $23 million, $14 million, and $9 million for 2006, 2005, and 2004, respectively. Deferred income taxes reflect the net tax effects of temporary differences between the bases of assets and liabilities for financial reporting and income tax purposes. The company's

(Exhibit continued on next page . . .)

EXHIBIT 4	(continued)

deferred tax assets and liabilities consist of the following as of the end of the periods shown below:

($ Millions)	2006	2005
Deferred tax assets:		
Net operating loss and credit carryforwards	$929	$1,202
Basis differences in investments in joint ventures	301	—
Deferred revenue	160	76
Accrued compensation	51	40
Accounts payable	43	25
Inventories	16	33
Accrued product and process technology	11	12
Other	36	87
Gross deferred assets	1,547	1,475
Less valuation allowance	(915)	(1,029)
Deferred tax assets, net of valuation allowance	632	446
Deferred tax liabilities:		
Excess tax over book depreciation	(308)	(315)
Receivables	(91)	—
Intangibles	(68)	—
Unremitted earnings on certain subsidiaries	(58)	(49)
Product and process technology	(45)	(39)
Other	(15)	(16)
Deferred tax liabilities	(585)	(419)
Net deferred tax assets	$47	$27
Reported as:		
Current deferred tax assets	$26	$32
Noncurrent deferred tax assets	49	30
Noncurrent deferred tax liabilities	(28)	(35)
Net deferred tax assets	$47	$27

The company has a valuation allowance against substantially all of its U.S. net deferred tax assets. As of 31 August 2006, the company had aggregate U.S. tax net operating loss carryforwards of $1.7 billion and unused U.S. tax credit carryforwards of $164 million. The company also has unused state tax net operating loss carryforwards of $1.4 billion and unused state tax credits of $163 million. During 2006, the company utilized approximately $1.1 billion of its U.S. tax net operating loss carryforwards as a result of IMFT, MP Mask, and related transactions.[5] Substantially all of the net operating loss carryforwards expire in 2022 to 2025 and substantially all of the tax credit carryforwards expire in 2013 to 2026.

The changes in valuation allowance of ($114) million and $25 million in 2006 and 2005, respectively, are primarily a result of uncertainties of realizing certain U.S. net operating losses and certain tax credit carryforwards. The change in the valuation allowance in 2006 and 2005 includes $12 million and $2 million, respectively, for stock plan deductions, which will be credited to additional capital if realized.

Provision has been made for deferred taxes on undistributed earnings of non-U.S. subsidiaries to the extent that dividend payments from such companies are expected to result in additional tax liability. Remaining undistributed earnings of $686 million as of 31 August 2006 have been indefinitely reinvested; therefore, no provision has been made for taxes due upon remittance of these earnings. Determination of the amount of unrecognized deferred tax liability on these unremitted earnings is not practicable.

EXAMPLE 6

Financial Analysis Example

Use the financial statement information and disclosures provided by MU in Exhibits 2, 3, and 4 to answer the following questions:

1. MU discloses a valuation allowance of $915 million (see Exhibit 4) against total deferred assets of $1,547 million in 2006. Does the existence of this valuation allowance have any implications concerning MU's future earning prospects?

2. How would MU's deferred tax assets and deferred tax liabilities be affected if the federal statutory tax rate was changed to 32 percent? Would a change in the rate to 32 percent be beneficial to MU?

3. How would reported earnings have been affected if MU were not using a valuation allowance?

4. How would MU's $929 million in net operating loss carryforwards in 2006 (see Exhibit 4) affect the valuation that an acquiring company would be willing to offer?

5. Under what circumstances should the analyst consider MU's deferred tax liability as debt or as equity? Under what circumstances should the analyst exclude MU's deferred tax liability from both debt and equity when calculating the debt-to-equity ratio?

Solution to 1: According to Exhibit 4, MU's deferred tax assets expire gradually until 2026 (2022 to 2025 for the net operating loss carryforwards and 2013 to 2026 for the tax credit carryforwards).

---

[5] Micron Technology entered into profitable joint ventures and acquired profitable companies in 2006. The company was able to apply its net operating tax loss carryforwards (NOLs) toward these profits thereby reducing the income tax payments that would otherwise have been made without the NOLs.

Because the company is relatively young, it is likely that most of these expirations occur toward the end of that period. Because cumulative federal net operating loss carryforwards total $1.7 billion, the valuation allowance could imply that MU is not reasonably expected to earn $1.7 billion over the next 20 years. However, as we can see in Exhibit 2, MU has earned profits for 2006, 2005, and 2004, thereby showing that the allowance could be adjusted downward if the company continues to generate profits in the future, making it more likely than not that the deferred tax asset would be recognized.

Solution to 2: MU's total deferred tax assets exceed total deferred tax liabilities by $47 million. A change in the federal statutory tax rate to 32 percent from the current rate of 35 percent would make these net deferred assets less valuable. Also, because it is possible that the deferred tax asset valuation allowance could be adjusted downward in the future (see discussion to solution 1), the impact could be far greater in magnitude.

Solution to 3: The disclosure in Exhibit 4 shows that the reduction in the valuation allowance reduced the income tax provision as reported on the income statement by $103 million in 2006. Additional potential reductions in the valuation allowance could similarly reduce reported income taxes (actual tax income taxes would not be affected by a valuation allowance established for financial reporting) in future years (see discussion to solution 1).

Solution to 4: If an acquiring company is profitable, it may be able to use MU's tax loss carryforwards to offset its own tax liabilities. The value to an acquirer would be the present value of the carryforwards, based on the acquirer's tax rate and expected timing of realization. The higher the acquiring company's tax rate, and the more profitable the acquirer, the sooner it would be able to benefit. Therefore, an acquirer with a high current tax rate would theoretically be willing to pay more than an acquirer with a lower tax rate.

Solution to 5: The analyst should classify the deferred tax liability as debt if the liability is expected to reverse with subsequent tax payment. If the liability is not expected to reverse, there is no expectation of a cash outflow and the liability should be treated as equity. By way of example, future company losses may preclude the payment of any income taxes, or changes in tax laws could result in taxes that are never paid. The deferred tax liability should be excluded from both debt and equity when both the amounts and timing of tax payments resulting from the reversals of temporary differences are uncertain.

COMPARISON OF IFRS AND U.S. GAAP   8

As mentioned earlier, though IFRS and U.S. GAAP follow similar conventions on many tax issues, there are some notable differences (such as revaluation). Exhibit 5 summarizes many of the key similarities and differences between IFRS and U.S. GAAP. Though both frameworks require a provision for deferred taxes, there are differences in the methodologies.

EXHIBIT 5	Deferred Income Tax Issues IFRS and U.S. GAAP Methodology Similarities and Differences	
Issue	**IFRS**	**U.S. GAAP**
General considerations:		
General approach	Full provision.	Similar to IFRS.
Basis for deferred tax assets and liabilities	Temporary differences—i.e., the difference between carrying amount and tax base of assets and liabilities (see exceptions below).	Similar to IFRS.
Exceptions (i.e., deferred tax is not provided on the temporary difference)	Nondeductible goodwill (that which is not deductible for tax purposes) does not give rise to taxable temporary differences.	Similar to IFRS, except no initial recognition exemption and special requirements apply in computing deferred tax on leveraged leases.
General considerations:		
	Initial recognition of an asset or liability in a transaction that: a) is not a business combination; and b) affects neither accounting profit nor taxable profit at the time of the transaction. Other amounts that do not have a tax consequence (commonly referred to as permanent differences) exist and depend on the tax rules and jurisdiction of the entity.	
Specific applications:		
Revaluation of plant, property, and equipment and intangible assets	Deferred tax recognized in equity.	Not applicable, as revaluation is prohibited.

(Exhibit continued on next page . . .)

EXHIBIT 5   (continued)

Issue	IFRS	U.S. GAAP
Foreign nonmonetary assets/liabilities when the tax reporting currency is not the functional currency	Deferred tax is recognized on the difference between the carrying amount, determined using the historical rate of exchange, and the tax base, determined using the balance sheet date exchange rate.	No deferred tax is recognized for differences related to assets and liabilities that are remeasured from local currency into the functional currency resulting from changes in exchange rates or indexing for tax purposes.
Investments in subsidiaries—treatment of undistributed profit	Deferred tax is recognized except when the parent is able to control the distribution of profit and it is probable that the temporary difference will not reverse in the foreseeable future.	Deferred tax is required on temporary differences arising after 1992 that relate to investments in domestic subsidiaries, unless such amounts can be recovered tax-free and the entity expects to use that method. No deferred taxes are recognized on undistributed profits of foreign subsidiaries that meet the indefinite reversal criterion. Deferred tax assets may be recorded only to the extent they will reverse in the foreseeable future.
Investments in joint ventures—treatment of undistributed profit	Deferred tax is recognized except when the venturer can control the sharing of profits and if it is probable that the temporary difference will not reverse in the foreseeable future.	Deferred tax is required on temporary differences arising after 1992 that relate to investment in domestic corporate joint ventures. No deferred taxes are recognized on undistributed profits of foreign corporate joint ventures that meet the indefinite reversal criterion. Deferred tax assets may be recorded only to the extent they will reverse in the foreseeable future.
Investment in associates—treatment of undistributed profit	Deferred tax is recognized except when the investor can control the sharing of profits and it is probable that the temporary difference will not reverse in the foreseeable future.	Deferred tax is recognized on temporary differences relating to investments in investees.
Uncertain tax positions	Reflects the tax consequences that follow from the manner in which the entity expects, at the balance sheet date, to be paid to (recovered from) the taxation authorities.	A tax benefit from an uncertain tax position may be recognized only if it is "more likely than not" that the tax position is sustainable based on its technical merits. The tax position is measured as the largest amount of tax benefit that is greater than 50 percent likely of being realized upon ultimate settlement.

(Exhibit continued on next page . . .)

EXHIBIT 5	(continued)

Issue	IFRS	U.S. GAAP
Measurement of deferred tax:		
Tax rates	Tax rates and tax laws that have been enacted or substantively enacted.	Use of substantively enacted rates is not permitted. Tax rate and tax laws used must have been enacted.
Recognition of deferred tax assets	A deferred tax asset is recognized if it is probable (more likely than not) that sufficient taxable profit will be available against which the temporary difference can be utilized.	A deferred tax asset is recognized in full but is then reduced by a valuation allowance if it is more likely than not that some or all of the deferred tax asset will not be realized.
Business combinations—Acquisitions:		
Step-up of acquired assets/liabilities to fair value	Deferred tax is recorded unless the tax base of the asset is also stepped up.	Similar to IFRS.
Previously unrecognized tax losses of the acquirer	A deferred tax asset is recognized if the recognition criteria for the deferred tax asset are met as a result of the acquisition. Offsetting credit is recorded in income.	Similar to IFRS, except the offsetting credit is recorded against goodwill.
Tax losses of the acquiree (initial recognition)	Similar requirements as for the acquirer except the offsetting credit is recorded against goodwill.	Similar to IFRS.
Subsequent resolution of income tax uncertainties in a business combination	If the resolution is more than one year after the year in which the business combination occurred, the result is recognized on the income statement.	The subsequent resolution of any tax uncertainty relating to a business combination is recorded against goodwill.
Subsequent recognition of deferred tax assets that were not "probable" at the time of the business combination	A deferred tax asset that was not considered probable at the time of the business combination but later becomes probable is recognized. The adjustment is to income tax expense with a corresponding adjustment to goodwill. The income statement shows a debit to goodwill expense and a credit to income tax expense. There is no time limit for recognition of this deferred tax asset.	The subsequent resolution of any tax uncertainty relating to a business combination is recorded first against goodwill, then noncurrent intangibles, and then income tax expense. There is no time limit for recognition of this deferred tax asset.
Presentation of deferred tax:		
Offset of deferred tax assets and liabilities	Permitted only when the entity has a legally enforceable right to offset and the balance relates to tax levied by the same authority.	Similar to IFRS.

(Exhibit continued on next page . . .)

EXHIBIT 5	(continued)	
Issue	IFRS	U.S. GAAP
Current/noncurrent	Deferred tax assets and liabilities are classified net as noncurrent on the balance sheet, with supplemental note disclosure for 1) the components of the temporary differences, and 2) amounts expected to be recovered within 12 months and more than 12 months from the balance sheet date.	Deferred tax assets and liabilities are either classified as current or noncurrent, based on the classification of the related non-tax asset or liability for financial reporting. Tax assets or liabilities not associated with an underlying asset or liability are classified based on the expected reversal period.
Reconciliation of actual and expected tax expense	Required. Computed by applying the applicable tax rates to accounting profit, disclosing also the basis on which the applicable tax rates are calculated.	Required for public companies only. Calculated by applying the domestic federal statutory tax rates to pre-tax income from continuing operations.

Sources: IFRS: IAS 1, IAS 12, and IFRS 3.
U.S. GAAP: FAS 109 and FIN 48.
"Similarities and Differences–A Comparison of IFRS and U.S. GAAP," PricewaterhouseCoopers, October 2006.

SUMMARY

Income taxes are a significant category of expense for profitable companies. Analyzing income tax expenses is often difficult for the analyst because there are many permanent and temporary timing differences between the accounting that is used for income tax reporting and the accounting that is used for financial reporting on company financial statements. The financial statements and notes to the financial statements of a company provide important information that the analyst needs to assess financial performance and to compare a company's financial performance with other companies. Key concepts in this reading are as follows:

▶ Differences between the recognition of revenue and expenses for tax and accounting purposes may result in taxable income differing from accounting profit. The discrepancy is a result of different treatments of certain income and expenditure items.

▶ The tax base of an asset is the amount that will be deductible for tax purposes as an expense in the calculation of taxable income as the company expenses the tax basis of the asset. If the economic benefit will not be taxable, the tax base of the asset will be equal to the carrying amount of the asset.

▶ The tax base of a liability is the carrying amount of the liability less any amounts that will be deductible for tax purposes in the future. With respect to revenue received in advance, the tax base of such a liability is the carrying amount less any amount of the revenue that will not be taxable in the future.

▶ Temporary differences arise from recognition of differences in the tax base and carrying amount of assets and liabilities. The creation of a deferred tax asset or liability as a result of a temporary difference will only be allowed if the difference reverses itself at some future date and to the extent that it is expected that the balance sheet item will create future economic benefits for the company.

▶ Permanent differences result in a difference in tax and financial reporting of revenue (expenses) that will not be reversed at some future date. Because it will not be reversed at a future date, these differences do not constitute temporary differences and do not give rise to a deferred tax asset or liability.

▶ Current taxes payable or recoverable are based on the applicable tax rates on the balance sheet date of an entity; in contrast, deferred taxes should be measured at the tax rate that is expected to apply when the asset is realized or the liability settled.

▶ All unrecognized deferred tax assets and liabilities must be reassessed on the appropriate balance sheet date and measured against their probable future economic benefit.

▶ Deferred tax assets must be assessed for their prospective recoverability. If it is probable that they will not be recovered at all or partly, the carrying amount should be reduced. Under U.S. GAAP, this is done through the use of a valuation allowance.

PRACTICE PROBLEMS FOR READING 38

1. Using the straight-line method of depreciation for reporting purposes and accelerated depreciation for tax purposes would *most likely* result in a:
   A. valuation allowance.
   B. deferred tax asset.
   C. temporary difference.

2. In early 2009 Sanborn Company must pay the tax authority €37,000 on the income it earned in 2008. This amount was recorded on the company's 31 December 2008 financial statements as:
   A. taxes payable.
   B. income tax expense.
   C. a deferred tax liability.

3. Income tax expense reported on a company's income statement equals taxes payable, plus the net increase in:
   A. deferred tax assets and deferred tax liabilities.
   B. deferred tax assets, less the net increase in deferred tax liabilities.
   C. deferred tax liabilities, less the net increase in deferred tax assets.

4. Analysts should treat deferred tax liabilities that are expected to reverse as:
   A. equity.
   B. liabilities.
   C. neither liabilities nor equity.

5. Deferred tax liabilities should be treated as equity when:
   A. they are not expected to reverse.
   B. the timing of tax payments is uncertain.
   C. the amount of tax payments is uncertain.

6. When both the timing and amount of tax payments are uncertain, analysts should treat deferred tax liabilities as:
   A. equity.
   B. liabilities.
   C. neither liabilities nor equity.

7. When accounting standards require recognition of an expense that is not permitted under tax laws, the result is a:
   A. deferred tax liability.
   B. temporary difference.
   C. permanent difference.

8. When certain expenditures result in tax credits that directly reduce taxes, the company will *most likely* record:
   A. a deferred tax asset.
   B. a deferred tax liability.
   C. no deferred tax asset or liability.

9. When accounting standards require an asset to be expensed immediately but tax rules require the item to be capitalized and amortized, the company will *most likely* record:

   A. a deferred tax asset.

   B. a deferred tax liability.

   C. no deferred tax asset or liability.

10. A company incurs a capital expenditure that may be amortized over five years for accounting purposes, but over four years for tax purposes. The company will *most likely* record:

   A. a deferred tax asset.

   B. a deferred tax liability.

   C. no deferred tax asset or liability.

11. A company receives advance payments from customers that are immediately taxable but will not be recognized for accounting purposes until the company fulfills its obligation. The company will *most likely* record:

   A. a deferred tax asset.

   B. a deferred tax liability.

   C. no deferred tax asset or liability.

The following information relates to Questions 12–14

Note I
Income Taxes

The components of earnings before income taxes are as follows ($ thousands):

	2007	2006	2005
Earnings before income taxes:			
United States	$ 88,157	$ 75,658	$ 59,973
Foreign	116,704	113,509	94,760
Total	$204,861	$189,167	$154,733

The components of the provision for income taxes are as follows ($ thousands):

	2007	2006	2005
Income taxes			
Current:			
Federal	$30,632	$22,031	$18,959
Foreign	28,140	27,961	22,263
	$58,772	$49,992	$41,222
Deferred:			
Federal	($4,752)	$5,138	$2,336
Foreign	124	1,730	621
	(4,628)	6,868	2,957
Total	$54,144	$56,860	$44,179

12. In 2007, the company's U.S. GAAP income statement recorded a provision for income taxes *closest* to:

A. $30,632.

B. $54,144.

C. $58,772.

13. The company's effective tax rate was *highest* in:

A. 2005.

B. 2006.

C. 2007.

14. Compared to the company's effective tax rate on U.S. income, its effective tax rate on foreign income was:

A. lower in each year presented.

B. higher in each year presented.

C. higher in some periods and lower in others.

15. Zimt AG presents its financial statements in accordance with U.S. GAAP. In 2007, Zimt discloses a valuation allowance of $1,101 against total deferred tax assets of $19,201. In 2006, Zimt disclosed a valuation allowance of $1,325 against total deferred tax assets of $17,325. The change in the valuation allowance *most likely* indicates that Zimt's:

A. deferred tax liabilities were reduced in 2007.

B. expectations of future earning power has increased.

C. expectations of future earning power has decreased.

16. Cinnamon, Inc. recorded a total deferred tax asset in 2007 of $12,301, offset by a $12,301 valuation allowance. Cinnamon *most likely*:

A. fully utilized the deferred tax asset in 2007.

B. has an equal amount of deferred tax assets and deferred tax liabilities.

C. expects not to earn any taxable income before the deferred tax asset expires.

The following information relates to Questions 17–19

The tax effects of temporary differences that give rise to deferred tax assets and liabilities are as follows ($ thousands):

	2007	2006
Deferred tax assets:		
Accrued expenses	$8,613	$7,927
Tax credit and net operating loss carryforwards	2,288	2,554
LIFO and inventory reserves	5,286	4,327
Other	2,664	2,109
Deferred tax assets	18,851	16,917
Valuation allowance	(1,245)	(1,360)
Net deferred tax assets	$17,606	$15,557
Deferred tax liabilities:		
Depreciation and amortization	$(27,338)	$(29,313)
Compensation and retirement plans	(3,831)	(8,963)
Other	(1,470)	(764)
Deferred tax liabilities	(32,639)	(39,040)
Net deferred tax liability	($15,033)	($23,483)

17. A reduction in the statutory tax rate would *most likely* benefit the company's:

   A. income statement and balance sheet.

   B. income statement but not the balance sheet.

   C. balance sheet but not the income statement.

18. If the valuation allowance had been the same in 2007 as it was in 2006, the company would have reported $115 *higher*:

   A. net income.

   B. deferred tax assets.

   C. income tax expense.

19. Compared to the provision for income taxes in 2007, the company's cash tax payments were:

   A. lower.

   B. higher.

   C. the same.

The following information relates to Questions 20–22

A company's provision for income taxes resulted in effective tax rates attributable to loss from continuing operations before cumulative effect of change in accounting principles that varied from the statutory federal income tax rate of 34 percent, as summarized in the table below.

Year Ended 30 June	2007	2006	2005
Expected federal income tax expense (benefit) from continuing operations at 34 percent	($112,000)	$768,000	$685,000
Expenses not deductible for income tax purposes	357,000	32,000	51,000
State income taxes, net of federal benefit	132,000	22,000	100,000
Change in valuation allowance for deferred tax assets	(150,000)	(766,000)	(754,000)
Income tax expense	$227,000	$56,000	$82,000

20. In 2007, the company's net income (loss) was *closest* to:

    A. ($217,000).

    B. ($329,000).

    C. ($556,000).

21. The $357,000 adjustment in 2007 *most likely* resulted in:

    A. an increase in deferred tax assets.

    B. an increase in deferred tax liabilities.

    C. no change to deferred tax assets and liabilities.

22. Over the three years presented, changes in the valuation allowance for deferred tax assets were *most likely* indicative of:

    A. decreased prospect for future profitability.

    B. increased prospects for future profitability.

    C. assets being carried at a higher value than their tax base.

SOLUTIONS FOR READING 38

1. C is correct. Because the differences between tax and financial accounting will correct over time, the resulting deferred tax liability, for which the expense was charged to the income statement but the tax authority has not yet been paid, will be a temporary difference. A valuation allowance would only arise if there was doubt over the company's ability to earn sufficient income in the future to require paying the tax.

2. A is correct. The taxes a company must pay in the immediate future are taxes payable.

3. C is correct. Higher reported tax expense relative to taxes paid will increase the deferred tax liability, whereas lower reported tax expense relative to taxes paid increases the deferred tax asset.

4. B is correct. If the liability is expected to reverse (and thus require a cash tax payment) the deferred tax represents a future liability.

5. A is correct. If the liability will not reverse, there will be no required tax payment in the future and the "liability" should be treated as equity.

6. C is correct. The deferred tax liability should be excluded from both debt and equity when both the amounts and timing of tax payments resulting from the reversals of temporary differences are uncertain.

7. C is correct. Accounting items that are not deductible for tax purposes will not be reversed and thus result in permanent differences.

8. C is correct. Tax credits that directly reduce taxes are a permanent difference, and permanent differences do not give rise to deferred tax.

9. A is correct. The capitalization will result in an asset with a positive tax base and zero carrying value. The amortization means the difference is temporary. Because there is a temporary difference on an asset resulting in a higher tax base than carrying value, a deferred tax asset is created.

10. B is correct. The difference is temporary, and the tax base will be lower (because of more rapid amortization) than the carrying value of the asset. The result will be a deferred tax liability.

11. A is correct. The advances represent a liability for the company. The carrying value of the liability exceeds the tax base (which is now zero). A deferred tax asset arises when the carrying value of a liability exceeds its tax base.

12. B is correct. The income tax provision in 2007 was $54,144, consisting of $58,772 in current income taxes, of which $4,628 were deferred.

13. B is correct. The effective tax rate of 30.1 percent ($56,860/$189,167) was higher than the effective rates in 2005 and 2007.

14. A is correct. In 2007 the effective tax rate on foreign operations was 24.2 percent [($28,140 + $124)/$116,704] and the effective U.S. tax rate was [($30,632 – $4,752)/$88,157] = 29.4 percent. In 2006 the effective tax rate on foreign operations was 26.2 percent and the U.S. rate was 35.9 percent. In 2005 the foreign rate was 24.1 percent and the U.S. rate was 35.5 percent.

15. B is correct. The valuation allowance is taken against deferred tax assets to represent uncertainty that future taxable income will be sufficient to fully utilize the assets. By decreasing the allowance, Zimt is signaling greater likelihood that future earnings will be offset by the deferred tax asset.

16. C is correct. The valuation allowance is taken when the company will "more likely than not" fail to earn sufficient income to offset the deferred tax asset. Because the valuation allowance equals the asset, by extension the company expects *no* taxable income prior to the expiration of the deferred tax assets.

17. A is correct. A lower tax rate would increase net income on the income statement, and because the company has a net deferred tax liability, the net liability position on the balance sheet would also improve (be smaller).

18. C is correct. The reduction in the valuation allowance resulted in a corresponding reduction in the income tax provision.

19. B is correct. The net deferred tax liability was smaller in 2007 than it was in 2006, indicating that in addition to meeting the tax payments provided for in 2007 the company also paid taxes that had been deferred in prior periods.

20. C is correct. The income tax provision at the statutory rate of 34 percent is a benefit of $112,000, suggesting that the pre-tax income was a loss of $112,000/0.34 = ($329,412). The income tax provision was $227,000. ($329,412) − $227,000 = ($556,412).

21. C is correct. Accounting expenses that are not deductible for tax purposes result in a permanent difference, and thus do not give rise to deferred taxes.

22. B is correct. Over the three-year period, changes in the valuation allowance reduced cumulative income taxes by $1,670,000. The reductions to the valuation allowance were a result of the company being "more likely than not" to earn sufficient taxable income to offset the deferred tax assets.

NON-CURRENT (LONG-TERM) LIABILITIES

by Elizabeth A. Gordon and Elaine Henry, CFA

LEARNING OUTCOMES

The candidate should be able to:	Mastery
a. determine the initial recognition and measurement and subsequent measurement of bonds;	☐
b. discuss the effective interest method and calculate interest expense, amortisation of bond discounts/premiums, and interest payments;	☐
c. discuss the derecognition of debt;	☐
d. explain the role of debt covenants in protecting creditors;	☐
e. discuss the financial statement presentation of and disclosures relating to debt;	☐
f. discuss the motivations for leasing assets instead of purchasing them;	☐
g. distinguish between a finance lease and an operating lease from the perspectives of the lessor and the lessee;	☐
h. determine the initial recognition and measurement and subsequent measurement of finance leases;	☐
i. compare and contrast the disclosures relating to finance and operating leases;	☐
j. describe defined contribution and defined benefit pension plans;	☐
k. compare and contrast the presentation and disclosure of defined contribution and defined benefit pension plans;	☐
l. calculate and interpret leverage and coverage ratios.	☐

INTRODUCTION   1

A **non-current** (long-term) **liability** broadly represents a probable sacrifice of economic benefits in periods generally greater than one year in the future. Common types of non-current liabilities reported in a company's financial statements include long-term debt (e.g., bonds payable, long-term notes payable),

Note:
New rulings and/or pronouncements issued after the publication of the readings on financial reporting and analysis may cause some of the information in these readings to become dated. Candidates are expected to be familiar with the overall analytical framework contained in the study session readings, as well as the implications of alternative accounting methods for financial analysis and valuation, as provided in the assigned readings. Candidates are not responsible for changes that occur after the material was written.

finance leases, pension liabilities, and deferred tax liabilities. This reading focuses on bonds payable and leases. Pension liabilities are also introduced.

This reading is organised as follows. Section 2 describes and illustrates the accounting for long-term bonds, including the issuance of bonds, the recording of interest expense and interest payments, the amortisation of any discount or premium, the derecognition of debt, and the disclosure of information about debt financings. In discussing the financial statement effects and analyses of these issues, we focus on solvency and coverage ratios. Section 3 discusses leases, including benefits of leasing and accounting for leases by both lessees and lessors. Section 4 provides an introduction to pension accounting and the resulting non-current liabilities. Section 5 discusses the use of leverage and coverage ratios in evaluating solvency. A summary of the reading is followed by practice problems in the CFA Institute format.

2   BONDS PAYABLE

This section discusses accounting for bonds payable—a common form of long-term debt. In some contexts (e.g., some government debt obligations), the word "bond" is used only for a debt security with a maturity of 10 years or longer; "note" refers to a debt security with a maturity between 2 and 10 years; and "bill" refers to a debt security with a maturity of less than 2 years. In this reading, we use the terms bond and note interchangeably because the accounting treatments of bonds payable and long-term notes payable are similar. In the following sections, we discuss bond issuance (initial recognition and measurement); bond amortisation, interest expense, and interest payments; market rates and fair value (subsequent measurement); repayment of bonds, including retirements and redemptions (derecognition); and other issues concerning disclosures related to debt. We also discuss debt covenants.

2.1 Accounting for Bond Issuance

Bonds are contractual promises made by a company (or other borrowing entity) to pay cash in the future to its lenders (i.e., bondholders) in exchange for receiving cash in the present. The terms of a bond contract are contained in a document called an indenture. The cash or sales proceeds received by a company when it issues bonds is based on the value (price) of the bonds at the time of issue; the price at the time of issue is determined as the present value of the future cash payments promised by the company in the bond agreement.

Ordinarily, bonds contain promises of two types of future cash payments: 1) the face value of the bonds, and 2) periodic interest payments. The **face value** of the bonds is the amount of cash payable by the company to the bondholders when the bonds mature. The face value is also referred to as the principal, par value, stated value, or maturity value. The date of maturity of the bonds (the date on which the face value is paid to bondholders) is stated in the bond contract and typically is a number of years in the future. Periodic interest payments are made based on the interest rate promised in the bond contract applied to the bonds' face value. The interest rate promised in the contract, which is the rate used to calculate the periodic interest payments, is referred to as the **coupon rate**, nominal rate, or stated rate. Similarly, the periodic interest payment is referred to as the coupon payment or simply the coupon. For fixed rate bonds (the primary focus of our discussion here), the coupon rate remains unchanged throughout the life of the bonds. The frequency with which interest payments are made is also stated in the bond contract. For example, bonds paying interest semi-annually will make two interest payments per year.[1]

The future cash payments are discounted to the present to arrive at the market value of the bonds. The **market rate of interest** is the rate demanded by purchasers of the bonds given the risks associated with future cash payment obligations of the particular bond issue. The market rate of interest at the time of issue often differs from the coupon rate because of interest rate fluctuations that occur between the time the issuer establishes the coupon rate and the day the bonds are actually available to investors. If the market rate of interest when the bonds are issued equals the coupon rate, the market value (price) of the bonds will equal the face value of the bonds. Thus, ignoring issuance costs, the issuing company will receive sales proceeds (cash) equal to the face value of the bonds. When a bond is issued at a price equal to its face value, the bond is said to have been issued at par.

If the coupon rate when the bonds are issued is higher than the market rate, the market value of the bonds—and thus the amount of cash the company receives—will be higher than the face value of the bonds. In other words, the bonds will sell at a premium to face value because they are offering an attractive coupon rate compared to current market rates. If the coupon rate is lower than the market rate, the market value and thus the sale proceeds from the bonds will be less than the face value of the bonds; the bond will sell at a discount to face value. The market rate at the time of issuance is the **effective interest rate** or borrowing rate that the company incurs on the debt. The effective interest rate is the discount rate that equates the present value of the two types of promised future cash payments to their selling price. For the issuing company, interest expense reported for the bonds in the financial statements is based on the effective interest rate.

On the issuing company's statement of cash flows, the cash received (sales proceeds) from issuing bonds is reported as a financing cash inflow. On the issuing company's balance sheet at the time of issue, bonds payable normally are measured and reported at the sales proceeds. In other words, the bonds payable are initially reported at the face value of the bonds minus any discount, or plus any premium.

Using a three-step approach, the following two examples illustrate accounting for bonds issued at face value and then accounting for bonds issued at a discount to face value. Accounting for bonds issued at a premium involves steps similar to the steps followed in the examples below. For simplicity, these examples assume a flat interest rate yield curve (i.e., that the market rate of interest is the same for each period). More-precise bond valuations use the interest rate applicable to each time period in which a payment of interest or principal occurs.

---

[1] Interest rates are stated on an annual basis regardless of the frequency of payment.

EXAMPLE 1

Bonds Issued at Face Value

Debond Corp. (a hypothetical company) issues £1,000,000 worth of five-year bonds, dated 1 January 2010, when the market interest rate on bonds of comparable risk and terms is 5 percent per annum. The bonds pay 5 percent interest annually on 31 December. What are the sales proceeds of the bonds when issued, and how is the issuance reflected in the financial statements?

Solution: Calculating the value of the bonds at issuance and thus the sales proceeds involves three steps: 1) identifying key features of the bonds and the market interest rate, 2) determining future cash outflows, and 3) discounting the future cash flows to the present.

First, identify key features of the bonds and the market interest rate necessary to determine sales proceeds:

Face value (principal):	£1,000,000
Time to maturity:	5 years
Coupon rate:	5%
Market rate at issuance:	5%
Frequency of interest payments:	annual
Interest payment:	£50,000

Interest payment: £50,000 — Each annual interest payment is the face value times the coupon rate (£1,000,000 × 5 %). If interest is paid other than annually, adjust the interest rate to match the interest payment period (e.g., divide the annual coupon rate by two for semi-annual interest payments).

Second, determine future cash outflows. Debond will pay bondholders £1,000,000 when the bonds mature in five years. On 31 December of each year until the bonds mature, Debond will make an interest payment of £50,000.

Third, sum the present value of the future payments of interest and principal to obtain the value of the bonds and thus the sales proceeds from issuing the bonds. In this example, the sum is £1,000,000 = (£216,474 + £783,526).

Date	Interest Payment	Present Value at Market Rate (5%)	Face Value Payment	Present Value at Market Rate (5%)	Total Present Value
31 December 2010	£50,000	£47,619			
31 December 2011	50,000	45,352			
31 December 2012	50,000	43,192			
31 December 2013	50,000	41,135			
31 December 2014	50,000	39,176	£1,000,000	£783,526	
Total		£216,474[2]		£783,526	£1,000,000
					Sales Proceeds

---

[2] Alternative ways to calculate the present value include 1) to treat the five annual interest payments as an annuity and use the formula for finding the present value of an annuity, and then add the present value of the principal payment, or 2) to use a financial calculator to calculate the total present value.

> The sales proceeds of the bonds when issued are £1,000,000. There is no discount or premium because these bonds are issued at face value. The issuance is reflected on the balance sheet as an increase of cash and an increase in a long-term liability, bonds payable, of £1,000,000. The issuance is reflected in the statement of cash flows as a financing cash inflow of £1,000,000.

The price of bonds is often expressed as a percentage of face value. For example, the price of bonds issued at par, as in Example 1, is 100 (i.e., 100 percent of face value). In Example 2, in which bonds are issued at a discount, the price is 95.79 (i.e., 95.79 percent of face value).

EXAMPLE 2

Bonds Issued at a Discount

Debond Corp. issues £1,000,000 worth of five-year bonds, dated 1 January 2010, when the market interest rate on bonds of comparable risk and terms is 6 percent. The bonds pay 5 percent interest annually on 31 December. What are the sales proceeds of the bonds when issued, and how is the issuance reflected in the financial statements?

Solution: The key features of the bonds and the market interest rate are:

Face value (principal):	£1,000,000
Time to maturity:	5 years
Coupon rate:	5%
Market rate at issuance:	6%
Frequency of interest payments:	annual
Interest payment:	£50,000 Each annual interest payment is the face value times the coupon rate (£1,000,000 × 5%).

The future cash outflows (interest payments and face value payment), the present value of the future cash outflows, and the total present value are:

Date	Interest Payment	Present Value at Market Rate (6%)	Face Value Payment	Present Value at Market Rate (6%)	Total Present Value
31 December 2010	£50,000	£47,170			
31 December 2011	50,000	44,500			
31 December 2012	50,000	41,981			
31 December 2013	50,000	39,605			
31 December 2014	50,000	37,363	£1,000,000	£747,258	
Total		£210,618		£747,258	£957,876
					Sales Proceeds

> The sales proceeds of the bonds when issued are £957,876. The bonds sell at a discount of £42,124 = (£1,000,000 − £957,876) because the market rate when the bonds are issued (6 percent) is greater than the bonds' coupon rate (5 percent). The issuance is reflected on the balance sheet as an increase of cash and an increase in a long-term liability, bonds payable, of £957,876. The bonds payable is composed of the face value of £1,000,000 minus a discount of £42,124. The issuance is reflected in the statement of cash flows as a financing cash inflow of £957,876.

In Example 2, the bonds were issued at a discount to face value because the bonds' coupon rate of 5 percent was less than the market rate. Bonds are issued at a premium to face value when the bonds' coupon rate exceeds the market rate.

Bonds issued with a coupon rate of zero (zero-coupon bonds) are always issued at a discount to face value. The value of zero-coupon bonds is based on the present value of the principal payment only because there are no periodic interest payments.

Such issuance costs as printing, legal fees, commissions, and other types of charges are costs incurred when bonds are issued. Under International Financial Reporting Standards (IFRS), all debt issuance costs are included in the measurement of the liability, bonds payable. Under U.S. generally accepted accounting principles (U.S. GAAP), companies generally show these debt issuance costs as an asset (a deferred charge), which is amortised on a straight-line basis to the relevant expense (e.g., legal fees) over the life of the bonds.[3] Under IFRS and U.S. GAAP, cash outflows related to bond issuance costs are included in the financing section of the statement of cash flows, usually netted against bond proceeds.

2.2 Accounting for Bond Amortisation, Interest Expense, and Interest Payments

In this section, we discuss accounting and reporting for bonds after they are issued. Most companies maintain the historical cost (sales proceeds) of the bonds after issuance, and they amortise any discount or premium over the life of the bond. The amount reported on the balance sheet for bonds is thus the historical cost plus or minus the cumulative amortisation, which is referred to as amortised cost. Companies also have the option to report the bonds at their current fair values.

The rationale for reporting the bonds at amortised historical cost is the company's intention to retain the debt until it matures. Therefore, changes in the underlying economic value of the debt are not relevant from the issuing company's perspective. From an investor's perspective, however, analysis of a company's underlying economic liabilities and solvency is more difficult when debt is reported at amortised historical cost. The rest of this section illustrates accounting and reporting of bonds at amortised historical cost. Section 2.3 discusses the alternative of reporting bonds at fair value.

---

[3] The Financial Accounting Standards Board (FASB), as part of the convergence project with the International Accounting Standards Board (IASB), has proposed that the treatment of issuance costs be amended to that under IFRS.

Companies initially report bonds as a liability on their balance sheet at the amount of the sales proceeds net of issuance costs under IFRS and at the amount of the sales proceeds under U.S. GAAP, ignoring any bond issuance costs. The amount at which bonds are reported on the company's balance sheet is referred to as the carrying amount, carrying value, book value, or net book value. If the bonds are issued at par, the initial carrying amount will be identical to the face value, and usually the carrying amount will not change over the life of the bonds.[4] For bonds issued at face value, the amount of periodic interest *expense* will be the same as the amount of periodic interest *payment* to bondholders.

If, however, the market rate differs from the bonds' coupon rate at issuance such that the bonds are issued at a premium or discount, the premium or discount is amortised systematically over the life of the bonds as a component of interest expense. For bonds issued at a premium to face value, the carrying amount of the bonds is initially greater than the face value. As the premium is amortised, the carrying amount (amortised cost) of the bonds will decrease to the face value. The reported interest expense will be less than the coupon payment. For bonds issued at a discount to face value, the carrying amount of the bonds is initially less than the face value. As the discount is amortised, the carrying amount (amortised cost) of the bonds will increase to the face value. The reported interest expense will be higher than the coupon payment.

The accounting treatment for bonds issued at a discount reflects the fact that the company essentially paid some of its borrowing costs at issuance by selling its bonds at a discount. Rather than there being an actual cash transfer in the future, this "payment" was made in the form of accepting less than the face value for the bonds at the date of issuance. The remaining borrowing cost occurs as a cash interest payment to investors each period. The total interest expense reflects both components of the borrowing cost: the periodic interest payments plus the amortisation of the discount. The accounting treatment for bonds issued at a premium reflects the fact that the company essentially received a reduction on its borrowing costs at issuance by selling its bonds at a premium. Rather than there being an actual reduced cash transfer in the future, this "reduction" was made in the form of receiving more than face value for the bonds at the date of issuance. The total interest expense reflects both components of the borrowing cost: the periodic interest payments less the amortisation of the premium. When the bonds mature, the carrying amount will be equal to the face value regardless of whether the bonds were issued at face value, a discount, or a premium.

Two methods for amortising the premium or discount of bonds that were issued at a price other than par are the effective interest rate method and the straight-line method. The effective interest rate method is required under IFRS and preferred under U.S. GAAP because it better reflects the economic substance of the transaction. The effective interest rate method applies the market rate in effect when the bonds were issued (historical market rate or effective interest rate) to the current amortised cost (carrying amount) of the bonds to obtain interest expense for the period. The difference between the interest expense (based on the effective interest rate and amortised cost) and the interest payment (based on the coupon rate and face value) is the **amortisation** of the discount or premium. The straight-line method of amortisation evenly amortises the premium or discount over the life of the bond, similar to straight-line depreciation on long-lived assets. Under either method, as the bond approaches maturity, the amortised cost approaches face value.

Example 3 illustrates both methods of amortisation for bonds issued at a discount. Example 4 shows amortisation for bonds issued at a premium.

---

[4] If a company reports debt at fair value, rather than amortised cost, the carrying value may change.

EXAMPLE 3

Amortising a Bond Discount

Debond Corp. issues £1,000,000 face value of five-year bonds, dated 1 January 2010, when the market interest rate is 6 percent. The sales proceeds are £957,876. The bonds pay 5 percent interest annually on 31 December.

1. What is the interest *payment* on the bonds each year?
2. What amount of interest *expense* on the bonds would be reported in 2010 and 2011 using the effective interest rate method?
3. Determine the reported value of the bonds (i.e., the carrying amount) at 31 December 2010 and 2011, assuming the effective interest rate method is used to amortise the discount.
4. What amount of interest expense on the bonds would be reported under the straight-line method of amortising the discount?

Solution to 1: The interest payment equals £50,000 annually (£1,000,000 × 5%).

Solution to 2: The sales proceeds of £957,876 are less than the face value of £1,000,000; the bonds were issued at a discount of £42,124. The bonds are initially reported as a long-term liability, bonds payable, of £957,876, which comprises the face value of £1,000,000 minus a discount of £42,124. The discount is amortised over time, ultimately, increasing the carrying amount (amortised cost) to face value.

Under the effective interest rate method, interest expense on the bonds is calculated as the bonds' carrying amount times the market rate in effect when the bonds are issued (effective interest rate). For 2010, interest expense is £57,473 = (£957,876 × 6%). The amount of the discount amortised in 2010 is the difference between the interest expense of £57,473 and the interest payment of £50,000 (i.e., £7,473). The bonds' carrying amount increases by the discount amortisation; at 31 December 2010, the bonds' carrying amount is £965,349 (beginning balance of £957,876 plus £7,473 discount amortisation). At this point, the carrying amount reflects a remaining unamortised discount of £34,651 (£42,124 discount at issuance minus £7,473 amortised).

For 2011, interest expense is £57,921 = (£965,349 × 6%), the carrying amount of the bonds on 1 January 2011 times the effective interest rate. The amount of the discount amortised in 2011 is the difference between the interest expense of £57,921 and the interest payment of £50,000 (i.e., £7,921). At 31 December 2011, the bonds' carrying amount is £973,270 (beginning balance of £965,349 plus £7,921 discount amortisation).

The following table illustrates interest expense, discount amortisation, and carrying amount (amortised cost) over the life of the bonds.

Year	Carrying Amount (Beginning of Year)	Interest Expense (at Effective Interest Rate of 6%)	Interest Payment (at Coupon Rate of 5%)	Amortisation of Discount	Carrying Amount (End of Year)
	(a)	(b)	(c)	(d)	(e)
2010	£957,876	£57,473	£50,000	£7,473	£965,349
2011	965,349	57,921	50,000	7,921	973,270
2012	973,270	58,396	50,000	8,396	981,666
2013	981,666	58,900	50,000	8,900	990,566
2014	990,566	59,434	50,000	9,434	1,000,000
Total		£292,124	£250,000	£42,124	

Solution to 3: The carrying amounts of the bonds at 31 December 2010 and 2011 are £965,349 and £973,270, respectively. Observe that the carrying amount of the bonds issued at a discount increases over the life of the bonds. At maturity, 31 December 2014, the carrying amount of the bonds equals the face value of the bonds. The carrying amount of the bonds will be reduced to zero when the principal payment is made.

Solution to 4: Under the straight-line method, the discount (or premium) is evenly amortised over the life of the bonds. In this example, the £42,124 discount would be amortised by £8,424.80 (£42,124 divided by 5 years) each year under the straight-line method. So, the annual interest expense under the straight-line method would be £58,424.80 (£50,000 plus £8,424.80).

The accounting and reporting for zero-coupon bonds is similar to the example above except that no interest payments are made; thus, the amount of interest expense each year is the same as the amount of the discount amortisation for the year.

EXAMPLE 4

Amortising a Bond Premium

Prembond Corp. issues £1,000,000 face value of five-year bonds, dated 1 January 2010, when the market interest rate is 4 percent. The sales proceeds are £1,044,518. The bonds pay 5 percent interest annually on 31 December.

1. What is the interest *payment* on the bonds each year?
2. What amount of interest *expense* on the bonds would be reported in 2010 and 2011 using the effective interest rate method?
3. Determine the reported value of the bonds (i.e., the carrying amount) at 31 December 2010 and 2011, assuming the effective interest rate method is used to amortise the premium.
4. What amount of interest expense on the bonds would be reported under the straight-line method of amortising the premium?

Solution to 1: The interest payment equals £50,000 annually (£1,000,000 × 5%).

Solution to 2: The sales proceeds of £1,044,518 are more than the face value of £1,000,000; the bonds were issued at a premium of £44,518. The bonds are initially reported as a long-term liability, bonds payable, of £1,044,518, which comprises the face value of £1,000,000 plus a premium of £44,518. The premium is amortised over time, ultimately decreasing the carrying amount (amortised cost) to face value.

Under the effective interest rate method, interest expense on the bonds is calculated as the bonds' carrying amount times the market rate in effect when the bonds are issued (effective interest rate). For 2010, interest expense is £41,781 = (£1,044,518 × 4%). The amount of the premium amortised in 2010 is the difference between the interest expense of £41,781 and the interest payment of £50,000 (i.e., £8,219). The bonds' carrying amount decreases by the premium amortisation; at 31 December 2010, the bonds' carrying amount is £1,036,299 (beginning balance of £1,044,518 less £8,219 premium amortisation). At this point, the carrying amount reflects a remaining unamortised premium of £36,299 (£44,158 premium at issuance minus £8,219 amortised).

For 2011, interest expense is £41,452 = (£1,036,299 × 4%). The amount of the premium amortised in 2011 is the difference between the interest expense of £41,452 and the interest payment of £50,000 (i.e., £8,548). At 31 December 2011, the bonds' carrying amount is £1,027,751 (beginning balance of £1,036,299 less £8,548 premium amortisation).

The following table illustrates interest expense, premium amortisation, and carrying amount (amortised cost) over the life of the bonds.

Year	Carrying Amount (Beginning of Year)	Interest Expense (at Effective Interest Rate of 6%)	Interest Payment (at Coupon Rate of 5%)	Amortisation of Discount	Carrying Amount (End of Year)
	(a)	(b)	(c)	(d)	(e)
2010	£1,044,518	£41,781	£50,000	£8,219	£1,036,299
2011	1,036,299	41,452	50,000	8,548	1,027,751
2012	1,027,751	41,110	50,000	8,890	1,018,861
2013	1,018,861	40,754	50,000	9,246	1,009,615
2014	1,009,615	40,385	50,000	9,615	1,000,000
Total				£44,518	

Solution to 3: The carrying amounts of the bonds at 31 December 2010 and 2011 are £1,036,299 and £1,027,751, respectively. Observe that the carrying amount of the bonds issued at a premium decreases over the life of the bonds. At maturity, 31 December 2014, the carrying amount of the bonds equals the face value of the bonds. The carrying amount of the bonds will be reduced to zero when the principal payment is made.

Solution to 4: Under the straight-line method, the premium is evenly amortised over the life of the bonds. In this example, the £44,518 premium would be amortised by £8,903.64 (£44,518 divided by 5 years) each year under the straight-line method. So, the annual interest expense under the straight-line method would be £41,096.36 (£50,000 less £8,903.64).

The reporting of interest payments on the statement of cash flows can differ under IFRS and U.S. GAAP. Under IFRS, interest payments on bonds can be included as an outflow in either the operating section or the financing section of the statement of cash flows. U.S. GAAP requires interest payments on bonds to be included as an operating cash outflow. (Some financial statement users consider the placement of interest payments in the operating section to be inconsistent with the placement of bond issue proceeds in the financing section of the statement of cash flows.) Typically, cash interest paid is not shown directly on the statement of cash flows, but companies are required to disclose interest paid separately.

Amortisation of a discount (premium) is a non-cash item and thus, apart from its effect on taxable income, has no affect on cash flow. In the section of the statement of cash flows that reconciles net income to operating cash flow, amortisation of a discount (premium) is added back to (subtracted from) net income.

2.3 Current Market Rates and Fair Value Reporting Option

Reporting bonds at amortised historical costs (historical cost plus or minus the cumulative amortisation) reflects the market rate at the time the bonds were *issued* (i.e., historical market rate or effective interest rate). As market interest rates change, the bonds' carrying amount diverges from the bonds' fair market value. When market interest rates decline, the fair value of a bond with a fixed coupon rate increases. As a result, a company's economic liabilities may be higher than its reported debt based on amortised historical cost. Conversely, when market interest rates increase, the fair value of a bond with a fixed coupon rate decreases and the company's economic liability may be lower than its reported debt. Using financial statement amounts based on amortised cost may underestimate (or overestimate) a company's debt-to-total-capital ratio and similar leverage ratios.

Companies recently have been given the option to report financial liabilities at fair values. Financial liabilities reported at fair value are designated as financial liabilities at fair value through profit or loss. Even if a company does not opt to report financial liabilities at fair value, the availability of fair value information in the financial statements has increased. IFRS and U.S. GAAP require fair value disclosures in the financial statements unless the carrying amount approximates fair value or the fair value cannot be reliably measured.[5]

A company selecting the fair value option for a liability with a fixed coupon rate will report gains (losses) when market interest rates increase (decrease). When market interest rates increase or other factors cause the fair value of a company's bonds to decline, the company reports a decrease in the fair value of its liability and a corresponding gain. When interest rates decrease or other factors cause the fair value of a company's bonds to increase, the company reports an increase in the fair value of its liability and a corresponding loss. The gains or losses resulting from changes in fair values are recognised in profit or loss.

Few companies have selected the option to report financial liabilities at fair value. Those that have are primarily companies in the financial sector. Reporting standards for financial investments and derivatives already required these companies to report a significant portion of their assets at fair values. Measuring financial liabilities at other than fair value, when financial assets are measured at

---

[5] IFRS (IAS 32, IAS 39, and IFRS 7) and U.S. GAAP (FASB ASC 820 and 825).

fair value, results in earnings volatility. This volatility is the result of using different bases of measurement for financial assets and financial liabilities. Goldman Sachs (NYSE:GS) elected to account for some financial liabilities at fair value under the fair value option. In its fiscal year 2008 10-K filing (page 74), Goldman explains this choice:

> The primary reasons for electing the fair value option are to reflect economic events in earnings on a timely basis, to mitigate volatility in earnings from using different measurement attributes and to address simplification and cost-benefit considerations.

Most companies, as required under IFRS and U.S. GAAP, disclose the fair values of financial liabilities. The primary exception to the disclosure occurs when fair value cannot be reliably measured. Example 5 illustrates Sony's fair value disclosures, including the fair values of long-term debt.

EXAMPLE 5

Fair Value Disclosures of Debt and Financial Instruments

The following are excerpts from Notes 2 and 13 of Sony Corporation's (NYSE:SNE) 20-F filing for the fiscal year ended 31 March 2009. These discuss the option for reporting fair values in the balance sheet and illustrate financial statement disclosures of fair values.

Note 2: *Summary of significant accounting policies (excerpt)*
. . . "The Fair Value Option for Financial Assets and Financial Liabilities." . . . permits companies to choose to measure, on an instrument-by-instrument basis, various financial instruments and certain other items at fair value that are not currently required to be measured at fair value. The fair value measurement election is irrevocable and subsequent changes in fair value must be recorded in earnings. . . . Sony did not elect the fair value option for any assets or liabilities that were not previously carried at fair value.

Note 13: *Fair value measurements (excerpt)*
The estimated fair values of Sony's financial instruments are summarised as follows. The following summary excludes cash and cash equivalents, call loans, time deposits, notes and accounts receivable, trade, call money, short-term borrowings, notes and accounts payable, trade and deposits from customers in the banking business because the carrying values of these financial instruments approximated their fair values due to their short-term nature.

	Yen in Millions			
	March 31, 2008		March 31, 2009	
	Carrying Amount	Estimated Fair Value	Carrying Amount	Estimated Fair Value
Long-term debt including the current portion	1,020,938	1,024,879	807,687	809,377
Investment contracts included in policyholders' account in the life insurance business	274,779	275,967	286,104	289,905

The fair values of long-term debt including the current portion and investment contracts included in policyholders' account in the life insurance business were estimated based on either the market value or the discounted future cash flows using Sony's current incremental borrowing rates for similar liabilities.

Use the excerpts from the notes to Sony's financial statements to address the following questions:

1. Does Sony report the fair values of its long-term debt on the balance sheet?
2. How does Sony measure the long-term debt reported on the balance sheet?
3. As of 31 March 2008 and 31 March 2009, what is the percent difference in the carrying amount and fair value of Sony's long-term debt?

Solution to 1: Sony does not report the fair values of its long-term debt on the balance sheet; Sony discloses that it did not elect the fair value option for any assets or liabilities that were not previously carried at fair value in Note 2. In Note 13, we also observe that Sony discloses the estimated fair value of long-term debt separately from its carrying amount.

Solution to 2: Notes 2 and 13 indicate that Sony did not elect the fair value option. Therefore, the carrying amount of its debt must be its amortised historical cost.

Solution to 3: In each year, the fair value of Sony's long-term debt is less than one half of one percent greater than its carrying amount: 0.4% [= (1,024,879/1,020,938) − 1] on 31 March 2008 and 0.2% [= (809,377/807,687) − 1] on 31 March 2009. Although the estimated fair values are higher, the difference is small and would most likely not materially affect an analysis of the company.

2.4 Derecognition of Debt

Once bonds are issued, a company may leave the bonds outstanding until maturity or redeem the bonds before maturity either by calling the bonds (if the bond issue includes a call provision) or by purchasing the bonds in the open market. If the bonds remain outstanding until the maturity date, the company pays bondholders the face value of the bonds at maturity. The discount or premium on the bonds would be fully amortised at maturity; the carrying amount would equal face value. Upon repayment, bonds payable is reduced by the carrying amount at maturity (face value) of the bonds and cash is reduced by an equal amount. Repayment of the bonds appears in the statement of cash flows as a financing cash outflow.

If a company decides to redeem bonds before maturity and thus extinguish the liability early, bonds payable is reduced by the carrying amount of the redeemed bonds. The difference between the cash required to redeem the bonds and the carrying amount of the bonds is a gain or loss on the extinguishment of debt. Under IFRS, debt issuance costs are included in the measurement of the liability and are thus part of its carrying amount. Under U.S. GAAP, debt issuance costs are accounted for separately from bonds payable and are amortised over the life of the bonds. Any unamortised debt issuance costs must be written off at the time of redemption and included in the gain or loss on debt extinguishment.

For example, a company reporting under IFRS has a £10 million bond issuance with a carrying amount equal to its face value and five years remaining until maturity. The company redeems the bonds at a call price of 103. The redemption cost is £10.3 million (= £10 million × 103%). The company's loss on redemption would be £300 thousand (£10 million carrying amount minus £10.3 million cash paid to redeem the callable bonds).

A gain or loss on the extinguishment of debt is disclosed on the income statement, in a separate line item, when the amount is material. A company typically discloses further detail about the extinguishment in the management discussion and analysis (MD&A) and/or notes to the financial statements.[6] In addition, in a statement of cash flows prepared using the indirect method, net income is adjusted to remove any gain or loss on the extinguishment of debt from operating cash flows and the cash paid to redeem the bonds is classified as cash used for financing activities. (Recall that the indirect method of the statement of cash flows begins with net income and makes necessary adjustments to arrive at cash from operations, including removal of gains or losses from non-operating activities.)

To illustrate the financial statement impact of the extinguishment of debt, consider the notes payable repurchase by B+H Ocean Carriers in Example 6 below.

EXAMPLE 6

Debt Extinguishment Disclosure

The following excerpts are from the 2008 20-F filing of B+H Ocean Carriers (NYSE Alternext: BHO). In its statement of cash flows, the company uses the indirect method to reconcile net income with net cash (used in) provided by operations.

---

[6] We use the term MD&A generally to refer to any management commentary provided on a company's financial condition, changes in financial condition, and results of operations. In the United States, the Securities and Exchange Commission (SEC) requires a management discussion and analysis for companies listed on U.S. public markets. Reporting requirements for such a commentary as the SEC-required MD&A vary across exchanges, but some are similar to the SEC requirements. Currently, the IASB is developing a standard for a management commentary that would be consistent for all companies reporting under IFRS.

Consolidated Statements of Income (excerpt)
For the Years Ended 31 December 2008, 2007, and 2006

	2008	2007	2006
Revenues:			
⋮	⋮	⋮	⋮
Total revenues	104,908,915	112,416,831	96,879,051
⋮	⋮	⋮	⋮
Total operating expenses	100,279,906	96,140,562	71,018,929
Income from vessel operations	4,629,009	16,276,269	25,860,122
Other income (expense):			
⋮	⋮	⋮	⋮
Gain on debt extinguishment	2,345,000	—	—
⋮	⋮	⋮	⋮
Total other income (expense), net	11,236,107	(14,257,092)	(7,085,809)
Net income	$15,865,116	$2,019,177	$18,774,313

Consolidated Statements of Cash Flows (excerpt)
For the Years Ended 31 December 2008, 2007, and 2006

	2008	2007	2006
CASH FLOWS FROM OPERATING ACTIVITIES:			
Net Income	$15,865,116	$2,019,177	$18,774,313
Adjustments to reconcile net income to net cash (used in) provided by operating activities:			
⋮	⋮	⋮	⋮
Gain on debt extinguishment	(2,345,000)	—	—
⋮	⋮	⋮	⋮
Total adjustments	(16,635,993)	38,842,386	19,815,773
Net cash (used in) provided by operating activities	(770,877)	40,861,563	38,590,086
⋮	⋮	⋮	⋮
CASH FLOWS FROM FINANCING ACTIVITIES:			
Payments for debt financing costs	(294,999)	(1,526,501)	(1,481,505)
⋮	⋮	⋮	⋮
Purchase of debt securities	(2,155,000)	—	(5,000,000)
⋮	⋮	⋮	⋮
Payments of unsecured debt	—	(31,402,960)	(1,356,092)

> **NOTE 2: SUMMARY OF SIGNIFICANT ACCOUNTING POLICIES (excerpt)**
>
> . . . The carrying amount of the Company's variable rate long-term debt approximates fair value.
>
> **NOTE 8: BONDS PAYABLE (excerpt)**
>
> On December 12, 2006, the Company issued $25 million of unsecured bonds. . . . Interest on the bonds is equal to LIBOR plus 4%, payable quarterly in arrears. . . . During the 4th quarter of 2008, the Company repurchased the unsecured bonds with a face value of $4.5 million and realized a $2.3 million gain.
>
> 1. The balance in bonds payable was reduced at redemption by:
>   A. $2,155,000.
>   B. $2,345,000.
>   C. $4,500,000.
>
> **Solution to 1:** C is correct. The bonds payable is reduced at redemption by the carrying amount of the bonds redeemed. The cash paid to extinguish the bonds plus the gain on redemption equals the carrying amount of the bonds. The carrying amount of the bonds was $4,500,000. In this case, the carrying amount equals the face value. The company recognized a gain of $2,345,000 when it extinguished the debt of $4,500,000 by paying only $2,155,000.

2.5 Debt Covenants

Borrowing agreements (the bond indenture) often include restrictions called covenants that protect creditors by restricting activities of the borrower. Debt covenants benefit borrowers to the extent that they lower the risk to the creditors and thus reduce the cost of borrowing. Affirmative covenants restrict the borrower's activities by requiring certain actions. For instance, covenants may require that the borrower maintain certain ratios above a specified amount or perform regular maintenance on real assets used as collateral. Negative covenants require that the borrower not take certain actions. Covenants may restrict the borrower's ability to invest, pay dividends, or make other operating and strategic decisions that might adversely affect the company's ability to pay interest and principal.

Common covenants include limitations on how borrowed monies can be used, maintenance of collateral pledged as security (if any), restrictions on future borrowings, requirements that limit dividends, and requirements to meet specific working capital requirements. Covenants may also specify minimum acceptable levels of financial ratios, such as debt-to-equity, current, or interest coverage.

When a company violates a debt covenant, it is a breach of contract. Depending on the severity of the breach and the terms of the contract, lenders may choose to waive the covenant, be entitled to a penalty payment or higher interest rate, renegotiate, or call for payment of the debt. Bond contracts typically require that the decision to call for immediate repayment be made, on behalf of all the bondholders, by holders of some minimum percentage of the principal amount of the bond issue.

Example 7 illustrates common disclosures related to debt covenants included in financial statement disclosures (notes to the financial statements).

EXAMPLE 7

Illustration of Debt Covenant Disclosures

The following excerpt is from TORM A/S (NASDAQ:TORM) from the Risk Factors section of Item 3, Key Information, in its fiscal year 2008 20-F filing. The excerpt illustrates debt covenants and their disclosure:

> Certain of our loan agreements contain restrictive covenants, which may limit our liquidity and corporate activities and prevent proper service of debt, which could result in the loss of our vessels.
>
> Some loan agreements impose operating and financial restrictions upon us. These restrictions may limit our ability to:
> ► change the management of our vessels without the lenders' consent (which they are not entitled to unreasonably withhold); and
> ► enter into mergers or corporate restructurings, or effect material divestments, if such would be materially adverse to the company.
>
> Our lenders' interests may be different from ours and we cannot guarantee that we will be able to obtain our lenders' permission when needed. This may prevent us from taking actions that are in our best interest.

The following excerpt is an additional excerpt from "Note 8: Bonds Payable" of B+H Ocean Carriers that was referenced in Example 6.

> The bond facility contains certain restrictive covenants which restrict the payment of dividends. The facility requires a minimum value adjusted equity ratio (as defined) of 25%. At December 31, 2008, the Company was in compliance with these covenants and is likely to remain in compliance throughout 2009. However, the bond agreement contains a cross default provision that essentially enables the lender to call the bonds if the Company defaults on a separate loan facility. The Company reclassified its long term debt because of a determination prospectively that certain covenants in certain long term agreements may be breached during 2009. As such, the Company has recorded the entire balance of the bonds as current as of December 31, 2008.

1. Which of the covenants described in the above excerpts is an affirmative covenant?

2. Based on the excerpt from B+H Ocean Carriers, what is the implied consequence of breaching certain covenants?

Solution to 1: The requirement that "a minimum value adjusted equity ratio (as defined) of 25 percent" be maintained by B+H Ocean Carriers is an example of an affirmative covenant. It requires the issuer to do something. The covenants on TORM A/S require that TORM not take certain actions (e.g., not change management of vessels without lenders' consent and not enter into mergers that would be materially adverse) and are negative covenants.

Solution to 2: If B+H Ocean Carriers breaches certain covenants, it seems that the entire balance of bonds payable becomes due. The bonds payable have been prospectively moved from non-current to current liabilities.

2.6 Presentation and Disclosure of Long-term Debt

The non-current (long-term) liabilities section of the balance sheet usually includes a single line item of the total amount of a company's long-term debt due after one year, with the portion of long-term debt due in the next twelve months shown as a current liability. Notes to the financial statements provide more information on the types and nature of a company's debt. These note disclosures can be used to determine the amount and timing of future cash outflows. The notes generally include stated and effective interest rates, maturity dates, restrictions imposed by creditors (covenants), and collateral pledged (if any). The amount of scheduled debt repayments for the next five years also is shown in the notes.

Example 8 contains an excerpt from Johnson & Johnson's 2008 10-K filing that illustrates common long-term debt disclosures.

EXAMPLE 8

Illustration of Long-Term Debt Disclosures

Exhibit 1 is an excerpt from Note 6 of Johnson & Johnson's (NYSE:JNJ) 2008 financial statements that illustrates financial statement disclosure for long-term debt, including type and nature of long-term debt, effective interest rates, and required payments over the next five years. Johnson & Johnson reports its debt at amortised cost.

EXHIBIT 1   Johnson & Johnson

6. Borrowings (excerpt)

The components of long-term debt are as follows:

(Dollars in Millions)	2008	Effective Rate %	2007	Effective Rate %
3% Zero Coupon Convertible Subordinated Debentures due 2020	$183	3	178	3
4.95% Debentures due 2033	500	4.95	500	4.95
3.80% Debentures due 2013	500	3.82	500	3.82

(Exhibit continued on next page . . .)

EXHIBIT 1	(continued)			

(Dollars in Millions)	2008	Effective Rate %	2007	Effective Rate %
6.95% Notes due 2029	294	7.14	294	7.14
6.73% Debentures due 2023	250	6.73	250	6.73
6.625% Notes due 2009	199	6.8	199	6.8
5.55% Debentures due 2017	1,000	5.55	1,000	5.55
5.95% Notes due 2037	995	5.99	995	5.99
5.50% Notes due 2024 (500 GBP1.4759)[2](500 GBP 1.9944)[3]	731	5.71	989	5.71
4.75% Notes due 2019 (1B Euro 1.4000)[2](1B Euro 1.4573)[3]	1,390	5.35	1,447	5.35
5.15% Debentures due 2012	599	5.18	599	5.18
5.86% Debentures due 2038	700	5.86		
5.15% Debentures due 2018	898	5.15		
Other (Includes Industrial Revenue Bonds)	102		132	
	8,341[4]	5.46[1]	7,083[4]	5.47[1]
Less current portion	221		9	—
	$8,120		**7,074**	

[1] Weighted average effective rate.

[2] Translation rate at December 28, 2008.

[3] Translation rate at December 30, 2007.

[4] The excess of the fair value over the carrying value of debt was $1.4 billion in 2008 and $0.3 billion in 2007.

The Company has access to substantial sources of funds at numerous banks worldwide. In September 2008, the Company secured a new 364-day and 5-year Credit Facility. Total credit available to the Company approximates $7.7 billion of which $6.3 billion expires September 24, 2009, and $1.4 billion expires September 25, 2013. Interest charged on borrowings under the credit line agreements is based on either bids provided by banks, the prime rate or London Interbank Offered Rates (LIBOR), plus applicable margins. Commitment fees under the agreements are not material.

. . .

Aggregate maturities of long-term obligations commencing in 2007 are (dollars in millions):

2009	2010	2011	2012	2013	After 2014
$ 221	22	18	620	507	6,953

Use the information in Exhibit 1 to answer the following questions:

1. Why are the effective interest rates unchanged from 2007 and 2008 for the first 11 borrowings listed?
2. Why does the carrying amount of the "4.95% debentures due 2033" remain the same in 2007 and 2008?
3. Why does the carrying amount of the "4.75% notes due 2019" decrease from 2007 to 2008?

Solution to 1: The effective interest rate is the market rate at which the bonds are issued and does not change from year to year.

Solution to 2: The carrying amount of the "4.95% debentures due 2033" remains the same because the effective interest rate at which the debentures were issued is the same as the coupon rate. The debentures were issued at par, and the carrying amount does not change.

Solution to 3: The notes are denominated in euros, with a face value of €1 billion. The dollar/euro translation exchange rate at the end of 2008 was lower than the exchange rate at the end of 2007 (1.4000 versus 1.4573). That decline explains the decrease in carrying value. Note that the face amount of the debt at the translation rate (at the end of 2008, €1 billion times 1.4000 = $1.4 billion) is higher than the carrying amount (at the end of 2008, $1.39 billion). The reason for this difference is that the notes were issued at a discount; the effective interest rate of 5.35 percent is higher than the 4.75 percent coupon rate. The carrying amount of the notes thus reflects the amortisation of the discount at issuance; the amortisation of the discount will increase the carrying amount.

In this reading, we focus on accounting for simple debt contracts. Debt contracts can take on additional features, which lead to more complexity. For instance, convertible debt and debt with warrants are more complex instruments that have both debt and equity features. Convertible debt gives the debt holder the option to exchange the debt for equity. Bonds issued with warrants give holders the right to purchase shares of the issuer's common stock at a specific price, similar to stock options. Issuance of bonds with warrants is more common by non-U.S. companies. Example 9 provides an example of a financial statement disclosure of bonds with warrants issued by a Chinese company.

EXAMPLE 9

Financial Statement Disclosure of Bonds with Warrants

The following excerpt is from the fiscal year 2008 Annual Report of the China Petroleum & Chemical Corporation (NYSE Euronext:SNP).

NOTE 29: DEBENTURES PAYABLE (excerpt)
On 26 February 2008, the Company issued convertible bonds with stock warrants due 2014 with an aggregate principal amount of RMB 30 billion in the PRC (the "Bonds with Warrants"). The Bonds with Warrants with fixed interest rate of 0.8% per annum and interest payable annually, were issued at par value of RMB 100. The Bonds with Warrants were guaranteed by Sinopec Group Company. Each lot of the Bonds with Warrants, comprising ten Bonds with Warrants are entitled to warrants (the "Warrants") to subscribe 50.5 A shares of the Company during the 5 trading days prior to 3 March 2010 at an initial exercise price of RMB 19.68 per share, subject to

adjustment for, amongst other things, cash dividends, subdivision or consolidation of shares, bonus issues, rights issues, capital distribution, change of control and other events which have a dilutive effect on the issued share capital of the Company.

If all warrants were exercised, how many shares would be subscribed for?

Solution: 1,515,000,000 shares would be subscribed for [aggregate principal amount divided by par value of a lot times shares subscribed per lot = (RMB 30,000,000,000/RMB 1,000) × 50.5 shares].

In addition to disclosures in the notes to the financial statements, an MD&A commonly provides other information about a company's capital resources, including debt financing and off-balance-sheet financing. In the MD&A, management often provides a qualitative discussion on any material trends, favorable or unfavorable, in capital resources and indicates any expected material changes in their mix and relative cost. Additional quantitative information is typically provided, including schedules summarising a company's contractual obligations (e.g., bond payables) and other commitments (e.g., lines of credit and guarantees) in total and over the next five years.

LEASES 3

A company wishing to obtain the use of an asset can either purchase the asset or lease the asset. Section 3.1 describes some advantages to leasing from the viewpoint of the **lessee** (the party obtaining the use of an asset through a lease). Section 3.2 describes the classification of leases. Section 3.2.1 describes the accounting treatments of different types of leases from the perspective of the lessee, and section 3.2.2 discusses leases from the perspective of the **lessor** (the owner of the asset).

3.1 Advantages of Leasing

A lease is a contract between the owner of an asset—the lessor—and another party seeking use of the asset—the lessee. Through the lease, the lessor grants the right to use the asset to the lessee. The right to use the asset can be for a long period, such as 20 years, or a much shorter period, such as a month. In exchange for the right to use the asset, the lessee makes periodic lease payments to the lessor. A lease, then, is a form of financing to the lessee provided by the lessor that enables the lessee to obtain the *use* of the leased asset.

There are several advantages to leasing an asset compared to purchasing it. Leases can provide less costly financing; they usually require little, if any, down payment and often are at lower fixed interest rates than those incurred if the asset was purchased. This financing advantage is the result of the lessor having advantages over the lessee and/or another lender. The lessor may be in a better position to take advantage of tax benefits of ownership, such as depreciation and interest. The lessor may be better able to value and bear the risks associated with ownership, such as obsolescence, residual value, and disposition of asset. The lessor may enjoy economies of scale for servicing assets. As a result of these advantages, the lessor may offer attractive lease terms and leasing the asset may be less costly for the lessee than owning the asset. Further, the negotiated lease contract may contain less-restrictive provisions than other forms of borrowing.

Companies also use certain types of leases because of perceived financial reporting and tax advantages. Although they provide a form of financing, certain types of leases are not shown as debt on the balance sheet. The items leased under these types of leases also do not appear as assets on the balance sheet. Therefore, no interest expense or depreciation expense is included in the income statement. In addition, in some countries—including the United States—because financial reporting rules differ from tax regulations, a company may own an asset for tax purposes (and thus obtain deductions for depreciation expense for tax purposes) while not reflecting the ownership in its financial statements. A lease that is structured to provide a company with the tax benefits of ownership while not requiring the asset to be reflected on the company's financial statements is known as a synthetic lease.

3.2 Finance (or Capital) Leases versus Operating Leases

There are two main classifications of leases: **finance** (or **capital**) and **operating leases**. [7] The economic substance of a finance (or capital) lease is very different from an operating lease, as are the implications of each for the financial statements for the lessee and lessor. In substance, a finance (capital) lease is equivalent to the purchase of some asset (lease to own) by the buyer (lessee) that is directly financed by the seller (lessor). An operating lease is an agreement allowing the lessee to use some asset for a period of time, essentially a rental.

Under IFRS, the classification of a lease as a finance lease or an operating lease depends on the transfer of the risks and rewards incidental to ownership of the leased asset.[8] If substantially *all* the risks and rewards are transferred to the lessee, the lease is classified as a finance lease and the lessee reports a leased asset and lease obligation on its balance sheet. Otherwise, the lease is reported as an operating lease, in which case the lessee reports neither an asset nor a liability; the lessee reports only the lease expense. Similarly, if the lessor transfers substantially *all* the risks and rewards incidental to legal ownership, the lease is reported as a finance lease and the lessor reports a lease receivable on its balance sheet and removes the leased asset from its balance sheet. Otherwise, the lease is reported as an operating lease, and the lessor keeps the leased asset on its balance sheet. Examples of situations that would normally lead to a lease being classified as a finance lease include the following:[9]

► The lease transfers ownership of the asset to the lessee by the end of the lease term.

► The lessee has the option to purchase the asset at a price that is expected to be sufficiently lower than the fair value at the date the option becomes exercisable for it to be reasonably certain, at the inception of the lease, that the option will be exercised.

► The lease term is for the major part of the economic life of the asset, even if the title is not transferred.

---

[7] "Finance lease" is IFRS terminology and "capital lease" is U.S. GAAP terminology.

[8] IAS 17 [Leases].

[9] Examples are from IAS 17, paragraph 10, and do not include all indicators that would lead to a lease being classified as a finance lease.

▶ At the inception of the lease, the present value of the minimum lease payments amounts to at least substantially all of the fair value of the leased asset.

▶ The leased assets are of such a specialised nature that only the lessee can use them without major modifications.

Although accounting for leases under U.S. GAAP is guided by a similar principle of the transfer of benefits and risks, U.S. GAAP is more prescriptive in its criteria for classifying capital and operating leases. Four criteria are specified to identify when a lease is a capital lease:[10]

1. Ownership of the leased asset transfers to the lessee at the end of the lease.
2. The lease contains an option for the lessee to purchase the leased asset cheaply (bargain purchase option).
3. The lease term is 75 percent or more of the useful life of the leased asset.
4. The present value of lease payments is 90 percent or more of the fair value of the leased asset.

Only one of these criteria has to be met for the lease to be considered a capital lease by the lessee. On the lessor side, satisfying at least one of these four criteria plus meeting revenue recognition requirements (that is, being reasonably assured of cash collection and having performed substantially under the lease) determine a capital lease. If none of the four criteria are met or if the revenue recognition requirement is not met, the lessor reports the lease as an operating lease.

3.2.1 Accounting and Reporting by the Lessee

Because a finance lease is economically similar to borrowing money and buying an asset, a company that enters into a finance lease as the lessee reports an asset (leased asset) and related debt (lease payable) on its balance sheet. The initial value of both the leased asset and lease payable is the lower of the present value of future lease payments and the fair value of the leased asset; in many cases, these will be equal. On the income statement, the company reports interest expense on the debt, and if the asset acquired is depreciable, the company reports depreciation expense. (The lessor, as we illustrate in the next section, reports the sale of an asset and a lease as receivable.)

Because an operating lease is economically similar to renting an asset, a company that enters into an operating lease as the lessee records a lease expense on its income statement during the period it uses the asset. No asset or liability is recorded on its balance sheet. The main accounting differences for a lessee between a finance lease and an operating lease, then, are that reported assets and debt are higher and expenses are generally higher in the early years under a finance lease. Because of the higher reported debt and expenses under a finance lease, lessees often prefer operating leases to finance leases. (Although classifying a lease as an operating lease can make reported profitability ratios and debt-to-equity ratios appear better, financial analysts are aware of this impact and typically adjust the reported numbers accordingly.)

On the lessee's statement of cash flows, for an operating lease, the full lease payment is shown as an operating cash outflow. For a finance lease, only the

---

[10] FASB ASC Topic 840 [Leases].

portion of the lease payment relating to interest expense reduces operating cash flow; the portion of the lease payment that reduces the lease liability appears as a cash outflow in the financing section.

Example 10 illustrates the accounting of a finance lease by a lessee.

EXAMPLE 10

Determining the Initial Recognition and Measurement and Subsequent Measurement of a Finance Lease for a Lessee

CAPBS Inc. enters into a lease agreement to acquire the use of a piece of machinery for four years beginning on 1 January 2010. The lease requires four annual payments of €28,679 starting on 1 January 2010. The useful life of the machine is four years, and its salvage value is zero. CAPBS accounts for the lease as a finance lease. The fair value of the machine is €100,000. The present value of the lease payments using the company's discount rate of 10 percent is €100,000. (A reminder is relevant for present value calculations: Lease payments are made at the beginning of each period.) The company uses straight-line depreciation.

1. Comment on the appropriateness of CAPBS treating the lease agreement as a finance lease under IFRS and a capital lease under U.S. GAAP.

2. What is the amount reported as a leased asset on the balance sheet on 1 January 2010? What depreciation expense is reported in fiscal year 2010?

3. What is the amount of the machinery reported as a leased asset on the balance sheet on 31 December 2010?

4. What is the amount of the lease liability reported on the balance sheet on 1 January 2010? What interest expense is reported in fiscal year 2010?

5. What is the amount of the lease liability reported on the balance sheet on 31 December 2010? What interest expense is reported in fiscal year 2011?

6. If CAPBS had determined that the above lease was an operating lease, what amount of expenses would be reported on the income statements in fiscal 2010 and 2011? How does this expense compare to the expenses reported under a capital lease?

Solution to 1: CAPBS should treat this lease as a finance lease under IFRS. The machine is leased for the major part of its useful life (the useful life of the machine and the lease are each four years). Also, the present value of lease payments equals substantially the fair value of the machine (both are €100,000). CAPBS should treat this lease as a capital lease under U.S. GAAP. The machine is leased for more than 75 percent of its useful life, and the present value of the lease payments exceeds 90 percent of the fair value of the leased asset.

Solution to 2: The amount initially reported as a leased asset on 1 January 2010 is €100,000. Depreciation expense each year is €25,000 [(€100,000 − €0)/4 years].

The table below shows CAPBS's depreciation expense and carrying amount for the leased asset by year.

Year	Initial Recognition Amount	Depreciation Expense	Accumulated Depreciation	Carrying Amount (Year-End)
	(a)	(b)	(c)	(d)
2010	€100,000	€25,000	€25,000	€75,000
2011	100,000	25,000	50,000	50,000
2012	100,000	25,000	75,000	25,000
2013	100,000	25,000	100,000	0
		€100,000		

► Column (a) is the lower of the fair value of the machinery and the present value (PV) of lease payments at lease inception. In this example, they are the same.

► Column (b) is the depreciation expense of €25,000 per year [straight-line depreciation = acquisition cost less salvage value divided by useful life = (€100,000 − €0)/4 years].

► Column (c) is the accumulated depreciation on the leased asset calculated as the prior year's accumulated depreciation plus the current year's depreciation expense.

► Column (d) is the carrying amount of the machine (the leased asset), which is the difference between the initial recognition amount and accumulated depreciation.

Solution to 3: From the table presented above, the carrying amount on 31 December 2010 is €75,000.

Solution to 4: The amount of the lease liability initially recognised on 1 January 2010 is €100,000, which is both the fair value of the leased asset and the present value of lease payments. However, the first lease payment of €28,679, due on 1 January 2010, immediately reduces the lease liability balance to €71,321. Interest expense in 2010 is based on the €71,321 carrying amount. Interest expense reported in fiscal year 2010 is €7,132 (€71,321 × 10%).

The table below shows CAPBS's lease payment, interest expense, and carrying values for its lease liability by year.[11]

Year	Lease Liability, 1 January	Annual Lease Payment, 1 January	Interest (at 10%; Accrued in Previous Year)	Reduction of Lease Liability, 1 January	Lease Liability on 31 December after Lease Payment on 1 January Same Year
	(a)	(b)	(c)	(d)	(e)
2010	€100,000	€28,679	€0	€28,679	€71,321
2011	71,321	28,679	7,132	21,547	49,774
2012	49,774	28,679	4,977	23,702	26,072
2013	26,072	28,679	2,607	26,072	0
		€114,717	€14,717	€100,000	

---

[11] The computations included throughout the example were made using an Excel worksheet; small apparent discrepancies in the calculations are because of rounding.

▶ Column (a) is the lease liability at the beginning of the year.

  ▶ 2010: €100,000

  ▶ Years thereafter: It is the lease liability at the end of the previous year.

▶ Column (b) is the annual lease payment made at the beginning of the year. A portion of the lease payment reduces interest accrued in the previous year, and the remainder of the lease payment reduces the carrying amount of the lease liability.

  ▶ For example, in 2011, the €28,679 paid on 1 January reduces the interest payable of €7,132 that accrued in 2010 (€71,321 × 10%) and then reduces the lease liability by €21,547.

▶ Column (c) is the interest portion of the 1 January lease payment made on that date. This amount of interest was accrued as interest payable during the *prior* year and is reported as the interest expense of the *prior* year. For example, at 31 December 2010, interest expense and interest payable in the amount of €7,132 was recognised.

▶ Column (d) is the reduction of the lease liability, which is the difference between the annual lease payment and the interest portion.

▶ Column (e) is the lease liability on 31 December of a given year just before the lease payment is made on the first day of the next year. It is equal to the lease liability on 1 January of the same year (column a) less the reduction of the lease liability (column d).

Solution to 5: From the table presented in *Solution to 4*, the interest expense in fiscal year 2011 is €4,977 (€49,744 × 10%).

Solution to 6: As an operating lease, a rent expense of €28,679 would be reported on the income statement each year. Under a capital lease, the expenses related to the lease are depreciation and interest expense. In 2010, the depreciation expense is €25,000 and the interest expense is €7,132. In 2011, the depreciation expense is €25,000 and the interest expense is €4,977.

A company reporting a lease as an operating lease will typically show higher profits in early years, higher return measures in early years, and a stronger solvency position than an identical company reporting an identical lease as a finance lease. However, the company reporting the lease as a finance lease will show higher operating cash flows because the portion of the lease payment that reduces the carrying amount of the lease liability will be reflected as a financing cash outflow rather than an operating cash outflow. The interest expense portion of the lease payment on the statement of cash flows can be treated as operating or financing cash outflow under IFRS and is treated as an operating cash outflow under U.S. GAAP.

The explicit standards in the United States that determine when a company should report a capital lease versus an operating lease make it easier for a company to structure a lease so that it is reported as an operating lease. The company structures the lease so that none of the four capital lease identifying criteria is met. Similar to debt disclosures, however, lease disclosures show payments under both capital and operating leases for the next five years and afterward. These disclosures can help to estimate the extent of a company's off-balance-sheet lease financing through operating leases. Example 11 illustrates the disclosures of operating and finance leases. Although these disclosures can be used to determine the effect on the financial statements if all operating leases were capitalized, this reading focuses solely on the information that is disclosed.

EXAMPLE 11

Financial Statement Disclosure of Leases by the Lessee

BASF Group (OTC: BASFY) has significant commitments under finance and operating leases. Presented below is selected note disclosure from its fiscal year 2008 financial statements.

27. LEASING
Leased assets
Property, plant and equipment include those assets which are considered to be economically owned through a finance lease. They primarily concern the following items:

Leased Assets (Millions €)	2008		2007	
	Acquisition Cost	Net Book Value	Acquisition Cost	Net Book Value
Land, land rights and buildings	20	13	26	18
Machinery and technical equipment	223	96	226	118
Miscellaneous equipment and fixtures	73	18	71	20
Advance payments and construction in progress	—	—	—	—
	316	127	323	156

Liabilities from Finance Leases (Millions €)	2008			2007		
	Minimum Lease Payments	Interest Portion	Leasing Liability	Minimum Lease Payments	Interest Portion	Leasing Liability
Following year 1	20	5	15	29	6	23
Following year 2	20	5	14	19	5	13
Following year 3	22	5	18	18	5	13
Following year 4	11	2	9	21	5	16
Following year 5	7	2	4	10	3	8
Over 5 years	29	10	20	35	12	23
	108	29	80	132	36	96

In the current business year and in 2007, no additional lease payments arising from contractual obligations were recognized in income above the minimum lease payments.

In 2008, leasing liabilities were not offset by any expected minimum lease payments from sub-leases.

In addition, BASF is a lessee under operating lease contracts. The resulting lease obligations totaling €1,449 million in 2008 and €1,272 in 2007 are due in the following years:

Commitments Due to Operating Lease Contracts (Millions €)

	Nominal Value of the Future Minimum Payments	
	Dec. 31, 2008	**Dec. 31, 2007**
Less than 1 year	**280**	292
1–5 years	**613**	505
Over 5 years	**556**	475
	1,449	1,272

1. At the end of fiscal year 2008, what is the total amount of finance lease liabilities BASF reports on its balance sheet?
2. Based on finance lease agreements in place at the end of fiscal year 2008, how much will BASF pay out on finance lease commitments in fiscal year 2009?
3. Based on finance lease agreements in place at the end of fiscal year 2008, what is the amount of interest expense that BASF will report in fiscal year 2009?
4. At the end of fiscal 2008, what are BASF's total commitments under operating leases?
5. Based on operating lease agreements in place at the end of fiscal year 2008, what is the minimum amount of rent expense that BASF will report in fiscal year 2009?
6. At the end of fiscal year 2008, what is the amount of leased assets (carrying amount) BASF reports on its balance sheet?

Solution to 1: €80 million—the total of the 2008 column "Leasing liability" in the "Liabilities from finance leases" table.

Solution to 2: €20 million—reported in the 2008 column "Minimum lease payments," row "Following year 1," in the "Liabilities from finance leases" table.

Solution to 3: €5 million—reported in the 2008 column "Interest portion," row "Following year 1," in the "Liabilities from finance leases" table.

Solution to 4: €1,449 million—the total of the 2008 column "Nominal value of the future minimum payments" in the "Commitments due to operating lease contracts" table.

Solution to 5: €280 million—reported in the 2008 column "Nominal value of the future minimum payments," row "Less than 1 year," in the "Commitments due to operating lease contracts" table.

Solution to 6: €127 million—the total of the 2008 column "Net book value" in the "Leased assets" table.

Example 12 contains information from Royal Dutch Shell's (LSE:RDSA) 2008 financial statements. As required by IFRS, the balance sheet presents finance lease obligations in the line items labeled "Debt." Additionally, IFRS require certain disclosures to be made in the notes; the layout of disclosure notes on debt varies across companies. For Royal Dutch, the disclosure note on debt, Note 18[A], first shows a breakdown of total debt reported on the balance sheet into two components: the amount of debt excluding finance lease obligations and the amount of finance lease obligations. Note 18[B] provides disclosures on the component of on-balance-sheet debt, excluding finance lease obligations. Next, Note 18[C] presents information about all the companies' lease obligations— both finance leases (which are a component of the on-balance-sheet total debt) and operating leases (for which no obligation appears on the balance sheet). This disclosure clearly illustrates that although finance leases and operating leases are both contractual obligations, only the finance leases are reported on the balance sheet. As mentioned above, a subsequent reading demonstrates how analysts adjust the total amount of debt as reported on the balance sheet to also include the off-balance-sheet obligations for operating leases. Analysts also should be aware that the International Accounting Standards Board (IASB) and the Financial Accounting Standards Board (FASB) are addressing the lease accounting standards, so these standards may change in the coming years.

EXAMPLE 12

Long-Term Debt and Lease Disclosures

Use the following excerpts taken from Royal Dutch Shell (LSE: RDSA) 2008 consolidated financial statements and notes to the consolidated financial statements to answer the questions below.

CONSOLIDATED BALANCE SHEET (excerpt)

$ Millions	Notes	Dec 31, 2008	Dec 31, 2007
LIABILITIES			
Non-current liabilities			
Debt	*18*	**13,772**	12,363
⋮		⋮	⋮
Current liabilities			
Debt	*18*	**9,497**	5,736
⋮		⋮	⋮
Total liabilities		**153,535**	143,502
EQUITY			
⋮		⋮	⋮
Total equity		**128,866**	125,968
Total liabilities and equity		**282,401**	269,470

CONSOLIDATED STATEMENT OF CASH FLOWS (excerpt)

	Dec 31, 2008	Dec 31, 2007
Net increase/(decrease) in debt with maturity period within three months	**4,161**	(455)
Other debt:		
New borrowings	**3,555**	4,565
Repayments	**(2,890)**	(2,796)

Note 1: Basis of Preparation (excerpt)

The Consolidated Financial Statements of Royal Dutch Shell plc (the Company) and its subsidiaries (collectively known as "Shell" or the "Shell group") have been prepared in accordance with the provisions of the Companies Act 1985, Article 4 of the International Accounting Standards (IAS) Regulation and with International Financial Reporting Standards (IFRS) as adopted by the European Union. As applied to Shell, there are no material differences with IFRS as issued by the International Accounting Standards Board (IASB), therefore the Consolidated Financial Statements have been prepared in accordance with IFRS as issued by the IASB.

Note 2: Accounting Policies (excerpt)
Financial liabilities

Debt and accounts payable are recognised initially at fair value based on amounts exchanged and subsequently at amortised cost, except for fixed rate debt subject to fair value hedging, which is remeasured for the hedged risk (see "Derivative contracts").

Interest on debt is accounted for using the effective interest method and, other than interest capitalised, is recognised in income.

Where fair value is not applied subsequent to initial recognition but is required for disclosure purposes, it is based on market prices where available, otherwise it is calculated as the net present value of expected future cash flows.

Note 18: Debt and Lease Arrangements (excerpt)

[A] DEBT						$ Millions
	Dec 31, 2008			Dec 31, 2007		
	Debt (Excluding Finance Lease Obligations)	Finance Lease Obligations	Total	Debt (Excluding Finance Lease Obligations)	Finance Lease Obligations	Total
Short-term debt	7,879	—	7,879	3,292	—	3,292
Long-term debt due within one year	1,314	304	1,618	2,290	154	2,444
Current debt	9,193	304	9,497	5,582	154	5,736
Non-current debt	10,061	3,711	13,772	8,533	3,830	12,363
Total	19,254	4,015	23,269	14,115	3,984	18,099

The fair value of debt approximates the carrying amount.

[B] DEBT (EXCLUDING FINANCE LEASE OBLIGATIONS)

The following tables compare contractual cash flows for debt (excluding finance lease obligations) owed by subsidiaries at December 31, by year of maturity, with the carrying amount in the Consolidated Balance Sheet. The carrying amount reflects the effects of discounting, premiums and fair value adjustments where hedging is applied.

2008 $ Millions, except where Otherwise Indicated

	Contractual Repayments (Excluding Interest)								
	2009	2010	2011	2012	2013	2014 and After	Total	Difference from Carrying Amount	Carrying Amount
Fixed rate dollar	6,821	506	1,001	503	1	3,539	12,371	290	12,661
Average interest rate	2.6%	5.2%	5.6%	5.0%	7.3%	5.4%			
Variable rate dollar debt	521	156	5	—	—	122	804	—	804
Average interest rate	1.8%	3.8%	6.3%	—	—	0.0%			
Fixed rate European debt	568	1,146	285	—	—	2,117	4,116	197	4,313
Average interest rate	2.9%	4.8%	2.0%	—	—	4.6%			
Variable rate European debt	237	—	—	—	—	—	237	—	237
Average interest rate	3.1%	—	—	—	—	—			
Other fixed rate debt	426	—	2	—	1	—	429	—	429
Average interest rate	18.4%	—	11.7%	—	12.4%	—			
Other variable rate debt	620	33	143	14	—	—	810	—	810
Average interest rate	9.4%	11.5%	7.8%	4.8%	—	—			
Total	9,193	1,841	1,436	517	2	5,778	18,767	487	19,254

The table above excludes interest estimated to be $827 million in 2009, $480 million in 2010, $389 million in 2011, $316 million in 2012, $290 million in 2013 and $290 million in 2014 and after (assuming interest rates with respect to variable rate debt remain constant and there is no change in aggregate principal amount of debt other than repayment at scheduled maturity as reflected in the table).

The weighted average interest rate on short-term debt excluding the short-term portion of long-term debt at December 31, 2008, was 4% (2007: 7%).

[C] LEASE ARRANGEMENTS

The future minimum lease payments for finance and operating leases and the present value of minimum finance lease payments at December 31, by maturity date are as follows:

2008				$ Millions
	Total Future Minimum Finance Lease Payments	Interest	Present Value of Minimum Finance Lease Payments	Total Future Minimum Operating Lease Payments
2009	608	304	304	4,648
2010–2013	2,008	1,094	914	9,905
2014 and after	4,076	1,279	2,797	4,712
Total	6,692	2,677	4,015	19,265

Operating lease expenses were as follows ($ Millions):

	2008	2007	2006
Minimum lease payments	3,339	3,091	2,571
Contingent rentals	68	63	59
Sub-lease income	(161)	(138)	(132)
Total	3,246	3,016	2,498

Use the above information to answer the following questions:

1. How does Royal Dutch Shell initially value its debt on the balance sheet? How is debt subsequently measured on the balance sheet?

2. What method does Shell use to calculate interest expense on its debt?

3. What is the total amount of debt appearing within current liabilities on the balance sheet at 31 December 2008, and what does it include?

4. What is the total amount of debt due after one year appearing on the balance sheet at 31 December 2008, and what does it include?

5. How does the interest rate in 2008 on short-term debt (excluding finance lease obligations and the short-term portion of long-term debt) compare to that in 2007?

6. What is the fair value of Royal Dutch Shell's debt at 31 December 2008?

7. What was Royal Dutch Shell's rent expense in fiscal year 2008 related to operating leases?

8. Comment on the relative magnitude of operating leases compared to finance leases?

9. What are Shell's debt-to-equity ratios for 2008 and 2007? Comment on year-to-year changes.

Solution to 1: From Note 2, debt is initially reported at fair value based on amounts exchanged. After issuance, debt is reported at amortised cost except for certain fixed rate debt that is subject to fair value hedging. That debt is remeasured to fair value.

Solution to 2: Note 2 indicates that Shell uses the effective interest rate method to calculate interest expense.

Solution to 3: The total amount of debt included in current liabilities on the balance sheet is $9,497. Note 18[A] shows that this amount comprises $7,879 short-term debt (excluding finance lease obligations), $1,314 long-term debt due within one year (excluding finance lease obligations), and $304 finance lease obligations. The finance lease obligations are those due within one year.

Solution to 4: The total amount of debt due after next year (non-current debt) is $13,722. Note 18[A] shows that this amount comprises $10,061 debt (excluding finance lease obligations) and $3,711 finance lease obligations.

Solution to 5: In Note 18 [B], Shell indicates that the interest rate on short-term debt has declined significantly. The weighted average interest rate at 31 December on short-term debt was 4 percent in 2008 and 7 percent in 2007.

Solution to 6: From Note 18 [A], Shell reports that the fair value of debt approximates its carrying amount. The carrying amount is $23,269.

Solution to 7: From Note 18 [C], rent expense on operating leases was $3,246 in 2008.

Solution to 8: Although operating and finance leases are accounted for differently, we can compare the undiscounted future minimum lease payments under operating leases and finance leases reported in Note 18 [C] to gain an initial understanding of their relative magnitude. The total future minimum lease payments under operating leases of $19,265 are more than two and one-half times the $6,692 under finance leases.

Solution to 9: Debt-to-equity ratios are calculated as follows ($ millions):

	2008	2007
Debt (included in non-current liabilities)	13,772	12,363
Debt (included in current liabilities)	9,497	5,736
Total current and non-current debt	23,269	18,099
Total equity	128,866	125,966
Debt-to-equity	18.06%	14.37%

The debt-to-equity ratio increased to 18.06 percent in 2008 from 14.37 percent in 2007. This increase is primarily attributable to an increase in short-term debt. From Note 18 [A] disclosures, short-term debt increased by $4,587 million (from $3,292 million in 2007 to $7,879 million in 2008), while the current portion of long-term debt decreased by $826 million (from $2,444 million to $1,618 million) and the non-current portion of debt increased by only $1,409 million (from $12,363 million to $13,772 million). The financing section excerpt of the statement of cash flows discloses that Shell issued $4,161 million in short-term debt in 2008, compared with repaying short-term debt in 2007.

3.2.2 Accounting and Reporting by the Lessor

Similar to accounting and reporting on the lessee side, the lessor also must determine whether a lease is classified as operating or finance. Under IFRS, the determination of a finance lease on the lessor's side mirrors that of the lessee's. That is, in a finance lease the lessor transfers substantially all the risks and rewards incidental to legal ownership.[12] Under U.S. GAAP, the lessor determines whether a lease is a capital or operating lease using the same four identifying criteria as a lessee, plus the additional revenue recognition criteria. That is, the lessor must be reasonably assured of cash collection and has performed substantially under the lease. From the lessor's perspective, U.S. GAAP distinguishes between types of capital leases. There are two main types of capital leases from a lessor's perspective: 1) **direct financing leases**, and 2) **sales-type leases**.[13]

Under IFRS and U.S. GAAP, if a lessor enters into an operating lease, the lessor records any lease revenue when earned. The lessor also continues to report the leased asset on the balance sheet and the asset's associated depreciation expense on the income statement.

Under IFRS, if a lessor enters into a finance lease, the lessor reports a receivable at an amount equal to the net investment in the lease (the present value of the minimum lease payments receivable and any estimated unguaranteed residual value accruing to the lessor).[14] The leased asset is derecognised; assets are reduced by the carrying amount of the leased asset. Initial direct costs incurred by a lessor, other than a manufacturer or dealer lessor, are added to the receivable and reduce the amount of income recognised over the lease term. The lease payment is treated as repayment of principal (reduces lease receivable) and finance income. The recognition of finance income should reflect a constant periodic rate of return on the lessor's net investment in the lease.

For lessors that are manufacturers or dealers, the initial direct costs are treated as an expense when the selling profit is recognised; typically, selling profit is recognised at the beginning of the lease term. Sales revenue equals the lower of the fair value of the asset or the present value of the minimum lease payments. The cost of sale is the carrying amount of the leased asset less the present value of the estimated unguaranteed residual value.

Under U.S. GAAP, a direct financing lease results when the present value of lease payments (and thus the amount recorded as a lease receivable) equals the carrying value of the leased asset. Because there is no "profit" on the asset itself, the lessor is essentially providing financing to the lessee and the revenues earned

---

[12] IAS 17, paragraph 36.

[13] A leveraged lease is a third type of capital lease from the lessor's perspective under U.S. GAAP. FASB ASC paragraph 840-30-05-4.

[14] Some lease contracts specify minimum lease payments with the potential for additional payments based upon some criteria.

by the lessor are financing in nature (i.e., interest revenue). If, however, the present value of lease payments (and thus the amount recorded as a lease receivable) exceeds the carrying amount of the leased asset, the lease is treated as a sales-type lease.

Both types of capital leases have similar effects on the balance sheet: The lessor reports a lease receivable based on the present value of future lease payments and derecognises the leased asset. The carrying value of the leased asset relative to the present value of lease payments distinguishes a direct financing lease from a sales-type lease. A direct financing lease is reported when the present value of lease payment is equal to the value of the leased asset to the lessor. When the present value of lease payments is greater than the value of the leased asset, the lease is a sales-type lease. The income statement effect will thus differ based on the type of lease.

In a direct financing lease, the lessor exchanges a lease receivable for the leased asset, no longer reporting the leased asset on its books. The lessor's revenue is derived from interest on the lease receivable. In a sales-type lease, the lessor "sells" the asset to the lessee and also provides financing on the sale. Therefore, in a sales-type lease, a lessor reports revenue from the sale, cost of goods sold (i.e., the carrying amount of the asset leased), profit on the sale, and interest revenue earned from financing the sale. The lessor will show a profit on the transaction in the year of inception and interest revenue over the life of the lease.

EXAMPLE 13

Determining Initial Recognition and Measurement and Subsequent Measurement of a Finance Lease when the Present Value of Lease Payments Equals the Value of the Leased Asset

DIRFIN Inc. owns a piece of machinery and plans to lease the machine on 1 January 2010. In the lease contract, DIRFIN requires four annual payments of €28,679 starting on 1 January 2010. DIRFIN is confident that the payments will be received. The useful life of the machine is four years, and its salvage value is zero. The present value of the lease payments and the fair value of the machine are each €100,000. The carrying amount for the machine also is €100,000. DIRFIN's discount rate is 10 percent.

1. Comment on the appropriateness of DIRFIN's treating the lease as a finance lease under IFRS and a capital lease under U.S. GAAP.

2. What is the amount of the lease receivable reported on the balance sheet on 1 January 2010? What is interest revenue reported in fiscal year 2010?

3. What is the carrying amount of the machine reported on the balance sheet on 1 January 2010?

4. What is the amount of the lease receivable reported on the balance sheet on 31 December 2010? What is interest income reported in fiscal year 2011?

5. If DIRFIN had determined the above lease was an operating lease, what amount of income would be reported on the income statement in fiscal year 2010?

Solution to 1: Treating this lease as a finance lease under IFRS and a capital lease under U.S. GAAP is appropriate. Under IFRS, the lease meets at least two of the suggested criteria for a finance lease: 1) The lease term is for the major part of the economic life of the asset, and 2) at inception of the lease, the present value of the minimum lease payments amounts to at least substantially all of the fair value of the leased asset. Under U.S. GAAP, the lease meets more than one of the required criteria for a capital lease: 1) The lease term is 75 percent or more of the useful life of the leased asset (the lease term and useful life are both four years), and 2) the present value is 90 percent or more of the fair value of the leased asset (the present value of lease payments approximately equals the fair value of the machine). The revenue recognition requirement also is met. Under U.S. GAAP, this capital lease is classified as a direct financing lease because the present value of lease payment is equal to the value of the leased asset.

Solution to 2: DIRFIN removes the leased asset from its records and records a lease receivable. On its income statement, DIRFIN reports interest revenues earned from financing the lease. The table below shows DIRFIN's interest revenue and carrying amounts for the lease receivable.

On 1 January 2010, the lease receivable is initially recorded at €100,000. Immediately after the first lease payment is received on 1 January 2010, the carrying amount of the lease receivable decreases to €71,321 and remains at this amount through 31 December 2010. Interest revenue for 2010 is €7,132 (10 percent interest rate times the loan receivable balance of €71,321 throughout 2010).

Year	Lease Receivable, 1 January	Annual Lease Payment Received, 1 January	Interest (at 10%; Accrued in Previous Year)	Reduction of Lease Receivable, 1 January	Lease Receivable on 31 December after Lease Payment on 1 January of Same Year
	(a)	(b)	(c)	(d)	(e)
2010	€100,000	€28,679	€0	€28,679	€71,321
2011	71,321	28,679	7,132	21,547	49,774
2012	49,774	28,679	4,977	23,702	26,072
2013	26,072	28,679	2,607	26,072	0
		€114,717	€14,717	€100,000	

► Column (a) is the lease receivable at the beginning of the year.

► Column (b) is the annual lease payment received at the beginning of the year, which is allocated to interest and reduction of the lease receivable.

► Column (c) is interest for the year calculated as the lease receivable outstanding for the year multiplied by the interest rate.

► Column (d) is the reduction of the lease receivable, which is the difference between the annual lease payments received and interest. Because the lease payment is due on 1 January, this amount of interest is a receivable at the end of the *prior* year and interest revenue of the *prior* year.

► Column (e) is the lease receivable after the lease payment is received and at the end of the year. It is the lease receivable at 1 January (column a) less the reduction of the lease receivable (column d).

Solution to 3: DIRFIN effectively sells the machine through the finance lease and so reports no carrying amount for the machine.

Solution to 4: The lease receivable is €71,321 at 31 December 2010. At 1 January 2011, the lease receivable decreases to €49,774 after the second lease payment is received on 1 January 2011. Interest revenue for 2011 is €4,977 (10 percent interest rate times the loan receivable balance of €49,774 throughout 2011).

Solution to 5: As an operating lease, rent income of €28,679 would be reported on the income statement.

When a lessor enters into a sales-type lease (a lease agreement where the present value of the future lease payments is greater than the value of the leased asset to the lessor), it will show a profit on the transaction in the year of lease inception and interest revenue over the life of the lease.

EXAMPLE 14

Determining the Financial Statement Impact of a Finance Lease by the Lessor when the Present Value of Lease Payments Is Greater than the Value of the Leased Asset

Assume a (hypothetical) company, Selnow, manufactures machinery and enters into an agreement to lease a machine on 1 January 2010. Under the lease, the company is to receive four annual payments of €28,679 starting on 1 January 2010. Selnow is confident that the payments will be received. The fair value of the machine and present value of the lease payments (using a 10 percent discount rate) are each €100,000, and the carrying amount of the machine is €90,000. The useful life of the machine is four years, and its salvage value is zero.

1. Comment on the appropriateness of Selnow's treatment of the lease agreement as a finance lease under IFRS and a capital lease under U.S. GAAP.
2. What is Selnow's income related to the lease in 2010? In 2011? Ignore taxes.

Solution to 1: Treating this lease as a finance lease under IFRS and a capital lease under U.S. GAAP is appropriate.

Under IFRS, the lease meets at least two of the suggested criteria for a finance lease: 1) The lease term is for the major part of the economic life of the asset (the lease term and useful life of the machine are both four years), and 2) at inception of the lease the present value of the minimum lease payments amounts to at least substantially all of the fair value of the leased asset (the present value of lease payments equals the fair value of the machine).

Under U.S. GAAP, the lease meets more than one of the required capital lease criteria, including the following: 1) The lease term is 75 percent or more of the useful life of the leased asset (the lease term and useful life of the machine are both four years), and 2) the present value is 90 percent or more of the fair value of the leased asset. The revenue recognition requirement also is met (Selnow is confident that the payments will be received). Further, under U.S. GAAP this lease is classified as a sales-type lease because the present value of the lease payments is greater than the carrying amount of the leased asset.

There is no difference, however, in accounting between IFRS and U.S. GAAP as a result of this additional classification under U.S. GAAP. The present value of the future lease payments is more than the lessor's carrying amount for the machine, and the difference is the lessor's profit from selling the machine. The lessor will record a profit of €10,000 on the sale of the machine in 2010 (€100,000 present value of lease payments receivable less €90,000 value of the machine).

Solution to 2: In 2010, Selnow shows income of €17,132 related to the lease. One part of this income is the €10,000 gain on the sale of the machine (sales revenues of €100,000 less costs of goods sold of €90,000). Selnow also shows interest revenue of €7,132 on its financing of the lease (lease receivable of €71,321 after the initial lease payment is received times the 10 percent discount rate). In 2011, Selnow reports only the interest revenue of €4,977 (lease receivable of €49,774 after the 1 January lease payment is received times the 10 percent discount rate). The table below shows lease payments received, interest revenue, and reduction of the lease receivable for Selnow's sales-type lease. Note that this table is the same as DIRFIN's table in Example 13 with the direct financing lease. They are the same because the present value of the lease payments in both cases is the same. It is the carrying amount of the machine that differs between the two examples.

Year	Lease Receivable, 1 January	Annual Lease Payment Received, 1 January	Interest (at 10%; Accrued in Previous Year)	Reduction of Lease Receivable, 1 January	Lease Receivable on 31 December after Lease Payment on 1 January of Same Year
	(a)	(b)	(c)	(d)	(e)
2010	€100,000	€28,679	€0	€28,679	€71,321
2011	71,321	28,679	7,132	21,547	49,774
2012	49,774	28,679	4,977	23,702	26,072
2013	26,072	28,679	2,607	26,072	0
		€114,717	€14,717	€100,000	

Exhibit 2 summarizes the financial statement impact of operating and financing leases on the lessee and lessor.

EXHIBIT 2	**Summary of Financial Statement Impact of Operating and Financing Leases on the Lessee and Lessor**		
	Balance Sheet	**Income Statement**	**Statement of Cash Flows**
Lessee			
Operating Lease	No effect	Reports rent expense	Rent payment is an operating cash outflow
Finance Lease under IFRS (capital lease under U.S. GAAP)	Recognises leased asset and lease liability	Reports depreciation expense on leased asset	Reduction of lease liability is a financing cash outflow
		Reports interest expense on lease liability	Interest portion of lease payment is either an operating or financing cash outflow under IFRS and an operating cash outflow under U.S. GAAP
Lessor			
Operating Lease	Retains asset on balance sheet	Reports rent income	Rent payments received are an operating cash inflow
		Reports depreciation expense on leased asset	
Finance Lease[a]			
When present value of lease payments equals the carrying amount of the leased asset (called a direct financing lease in U.S. GAAP)	Removes asset from balance sheet Recognises lease receivable	Reports interest revenue on lease receivable	Interest portion of lease payment received is either an operating or investing cash inflow under IFRS and an operating cash outflow under U.S. GAAP
			Receipt of lease principal is an investing cash inflow[b]
When present value of lease payments exceeds the carrying amount of the leased asset (called a sales-type lease in U.S. GAAP)	Removes asset Recognises lease receivable	Reports profit on sale Reports interest revenue on lease receivable	Interest portion of lease payment received is either an operating or investing cash inflow under IFRS and an operating cash outflow under U.S. GAAP
			Receipt of lease principal is an investing cash inflow[b]

[a] U.S. GAAP distinguishes between a direct financing lease and a sales-type lease, but IFRS does not. The accounting is the same for IFRS and U.S. GAAP despite this additional classification under U.S. GAAP.

[b] If providing leases is part of a company's normal business activity, the cash flows related to the leases are classified as operating cash.

INTRODUCTION TO PENSIONS AND OTHER POST-EMPLOYMENT BENEFITS

Pensions and other post-employment benefits are non-current liabilities reported by many companies. Companies may offer various types of benefits to their employees following retirement, such as pension plans, health care plans, medical insurance, and life insurance. Pension plans often are the most significant post-employment benefits provided to retired employees.

The accounting and reporting depends on the type of pension plan offered. Two common pension plans are the **defined contribution plan** and the **defined benefit plan**. Under a defined contribution plan, a company contributes an agreed upon (defined) amount into the plan. The agreed upon amount is the pension expense. The only impact on the balance sheet is a decrease in cash; however, if some portion of the agreed upon amount has not been paid by fiscal year-end, a liability would be recognised on the balance sheet. The amount paid (contributed to the plan) is treated as an operating cash outflow. Because the amount of the contribution is defined and the company has no further obligation once the contribution has been made, accounting for a defined contribution plan is fairly straightforward.

Accounting for a defined benefit plan is more complicated. Under a defined benefit plan, a company makes promises of future benefits to be paid to the employee during retirement. For example, a company could promise an employee annual pension payments of 70 percent of his final salary at retirement until death. To determine the amount of the obligation for the promise to pay the employee the pension during retirement, many assumptions have to be made, such as the employee's expected salary at retirement and the number of years the employee is expected to live beyond retirement. The future amounts the company will pay out are estimated and discounted to a present value to determine the pension obligation. The pension obligation is allocated over the employee's employment as part of pension expense.

The company's reported pension expense includes five common components: a) employees' service costs incurred during the period; b) interest expense accrued on the beginning pension obligation; c) actuarial gains and losses; d) changes to the terms of a pension plan that increase the benefit obligation applicable to employees' service during previous periods (past service costs); and e) expected return on plan assets.

The service cost during the period for an employee is the present value of the increase in the pension benefit earned by the employee as a result of providing one more year of service. Interest costs are included in pension expense because a defined benefit pension plan can be considered a long-term borrowing from employees. Instead of paying employees for the services they provide this year, a company is deferring payment until future periods. Because the employees have provided the service to earn their pensions, the company has an obligation to them. Like other borrowings, interest accrues on the amount of the pension obligation outstanding.

Most defined benefit pension plans are funded through a separate legal entity, typically a pension trust fund. A company makes payments into the pension fund, and retirees are paid from the fund. The payments the company makes into the fund are invested until they are needed to pay the retirees. Expected earnings on the investments are subtracted from other pension costs to get the reported pension expense. Because of year-to-year fluctuations in market returns, standard setters allow companies to use an expected rather an actual return to reduce the volatility of reported pension expense. Pension plan assets are intended as long-term investments; if the expected returns are accurately estimated, differences between the actual return and the expected return should offset over the long run. If the difference between the expected return and actual return becomes large, however, companies are required to amortise a portion into pension expense.

Actuarial gains and losses can occur when changes are made to the assumptions on which a company's estimated pension obligation has been based (e.g., employee turnover, mortality rates, retirement ages, compensation increases). Prior service costs arise because of changes in benefits promised. Some actuarial gains and losses, and past service costs, might not yet be recognised in pension expense or the pension obligation because IFRS and U.S. GAAP allow companies to "smooth" the effects of these two items over time rather than immediately reflect the total amount of the effect as income or expense.

Similar to other forms of employee compensation for a manufacturing company, the pension expense related to production employees is added to inventory and expensed through cost of sales (cost of goods sold). For employees not involved directly in the production process, the pension expense is included with salaries and other administrative expenses. Therefore, pension expense is not directly reported on the income statement. Rather, extensive disclosures are included in the notes to the financial statements.

Under IFRS, companies can choose how to measure the net pension obligation (or asset) reported on the balance sheet. Companies can choose to measure the net pension obligation (or asset) as the pension obligation less plan assets. If the pension obligation is greater than plan assets, a net pension obligation is shown and the pension fund is underfunded. If the plan assets are greater than the plan liabilities, a net pension asset is reported. Alternatively, companies can choose to exclude the unrecognised smoothed amounts of actuarial gains or losses or past service costs from the balance sheet. Under U.S. GAAP, companies are required to measure the net pension obligation (or asset) as the pension obligation less plan assets.

Example 15 presents excerpts of pension-related disclosures from Novo Nordisk's 2008 Annual Report.

EXAMPLE 15

Pension-Related Disclosures

The following are excerpts of pension-related disclosures from Novo Nordisk's (NYSE:NVO) 2008 Annual Report:

1 Summary of significant accounting policies
Pensions
The Group operates a number of defined contribution plans throughout the world. In a few countries the group still operates defined benefit plans. The costs for the year for defined benefit plans are determined using the projected unit credit method. This reflects services rendered by employees to the dates of valuation and is based on actuarial assumptions primarily regarding discount rates used in determining the present value of benefits, projected rates of remuneration growth and long-term expected rates of return for plan assets. Discount rates are based on the market yields of high-rated corporate bonds in the country concerned.

Actuarial gains and losses are recognised as income or expense when the net cumulative unrecognised actuarial gains and losses for each individual plan at the end of the previous reporting period exceeded 10% of the higher of the defined benefit obligation and the fair value of plan assets at that date. These gains or losses are recognised over the expected average remaining working lives of the employees participating in the plans. Past service costs are allocated over the average period until the benefits become vested.

6 Employee Costs

DKK million	2008	2007	2006
Wages and salaries	10,541	9,792	9,225
Share-based payment costs (refer to note 33)	331	130	113
Pensions — defined contribution plans	745	724	670
Retirement benefit obligations (refer to note 24)	128	109	111
Other contributions to social security	714	709	645
Other employee costs	1,169	1,094	911
Total employee costs	13,628	12,558	11,675

24 Retirement Benefit Obligations

DKK million	2008	2007	2006
Retirement obligations	1,103	885	938
Plan assets	(649)	(566)	(495)
Deficit/(surplus)	454	319	443
Unrecognised gains/(loss)	(35)	43	(113)
Retirement obligations recognised in the balance sheet	419	362	330

Amounts Recognised in the Income Statement for the Year

Current service cost	112	91
Interest cost on pension obligation	41	32
Expected return on plan assets	(24)	(18)
Actuarial (gains)/losses recognised in the year	(2)	1
Past service cost	1	3
Total income statement charge	128	109

Use information in the excerpts to answer the following questions:

1. What type(s) of pension plans does Novo Nordisk have?
2. What amount of pension expense did Novo Nordisk report in 2008?
3. What is reported on Novo Nordisk's 2008 balance sheet with respect to pensions?
4. If Novo Nordisk had chosen the pension reporting alternative consistent with U.S. GAAP, what would have been reported on Novo Nordisk's 2008 balance sheet with respect to pensions?

Solution to 1: Note 1 "Summary of significant accounting policies" indicates that the company has both defined contribution and defined benefit pension plans. The note indicates that the company continues to operate defined benefit plans in only a few countries.

Solution to 2: Note 6 "Employee costs" shows that the pension expense related to the defined contribution pension plans was DKK745 million and that related to the retirement benefit obligations of the defined benefit plans was DKK128 million. Details of the DKK128 million pension expense (income statement charge) of the defined benefit plans are shown in Note 24 under "Amounts recognised in the income statement for the year." The total pension expense reported for 2008 was DKK873 million.

Solution to 3: Note 24 "Retirement benefit obligations" shows the net pension obligation recognised in the balance sheet for fiscal year 2008 to be DKK419 million. This amount is the retirement obligation less plan assets, after adjusting for the unrecognised gain or loss related to the smoothed items. By subtracting unrecognised losses, Novo Nordisk uses the alternative treatment allowed under IFRS.

Solution to 4: If Novo Nordisk chose the treatment consistent with U.S. GAAP, its net pension obligation would have been DKK454 million:

(DKK Million)	2008
Retirement obligations	1,103
Plan assets	(649)
Deficit/(surplus)	454

EVALUATING SOLVENCY: LEVERAGE AND COVERAGE RATIOS

5

Solvency refers to a company's ability to meet its long-term debt obligations, including both principal and interest payments. In evaluating a company's solvency, ratio analyses can provide information about the relative amount of debt in the company's capital structure and the adequacy of earnings and cash flow to cover interest expense and other fixed charges (such as lease or rental payments) as they come due. Ratios are useful to evaluate a company's performance over time compared to the performance of other companies and industry norms. Ratio analysis has the advantage of allowing the comparison of companies regardless of their size and reporting currency.

The two primary types of solvency ratios are leverage ratios and coverage ratios. Leverage ratios focus on the balance sheet and measure the extent to which a company uses liabilities rather than equity to finance its assets. Coverage ratios focus on the income statement and cash flows and measure the ability of a company to cover its debt-related payments.

Exhibit 3 describes the two types of commonly used solvency ratios. The first three leverage ratios use total debt in the numerator.[15] The *debt-to-assets ratio* expresses the percentage of total assets financed with debt. Generally, the higher the ratio, the higher the financial risk and thus the weaker the solvency. The *debt-to-capital ratio* measures the percentage of a company's total capital (debt plus equity) financed through debt. The *debt-to-equity ratio* measures the amount of debt financing relative to equity financing. A *debt-to-equity ratio* of 1.0 indicates equal amounts of debt and equity, which is the same as a debt-to-capital ratio of 50 percent. Interpretations of these ratios are similar. Higher debt-to-capital or debt-to-equity ratios imply weaker solvency. A caveat must be made when comparing debt ratios of companies in different countries. Within certain countries, companies historically have obtained more capital from debt than equity financing, so debt ratios tend to be higher for companies in these countries.

EXHIBIT 3	Definitions of Commonly Used Solvency Ratios	
Solvency Ratios	**Numerator**	**Denominator**
<u>Leverage Ratios</u>		
Debt-to-assets ratio	Total debt[a]	Total assets
Debt-to-capital ratio	Total debt[a]	Total debt[a] + Total shareholders' equity
Debt-to-equity ratio	Total debt[a]	Total shareholders' equity
Financial leverage ratio	Average total assets	Average shareholders' equity
<u>Coverage Ratios</u>		
Interest coverage ratio	EBIT[b]	Interest payments
Fixed charge coverage ratio	EBIT[b] + Lease payments	Interest payments + Lease payments

[a] In this reading, debt is defined as the sum of interest-bearing short-term and long-term debt.

[b] EBIT is earnings before interest and taxes.

---

[15] For calculations in this reading, total debt is the sum of interest-bearing short-term and long-term debt, excluding non-interest-bearing liabilities, such as accrued expenses, accounts payable, and deferred income taxes. This definition of total debt differs from other definitions that are more inclusive (e.g., all liabilities) or more restrictive (e.g., long-term debt only). If the use of different definitions of total debt materially changes conclusions about a company's solvency, the reasons for the discrepancies should be further investigated.

The *financial leverage ratio* (also called the 'leverage ratio' or 'equity multiplier') measures the amount of total assets supported by one money unit of equity. For example, a value of 4 for this ratio means that each €1 of equity supports €4 of total assets. The higher the financial leverage ratio, the more leveraged the company in the sense of using debt and other liabilities to finance assets. This ratio often is defined in terms of average total assets and average total equity and plays an important role in the DuPont decomposition of return on equity.[16]

The *interest coverage ratio* measures the number of times a company's EBIT could cover its interest payments. A higher interest coverage ratio indicates stronger solvency, offering greater assurance that the company can service its debt from operating earnings. The *fixed charge coverage ratio* relates fixed financing charges, or obligations, to the cash flow generated by the company. It measures the number of times a company's earnings (before interest, taxes, and lease payments) can cover the company's interest and lease payments.

Example 16 demonstrates the use of solvency ratios in evaluating the creditworthiness of a company.

EXAMPLE 16

Evaluating Solvency Ratios

A credit analyst is evaluating and comparing the solvency of two companies—Nokia Corporation (NYSE: NOK) and LM Ericsson Telephone Company (NYSE: ERIC)—at the beginning of 2009. The following data are gathered from the companies' 2008 annual reports and 20-F filings:

	Nokia (€ Millions)		Ericsson (SEK Millions)	
	2008	**2007**	**2008**	**2007**
Short-term borrowings	3,578	714	1,639	2,831
Current portion of long-term interest bearing debt	13	173	3,903	3,068
Long-term interest bearing debt	861	203	24,939	21,320
Total shareholders' equity	14,208	14,773	140,823	134,112
Total assets	39,582	37,599	285,684	245,117
EBIT	4,966	7,985	16,252	30,646
Interest payments	155	59	1,689	1,513

---

[16] The basic DuPont decomposition is: Return on equity = Net income/Average shareholders' equity = (Sales/Average total assets) × (Net income/Sales) × (Average total assets/Average shareholders' equity).

Use this information to answer the following questions:

1. **A.** What are each company's debt-to-assets, debt-to-capital, and debt-to-equity ratios for 2008 and 2007?

   B. Comment on any changes in the calculated leverage ratios from year-to-year for both companies.

   C. Comment on the calculated leverage ratios of Nokia compared to Ericsson.

2. **A.** What is each company's interest coverage ratio for 2008 and 2007?

   B. Comment on any changes in the interest coverage ratio from year to year for both companies.

   C. Comment on the interest coverage ratio of Nokia compared to Ericsson.

Solution to 1:

A. <u>For Nokia</u>

Debt-to-assets for 2008: 11.2% = (3,578+13+861)/39,582
Debt-to-assets for 2007: 2.9% = (714+173+203)/37,599

Debt-to-capital for 2008: 23.9% =
(3,578+13+861)/(3,578+13+861+14,208)
Debt-to-capital for 2007: 6.9% =
(714+173+203)/(714+173+203+14,773)

Debt-to-equity for 2008: 31.3% = (3,578+13+861)/(14,208)
Debt-to-equity for 2007: 7.4% = (714+173+203)/(14,773)

<u>For Ericsson</u>

Debt-to-assets for 2008: 10.7% = (1,639+3,903+24,939)/(285,684)
Debt-to-assets for 2007: 11.1% = (2,831+3,068+21,320)/(245,117)

Debt-to-capital for 2008: 17.8% =
(1,639+3,903+24,939)/(1,639+3,903+24,939+140,823)
Debt-to-capital for 2007: 16.9% =
(2,831+3,068+21,320)/(2,831+3,068+21,320+134,112)

Debt-to-equity for 2008: 21.6% = (1,639+3,903+24,939)/(140,823)
Debt-to-equity for 2007: 20.3% = (2,831+3,068+21,320)/(134,112)

B. Nokia's leverage ratios all increased from 2007 to 2008, suggesting weakening solvency. Comparing debt year to year, we observe that leverage ratios increased because of a significant increase in short-term borrowings and an increase in long-term interest bearing debt without a similar increase in shareholders' equity. In fact, shareholders' equity declined.

   On the other hand, Ericsson's leverage ratios appear fairly similar for 2007 and 2008. During 2008, it appears as though Ericsson shifted away from short borrowings to long-term debt.

C. In 2007, all three of Nokia's leverage ratios were lower than Ericsson's. In 2008, the opposite was true. Ericsson's capital structure seems fairly constant over the two years, whereas Nokia's capital structure has shifted toward more debt.

Solution to 2:

A. <u>For Nokia</u>

Interest coverage ratio for 2008: 32.0 = (4,966/155)
Interest coverage ratio for 2007: 135.3 = (7,985/59)

<u>For Ericsson</u>

Interest coverage ratio for 2008: 9.6 = (16,252/1,689)
Interest coverage ratio for 2007: 20.3 = (30,646/1,513)

B. Nokia's interest coverage ratio decreased from 2007 to 2008 because of a decrease in EBIT and an increase in interest payments. Even with the decrease, Nokia appears to have sufficient operating earnings to cover interest payments. Similarly, Ericsson's interest coverage ratio decreased from 2007 to 2008, primarily because of a decrease in EBIT. Ericsson also appears to have sufficient operating earnings to cover interest payments.

C. Nokia's ability to cover interest payments is greater than Ericsson's, although both companies appear to have sufficient operating earnings to cover interest payments.

SUMMARY

Non-current liabilities arise from different sources of financing and different types of creditors. Bonds are a common source of financing from debt markets. Bonds are initially valued at fair value when issued, and then companies have the choice of whether to subsequently measure bonds at fair value or amortised cost.

Leases are related to the use of specific assets. In a finance lease, the lessee assumes substantially all the risks and benefits of ownership of the leased asset so the lessee reports an asset and related obligation. Typically, the lessor will report a lease receivable and derecognise the asset. In an operating lease, the lessee secures the right to use the leased asset but substantially all the risk and rewards of ownership are not transferred. The lessor does not derecognise the asset and reports lease (rent) income, and the lessee reports lease (rent) expense.

Pensions and other post-employment benefits are additional forms of compensation. Employees work currently to earn benefits for retirement or post-employment as well as to earn current salaries and wages. Companies with defined contribution plans report the agreed upon contribution paid into a plan as an expense. Defined benefit plans provide for agreed upon future benefits. Understanding the reporting of non-current liabilities when they arise and how they are subsequently valued is important in assessing a company's solvency and potential changes in its solvency.

Key points in accounting and reporting of non-current liabilities include the following:

▶ The sales proceeds of a bond issue are determined by discounting future cash payments using the market rate of interest at the time of issuance (effective interest rate). The reported interest expense on bonds is based on the effective interest rate.

▶ Future cash payments on bonds usually include periodic interest payments (made at the stated interest rate or coupon rate) and the principal amount at maturity.

▶ When the market rate of interest equals the coupon rate for the bonds, the bonds will sell at par (i.e., at a price equal to the face value). When the market rate of interest is higher than the bonds' coupon rate, the bonds will sell at a discount. When the market rate of interest is lower than the bonds' coupon rate, the bonds will sell at a premium.

▶ An issuer amortises any issuance discount or premium on bonds over the life of the bonds.

▶ If a company redeems bonds before maturity, it reports a gain or loss on debt extinguishment computed as the net carrying amount of the bonds (including bond issuance costs under IFRS) less the amount required to redeem the bonds.

▶ Debt covenants impose restrictions on borrowers, such as limitations on future borrowing or requirements to maintain a minimum debt-to-equity ratio.

▶ The carrying amount of bonds is typically amortised historical cost, which can differ from their fair value.

▶ Companies are required to disclose the fair value of financial liabilities, including debt. Although permitted to do so, few companies opt to report debt at fair values on the balance sheet.

▶ Accounting standards require leases to be classified as either operating leases or finance (capital) leases. Leases are classified as finance leases when substantially all the risks and rewards of legal ownership are transferred to the lessee.

▶ When a lessee reports a lease as an operating lease rather than a finance lease, the lessee usually appears more profitable in the early years of the lease and less so later, and it appears more solvent over the whole period.

▶ When a lessor reports a lease as a finance lease rather than an operating lease, the lessor usually appears more profitable in the early years of the lease.

▶ In a finance lease where the present value of lease payments equals the carrying amount of the leased asset, a lessor earns only interest revenue. In a finance lease where the present value of lease payments exceeds the carrying amount of the leased asset, a lessor earns both interest revenue and a profit (or loss) on the sale of the leased asset.

▶ Two types of pension plans are defined contribution plans and defined benefits plans. Under a defined contribution plan, the cash payment made into the plan is recognised as pension expense. Pension expense under the defined benefit plan typically includes five components: a) service costs incurred during the period; b) interest expense accrued on the beginning pension obligation; c) actuarial gains and losses; d) changes to the terms of a pension plan that increase the benefit obligation applicable to employees' service during previous periods (past service cost); and e) expected return on plan assets.

▶ Under IFRS, companies have a choice between reporting the net pension liability (or asset) as either the full amount of the pension obligation less plan assets or excluding any cumulative actuarial gains or losses or past service costs from the balance sheet. Under U.S. GAAP, companies must report the difference between the pension obligation and the pension assets as an asset or liability on the balance sheet.

▶ Solvency refers to a company's ability to meet its long-term debt obligations.

▶ In evaluating solvency, leverage ratios focus on the balance sheet and measure the amount of debt financing relative to equity financing.

▶ In evaluating solvency, coverage ratios focus on the income statement and cash flows and measure the ability of a company to cover its interest payments.

PRACTICE PROBLEMS FOR READING 39

1. A company issues €1 million of bonds at face value. When the bonds are issued, the company will record a:
   A. cash inflow from investing activities.
   B. cash inflow from financing activities.
   C. cash inflow from operating activities.

2. At the time of issue of 4.50% coupon bonds, the effective interest rate was 5.00%. The bonds were *most likely* issued at:
   A. par.
   B. a discount.
   C. a premium.

3. Oil Exploration LLC paid $45,000 in printing, legal fees, commissions, and other costs associated with its recent bond issue. It is most likely to record these costs on its financial statements as:
   A. an asset under U.S. GAAP and reduction of the carrying value of the debt under IFRS.
   B. a liability under U.S. GAAP and reduction of the carrying value of the debt under IFRS.
   C. a cash outflow from investing activities under both U.S. GAAP and IFRS.

4. On 1 January 2010, Elegant Fragrances Company issues £1,000,000 face value, five-year bonds with annual interest payments of £55,000 to be paid each 31 December. The market interest rate is 6.0 percent. Using the effective interest rate method of amortisation, Elegant Fragrances is *most likely* to record:
   A. an interest expense of £55,000 on its 2010 income statement.
   B. a liability of £982,674 on the 31 December 2010 balance sheet.
   C. a £58,736 cash outflow from operating activity on the 2010 statement of cash flows.

5. Consolidated Enterprises issues €10 million face value, five-year bonds with a coupon rate of 6.5 percent. At the time of issuance, the market interest rate is 6.0 percent. Using the effective interest rate method of amortisation, the carrying value after one year will be *closest* to:
   A. €10.17 million.
   B. €10.21 million.
   C. €10.28 million.

6. The management of Bank EZ repurchases its own bonds in the open market. They pay €6.5 million for bonds with a face value of €10.0 million and a carrying value of €9.8 million. The bank will *most likely* report:
   A. other comprehensive income of €3.3 million.
   B. other comprehensive income of €3.5 million.
   C. a gain of €3.3 million on the income statement.

7. Innovative Inventions, Inc. needs to raise €10 million. If the company chooses to issue zero-coupon bonds, its debt-to-equity ratio will *most likely*:

   A. rise as the maturity date approaches.

   B. decline as the maturity date approaches.

   C. remain constant throughout the life of the bond.

8. Fairmont Golf issued fixed rate debt when interest rates were 6 percent. Rates have since risen to 7 percent. Using only the carrying amount (based on historical cost) reported on the balance sheet to analyze the company's financial position would *most likely* cause an analyst to:

   A. overestimate Fairmont's economic liabilities.

   B. underestimate Fairmont's economic liabilities.

   C. underestimate Fairmont's interest coverage ratio.

9. Debt covenants are *least likely* to place restrictions on the issuer's ability to:

   A. pay dividends.

   B. issue additional debt.

   C. issue additional equity.

10. Compared to using a finance lease, a lessee that makes use of an operating lease will *most likely* report higher:

   A. debt.

   B. rent expense.

   C. cash flow from operating activity.

11. Which of the following is *most likely* a lessee's disclosure about operating leases?

   A. Lease liabilities.

   B. Future obligations by maturity.

   C. Net carrying amounts of leased assets.

12. For a lessor, the leased asset appears on the balance sheet and continues to be depreciated when the lease is classified as a(n):

   A. sales-type lease.

   B. operating lease.

   C. financing lease.

13. Under U.S. GAAP, a lessor's reported revenues at lease inception will be *highest* if the lease is classified as a(n):

   A. sales-type lease.

   B. operating lease.

   C. direct financing lease.

14. A lessor will record interest income if a lease is classified as:

   A. a capital lease.

   B. an operating lease.

   C. either a capital or an operating lease.

15. Cavalier Copper Mines has $840 million in total liabilities and $520 million in shareholders' equity. It discloses operating lease commitments over the next five years with a present value of $100 million. If the lease commitments are treated as debt, the debt-to-total-capital ratio is *closest* to:

   A. 0.58.

   B. 0.62.

   C. 0.64.

16. Penben Corporation has a defined benefit pension plan. At 31 December, its pension obligation is €10 million and pension assets are €9 million. If Penben chooses to report under a method consistent with both IFRS and U.S. GAAP, the reporting on the balance sheet would be *closest* to which of the following?

   A. €10 million is shown as a liability, and €9 million appears as an asset.

   B. €1 million is shown as a net pension obligation.

   C. There is no choice that reports pension assets and obligations on the balance sheet consistently under IFRS and U.S. GAAP.

SOLUTIONS FOR READING 39

1. B is correct. The company receives €1 million in cash from investors at the time the bonds are issued, which is recorded as a financing activity.

2. B is correct. The effective interest rate is greater than the coupon rate and the bonds will be issued at a discount.

3. A is correct. Under U.S. GAAP, expenses incurred when issuing bonds are generally recorded as an asset and amortised to the related expense (legal, etc.) over the life of the bonds. Under IFRS, they are included in the measurement of the liability. The related cash flows are financing activities.

4. B is correct. The bonds will be issued at a discount because the market interest rate is higher than the stated rate. Discounting the future payments to their present value indicates that at the time of issue, the company will record £978,938 as both a liability and a cash inflow from financing activities. Interest expense in 2009 is £58,736 (£978,938 times 6.0 percent). During the year, the company will pay cash of £55,000 related to the interest payment, but interest expense on the income statement will also reflect £3,736 related to amortisation of the initial discount (£58,736 interest expense less the £55,000 interest payment). Thus, the value of the liability at 31 December 2010 will reflect the initial value (£978,938) plus the amortised discount (£3,736), for a total of £982,674. The cash outflow of £55,000 may be presented as either an operating or financing activity under IFRS.

5. A is correct. The coupon rate on the bonds is higher than the market rate, which indicates that the bonds will be issued at a premium. Taking the present value of each payment indicates an issue date value of €10,210,618. The interest expense is determined by multiplying the carrying amount at the beginning of the period (€10,210,618) by the market interest rate at the time of issue (6.0 percent) for an interest expense of €612,637. The value after one year will equal the beginning value less the amount of the premium amortised to date, which is the difference between the amount paid (€650,000) and the expense accrued (€612,637) or €37,363. €10,210,618 − €37,363 = €10,173,255 or €10.17 million.

6. C is correct. A gain of €3.3 million (carrying amount less amount paid) will be reported on the income statement.

7. A is correct. The value of the liability for zero-coupon bonds increases as the discount is amortised over time. Furthermore, the amortised interest will reduce earnings at an increasing rate over time as the value of the liability increases. Higher relative debt and lower relative equity (through retained earnings) will cause the debt-to-equity ratio to increase as the zero-coupon bonds approach maturity.

8. A is correct. When interest rates rise, bonds decline in value. Thus, the carrying amount of the bonds being carried on the balance sheet is higher than the market value. The company could repurchase the bonds for less than the carrying amount, so the economic liabilities are overestimated. Because the bonds are issued at a fixed rate, there is no effect on interest coverage.

9. C is correct. Covenants protect debtholders from excessive risk taking, typically by limiting the issuer's ability to use cash or by limiting the overall levels of debt relative to income and equity. Issuing additional equity would increase the company's ability to meet its obligations, so debtholders would not restrict that ability.

10. B is correct. An operating lease is not recorded on the balance sheet (debt is lower), and lease payments are entirely categorised as rent (interest expense is lower.) Because the rent expense is an operating outflow but principal repayments are financing cash flows, the operating lease will result in lower cash flow from operating activity.

11. B is correct. The lessee will disclose the future obligation by maturity of its operating leases. The future obligations by maturity, leased assets, and lease liabilities will all be shown for finance leases.

12. B is correct. When a lease is classified as an operating lease, the underlying asset remains on the lessor's balance sheet. The lessor will record a depreciation expense that reduces the asset's value over time.

13. A is correct. A sales-type lease treats the lease as a sale of the asset, and revenue is recorded at the time of sale equal to the present value of future lease payments. Under a direct financing lease, only interest income is reported as earned. Under an operating lease, revenue from rent is reported when collected.

14. A is correct. A portion of the payments for capital leases, either direct financing or sales-type, is reported as interest income. With an operating lease, all revenue is recorded as rental revenue.

15. C is correct. The current debt-to-total-capital ratio is $840/($840+$520) = 0.62. To adjust for the lease commitments, an analyst should add $100 to both the numerator and denominator: $940/($940+$520) = 0.64.

16. B is correct. Under both IFRS and U.S. GAAP, a company can choose to report net pension obligation as the pension obligation less the plan assets. Under IFRS, the company also has the option to exclude any cumulative actuarial gains or losses or past service costs from the balance sheet.

STUDY SESSION 10
FINANCIAL REPORTING AND ANALYSIS:
Applications and International Standards Convergence

The readings in this study session discuss financial statement analysis applications and the international convergence of accounting standards.

The most frequently used tools and techniques to evaluate companies include common size analysis, cross-sectional analysis, trend analysis, and ratio analysis. Beyond mere knowledge of these tools, however, the analyst must recognize the implications of accounting choices on the quality of a company's reported financial results. Then the analyst can apply these financial analysis techniques to major analyst tasks including the evaluation of past and future financial performance, credit risk, and the screening of potential equity investments. The readings also discuss analyst adjustments to reported financials. Such adjustments are often needed to put companies' reported results on a comparable basis.

This study session concludes with a reading on convergence of international and U.S. accounting standards. Although there has been much progress in harmonizing accounting standards globally, as this reading discusses, significant variations still exist among generally accepted accounting principles from one country to another.

Note:
New rulings and/or pronouncements issued after the publication of the readings on financial reporting and analysis may cause some of the information in these readings to become dated. Candidates are expected to be familiar with the overall analytical framework contained in the study session readings, as well as the implications of alternative accounting methods for financial analysis and valuation, as provided in the assigned readings. Candidates are not responsible for changes that occur after the material was written.

READING ASSIGNMENTS

FINANCIAL REPORTING QUALITY: RED FLAGS AND ACCOUNTING WARNING SIGNS

by Thomas R. Robinson, CFA and Paul Munter

LEARNING OUTCOMES

The candidate should be able to:	Mastery
a. describe incentives that might induce a company's management to overreport or underreport earnings;	☐
b. describe activities that will result in a low quality of earnings;	☐
c. describe the "fraud triangle";	☐
d. describe the risk factors that may lead to fraudulent accounting related to 1) incentives and pressures, 2) opportunities, and 3) attitudes and rationalizations;	☐
e. describe common accounting warning signs and methods for detecting each.	☐

Note:
New rulings and/or pronouncements issued after the publication of the readings on financial reporting and analysis may cause some of the information in these readings to become dated. Candidates are expected to be familiar with the overall analytical framework contained in the study session readings, as well as the implications of alternative accounting methods for financial analysis and valuation, as provided in the assigned readings. Candidates are not responsible for changes that occur after the material was written.

INTRODUCTION 1

Recent years have seen numerous accounting scandals, some resulting in bankruptcies and even the demise of a major CPA firm. Unfortunately, these scandals are not a new phenomenon. Looking back, we see that scandals such as these have occurred from time to time, in particular when there is a downturn in the economy and managers have felt pressure to meet market earnings expectations or debt covenants or to maintain or increase their personal wealth. By examining recent scandals, we can learn more about warning signs of danger and the techniques used to manipulate reported financial results.

555

This reading takes a look at red flags and aggressive accounting techniques that have resulted in a reduction of the financial reporting quality of corporate financial statements. Financial reporting quality goes beyond the traditional view of conservatism and earnings quality. Financial reporting quality relates the overall quality of the financial statements and related disclosures to ask how well the reported results fairly present the operations and financial position of a company. In the United States, audits are intended to ensure this fair presentation in accordance with U.S. generally accepted accounting principles (GAAP). Similarly, in the United Kingdom and in the international accounting standards (IAS), there is a desire to achieve a true and fair view of the company. Additionally, CEOs and CFOs of public companies are now required by Section 302 of the Sarbanes-Oxley Act (SOA) to provide quarterly certifications that the information included in Securities and Exchange Commission (SEC) filings represents a fair presentation of operations and financial position.[1]

This reading discusses financial reporting quality and activities that result in low financial reporting quality. We describe some prominent accounting scandals over the years, SEC studies, and related auditing literature to identify nonaccounting red flags that can be used to identify potential problem areas. We also discuss a variety of accounting warning signs, such as aggressive reporting of revenues or off-balance sheet activities. Finally, we show how the red flags can be applied to accounting scandals, using Enron and Sunbeam as examples.

2 FINANCIAL REPORTING QUALITY

The concept of financial reporting quality is not new. The Association for Investment Management and Research (AIMR) has periodically published surveys and other documents on the subject. In a recent survey, AIMR found that a vast majority of portfolio managers and securities analysts surveyed found corporate disclosures and the quality of financial reporting to be very important (43 percent), extremely important (30 percent), or somewhat important (22 percent). Unfortunately, on a 5.0-point scale, these same analysts rated public companies they follow on average 3.4 (C+).[2]

A principal concern of many users of financial statements has been whether or not earnings are overstated. There is a preference by some for the use of conservative accounting practices; those that result in lower earnings in early periods relative to later periods. This is certainly an important consideration, but it is not the only factor that should be used in evaluating financial reporting quality. Companies may be motivated to increase earnings in a particular period to meet analysts' earnings expectations, to meet debt covenants, or to improve

---

[1] *See also* SEC Release No. 33-8124, *Certification of Disclosure in Companies' Quarterly and Annual Reports,* August 29, 2002.

[2] 2003 AIMR Member Survey of Global Corporate Financial Reporting Quality and Corporate Communications and Disclosure Practices, October 2003, www.aimr.org.

incentive compensation. Importantly, management also may have incentives to lower reported earnings in a particular period. For example, management may be motivated to report lower earnings to obtain trade relief, negotiate lower payments to other counterparties from a prior business transaction, or negotiate concessions from unions or others.

In addition to making sure earnings are presented fairly, it also is important that the financial position of the company is presented fairly, particularly from the standpoint of creditors. Just as management might be motivated to overstate earnings, it may have an incentive to overstate assets or understate liabilities to make the company's financial position appear to be more solvent. Conversely, management may want to understate assets to improve certain ratios, such as return on assets. Likewise, it may want to appear less solvent in a quest to negotiate concessions from creditors, vendors, and employees.

The quality of reported cash flow is another factor that needs to be examined. In some recent scandals, companies have been creative in generating operating cash flow from borrowing activities.[3] Financial disclosures or lack thereof also are important.[4] For example, when a company enters into a guarantee to others, this is an obligation that is important to creditors. Some guarantees are required to be measured and reported on the balance sheet as a liability. Other guarantees are not required to be measured and reported, but must be disclosed.[5] Clearly, the adequacy of these disclosures affects financial reporting quality.

Further, a simultaneous examination of all of the financial statements is a useful tool in detecting financial irregularities. For example, a combination of increasing earnings and decreasing operating cash flow may indicate aggressive reporting of earnings. Similarly, fraudulent activities to inflate sales and understate expenses generally lead to a buildup in assets on the balance sheet (often assets, such as receivables and inventory, but, as in the case of WorldCom, it can involve long-lived assets, as well).

We define high financial reporting quality as overall financial reporting, including disclosures, which results in a fair presentation of a company's operations (including both earnings and cash flow) and financial position. Low financial reporting quality, on the other hand, can result from a variety of activities, including the following:

▶ Following GAAP but selecting alternatives within GAAP that bias or distort reported results to achieve a desired outcome (e.g., selecting a depreciation method that results in higher earnings than the economic depreciation of the assets warrant).

▶ Using loopholes or bright-lines in accounting principles (e.g., the lessee has a capital lease if the present value of the lease payments is 90 percent or more of the fair value of the property) to structure transactions to achieve a desired outcome that differs from the economic structure of the transaction (e.g., that allows a lessor to structure a lease solely to qualify for immediate sales treatment while still allowing the lessee to treat it as an off-balance sheet arrangement).

---

[3] See, e.g., SEC Accounting and Auditing Enforcement Release No. 1631, *In the Matter of Dynegy, Inc.*, September 24, 2002.

[4] See, e.g., SEC Accounting and Auditing Enforcement Release No. 1555, *In the Matter of Edison Schools, Inc.*, May 14, 2002, in which the SEC determined that, even though the company's accounting was appropriate, its disclosures were lacking.

[5] See SEC Release No. 33-8182, *Disclosure in Management's Discussion and Analysis about Off-Balance Sheet Arrangements and Aggregate Contractual Obligations*, January 27, 2003.

► Using unrealistic or inappropriate estimates and assumptions to achieve a desired outcome (e.g., using extraordinarily long depreciable lives for assets or unrealistically optimistic assumptions about collectibility of receivables and loans).

► Stretching accounting principles to achieve a desired outcome (e.g., using a narrowly defined rule on consolidation of special-purpose entities (SPEs) for a leasing transaction to justify nonconsolidation of SPEs in other types of transactions).

► Engaging in fraudulent financial reporting. Rather than low financial reporting quality, this category actually has no financial reporting quality.

3   RED FLAGS AND ACCOUNTING WARNING SIGNS

The auditing literature can help an analyst, creditor, or investor to begin to identify red flags. In October 2002, the American Institute of Certified Public Accountants (AICPA) published the Statement on Auditing Standards (SAS) No. 99, *Consideration of Fraud in a Financial Statement Audit* (SAS-99). SAS-99 warns practitioners to be alert for the "fraud triangle," or three conditions that are generally present when fraud occurs:

1. *Incentives or pressures* exist that can lead to fraudulent financial reporting, such as pressure to meet debt covenants or analysts' earnings expectations.
2. *Opportunities* to commit fraud exist, such as poor internal control.
3. The individuals themselves are able to *rationalize* their behavior, such as a desire to get the company through a difficult time, after which they plan to undo their accounting games.

Management has a unique ability to perpetrate fraud because it frequently is in a position to directly or indirectly manipulate accounting records and present fraudulent financial information. Fraudulent financial reporting often involves management override of controls that otherwise may appear to be operating effectively. Management can either direct employees to perpetrate fraud or solicit help in carrying it out. In addition, management personnel at a component of the entity may be in a position to manipulate the accounting records of the component in a manner that causes a material misstatement in the consolidated financial statements of the entity. Management override of controls can occur in unpredictable ways.

SAS-99 provides examples of fraud risk factors for each of the conditions of the fraud triangle, as set forth in Exhibits 1, 2, and 3. While these were written with auditors in mind, analysts and others can easily use them as red flags. For example, as shown in Exhibit 3, one risk factor is disputes with auditors. Significant disputes must be reported to the company's audit committee and in SEC filings so that the audit committee and analysts can have access to information for this red flag.

It is important that we learn from previous scandals. In fact, there is much to be learned from reviewing prior accounting scandals. Such postmortem reviews can be very useful in identifying common accounting warning signs that can serve as contemporaneous red flags that help auditors, analysts, and others identify future fraud schemes. In response to the mandate of Section 704 of the SOA, the SEC conducted a study to examine the root causes of recent enforcement actions.[6] In addition, the AICPA and others have examined the frequency of

---

[6] SEC, *Report Pursuant to Section 704 of the Sarbanes-Oxley Act of 2002,* January 2003.

EXHIBIT 1	Risk Factors Related to Incentives/Pressures

► Financial stability or profitability is threatened by economic, industry, or entity operating conditions, such as (or as indicated by):

   ► high degree of competition or market saturation, accompanied by declining margins

   ► high vulnerability to rapid changes, such as changes in technology, product obsolescence, or interest rates

   ► significant declines in customer demand and increasing business failures in either the industry or overall economy

   ► operating losses making the threat of bankruptcy, foreclosure, or hostile takeover imminent

   ► recurring negative cash flows from operations or an inability to generate cash flows from operations while reporting earnings and earnings growth

   ► rapid growth or unusual profitability, especially compared to that of other companies in the same industry

   ► new accounting, statutory, or regulatory requirements

► Excessive pressure exists for management to meet the requirements or expectations of third parties due to the following:

   ► profitability or trend-level expectations of investment analysts, institutional investors, significant creditors, or other external parties (particularly expectations that are unduly aggressive or unrealistic), including expectations created by management in, for example, overly optimistic press releases or annual report messages

   ► need to obtain additional debt or equity financing to stay competitive— including financing of major research and development or capital expenditures

   ► marginal ability to meet exchange listing requirements or debt repayment or other debt covenant requirements

   ► perceived or real adverse effects of reporting poor financial results on significant pending transactions, such as business combinations or contract awards

► Information available indicates that management or the board of directors' personal financial situation is threatened by the entity's financial performance arising from the following:

   ► significant financial interests in the entity

   ► significant portions of their compensation (e.g., bonuses, stock options, and earn-out arrangements) being contingent upon achieving aggressive targets for stock price, operating results, financial position, or cash flow

   ► personal guarantees of debts of the entity

► There is excessive pressure on management or operating personnel to meet financial targets set up by the board of directors or management, including sales or profitability incentive goals.

Source: AICPA, SAS No. 99, Consideration of Fraud in a Financial Statement Audit, October 2002.

EXHIBIT 2	Risk Factors Related to Opportunities

► The nature of the industry or the entity's operations provides opportunities to engage in fraudulent financial reporting that can arise from the following:

  ► significant related-party transactions not in the ordinary course of business or with related entities not audited or audited by another firm

  ► a strong financial presence or ability to dominate a certain industry sector that allows the entity to dictate terms or conditions to suppliers or customers that may result in inappropriate or non-arm's-length transactions

  ► assets, liabilities, revenues, or expenses based on significant estimates that involve subjective judgments or uncertainties that are difficult to corroborate

  ► significant, unusual, or highly complex transactions, especially those close to period end that pose difficult "substance over form" questions

  ► significant operations located or conducted across international borders in jurisdictions where differing business environments and cultures exist

  ► significant bank accounts or subsidiary or branch operations in tax-haven jurisdictions for which there appear to be no clear business justification

► There is ineffective monitoring of management as a result of the following:

  ► domination of management by a single person or small group (in a non-owner-managed business) without compensating controls

  ► ineffective board of directors or audit committee oversight over the financial reporting process and internal control

► There is a complex or unstable organizational structure, as evidenced by the following:

  ► difficulty in determining the organization or individuals that have controlling interest in the entity

  ► overly complex organizational structure involving unusual legal entities or managerial lines of authority

  ► high turnover of senior management, counsel, or board members

► Internal control components are deficient as a result of the following:

  ► inadequate monitoring of controls, including automated controls and controls over interim financial reporting (when external reporting is required)

  ► high turnover rates or employment of ineffective accounting, internal audit, or information technology staff

  ► ineffective accounting and information systems, including situations involving reportable conditions

Source: AICPA, SAS No. 99, Consideration of Fraud in a Financial Statement Audit, October 2002.

financial statement restatements by SEC registrants in recent years. Those studies show a disturbing trend of steadily increasing restatements:

► 157 in 2000;

► 270 in 2001;

► 330 in 2002;

► more than 350 in 2003 (as of September 30).

EXHIBIT 3	Risk Factors Related to Attitudes/ Rationalizations

Risk factors reflective of attitudes/rationalizations by board members, management, or employees that allow them to engage in and/or justify fraudulent financial reporting may not be susceptible to observation by the auditor. Nevertheless, the auditor who becomes aware of the existence of such information should consider it in identifying the risks of material misstatement arising from fraudulent financial reporting. For example, auditors may become aware of the following information that may indicate a risk factor:

► ineffective communication, implementation, support, or enforcement of the entity's values or ethical standards by management or the communication of inappropriate values or ethical standards

► nonfinancial management's excessive participation in or preoccupation with the selection of accounting principles or the determination of significant estimates

► known history of violations of securities laws or other laws and regulations or claims against the entity, its senior management, or board members alleging fraud or violations of laws and regulations

► excessive interest by management in maintaining or increasing the entity's stock price or earnings trend

► a practice by management of committing to analysts, creditors, and other third parties to achieve aggressive or unrealistic forecasts

► management failing to correct known reportable conditions on a timely basis

► an interest by management in employing inappropriate means to minimize reported earnings for tax-motivated reasons

► recurring attempts by management to justify marginal or inappropriate accounting on the basis of materiality

► the relationship between management and the current or predecessor auditor is strained, as exhibited by the following:

   ► frequent disputes with the current or predecessor auditor on accounting, auditing, or reporting matters

   ► unreasonable demands on the auditor, such as unreasonable time constraints regarding the completion of the audit or the issuance of the auditor's report

   ► formal or informal restrictions on the auditor that inappropriately limit access to people or information or the ability to communicate effectively with the board of directors or audit committee

   ► domineering management behavior in dealing with the auditor, especially involving attempts to influence the scope of the auditor's work or the selection or continuance of personnel assigned to or consulted on the audit engagement

Source: AICPA, SAS No. 99, Consideration of Fraud in a Financial Statement Audit, October 2002.

The SEC study, *Report Pursuant to Section 704 of the Sarbanes-Oxley Act of 2002,* reviews 515 enforcement actions between July 31, 1997, and July 30, 2002. The study classified improper accounting practices into four categories:

1. Improper revenue recognition (126 cases), including reporting revenue in advance through techniques, such as holding the accounting period open, billing without shipping (bill and hold), fictitious revenue, and improper valuation of revenue.

2. Improper expense recognition (101 cases), including improper capitalization, overstating inventory, understating bad debts/loan losses, improper use of restructuring reserves, and failure to record asset impairments.

3. Improper accounting in connection with business combinations (23 cases).

4. Other accounting and reporting issues (130 cases), including inadequate disclosures, failure to disclose related party transactions, inappropriate accounting for nonmonetary and round-trip transactions, improper accounting for foreign payments in violation of the Foreign Corrupt Practices Act, improper use of off-balance sheet arrangements, and improper use of non-GAAP financial measures.

Based on these studies and a review of accounting scandals, several common accounting warning signs are apparent:

▶ **Aggressive revenue recognition**. More than half of the restatements and SEC enforcement cases involve inappropriate revenue recognition practices. Companies are required to disclose in the financial statement footnotes their revenue recognition practices. These disclosures and any other information available about a company's revenue recognition policies should be scrutinized. Aggressive techniques are those that result in the reporting of revenue earlier than may be appropriate (even though they may not technically violate GAAP). These include:

  ▶ Bill-and-hold sales arrangements (invoicing a sale without shipping merchandise);

  ▶ Sales-type leases (lessor reporting leases as a sale, particularly when the lessee is treating the transaction as an operating lease);

  ▶ Recording revenue at the time a contract is signed but before delivery of goods or services;

  ▶ Recording revenue prior to fulfilling all of the terms of contracts (e.g., installation or verification that computer equipment/software is functioning according to contract terms); and

  ▶ Using swaps or barter arrangements to generate sales.

▶ **Operating cash flow out of line with reported earnings**. If a company is reporting positive and perhaps growing earnings but operating cash flow is negative or declining, this could indicate accounting irregularities. A cash flow earnings index (operating cash flow divided by net income) is useful in identifying potential problems (a ratio consistently below 1.0 or a ratio that is declining from one period to the next).

▶ **Growth in revenues out of sync with economy, industry, or peer companies and with growth in receivables**. If a company is reporting high revenue growth that is inconsistent with other companies in its industry or peer group, this could be the result of superior management or products, but also could indicate that the analyst should pay close attention to the quality of these revenues. Particular attention should be paid when receivables are growing faster than revenues or days' receivables are increasing over time. This could indicate nonexistent sales.

▶ **Growth in inventory out of line with sales growth or days inventory increasing over time**. This could indicate problems with:

  ▶ inventory management;

  ▶ potentially obsolete inventory; or, in some cases

  ▶ inappropriate overstatement of inventory to increase gross and net profits.

▶ **Classification of nonoperating or nonrecurring income as revenue**. Some companies may attempt to move income items up the income statement to mask deteriorating revenues or show higher revenue growth.

▶ **Deferral of expenses**. The accounting policies of a company may indicate that current expenditures are being capitalized and deferred to future years through amortization or some other means (e.g., WorldCom). It is important to identify if this is a common industry practice or if the company is boosting current period profits. This often results in an increase in assets with terms, such as "deferred customer acquisition costs," so any assets that appear unusual also can be scrutinized to identify this activity.

▶ **Excessive use of operating leases by lessees**. While there are legitimate reasons for leasing assets and use of leasing does not violate GAAP, some companies structure equipment acquisitions in the form of operating leases to achieve desirable financial ratios (low debt ratios, higher return on assets). If a company is using these to a greater extent than its peers, this is a potential red flag. It is usually best to adjust the financial statements to see what the ratios would look like if the equipment had been purchased.

▶ **Classification of expenses or losses as extraordinary or nonrecurring**. While some companies try to move income up the income statement to report certain gains as revenues, the opposite occurs for expenses. If a company has "special" charges year after year, it is usually best to classify them as ordinary operating expenses for evaluation purposes.

▶ **LIFO liquidations**. For companies using the last-in, first-out (LIFO) method of inventory, they can get an artificial boost to earnings by running the inventory balance low at year-end. Unfortunately, this results in a higher tax bill. This red flag can be identified by reviewing the inventory footnotes for a decline in the LIFO reserve.

▶ **Gross margins or operating margins out of line with peer companies**. While indicative of good management and cost control, this also can indicate that accounting methods are being selected to improve financial results relative to peers. It is useful to compare the accounting methods in the footnotes to see if they are more or less conservative than peer companies. This also could indicate use of other techniques described previously, such as overstatement of inventory or capitalization of costs.

▶ **Use of long useful lives for depreciation and amortization**. These should be compared with other peer companies to see if they are reasonable.

▶ **Use of aggressive pension plan assumptions**. This can result in a misstatement of both earnings and financial leverage. Particularly watch for high discount rates (lowers pension expense and liability) and high expected return on plan assets (lowers pension expense).

- ▶ **Common use of fourth-quarter surprises.** Unusually high revenues or low expenses in the final quarter of the year that cannot be attributed to seasonality.

- ▶ **Equity method of accounting/frequent use of off-balance sheet SPEs or variable-interest entities.** Use of investments and entities that result in nonconsolidation, particularly if the arrangement is not normal in the industry.

- ▶ **Other off-balance sheet financing or guarantees.** Recent SEC rules require additional disclosure of these types of activities that should be scrutinized carefully.

The existence of these red flags (the risk factors) and accounting warning signs does not mean that the company is engaged in accounting fraud. The analyst should take care, however, when performing due diligence on companies with multiple red flags. If too many red flags exist, it is certainly appropriate to tread with caution and it may be best to walk away.

4 ACCOUNTING SCANDALS: ENRON

A number of red flags were available in the Enron accounting scandals.[7] We chose Enron to demonstrate warning signs to investors, creditors, and analysts. While Enron engaged in a variety of sophisticated accounting techniques, as documented by the bankruptcy examiner, and these techniques may have been difficult for an outsider to uncover, there were red flags before the collapse of the stock in November 2001. A number of warning signs were available in Enron's calendar year 2000 Form 10K, filed in early April 2001.

In Enron's case, operating cash flow exceeded net income; however, there were items of concern related to cash flow disclosures. Exhibit 4 contains an excerpt from the section on Financial Condition.[8]

Note that investing cash flows exceed operating cash flows by a wide margin in 1998 and 1999, requiring a need for heavy financing. Further, the large increase in operating cash flow for 2000 is in part explained by the "receipt of cash associated with the assumption of a contractual obligation," which sounds more like financing than operating activities. The importance of obtaining financing to support investing cash flows in excess of operating cash flows is apparent in several sections of the 10K, such as:[9]

> Enron is a party to certain financial contracts which contain provisions for early settlement in the event of a significant market price decline in which Enron's common stock falls below certain levels (prices ranging from $28.20 to $55.00 per share) or if the credit ratings for Enron's unsecured, senior long-term debt obligations fall below investment grade. The impact of this early settlement could include the issuance of additional shares of Enron common stock.

---

[7] A number of excellent books document other accounting scandals. *See, e.g.,* Charles W. Mulford and Eugene E. Comiskey, The Financial Numbers Game: Detecting Creative Accounting Practices (John Wiley & Sons, January 2002), and Howard M. Schilit, Financial Shenanigans, 2nd ed. (McGraw-Hill Trade, March 2002).

[8] Enron, Form 10K, Management's Discussion and Analysis, Financial Condition, 2000.

[9] *Id.*

EXHIBIT 4	Enron Disclosures of Cash Flows (Excerpt from the Annual Report Section on Financial Condition, 2000)		
(in Millions)	**2000**	**1999**	**1998**
Cash provided by (used in)			
Operating activities	$4,779	$1,228	$1,640
Investing activities	(4,264)	(3,507)	(3,965)
Financing activities	571	2,456	2,266

Net cash provided by operating activities increased $3,551 million in 2000, primarily reflecting decreases in working capital, positive operating results, and a receipt of cash associated with the assumption of a contractual obligation. Net cash provided by operating activities decreased $412 million in 1999, primarily reflecting increases in working capital and net assets from price risk management activities, partially offset by increased earnings and higher proceeds from sales of merchant assets and investments. The 1998 amount reflects positive operating cash flow from Enron's major business segments, proceeds from sales of interests in energy-related merchant assets, and cash from timing and other changes related to Enron's commodity portfolio, partially offset by new investments in merchant assets and investments.

Enron's senior unsecured long-term debt is currently rated BBB+ by Standard & Poor's Corporation and Fitch IBCA and Baa1 by Moody's Investor Service. Enron's continued investment grade status is critical to the success of its wholesale businesses as well as its ability to maintain adequate liquidity. Enron's management believes it will be able to maintain its credit rating.

Here we can see that Enron's management was under pressure to support both the stock price and debt rating, providing an incentive for earnings management behavior.

Enron used a market-value method for reporting revenues. In footnote 1 to the financial statements, Enron reported the use of market value for inventories, which it stated consists primarily of commodities. This is permitted under GAAP, and the amount of inventory on Enron's balance sheet was not large. Enron extended this method, however, to other types of contracts:[10]

Accounting for Price Risk Management. Enron engages in price risk management activities for both trading and nontrading purposes. Instruments utilized in connection with trading activities are accounted for using the mark-to-market method. Under the mark-to-market method of accounting, forwards, swaps, options, energy transportation contracts utilized for trading activities, and other instruments with third parties are reflected at fair value and are shown as "Assets and Liabilities from Price Risk Management Activities" in the Consolidated Balance Sheet. These activities also include the commodity risk management component embedded in energy outsourcing contracts. Unrealized gains and losses from newly originated contracts, contract restructurings and the impact of price

---

[10] *Id.* at n.1.

EXHIBIT 5	Enron 10K, 2000 (Summary of Footnote 19)	
Quarter	**1999 (Millions)**	**2000 (Millions)**
First	$7,632	$13,145
Second	9,672	16,886
Third	11,835	30,007
Fourth	10,973	40,751
Total	$40,112	$100,789

movements are recognized as "Other Revenues." Changes in the assets and liabilities from price risk management activities result primarily from changes in the valuation of the portfolio of contracts, newly originated transactions and the timing of settlement relative to the receipt of cash for certain contracts. The market prices used to value these transactions reflect management's best estimate considering various factors including closing exchange and over-the-counter quotations, time value and volatility factors underlying the commitments.

The use of the mark-to-market method for other types of contracts is somewhat unusual and presents ample opportunities to report revenues and income in any amount that management desires. The bankruptcy examiner's report notes that at least one analyst raised this issue as early as 1999. The analyst pointed out that Enron could recognize revenue from projects before they became operational, and this front-end loading of revenue and profits was limited only by Enron's "financial engineering skills."[11] The market-to-market gains were reported as other revenue on Enron's income statement as follows:

▶ 1998: $4,045 million
▶ 1999: $5,338 million
▶ 2000: $7,232 million

These amounts exceeded 10 percent of total revenues in 1998 and 1999. Further, without these "other revenues," operating income would have been negative. Enron's risk-management activities were reported as part of its wholesale services business segment, which comprised $94,906 million of revenue out of Enron's total revenue of $100,789 million. Adding to the red flags concerning revenue is the quarterly revenue reported in footnote 19 of Form 10K, as shown in Exhibit 5. In 2000, a disproportionate amount of revenues were reported in the third and fourth quarters, which is out of line with the seasonal trend.

Enron also engaged in securitizations of assets in its so-called price-risk-management business. In some cases, these resulted in sales to SPEs of assets with inflated values, which were really financing-type activities. In one case, Enron reported a gain on the sale of a portion of a joint venture with a major video rental company, when the technology for the venture did not exist.[12]

---

[11] Second Interim Report of Neal Batson, Court Appointed Examiner, US Bankruptcy Court, Southern District of New York, January 21, 2003, p. 26, discussing June 1999 report of JPMorgan.

[12] *Id* at pp. 29–31.

Enron's footnotes indicate that in some cases Enron effectively protected investors in these SPEs from risk:[13]

> Securitizations. From time to time, Enron sells interests in certain of its financial assets. Some of these sales are completed in securitizations, in which Enron concurrently enters into swaps associated with the underlying assets which limits the risks assumed by the purchaser. Such swaps are adjusted to fair value using quoted market prices, if available, or estimated fair value based on management's best estimate of the present value of future cash flow. These swaps are included in Price Risk Management activities above as equity investments. During 2000, gains from sales representing securitizations were $381 million and proceeds were $2,379 million ($545 million of the proceeds related to sales to Whitewing Associates, L.P.).

Assets related to price-risk-management activities when mark-to-market accounting was used increased drastically on the balance sheet during 2000 by $15,872 million. The scope and unusual accounting for these transactions should have been cause for concern.

Enron extended its mark-to-market accounting to equity-method investments. As noted previously, the equity method enables companies to keep assets and liabilities off of the balance sheet. Under the equity method of accounting, Enron should report its percentage share of GAAP income on its income statements. Enron, however, used the market-value method for some equity investees.[14]

> Investments in Unconsolidated Affiliates. Investments in unconsolidated affiliates are accounted for by the equity method, except for certain investments resulting from Enron's merchant investment activities which are included at market value in "Other Investments" in the Consolidated Balance Sheet.

Overall, Enron's disclosures of significant equity-method investment are another red flag, particularly since the income-sharing ratios differ from the voting interests and some entities were valued at fair value, as shown in Exhibit 6.[15]

Enron's net trade receivables on the balance sheet grew from $3,030 million in 1999 to $10,396 million in 2000. The allowance for doubtful accounts grew from $40 million to only $130 million, which calls into question the quality of the receivables and underlying revenues. Other transactions, such as barter of cable capacity, are also recorded, but probably the most disturbing disclosure is that about related-party transactions:

Related Party Transactions

In 2000 and 1999, Enron entered into transactions with limited partnerships (the Related Party) whose general partner's managing member is a senior officer of Enron. The limited partners of the Related Party are unrelated to Enron. Management believes that the terms of the transactions with the Related Party were reasonable compared to those which could have been negotiated with unrelated third parties.

---

[13] Enron, Form 10K, December 31, 2000, n.3.

[14] *Id.* at n.1.

[15] *Id.* at n.9.

EXHIBIT 6	Enron Annual Report, 2000 (Unconsolidated Equity Affiliates)

Enron's investment in and advances to unconsolidated affiliates that are accounted for by the equity method is as follows (in millions):

	Net Voting Interest[a]	December 31, 2000	December 31, 1999
Azurix Corp.	34%	$ 325	$ 762
Bridgeline Holdings	40%	229	—
Citrus Corp.	50%	530	480
Dabhol Power Company	50%	693	466
Joint Energy Development Investments L.P. (JEDI)[b]	50%	399	211
Joint Energy Development Investments II L.P. (JEDI II)[b]	50%	220	162
SK—Enron Co. Ltd.	50%	258	269
Transportadora de Gas del Sur S.A.	35%	479	452
Whitewing Associates, L.P.[b]	50%	558	662
Other		1,603	1,572
		$5,294	$5,036

[a] Certain investments have income sharing ratios that differ from Enron's voting interests.
[b] JEDI and JEDI II account for their investments at fair value. Whitewing accounts for certain of its investments at fair value. These affiliates held fair value investments totaling $1,823 million and $1,128 million, respectively, at December 31, 2000, and 1999.

In 2000, Enron entered into transactions with the Related Party to hedge certain merchant investments and other assets. As part of the transactions, Enron i) contributed to newly-formed entities (the Entities) assets valued at approximately $1.2 billion, including $150 million in Enron notes payable, 3.7 million restricted shares of outstanding Enron common stock and the right to receive up to 18.0 million shares of outstanding Enron common stock in March 2003 (subject to certain conditions) and ii) transferred to the Entities assets valued at approximately $309 million, including a $50 million note payable and an investment in an entity that indirectly holds warrants convertible into common stock of an Enron equity method investee. In return, Enron received economic interests in the Entities, $309 million in notes receivable, of which $259 million is recorded at Enron's carryover basis of zero, and a special distribution from the Entities in the form of $1.2 billion in notes receivable, subject to changes in the principal for amounts payable by Enron in connection with the execution of additional derivative instruments. Cash in these Entities of $172.6 million is invested in Enron demand notes. In addition, Enron paid $123 million to purchase share-settled options from the Entities on 21.7 million shares of Enron common stock. The Entities paid Enron $10.7 million to terminate the share-settled options on 14.6 million shares of Enron common stock outstanding. In late 2000,

Enron entered into share-settled collar arrangements with the Entities on 15.4 million shares of Enron common stock. Such arrangements will be accounted for as equity transactions when settled.

In 2000, Enron entered into derivative transactions with the Entities with a combined notional amount of approximately $2.1 billion to hedge certain merchant investments and other assets. Enron's notes receivable balance was reduced by $36 million as a result of premiums owed on derivative transactions. Enron recognized revenues of approximately $500 million related to the subsequent change in the market value of these derivatives, which offset market value changes of certain merchant investments and price risk management activities. In addition, Enron recognized $44.5 million and $14.1 million of interest income and interest expense, respectively, on the notes receivable from and payable to the Entities.

It appears that the assets of this related party consisted primarily of receivables from Enron and other Enron securities. Further, Enron engaged in billions of dollars of "derivatives" transactions with the related party. We have only included a portion of the related-party disclosure here. The footnotes go on to describe sales of assets to the related parties on which revenues and income were recognized. This type of self-dealing amounting to billions of dollars is what ultimately led to the collapse of Enron when potential write-downs related to these activities were announced in October 2001.

There were ample red flags outside of SEC filings. In May 2001, Enron's vice chairman resigned; in August 2001, the president resigned. The proxy statement shows that top management pay was largely from bonus and stock awards. The chairman of the board, for example, received more than 90 percent of his compensation from bonus and stock awards and only a small portion from salary.

ACCOUNTING SCANDALS: SUNBEAM   5

As noted previously, the most common improper accounting techniques have involved the recognition of revenue. Sunbeam provides a good case study in accelerating revenue and the accounting warning signs that indicate its presence. In July 1996, Sunbeam's board of directors hired Albert J. Dunlap to turn the company around. According to the SEC, Dunlap and his colleagues engaged in a variety of improper activities to achieve promised sales and earnings targets, as well as to increase the stock price for a sale of the company.[16] The SEC charged that Sunbeam in 1996, 1997, and the first quarter of 1998:

▶ created "cookie jar" reserves in 1996 to draw on in future years to improve earnings;

▶ recorded revenue from contingent sales;

▶ accelerated sales from later periods into the present quarter;

▶ used improper bill-and-hold transactions.

---

[16] SEC Release No. 2001-49, *SEC Sues Former CEO, CFO, Other Top Former Officers of Sunbeam Corporation in Massive Financial Fraud*, May 15, 2001.

EXHIBIT 7	Sunbeam (Relative Growth in Sales, Receivables, and Inventory)	
	1996	**1997**
Sales	−3.21%	18.69%
Inventory	−22.41%	57.89%
Receivables	−1.28%	38.47%

To uncover accounting warning signs, we examined financial data reported in Sunbeam's Form 10K for 1996 and 1997. As noted previously, increases in sales, receivables, and inventory should generally be in line. Exhibit 7 shows the relative growth in these amounts for Sunbeam for 1996 and 1997.

Note that for 1996, when the new management came in, sales declined slightly, as did receivables. This relationship would be expected. The larger decline in inventory is not usual. It is potentially the result of restructuring charges taken by new management in 1996, as shown in Exhibit 8.[17]

These are the cookie jar reserves referred to by the SEC. By expensing these in 1996, Sunbeam recorded a loss in the current year but set the stage for increasing income in future years. For example, if the cost of sales write-off included some write-offs of inventory, the company would have a higher profit when that inventory was sold in future years. The increase in revenues in 1997 is about 19 percent, but receivables increased by 38 percent, calling into question the quality of both the receivables and sales. Further, the increase in inventory is out of line at 58 percent, which could result from the prior year write-off and subsequent return to more normal levels. It could also indicate an overstatement of inventory to boost profits. The company reported an increase in gross margin in 1997 in spite of the need for a turnaround of the business.

Another indicator of problems with sales and cookie jar reserves is an examination of Sunbeam's cash flow compiled from Form 10K filings, as shown in Exhibit 9. The relationship of net income and operating cash flow in 1994 and 1995 is not unusual. In 1996, net income is a large negative number, yet operating cash flow is positive. The primary reason for this is the large noncash restructuring charges, which reduced 1996 income but not cash flow. In 1997, net income reached record levels for recent years, yet operating cash flow was

EXHIBIT 8	Sunbeam (Restructuring Charges, 1996)
	Pretax Dollar Amount
Restructuring, Impairment, and Other Costs	$154.9
Cost of Sales	92.3
Selling, General, and Administrative	42.5
Estimated Loss from Discontinued Operations	47.9
Total	**$337.6**

---

[17] Sunbeam, Form 10K, 1996, p. 14.

EXHIBIT 9	Sunbeam (Cash Flow Compiled from Form 10K Filings)			
Thousands of Dollars	**1994**	**1995**	**1996**	**1997**
Net Income	107,011	50,511	(228,262)	109,415
Operating Cash Flow	80,835	81,516	14,163	(8,249)

negative. This was primarily due to the increase in receivables and inventory. The difference would have been greater if not for a sale of receivables that increased operating cash flow by $59 million in 1997.[18]

An additional warning sign comes in a change in the company's revenue recognition policy footnote from 1996 to 1997:

▶ 1996: "The Company recognizes revenue from product sales at the time of shipment. Net sales is comprised of gross sales less provisions for expected customer returns, discounts, promotional allowances and cooperative advertising."

▶ 1997: "The Company recognizes revenues from product sales principally at the time of shipment to customers. In limited circumstances, at the customers' request, the Company may sell seasonal product on a bill and hold basis provided that the goods are completed, packaged and ready for shipment, such goods are segregated and the risks of ownership and legal title have passed to the customer. The amount of such bill and hold sales at December 29, 1997, was approximately 3 percent of consolidated revenues. Net sales is comprised of gross sales less provisions for expected customer returns, discounts, promotional allowances and cooperative advertising."

Further, it appears that the company reduced its bad-debt reserves relative to the increase in receivables. The allowance for doubtful accounts only increased about $1 million from 1996 to 1997, in spite of the large increase in receivables ($82 million). The company's bad-debt expense was about $23.4 million in 1996, but only 8.4 million in 1997.[19]

The company reports in its footnotes that its business is not seasonal, stating:[20]

On a consolidated basis, Sunbeam sales do not exhibit substantial seasonality. However, sales of outdoor cooking products are strongest in the first half of the year, while sales of appliances and personal care and comfort products are strongest in the second half of the year. In addition, sales of a number of the Company's products, including warming blankets, vaporizers, humidifiers and grills may be impacted by unseasonable weather conditions. During 1997, the Company initiated early buy programs for highly seasonal products such as grills and warming blankets in order to more levelize production and distribution activities.

---

[18] Sunbeam, Form 10K, 1997, p. 18.

[19] *Id.* at p. F-29.

[20] *Id.* at p. 6.

EXHIBIT 10	Sunbeam (Fourth-Quarter Sales Boost Suggests Aggressive Revenue Recognition)	
Percentage of Revenue in Each Quarter	**1996**	**1997**
First Quarter	23.34%	21.70%
Second Quarter	25.80%	24.62%
Third Quarter	23.55%	24.74%
Fourth Quarter	27.31%	28.94%

This provides a hint about the use of aggressive techniques to accelerate revenue into the fourth quarter. Exhibit 10 was compiled from quarterly disclosures in Sunbeam's 1996 and 1997 Form 10K filings. The increase in fourth-quarter revenues in a nonseasonal business is a warning sign.

6   BE ALERT FOR WARNING SIGNS

Studies of prior accounting scandals give us clues to evaluating other companies. While companies may look for more sophisticated methods to manage earnings, many of the recent scandals have involved the same techniques employed in the early years of U.S. capital markets. For example, in the 1930s, McKesson & Robbins created fictitious revenues, overstating receivables and inventory. In the 1980s, Crazy Eddie, Inc., engaged in much the same activities as did Sunbeam in the 1990s. Being alert for red flags that have occurred in past accounting scandals can help to identify potential problems early.

PRACTICE PROBLEMS FOR READING 40

1. Management may be under pressure to misstate earnings, and there are many incentives to do so. Which one of the following is *most likely not* an incentive to overreport earnings?

   A. To negotiate concessions from unions.

   B. To meet analysts' earnings expectations.

   C. To improve managements' incentive compensation.

2. Which of the following will *most likely* result in lower financial reporting quality?

   A. Engaging in fraudulent financial reporting.

   B. A low allowance for uncollectable accounts receivables.

   C. Selecting alternatives within accepted accounting principles that distort results to achieve a desired outcome.

3. Accordingly to Statement on Auditing Standards No. 99, *Considerations of Fraud in a Financial Statement Audit,* the three conditions that are generally present when fraud occurs (also known as the "fraud triangle") are incentives that can lead to fraudulent reporting, opportunities to commit fraud, and:

   A. poor firm financial performance.

   B. rationalizations to justify behavior.

   C. ineffective monitoring of management.

4. Accordingly to Statement on Auditing Standards No. 99, *Considerations of Fraud in a Financial Statement Audit,* which of the following statements is *most likely* an indication that excessive pressure exists on management to meet third parties' requirements or expectations?

   A. A marginal ability to meet debt repayments or covenants.

   B. Significant operations located across international borders.

   C. A complex organizational structure with unusual legal entities.

5. Accordingly to Statement on Auditing Standards No. 99, *Considerations of Fraud in a Financial Statement Audit,* which of the following risk factors *most likely* represents an opportunity for management to commit fraud?

   A. Revenue estimates that are based on subjective judgments.

   B. Excessive interest by management in increasing the stock price.

   C. Excessive competition in the industry resulting in declining margins.

6. Accordingly to Statement on Auditing Standards No. 99, *Considerations of Fraud in a Financial Statement Audit,* which of the following *most likely* indicates a risk factor reflective of managements' attitudes that may allow them to rationalize accounting fraud?

   A. New regulatory requirements.

   B. The dependence of managements' compensation upon meeting aggressive stock price targets.

   C. Managements' repeated attempts to justify inappropriate accounting on the basis of materiality.

7. An analyst is *most likely* to detect financial irregularities regarding a company's guarantee to others under an off-balance sheet arrangement through an examination of:

   A.   the financial disclosures.

   B.   the cash flow statement.

   C.   simultaneous examination of all the financial statements.

8. During the period between 31 July 1997 to 30 July 2002, the *most significant* category of enforcement actions by the SEC was improper:

   A.   revenue recognition.

   B.   accounting for business combinations.

   C.   accounting for foreign payments in violation of the Foreign Corrupt Practices Act.

9. Which of the following red flags were present in Enron's 2000 Form 10K?

   A.   "Cookie jar" reserves.

   B.   Recognizing revenue on a bill-and-hold basis.

   C.   Sales to SPEs under its price-risk management business.

10. Which of the following accounting warning signs was present at Sunbeam Corporation over the 1996 to 1997 period?

   A.   A decrease in gross margins.

   B.   Increasing revenues and decreasing receivables.

   C.   Positive operating cash flow that was out of line with its reported earnings.

11. The accounting warning signs of early revenue recognition for Sunbeam included:

   A.   significant sales to related parties.

   B.   the use of bill-and-hold transactions.

   C.   the use of marked-to-market method for contracts.

SOLUTIONS FOR READING 40

1. A is correct. Negotiating concessions from unions would likely be an incentive for management to *underreport* rather than *overreport* earnings.

2. C is correct. Selecting alternatives within GAAP that bias or distort reported results to achieve a desired outcome that differs from the economic structure of the transaction can result in lower financial reporting quality.

3. B is correct. In addition to incentives and opportunities for fraud, when it occurs, individuals typically rationalize their behavior, such as a desire to get the company through a difficult time, after which they plan to undo their accounting games.

4. A is correct. A marginal ability to meet debt repayments or covenants, if known, will likely result in some adverse actions by the holder of the debt as they try to secure their investment.

5. A is correct. The need for significant estimates and judgments in the preparation of financial statements provides opportunities to commit fraud.

6. C is correct. Recurring attempts by management to justify marginal or inappropriate accounting on the basis of materiality may indicate a risk factor reflective of attitudes by management that allow them to engage in fraudulent financial reporting.

7. A is correct. While some guarantees may not be reported on the balance sheet as a liability, such guarantees should be disclosed.

8. A is correct. As reported in the SEC study, *Report Pursuant to Section 704 of the Sarbanes-Oxley Act of 2002*, improper revenue recognition accounted for 126 of the 515 enforcement cases.

9. C is correct. The so-called price-risk-management business, in some cases, resulted in sales to SPEs of assets with inflated values which were really financing-type activities.

10. C is correct. There was a positive operating cash flow of $14.2 million compared to a net loss of $228.3 million in 1996. (See Exhibit 9.)

11. B is correct. Sunbeam used bill-and-hold transactions. Enron used the other two methods.

ACCOUNTING SHENANIGANS ON THE CASH FLOW STATEMENT

by Marc A. Siegel

LEARNING OUTCOME

The candidate should be able to analyze and discuss the following ways to manipulate the cash flow statement:

Mastery ☐

▶ stretching out payables;

▶ financing of payables;

▶ securitization of receivables; and

▶ using stock buybacks to offset dilution of earnings.

INTRODUCTION   1

CPAs typically focus on uncovering items that would impact the reported earnings or the balance sheet of a company. Knowing that investors use the balance sheet and the income statement to make investment decisions, companies sometimes engage in unusual or aggressive accounting practices in order to flatter their reported figures, especially earnings.

In the wake of recent high-profile scandals, the landscape is beginning to change. The majority of investors are now keenly aware of the concept of quality of earnings. It is now fairly common knowledge in the investment community that corporate management can in various ways manipulate earnings as reflected on the income statement. As a result, certain investors shun reported earnings and instead focus more attention on other metrics to evaluate the operational health of a business. Some metrics are non-GAAP, such as backlog, same-store

Note:
New rulings and/or pronouncements issued after the publication of the readings on financial reporting and analysis may cause some of the information in these readings to become dated. Candidates are expected to be familiar with the overall analytical framework contained in the study session readings, as well as the implications of alternative accounting methods for financial analysis and valuation, as provided in the assigned readings. Candidates are not responsible for changes that occur after the material was written.

Marc A. Siegel, CPA, is director of research of the Center for Financial Research & Analysis (www.cfraonline.com).

577

sales, and bookings. Many analysts have also embraced cash flow measurements. These analysts believe that, notwithstanding the fraud at Parmalat Finanziaria SpA, cash cannot be manipulated. But this, too, is a misconception. While quality of earnings is now a buzzword, it may be another 10 years before it is as widely understood that the quality of cash flows is just as valid a concern.

Most conceptual definitions of materiality include the concept of factors that affect an investment decision. As Wall Street analysts have lost faith in earnings-based metrics in the wake of Enron, WorldCom, and others, many have gravitated toward the cash flow statement. Companies are regularly evaluated on the basis of free cash flow yield and other measures of cash generation. The focus of audits must change in order to devote more attention to the cash flow statement; the users of financial statements demand it.

2   DISPELLING THE MYTH ABOUT CASH FLOWS

Investors' increased focus on the cash flow statement is beneficial. Analyzing the cash flow statement is integral to understanding a company's financial performance and position because it often provides a check to the quality of the earnings shown in the income statement. Certain accounting shenanigans can, however, either artificially boost reported operating cash flow or present unsustainable cash flows. The increased scrutiny has alerted people to how some companies mask declines in operating cash flow. For example, after WorldCom's reverse-engineering subterfuge, many have learned to look for excessive capitalization of cash expenditures. Others now scrutinize the cash flow statement for nonrecurring sources of cash, such as the receipt of an income tax refund. Certain complex situations can arise that cause reported cash flow from operations to appear higher than it would have otherwise.

As the investment community begins to focus on this metric, auditors should adapt as well. Auditors have little to work with, however; only SFAS 95, Statement of Cash Flows, specifically addresses the cash flow statement, and only 15 paragraphs within SFAS 95 discuss the appropriate categorization of cash expenditures within the cash flow statement. On the other hand, a plethora of authoritative guidance surrounds the calculation and presentation of earnings. The following examples show how companies can employ certain techniques (many of which are within GAAP) to show improved reported cash flows.

3   STRETCHING OUT PAYABLES

The simplest thing that companies can do to improve reported operating cash flow is to slow down the rate of payments to their vendors. Extending out vendors used to be interpreted as a sign that a company was beginning to struggle with its cash generation. Companies now "spin" this as a prudent cash-management strategy. Another consequence of this policy is to boost the reported growth in cash flows from operations. In other words, reported operating cash flows can be improved due solely to a change in policy to slow the payment rate to vendors. If analysts or investors expect the current period improvement to continue, they may be mistaken; vendors will eventually put increasing pressure on the company to pay more timely. Therefore, any benefit may be unsustainable or, at minimum, any year-over-year improvement in operating cash flow may be unsustainable.

EXHIBIT 1	General Electric: Days Sales Payable, Annual Trend			
Year Ending December 31,	2003	2002	2001	2000
Days Sales Payable (DSP)	53.1	51.5	47.7	40.2

The extension of payables can be identified by monitoring days sales in payables (DSP). This metric is calculated as the end-of-period accounts-payable balance divided by the cost of goods sold and multiplied by the number of days in the period. As DSP grow, operating cash flows are boosted. As Exhibit 1 shows, General Electric Corporation began stretching out its payables in 2001 and therefore received boosts to operating cash flow. The figures show, however, that while the company received a significant benefit to cash flows from operations in 2001, that benefit began to slow in subsequent periods, indicating that GE will probably be unable to continue to fuel growth in operating cash flow using this method. Interestingly, GE modified some executive compensation agreements to include cash flow from operations as a metric on which management is evaluated.

FINANCING OF PAYABLES

4

A more complicated version of stretching out payables is the financing of payables. This occurs when a company uses a third-party financial institution to pay the vendor in the current period, with the company then paying back the bank in a subsequent period. An arrangement between Delphi Corporation and General Electric Capital Corporation shows how seemingly innocuous ventures can affect operating cash flows. The arrangement allowed Delphi to finance its accounts payable through GE Capital. Specifically, GE Capital would pay Delphi's accounts payable each quarter. In return, Delphi would reimburse GE Capital the following quarter and pay a fee for the service.

This agreement provided Delphi with a means to change the timing of its operating cash flows. In the first quarter of the venture, Delphi did not have to expend any cash with respect to accounts payable to vendors. The impact to operating cash flows can be seen in Delphi's accounting for the agreement with GE Capital. After GE Capital paid the amounts due from Delphi to its vendors, Delphi reclassified these items from accounts payable to short-term loans due to GE Capital. Delphi did this in a quarter in which cash flows were seasonally strong and it had access to the accounts-receivable securitization facilities. The reclassification resulted in a decrease to operating cash flow in that quarter, and an increase in financing cash flows. In the subsequent quarter, when Delphi paid GE Capital, the cash outflow was accounted for as a financing activity because it was a repayment of a loan. Normally, cash expenditures for accounts payable are included in operating activities. Therefore, because of the arrangement, Delphi was able to manage the timing of reported operating cash flows each period because the timing and extent of the vendor financing (and offsetting receivables securitizations) was at the discretion of company management.

Another example shows that the accounting profession has been slow to adapt to these types of transactions. During 2004, three companies in the same industry—AutoZone, Pep Boys, and Advance Auto Parts—all financed payments to vendors through a third-party financial institution. In other words, similar to Delphi above, the financial institution paid the vendors on behalf of the respective automotive company. Subsequently, the company paid back the bank, thereby slowing down its rate of payment to the vendors and boosting its operating cash flow. While each of these auto parts companies used a similar process for financing payables, each reflected it differently on its cash flow statement. Interestingly, two of these companies had the same auditor. This disparity in accounting treatment made analysts' comparisons of free cash flow yields for each of these companies irrelevant.

The lesson here is that auditors should ask questions whenever financial intermediaries are inserted in between parties that usually have no financial intermediary.

5   SECURITIZATIONS OF RECEIVABLES

A particularly significant item that could obfuscate both true cash flows and earnings is the securitization of receivables. Securitizations of receivables occur when companies package their receivables, most often those that have a longer term and higher credit quality, and transfer them to a financial institution or a variable interest entity (VIE). If the VIE is bankruptcy-remote (i.e., creditors cannot attach the assets of the VIE if the VIE sponsor files for bankruptcy), then GAAP indicates that the receivables have effectively been sold and the proceeds received should be reflected in the operating section of the cash flow statement.

The issue relates to nonfinancial companies, which are in effect able to boost reported operating cash flow by deciding how much and when to securitize accounts receivable. To the extent that proceeds received from the securitizations increase, any reported improvement in cash flow from operations should be considered unsustainable, because there is a limit to how much a company can securitize.

An interesting corollary to the impact on operating cash flow from securitizations is the impact on earnings. Specifically, in many cases companies can report gains when long-term accounts receivable are securitized. This occurs because the book value of the receivables at the time they are securitized does not include all the future interest income that is to be earned, yet the entity purchasing the receivables will have to pay for that interest. As a result, in this simplified example, because the amount received for the receivables is greater than the book value, a gain is generated. The amount of the gain can be affected as well by a variety of management assumptions, such as the expected default rate of the receivables securitized, the expected prepayment rate, and the discount rate used.

GAAP does not prescribe where on the income statement this gain is to be recorded. While one company may report the gain on sale of the receivables within revenues (the most aggressive approach), another might record it as an offset to selling, general, or administrative expenses. Another company might report the gain "below the line" in other nonoperating income. Marriott Corporation used to record the gain on securitizations of timeshare notes receivables within revenue. Specifically, in 2000, Marriott reported a gain on sale of $20 million within revenue from the securitization of these receivables. In 2001, the company reflected a $40 million gain on sale within revenues, helping to boost both reported revenues growth and pretax earnings growth. In 2002, Marriott's gain on sale was $60 million, again included in revenues, which further fueled reported revenues and earnings growth. In 2003, however, the gain on sale was flat at $60 million. Perhaps coincidentally, Marriott changed its accounting for these gains in 2003 and reported the gains on sale for all years presented as a component of "other" (nonoperating) income.

TAX BENEFITS FROM STOCK OPTIONS 　　　6

Most companies currently follow Accounting Principles Board (APB) Opinion 25, which generally allows companies to avoid recording stock options as an expense when granted. Current IRS rules do not allow a company to take a deduction on its tax return when options are granted. At the time the stock option is exercised, however, the company is permitted to take a deduction on its tax return for that year reflecting the difference between the strike price and the market price of the option. On the external financial statements reported to investors, that deduction reduces (debits) taxes payable on the balance sheet, with the corresponding credit going to increase the equity section (additional paid-in-capital). Exhibit 2 shows the growing benefit that Cisco Corporation's operating cash flow received from this tax benefit.

| EXHIBIT 2 | Cisco Corporation's Statement of Cash Flows for Three Years Ended July 30, 2004 |

Cisco Corporation Consolidated Statements of Cash Flows

Years Ended	July 31, 2004	July 28, 2003	July 27, 2002
Cash flows from operating activities:			
Net income	$ 4,401	$ 3,578	$ 1,893
Adjustments to reconcile net income to net cash provided by operating activities:			
Cumulative effect of accounting change, net of tax	567	—	—
Depreciation and amortization	1,443	1,591	1,957
Provision for doubtful accounts	19	(59)	91
Provision for inventory	205	70	131
Deferred income taxes	552	(14)	(573)
Tax benefits from employee stock option plans	537	132	61
In-process research and development	3	4	53
Net (gains) losses and impairment charges on investments	(155)	520	1,127
Change in operating assets and liabilities:			
Accounts receivable	(488)	(125)	270
Inventories	(538)	(17)	673

(Exhibit continued on next page . . .)

EXHIBIT 2   (continued)

Prepaid expenses and other current assets	**(42)**	(61)	(28)
Accounts payable	**54**	35	(174)
Income taxes payable	**260**	(125)	389
Accrued compensation	**(7)**	104	307
Deferred revenue	**688**	(84)	678
Other accrued liabilities	**(378)**	(309)	(268)
Net cash provided by operating activities	**7,121**	5,240	6,587
Cash flows from investing activities:			
Purchases of short-term investments	**(12,206)**	(9,396)	(5,473)
Proceeds from sales and maturities of short-term investments	**13,570**	10,319	5,868
Purchases of investments	**(20,848)**	(18,063)	(15,760)
Proceeds from sales and maturities of investments	**20,757**	12,497	15,317
Purchases of restricted investments	—	—	(291)
Proceeds from sales and maturities of restricted investments	—	—	1,471
Acquisition of property and equipment	**(613)**	(717)	(2,641)
Acquisition of businesses, net of cash and cash equivalents	**(104)**	33	16
Change in lease receivables, net	**(159)**	79	380
Change in investments in privately held companies	**(13)**	(223)	(58)
Lease deposits	—	—	320
Purchase of minority interest of Cisco Systems, K.K. (Japan)	**(71)**	(59)	(115)
Other	**153**	94	159
Net cash provided by (used in) investing activities	**466**	(5,436)	(807)
Cash flows from financing activities:			
Issuance of common stock	**1,257**	578	655
Repurchase of common stock	**(9,080)**	(5,984)	(1,854)
Other	**33**	43	30
Net cash used in financing activities	**(7,790)**	(5,363)	(1,169)
Net (decrease) increase in cash and cash equivalents	**(203)**	(5,559)	4,611
Cash and cash equivalents, beginning of fiscal year	**3,925**	9,484	4,873
Cash and cash equivalents, end of fiscal year	**$ 3,722**	$ 3,925	$ 9,484

A question developed over how to classify this tax benefit (reduction of the taxes payable) on the cash flow statement. Some companies had been including it as an addback to net income in the operating section of the cash flow statement; others included it as a financing activity. FASB's Emerging Issues Task Force (EITF) Issue 00-15, released in July 2000, specifically indicated that a reduction in taxes payable should, if significant, be shown as a separate line item on the cash flow statement in the operating section (i.e., as a source of cash). [SFAS 123(R), Share-Based Payment, which requires options to be expensed, also relegates the excess tax benefit to the financing section of the cash flow statement. SFAS 123(R) takes effect for fiscal years beginning after June 15, 2005.] If the company does not disclose the tax benefit in the operating section or in the statement of changes in stockholders equity, then EITF 00-15 provided that the company should disclose any material amounts in the notes to the financial statements. The tax benefit is sometimes disclosed only in the annual statement of stockholders equity, rather than as a separate line item in the operating section of the cash flow statement for investors to analyze.

To the extent that operating cash flow is affected by a growing impact from the tax benefit on stock options, an investor should question whether the reported operating cash flow growth is in fact sustainable and is indicative of improved operations. In fact, the boost to operating cash flow is often greatest in a period when the stock price has increased. In other words, when the stock is performing well, more stock options are exercised, resulting in a higher tax benefit, which is included as a source of operating cash flow, implying improving growth of operating cash flow. Because companies in the technology sector use stock options to a higher degree, these entities may require more-careful scrutiny. (This is an issue, however, only when a company has taxable income and the taxes that it would have paid are avoided by this tax benefit. If a company has a loss, there is no boost to operating cash flow.) Analysts and investors should thoroughly review the cash flow statement, the stockholders equity statement, and the notes to the financial statements to glean the volume of options exercised during the period, and the related tax benefit included as a source of operating cash flow.

STOCK BUYBACKS TO OFFSET DILUTION　　7

A second issue related to stock options that affects reported cash flows is the buyback of company stock. A large number of companies have, in recent periods, been buying back their own stock on the open market. In a majority of cases, this activity is due to stock-option activity. Specifically, as stock prices generally increased in 2003, many of those who held stock options exercised those relatively cheap options. If companies did nothing to offset the larger number of outstanding shares that existed as a result of the growing number of in-the-money options, earnings per share would be negatively affected. Management of such companies therefore face a choice: They can allow earnings per share to be diluted by the growing share count or they can buy back company stock to offset that dilution.

From an accounting standpoint, the impact of options on the income statement is usually minimal, as discussed above. On the cash flow statement, the tax benefit of option exercises is a source of operating cash flow, benefiting those companies whose option exercises grow. Cash expended by a company for the buyback of corporate stock, however, is considered a financing activity on the cash flow statement. Consequently, as option exercises grow, so does the boost to operating cash flows for the tax benefit, but the outflows for stock buybacks to offset dilution of earnings are recorded in the financing section of the cash flow statement.

Interestingly, as a company's stock price rises, more options are generally exercised and the company must buy back more stock at the ever-higher market prices. In some cases, the entire amount of cash flow generated by operations in recent periods could be expended to buy back company stock to offset the dilution from in-the-money options. (See Cisco's cash flow statements in Exhibit 2.) Therefore, when analyzing the true earnings power of a company as measured by cash flows, it is important to consider the cash expended to buy back stock to offset dilution. This cash outflow should be subtracted from the operating cash flow in order to calculate the true free cash flow the company generated in the period in question.

8   OTHER MEANS

Many other means exist by which companies can influence the timing or the magnitude of reported free cash flows. Increasing the use of capital lease transactions as a way to acquire fixed assets obfuscates free cash flow because capital expenditures may be understated on a year-over-year basis. The accounting for outstanding checks and financing receivables are additional examples. In fact, General Motors and others have restated prior years' reported cash flow results in order to reflect the SEC's increased scrutiny of finance receivables. The restatement amounted to a downward revision of almost half of the reported operating cash flow.

Some companies have pointed analysts toward different metrics, such as operating cash flows, which are believed to be a more transparent indicator of a company's performance. The quality of a company's cash flows must be assessed, as highly motivated and intelligent management teams have created new ways to obfuscate the true picture of a company's operations. Auditors must be aware of the new focus by users of financial statements on operating cash flows, and adjust their work accordingly in order to provide the most value to the public.

PRACTICE PROBLEMS FOR READING 41

1. Which of the following financial statements are commonly misconceived by analysts as the *least* susceptible to manipulation?

    A. Balance sheet.

    B. Income statement.

    C. Cash flow statement.

2. Which of the following will be the *most likely* consequence if a company with constant sales slows down the rate of payments to its vendors?

    A. Cost of goods sold will increase.

    B. Days sales payable will increase.

    C. Accounts payables will decrease.

3. Gill Co. has cost of goods sold of $100 million with an accounts payable balance of $92 million at the end of the first quarter. In the second quarter, the company has cost of goods sold of $100 million with an accounts payable balance of $90 million at the end of the quarter. Assuming that the first and second quarters have 90 and 92 days respectively, which of the following is the most likely conclusion from this data? Gill Co. has:

    A. slowed its rate of payment to vendors.

    B. accelerated its rate of payment to vendors.

    C. maintained its rate of payment to vendors.

4. If a firm's annual days sales in payables (DSP) was 60 days, and the annual cost of goods sold is expected to increase by 22% (and the number of days remain constant), which of the following changes in the end-of-period accounts payable balance will *most likely* improve (increase) the operating cash flow?

    A. 24% decrease.

    B. 20% increase.

    C. 24% increase.

5. Analysts should identify instances where payments to vendors are financed through third-party financial institutions because there have been instances where the cash outflow for repayments to these institutions have been classified as a(n):

    A. financing activity.

    B. investing activity.

    C. operating cash flow activity.

6. The ability to improve operating cash flow through securitization activities is *most likely* problematic because:

    A. the benefit tends to understate reported earnings.

    B. no provisions are made for defaults or prepayments.

    C. the benefit is unsustainable on a consistent basis in the future.

7. If accounts receivable are securitized at a value that is more than book value, the *most* aggressive means of reporting the gain on the income statement is within:

   A. revenue.

   B. nonoperating income.

   C. selling, general, and administrative expenses.

8. What is *least likely* to cause a distortion in the true free cash flow of a company assuming that a large stock buyback has taken place to offset the dilutions from options exercised?

   A. Stock bought back on the open market.

   B. Classifying the cash expended to buy back stock as a financing activity.

   C. Classifying the tax benefit of option exercises as an operating cash flow.

9. Which of the following is the *least important* reason why an analyst should review the cash flow statement, the stockholders' equity statement, and the notes to the financial statements for information regarding stock options? To determine:

   A. the volume of options exercised in the period.

   B. the extent to which cash flows are affected by the tax benefit on stock options.

   C. whether the company follows APB No. 25 or SFAS 123(R) to account for stock options.

10. Which of the following is *least likely* to be a reason a company would securitize its accounts receivable? To increase:

   A. net income.

   B. operating cash flows.

   C. financing cash flows.

SOLUTIONS FOR READING 41

1. C is correct. Analysts typically focus on the reported earnings (income statement) or the balance sheet of a company believing that "cash cannot be manipulated."

2. B is correct. Days sales payable (DSP) is a metric that measures the extension of payables. The metric is calculated by taking the end-of-period accounts payables divided by the cost of goods sold, multiplied by the number of days in the period. As a company slows down payments, accounts payables increase while costs of goods sold and number of days in the period remain constant. Consequently, DSP will increase.

3. C is correct. The days sales payable (DSP) for both periods is the same at 82.8 days. Quarter 1: ($92 million / $100 million) × 90 days = 82.8 days and Quarter 2: ($90 million / $100 million) × 92 days = 82.8 days. [DSP = (Accounts payable / Costs of goods sold) × (Number of days)]

4. C is correct. If the accounts payable balance increases by 24%, the days sales payable (DSP) becomes 61 days = (60 days) × (1 + 24%) / (1 + 22%). Thus, the DSP has increased from 60 to 61 days, meaning the company has slowed its payments to vendors, increased accounts payable and thereby increased its operating cash flow. [DSP = (Accounts payable / Costs of goods sold) × (Number of days)].

5. A is correct. By classifying these repayments as a financing activity and not part of operating cash flow, management has changed the timing of its operating cash flows.

6. C is correct. The practice is unsustainable due to the limit on the amount of accounts receivable that can be securitized.

7. A is correct. This is the most aggressive approach for recording the gain on the income statement.

8. A is correct. Most stock buy backs occur in the open market and do not result in any distortion of cash flow.

9. C is correct. Since 2005, U.S. GAAP require all companies to follow SFAS 123(R) which requires options to be expensed.

10. C is correct. The securitization of accounts receivable results in an increase in operating cash flows (as receivables decrease), and they are frequently sold at a gain, which increases net income. Financing cash flows are not affected.

FINANCIAL STATEMENT ANALYSIS: APPLICATIONS

by Thomas R. Robinson, CFA, Jan Hendrik van Greuning, CFA, Elaine Henry, CFA, and Michael A. Broihahn, CFA

LEARNING OUTCOMES

The candidate should be able to:	Mastery
a. evaluate a company's past financial performance and explain how a company's strategy is reflected in past financial performance;	☐
b. prepare a basic projection of a company's future net income and cash flow;	☐
c. describe the role of financial statement analysis in assessing the credit quality of a potential debt investment;	☐
d. discuss the use of financial statement analysis in screening for potential equity investments;	☐
e. determine and justify appropriate analyst adjustments to a company's financial statements to facilitate comparison with another company.	☐

INTRODUCTION   1

This reading presents several important applications of financial statement analysis. Among the issues we will address are the following:

▶ What are the key questions to address in evaluating a company's past financial performance?

▶ How can an analyst approach forecasting a company's future net income and cash flow?

▶ How can financial statement analysis be used to evaluate the credit quality of a potential fixed-income investment?

Note:
New rulings and/or pronouncements issued after the publication of the readings on financial reporting and analysis may cause some of the information in these readings to become dated. Candidates are expected to be familiar with the overall analytical framework contained in the study session readings, as well as the implications of alternative accounting methods for financial analysis and valuation, as provided in the assigned readings. Candidates are not responsible for changes that occur after the material was written.

▶ How can financial statement analysis be used to screen for potential equity investments?

▶ How can differences in accounting methods affect financial ratio comparisons between companies, and what are some adjustments analysts make to reported financials in the interests of comparability?

Prior to undertaking any analysis, an analyst should explore the purpose and context of the analysis because purpose and context guide further decisions about the approach, the tools, the data sources, and the format in which to report results of the analysis, and also suggest which aspects of the analysis are most important. The analyst should then be able to formulate the key questions that the analysis must address. The questions will suggest the data the analyst needs to collect to objectively address the questions. The analyst then processes and analyzes the data to answer these questions. Conclusions and decisions based on the analysis are communicated in a format appropriate to the context, and follow-up is undertaken as required. Although this reading will not formally present applications as a series of steps, the process just described is generally applicable.

Section 2 describes the use of financial statement analysis to evaluate a company's past financial performance, and Section 3 describes basic approaches to projecting a company's future financial performance. Section 4 presents the use of financial statement analysis in assessing the credit quality of a potential debt investment. Section 5 concludes the survey of applications by describing the use of financial statement analysis in screening for potential equity investments. Analysts often encounter situations in which they must make adjustments to a company's reported financial results to increase their accuracy or comparability with the financials of other companies. Section 6 illustrates several typical types of analyst adjustments. A summary of the key points and practice problems in the CFA Institute multiple-choice format conclude the reading.

2   APPLICATION: EVALUATING PAST FINANCIAL PERFORMANCE

Analysts often analyze a company's past financial performance to determine the comparability of companies for a market-based valuation,[1] to provide a basis for a forward-looking analysis of the company, or to obtain information for evaluating the company's management.

---

[1] Stowe, Robinson, Pinto, and McLeavey (2002) describe market-based valuation as using price multiples ratios of a stock's market price to some measure of value per share (e.g., price-to-earnings ratios). Although the valuation method may be used independently of an analysis of a company's past financial performance, such an analysis may explain reasons for differences in companies' price multiples.

An evaluation of a company's past performance addresses not only *what* happened (i.e., how the company performed) but also *why* it happened—the causes behind the performance and how the performance reflects the company's strategy. Evaluative judgments assess whether the performance is better or worse, compared with a relevant benchmark such as the company's own historical performance, a competitor's performance, or market expectations. Some of the key analytical questions include:

▶ How have corporate measures of profitability, efficiency, liquidity, and solvency changed over the period being analyzed? Why?

▶ How do the level and trend in a company's profitability, efficiency, liquidity, and solvency compare with the corresponding results of other companies in the same industry? What explains any differences?

▶ What aspects of performance are critical for a company to successfully compete in its industry, and how did the company perform relative to those critical performance aspects?

▶ What are the company's business model and strategy, and how did they influence the company's performance as reflected, for example, in its sales growth, efficiency, and profitability?

Data available to answer these questions include the company's (and its competitors') financial statements, materials from the company's investor relations department, corporate press releases, and nonfinancial statement regulatory filings, such as proxies. Useful data also include industry information (e.g., from industry surveys, trade publications, and government sources), consumer information (e.g., from consumer satisfaction surveys), and information that is gathered by the analyst firsthand (e.g., through on-site visits). Processing the data will typically involve creating common-size financial statements, calculating financial ratios, and reviewing or calculating industry-specific metrics. Example 1 illustrates the effects of strategy on performance and the use of basic economic reasoning in interpreting results.

EXAMPLE 1

A Change in Strategy Reflected in a Change in Financial Performance

In analyzing the historical performance of Motorola (NYSE: MOT) as of the beginning of 2006, an analyst might refer to the information presented in Exhibit 1. Panel A presents selected data for Motorola from 2003 to 2005. Panel B presents an excerpt from the segment footnote, giving data for Motorola's mobile device business segment (the segment that manufactures and sells cellular phones). Panel C presents excerpts from the Management Discussion and Analysis (MD&A) describing the results of the segment.

Looking back to 1996, Motorola was the market leader with its Star-TAC cellular phone, but since 1998, Nokia had become the largest player in the global mobile phone market. "The mood inside Motorola was grim in early 2003. Nokia, whose 'candy bar' phone designs were all the rage had snatched Motorola's No. 1 worldwide market share" (*Fortune*, 12 June 2006, p. 126).

Following the arrival of new CEO Edward Zander at the end of 2003, Motorola radically revamped its strategy for new products: "Design leads, and engineering follows" (*Business Week*, 8 August 2005, p. 68). Motorola's strategy thereafter evolved to include a strong consumer marketing orientation to complement its historically strong technological position. The company launched 60 new products in 2004, an important one of which was the RAZR cellular phone with an ultra-thin profile that served to differentiate it from competitors' offerings. The successful introduction of new products in 2004 enabled the company to gain market share and increase profitability.

The changes at Motorola extended beyond the product strategy. An article in *Barron's* noted that in addition to the shift in product strategy, "Motorola has undergone a financial overhaul . . . The company has reduced the percentage of working capital to sales to less than 12 percent from about 22 percent, a sign of increased efficiency" (*Barron's* 25 July 2005, p. 23).

EXHIBIT 1	Selected Data for Motorola (Years Ended 31 December)

Panel A: Data for Motorola

(Dollars in Millions)	2005	2004	2003
Net sales	36,843	31,323	23,155
Gross margin	11,777	10,354	7,503
Operating earnings	4,696	3,132	1,273
Total assets	35,649	30,922	26,809

Panel B: Data for Motorola's Mobile Device Segment from Segment Footnote

(Dollars in Millions)	2005	2004	2003
Net sales	21,455	17,108	11,238
Operating earnings	2,198	1,728	511
Assets	7,548	5,442	3,900

Panel C: Excerpt from MD&A

2004 Our wireless handset business had a very strong year in 2004, reflected by a 53% increase in net sales, a 257% increase in operating earnings and increased market share. The increase in net sales was driven by an increase in unit shipments, which increased 39% in 2004 compared to 2003, and improved ASP [average selling price], which increased 15% in 2004 compared to 2003 . . . This increase in net sales, accompanied by process improvements in the supply chain and benefits from ongoing

(Exhibit continued on next page . . .)

> **EXHIBIT 1**   **(continued)**
>
> cost reduction activities resulted in increased gross margin, which drove the increase in overall operating earnings for the business. . . .
>
> **2005**   Net sales increased by $4.3 billion, or 25%, to $21.5 billion and operating earnings increased by 27% to $2.2 billion. We shipped 146 million handsets in 2005, up 40% from 2004 . . . The increase in unit shipments was attributed to an increase in the size of the total market and a gain in the segment's market share. The gain in market share reflected strong demand for GSM handsets and consumers' desire for the segment's compelling products that combine innovative style and leading technology. The segment had increased net sales in all regions of the world as a result of an improved product portfolio, strong market growth in emerging markets, and high replacement sales in more mature markets. Average selling price ("ASP") decreased approximately 10% compared to 2004, driven primarily by a higher percentage of lower-tier, lower-priced handsets in the overall sales mix.
>
> *Source*: Motorola's 2005 10-K filed 2 March 2006 and 2004 10-K filed 4 March 2005.

Using the information provided, address the following:

1. Typically, products that are differentiated either through recognizable brand names, proprietary technology, or both can be sold at a higher price than commodity products.

   A. In general, would the selling prices of differentiated products be more directly reflected in a company's operating profit margin or gross profit margin?

   B. Does Motorola's segment footnote (Panel B) reflect a successful differentiation strategy in its mobile devices business?

   C. Based on the excerpts from Motorola's MD&A (Panel C), compare and contrast the drivers of the growth in sales in Motorola's mobile device business in 2005 with the drivers in 2004.

2. The *Barron's* article refers to working capital as a percentage of sales, an indicator of efficiency.

   A. In general, what other ratios indicate a company's efficiency?

   B. Does the financial data for Motorola shown in this example reflect increased efficiency?

Solution to 1:

A. Sales of differentiated products at premium prices would generally be reflected more directly in the gross profit margin, increasing it, all else equal. The effect of premium pricing generally would also be reflected in a higher operating margin. However, expenditures on advertising and/or research in support of differentiating features mean that the effect on operating profit margins is often weaker than the effect on gross profit margins.

B. Although Motorola's segment footnote does not include information on gross margins by segment, it does include sufficient information for calculating operating profit margins, which should also be positively correlated with premium pricing. Dividing operating earnings by net sales, we find that operating margins in the mobile devices business increased from 4.5 percent ($511/11,238) in 2003 to 10.1 percent ($1,728/17,108) in 2004 and 10.2 percent ($2,198/21,455) in 2005. The data indicate successful results from the differentiation strategy in 2004, but no further meaningful improvement in 2005.

C. In both years, the MD&A attributes sales growth to an increase in Motorola's share of the handset market. The 2005 MD&A explicitly mentions growth of the total wireless handset market as another factor in sales growth for that year. The 2004 results benefited from both a 39 percent increase in units sales (compared with 2003) and a 15 percent increase in ASP. The sources of growth shifted somewhat from 2004 to 2005. Lower-tier, lower-price handsets became a larger part of Motorola's product mix in 2005, and ASP declined by 10 percent. Because sales grew by 25.4 percent [= (21,455 − 17,108)/17,108] in 2005, it is clear, however, that the growth in handset unit sales more than overcame the decline in ASP.

Solution to 2:

A. Other ratios that indicate a company's efficiency include asset turnover, fixed asset turnover, working capital turnover, receivables turnover, and inventory turnover. In addition, efficiency is indicated by days of inventory on hand, days of sales outstanding, and days of payables.

B. Yes, they do indicate increased efficiency. The data given permit the calculation of one efficiency ratio, total asset turnover. Motorola's total asset turnover improved from 0.864 (23,155/26,809) for 2003 to 1.013 (31,323/30,922) for 2004 to 1.033 (36,843/35,649) for 2005.

In calculating financial statement ratios, an analyst needs to be aware of the potential impact of companies reporting under different accounting standards, such as U.S. generally accepted accounting principles (U.S. GAAP) and international financial reporting standards (IFRS). Furthermore, even within a given set of accounting standards, companies still have discretion to choose among acceptable methods and also must make certain estimates even when applying the same method. Therefore, it may be useful to make selected adjustments to a company's financial statement data in order to facilitate comparisons with other companies or with the industry overall. Examples of such analyst adjustments will be discussed in Section 6. Example 2 illustrates how differences in accounting standards can affect financial ratio comparisons.

EXAMPLE 2

The Effect of U.S. GAAP versus IFRS on ROE Comparisons

Despite convergence between U.S. GAAP and IFRS, differences remain. Non-U.S. companies that use IFRS (or any other acceptable body of accounting standards) and file with the U.S. Securities and Exchange Commission (because their shares or depositary receipts based on their shares trade in the United States) are required to reconcile their net income and shareholders' equity accounts to U.S. GAAP. In comparing the historical performance of Motorola and Nokia, you have prepared Exhibit 2 to evaluate whether the difference in accounting standards affects the comparison of the two companies' return on equity (ROE). Panel A presents selected data for Motorola for 2004 and 2005, and Panel B presents data for Nokia under IFRS and under U.S. GAAP.[2]

EXHIBIT 2	Data for Motorola and Nokia for a ROE Calculation (Years Ended 31 December)

Panel A: Selected Data for Motorola

(Dollars in Millions)	2005	2004
U.S. GAAP		
Net income	4,599	2,191
Shareholders' equity	16,676	13,331

Panel B: Selected Data for Nokia Corporation

(Euros in Millions)	2005	2004
IFRS		
Net income	3,616	3,192
Shareholders' equity	12,155	14,231
U.S. GAAP		
Net income	3,582	3,343
Shareholders' equity	12,558	14,576

Sources: Motorola's 10-K and Nokia's 20-F, both filed 2 March 2006.

Does the difference in accounting standards affect the ROE comparison?

Solution: Motorola's return on average shareholders' equity for 2005 at 30.7 percent [net income of $4,599 divided by average shareholders' equity, calculated as ($16,676 + $13,331)/2] was higher than Nokia's, whether calculated under IFRS or U.S. GAAP. The difference in accounting standards does *not* affect the conclusion, though it does affect the magnitude of the difference in profitability. Under IFRS, Nokia's ROE was 27.4 percent [net income of €3,616 divided by

---

[2] In 2008, the Securities and Exchange Commission adopted rules to accept from foreign private issuers financial statements prepared in accordance with IFRS as issued by the IASB. These financial statements no longer need to be reconciled to U.S. GAAP.

average shareholders' equity, calculated as (€12,155+ €14,231)/2].
Under U.S. GAAP, Nokia's ROE was slightly lower at 26.4 percent [net
income of €3,582 divided by average shareholders' equity, calculated as
(€12,558 + €14,576)/2]. Results of the calculations are summarized in
the following table:

Panel A: Motorola

U.S. GAAP

Return on average shareholders' equity	30.7%

Panel B: Nokia Corporation

IFRS

Return on average shareholders' equity	27.4%

U.S. GAAP

Return on average shareholders' equity	26.4%

In Example 2, Nokia's ROE for 2005 under IFRS and U.S. GAAP differed only
slightly. In some cases, the effect of applying IFRS and U.S. GAAP on ROE and
other profitability ratios can be substantial. For example, the Swiss drug company
Novartis, which has undertaken historically numerous business combinations,
shows a return on average shareholders' equity of 19.0 percent in 2005 under IFRS
compared with 13.7 percent under U.S. GAAP; the differences are largely due to
differences in accounting for business combinations.[3] Research indicates that for
most non-U.S. companies filing with the U.S. Securities and Exchange Commission (SEC), differences between U.S. GAAP and home-country GAAP net income
average around 1 to 2 percent of market value of equity, but with large variation.[4]

Comparison of the levels and trends in the company's performance provide
information for statements about *how* the company performed. The company's
management presents its view about causes underlying its performance in the
MD&A section of its annual report and during periodic conference calls. To gain
additional understanding on the causes underlying a company's performance, an
analyst can review industry information or seek additional sources of information.

The results of an analysis of past performance provide a basis for reaching
conclusions and making recommendations. For example, an analysis undertaken
as the basis for a forward-looking study might result in conclusions about whether
a company's future performance is likely to reflect continuation of recent historical trends or not. As another example, an analysis to support a market-based valuation of a company might focus on whether the company's better (worse)
profitability and growth outlook compared with the peer group median justify its
relatively high (low) valuation, as judged by market multiples such as price-to-
earnings ratio (P/E), market-to-book ratio (MV/BV), and total invested capital to

---

[3] Henry and Yang (2006).

[4] Pownall and Schipper (1999). "Home country GAAP" can refer to IFRS in addition to non-IFRS
GAAP other than U.S. GAAP.

earnings before interest, taxes, depreciation, and amortization (TIC/EBITDA).[5] As another example, an analysis undertaken as a component of an evaluation of the company's management might result in conclusions about whether the company has grown as fast as another company, or as the industry overall, and whether the company has maintained profitability while growing.

APPLICATION: PROJECTING FUTURE FINANCIAL PERFORMANCE

3

In some cases, evaluating a company's past performance provides a basis for forward-looking analyses. An evaluation of a company's environment and history may persuade the analyst that historical data constitute a valid basis for such analyses and that the analyst's projections may be based on the continuance of past trends, perhaps with some adjustments. Alternatively, in the case of a major acquisition or divestiture, or for a start-up company, or for a company operating in a volatile industry, past performance may be less relevant to future performance.

Projections of future financial performance are used in determining the value of a company or of its equity component. Projections of future financial performance are also used in credit analysis—particularly in project finance or acquisition finance—to determine whether a company's cash flows will be adequate to pay the interest and principal on its debt and to evaluate whether a company will likely be in compliance with its financial covenants.

Sources of data for analysts' projections include some or all of the following: the company's projections; the company's previous financial statements; industry structure and outlook; and macroeconomic forecasts.

Projections of a company's near-term performance may be used as an input to market-based valuation (valuation based on price multiples). Such projections may involve projecting next years' sales and using the common-size income statement to project major expense items or particular margins on sales (e.g., gross profit margin or operating profit margin). More complex projections of a company's future performance involve developing a more detailed analysis of components across multiple periods—for example, projections of sales and gross margin by product line, projection of operating expenses based on historical patterns, and projection of interest expense based on requisite debt funding, interest rates, and applicable taxes. Furthermore, a projection should include sensitivity analyses related to the major assumptions.

3.1 Projecting Performance: An Input to Market-Based Valuation

One application of financial statement analysis involves projecting a company's near-term performance as an input to market-based valuation. For example, one might project a company's sales and profit margin to estimate earnings per share (EPS) and then apply a projected P/E to establish a target price for a company's stock.

Analysts often take a top-down approach to projecting a company's sales.[6] First, industry sales are projected based on their historical relation with some

---

[5] **Total invested capital** is the sum of market value of common equity, book value of preferred equity, and face value of debt.

[6] The discussion in this paragraph is indebted to Benninga and Sarig (1997).

macroeconomic indicator or indicators such as real gross domestic product. In researching the automobile industry, for example, the analyst may find that the industry's annual domestic unit automobile sales (numbers of cars sold in domestic markets) bears a relation to annual changes in real GDP. Regression analysis is often used in establishing the parameters of such relations. Other factors in projecting sales may include consumer income or tastes, technological developments, and the availability of substitute products or services. After industry sales are projected, a company's market share is projected. Company-level market share projections may be based on historical market share and a forward-looking assessment of the company's competitive position. The company's sales are then estimated as its projected market share multiplied by projected total industry sales.

After developing a sales forecast for a company, an analyst can choose among various methods for forecasting income and cash flow. One decision is the level of detail in forecasts. For example, separate forecasts may be made for individual expense items or for more aggregated expense items, such as total operating expenses. Rather than stating a forecast in terms of expenses, the forecast might be stated in terms of a forecasted profit margin (gross, operating, or net). The net profit margin, in contrast to the gross or operating profit margins, is affected by financial leverage and tax rates, which are subject to managerial and legal/regulatory revisions; therefore, historical data may sometimes be more relevant for projecting gross or operating margins. Whatever the margin used, the forecasted amount of profit for a given period is the product of the forecasted amount of sales and the forecast of the selected profit margin.

As Example 3 illustrates, for relatively mature companies operating in non-volatile product markets, historical information on operating profit margins can provide a useful starting point for forecasting future operating profits (at least over short forecasting horizons). For a new or relatively volatile business, or one with significant fixed costs (which can magnify the volatility of operating margins), historical operating profit margins are typically less reliable for projecting future margins.

EXAMPLE 3

Using Historical Operating Profit Margins to Forecast Operating Profit

One approach to projecting operating profit is to determine a company's average operating profit margin over the previous three years and apply that margin to a forecast of the company's sales. Consider the following three companies:

▶ Johnson & Johnson (JNJ). This U.S. health care conglomerate founded in 1887 had 2005 sales of around $50.5 billion from its three main businesses: pharmaceuticals, medical devices and diagnostics, and consumer products.

▶ BHP Billiton (BHP). This company, with group headquarters in Australia and secondary headquarters in London, is the world's largest natural resources company, reporting revenue of approximately US$32 billion for the fiscal year ended June 2006. The company mines, processes, and markets coal, copper, nickel, iron, bauxite, and silver and also has substantial petroleum operations.

► TomTom. This Dutch company, which went public on the Amsterdam Stock Exchange in 2005, provides personal navigation products and services in Europe, North America, and Australia. The company's revenues for 2005 were €720 million, an increase of 275 percent from 2004 and more than 18 times greater than revenues in 2003.

Address the following problems:

1. For each of the three companies given, state and justify whether the suggested forecasting method would be a reasonable starting point for projecting future operating profit.

2. Assume the suggested approach was applied to each of the three companies based on the realized level of sales provided. Consider the following additional information:

   ► JNJ: For the three years prior to 2005, JNJ's average operating profit margin was approximately 26.6 percent. The company's actual operating profit for 2005 was $13.4 billion.

   ► BHP: For the three years prior to the year ending June 2006, BHP's average operating profit margin was approximately 22.5 percent, based on data from Thompson Financial. The company's actual operating profit for the year ended June 2006, excluding profits from a jointly controlled entity, was $9.7 billion.

   ► TomTom: Over the three years prior to 2005, TomTom's average operating profit margin was approximately 23.5 percent. The company's actual operating profit for 2005 was €195 million.

   Using the additional information given, state and justify whether actual results supported the usefulness of the stable operating margin assumption.

Solution to 1:

JNJ. Because JNJ is an established company with diversified operations across relatively stable businesses, the suggested approach to projecting the company's operating profit might provide a reasonable starting point.

BHP. Because commodity prices tend to be volatile and the mining industry is relatively capital intensive, the suggested approach to projecting BHP's operating profit would probably not have provided a useful starting point.

TomTom. A new company such as TomTom has little operating history on which to judge stability of margins. Two aspects about the company suggest that the broad approach to projecting operating profit would not be a useful starting point for TomTom. First, the company operates in an area of rapid technological change, and second, the company appears to be in a period of rapid growth.

Solution to 2:

JNJ. JNJ's actual operating profit margin for 2005 was 26.5 percent ($13.4 billion divided by sales of $50.5 billion), which is very close to the company's three-year average operating profit margin of approximately 26.6 percent. If the average operating profit margin had been applied to perfectly forecasted 2005 sales to obtain forecasted operating profit, the forecasting error would have been minimal.

BHP. BHP's actual operating profit margin for the year ended June 2006 was 30.3 percent ($9.7 billion divided by sales of $32 billion). If the company's average profit margin of 22.5 percent had been applied to perfectly forecasted sales, the forecasted operating profit would have been approximately $7.2 billion, 26 percent less than actual operating profit.

TomTom. TomTom's actual operating profit margin for 2005 was 27.1 percent (€195 million divided by sales of €720 million). If the average profit margin of 23.5 percent had been applied to perfectly forecasted sales, the forecasted operating profit would have been approximately €169 million, or 13 percent below TomTom's actual operating profit.

Although prior years' profit margins can provide a useful starting point in projections for companies with relatively stable business, the underlying data should, nonetheless, be examined to identify items that are not likely to reoccur. Such nonrecurring (i.e., transitory) items should be removed from computations of any profit amount or profit margin that will be used in projections. Example 4 illustrates this principle.

EXAMPLE 4

Issues in Forecasting

In reviewing Motorola's 2005 performance, an analyst notes the following items. What is the relevance of each item in forecasting the item given in italics?

1. Of Motorola's $4,696 million of operating earnings, $458 million was from other income, primarily payment received from a former customer that had defaulted several years ago on obligations to Motorola. *Operating earnings.*
2. Motorola's income included $1.9 billion from gains on sales of investments. Investments at the end of 2005 were $1.6 billion compared with $3.2 billion at the end of 2004. *Net income.*
3. Motorola's effective tax rate for 2005 was 29.5 percent compared with 32.6 percent for each of the previous two years. A main reason

for the lower effective tax rate was a one-time tax incentive for U.S. multinational companies to repatriate accumulated earnings from their foreign subsidiaries. *Net income.*

4. Motorola had losses from discontinued operations of $21 million and $659 million for the years 2005 and 2004, respectively. *Net income.*

Solution to 1: This item related to a specific former customer and is not an ongoing source of operating earnings. Therefore, it is not relevant in forecasting operating earnings.

Solution to 2: Gains on sales of investments are not a core part of Motorola's business, and the sale in 2005 halved the amount of Motorola's investments. Thus, this item should not be viewed as an ongoing source of earnings, and it is, therefore, not relevant to forecasting net income.

Solution to 3: The lower tax rate does not appear to reflect an ongoing change and, therefore, a projection would probably consider the previous years' higher rate as more representative and more useful in forecasting net income.

Solution to 4: Results of discontinued items should not be included either when assessing past performance or when forecasting future net income.

In general, when earnings projections are used as a basis for market-based valuations, an analyst will make appropriate allowance for transitory components of past earnings.

3.2 Projecting Multiple-Period Performance

Projections of future financial performance over multiple periods are needed in valuation models that estimate the value of a company or its equity by discounting future cash flows. The value of a company or its equity developed in this way can then be compared with the market price as a basis for investment decisions.

Projections of future performance are also used for credit analysis, in which case conclusions include an assessment of a borrower's ability to repay interest and principal of debt obligations. Investment recommendations depend on the needs and objectives of the client and on an evaluation of the risk of the investment relative to its expected return—both of which are a function of the terms of the debt obligation itself as well as financial market conditions. Terms of the debt obligation include amount, interest rate, maturity, financial covenants, and collateral.

Example 5 presents an elementary illustration of net income and cash flow forecasting to illustrate a format for analysis and some basic principles. In Example 5, assumptions are shown first and the period-by-period abbreviated financial statement that results from the assumption is shown below.

Depending on the use of the forecast, an analyst may choose to compute further, specific cash flow metrics. For example, free cash flow to equity, used in discounted cash flow approaches to equity valuation, can be found as net income adjusted for noncash items, minus investment in net working capital and in net fixed assets, plus net borrowing.[7]

EXAMPLE 5

Basic Example of Financial Forecasting

Assume a company is formed with $100 of equity capital, all of which is immediately invested in working capital. Assumptions are as follows:

Dividends	Nondividend paying
First-year sales	$100
Sales growth	10% per annum
Cost of goods sold/sales	20%
Operating expense/sales	70%
Interest income rate	5%
Tax rate	30%
Working capital as percent of sales	90%

Based on the above information, forecast the company's net income and cash flow for five years.

Solution: Exhibit 3 below shows the net income forecasts in Line 7 and cash flow forecasts ("change in cash") in Line 18.

EXHIBIT 3   Basic Financial Forecasting

	Time					
	0	1	2	3	4	5
1) Sales		100.0	110.0	121.0	133.1	146.4
2) Cost of goods sold		(20.0)	(22.0)	(24.2)	(26.6)	(29.3)
3) Operating expenses		(70.0)	(77.0)	(84.7)	(93.2)	(102.5)
4) Interest income		0.0	0.9	0.8	0.8	0.7
5) Income before tax		10.0	11.9	12.9	14.1	15.3
6) Taxes		(3.0)	(3.6)	(3.9)	(4.2)	(4.6)
7) Net income		7.0	8.3	9.0	9.9	10.7
8) Cash/Borrowing	0.0	17.0	16.3	15.4	14.4	13.1
9) Working capital (non cash)	100.0	90.0	99.0	108.9	119.8	131.8
10) Total assets	100.0	107.0	115.3	124.3	134.2	144.9
11) Liabilities	0.0	0.0	0.0	0.0	0.0	0.0
12) Equity	100.0	107.0	115.3	124.3	134.2	144.9
13) Total liabilities + Equity	100.0	107.0	115.3	124.3	134.2	144.9
14) Net income		7.0	8.3	9.0	9.9	10.7

(Exhibit continued on next page . . .)

---

[7] See Stowe et al. (2002) for further information.

EXHIBIT 3	(continued)					
		Time				
	0	**1**	**2**	**3**	**4**	**5**
15) Plus noncash items		0.0	0.0	0.0	0.0	0.0
16) Less: investment in working capital		−10.0	9.0	9.9	10.9	12.0
17) Less: investment in fixed capital		0.0	0.0	0.0	0.0	0.0
18) Change in cash		17.0	−0.7	−0.9	−1.0	−1.3
19) Beginning cash		0.0	17.0	16.3	15.4	14.4
20) Ending cash		17.0	16.3	15.4	14.4	13.1

To explain the exhibit, at time zero, the company is formed with $100 of equity capital (Line 12). All of the company's capital is assumed to be immediately invested in working capital (Line 9). In future periods, because it is assumed that no dividends are paid, equity increases each year by the amount of net income. Future periods' working capital is assumed to be 90 percent of annual sales.

Sales are assumed to be $100 in the first period and to grow at a constant rate of 10 percent per annum (Line 1). The cost of goods sold is assumed constant at 20 percent of sales (Line 2), so the gross profit margin is 80 percent. Operating expenses are assumed to be 70 percent of sales each year (Line 3). Interest income (Line 4) is calculated as 5 percent of the beginning cash/borrowing balance (Line 8) and is an income item when there is a cash balance, as it is in this example. (If available cash is inadequate to cover required cash outflows, the shortfall is presumed to be covered by borrowing. This borrowing would be shown as a negative balance on Line 8 and an associated interest expense on Line 4. Alternatively, a forecast can be presented with separate lines for cash and borrowing.) Taxes of 30 percent are deducted to obtain net income (Line 7).

To calculate each period's cash flow, we begin with net income (Line 7 = Line 14), add back any noncash items such as depreciation (Line 15), deduct investment in working capital (Line 16), and deduct investment in fixed capital (Line 17).[8] In this simple example, we are assuming that the company does not invest in any fixed capital (long-term assets) but, rather, rents furnished office space. Therefore, there is no depreciation, and thus noncash items are zero. Each period's change in cash (Line 18) is added to the beginning cash balance (Line 19) to obtain the ending cash balance (Line 20 = Line 8).

Example 5 is simplified to demonstrate some principles of forecasting. In practice, each aspect of a forecast presents substantial challenges. Sales forecasts may be very detailed, with separate forecasts for each year of each product line, and/or each geographical or business segment. Sales forecasts may be based on past results (for relative stable businesses), management forecasts, industry studies,

---

[8] Working capital represents funds that must be invested in the daily operations of a business such as to carry inventory and accounts receivable. The term "investment" in this context means "the addition to" or "increase." The "investment in fixed capital" is also referred to as "capital expenditure" or "capex." See Stowe et al. (2002), Chapter 3, for further information.

and/or macroeconomic forecasts. Similarly, gross margins may be detailed and may be based on past results or forecast relationships. Expenses other than cost of goods sold may be broken down into more detailed line items, each of which may be forecasted based on its relationship with sales (if variable) or on its historical levels. Working capital requirements may be estimated as a proportion of the amount of sales (as in the example) or the change in sales, or as a compilation of specific forecasts for inventory, receivables, and payables. Most forecasts will involve some investment in fixed assets, in which case depreciation amounts affect taxable income and net income but not cash flow. Example 5 makes the simplifying assumption that interest is paid on the beginning-of-year cash balance.

Example 5 developed a series of point estimates for future net income and cash flow. In practice, forecasting generally includes an analysis of the risk in forecasts—in this case, an assessment of the impact on income and cash flow if the realized values of variables differ significantly from the assumptions used in the base case or if actual sales are much different from forecasts. Quantifying the risk in forecasts requires an analysis of the economics of the company's businesses and expense structures, and the potential impact of events affecting the company, the industry, and the economy in general. That investigation done, the analyst can assess risk using scenario analysis or Monte Carlo simulation. Scenario analysis involves specifying assumptions that differ from those included as the base case assumptions. In the above example, the projections of net income and cash flow could be recast using a more pessimistic scenario, with assumptions changed to reflect slower sales growth and higher costs. A Monte Carlo simulation involves specifying probability distributions of values for variables and random sampling from those distributions. In the above analysis, the projections would be repeatedly recast using randomly selected values for the drivers of net income and cash flow, thus permitting the analyst to evaluate the range of results possible and the probability of simulating the possible actual outcomes.

An understanding of financial statements and ratios can enable an analyst to make more detailed projections of income statement, balance sheet, and statement of cash flows items. For example, an analyst may collect information on normal inventory and receivables turnover ratios and use this information to forecast accounts receivable, inventory, and cash flows based on sales projections rather than use a composite working capital investment assumption, as in the above example.

As the analyst makes detailed forecasts, he or she must ensure that they are mutually consistent. For instance, in Example 6, the analyst's forecast concerning days of sales outstanding (which is an estimate of the average time to collect payment from sales made on credit) should flow from a model of the company that yields a forecast of the change in the average accounts receivable balance given as the solution to the problem. Otherwise, predicted days of sales outstanding and accounts receivable would not be mutually consistent.

EXAMPLE 6

Consistency of Forecasts[9]

Brown Corporation had an average days-of-sales-outstanding (DSO) period of 19 days in 2005. An analyst thinks that Brown's DSO will decline to match the industry average of 15 days in 2006. Total sales (all on credit) in 2005 were $300 million, and Brown expects total sales (all

---

[9] Adapted from a past CFA Institute examination question.

on credit) to increase to \$320 million in 2006. To achieve the lower DSO, the change in the average accounts receivable balance from 2005 to 2006 that must occur is *closest* to:

A. −\$3.51 million.

B. −\$2.46 million.

C. \$2.46 million.

D. \$3.51 million.

Solution: B is correct. The first step is to calculate **accounts receivable turnover** from the DSO collection period. Receivable turnover equals 365/19 (DSO) = 19.2 for 2005, and 365/15 = 24.3 in 2006. Next, we use the fact that the average accounts receivable balance equals sales/receivable turnover to conclude that for 2005, average accounts receivable was \$300,000,000/19.2 = \$15,625,000, and for 2006, it must equal \$320,000,000/24.3 = \$13,168,724. The difference is a reduction in receivables of \$2,456,276.

The next section illustrates the application of financial statement analysis to credit risk analysis.

APPLICATION: ASSESSING CREDIT RISK

4

Credit risk is the risk of loss caused by a counterparty's or debtor's failure to make a promised payment. For example, credit risk with respect to a bond is the risk that the obligor (the issuer of the bond) is not able to pay interest and principal according to the terms of the bond indenture (contract). **Credit analysis** is the evaluation of credit risk. Credit analysis may relate to the credit risk of an obligor in a particular transaction or to an obligor's overall credit-worthiness.

In assessing an obligor's overall credit-worthiness, one general approach is credit scoring, a statistical analysis of the determinants of credit default. As noted above, credit analysis for specific types of debt (e.g., acquisition financing and other highly leveraged financing) typically involves projections of period-by-period cash flows.

Whatever the techniques adopted, the analytical focus of credit analysis is on debt-paying ability. Unlike payments to equity investors, payments to debt investors are limited by the agreed contractual interest. If a company experiences financial success, its debt becomes less risky, but its success does not increase the amount of payments to its debtholders. In contrast, if a company experiences financial distress, it may be unable to pay interest and principal on its debt obligations. Thus, credit analysis has a special concern with the sensitivity of debt-paying ability to adverse events and economic conditions—cases in which the creditor's promised returns may be most at risk. Because those returns are generally paid in cash, credit analysis usually focuses on cash flow rather than accrual-income returns. Typically, credit analysts use return measures related to operating cash flow because it represents cash generated internally, which is available to pay creditors.

These themes are reflected in Example 7, which illustrates the application of four groups of quantitative factors in credit analysis to an industry group: scale and diversification, tolerance for leverage, operational efficiency, and margin stability. Scale and diversification relate to a company's sensitivity to adverse events and economic conditions as well as to other factors—such as market leadership, purchasing power with suppliers, and access to capital markets—that can affect debt-paying ability. Financial policies or tolerance for leverage relates to the obligor's ability to service its indebtedness (i.e., make the promised payments on debt). In the example, various solvency ratios are used to measure tolerance for leverage. One set of tolerance-for-leverage measures is based on retained cash flow (RCF). RCF is defined by Moody's as operating cash flow before working capital changes less dividends. A ratio of RCF/total debt of 0.5, for example, indicates that the company may be able to pay off debt in approximately 1/0.5 = 2 years from cash flow retained in the business (at current levels of RCF and debt), assuming no capital expenditures; a ratio adjusting for capital expenditures is also used. Other factors include interest coverage ratios based on EBITDA, which is also chosen by Moody's in specifying factors for operational efficiency and margin stability. "Operational efficiency" as defined by Moody's relates to cost structure: Companies with lower costs are better positioned to deal with financial stress. "Margin stability" relates to the past volatility of profit margins: Higher stability should be associated with lower credit risk.

EXAMPLE 7

Moody's Evaluation of Quantifiable Rating Factors[10]

Moody's Investors Service indicates that when assigning credit ratings for the global paper and forest products industry, they look at a number of factors, including quantitative measures of four broad factors. These factors are weighted and aggregated in determining the overall credit rating assigned. The four broad factors, the subfactors, and weightings are as follows:

Broad Factor	Subfactors	Subfactor Weighting (%)	Broad Factor Weighting (%)
Scale and diversification	Average annual revenues	6.00	15
	Segment diversification	4.50	
	Geographic diversification	4.50	
Financial policies (tolerance for leverage)	Retained cash flow (RCF)/Total debt	11.00	55
	(RCF − Capital expenditures)/Total debt	11.00	
	Total debt/EBITDA	11.00	
	(EBITDA − Capital expenditures)/Interest	11.00	
	EBITDA/Interest	11.00	
Operational efficiency	Vertical integration	5.25	15
	EBITDA margin	5.25	
	EBITDA/Average assets	4.50	
Margin stability	Average percentage change in EBITDA margin	15.00	15
Total		100.00	100

[10] Moody's Investors Service, "Rating Methodology: Global Paper & Forest Products Industry," June 2006, pp. 8–19.

1. What are some reasons why Moody's may have selected these four broad factors as being important in assigning a credit rating?

2. Why might financial policies be weighted so heavily?

Solution to 1:

Scale and Diversification:

▶ Large scale can result in purchasing power over suppliers, leading to cost savings.

▶ Product and geographic diversification should lower risk.

Financial Policies:

▶ Strong financial policies should be associated with the ability of cash flow to service debt.

Operational Efficiency:

▶ Companies with high operational efficiency should have lower costs and higher margins than less efficient companies and so be able to withstand a downturn easier.

Margin Stability:

▶ Lower volatility in margins would imply lower risk relative to economic conditions.

Solution to 2: The level of debt relative to earnings and cash flow is a critical factor in assessing credit-worthiness. The higher the current level of debt, the higher the risk of default.

A point to note regarding Example 7 is that the rating factors and the metrics used to represent each can vary by industry group. For example, for heavy manufacturing (manufacturing of the capital assets used in manufacturing and production processes), Moody's distinguishes order trends and quality as distinctive credit factors affecting future revenues, factory load, and profitability patterns.

Analyses of a company's historical and projected financial statements are an integral part of the credit evaluation process. As noted by Moody's, the rating process makes:

> . . . extensive use of historic financial statements. Historic results help with understanding the pattern of a company's results and how the company compares to others. They also provide perspective, helping to ensure that estimated future results are grounded in reality.[11]

As noted in the above example, Moody's computes a variety of ratios in assessing credit-worthiness. A comparison of a company's ratios to its peers is informative in evaluating relative credit-worthiness, as demonstrated in Example 8.

---

[11] Ibid., p. 6.

EXAMPLE 8

Peer Comparison of Ratios

A credit analyst is assessing the tolerance for leverage for two paper companies based on the following subfactors identified by Moody's:[12]

	International Paper	**Louisiana-Pacific**
RCF/Debt	8.2 %	59.1%
(RCF − Capital expenditures)/Debt	0.2%	39.8%
Debt/EBITDA	5.6x	1.0x
(EBITDA − Capital expenditures)/Interest	1.7x	8.1x
EBITDA/Interest	3.1x	10.0x

Based solely on the data given, which company is more likely to be assigned a higher credit rating?

Solution: The ratio comparisons are all in favor of Louisiana-Pacific. Louisiana-Pacific has a much higher level of retained cash flow relative to debt whether capital expenditures are netted from RCF or not. Louisiana-Pacific has a lower level of debt relative to EBITDA and a higher level of EBITDA relative to interest expense. Louisiana-Pacific is likely to be assigned a higher credit rating.

Before calculating ratios such as those presented in Example 8, rating agencies make certain adjustments to reported financial statements, such as adjusting debt to include off-balance sheet debt in a company's total debt.[13] A later section will describe some common adjustments. Financial statement analysis, especially financial ratio analysis, can also be an important tool used in selecting equity investments, as discussed in the next section.

5   APPLICATION: SCREENING FOR POTENTIAL EQUITY INVESTMENTS

Ratios using financial statement data and market data are used to screen for potential equity investments. **Screening** is the application of a set of criteria to reduce a set of potential investments to a smaller set having certain desired characteristics. Criteria involving financial ratios generally involve comparing one or more ratios with some prespecified cutoff values.

---

[12] Ibid., p. 12; the values reported are based on average historical data.

[13] Ibid., p. 6.

A security selection approach incorporating financial ratios may be used whether the investor uses top-down analysis or bottom-up analysis. **Top-down analysis** involves identifying attractive geographic segments and/or industry segments and then the most attractive investments within those segments. **Bottom-up analysis** involves selection from all companies within a specified investment universe. Regardless of the direction, screening for potential equity investments aims to identify companies that meet specific criteria. An analysis of this type may be used as the basis for directly forming a portfolio, or it may be undertaken as a preliminary part of a more thorough analysis of potential investment targets.

Fundamental to this type of analysis are decisions about which metrics to use as screens, how many metrics to include, what values of those metrics to use as cutoff points, and what weighting to give each metric. Metrics can include not only financial ratios but also characteristics such as market capitalization or membership as a component security in a specified index. Exhibit 4 is an example of a hypothetical simple stock screen based on the following criteria: a valuation ratio (price-to-sales) less than a specified value; a solvency ratio measuring financial leverage (total assets/equity) not exceeding a specified value; dividend payments; and positive one-year-ahead forecast EPS. The exhibit shows the results of applying the screen to a set of 4,203 U.S. securities that comprise a hypothetical equity manager's investment universe.

EXHIBIT 4	Example of a Stock Screen	
	Stocks Meeting Criterion	
Criterion	**Number**	**Percent of Total**
Price per share/Sales per share < 1.5	1,560	37.1
Total assets/Equity ≤ 2.0	2,123	50.5
Dividends > 0	2,497	59.4
Consensus forecast EPS > 0	2,956	70.3
Meeting all four criteria simultaneously	473	11.3

Source: http://finance.yahoo.com.

Several points about the screen in Exhibit 4 are observed in many screens seen in practice:

▶ Some criteria serve as checks on the interpretation of other criteria. In this hypothetical example, the first criterion selects stocks that are relatively cheaply valued. However, the stocks might be cheap for a good reason, such as poor profitability or excessive financial leverage. So, the criteria requiring forecast EPS and dividends to be positive serve as checks on profitability, and the criterion limiting financial leverage serves as a check on financial risk. Of course, financial ratios or other statistics cannot generally control for exposure to certain types of risk (e.g., related to regulatory developments or technological innovation).

▶ If all the criteria were completely independent of each other, the set of stocks meeting all four criteria would be 329, equal to 4,203 times 7.8 percent—the product of the fraction of stocks satisfying the four criteria individually (i.e., $0.371 \times 0.505 \times 0.594 \times 0.703 = 0.078$, or 7.8 percent). As the screen illustrates, criteria are often not independent, and the result is more securities passing the screen. In this example, 473 (or 11.3 percent) of the securities passed all four screens. As an example of the lack of independence, dividend-paying status is probably positively correlated with the ability to generate positive earnings and the value of the fourth criterion. If stocks that pass one test tend to also pass the other, fewer would be eliminated after the application of the second test.

▶ The results of screens can sometimes be relatively concentrated in a subset of the sectors represented in the benchmark. The financial leverage criterion in Exhibit 4 would exclude all banking stocks, for example. What constitutes a high or low value of a measure of a financial characteristic can be sensitive to the industry in which a company operates.

Screens can be used by both **growth investors** (focused on investing in high-earnings-growth companies), **value investors** (focused on paying a relatively low share price in relation to earnings or assets per share), and **market-oriented investors** (an intermediate grouping for investors whose investment disciplines cannot be clearly categorized as value or growth). The criteria of growth screens would typically feature criteria related to earnings growth and/or momentum. Value screens, as a rule, feature criteria setting upper limits for the value of one or more valuation ratios. Market-oriented screens would not strongly emphasize valuation or growth criteria. The use of screens involving financial ratios may be most common among value investors.

There have been many studies researching the most effective items of accounting information for screening equity investments. Some research suggests that certain items of accounting information can help explain (and potentially predict) market returns (e.g., Chan et al. 1991; Lev and Thiagarajan 1993; Lakonishok et al. 1994; Davis 1994; Arbanell and Bushee 1998). Representative of such investigations is Piotroski (2000), whose screen uses nine accounting-based fundamentals that aim to identify financially strong and profitable companies among those with high book value/market value ratios. For example, the profitability measures relate to whether the company reported positive net income, positive cash flow, and an increase in return on assets (ROA).

An analyst may want to evaluate how a portfolio based on a particular screen would have performed historically, using a process known as "backtesting." **Backtesting** applies the portfolio selection rules to historical data and calculates what returns would have been earned if a particular strategy had been used. The relevance of backtesting to investment success in practice can, however, be limited. Haugen and Baker (1996) describe some of these limitations:

▶ Survivorship bias: If the database used in backtesting eliminates companies that cease to exist because of a merger or bankruptcy, then the remaining companies collectively will appear to have performed better.

▶ Look-ahead bias: If a database includes financial data updated for restatements (where companies have restated previously issued financial statements to correct errors or reflect changes in accounting principles),[14]

---

[14] In the United States, restatements of previously issued financial statements have increased in recent years. The U.S. Government Accounting Office (2002) reports 919 restatements by 834 public companies in the period from January 1997 to June 2002. The number of restatements increased from 613 in 2004 to 1,195 in 2005 (*Wall Street Journal*, 2006).

then there is a mismatch between what investors would have actually known at the time of the investment decision and the information used in backtesting.

▶ Data-snooping bias: If researchers build models based on previous researchers' findings, then using the same database to test the model is not actually a test. Under this scenario, the same rules may or may not produce similar results in the future. One academic study argues that the apparent ability of value strategies to generate excess returns is largely explainable as the result of collective data snooping (Conrad, Cooper, and Kaul, 2003).

EXAMPLE 9

Ratio-Based Screening for Potential Equity Investments

Below are two alternative strategies under consideration by an investment firm:

> *Strategy A* invests in stocks that are components of a global equity index, have a ROE above the median ROE of all stocks in the index, and a P/E ratio less than the median P/E.
>
> *Strategy B* invests in stocks that are components of a broad-based U.S. equity index, have price to operating cash flow in the lowest quartile of companies in the index, and have shown increases in sales for at least the past three years.

Both strategies were developed with the use of backtesting.

1. How would you characterize the two strategies?
2. What concerns might you have about using such strategies?

Solution to 1: Strategy A appears to aim for global diversification and combines a requirement for profitability with a traditional measure of value (low P/E). Strategy B focuses on both large and small companies in a single market and apparently aims to identify companies that are growing and yet managing to generate positive cash flow from operations.

Solution to 2: The use of *any* approach to investment decisions depends on the objectives and risk profile of the investor. With that crucial consideration in mind, ratio-based benchmarks can offer an efficient way to screen for potential equity investments. However, in doing so, many types of questions arise.

First, unintentional selections can be made if criteria are not specified carefully. For example, Strategy A might unintentionally select a loss-making company with negative shareholders' equity because negative net income divided by negative shareholders' equity would arithmetically result in a positive ROE. Strategy B might unintentionally select a company with negative operating cash flow because price to operating cash flow would be negative and thus very low in the ranking. In both cases, the analyst can add additional screening criteria to avoid unintentional selection (e.g., criteria requiring positive shareholders' equity and operating cash flow).

> Second, the inputs to ratio analysis are derived from financial statements, and companies may differ in the financial standards applied (e.g., IFRS versus U.S. GAAP); the specific accounting method chosen within those allowed under any body of reporting standards; and/or the estimates made in applying an accounting method.
>
> Third, backtesting may not provide a reliable indication of future performance because of survivorship bias, look-ahead bias, or data snooping; furthermore, as suggested by finance theory and by common sense, the past is not necessarily indicative of the future. Fourth, implementation decisions can crucially affect returns. For example, decisions about frequency and timing of portfolio selection and reevaluation affect transaction costs and taxes paid out of the portfolio.

6 ANALYST ADJUSTMENTS TO REPORTED FINANCIALS

When comparing companies that use different accounting methods or estimate key accounting inputs in different ways, analysts frequently adjust a company's financials. In this section, we first provide a framework for considering potential analyst adjustments to facilitate such comparisons and then provide examples of such adjustments. In practice, required adjustments vary widely. The examples presented here are not intended to be comprehensive, but rather to illustrate the use of adjustments to facilitate comparison.

6.1 A Framework for Analyst Adjustments

In this discussion of potential analyst adjustments to a company's financial statements, we employ a balance sheet focused framework. Of course, because the financial statements are interrelated, adjustments to items reported on one statement must also be reflected in adjustments to items on another statement. For example, an analyst adjustment to the balance sheet item inventory affects the income statement item cost of goods sold; and the owners' equity amount is affected by analyst adjustments relating to expense or revenue recognition.

Regardless of the particular order in which an analyst considers the items that may require adjustment for comparability, the following considerations are appropriate:

▶ *Importance.* Is an adjustment to this item likely to affect my conclusions? In other words, does it matter? For example, in an industry where companies require minimal inventory, does it matter that two companies use different inventory accounting methods?

▶ *Body of standards.* Is there a difference in the body of standards being used (U.S. GAAP versus IFRS)? If so, in which areas is the difference likely to affect a comparison?

▶ *Methods.* Is there a difference in methods?

▶ *Estimates.* Is there a difference in important estimates?

The following sections illustrate analyst adjustments—first those relating to the asset side of the balance sheet and then those relating to the liability side.

6.2 Analyst Adjustments Related to Investments

Accounting for investments in the debt and equity securities of other companies (other than investments accounted for under the equity method and investments in consolidated subsidiaries) depends on management's intention (i.e., to actively trade the securities, make them available for sale, or, in the case of debt securities, to hold them to maturity). When securities are classified as "trading" securities, unrealized gains and losses are reported in the income statement. When securities are classified as "available-for-sale" securities, unrealized gains and losses are not reported in the income statement and instead are recognized in equity. If two otherwise comparable companies have significant differences in the classification of investments, analyst adjustments may be useful to facilitate comparison.

Also, IFRS requires that those unrealized gains and losses on available-for-sale debt securities that arise due to exchange rate movements be recognized in the income statement, whereas U.S. GAAP does not. To facilitate comparison across companies, increases (decreases) in the value of available-for-sale debt securities arising from exchange rate movements can be deducted from (added to) the amount of income reported by the IFRS-reporting company.

6.3 Analyst Adjustments Related to Inventory

With inventory, adjustments may be required for different accounting methods. As described in previous readings, a company's decision about the inventory method will affect the value of inventory shown on the balance sheet as well as the value of inventory that is sold (cost of goods sold). If one company, not reporting under IFRS,[15] uses LIFO (last in, first out) and another uses FIFO (first in, first out), comparison of the two companies may be difficult. However, companies that use the LIFO method must also disclose the value of their inventory under the FIFO method. To place inventory values for a company using LIFO reporting on a FIFO basis, the analyst would add the ending balance of the LIFO reserve to the ending value of inventory under LIFO accounting; to adjust cost of goods sold to a FIFO basis, the analyst would subtract the change in the LIFO reserve from the reported cost of goods sold under LIFO accounting. Example 10 illustrates the use of a disclosure of the value of inventory under the FIFO method to make a valid current ratio comparison between companies reporting on a LIFO and FIFO basis.

EXAMPLE 10

Adjustment for a Company Using LIFO Method of Accounting for Inventories

An analyst is comparing the financial performance of SL Industries (AMEX: SLI), a U.S. company operating in the electric lighting and wiring industry, with a company that reports using IFRS. The IFRS company uses the FIFO method of inventory accounting, and you therefore must convert SLI's results to a comparable basis.

---

[15] IAS No. 2 does not permit the use of LIFO.

EXHIBIT 5	**Data for SL Industries**	

	31 December	
	2005	**2004**
Total current assets	$44,194,000	$37,990,000
Total current liabilities	18,387,000	18,494,000

NOTE 6. INVENTORIES

Inventories consist of the following ($ in thousands):

	31 December	
	2005	**2004**
Raw materials	$ 9,774	$ 9,669
Work in process	4,699	5,000
Finished goods	1,926	3,633
	16,399	18,302
Less: Allowances	(1,829)	(2,463)
	$14,570	$15,839

The above includes certain inventories that are valued using the LIFO method, which aggregated $4,746,000 and $3,832,000 as of December 31, 2005 and December 31, 2004, respectively. The excess of FIFO cost over LIFO cost as of December 31, 2005 and December 31, 2004 was approximately $502,000 and $565,000, respectively.

Source: 10-K for SL Industries, Inc. for the year ended 31 December 2005; filed with the SEC 24 March 2006.

---

1. Based on the information in Exhibit 5, calculate SLI's current ratio under FIFO and LIFO for 2004 and 2005.

2. Interpret the results of adjusting the current ratio to be consistent with inventory on a FIFO basis.

Solution to 1: The calculations of SLI's current ratio (current assets divided by current liabilities) are given below.

	2005	**2004**
I. Current Ratio (Unadjusted)		
Total current assets	$44,194,000	$37,990,000
Total current liabilities	18,387,000	18,494,000
Current ratio (unadjusted)	2.40	2.05

	2005	2004
II. Current Ratio (Adjusted)		
Adjust the inventory to FIFO, add	502,000	565,000
Total current assets (adjusted)	$44,696,000	$38,555,000
Total current liabilities	18,387,000	18,494,000
Current ratio (adjusted)	2.43	2.08

To adjust the LIFO inventory to FIFO, the excess amounts of FIFO cost over LIFO cost are added to LIFO inventory, increasing current assets by an equal amount. The effect of adjusting inventory on the current ratio is to increase it from 2.05 to 2.08 in 2004 and from 2.40 to 2.43 in 2005.

Solution to 2: SLI appears to be somewhat more liquid based on the adjusted current ratio. However, the year-over-year improvement in the current ratio on an adjusted basis at 16.8 percent (2.43/2.08 − 1) was slightly less favorable than the improvement of 17.1 percent (2.40/2.05 − 1) on an unadjusted basis.

In summary, the information disclosed by companies using LIFO allows an analyst to calculate the value of the company's inventory as if it were using the FIFO method. In the example above, the portion of inventory valued using the LIFO method was a relatively small portion of total inventory, and the LIFO reserve (excess of FIFO cost over LIFO) was also relatively small. However, if the LIFO method is used for a substantial part of a company's inventory and the LIFO reserve is large relative to reported inventory, the adjustment to a FIFO basis can be important for comparison of the LIFO-reporting company with another company that uses the FIFO method of inventory valuation. Example 11 illustrates a case in which such an adjustment would have a major impact on an analyst's conclusions.

EXAMPLE 11

Analyst Adjustment to Inventory Value for Comparability in a Current Ratio Comparison

Company A reports under IFRS and uses the FIFO method of inventory accounting for its entire inventory. Company B reports under U.S. GAAP and uses the LIFO method. Exhibit 6 gives data pertaining to current assets, LIFO reserves, and current liabilities of these companies.

Based on the data given in Exhibit 6, compare the liquidity of the two companies as measured by the current ratio.

EXHIBIT 6	Data for Companies Accounting for Inventory on Different Bases	
	Company A (FIFO)	**Company B (LIFO)**
Current assets (includes inventory)	$ 300,000	$ 80,000
LIFO reserve	N/A	$ 20,000
Current liabilities	$ 150,000	$ 45,000

Solution: Company A's current ratio is 2.0. Based on unadjusted balance sheet data, Company B's current ratio is 1.78. Company A's higher current ratio indicates that Company A appears to be more liquid than Company B; however, the use of unadjusted data for Company B is not appropriate for making comparisons with Company A.

After adjusting Company B's inventory to a comparable basis (i.e., to a FIFO basis), the conclusion changes. The table below summarizes the results when Company B's inventory is left on a LIFO basis and when it is placed on a FIFO basis for comparability with Company A.

		Company B	
	Company A (FIFO)	**Unadjusted (LIFO Basis)**	**Adjusted (FIFO Basis)**
Current assets (includes inventory)	$ 300,000	$ 80,000	$ 100,000
Current liabilities	$ 150,000	$ 45,000	$ 45,000
Current ratio	2.00	1.78	2.22

When both companies' inventories are stated on a FIFO basis, Company B appears to be more liquid, as indicated by its current ratio of 2.22 versus Company A's ratio of 2.00. The adjustment to place Company B's inventory on a FIFO basis was significant because Company B was assumed to use LIFO for its entire inventory and its inventory reserve was $20,000/$80,000 = 0.25, or 25 percent of its reported inventory.

As mentioned earlier, an analyst can also adjust the cost of goods sold for a company using LIFO to a FIFO basis by subtracting the change in the amount of the LIFO reserve from cost of goods sold. Such an adjustment would be appropriate for making profitability comparisons with a company reporting on a FIFO basis and would be important to make when the impact of the adjustment would be material.

6.4 Analyst Adjustments Related to Property, Plant, and Equipment

Management generally has considerable discretion in the determination of depreciation expense. Depreciation expense affects reported net income and reported net fixed asset values. Analysts often consider management's choices related to depreciation as one qualitative factor in evaluating the quality of a company's financial reporting and, in some cases, they may adjust reported depreciation expense for a specific analytic purpose.

The amount of depreciation expense depends on both the accounting method and the estimates used in the calculations. Companies can depreciate fixed assets (other than land) using the straight-line method, an accelerated method, or a usage method. The straight-line method reports an equal amount of depreciation expense each period, computed as the depreciable cost divided by the estimated useful life of the asset (when acquired, an asset's depreciable cost is calculated as its total cost minus its estimated salvage value). Accelerated methods depreciate the asset more quickly, apportioning a greater amount of the depreciable cost to depreciation expense in the earlier periods. Usage-based methods depreciate an asset in proportion to its usage. Apart from selecting a depreciation method, companies must estimate an asset's salvage value and useful life to compute depreciation.

Disclosures required for depreciation often do not facilitate specific adjustments, so comparisons across companies concerning their decisions in depreciating assets are often qualitative and general. The accounts that are associated with depreciation include the balance sheet accounts for gross property, plant, and equipment (gross PPE); accumulated depreciation; the income statement account for depreciation expense; and the statement of cash flows disclosure of capital expenditure (capex) and asset disposals. The relationships between these items can reveal various pieces of information:

- ▶ accumulated depreciation divided by gross PPE, from the balance sheet, suggests how much of its useful life the company's overall asset base has passed;

- ▶ accumulated depreciation divided by depreciation expense suggests how many years' worth of depreciation expense has already been recognized (i.e., the average age of the asset base);

- ▶ net PPE (net of accumulated depreciation) divided by deprecation expense is an approximate indicator of how many years of useful life remain for the company's overall asset base;

- ▶ gross PPE divided by depreciation expense can suggest the average life of the assets at installation;

- ▶ capex divided by the sum of gross PPE plus capex can suggest what percentage of the asset base is being renewed through new capital investment; and

- ▶ capex in relation to asset disposal provides information on growth of the asset base.

These relationships can be evaluated across companies in an industry to suggest differences in strategies for asset utilization or areas for further investigation.

EXAMPLE 12

Differences in Depreciation

An analyst is evaluating the financial statements for two companies in the same industry. The companies have similar strategies with respect to the use of equipment in manufacturing their products. The following information is provided (amounts in millions):

	Company A ($)	Company B ($)
Net PPE	1,200	750
Depreciation expense	120	50

1. Based on the information given, estimate the average remaining useful lives of the asset bases of Company A and Company B.

2. Suppose that, based on a physical inspection of the companies' plants and other industry information, the analyst believes that the actual remaining useful lives of Company A's and Company B's assets is roughly equal at 10 years. Based only on the facts given, what might the analyst conclude concerning Company B's reported net income?

Solution to 1: The estimated average remaining useful life of Company A's asset base, calculated as net PPE divided by depreciation expense, is $1,200/$120 = 10 years. For Company B, the average remaining useful life of the asset base appears to be far longer at 15 years ($750/$50).

Solution to 2: If Company B's depreciation expense were calculated using 10 years, it would be $75 million (i.e., $25 million higher than reported) and higher depreciation expense would decrease net income. The analyst might conclude that Company B's reported net income reflects relatively aggressive accounting estimates compared with Company A's reported net income.

6.5 Analyst Adjustments Related to Goodwill

Goodwill is an example of an intangible asset (i.e., one without physical substance). Goodwill arises when one company purchases another for a price that exceeds the fair value of the assets acquired. Goodwill is recorded as an asset. For example, assume ParentCo purchases TargetCo for a purchase price of $400 million, the fair value of TargetCo's identifiable assets is $300 million, and the excess of the purchase price is attributed to TargetCo's valuable brands and well-trained workforce. ParentCo will record total assets of $400 million, consisting of $300 million in identifiable assets and $100 million of goodwill. The goodwill is tested annually for impairment, and if its value has declined, ParentCo will reduce the amount of the asset and report a write-off due to impairment.

One of the conceptual difficulties with goodwill arises in comparative financial statement analysis. Consider, for example, two hypothetical U.S. companies, one of which has grown by making an acquisition and the other one of which has grown internally. Assume that the economic value of the two companies is identical: Each has an identically valuable branded product, well-trained workforce, and proprietary technology. The company that has grown by acquisition will incur a related expenditure and will report assets on its balance sheet equal to the amount of the expenditure (assuming no write-offs). The company that has grown internally will have done so by incurring expenditures for advertising, staff training, and research, all of which are expensed as incurred under U.S. GAAP and are thus not directly reflected on the company's balance sheet. Ratios based on asset values and/or income, including profitability ratios such as return on assets and MV/BV, will generally differ for the two companies because of differences in the accounting values of assets and income related to goodwill, although by assumption the economic value of the companies is identical.

EXAMPLE 13

Ratio Comparisons for Goodwill

Miano Marseglia is an analyst who is evaluating the relative valuation of two footwear manufacturing companies: Phoenix Footwear Group (AMEX: PXG) and Rocky Brands (NASDAQ: RCKY). As one part of an overall analysis, Marseglia would like to see how the two companies compare with each other and with the industry based on price/book (P/B) ratios.[16] Because both companies are nondiversified, are small, and have high risk relative to larger, more diversified companies in the industry, Marseglia expects them to sell at a lower P/B ratio than the industry average of 3.68. Marseglia collects the following data on the two companies.

	PXG ($)	RCKY ($)
Market capitalization at 11 October 2006 (Market price per share times the number of shares outstanding)	37.22 million	67.57 million
Total shareholders' equity as of the most recent quarter (MRQ)	54.99 million	100.35 million
Goodwill	33.67 million	24.87 million
Other intangible assets	33.22 million	38.09 million

Marseglia computes the P/B ratios as follows:

PXG $37.22/$54.99 = 0.68

RCKY $67.57/$100.35 = 0.67

The companies have similar P/B ratios (i.e., they are approximately equally valued relative to MRQ shareholders' equity). As expected, each company also appears to be selling at a significant discount to the industry average P/B multiple of 3.68. Marseglia is concerned, however, because he notes that both companies have significant intangible assets, particularly goodwill. He wonders what the relative value would be if the P/B ratio were computed after adjusting book value first to remove goodwill and then to remove all intangible assets. Book value reduced by all intangible assets is known as "tangible book value." The average price/tangible book value for the industry is 4.19.

1. Compute the P/B ratio adjusted for goodwill and the price/tangible book value ratio for each company.

---

[16] Price/book, or P/B, is the price per share divided by stockholders' equity per share. It is also referred to as a market/book, or MV/BV, ratio because it can also be calculated as total market value of the stock (market capitalization) divided by total stockholders' equity.

2. Which company appears to be a better value based *solely* on this data? (Note that the P/B ratio is only one part of a broader analysis. Much more evidence on the valuation and the comparability of the companies would be required to reach a conclusion about whether one company is a better value.)

Solution to 1:

	PXG ($)	RCKY ($)
Total stockholders' equity	54.99 million	100.35 million
Less: Goodwill	33.67 million	24.87 million
Book value, adjusted	21.32 million	75.48 million
Adjusted P/B ratio	37.22/21.32 = 1.75	67.57/75.48 = 0.90

	PXG ($)	RCKY ($)
Total stockholders' equity	54.99 million	100.35 million
Less: Goodwill	33.67 million	24.87 million
Less: Other intangible assets	33.22 million	38.09 million
Tangible book value	(11.90) million	37.39 million
Price/tangible book value ratio	NM (not meaningful)	67.57/37.39 = 1.81

Solution to 2: Based on an adjustment for goodwill accumulated in acquisitions, RCKY appears to be selling for a lower price relative to book value than PXG (0.90 versus 1.75). Both companies are selling at a significant discount to the industry, even after adjusting for goodwill.

Based on price/tangible book value, RCKY is also selling for a lower multiple than the industry (1.81 versus 4.19). PXG has a negative tangible book value, and its price/tangible book value ratio is not meaningful with a negative denominator. Based on this interpretation and based *solely* on this information, PXG appears relatively expensive compared with RCKY.

6.6 Analyst Adjustments Related to Off-Balance Sheet Financing

A number of business activities give rise to obligations which, although they are economically liabilities of a company, are not required to be reported on a company's balance sheet. Including such off-balance sheet obligations in a company's liabilities can affect ratios and conclusions based on such ratios. In this section, we describe adjustments to financial statements related to one type of off-balance sheet obligation, the operating lease.

The rights of a lessee (the party that is leasing some asset) may be very similar to the rights of an owner, but if the terms of the lease can be structured so it can be accounted for as an operating lease, the lease is treated like a rental contract, and neither the leased asset nor the associated liability is reported on the balance sheet.[17] The lessee simply records the periodic lease payment as a rental expense in its income statement. In contrast, when a company actually owns an asset, the asset is shown on the balance sheet along with any corresponding liability, such as financing for the asset. Similarly, if a lease is accounted for as a capital lease—essentially equivalent to ownership—the leased asset and associated liability appear on the lessee's balance sheet. The issue of concern to analysts arises when a lease conveys to the lessee most of the benefits and risks of ownership, but the lease is accounted for as an operating lease—the case of off-balance sheet financing. International accounting standard setters have stated that the entities should not avoid balance sheet recording of leases through artificial leasing structures, seeking to avoid the substance of the transaction.

A 2005 report by the U.S. SEC on off-balance sheet financing estimates that more than 63 percent of companies in the United States report having an operating lease. The SEC estimate of total future lease payments under operating leases was $1.2 trillion.

Because companies are required to disclose in their financial statements the amount and timing of lease payments, an analyst can use this information to answer the question: How would a company's financial position look if operating lease obligations were included in its total liabilities?

Exhibit 7 presents selected items from the balance sheet of AMR Corporation (the parent of American Airlines) and the text of the footnote from the financial statements about the company's leases. We can use the information in this exhibit to illustrate analyst adjustments:

EXHIBIT 7	Lease Arrangements of AMR Corporation (NYSE: AMR) Selected Items from Balance Sheet ($ Millions)	

	31 December	
	2005	**2004**
Total Assets	**$29,495**	**$28,773**
Current maturities of long-term debt	$ 1,077	$ 659
Long-term debt, less current maturities	12,530	12,436
Total long-term debt	13,607	13,095
Current obligations under capital leases	162	147
Obligations under capital leases, less current obligations	926	1,088
Total long-term debt and capital leases	$14,695	$14,330

From Footnote 5. Leases

AMR's subsidiaries lease various types of equipment and property, primarily aircraft and airport facilities. The future minimum lease payments required under capital leases, together with the present value of such payments, and future minimum lease payments required under operating leases that have initial or

(Exhibit continued on next page . . .)

---

[17] A lessee classifies a lease as an operating lease if certain guidelines concerning the term of the lease, the present value of the lease payments, and the ownership of the asset at the end of the lease term are satisfied. Under U.S. GAAP, FASB ASC Section 840-10-25 [Leases–Overall–Recognition] specifies the criteria for classification.

EXHIBIT 7   (continued)

remaining non-cancelable lease terms in excess of one year as of December 31, 2005, were (in millions):

Year Ending December 31	Capital Leases	Operating Leases
2006	$263	$1,065
2007	196	1,039
2008	236	973
2009	175	872
2010	140	815
2011 and thereafter	794	7,453
	$1,804	$12,217[a]
Less amount representing interest	716	
Present value of net minimum lease payments	$1,088	

[a] As of December 31, 2005, included in Accrued liabilities and Other liabilities and deferred credits on the accompanying consolidated balance sheet is approximately $1.4 billion relating to rent expense being recorded in advance of future operating lease payments.

Source: AMR Corporation's Form 10-K for period ending 31 December 2005, filed 24 February 2006.

To evaluate the company's solvency position, we can calculate the debt-to-assets ratio, defined in the reading on financial analysis techniques as the ratio of total debt to total assets. Excluding obligations under capital leases (amounting to $1,088 in 2005) from the definition of total debt, we would calculate the ratio for 2005 as 46.1 percent (total long-term debt/total assets = $13,607/$29,495). Properly including obligations under capital leases in the definition of total debt, we would calculate the ratio as 49.8 percent ($14,695/$29,495).

The company's footnote on leases discloses a total of $12.2 billion of future payments for operating leases on an undiscounted basis. The footnote also indicates that, of this amount, only $1.4 billion is shown on the balance sheet. To determine the impact of including operating lease obligations in the total liabilities, we will calculate the present value of the future operating lease payments. Calculating the present value of the future operating lease payments requires a discount rate. We can estimate an appropriate discount rate from the information about the present value of the capital lease payments. The discount rate is the internal rate of return implied by the stream of lease payments and their present value.

For AMR, the present value of the capital lease payments is $1,088 million. Using the stream of payments shown in the footnote and assuming that all of the $794 million payments are made in the year 2011 would give an internal rate of return of 13.7 percent. However, based on the schedule of payments shown, a better assumption is that the $794 million payments do not all occur in a single year. One approach to estimating the timing of these payments is to assume that the payments in 2011 and subsequent years equal the average annual payments in years 2006 to 2010 of $202 = ($263 + $196 + $236 + $175 + $140)/5. Using this approach, there are four annual payments in 2011 and thereafter, and the internal rate of return of the capital lease is 12.1 percent. Given that lease payments have been generally declining over 2006 to 2010, another approach resulting in lower lease payments after 2010 would be to assume that the $794 million is paid equally over some longer time span, such as 10 years. Using this assumption, the internal rate of return of the capital lease payments is 10.0 percent.[18]

EXHIBIT 8	**Present Value of Operating Lease Payments Using Discount Rate Derived from Present Value of Capital Lease Payments ($Millions)**				
	Capital Lease			**Operating Lease**	
	Payments (as Given)	**Payments Incl. Estimated Annual Payments for 2011 and Thereafter**	**Payments Incl. Estimated Annual Payments for 2011 and Thereafter**	**Payments (as Given)**	**Payments Incl. Estimated Annual Payments for 2011 and Thereafter**
Present value, *given*	−$1,088	−$1,088	−$1,088		
Year 2006	$263	$263	$263	$1,065	$1,065
2007	$196	$196	$196	$1,039	$1,039
2008	$236	$236	$236	$973	$973
2009	$175	$175	$175	$872	$872
2010	$140	$140	$140	$815	$815
2011 and thereafter	$794	$202	$79	$7,453	$953
		$202	$79		$953
		$202	$79		$953
		$188	$79		$953
			$79		$953
			$79		$953
			$79		$953
			$79		$782
			$79		
			$79		
Internal rate of return	13.7%	12.1%	10.0%		
Present value of operating lease payments using a 13.7% discount rate:					$5,671
Present value of operating lease payments using a 12.1% discount rate:					$6,106
Present value of operating lease payments using a 10.0% discount rate:					$6,767

---

[18] If the term structure of the capital and operating leases can be assumed to be similar, an alternative, shortcut, way to estimate the present value of future operating lease payments that do not appear on the balance sheet is to assume that the relationship between the discounted and undiscounted operating lease payments is approximately the same as the relationship between the discounted and undiscounted capital lease payments. The discounted capital lease payments of $926 million as reported on the balance sheet are 56.4 percent of the undiscounted noncurrent capital lease payments of $1,642 million ($1,804 million total minus $162 million current payments). Applying the same relationship to operating lease payments, 56.4 percent of the undiscounted noncurrent operating lease payments of $10,817 million ($12,217 million total minus $1,400 million current) equals $6.1 billion, yielding $7.5 billion as the present value of operating lease payments including the current obligation of $1.4 billion.

Having estimated an appropriate discount rate, we can calculate the present value of the future operating lease payments. Exhibit 8 presents the results of these calculations and illustrates the sensitivity of the analysis to assumptions about the timing of cash flows. We developed discount rate estimates of 12.1 percent and 10 percent. Using a discount rate of 12.1 percent, the present value of future operating lease payments would be roughly $6.1 billion, and using a discount rate of 10.0 percent, the present value would be around $6.8 billion. Because $1.4 billion of the amounts related to operating leases already appear on the balance sheet (as disclosed in the company's lease footnote), the value of the future operating lease payments that do not appear on the balance sheet are estimated to be in the range of $6,106 million − $1,400 million = $4,706 million, or about $4.7 billion, to $6,767 million − $1,400 million = $5,367 million, or about $5.4 billion. The lower the assumed discount rate, the higher the present value of the lease payments.

We now add the present value of the off-balance sheet future operating lease payments to the company's total assets and total debt. Making this adjustment increases the debt-to-assets ratio to an amount between ($14,695 + $4,706)/($29,495 + $4,706) = 56.7 percent and ($14,695 + $5,367)/($29,495 + $5,367) = 57.5 percent. If a point estimate of the debt-to-assets ratio were needed, in this case, the analyst might select the 57.5 percent estimate based on the lower discount rate because that discount rate is more consistent with yields on investment-grade bonds as of the date of the example.

EXAMPLE 14

Analyst Adjustment to Debt for Operating Lease Payments

An analyst is evaluating the capital structure of two (hypothetical) companies, Koller Semiconductor and MacRae Manufacturing, as of the beginning of 2006. Koller Semiconductor makes somewhat less use of operating leases than MacRae Manufacturing. The analyst has the following additional information:

	Koller Semiconductor	MacRae Manufacturing
Total debt	$1,200	$2,400
Total equity	$2,000	$4,000
Average interest rate on debt	10%	8%
Lease payments on operating leases:		
2006	10	90
2007	18	105
2008	22	115
2009	25	128
2010 and thereafter	75	384

Based on the information given, discuss how adjusting for operating leases affects the companies' solvency based on their debt to debt-plus-equity ratios, assuming no adjustment to equity. (Assume payments after 2009 occur at the same rate as for 2009. For example, for Koller Semiconductor, the payments for 2010 through 2012 are assumed to be $25 each year.)

Solution: Before making the adjustment, the companies' debt to debt-plus-equity ratios are identical, both at 37.5 percent. To make the adjustment for operating leases, the first step is to calculate the present value of the operating lease payments. Assuming that payments after 2009 occur at the same rate as for 2009, Koller's payment would be $25 in 2010, 2011, and 2012. The present value of $25 discounted for five years at 10 percent is $15.52. MacRae's payment is assumed to be $128 in each of 2010, 2011, and 2012. The present value of $128 discounted for five years at 8 percent is $87.11. Calculations for the following two years are made in the same manner, resulting in the present values shown in the following table:

	Koller Semiconductor ($)	MacRae Manufacturing ($)
2006	9.09	83.33
2007	14.88	90.02
2008	16.53	91.29
2009	17.08	94.08
2010	15.52	87.11
2011	14.11	80.66
2012	12.83	74.69
Total present value (PV)	100.04	601.18

After adding the present value of capitalized lease obligations to total debt, MacRae Manufacturing's debt to debt-plus-equity ratio is significantly higher, at 42.9 percent, as shown in the following table. The higher ratio reflects the impact of lease obligations on MacRae's solvency:

	Koller Semiconductor		MacRae Manufacturing	
	Before Capitalizing	After Capitalizing	Before Capitalizing	After Capitalizing
Total debt	$1,200	$1,300	$2,400	$3,001
Total equity	$2,000	$2,000	$4,000	$4,000
Debt/ (Debt + Equity)	37.5%	39.4%	37.5%	42.9%

The adjustment for operating leases essentially treats the transaction as if the asset had been purchased rather than leased. The present value of the capitalized lease obligations is the amount owed and the amount at which the asset is valued. Further adjustments reflect the reduction of rent expenses (if the asset is owned, rent would not be paid), the related interest expense on the amount owed, and a depreciation expense for the asset. The reduction of rent expense can be estimated as the average of two years of rent expense. Interest expense is estimated as the interest rate times the PV of the lease payments. Depreciation is estimated on a straight-line basis based on the number of years of future lease payments.

EXAMPLE 15

Stylized Example of Effect on Coverage Ratio for Operating Lease Adjustment

The analyst is also evaluating the interest coverage ratio of the companies in the previous example, Koller Semiconductor and MacRae Manufacturing.

	Koller Semiconductor ($)	MacRae Manufacturing ($)
EBIT before adjustment	850	1,350
Interest expense before adjustment	120	192

The prior-year (2005) rent expense was $11 for Koller Semiconductor and $90 for MacRae Manufacturing.

Using the information in Example 14 and the additional information given above, discuss how adjustment for operating leases affects the companies' solvency as measured by their coverage ratios.

Solution: Interest coverage is calculated as EBIT divided by interest. For the adjustments, rent expense is the average of two years' rent. For Koller Semiconductor, rent expense is calculated as ($11 + $10)/2. The cost of interest on lease obligations is estimated as the interest rate multiplied by the present value of the lease payments. For Koller Semiconductor, this interest expense is calculated as 10% × $100.04, and for MacRae Manufacturing, it is calculated as 8% × $601.18. Depreciation is estimated on a straight-line basis by dividing the PV of lease payments by the number of years of lease payments (seven years). After the adjustment, both companies show a decline in interest coverage ratio, reflecting the increased obligation associated with the operating lease obligations. There is also a larger apparent difference in the coverage between the two companies.

	Koller Semiconductor	MacRae Manufacturing
Interest coverage before adjustment	**7.1**	**7.0**
EBIT before adjustment	**850**	**1,350**
Rent expense; an add-back to EBIT	10.5	90.0
Depreciation; a deduction from EBIT	(14.3)	(85.9)
EBIT after adjustment	846.2	1354.1
Interest expense before adjustment	120	192
Assumed cost of interest on lease obligation (to add to interest)	10.0	48.1
Interest expense after adjustment	130.0	240.1
Interest coverage after adjustment	**6.5**	**5.6**

In summary, adjusting a company's financial statements to include amounts of lease payments gives a more complete picture of the company's financial condition and enables the comparison of companies with varying arrangements for financing assets. It may additionally be necessary to adjust for amounts associated with other off-balance sheet financing arrangements.

SUMMARY

This reading described selected applications of financial statement analysis, including the evaluation of past financial performance, the projection of future financial performance, the assessment of credit risk, and the screening of potential equity investments. In addition, the reading introduced analyst adjustments to reported financials. In all cases, the analyst needs to have a good understanding of the financial reporting standards under which financial statements are prepared. Because standards evolve over time, analysts must stay current in order to make good investment decisions. The main points in the reading include the following:

▶ Evaluating a company's historical performance addresses not only what happened but also the causes behind the company's performance and how the performance reflects the company's strategy.

▶ The projection of a company's future net income and cash flow often begins with a top-down sales forecast in which the analyst forecasts industry sales and the company's market share. By projecting profit margins or expenses and the level of investment in working and fixed capital needed to support projected sales, the analyst can forecast net income and cash flow.

▶ Projections of future performance are needed for discounted cash flow valuation of equity and are often needed in credit analysis to assess a borrower's ability to repay interest and principal of a debt obligation.

▶ Credit analysis uses financial statement analysis to evaluate credit-relevant factors, including tolerance for leverage, operational efficiency, and margin stability.

▶ When ratios using financial statement data and market data are used to screen for potential equity investments, fundamental decisions include which metrics to use as screens, how many metrics to include, what values of those metrics to use as cutoff points, and what weighting to give each metric.

▶ Analyst adjustments to a company's reported financial statements are sometimes necessary (e.g., when comparing companies that use different accounting methods or assumptions). Adjustments include those related to investments; inventory; property, plant, and equipment; goodwill; and off-balance sheet financing.

PRACTICE PROBLEMS FOR READING 42

1. Projecting profit margins into the future on the basis of past results would be *most* reliable when the company:

   A. is a large, diversified company operating in mature industries.

   B. is in the commodities business.

   C. operates in a single business segment.

2. Galambos Corporation had an average receivable collection period of 19 days in 2003. Galambos has stated that it wants to decrease its collection period in 2004 to match the industry average of 15 days. Credit sales in 2003 were $300 million, and analysts expect credit sales to increase to $400 million in 2004. To achieve the company's goal of decreasing the collection period, the change in the average accounts receivable balance from 2003 to 2004 that must occur is *closest* to:

   A. −$420,000.

   B. $420,000.

   C. $836,000.

3. Credit analysts are likely to consider which of the following in making a rating recommendation?

   A. Business risk, but not financial risk.

   B. Financial risk, but not business risk.

   C. Both business risk and financial risk.

4. When screening for potential equity investments based on return on equity, to control risk an analyst would be *most likely* to include a criterion that requires:

   A. positive net income.

   B. negative net income.

   C. negative shareholders' equity.

5. One concern when screening for low price-to-earnings stocks is that companies with low price-to-earnings ratios may be financially weak. What criteria might an analyst include to avoid inadvertently selecting weak companies?

   A. Current-year sales growth lower than prior-year sales growth.

   B. Net income less than zero.

   C. Debt-to-total assets ratio below a certain cutoff point.

6. When a database eliminates companies that cease to exist because of a merger or bankruptcy, this can result in:

   A. look-ahead bias.

   B. backtesting bias.

   C. survivorship bias.

7. In a comprehensive financial analysis, financial statements should be:

   A. used as reported without adjustment.

   B. adjusted after completing ratio analysis.

   C. adjusted for differences in accounting standards, such as international financial reporting standards and U.S. generally accepted accounting principles.

8. When comparing financial statements prepared under IFRS with those prepared under U.S. generally accepted accounting principles, analysts may need to make adjustments related to:

   A. realized losses.

   B. unrealized gains and losses for trading securities.

   C. unrealized gains and losses for available-for-sale securities.

9. When comparing a U.S. company using the last in, first out (LIFO) method of inventory to companies preparing their financial statements under international financial reporting standards (IFRS), analysts should be aware that according to IFRS, the LIFO method of inventory:

   A. is never acceptable.

   B. is always acceptable.

   C. is acceptable when applied to finished goods inventory only.

10. An analyst is evaluating the balance sheet of a U.S. company that uses last in, first out (LIFO) accounting for inventory. The analyst collects the following data:

	31 Dec 05	31 Dec 06
Inventory reported on balance sheet	$500,000	$600,000
LIFO reserve	$50,000	$70,000
Average tax rate	30%	30%

After adjustment to convert to first in, first out (FIFO), inventory at 31 December 2006 would be *closest* to:

   A. $600,000.

   B. $620,000.

   C. $670,000.

11. An analyst gathered the following data for a company ($ in millions):

	31 Dec 2000	31 Dec 2001
Gross investment in fixed assets	$2.8	$2.8
Accumulated depreciation	$1.2	$1.6

The average age and average depreciable life, respectively, of the company's fixed assets at the end of 2001 are *closest* to:

	Average Age	Average Depreciable Life
A.	1.75 years	7 years
B.	1.75 years	14 years
C.	4.00 years	7 years

12. To compute tangible book value, an analyst would:

 A. add goodwill to stockholders' equity.

 B. add all intangible assets to stockholders' equity.

 C. subtract all intangible assets from stockholders' equity.

13. Which of the following is an off-balance sheet financing technique? The use of:

 A. the LIFO inventory method.

 B. capital leases.

 C. operating leases.

14. To better evaluate the solvency of a company, an analyst would most likely add to total liabilities:

 A. the present value of future capital lease payments.

 B. the total amount of future operating lease payments.

 C. the present value of future operating lease payments.

SOLUTIONS FOR READING 42

1. A is correct. For a large, diversified company, margin changes in different business segments may offset each other. Furthermore, margins are most likely to be stable in mature industries.

2. C is correct. Accounts receivable turnover is equal to 365/19 (collection period in days) = 19.2 for 2003 and needs to equal 365/15 = 24.3 in 2004 for Galambos to meet its goal. Sales/turnover equals the accounts receivable balance. For 2003, $300,000,000/19.2 = $15,625,000, and for 2004, $400,000,000/24.3 = $16,460,905. The difference of $835,905 is the increase in receivables needed for Galambos to achieve its goal.

3. C is correct. Credit analysts consider both business risk and financial risk.

4. A is correct. Requiring that net income be positive would avoid selecting companies that report positive return on equity because both net income and shareholders' equity are negative.

5. C is correct. A lower debt-to-total assets ratio indicates greater financial strength. Requiring that a company's debt-to-total assets ratio be below a certain cutoff point would allow the analyst to screen out highly leveraged and, therefore, potentially financially weak companies. Requiring declining sales growth (answer A) or negative income (answer B) would not be appropriate for screening out financially weak companies.

6. C is correct. Survivorship bias exists when companies that merge or go bankrupt are dropped from the database and only surviving companies remain. Look-ahead bias involves using updated financial information in backtesting that would not have been available at the time the decision was made. Backtesting involves testing models in prior periods and is not a bias itself.

7. C is correct. Financial statements should be adjusted for differences in accounting standards (as well as accounting and operating choices). These adjustments should be made prior to ratio analysis.

8. C is correct. IFRS makes a distinction between unrealized gains and losses on available-for-sale debt securities that arise due to exchange rate movements and requires these changes in value to be recognized in the income statement, whereas U.S. GAAP does not make this distinction.

9. A is correct. LIFO is not permitted under international financial reporting standards.

10. C is correct. To convert LIFO inventory to FIFO inventory, the entire LIFO reserve must be added back: $600,000 + $70,000 = $670,000.

11. C is correct. There were no additions or deletions to the fixed asset account during the year, so depreciation expense is equal to the difference in accumulated depreciation at the beginning of the year and the end of the year, or 0.4 million. Average age is equal to accumulated depreciation/depreciation expense, or 1.6/0.4 = 4 years. Average depreciable life is equal to ending gross investment/depreciation expense = 2.8/0.4 = 7 years.

12. C is correct. Tangible book value removes all intangible assets, including goodwill, from the balance sheet.

13. C is correct. Operating leases can be used as an off-balance sheet financing technique because neither the asset nor liability appears on the balance sheet. Inventory and capital leases are reported on the balance sheet.

14. C is correct. The present value of future operating lease payments would be added to total assets and total liabilities.

INTERNATIONAL STANDARDS CONVERGENCE

by Thomas R. Robinson, CFA, Jan Hendrik van Greuning, CFA, Elaine Henry, CFA, and Michael A. Broihahn, CFA

LEARNING OUTCOMES

The candidate should be able to:	Mastery
a. identify and explain the major international accounting standards for each asset and liability category on the balance sheet and the key differences from U.S. generally accepted accounting principles (GAAP);	☐
b. identify and explain the major international accounting standards for major revenue and expense categories on the income statement and the key differences from U.S. GAAP;	☐
c. identify and explain the major differences between international and U.S. GAAP accounting standards concerning the treatment of interest and dividends on the statement of cash flows;	☐
d. interpret the effect of differences between international and U.S. GAAP accounting standards on the balance sheet, income statement, and the statement of changes in equity for some commonly used financial ratios.	☐

INTRODUCTION 1

The International Accounting Standards Board (IASB) is the standard-setting body of the International Accounting Standards Committee (IASC) Foundation. The objectives of the IASC Foundation are to develop a single set of global financial reporting standards and to promote the use of those standards. In accomplishing these objectives, the IASC Foundation explicitly aims to bring about convergence between national standards and international standards.

Note:
New rulings and/or pronouncements issued after the publication of the readings on financial reporting and analysis may cause some of the information in these readings to become dated. Candidates are expected to be familiar with the overall analytical framework contained in the study session readings, as well as the implications of alternative accounting methods for financial analysis and valuation, as provided in the assigned readings. Candidates are not responsible for changes that occur after the material was written.

International Financial Statement Analysis, by Thomas R. Robinson, CFA, Jan Hendrik van Greuning, CFA, Elaine Henry, CFA, and Michael A. Broihahn, CFA. Copyright © 2007 by CFA Institute. Reprinted with permission.

Around the world, many national accounting standard setters have adopted, or are in the process of adopting, the standards issued by the IASB: International Financial Reporting Standards, or IFRS.[1]

Over the past few years, convergence between IFRS and U.S. generally accepted accounting principles (U.S. GAAP), which are issued by the Financial Accounting Standards Board (FASB), has increased significantly. The two accounting standards boards now issue joint exposure drafts for a number of standards. In February 2006, the FASB and IASB published a memorandum of understanding outlining a "roadmap for convergence" over the next several years.

The IFRS *Framework for the Preparation and Presentation of Financial Statements* (referred to here as the "Framework") was introduced in the reading on financial reporting standards. In this reading, we review certain key aspects of the *Framework*. Section 2 provides an overview of the *Framework*. Sections 3, 4, and 5 provide additional descriptions of the IFRS relevant to each of the financial statements, noting some of the differences currently remaining between IFRS and U.S. GAAP. Section 6 summarizes the standard setters' agenda for convergence. Section 7 describes the effect on selected financial ratios of current differences between U.S. and international standards. A summary of key points and practice problems in the CFA Institute multiple-choice format conclude the reading.

A note of caution: The stated objective of the IASB/FASB convergence project is to eliminate differences between IFRS and U.S. GAAP. The convergence project implies that frequent changes to accounting standards are bound to continue for a number of years. Because a detailed comparison of current differences between IFRS and U.S. GAAP would be of limited practical value, this reading aims to present basic principles and issues. Analysts should be aware of resources available to find the timeliest information on IFRS, including the website of the IASB (www.iasb.org) and the website of the FASB (www.fasb.org).

2 THE IFRS *FRAMEWORK*

The IFRS *Framework*, which is currently being re-examined as part of the international convergence project, was originally published in 1989 and was designed to assist the IASB in developing standards as well as to assist users of financial statements in interpreting the information contained therein. The *Framework* sets forth the concepts that underlie the preparation and presenta-

---

[1] International accounting standards also include standards with a numbering system identified as "IAS" (international accounting standards), which were issued by the board of the IASC prior to the formation of the IASB in 2001 and the hand-over of standard-setting functions from the IASC's board to the IASB.

tion of financial statements and provides guidance on the definition, recognition, and measurement of the elements from which financial statements are constructed. In addition, the *Framework* discusses the concepts of capital and capital maintenance.

2.1 Key Aspects of the IFRS *Framework*

The objectives of financial statements, as stated in the *Framework*, are "to provide information about the financial position, performance, and changes in financial position of an entity; this information should be useful to a wide range of users for the purpose of making economic decisions."[2] The definition, therefore, covers the balance sheet (including the statement of changes in equity), income statement, and statement of cash flows.

To achieve the objective of providing useful information, financial statements should have certain characteristics. Recent IASB updates emphasize the following qualitative characteristics related to the usefulness of information in financial statements:

▶ relevance;

▶ predictive value;

▶ faithful representation (an emphasis on economic substance over form, reliability, and completeness);

▶ neutrality (absence of bias);

▶ verifiability.

Financial statements provide information on the financial position and performance of an entity by grouping the effects of transactions and other events into the following five broad classes or elements:

Balance Sheet Elements (Financial Position):

▶ Assets. Resources controlled by an entity as a result of past events and from which future economic benefits are expected to flow to the entity.

▶ Liabilities. Present obligations of an entity arising from past events, the settlement of which is expected to result in an outflow of resources from the entity.

▶ Equity. Assets less liabilities (for companies, shareholders' equity), which is the residual interest in the assets of the entity.

Income Statement Elements (Performance):

▶ Income. Increases in economic benefits that result in an increase in equity, other than increases resulting from contributions by owners. The increases in economic benefits may be in the form of inflows of assets, enhancements to assets, or decreases in liabilities. Income includes both revenues and gains. Revenues are income from the ordinary activities of the entity (e.g., the sale of products). Gains result from activities other than ordinary activities (e.g., the sale of equipment no longer needed).

---

[2] *Framework for the Preparation and Presentation of Financial Statements*, IASC, 1989, adopted by IASB 2001, paragraph 12.

▶ Expenses. Decreases in economic benefits that result in decreases in equity, other than decreases because of distributions to owners. The decreases in economic benefits may be in the form of outflows of assets, depletions of assets, or increases in liabilities. (Expenses include losses as well as those items normally thought of as expenses, such as the cost of goods sold or wages.)

Changes in these five basic elements are portrayed in the statement of cash flow and the statement of changes in equity.

2.2 Challenges in Financial Statement Preparation: Timing and Amounts

Two key challenges for preparers of financial statements are determining when to recognize financial events and how to measure the financial effect of these events.

Recognition is the process of incorporating into the financial statement an item that meets the definition of a financial statement element (i.e., assets, liabilities, equity, income, and expenses) and satisfies the criteria for recognition. The IFRS criteria for recognition of an item are that it should be recognized in the financial statements if:

▶ it is *probable* that any future economic benefit associated with the item will flow to or from the entity, and

▶ the item has a cost or value that can be *measured with reliability*.

Measurement is the process of determining the monetary effect of financial events and thus the amounts that are to be recognized and presented in the financial statements.

In meeting the challenges of recognition and measurement, financial statement preparers employ judgment about appropriate methods—many of which are constrained by IFRS requirements to use specific methods—and the estimation of relevant parameters. Such judgments and estimates can vary across companies and across time; therefore, analysts should develop awareness of the potential effect of these variations on financial statements.

3   THE BALANCE SHEET

A number of standards, including the *Framework* described above, apply to the majority of the components of the balance sheet. These include standards describing requirements for companies adopting international financial standards for the first time,[3] requirements for presenting financial statements under international financial standards,[4] and accounting for changes in accounting principles and estimates.[5]

---

[3] IFRS No. 1.
[4] IAS No. 1.
[5] IAS No. 8.

Other standards apply more directly to specific components of the balance sheet. The sections below describe the key aspects of the standards relevant to each component of the balance sheet.

3.1 Marketable Securities

The international standards of accounting for marketable securities, contained in IAS No. 39, require that companies recognize securities initially at fair market value; for investments in marketable securities, this is typically the cost to acquire securities.

The fair market value of securities changes over time, and the central issue in accounting for securities is: Should securities continue to be presented at cost or adjusted as changes occur in their fair market value? Under the accounting standards, the answer depends on how the security is categorized.

Securities with fixed maturities and payments (e.g., bonds) that the company intends to hold until maturity (and has the ability to do so) can be categorized as "held to maturity." Held-to-maturity securities are presented at their original cost, updated for any amortization of discount or premium. A debt security purchased for an amount greater than its principal value is said to have been purchased at a premium; if purchased for an amount less than its principal value, it is said to have been purchased at a discount. Any premium or discount is amortized (i.e., reduced) over the remaining life of the security so that at maturity, the value of the security in the accounting records equals the principal value.

Securities that do not have fixed maturities (e.g., equity) and bonds that a company does not intend to hold until maturity are presented at their fair market value, and the reported value continues to be adjusted as changes occur in the fair market value. Such changes in a security's fair market value during an accounting period, assuming the security is not sold, give rise to unrealized gains or losses. An unrealized gain results from an increase in a security's value over the accounting period, and an unrealized loss results from a decrease in a security's value. If the security is sold, the gain or loss is said to be realized. When securities are sold, a company realizes a gain (loss) if the sale price is greater than (less than) the value of the security in the company's books.

The accounting for unrealized holding gains or losses differs for **held-for-trading securities** (trading securities) versus available-for-sale securities. Trading securities are simply those securities that the company intends to trade, and available-for-sale securities are those that do not fall into any other category. The category "trading securities" also includes derivatives.

Unrealized holding gains or losses on trading securities are recorded in the income statement. Unrealized holding gains or losses on available-for-sale securities are recorded in equity (as part of other comprehensive income) until the securities are sold. So, both trading and available-for-sale securities are valued at market value, but only the unrealized holding gains or losses on trading securities flow directly through the income statement. As a result, the performance of trading securities portfolios is more transparently reflected in the financial statements.

Exhibit 1 summarizes the different categories of marketable securities and their accounting treatment.

EXHIBIT 1	Categories of Marketable Securities and Accounting Treatment		
Category	How Measured	Unrealized and Realized Gains and Losses	Income (Interest and Dividends) Reported
Held to maturity	Amortized cost	Unrealized: not reported Realized: reported in income statement	In income statement
Trading	Fair value	Unrealized: reported in income statement Realized: reported in income statement	In income statement
Available for sale	Fair value	Unrealized: reported in equity Realized: reported in income statement	In income statement

EXAMPLE 1

Accounting for Marketable Securities

Assume a company has the following portfolio of marketable securities:

Category	Value at Fiscal Year End 2005 ($)	Value at Fiscal Year End 2006 ($)
Held to maturity	10,000,000	10,000,000
Held for trading	5,000,000	5,500,000
Available for sale	8,000,000	7,000,000

1. What amount of unrealized holding gains or losses would the company report in total?

2. How much unrealized holding gains or losses would the company report in its income statement?

Solution to 1: The total amount of unrealized holding gains or losses that the company would report is determined by comparing the end-of-period value of held-for-trading and available-for-sale securities with their values as reported at the end of the previous period. In this example, the company would report a total of $500,000 as unrealized holding *losses*, calculated as the value of the held-for-trading and available-for-sale securities at the end of the period ($12,500,000) minus their value at the beginning of the period ($13,000,000).

Solution to 2: The company would report an unrealized holding *gain* of $500,000 in its income statement. The change in the market value of the available-for-sale securities (the unrealized loss of $1,000,000) would not be reported in the income statement. Instead, it would be shown as part of comprehensive income.

An analyst should obtain an understanding of management's rationale for categorizing securities as "trading securities" or as "available for sale." The performance of trading securities portfolios is more transparently reflected in the financial statements because the income statement shows both income (interest and dividends) and changes in value, whether realized or unrealized. In contrast, with available-for-sale securities, there is an asymmetrical treatment of income and changes in value. This asymmetrical treatment can cause an unsophisticated user of financial statements to misinterpret the performance of a company's marketable securities portfolio. It is possible, for example, that unrealized losses could accumulate in equity without affecting the income statement.

An additional standard relevant to marketable securities is the requirement that risk exposures arising from financial instruments be disclosed; requirements include specified minimum qualitative and quantitative disclosures about credit risk, liquidity risk, and market risk.[6] Qualitative disclosures require a description of management's objectives, policies, and processes for managing those risks. Quantitative disclosures refer to the provision of information regarding the *extent* to which an entity is exposed to risk. Together, these disclosures provide an overview of the entity's use of financial instruments and the resulting risk exposures.

3.2 Inventories

The reading on balance sheets describes various methods by which companies determine the cost of goods in inventory. Unlike U.S. GAAP, international accounting standards[7] require that the choice of the accounting method used to value inventories should be based upon the order in which products are sold, relative to when they are put into inventory. Therefore, whenever possible, the cost of a unit of inventory should be assigned by specific identification of the unit's costs. In many cases, however, it is necessary to use a formula to calculate inventory costs.

International standards permit the use of two alternative formulas for assigning the cost of inventory: 1) weighted average cost, in which the cost per unit of inventory is determined as a weighted average of the cost of all units of inventory, and 2) first in, first out (FIFO), in which it is assumed that the costs associated with the first units purchased (first in) are considered to be the cost of the first units sold (first out).

---

[6] IFRS No. 7.

[7] IAS No. 2.

Unlike U.S. GAAP, international standards do not allow the use of the LIFO (last in, first out) method to calculate the cost of inventory because the method is not considered a faithful model of inventory flows. The IASB has noted that the use of LIFO is often tax driven because this method results in lower taxable income during periods of rising prices; however, they concluded that tax considerations do not provide a conceptual basis for selecting an appropriate treatment.

Like U.S. GAAP, international standards require inventory to be reported at the lower of cost or net realizable value. However, IFRS permits the reversal of inventory write-downs, but no such provision exists in U.S. GAAP.

3.3 Property, Plant, and Equipment

The international standards of accounting for property, plant, and equipment, contained in IAS No. 16, require companies to recognize these assets initially at cost.

Like U.S. GAAP, international standards allow property, plant, and equipment to be reported in the financial statements at cost less accumulated depreciation. "Depreciation" is the systematic allocation of the cost of the asset over its useful life, and "accumulated depreciation" is the cumulative amount of depreciation expense recorded in relation to the asset.

Unlike U.S. GAAP, international accounting standards allow another alternative: reporting property, plant, and equipment at a revalued amount. When property, plant, and equipment are revalued, they are reported in the financial statements at fair value as of the revaluation date, less accumulated depreciation subsequent to the revaluation. Any revaluation increase is reported as part of equity, unless it is reversing a previous revaluation decrease. (The reason for this is that the previous decrease was reported as a reduction in the company's net income.) Any revaluation decrease is reported in profit and loss unless it is reversing a previous revaluation increase.

3.4 Long-Term Investments

The overall IFRS *Framework* for accounting for a company's investments in the securities of another company is based on the extent of control that the investing company has on the investee company. In the discussion of marketable securities above, it was assumed that the equity investment gave the investing company no control over the investee. As discussed, in such cases, the investments are designated as "trading" or "available for sale" and reflected at fair value.

If, however, an equity investment *did* give the investing company some control over the investee, the accounting standards require a different treatment. The specific treatment depends on the amount of control. If an investor owns 20 percent or more of the voting power of an investee, such an ownership stake would provide significant influence, where significant influence is defined as "power to participate in financial and operating policy decisions of the investee but is not control or joint control over those policies."[8] When an investor has significant influence, international standards require that the investment be reported using the equity method of accounting. The equity method of accounting means that the investor reports its pro rata share of the investee's profits as an increase in the amount of investment.

---

[8] IAS No. 28.

If an investor owns more than 50 percent of the voting power of the investee, such an ownership stake would provide significant control and the investee's financial statements would be consolidated with those of the investor. Consolidation roughly means that the investee's assets, liabilities, and income are combined into those of the investor. *Note*: The IFRS standard on business combinations is an active agenda item of the convergence project and is, therefore, subject to change during coming years.

When an investor shares the ownership of an investee, as in a joint venture, control is shared and the investor would account for the investment using either the proportionate consolidation method or the equity method. Proportionate consolidation roughly means that the investor's financial statements include its proportionate share of the investee's assets, liabilities, and income.

Exhibit 2 summarizes the different levels of control associated with each level of ownership and the accounting treatment used in each situation.

EXHIBIT 2	Accounting Treatment for Different Levels of an Investor's Percentage Ownership in an Investee and Related Extent of Control		
Extent of Control	**Percent Ownership**	**Accounting Treatment**	**IFRS Reference**
Significant influence	Between 20–50%	Equity accounting	IAS No. 28
Control	More than 50%	Business combinations/ consolidation	IAS No. 27/IFRS No. 3/SIC 12
Joint control	Shared	Joint ventures/ proportionate consolidation or equity accounting	IAS No. 31/ SIC 13

Note: SIC = Standing Interpretations Committee.

Like U.S. GAAP, international standards use extent of control as a factor determining whether an investee should be consolidated. U.S. GAAP differs from IFRS in that it allows a dual model: one model based on extent of voting control and one model based on an alternative assessment of economic control. The model based on economic control depends first on the economic substance of the investee and second on the investor's economic interests in the investee (liability for the investee's losses and opportunity to benefit from the investee's gains).

Unlike U.S. GAAP, international standards permit that interests in joint ventures may be accounted for using the proportionate consolidation method or the equity method,[9] whereas U.S. GAAP requires the equity method of accounting.

3.5 Goodwill

IFRS defines **goodwill** as the amount an acquirer pays to buy another company, minus the fair value of the net identifiable assets acquired. Goodwill is intended to represent future economic benefits arising from assets that are not capable of

---

[9] IAS No. 31.

being individually identified and separately recognized. Goodwill is considered an **intangible asset** (i.e., an asset without physical substance). Whereas some intangible assets—so-called identifiable intangible assets, such as patents and trademarks—can be bought and sold individually, goodwill cannot. Goodwill is an **unidentifiable intangible**.

Under IFRS No. 3, goodwill is capitalized as an asset and tested for impairment annually. **Impairment** means diminishment in value. Impairment of goodwill is a noncash expense; however, the impairment of goodwill does affect reported net income. When impairment of goodwill is charged against income in the current period, current reported income decreases. This charge against income also leads to reduced net assets and reduced shareholders' equity, but potentially improved return on assets, asset turnover ratios, return on equity, and equity turnover ratios because equity, the denominator in these ratios, is smaller. Even if the market reacts indifferently to an impairment write-off, an analyst should understand the implications of a goodwill write-off and, more generally, evaluate whether reported goodwill has been impaired. Example 2 presents a partial goodwill impairment footnote for Prudential PLC.

EXAMPLE 2

Goodwill Impairment Testing

Susan Lee is examining the financial statements of Prudential PLC and notes that the income statement shows a goodwill impairment charge of £120 million. Lee finds the following footnote to Prudential's financial statements.

Prudential PLC
2005 Annual Report Footnote H1

Impairment Testing

Goodwill does not generate cash flows independently of other groups of assets and thus is assigned to cash generating units (CGUs) for the purposes of impairment testing. These CGUs are based upon how management monitors the business and represent the lowest level to which goodwill can be allocated on a reasonable basis. An allocation of the Group's goodwill to CGUs is shown below:

	2005 £ Millions	2004 £ Millions
M&G	1,153	1,153
Japan life company	—	120
Venture investment subsidiaries of the PAC with-profits fund	607	784
Other	188	188
	1,948	2,245

'Other' represents goodwill amounts allocated across cash generating units in Asia and U.S. operations. These goodwill amounts are not individually material. There are no other intangible assets with indefinite useful lives other than goodwill.

Assessment of Whether Goodwill May Be Impaired

With the exception of M&G and venture investment subsidiaries of the PAC with-profits fund, the goodwill in the balance sheet relates to acquired life businesses. The Company routinely compares the aggregate of net asset value and acquired goodwill on an IFRS basis of acquired life business with the value of the business as determined using the EEV methodology, as described in section D1. Any excess of IFRS over EEV carrying value is then compared with EEV basis value of current and projected future new business to determine whether there is any indication that the goodwill in the IFRS balance sheet may be impaired.

Goodwill is tested for impairment by comparing the CGUs carrying amount, excluding any goodwill, with its recoverable amount.

M&G

The recoverable amount for the M&G CGU has been determined by calculating its value in use. This has been calculated by aggregating the present value of future cash flows expected to be derived from the component businesses of M&G (based upon management projections) and its current surplus capital.

The discounted cash flow valuation has been based on a three-year plan prepared by M&G, and approved by the directors of Prudential plc, and cash flow projections for later years.

As a cross check to the discounted cash flow analysis, a review was undertaken of publicly available information for companies engaged in businesses comparable to the component businesses, including reported market prices for such companies' shares. In addition, a review was undertaken of publicly available terms of transactions involving companies comparable to the component businesses. In particular, comparison has been made of the valuation multiples implied by the discounted cash flow analysis to current trading multiples of companies comparable to the component businesses, as well as to multiples achieved in precedent transactions.

The value in use is particularly sensitive to a number of key assumptions, as follows:

i. The assumed growth rate on forecast cash flows beyond the terminal year of the budget. A growth rate of 2.5 percent has been used to extrapolate beyond the plan period.

ii. The risk discount rate. Differing discount rates have been applied in accordance with the nature of the individual component businesses. For retail and institutional business a risk discount rate of 12 percent has been applied. This represents the average implied discount rate for comparable UK listed asset managers calculated by reference to risk-free rates, equity risk premiums of 5 percent and an average 'beta' factor for relative market risk of comparable UK listed asset managers. A similarly granular approach has been applied for the other component businesses of M&G.

iii. That asset management contracts continue on similar terms.

Management believes that any reasonable change in the key assumptions would not cause the carrying amount of M&G to exceed its recoverable amount.

Japanese Life Company

As noted above, the entire goodwill relating to the Japanese life operation of £120 million has been deemed to be impaired following impairment testing carried out in 2005. This testing was based on a recoverable amount for the Japanese company that was determined by calculating its value in use based on net present value cash flow projections. Such projections reflected existing business over the expected duration of the contracts and expected new business. A risk discount rate of 5 percent was applied to the projected cash flows. On the basis of the results of this exercise it was determined that all goodwill held in relation to the Japanese business should be written off in 2005.

PAC With-Profits Fund Venture Investment Subsidiaries

The recoverable amount for the ventures entities controlled by the Group through PPM Capital has been determined on a portfolio CGU basis by aggregating fair values calculated for each entity less costs to sell these entities.

The fair value of each entity is calculated by PPM Capital in accordance with the International Private Equity and Venture Capital Valuation Guidelines which set out industry best practice for determining the fair value of private equity investments. The guidelines require that an enterprise value is calculated for each investment, typically using an appropriate multiple applied to the Company's maintainable earnings. All amounts relating to financial instruments ranking higher in a liquidation than those controlled by PPM Capital are then deducted from the enterprise value and a marketability discount applied to the result to give a fair value attributable to the instruments controlled by PPM Capital. The marketability discount ranges from 10 percent to 30 percent, depending on PPM Capital's level of control over a realization process.

Management believes that any reasonable change in the key assumptions would not give rise to an impairment charge.

---

1. What operating unit resulted in a goodwill impairment charge, and how was the charge computed?
2. For the operating unit identified in Part 1, would an analyst anticipate subsequent goodwill impairments?

Solution to 1: The entire impairment charge for 2005 was related to the Japanese life company operating unit. The loss was determined by projecting future cash flows for this unit and discounting them at a rate of 5 percent.

Solution to 2: Because the impairment charge for 2005 represented all of the goodwill of the Japanese life company operating unit, subsequent goodwill impairments for this operating unit should not occur.

Because goodwill can significantly influence the comparability of financial statements between companies using different accounting methods, analysts sometimes make certain goodwill-related adjustments to a company's financial statements. The objective of such adjustments is to remove any distortion that goodwill and its recognition, amortization, and impairment might create. Adjustments include the following:

▶ subtracting goodwill from assets and use of this adjusted data to compute financial ratios;

▶ excluding goodwill impairment charges from income and use of this adjusted data when reviewing operating trends; and

▶ evaluating future business acquisitions by taking into account the purchase price paid relative to the net assets and earnings prospects of the acquired company.

If the amount an acquirer pays to buy another company is less than the fair value of the net identifiable assets acquired, it is not recognized as "negative goodwill." Instead, a gain is recognized. However, before any gain is recognized, the acquirer should reassess the cost of acquisition and the fair values attributed to the acquiree's identifiable assets, liabilities, and contingent liabilities.

As noted, goodwill arises in connection with acquisitions. Several other aspects of international accounting for acquisitions may be noted. Under the acquisition method of accounting,[10] the acquisition price must be allocated to all of the acquired company's identifiable tangible and intangible assets, liabilities, and contingent liabilities. The assets and liabilities of the acquired entity are combined into the financial statements of the acquiring company at their fair values on the acquisition date. Because the acquirer's assets and liabilities, measured at their historical costs, are combined with the acquired company's assets and liabilities, measured at their fair market value on the acquisition date, the acquirer's pre- and post-merger balance sheets are often not easily compared.

Furthermore, under the acquisition method, the income statement and the statement of cash flows include the operating performance of the acquiree from the date of the acquisition forward. Operating results prior to the acquisition are not restated and remain the same as historically reported by the acquirer. Consequently, although the financial statements of the acquirer will reflect the reality of the acquisition, they will not be comparable before and after the acquisition.

3.6 Intangible Assets Other than Goodwill

IAS No. 38 includes standards for reporting certain intangible assets other than goodwill. These intangible assets are referred to as "identifiable intangible assets." Identifiable intangible assets arise either from contractual or other legal rights, or must be capable of being separated from the company and sold, transferred, licensed, rented, or exchanged.

The standards for reporting identifiable intangible assets, contained in IAS No. 38, provide that an intangible asset is recognized—at cost—if it is probable

---

[10] IFRS No. 3.

that the future economic benefits attributable to the asset will flow to the company and if the cost of the asset can be measured reliably. Only those intangibles that have been purchased or manufactured (in limited instances) may be recognized as assets. Internally produced items, such as customer lists, are not recognized as assets.

Given that it meets the criteria for recognition, an intangible asset with a finite useful life is amortized on a systematic basis over the best estimate of its useful life. In other words, the cost of the identifiable intangible asset is allocated systematically over the asset's useful life. If the identifiable intangible asset does not have a finite useful life, it is not amortized. Instead, the asset is tested at least annually for impairment as with goodwill. Testing for impairment involves evaluating whether the current value of an asset is materially lower than its carrying value.

Like U.S. GAAP, international standards allow identifiable intangibles to be reported in the financial statements at cost less amortization and less any impairment charges.

Unlike U.S. GAAP, international accounting standards allow another alternative: reporting identifiable intangible assets at a revalued amount. When identifiable intangible assets are revalued, they are reported in the financial statements at fair value as of the revaluation date, less accumulated amortization subsequent to the revaluation. Any revaluation increase is reported as part of equity, unless it is reversing a previous revaluation decrease. Any revaluation decrease is reported in profit and loss unless it is reversing a previous revaluation increase. U.S. GAAP prohibits revaluations.

Companies also have intangible assets that accounting rules do not include as items that can be recorded in financial statements; these intangible assets include management skill, a positive corporate culture, trademarks, name recognition, a good reputation, proprietary products, and so forth. However, the costs related to these intangible assets—such as training, advertising, and research—must be expensed. An analyst must be aware of the potential value of such unrecorded assets.

3.7 Provisions (Nonfinancial Liabilities)

Nonfinancial liabilities include **provisions**, which are liabilities of uncertain timing or amount, such as warranty obligations, and contingent liabilities, which are liabilities contingent on the occurrence of some event. The standards for reporting nonfinancial liabilities, contained in IAS No. 37, provide that a company should recognize nonfinancial liabilities when it has a present obligation as a result of a past event and the company can reliably estimate the cost to settle the obligation.

The amount recognized as a nonfinancial liability should be the best estimate, as of the balance sheet date, of the cost that will be required to settle the obligation.

4   THE INCOME STATEMENT

A number of standards, including the *Framework* (described above), apply to the majority of the components of the income statement. These include standards describing requirements for companies adopting international financial standards for the first time, requirements for presenting financial statements under international financial standards, and accounting for changes in accounting principles and estimates.[11]

Other standards apply more directly to specific components of the income statement. The sections below describe the key aspects of the standards relevant to each component in the same order as the components described in the reading discussing the income statement.

4.1 Revenue Recognition: General

The IASB *Framework* defines income as including both revenue and gains. In IAS No. 18, revenue is defined as the gross inflow of economic benefits during the period, arising in the ordinary course of activities, or resulting in increases in equity other than contributions by equity participants.

IAS No. 18 addresses how revenue is to be measured, namely, at the fair value of consideration received. The standard also addresses the timing of revenue recognition.

Some criteria for recognizing revenue are common to both the sale of goods and the provision of services: It must be possible to reliably measure the amount of revenue and costs of the transaction, and it must be probable that economic benefits of the transaction will flow to the seller. In addition, to recognize revenue from the sale of goods, it is necessary that the risks and rewards of ownership pass to the buyer and that the seller not have continued control over the goods sold. To recognize revenue from the provision of services, it is necessary that the stage of completion of the service can be measured reliably.

U.S. GAAP defines revenue in terms of actual or expected cash flows, and, for revenue recognition, U.S. GAAP focuses extensively on realization and earned status. U.S. GAAP also provides more extensive guidance than IFRS regarding industry-specific issues. Despite such differences, the key principles are similar in U.S. GAAP and IFRS.

4.2 Revenue Recognition for Construction Contracts

IAS No. 11 deals with the recognition of construction contract revenue and costs—in particular, the allocation of contract revenue and costs to the accounting periods in which construction work is performed. The standard applies to the accounting for construction contracts in the financial statements of contractors.

A construction contract is a contract specifically negotiated for the construction of an asset or a combination of assets that are closely interrelated or interdependent in terms of their design, technology, and function, or their ultimate purpose or use. Construction contracts include those for the construction or restoration of assets and the restoration of the environment.

When the outcome of a construction contract can be estimated reliably, revenue and costs (and, therefore, profit) should be recognized based on the stage of completion (percentage of completion method). When the outcome of a contract *cannot* be reliably estimated, revenue should be recognized to the extent that it is probable to recover contract costs. This requirement differs from U.S. GAAP, which requires that the completed contract method be used in such cases.

---

[11] IFRS No. 1, IAS No. 1, and IAS No. 8, respectively.

4.3 Cost of Sales

Two international accounting standards, IAS No. 2 (accounting for the cost of inventories) and IAS No. 18 (revenue recognition), have an effect on cost of sales. As noted, under international standards, LIFO is not an acceptable method for the valuation of inventory. Consequently, financial statements prepared according to U.S. GAAP may differ significantly from those prepared under IFRS.

U.S. GAAP does, however, require that companies using LIFO disclose the information required to enable a user of financial statements to adjust the inventory and cost of sales figures to a basis comparable with financial statements prepared using IFRS.

4.4 Administrative Expenses (Including Employee Benefits)

Administrative (or operating) expenses typically include overheads related to employee costs. The IASB *Framework* defines expenses to include losses because expenses are decreases in economic benefits that result in a decrease in equity. The inclusion of losses as expenses contrasts with U.S. GAAP, which differentiates expenses from losses by restricting the term "expenses" to refer to those outflows (of cash or the equivalent) that relate to the entity's ongoing primary business operations.

One type of administrative expense with specific international accounting principles is the expense related to employee benefits, such as salaries, bonuses, post-employment benefits, and termination benefits. Recognition and measurement principles, as well as the disclosure requirements, are provided in IAS No. 19. IFRS No. 2 deals with equity compensation benefits, such as share options.

4.5 Depreciation Expenses

As discussed above, depreciation is the process of recognizing the costs of fixed assets over time by systematically decreasing the assets' value and reporting a commensurate expense on the income statement. The term "depletion" is used for this process when the asset is a natural resource, and the term "amortization" is used for this process when the asset is an intangible asset. The cost of acquiring land is not depreciated.

International standards require companies to review the depreciation method applied to an asset at least at each financial year-end. If there has been a significant change in the expected pattern of consumption of the future economic benefits embodied in the asset, companies must change the depreciation method to reflect the changed pattern. Similar to U.S. GAAP, such a change is accounted for as a change in accounting estimate[12] and thus reflected on future financial statements.

Various depreciation methods exist, including the straight-line method (which allocates evenly the cost of a long-lived asset over its estimated useful life) and accelerated methods (which allocate a greater proportion of the

---

[12] IAS No. 8.

asset's cost in the earlier years of its useful life, thus accelerating the timing of the depreciation expense). In choosing the appropriate depreciation method, IFRS requires:

► the depreciable amount is allocated on a *systematic* basis over the useful life, and

► the method used must reflect the pattern of expected *consumption*.

Whether the straight-line depreciation method or an accelerated method is used, the method complies with IFRS *only* if it reflects the pattern of the expected consumption of the assets.

4.6 Finance Costs

In general, borrowing costs—defined as interest and other costs incurred by an entity in connection with the borrowing of funds—are expensed in the period incurred.

IFRS offers an alternative to expensing borrowing costs immediately. When borrowing costs are incurred in connection with the acquisition, construction, or production of an asset that takes a long time to be ready for its intended use, such borrowing costs can be added to the total cost of the asset.[13] In other words, rather than expensing these costs immediately, a company has the alternative to capitalize these borrowing costs and depreciate them over time. This topic is an item on the list of IASB's short-term convergence projects as of December 2006.

U.S. GAAP requires the capitalization of interest costs for assets that take a substantial time to complete.

4.7 Income Tax Expense

IAS No. 12 prescribes the accounting treatment for income taxes and specifically addresses issues relating to the carrying amount of assets as well as transactions and other events of the current period, which are recognized in the entity's financial statements.

As with U.S. GAAP, international standards provide for the accounting treatment when differences exist between accounting methods allowed by the relevant taxing authority and accounting methods allowed for financial statement reporting (i.e., IFRS). Where differences exist between methods allowable by taxing authorities and by IFRS, differences will exist between taxable profit and financial statement pretax profit (also referred to as "accounting profit"). Such differences give rise to differences in the value of a company's assets and liabilities recorded in its financial statements (balance sheet) and the tax bases of those assets and liabilities. In turn, these differences can result in future taxes payable or receivable, so-called deferred tax liabilities and deferred tax assets.

The primary differences between U.S. GAAP and IFRS are attributable to differences in exceptions to the application of the principles (i.e., differences in the scope of coverage of the principles).

---

[13] IAS No. 23.

4.8 Nonrecurring Items

Nonrecurring items generally include discontinued operations, accounting changes, and unusual or infrequent items. As noted, analysts typically find it useful to break reported earnings down into recurring and nonrecurring components. Recurring earnings are viewed as permanent or sustainable, whereas nonrecurring earnings are considered to be somewhat random and unsustainable. Therefore, analysts often exclude the effects of nonrecurring items when performing a short-term analysis of an entity (e.g., estimating next year's earnings). However, even so-called nonrecurring events, such as sales of a part of a business, tend to recur from time to time, so analysts may include some average (per year) amount of nonrecurring items for longer-term analyses.

IFRS and U.S. GAAP differ in their treatment of these issues, although as with other areas, convergence is occurring.[14]

For discontinued operations, IFRS changed to align with U.S. GAAP. IFRS No. 5 generally converges with SFAS No. 144.[15] The new international guidance, like the U.S. standards, requires that discontinued operations be reported when a company disposes of one of its business components (or when the component is being held for sale) and will no longer have management involvement.

For accounting changes, U.S. GAAP changed to align with IFRS. SFAS No. 154,[16] issued in June 2005, generally converges with IAS No. 8. Changes in accounting principles are accounted for retrospectively, and changes in accounting estimates are accounted for prospectively.

For extraordinary items, convergence has not yet been achieved. U.S. GAAP continues to allow extraordinary items (i.e., items that are both unusual in nature and infrequent in occurrence) to be reported separately from net income.

Unlike U.S. GAAP, IFRS do not distinguish between items that are and are not likely to recur. Furthermore, IFRS do not permit any items to be classified as "extraordinary items." However, IFRS do require the disclosure of all material information that is relevant to understanding a company's performance. The analyst generally can use this information, together with information from outside sources, to estimate amounts of recurring and nonrecurring items.

5

THE STATEMENT OF CASH FLOWS

Both international standards and U.S. GAAP require that a statement of cash flows be included among a company's full set of financial statements (FASB Statement No. 95, *Statement of Cash Flows*,[17] and IAS No. 7, *Cash Flow Statements*) showing the changes in cash and cash equivalents over an accounting period.

Both sets of standards require that the statement of cash flows include sections covering operating, investing, and financing activities of the company. The differences between international and U.S. standards arise in the classification of certain cash flows.

International standards allow companies to report cash inflows from interest and dividends as either operating or investing activities and cash outflows for

---

[14] This topic is discussed in "Convergence: In Search of the Best," D. Herrmann and I.P.N. Hauge, *Journal of Accountancy* online edition, January 2006: www.aicpa.org/PUBS/JOFA/jan2006/herrmann.htm.

[15] FASC ASC Subtopic 205-20 [Presentation of Financial Statements–Discontinued Operations].

[16] FASC ASC Topic 250 [Accounting Changes and Error Corrections].

[17] FASC ASC Topic 230 [Statement of Cash Flows].

interest and dividends as either operating or financing activities (see Exhibit 3). In contrast, U.S. standards require the following: Interest and dividends received are classified as inflows from operating activities; interest paid is classified as an outflow for operating activities; and dividends paid are classified as financing activities.

EXHIBIT 3	Statement of Cash Flows

Classification of Interest and Dividends under International and U.S. Standards

Category	Classification in IFRS vs. U.S. GAAP

Cash Flows from *Operating* Activities

Cash from principal revenue-producing activities of the entity (i.e., cash receipts from customers less cash payments to suppliers and employees).

Interest received	IFRS alternatives: operating or investing section
	U.S. GAAP: mandated operating section
Dividends received	IFRS alternatives: operating or investing section
	U.S. GAAP: mandated operating section
Interest paid	IFRS alternatives: operating or financing section
	U.S. GAAP: mandated operating section
Dividends paid (IFRS only)	IFRS alternatives: operating or financing section

Cash Flows from *Investing* Activities

Purchases of long-term assets and other investments not included in cash equivalents; proceeds on sale.

Interest received (IFRS only)	IFRS alternatives: operating or investing section
Dividends received (IFRS only)	IFRS alternatives: operating or investing section

Cash Flows from *Financing* Activities

Cash from issuance or repayment of equity capital and/or long-term debt.

Dividends paid	IFRS alternatives: operating or financing section
	U.S. GAAP: mandated financing section
Interest paid	IFRS alternatives: operating or financing section

6   STANDARD SETTERS' AGENDA FOR CONVERGENCE

As noted in the introduction to this reading, in February 2006, the FASB and IASB published a memorandum of understanding outlining a "roadmap for convergence" over the next several years. This section summarizes the standard setters' agenda for convergence over the period 2006 to 2008.

By 2008, the IASB and FASB aim to conclude whether any major differences should be eliminated in the following topics for short-term convergence, and if so, to complete the work to do so: fair value option (allow companies to report financial assets and liabilities at fair value on a contract-by-contract basis, converging to IFRS); borrowing costs (eliminate alternative to expense immediately when in connection with longer-term projects, converging to U.S. GAAP); research and development; impairment; segment reporting; subsequent events; and income taxes.

Topics that are already on an active agenda for IASB and/or FASB include business combinations, consolidations, fair value measurement guidance, liabilities and equity distinctions, performance reporting, post-retirement benefits (including pensions), and revenue recognition. Joint IASB and FASB goals for 2008 have been established for each of these topics.

7   EFFECT OF DIFFERENCES BETWEEN ACCOUNTING STANDARDS

As we note throughout this reading, differences between international and U.S. accounting standards are decreasing as convergence between the two sets of standards occurs. Differences that do exist have an effect on commonly used financial ratios. We discuss several major differences here.

If comparing a U.S. company that uses LIFO accounting with an international company for whom this method is not allowable, an analyst will make adjustments. Specifically, using financial statement note disclosures, the analyst will adjust the U.S. company's profits (gross, operating, and net), ending inventory, and total assets. These adjustments will affect certain profitability, solvency, liquidity, and activity ratios. For comparison purposes, inventory is adjusted from LIFO to FIFO by adding the LIFO reserve to the LIFO inventory value on the balance sheet. Under U.S. GAAP, a company must disclose the LIFO reserve amount in the financial statement notes if the LIFO method is followed. In addition, cost of goods sold is adjusted from LIFO to FIFO by subtracting the net increase in the LIFO reserve that occurred during the fiscal year. Example 3 illustrates a LIFO to FIFO conversion.

EXAMPLE 3

LIFO Effects on Financial Statements and Ratios

Buccaneer Corporation prepares its financial statements (Exhibits 4 and 5) in accordance with U.S. GAAP and uses the LIFO inventory method. During the year, Buccaneer's LIFO reserve increased from $40 million to $64 million. The income tax rate is 30 percent.

EXHIBIT 4	Income Statement and Balance Sheet under LIFO and FIFO Inventory Accounting ($ Millions)		
Account	LIFO Method	LIFO to FIFO Adjustment	FIFO Method
Sales	1,800.0	—	1,800.0
Cost of sales	1,060.0	(24.0)	1,036.0
Gross profit	740.0	24.0	764.0
Operating expenses	534.0	—	534.0
Income before taxes	206.0	24.0	230.0
Income taxes	61.8	(7.2)	69.0
Net income	144.2	(16.8)	161.0
Cash	80.0	—	80.0
Inventory	356.0	64.0	420.0
Other current assets	344.0	—	344.0
Fixed assets, net	1,120.0	—	1,120.0
Total assets	1,900.0	64.0	1,964.0
Current liabilities	200.0	—	200.0
Noncurrent liabilities	424.0	19.2	443.2
Common stock	840.0	—	840.0
Retained earnings	436.0	44.8	480.8
Total liabilities and equity	1,900.0	64.0	1,964.0

The net increase in Buccaneer's LIFO reserve during the fiscal year was $24 million ($64 million − $40 million). To adjust from LIFO to FIFO, the net increase in the LIFO reserve must be subtracted from the LIFO reported cost of sales. (A net decrease in the LIFO reserve during the year would be added to LIFO reported cost of sales in a LIFO to FIFO conversion.) Accordingly, because reported gross profits are $24 million higher after the FIFO conversion, income tax expense will increase by $7.2 million ($24 million × 30% income tax rate), resulting in an increase to net income of $16.8 million. For the balance sheet conversion, the year-end LIFO reserve of $64 million is added to the LIFO reported inventory, resulting in an increase of $64 million to both inventory and total assets under FIFO. In addition, the deferred income tax liabilities will increase by $19.2 million ($64 million × 30% income tax rate), and retained earnings will increase by $44.8 million ($64 million × 70% after-tax retention).

Comparative selected profitability, solvency, liquidity, and activity ratios for Buccaneer Corporation under the two inventory methods are given in Exhibit 5.

EXHIBIT 5	Financial Ratios under LIFO and FIFO Inventory Accounting		
Ratio	**Formula**	**LIFO Method**	**FIFO Method**
Net profit margin	Net income ÷ Net sales	8.01%	8.94%
Financial leverage	Total assets ÷ Total equity	1.489	1.487
Current ratio	Current assets ÷ Current liabilities	3.90	4.22
Inventory turnover	Cost of sales ÷ Ending inventory	2.98 turns	2.47 turns

If comparing an IFRS company with a U.S. company that reports extraordinary items separately from net income but which reports certain unusual items as part of operating income, an analyst will examine the financial statement notes to identify similar items that have received different reporting treatment.

If comparing an IFRS company, which has written up the value of its intangible or tangible long-term assets, with a U.S. company, an analyst will eliminate the effect of the write-ups in calculating asset-based ratios. Example 4 illustrates a revaluation adjustment conversion.

EXAMPLE 4

Analyst Adjustments to Revaluations in IFRS/U.S. GAAP Comparisons

Aramis Ltd. prepares its financial statements in accordance with IFRS. During the current year, Aramis revalued its fixed assets upward by a total of €75 million to better reflect its present fair market value.

The analyst must reverse the revaluation adjustments that Aramis has made if Aramis is to be compared with a company that complies with U.S. GAAP. For Aramis, the analyst will reduce both fixed assets and other equity by the upward revaluation of €75 million. Exhibit 6 shows these adjustments.

EXHIBIT 6	Analyst Adjustments to Revaluation (€ Millions)		
Account	**Unadjusted**	**Reversal of Revaluation**	**Post-Adjustment**
Sales	1,700.0	—	1,700.0
Cost of sales	1,040.0	—	1,040.0
Gross profit	660.0	—	660.0
Operating expenses	475.0	—	475.0
Income before taxes	185.0	—	185.0
Income taxes	74.0	—	74.0
Net income	111.0	—	111.0

(Exhibit continued on next page . . .)

EXHIBIT 6	(continued)		
Account	**Unadjusted**	**Reversal of Revaluation**	**Post-Adjustment**
Fixed assets, net	1,150.0	(75.0)	1,075.0
Inventory	310.0	—	310.0
Other current assets	120.0	—	120.0
Cash	20.0	—	20.0
Total assets	1,600.0	(75.0)	1,525.0
Noncurrent liabilities	370.0	—	370.0
Current liabilities	225.0	—	225.0
Contributed capital	550.0	—	550.0
Earned and other equity	455.0	(75.0)	380.0
Total liabilities and equity	1,600.0	(75.0)	1,525.0

Selected comparative performance ratios for Aramis under the two approaches are given in Exhibit 7.

EXHIBIT 7	Financial Ratios Pre- and Post-Adjustment		
Ratio	**Formula**	**Unadjusted**	**Post-Adjustment**
Return on assets	Net income ÷ Total assets	6.94%	7.28%
Return on equity	Net income ÷ Total equity	11.04%	11.94%
Asset turnover	Net sales ÷ Total assets	1.063 turns	1.115 turns
Equity turnover	Net sales ÷ Total equity	1.692 turns	1.828 turns
Financial leverage	Total assets ÷ Total equity	1.592	1.640

SUMMARY

The IASB is the standard-setting body of the IASC Foundation. The objectives of the IASC Foundation are to develop a single set of global financial reporting standards and to promote the use of those standards. In accomplishing these objectives, the IASC Foundation explicitly aims to bring about convergence between national standards and international standards. Many national accounting standard setters have adopted, or are in the process of adopting, the IFRS.

This reading discussed both the IFRS *Framework* and the IFRS standards for reporting accounting items on the balance sheet, income statement, and cash flow statement. Key points include the following:

▶ The objectives of financial statements, as stated in the *Framework*, are "to provide information about the financial position, performance, and changes in financial position of an entity; this information should be useful to a wide range of users for the purpose of making economic decisions."

▶ To achieve the objective of providing useful information, financial statements should have the following qualitative characteristics: relevance, predictive value, faithful representation, neutrality, and verifiability.

▶ Financial statements provide information on the financial position and performance of an entity by grouping the effects of transactions and other events into the following five broad elements: assets, liabilities, equity, income, and expenses.

▶ Both IFRS and U.S. GAAP require companies to present basic financial statements: balance sheet, income statement, statement of cash flows, and statement of changes in equity.

▶ One major difference between IFRS and U.S. GAAP affecting all three statements involves inventories: U.S. GAAP allows the LIFO method for inventory costing, whereas IFRS does not.

▶ Another major balance sheet difference between IFRS and U.S. GAAP is that IFRS allows companies to revalue property, plant, and equipment as well as intangible assets.

▶ Accounting for investments is another area of difference: IFRS uses a voting control model to determine need for consolidation, whereas U.S. GAAP uses a dual model based on voting control and economic control.

▶ An important difference between IFRS and U.S. GAAP is the treatment of some nonrecurring items. IFRS does not permit any items to be classified as "extraordinary items."

▶ International standards allow companies to report cash inflows from interest and dividends as relating to either "operating" or "investing activities," and cash outflows for interest and dividends as relating to either "operating" or "financing activities."

▶ Convergence between IFRS and U.S. GAAP has increased significantly over the past few years and is continuing.

▶ Analysts should know how to make financial statement adjustments to better compare IFRS reporting companies with those companies reporting under U.S. GAAP.

PRACTICE PROBLEMS FOR READING 43

1. According to the IFRS *Framework*, which of the following is a qualitative characteristic related to the usefulness of information in financial statements?
   A. Neutrality.
   B. Timeliness.
   C. Accrual basis.

2. Under the IFRS *Framework*, changes in the elements of financial statements are *most likely* portrayed in the:
   A. balance sheet.
   B. income statement.
   C. statement of cash flows.

3. Under IASB standards, which of the following categories of marketable securities is *most likely* to incur an asymmetrical treatment of income and changes in value?
   A. Held for trading.
   B. Held to maturity.
   C. Available for sale.

4. According to IASB standards, which of the following inventory methods is *most preferred*?
   A. Specific identification.
   B. Weighted average cost.
   C. First in, first out (FIFO).

5. According to IASB standards, which of the following inventory methods is not acceptable?
   A. Weighted average cost.
   B. First in, first out (FIFO).
   C. Last in, first out (LIFO).

6. Under IASB standards, inventory write-downs are:
   A. not allowed.
   B. allowed but not reversible.
   C. allowed and subject to reversal.

7. According to IASB standards, property, plant, and equipment revaluations are:
   A. not allowed.
   B. allowed for decreases only.
   C. allowed for both increases and decreases.

8. Under IASB standards, a joint venture interest is accounted for by using:
   A. consolidation.
   B. the equity method or consolidation.
   C. the equity method or proportionate consolidation.

9. Under IASB standards, goodwill:
    A. may be written off when acquired.
    B. is subject to an annual impairment test.
    C. is amortized over its expected useful life.

10. Under IASB standards, negative goodwill:
    A. must be recorded as a gain.
    B. is prorated to the noncurrent assets.
    C. is accounted for as an extraordinary item.

11. Under IASB standards, an identifiable intangible asset with an indefinite life:
    A. may be written off when acquired.
    B. is amortized over a 20-year period.
    C. is accounted for in the same manner as goodwill.

12. Under IASB standards, identifiable intangible assets are:
    A. only revalued downward, with the decrease reported to profit and loss.
    B. revalued upward and reported to equity when reversing a previous revaluation decrease.
    C. revalued upward and reported to profit and loss when reversing a previous revaluation decrease.

13. Under IASB standards, when the outcome of a construction contract cannot be estimated reliably, revenue and costs should be:
    A. recognized by using the completed contract method.
    B. recognized by using the percentage of completion contract method.
    C. recognized to the extent that it is probable to recover contract costs.

14. Under IASB standards, fixed asset depreciation methods must be:
    A. rational and systematic.
    B. rational and reviewed at least annually.
    C. systematic and reflect the pattern of expected consumption.

15. Under IASB standards, cash inflows for the receipt of interest and dividends are:
    A. operating cash flows.
    B. either operating or investing cash flows.
    C. either investing or financing cash flows.

16. Under IASB standards, cash outflows for the payment of interest are:
    A. operating cash flows.
    B. either investing or financing cash flows.
    C. either operating or financing cash flows.

17. Under IASB standards, cash outflows for the payment of dividends are:
    A. financing cash flows.
    B. either operating or investing cash flows.
    C. either operating or financing cash flows.

18. When comparing a U.S. company that uses LIFO accounting with an IFRS company that uses FIFO accounting, an analyst will:

   A. make no adjustment if the adjustment data are unavailable.

   B. adjust either company to achieve comparability with the other.

   C. adjust the U.S. company to achieve comparability with the IFRS company.

19. When comparing an IFRS company that has written up the value of its intangible assets with a U.S. company, an analyst will eliminate the effect of the write-ups in calculating the:

   A. gross margin.

   B. earnings per share.

   C. financial leverage multiplier.

SOLUTIONS FOR READING 43

1. A is correct. Neutrality is a qualitative characteristic. (Timeliness is a constraint and accrual basis is an assumption.)

2. C is correct. Changes in the five basic elements (assets, liabilities, equity, income, and expenses) are portrayed in the statement of cash flows and the statement of changes in equity.

3. C is correct. For available-for-sale securities, there is an asymmetrical treatment of income and changes in value. Under this classification, unrealized gains and losses can accumulate in equity without affecting the income statement.

4. A is correct. Whenever possible, the cost of inventory should be assigned by specific identification of the unit's costs. Two alternative formulas for assigning the cost of inventory are weighted average cost and FIFO.

5. C is correct. LIFO is not an acceptable inventory costing method.

6. C is correct. Like U.S. GAAP, international standards require inventory to be reported at the lower of cost or net realizable value. However, IFRS permit the reversal of inventory write-downs, but no such provision exists in U.S. GAAP.

7. C is correct. Unlike U.S. GAAP, international accounting standards allow revaluations (both increases and decreases) for property, plant, and equipment.

8. C is correct. When an investor shares the ownership of an investee, as in a joint venture, control is shared and the investor would account for the investment using a proportionate consolidation method, with the equity method as an alternative.

9. B is correct. Under IFRS No. 3, goodwill is capitalized and tested for impairment annually.

10. A is correct. A gain is recognized if the amount an acquirer pays to buy another company is less than the fair value of the identifiable net assets acquired. Extraordinary gains are not allowed under IASB.

11. C is correct. If an intangible asset does not have a finite life, it is not amortized. Instead, the asset is tested at least annually for impairment (like goodwill).

12. C is correct. Any upward revaluation is reported as part of equity, unless it is reversing a previous revaluation decrease.

13. C is correct. When the outcome of a contract cannot be reliably estimated, revenue should be recognized to the extent that it is probable to recover contract costs. This differs from U.S. GAAP, which requires that the completed contract method be used in such cases.

14. C is correct. In choosing the appropriate depreciation method, IFRS requires that 1) the depreciable amount is allocated on a systematic basis over the useful life, and 2) the method used must reflect the pattern of expected consumption.

15. B is correct. IASB allows cash flows from interest and dividends to be reported as either "operating" or "investing cash inflows." Under U.S. GAAP, these must be reported as "operating cash inflows."

16. C is correct. IASB allows cash payments for interest to be reported as either "operating" or "financing cash outflows." Under U.S. GAAP, these must be reported as "operating cash outflows."

17. C is correct. IASB allows cash payments for dividends to be reported as either "operating" or "financing cash outflows." Under U.S. GAAP, these must be reported as "financing cash outflows."

18. C is correct. If comparing a U.S. company that uses LIFO accounting with an international company for whom this method is not allowable, an analyst will make adjustments. Specifically, using LIFO reserve note disclosures, the analyst will adjust the U.S. company's profits, ending inventory, and total assets.

19. C is correct. If comparing an IFRS company, which has written up the value of its intangible assets, with a U.S. company, an analyst will eliminate the effect of the write-ups in calculating any affected asset-based ratios, which, in this case, includes the financial leverage multiplier (Total assets ÷ Total common equity).

A priori probability   A probability based on logical analysis rather than on observation or personal judgment.

Abandonment option   The ability to terminate a project at some future time if the financial results are disappointing.

Abnormal return   The amount by which a security's actual return differs from its expected return, given the security's risk and the market's return.

Above full-employment equilibrium A macroeconomic equilibrium in which real GDP exceeds potential GDP.

Absolute dispersion   The amount of variability present without comparison to any reference point or benchmark.

Absolute frequency   The number of observations in a given interval (for grouped data).

Accelerated book build   An offering of securities by an investment bank acting as principal that is accomplished in only one or two days.

Accelerated methods of depreciation   Depreciation methods that allocate a relatively large proportion of the cost of an asset to the early years of the asset's useful life.

Account   With the accounting systems, a formal record of increases and decreases in a specific asset, liability, component of owners' equity, revenue, or expense.

Account format   A method of presentation of accounting transactions in which effects on assets appear at the left and effects on liabilities and equity appear at the right of a central dividing line; also known as T-account format.

Accounting profit (income before taxes or pretax income)   Income as reported on the income statement, in accordance with prevailing accounting standards, before the provisions for income tax expense.

Accounting risk   The risk associated with accounting standards that vary from country to country or with any uncertainty about how certain transactions should be recorded.

Accounts payable   Amounts that a business owes to its vendors for goods and services that were purchased from them but which have not yet been paid.

Accounts receivable turnover   Ratio of sales on credit to the average balance in accounts receivable.

Accrual basis   Method of accounting in which the effect of transactions on financial condition and income are recorded when they occur, not when they are settled in cash.

Accrued expenses (accrued liabilities)   Liabilities related to expenses that have been incurred but not yet paid as of the end of an accounting period—an example of an accrued expense is rent that has been incurred but not yet paid, resulting in a liability "rent payable."

Accrued interest   Interest earned but not yet paid.

Accumulated benefit obligation   Under U.S. GAAP, a measure used in estimating a defined-benefit pension plan's liabilities, defined as "the actuarial present value of benefits (whether vested or non-vested) attributed by the pension benefit formula to employee service rendered before a specified date and based on employee service and compensation (if applicable) prior to that date."

Accumulated depreciation   An offset to property, plant, and equipment (PPE) reflecting the amount of the cost of PPE that has been allocated to current and previous accounting periods.

Acquiring company, or acquirer   The company in a merger or acquisition that is acquiring the target.

Acquisition   The purchase of some portion of one company by another; the purchase may be for assets, a definable segment of another entity, or the purchase of an entire company.

Acquisition method   A method of accounting for a business combination where the acquirer is required to measure each identifiable asset and liability at fair value. This method was the result of a joint project of the IASB and FASB aiming at convergence in standards for the accounting of business combinations.

Active factor risk   The contribution to active risk squared resulting from the portfolio's different-than-benchmark exposures relative to factors specified in the risk model.

Active investment   An approach to investing in which the investor seeks to outperform a given benchmark.

Active return   The return on a portfolio minus the return on the portfolio's benchmark.

Active risk   The standard deviation of active returns.

Active risk squared   The variance of active returns; active risk raised to the second power.

Active specific risk or asset selection risk   The contribution to active risk squared resulting from the portfolio's active weights on individual assets as those weights interact with assets' residual risk.

Active strategy   In reference to short-term cash management, an investment strategy characterized by monitoring and attempting to capitalize on market conditions to optimize the risk and return relationship of short-term investments.

Activity ratios (asset utilization or operating efficiency ratios)   Ratios that measure how efficiently a company performs day-to-day tasks, such as the collection of receivables and management of inventory.

Addition rule for probabilities   A principle stating that the probability that A or B occurs (both occur) equals the probability that A occurs, plus the probability that B occurs, minus the probability that both A and B occur.

Add-on interest   A procedure for determining the interest on a bond or loan in which the interest is added onto the face value of a contract.

Adjusted beta   Historical beta adjusted to reflect the tendency of beta to be mean reverting.

Adjusted R^2   A measure of goodness-of-fit of a regression that is adjusted for degrees of freedom and hence does not automatically increase when another independent variable is added to a regression.

Agency costs   Costs associated with the conflict of interest present when a company is managed by non-owners. Agency costs result from the inherent conflicts of interest between managers and equity owners.

Agency costs of equity   The smaller the stake that managers have in the company, the less is their share in bearing the cost of excessive perquisite consumption or not giving their best efforts in running the company.

Agency problem, or principal-agent problem   A conflict of interest that arises when the agent in an agency relationship has goals and incentives that differ from the principal to whom the agent owes a fiduciary duty.

Agency relationships   An arrangement whereby someone, an agent, acts on behalf of another person, the principal.

Aggregate demand The relationship between the quantity of real GDP demanded and the price level.

G-1

Aggregate hours The total number of hours worked by all the people employed, both full time and part time, during a year.

Aging schedule A breakdown of accounts into categories of days outstanding.

Allocationally efficient Said of a market, a financial system, or an economy that promotes the allocation of resources to their highest value uses.

Allowance for bad debts An offset to accounts receivable for the amount of accounts receivable that are estimated to be uncollectible.

All-or-nothing (AON) orders An order that includes the instruction to trade only if the trade fills the entire quantity (size) specified.

Alternative hypothesis The hypothesis accepted when the null hypothesis is rejected.

Alternative investment markets Market for investments other than traditional securities investments (i.e., traditional common and preferred shares and traditional fixed income instruments). The term usually encompasses direct and indirect investment in real estate (including timberland and farmland) and commodities (including precious metals); hedge funds, private equity, and other investments requiring specialized due diligence.

Alternative trading systems (electronic communications networks or multilateral trading facilities) Trading venues that function like exchanges but that do not exercise regulatory authority over their subscribers except with respect to the conduct of the subscribers' trading in their trading systems.

American depository receipt A U.S. dollar-denominated security that trades like a common share on U.S. exchanges.

American depository shares The underlying shares on which American depository receipts are based. They trade in the issuing company's domestic market.

American option An option that can be exercised at any time until its expiration date.

Amortization The process of allocating the cost of intangible long-term assets having a finite useful life to accounting periods; the allocation of the amount of a bond premium or discount to the periods remaining until bond maturity.

Amortizing and accreting swaps A swap in which the notional principal changes according to a formula related to changes in the underlying.

Analysis of variance (ANOVA) The analysis of the total variability of a dataset (such as observations on the dependent variable in a regression) into components representing different sources of variation; with reference to regression, ANOVA provides the inputs for an F-test of the significance of the regression as a whole.

Annual percentage rate The cost of borrowing expressed as a yearly rate.

Annuity A finite set of level sequential cash flows.

Annuity due An annuity having a first cash flow that is paid immediately.

Anticipation stock Excess inventory that is held in anticipation of increased demand, often because of seasonal patterns of demand.

Antidilutive With reference to a transaction or a security, one that would increase earnings per share (EPS) or result in EPS higher than the company's basic EPS—antidilutive securities are not included in the calculation of diluted EPS.

Arbitrage 1) The simultaneous purchase of an undervalued asset or portfolio and sale of an overvalued but equivalent asset or portfolio, in order to obtain a riskless profit on the price differential. Taking advantage of a market inefficiency in a risk-free manner. 2) The condition in a financial market in which equivalent assets or combinations of assets sell for two different prices, creating an opportunity to profit at no risk with no commitment of money. In a well-functioning financial market, few arbitrage opportunities are possible. 3) A risk-free operation that earns an expected positive net profit but requires no net investment of money.

Arbitrage opportunity An opportunity to conduct an arbitrage; an opportunity to earn an expected positive net profit without risk and with no net investment of money.

Arbitrage portfolio The portfolio that exploits an arbitrage opportunity.

Arbitrageurs Traders who engage in arbitrage (see *arbitrage*).

Arithmetic mean The sum of the observations divided by the number of observations.

Arms index, also called **TRIN** A flow of funds indicator applied to a broad stock market index to measure the relative extent to which money is moving into or out of rising and declining stocks.

Arrears swap A type of interest rate swap in which the floating payment is set at the end of the period and the interest is paid at that same time.

Asian call option A European-style option with a value at maturity equal to the difference between the stock price at maturity and the average stock price during the life of the option, or $0, whichever is greater.

Ask (offer) The price at which a dealer or trader is willing to sell an asset, typically qualified by a maximum quantity (ask size).

Ask size The maximum quantity of an asset that pertains to a specific ask price from a trader. For example, if the ask for a share issue is $30 for a size of 1,000 shares, the trader is offering to sell at $30 up to 1,000 shares.

Asset allocation The process of determining how investment funds should be distributed among asset classes.

Asset beta The unlevered beta; reflects the business risk of the assets; the asset's systematic risk.

Asset class A group of assets that have similar characteristics, attributes, and risk/return relationships.

Asset purchase An acquisition in which the acquirer purchases the target company's assets and payment is made directly to the target company.

Asset retirement obligations (AROs) The fair value of the estimated costs to be incurred at the end of a tangible asset's service life. The fair value of the liability is determined on the basis of discounted cash flows.

Asset-based loan A loan that is secured with company assets.

Asset-based valuation models Valuation based on estimates of the market value of a company's assets.

Assets Resources controlled by an enterprise as a result of past events and from which future economic benefits to the enterprise are expected to flow.

Assignment of accounts receivable The use of accounts receivable as collateral for a loan.

Asymmetric information The differential of information between corporate insiders and outsiders regarding the company's performance and prospects. Managers typically have more information about the company's performance and prospects than owners and creditors.

At the money An option in which the underlying value equals the exercise price.

Autocorrelation The correlation of a time series with its own past values.

Automated Clearing House An electronic payment network available to businesses, individuals, and financial institutions in the United States, U.S. Territories, and Canada.

Automatic fiscal policy A fiscal policy action that is triggered by the state of the economy.

Automatic stabilizers Mechanisms that stabilize real GDP without explicit action by the government.

Autonomous tax multiplier The magnification effect of a change in taxes on aggregate demand.

Autoregressive (AR) model A time series regressed on its own past values, in which the independent variable is a lagged value of the dependent variable.

Available-for-sale investments Debt and equity securities not classified as either held-to-maturity or held-for-trading securities. The investor is willing to sell but not actively planning to sell. In general, available-for-sale securities are reported at fair value on the balance sheet.

Average cost pricing rule A rule that sets price to cover cost including normal profit, which means setting the price equal to average total cost.

Average fixed cost Total fixed cost per unit of output.

Average product The average product of a factor of production. It equals total product divided by the quantity of the factor employed.

Average total cost Total cost per unit of output.

Average variable cost Total variable cost per unit of output.

Backtesting With reference to portfolio strategies, the application of a strategy's portfolio selection rules to historical data to assess what would have been the strategy's historical performance.

Backward integration A merger involving the purchase of a target ahead of the acquirer in the value or production chain; for example, to acquire a supplier.

Backwardation A condition in the futures markets in which the benefits of holding an asset exceed the costs, leaving the futures price less than the spot price.

Balance sheet (statement of financial position or statement of financial condition) The financial statement that presents an entity's current financial position by disclosing resources the entity controls (its assets) and the claims on those resources (its liabilities and equity claims), as of a particular point in time (the date of the balance sheet).

Balance sheet ratios Financial ratios involving balance sheet items only.

Balanced budget A government budget in which tax revenues and outlays are equal.

Balanced budget multiplier The magnification effect on aggregate demand of a simultaneous change in government expenditure and taxes that leaves the budget balanced.

Balance-sheet-based accruals ratio The difference between net operating assets at the end and the beginning of the period compared to the average net operating assets over the period.

Balance-sheet-based aggregate accruals The difference between net operating assets at the end and the beginning of the period.

Bank discount basis A quoting convention that annualizes, on a 360-day year, the discount as a percentage of face value.

Bar chart A price chart with four bits of data for each time interval—the high, low, opening, and closing prices. A vertical line connects the high and low. A cross-hatch left indicates the opening price and a cross-hatch right indicates the close.

Bargain purchase When a company is acquired and the purchase price is less than the fair value of the net assets. The current treatment of the excess of fair value over the purchase price is different under IFRS and U.S. GAAP. The excess is never accounted for as negative goodwill.

Barriers to entry Legal or natural constraints that protect a firm from potential competitors.

Barter The direct exchange of one good or service for other goods and services.

Basic EPS Net earnings available to common shareholders (i.e., net income minus preferred dividends) divided by the weighted average number of common shares outstanding.

Basis point value (BPV) Also called *present value of a basis point* or *price value of a basis point* (PVBP), the change in the bond price for a 1 basis point change in yield.

Basis swap 1) An interest rate swap involving two floating rates. 2) A swap in which both parties pay a floating rate.

Basket of listed depository receipts An exchange-traded fund (ETF) that represents a portfolio of depository receipts.

Bayes' formula A method for updating probabilities based on new information.

Bear hug A tactic used by acquirers to circumvent target management's objections to a proposed merger by submitting the proposal directly to the target company's board of directors.

Bear spread An option strategy that involves selling a put with a lower exercise price and buying a put with a higher exercise price. It can also be executed with calls.

Behavioral finance A field of finance that examines the psychological variables that affect and often distort the investment decision making of investors, analysts, and portfolio managers.

Behind the market Said of prices specified in orders that are worse than the best current price; e.g., for a limit buy order, a limit price below the best bid.

Below full-employment equilibrium A macroeconomic equilibrium in which potential GDP exceeds real GDP.

Benchmark A comparison portfolio; a point of reference or comparison.

Benchmark error The use of an inappropriate or incorrect benchmark to assess and compare portfolio returns and management.

Benchmark portfolio A comparison portfolio or index that represents the persistent and prominent investment characteristics of the securities in an actual portfolio.

Bernoulli random variable A random variable having the outcomes 0 and 1.

Bernoulli trial An experiment that can produce one of two outcomes.

Best bid The highest bid in the market.

Best efforts offering An offering of a security using an investment bank in which the investment bank, as agent for the issuer, promises to use its best efforts to sell the offering but does not guarantee that a specific amount will be sold.

Best offer The lowest offer (ask price) in the market.

Beta A measure of systematic risk that is based on the covariance of an asset's or portfolio's return with the return of the overall market.

Bid price The price at which a dealer or trader is willing to buy an asset, typically qualified by a maximum quantity.

Bid size The maximum quantity of an asset that pertains to a specific bid price from a trader.

Big tradeoff The conflict between equality and efficiency.

Bilateral monopoly A situation in which a single seller (a monopoly) faces a single buyer (a monopsony).

Binomial model A model for pricing options in which the underlying price can move to only one of two possible new prices.

Binomial random variable The number of successes in n Bernoulli trials for which the probability of success is constant for all trials and the trials are independent.

Binomial tree The graphical representation of a model of asset price dynamics in which, at each period, the asset moves up with probability p or down with probability $(1 - p)$.

Black market   An illegal market in which the price exceeds the legally imposed price ceiling.

Block   Orders to buy or sell that are too large for the liquidity ordinarily available in dealer networks or stock exchanges.

Block brokers   A broker (agent) that provides brokerage services for large-size trades.

Blue chip companies   Widely held large market capitalization companies that are considered financially sound and are leaders in their respective industry or local stock market.

Bollinger Bands   A price-based technical analysis indicator consisting of a moving average plus a higher line representing the moving average plus a set number of standard deviations from average price (for the same number of periods as used to calculate the moving average) and a lower line that is a moving average minus the same number of standard deviations.

Bond equivalent yield   A calculation of yield that is annualized using the ratio of 365 to the number of days to maturity. Bond equivalent yield allows for the restatement and comparison of securities with different compounding periods.

Bond option   An option in which the underlying is a bond; primarily traded in over-the-counter markets.

Bond yield plus risk premium approach   An estimate of the cost of common equity that is produced by summing the before-tax cost of debt and a risk premium that captures the additional yield on a company's stock relative to its bonds. The additional yield is often estimated using historical spreads between bond yields and stock yields.

Bond-equivalent basis   A basis for stating an annual yield that annualizes a semiannual yield by doubling it.

Bond-equivalent yield   The yield to maturity on a basis that ignores compounding.

Bonding costs   Costs borne by management to assure owners that they are working in the owners' best interest (e.g., implicit cost of non-compete agreements).

Book building   Investment bankers' process of compiling a "book" or list of indications of interest to buy part of an offering.

Book value (or **carrying value**)   The net amount shown for an asset or liability on the balance sheet; book value may also refer to the company's excess of total assets over total liabilities.

Book value equity per share   The amount of book value (also called carrying value) of common equity per share of common stock, calculated by dividing the book value of shareholders' equity by the number of shares of common stock outstanding.

Bootstrapping earnings   An increase in a company's earnings that results as a consequence of the idiosyncrasies of a merger transaction itself rather than because of resulting economic benefits of the combination.

Bottom-up analysis   With reference to investment selection processes, an approach that involves selection from all securities within a specified investment universe, i.e., without prior narrowing of the universe on the basis of macroeconomic or overall market considerations.

Box spread   An option strategy that combines a bull spread and a bear spread having two different exercise prices, which produces a risk-free payoff of the difference in the exercise prices.

Break point   In the context of the weighted average cost of capital (WACC), a break point is the amount of capital at which the cost of one or more of the sources of capital changes, leading to a change in the WACC.

Breakeven point   The number of units produced and sold at which the company's net income is zero (revenues = total costs).

Breakup value   The value that can be achieved if a company's assets are divided and sold separately.

Breusch–Pagan test   A test for conditional heteroskedasticity in the error term of a regression.

Broker   1) An agent who executes orders to buy or sell securities on behalf of a client in exchange for a commission. 2) *See* Futures commission merchants.

Broker–dealer   A financial intermediary (often a company) that may function as a principal (dealer) or as an agent (broker) depending on the type of trade.

Brokered market   A market in which brokers arrange trades among their clients.

Budget deficit   A government's budget balance that is negative—outlays exceed tax revenues.

Budget surplus   A government's budget balance that is positive—tax revenues exceed outlays.

Bull spread   An option strategy that involves buying a call with a lower exercise price and selling a call with a higher exercise price. It can also be executed with puts.

Business risk   The risk associated with operating earnings. Operating earnings are uncertain because total revenues and many of the expenditures contributed to produce those revenues are uncertain.

Butterfly spread   An option strategy that combines two bull or bear spreads and has three exercise prices.

Buy side firm   An investment management company or other investor that uses the services of brokers or dealers (i.e., the client of the sell side firms).

Buyout fund   A fund that buys all the shares of a public company so that, in effect, the company becomes private.

Call   An option that gives the holder the right to buy an underlying asset from another party at a fixed price over a specific period of time.

Call market   A market in which trades occur only at a particular time and place (i.e., when the market is called).

Call money rate   The interest rate that buyers pay for their margin loan.

Callable (or redeemable) **common shares**   Shares that give the issuing company the option (or right), but not the obligation, to buy back the shares from investors at a call price that is specified when the shares are originally issued.

Candlestick chart   A price chart with four bits of data for each time interval. A candle indicates the opening and closing price for the interval. The body of the candle is shaded if the opening price was higher than the closing price, and the body is clear if the opening price was lower than the closing price. Vertical lines known as wicks or shadows extend from the top and bottom of the candle to indicate the high and the low prices for the interval.

Cannibalization   Cannibalization occurs when an investment takes customers and sales away from another part of the company.

Cap   1) A contract on an interest rate, whereby at periodic payment dates, the writer of the cap pays the difference between the market interest rate and a specified cap rate if, and only if, this difference is positive. This is equivalent to a stream of call options on the interest rate. 2) A combination of interest rate call options designed to hedge a borrower against rate increases on a floating-rate loan.

Capital allocation line (CAL)   A graph line that describes the combinations of expected return and standard deviation of return available to an investor from combining the optimal portfolio of risky assets with the risk-free asset.

Capital asset pricing model (CAPM)   An equation describing the expected return on any asset (or portfolio) as a linear function of its beta relative to the market portfolio.

Capital budgeting   The allocation of funds to relatively long-range projects or investments.

Capital market expectations   An investor's expectations concerning the risk and return prospects of asset classes.

Capital market line (CML) The line with an intercept point equal to the risk-free rate that is tangent to the efficient frontier of risky assets; represents the efficient frontier when a risk-free asset is available for investment.

Capital markets Financial markets that trade securities of longer duration, such as bonds and equities.

Capital rationing A capital rationing environment assumes that the company has a fixed amount of funds to invest.

Capital structure The mix of debt and equity that a company uses to finance its business; a company's specific mixture of long-term financing.

Capitalized inventory costs Costs of inventories including costs of purchase, costs of conversion, other costs to bring the inventories to their present location and condition, and the allocated portion of fixed production overhead costs.

Caplet Each component call option in a cap.

Capped swap A swap in which the floating payments have an upper limit.

Captive finance subsidiary A wholly-owned subsidiary of a company that is established to provide financing of the sales of the parent company.

Carrying amount (book value) The amount at which an asset or liability is valued according to accounting principles.

Cartel A group of firms that has entered into a collusive agreement to restrict output and increase prices and profits.

Cash In accounting contexts, cash on hand (e.g., petty cash and cash not yet deposited to the bank) and demand deposits held in banks and similar accounts that can be used in payment of obligations.

Cash basis Accounting method in which the only relevant transactions for the financial statements are those that involve cash.

Cash conversion cycle (net operating cycle) A financial metric that measures the length of time required for a company to convert cash invested in its operations to cash received as a result of its operations; equal to days of inventory on hand + days of sales outstanding – number of days of payables.

Cash equivalents Very liquid short-term investments, usually maturing in 90 days or less.

Cash flow additivity principle The principle that dollar amounts indexed at the same point in time are additive.

Cash flow at risk (CFAR) A variation of VAR that reflects the risk of a company's cash flow instead of its market value.

Cash flow from operations (cash flow from operating activities or operating cash flow) The net amount of cash provided from operating activities.

Cash flow statement (statement of cash flows) A financial statement that reconciles beginning-of-period and end-of-period balance sheet values of cash; consists of three parts: cash flows from operating activities, cash flows from investing activities, and cash flows from financing activities.

Cash offering A merger or acquisition that is to be paid for with cash; the cash for the merger might come from the acquiring company's existing assets or from a debt issue.

Cash price or spot price The price for immediate purchase of the underlying asset.

Cash ratio A liquidity ratio calculated as (cash + short-term marketable investments) divided by current liabilities; measures a company's ability to meet its current obligations with just the cash and cash equivalents on hand.

Cash settlement A procedure used in certain derivative transactions that specifies that the long and short parties engage in the equivalent cash value of a delivery transaction.

Cash-flow-statement-based accruals ratio The difference between reported net income on an accrual basis and the cash flows

from operating and investing activities compared to the average net operating assets over the period.

Cash-flow-statement-based aggregate accruals The difference between reported net income on an accrual basis and the cash flows from operating and investing activities.

CBOE Volatility Index A measure of near-term market volatility as conveyed by S&P 500 stock index option prices.

Central bank A bank's bank and a public authority that regulates the nation's depository institutions and controls the quantity of money.

Central limit theorem A result in statistics that states that the sample mean computed from large samples of size n from a population with finite variance will follow an approximate normal distribution with a mean equal to the population mean and a variance equal to the population variance divided by n.

Centralized risk management or companywide risk management When a company has a single risk management group that monitors and controls all of the risk-taking activities of the organization. Centralization permits economies of scale and allows a company to use some of its risks to offset other risks. (See also *enterprise risk management*.)

Chain rule of forecasting A forecasting process in which the next period's value as predicted by the forecasting equation is substituted into the right-hand side of the equation to give a predicted value two periods ahead.

Change in polarity principle A tenet of technical analysis that once a support level is breached, it becomes a resistance level. The same holds true for resistance levels; once breached, they become support levels.

Chart of accounts A list of accounts used in an entity's accounting system.

Cheapest to deliver A bond in which the amount received for delivering the bond is largest compared with the amount paid in the market for the bond.

Cherry-picking When a bankrupt company is allowed to enforce contracts that are favorable to it while walking away from contracts that are unfavorable to it.

Classical A macroeconomist who believes that the economy is self-regulating and that it is always at full employment.

Classified balance sheet A balance sheet organized so as to group together the various assets and liabilities into subcategories (e.g., current and noncurrent).

Clean-surplus accounting The bottom-line income reflects all changes in shareholders' equity arising from other than owner transactions. In the absence of owner transactions, the change in shareholders' equity should equal net income. No adjustments such as translation adjustments bypass the income statement and go directly to shareholders equity.

Clearing instructions Instructions that indicate how to arrange the final settlement ("clearing") of a trade.

Clearinghouse An entity associated with a futures market that acts as middleman between the contracting parties and guarantees to each party the performance of the other.

Clientele effect The preference some investors have for shares that exhibit certain characteristics.

Closed-end fund A mutual fund in which no new investment money is accepted. New investors invest by buying existing shares, and investors in the fund liquidate by selling their shares to other investors.

Closeout netting Netting the market values of *all* derivative contracts between two parties to determine one overall value owed by one party to another in the event of bankruptcy.

Coefficient of variation (CV) The ratio of a set of observations' standard deviation to the observations' mean value.

Cointegrated   Describes two time series that have a long-term financial or economic relationship such that they do not diverge from each other without bound in the long run.

Collar   An option strategy involving the purchase of a put and sale of a call in which the holder of an asset gains protection below a certain level, the exercise price of the put, and pays for it by giving up gains above a certain level, the exercise price of the call. Collars also can be used to provide protection against rising interest rates on a floating-rate loan by giving up gains from lower interest rates.

Collusive agreement   An agreement between two (or more) producers to restrict output, raise the price, and increase profits.

Combination   A listing in which the order of the listed items does not matter.

Command system   A method of allocating resources by the order (command) of someone in authority. In a firm a managerial hierarchy organizes production.

Commercial paper   Unsecured short-term corporate debt that is characterized by a single payment at maturity.

Committed lines of credit   A bank commitment to extend credit up to a pre-specified amount; the commitment is considered a short-term liability and is usually in effect for 364 days (one day short of a full year).

Commodity forward   A contract in which the underlying asset is oil, a precious metal, or some other commodity.

Commodity futures   Futures contracts in which the underlying is a traditional agricultural, metal, or petroleum product.

Commodity option   An option in which the asset underlying the futures is a commodity, such as oil, gold, wheat, or soybeans.

Commodity swap   A swap in which the underlying is a commodity such as oil, gold, or an agricultural product.

Common shares   A type of security that represent an ownership interest in a company.

Common size statements   Financial statements in which all elements (accounts) are stated as a percentage of a key figure such as revenue for an income statement or total assets for a balance sheet.

Common-size analysis   The restatement of financial statement items using a common denominator or reference item that allows one to identify trends and major differences; an example is an income statement in which all items are expressed as a percent of revenue.

Company analysis   Analysis of an individual company.

Company fundamental factors   Factors related to the company's internal performance, such as factors relating to earnings growth, earnings variability, earnings momentum, and financial leverage.

Company share-related factors   Valuation measures and other factors related to share price or the trading characteristics of the shares, such as earnings yield, dividend yield, and book-to-market value.

Comparable company   A company that has similar business risk; usually in the same industry and preferably with a single line of business.

Competitive strategy   A company's plans for responding to the threats and opportunities presented by the external environment.

Complement   In probability, with reference to an event *S*, the event that *S* does not occur; in economics, a good that is used in conjunction with another good.

Complete markets   Informally, markets in which the variety of distinct securities traded is so broad that any desired payoff in a future state-of-the-world is achievable.

Completed contract   A method of revenue recognition in which the company does not recognize any revenue until the contract is completed; used particularly in long-term construction contracts.

Component cost of capital   The rate of return required by suppliers of capital for an individual source of a company's funding, such as debt or equity.

Compounding   The process of accumulating interest on interest.

Comprehensive income   The change in equity of a business enterprise during a period from nonowner sources; includes all changes in equity during a period except those resulting from investments by owners and distributions to owners; comprehensive income equals net income plus other comprehensive income.

Conditional expected value   The expected value of a stated event given that another event has occurred.

Conditional heteroskedasticity   Heteroskedasticity in the error variance that is correlated with the values of the independent variable(s) in the regression.

Conditional probability   The probability of an event given (conditioned on) another event.

Conditional variances   The variance of one variable, given the outcome of another.

Confidence interval   A range that has a given probability that it will contain the population parameter it is intended to estimate.

Conglomerate merger   A merger involving companies that are in unrelated businesses.

Consistency   A desirable property of estimators; a consistent estimator is one for which the probability of estimates close to the value of the population parameter increases as sample size increases.

Consistent   With reference to estimators, describes an estimator for which the probability of estimates close to the value of the population parameter increases as sample size increases.

Consolidation   The combining of the results of operations of subsidiaries with the parent company to present financial statements as if they were a single economic unit. The asset, liabilities, revenues and expenses of the subsidiaries are combined with those of the parent company, eliminating intercompany transactions.

Constant maturity swap or CMT swap   A swap in which the floating rate is the rate on a security known as a constant maturity treasury or CMT security.

Constant maturity treasury or CMT   A hypothetical U.S. Treasury note with a constant maturity. A CMT exists for various years in the range of 2 to 10.

Constant returns to scale   Features of a firm's technology that lead to constant long-run average cost as output increases. When constant returns to scale are present, the *LRAC* curve is horizontal.

Constituent securities   With respect to an index, the individual securities within an index.

Consumer Price Index (CPI)   An index that measures the average of the prices paid by urban consumers for a fixed "basket" of the consumer goods and services.

Consumer surplus   The value (or marginal benefit) of a good minus the price paid for it, summed over the quantity bought.

Contango   A situation in a futures market where the current futures price is greater than the current spot price for the underlying asset.

Contestable market   A market in which firms can enter and leave so easily that firms in the market face competition from potential entrants.

Contingent claims   Derivatives in which the payoffs occur if a specific event occurs; generally referred to as options.

Continuation patterns   A type of pattern used in technical analysis to predict the resumption of a market trend that was in place prior to the formation of a pattern.

Continuous market   A market where stocks are priced and traded continuously by an auction process or by dealers when the market is open.

Continuous random variable   A random variable for which the range of possible outcomes is the real line (all real numbers between $-\infty$ and $+\infty$ or some subset of the real line).

Continuous time   Time thought of as advancing in extremely small increments.

Continuous trading market   A market in which trades can be arranged and executed any time the market is open.

Continuously compounded return   The natural logarithm of 1 plus the holding period return, or equivalently, the natural logarithm of the ending price over the beginning price.

Contra account   An account that offsets another account.

Contribution margin   The amount available for fixed costs and profit after paying variable costs; revenue minus variable costs.

Controlling interest   An investment where the investor exerts control over the investee, typically by having a greater than 50 percent ownership in the investee.

Convenience yield   The nonmonetary return offered by an asset when the asset is in short supply, often associated with assets with seasonal production processes.

Conventional cash flow   A conventional cash flow pattern is one with an initial outflow followed by a series of inflows.

Convergence   In technical analysis, a term that describes the case when an indicator moves in the same manner as the security being analyzed.

Conversion factor   An adjustment used to facilitate delivery on bond futures contracts in which any of a number of bonds with different characteristics are eligible for delivery.

Convertible debt   Debt with the added feature that the bondholder has the option to exchange the debt for equity at pre-specified terms.

Convertible preference shares   A type of equity security that entitles shareholders to convert their shares into a specified number of common shares.

Cooperative equilibrium   The outcome of a game in which the players make and share the monopoly profit.

Core inflation rate   A measure of inflation based on the core CPI—the CPI excluding food and fuel.

Corporate governance   The system of principles, policies, procedures, and clearly defined responsibilities and accountabilities used by stakeholders to overcome the conflicts of interest inherent in the corporate form.

Corporate raider   A person or organization seeking to profit by acquiring a company and reselling it, or seeking to profit from the takeover attempt itself (e.g. greenmail).

Corporation   A legal entity with rights similar to those of a person. The chief officers, executives, or top managers act as agents for the firm and are legally entitled to authorize corporate activities and to enter into contracts on behalf of the business.

Correlation   A number between -1 and $+1$ that measures the co-movement (linear association) between two random variables.

Correlation analysis   The analysis of the strength of the linear relationship between two data series.

Correlation coefficient   A number between -1 and $+1$ that measures the consistency or tendency for two investments to act in a similar way. It is used to determine the effect on portfolio risk when two assets are combined.

Cost averaging   The periodic investment of a fixed amount of money.

Cost of capital   The rate of return that suppliers of capital require as compensation for their contribution of capital.

Cost of carry   The cost associated with holding some asset, including financing, storage, and insurance costs. Any yield received on the asset is treated as a negative carrying cost.

Cost of carry model   A model for pricing futures contracts in which the futures price is determined by adding the cost of carry to the spot price.

Cost of debt   The cost of debt financing to a company, such as when it issues a bond or takes out a bank loan.

Cost of goods sold   For a given period, equal to beginning inventory minus ending inventory plus the cost of goods acquired or produced during the period.

Cost of preferred stock   The cost to a company of issuing preferred stock; the dividend yield that a company must commit to pay preferred stockholders.

Cost recovery method   A method of revenue recognition in which the seller does not report any profit until the cash amounts paid by the buyer—including principal and interest on any financing from the seller—are greater than all the seller's costs for the merchandise sold.

Cost structure   The mix of a company's variable costs and fixed costs.

Cost-push inflation   An inflation that results from an initial increase in costs.

Council of Economic Advisers   The President's council whose main work is to monitor the economy and keep the President and the public well informed about the current state of the economy and the best available forecasts of where it is heading.

Counterparty risk   The risk that the other party to a contract will fail to honor the terms of the contract.

Coupon rate   The interest rate promised in a contract; this is the rate used to calculate the periodic interest payments.

Covariance   A measure of the co-movement (linear association) between two random variables.

Covariance matrix   A matrix or square array whose entries are covariances; also known as a variance–covariance matrix.

Covariance stationary   Describes a time series when its expected value and variance are constant and finite in all periods and when its covariance with itself for a fixed number of periods in the past or future is constant and finite in all periods.

Covered call   An option strategy involving the holding of an asset and sale of a call on the asset.

Covered interest arbitrage   A transaction executed in the foreign exchange market in which a currency is purchased (sold) and a forward contract is sold (purchased) to lock in the exchange rate for future delivery of the currency. This transaction should earn the risk-free rate of the investor's home country.

Credit   With respect to double-entry accounting, a credit records increases in liability, owners' equity, and revenue accounts or decreases in asset accounts; with respect to borrowing, the willingness and ability of the borrower to make promised payments on the borrowing.

Credit analysis   The evaluation of credit risk; the evaluation of the creditworthiness of a borrower or counterparty.

Credit derivatives   A contract in which one party has the right to claim a payment from another party in the event that a specific credit event occurs over the life of the contract.

Credit risk or default risk   The risk of loss caused by a counterparty's or debtor's failure to make a promised payment.

Credit scoring model   A statistical model used to classify borrowers according to creditworthiness.

Credit spread option   An option on the yield spread on a bond.

Credit swap   A type of swap transaction used as a credit derivative in which one party makes periodic payments to the other and receives the promise of a payoff if a third party defaults.

Credit VAR, Default VAR, or Credit at Risk   A variation of VAR that reflects credit risk.

Credit-linked notes   Fixed-income securities in which the holder of the security has the right to withhold payment of the full amount due at maturity if a credit event occurs.

Credit-worthiness   The perceived ability of the borrower to pay what is owed on the borrowing in a timely manner; it represents the ability of a company to withstand adverse impacts on its cash flows.

Cross elasticity of demand   The responsiveness of the demand for a good to a change in the price of a substitute or complement, other things remaining the same. It is calculated as the percentage change in the quantity demanded of the good divided by the percentage change in the price of the substitute or complement.

Crossing networks   Trading systems that match buyers and sellers who are willing to trade at prices obtained from other markets.

Cross-product netting   Netting the market values of all contracts, not just derivatives, between parties.

Cross-sectional analysis   Analysis that involves comparisons across individuals in a group over a given time period or at a given point in time.

Cross-sectional data   Observations over individual units at a point in time, as opposed to time-series data.

Crowding-out effect   The tendency for a government budget deficit to decrease investment.

Cumulative distribution function   A function giving the probability that a random variable is less than or equal to a specified value.

Cumulative preference shares   Preference shares for which any dividends that are not paid accrue and must be paid in full before dividends on common shares can be paid.

Cumulative relative frequency   For data grouped into intervals, the fraction of total observations that are less than the value of the upper limit of a stated interval.

Cumulative voting   Voting that allows shareholders to direct their total voting rights to specific candidates, as opposed to having to allocate their voting rights evenly among all candidates.

Currency   The notes and coins held by individuals and businesses.

Currency drain ratio   The ratio of currency to deposits.

Currency forward   A forward contract in which the underlying is a foreign currency.

Currency option   An option that allows the holder to buy (if a call) or sell (if a put) an underlying currency at a fixed exercise rate, expressed as an exchange rate.

Currency swap   A swap in which each party makes interest payments to the other in different currencies.

Current assets, or liquid assets   Assets that are expected to be consumed or converted into cash in the near future, typically one year or less.

Current cost   With reference to assets, the amount of cash or cash equivalents that would have to be paid to buy the same or an equivalent asset today; with reference to liabilities, the undiscounted amount of cash or cash equivalents that would be required to settle the obligation today.

Current credit risk   The risk associated with the possibility that a payment currently due will not be made.

Current exchange rate   For accounting purposes, the spot exchange rate on the balance sheet date.

Current liabilities   Short-term obligations, such as accounts payable, wages payable, or accrued liabilities, that are expected to be settled in the near future, typically one year or less.

Current rate method   Approach to translating foreign currency financial statements for consolidation in which all assets and liabilities are translated at the current exchange rate. The current rate method is the prevalent method of translation.

Current ratio   A liquidity ratio calculated as current assets divided by current liabilities.

Current taxes payable   Tax expenses that have been recognized and recorded on a company's income statement but which have not yet been paid.

Cyclical company   A company whose profits are strongly correlated with the strength of the overall economy.

Cyclical stock   The shares (stock) of a company whose earnings have above-average sensitivity to the business cycle.

Cyclical surplus or deficit   The actual surplus or deficit minus the structural surplus or deficit.

Cyclical unemployment   The fluctuating unemployment over the business cycle.

Daily settlement   See *Marking to market.*

Dark pools   Alternative trading systems that do not display the orders that their clients send to them.

Data mining (or **data snooping**)   The practice of determining a model by extensive searching through a dataset for statistically significant patterns.

Day order   An order that is good for the day on which it is submitted. If it has not been filled by the close of business, the order expires unfilled.

Day trader   A trader holding a position open somewhat longer than a scalper but closing all positions at the end of the day.

Days of inventory on hand (DOH)   An activity ratio equal to the number of days in the period divided by inventory turnover over the period.

Days of sales outstanding (DSO)   An activity ratio equal to the number of days in the period divided by receivables turnover.

Dead cross   A technical analysis term that describes a situation where a short-term moving average crosses from above a longer-term moving average to below it; this movement is considered bearish.

Dead-hand provision   A poison pill provision that allows for the redemption or cancellation of a poison pill provision only by a vote of continuing directors (generally directors who were on the target company's board prior to the takeover attempt).

Deadweight loss   A measure of inefficiency. It is equal to the decrease in total surplus that results from an inefficient level of production.

Dealers   A financial intermediary that acts as a principal in trades.

Dealing securities   Securities held by banks or other financial intermediaries for trading purposes.

Debit   With respect to double-entry accounting, a debit records increases of asset and expense accounts or decreases in liability and owners' equity accounts.

Debt covenants   Agreements between the company as borrower and its creditors.

Debt incurrence test   A financial covenant made in conjunction with existing debt that restricts a company's ability to incur additional debt at the same seniority based on one or more financial tests or conditions.

Debt rating approach   A method for estimating a company's before-tax cost of debt based upon the yield on comparably rated bonds for maturities that closely match that of the company's existing debt.

Debt ratings   An objective measure of the quality and safety of a company's debt based upon an analysis of the company's ability to pay the promised cash flows, as well as an analysis of any indentures.

Debt with warrants   Debt issued with warrants that give the bondholder the right to purchase equity at prespecified terms.

Debt-to-assets ratio A solvency ratio calculated as total debt divided by total assets.

Debt-to-capital ratio A solvency ratio calculated as total debt divided by total debt plus total shareholders' equity.

Debt-to-equity ratio A solvency ratio calculated as total debt divided by total shareholders' equity.

Decentralized risk management A system that allows individual units within an organization to manage risk. Decentralization results in duplication of effort but has the advantage of having people closer to the risk be more directly involved in its management.

Deciles Quantiles that divide a distribution into 10 equal parts.

Decision rule With respect to hypothesis testing, the rule according to which the null hypothesis will be rejected or not rejected; involves the comparison of the test statistic to rejection point(s).

Declaration date The day that the corporation issues a statement declaring a specific dividend.

Deductible temporary differences Temporary differences that result in a reduction of or deduction from taxable income in a future period when the balance sheet item is recovered or settled.

Deep in the money Options that are far in-the-money.

Deep out of the money Options that are far out-of-the-money.

Default risk premium An extra return that compensates investors for the possibility that the borrower will fail to make a promised payment at the contracted time and in the contracted amount.

Defensive company A company whose revenues and profits are least affected by fluctuations in the overall economic activity.

Defensive interval ratio A liquidity ratio that estimates the number of days that an entity could meet cash needs from liquid assets; calculated as (cash + short-term marketable investments + receivables) divided by daily cash expenditures.

Defensive stock The shares (stock) of a company whose earnings have below-average sensitivity to the business cycle.

Deferred tax assets A balance sheet asset that arises when an excess amount is paid for income taxes relative to accounting profit. The taxable income is higher than accounting profit and income tax payable exceeds tax expense. The company expects to recover the difference during the course of future operations when tax expense exceeds income tax payable.

Deferred tax liabilities A balance sheet liability that arises when a deficit amount is paid for income taxes relative to accounting profit. The taxable income is less than the accounting profit and income tax payable is less than tax expense. The company expects to eliminate the liability over the course of future operations when income tax payable exceeds tax expense.

Defined-benefit pension plans Plan in which the company promises to pay a certain annual amount (defined benefit) to the employee after retirement. The company bears the investment risk of the plan assets.

Defined-contribution pension plans Individual accounts to which an employee and typically the employer makes contributions, generally on a tax-advantaged basis. The amounts of contributions are defined at the outset, but the future value of the benefit is unknown. The employee bears the investment risk of the plan assets.

Definitive merger agreement A contract signed by both parties to a merger that clarifies the details of the transaction, including the terms, warranties, conditions, termination details, and the rights of all parties.

Degree of confidence The probability that a confidence interval includes the unknown population parameter.

Degree of financial leverage (DFL) The ratio of the percentage change in net income to the percentage change in operating income; the sensitivity of the cash flows available to owners when operating income changes.

Degree of operating leverage (DOL) The ratio of the percentage change in operating income to the percentage change in units sold; the sensitivity of operating income to changes in units sold.

Degree of total leverage The ratio of the percentage change in net income to the percentage change in units sold; the sensitivity of the cash flows to owners to changes in the number of units produced and sold.

Degrees of freedom (df) The number of independent observations used.

Delivery A process used in a deliverable forward contract in which the long pays the agreed-upon price to the short, which in turn delivers the underlying asset to the long.

Delivery option The feature of a futures contract giving the short the right to make decisions about what, when, and where to deliver.

Delta The relationship between the option price and the underlying price, which reflects the sensitivity of the price of the option to changes in the price of the underlying.

Delta hedge An option strategy in which a position in an asset is converted to a risk-free position with a position in a specific number of options. The number of options per unit of the underlying changes through time, and the position must be revised to maintain the hedge.

Delta-normal method A measure of VAR equivalent to the analytical method but that refers to the use of delta to estimate the option's price sensitivity.

Demand for money The relationship between the quantity of money demanded and the interest rate when all other influences on the amount of money that people wish to hold remain the same.

Demand-pull inflation An inflation that results from an initial increase in aggregate demand.

Dependent With reference to events, the property that the probability of one event occurring depends on (is related to) the occurrence of another event.

Dependent variable The variable whose variation about its mean is to be explained by the regression; the left-hand-side variable in a regression equation.

Depository institution A firm that takes deposits from households and firms and makes loans to other households and firms.

Depository institutions Commercial banks, savings and loan banks, credit unions, and similar institutions that raise funds from depositors and other investors and lend it to borrowers.

Depository receipt A security that trades like an ordinary share on a local exchange and represents an economic interest in a foreign company.

Depreciation The process of systematically allocating the cost of long-lived (tangible) assets to the periods during which the assets are expected to provide economic benefits.

Derivative A financial instrument whose value depends on the value of some underlying asset or factor (e.g., a stock price, an interest rate, or exchange rate).

Derivative pricing rule A pricing rule used by crossing networks in which a price is taken (derived) from the price that is current in the asset's primary market.

Derivatives dealers Commercial and investment banks that make markets in derivatives.

Derived demand Demand for a factor of production, which is derived from the demand for the goods and services produced by that factor.

Descriptive statistics The study of how data can be summarized effectively.

Designated fair value instruments Financial instruments that an entity chooses to measure at fair value per IAS 39 or SFAS 159. Generally, the election to use the fair value option is irrevocable.

Desired reserve ratio The ratio of reserves to deposits that banks want to hold.

Diff swaps A swap in which the payments are based on the difference between interest rates in two countries but payments are made in only a single currency.

Diffuse prior The assumption of equal prior probabilities.

Diluted EPS The EPS that would result if all dilutive securities were converted into common shares.

Diluted shares The number of shares that would be outstanding if all potentially dilutive claims on common shares (e.g., convertible debt, convertible preferred stock, and employee stock options) were exercised.

Diminishing balance method An accelerated depreciation method, i.e., one that allocates a relatively large proportion of the cost of an asset to the early years of the asset's useful life.

Diminishing marginal returns The tendency for the marginal product of an additional unit of a factor of production to be less than the marginal product of the previous unit of the factor.

Direct debit program An arrangement whereby a customer authorizes a debit to a demand account; typically used by companies to collect routine payments for services.

Direct financing lease A type of finance lease, from a lessor perspective, where the present value of the lease payments (lease receivable) equals the carrying value of the leased asset. The revenues earned by the lessor are financing in nature.

Direct format (direct method) With reference to the cash flow statement, a format for the presentation of the statement in which cash flow from operating activities is shown as operating cash receipts less operating cash disbursements.

Direct write-off method An approach to recognizing credit losses on customer receivables in which the company waits until such time as a customer has defaulted and only then recognizes the loss.

Dirty-surplus accounting Accounting in which some income items are reported as part of stockholders' equity rather than as gains and losses on the income statement; certain items of comprehensive income bypass the income statement and appear as direct adjustments to shareholders' equity.

Dirty-surplus items Direct adjustments to shareholders' equity that bypass the income statement.

Disbursement float The amount of time between check issuance and a check's clearing back against the company's account.

Discount To reduce the value of a future payment in allowance for how far away it is in time; to calculate the present value of some future amount. Also, the amount by which an instrument is priced below its face value.

Discount interest A procedure for determining the interest on a loan or bond in which the interest is deducted from the face value in advance.

Discount rate The interest rate at which the Fed stands ready to lend reserves to depository institutions.

Discounted cash flow analysis In the context of merger analysis, it is an estimate of a target company's value found by discounting the company's expected future free cash flows to the present.

Discouraged workers People who are available and willing to work but have not made specific effort to find a job in the previous four weeks.

Discrete random variable A random variable that can take on at most a countable number of possible values.

Discrete time Time thought of as advancing in distinct finite increments.

Discretionary fiscal policy A fiscal action that is initiated by an act of Congress.

Discriminant analysis A multivariate classification technique used to discriminate between groups, such as companies that either will or will not become bankrupt during some time frame.

Discriminatory pricing rule A pricing rule used in continuous markets in which the limit price of the order or quote that first arrived determines the trade price.

Diseconomies of scale Features of a firm's technology that lead to rising long-run average cost as output increases.

Dispersion The variability around the central tendency.

Display size The size of an order displayed to public view.

Disposable income Aggregate income minus taxes plus transfer payments.

Divergence In technical analysis, a term that describes the case when an indicator moves differently from the security being analyzed.

Diversification ratio The ratio of the standard deviation of an equally weighted portfolio to the standard deviation of a randomly selected security.

Divestiture The sale, liquidation, or spin-off of a division or subsidiary.

Dividend A distribution paid to shareholders based on the number of shares owned.

Dividend discount model (DDM) A present value model that estimates the intrinsic value of an equity share based on the present value of its expected future dividends.

Dividend discount model based approach An approach for estimating a country's equity risk premium. The market rate of return is estimated as the sum of the dividend yield and the growth rate in dividends for a market index. Subtracting the risk-free rate of return from the estimated market return produces an estimate for the equity risk premium.

Dividend payout policy The strategy a company follows with regard to the amount and timing of dividend payments.

Dividend payout ratio The ratio of cash dividends paid to earnings for a period.

Dividend yield Annual dividends per share divided by share price.

Dividends per share The dollar amount of cash dividends paid during a period per share of common stock.

Divisor A number (denominator) used to determine the value of a price return index. It is initially chosen at the inception of an index and subsequently adjusted by the index provider, as necessary, to avoid changes in the index value that are unrelated to changes in the prices of its constituent securities.

Dominant strategy equilibrium A Nash equilibrium in which the best strategy for each player is to cheat (deny) regardless of the strategy of the other player.

Double bottoms In technical analysis, a reversal pattern that is formed when the price reaches a low, rebounds, and then sells off back to the first low level; used to predict a change from a downtrend to an uptrend.

Double declining balance depreciation An accelerated depreciation method that involves depreciating the asset at double the straight-line rate. This rate is multiplied by the book value of the asset at the beginning of the period (a declining balance) to calculate depreciation expense.

Double taxation Corporate earnings are taxed twice when paid out as dividends. First, corporate earnings are taxed regardless of whether they will be distributed as dividends or retained at the corporate level, and second, dividends are taxed again at the individual shareholder level.

Double top   In technical analysis, a reversal pattern that is formed when an uptrend reverses twice at roughly the same high price level; used to predict a change from an uptrend to a downtrend.

Double-entry accounting   The accounting system of recording transactions in which every recorded transaction affects at least two accounts so as to keep the basic accounting equation (assets = liabilities + owners' equity) in balance.

Down transition probability   The probability that an asset's value moves down in a model of asset price dynamics.

Downstream   A transaction between two affiliates, an investor company and an associate company such that the investor company records a profit on its income statement. An example is a sale of inventory by the investor company to the associate.

Drag on liquidity   When receipts lag, creating pressure from the decreased available funds.

Dummy variable   A type of qualitative variable that takes on a value of 1 if a particular condition is true and 0 if that condition is false.

Duopoly   A market structure in which two producers of a good or service compete.

DuPont analysis   An approach to decomposing return on investment, e.g., return on equity, as the product of other financial ratios.

Duration   A measure of an option-free bond's average maturity. Specifically, the weighted average maturity of all future cash flows paid by a security, in which the weights are the present value of these cash flows as a fraction of the bond's price. A measure of a bond's price sensitivity to interest rate movements.

Dutch Book theorem   A result in probability theory stating that inconsistent probabilities create profit opportunities.

Dynamic hedging   A strategy in which a position is hedged by making frequent adjustments to the quantity of the instrument used for hedging in relation to the instrument being hedged.

Earnings at risk (EAR)   A variation of VAR that reflects the risk of a company's earnings instead of its market value.

Earnings expectation management   Attempts by management to influence analysts' earnings forecasts.

Earnings game   Management's focus on reporting earnings that meet consensus estimates.

Earnings management activity   Deliberate activity aimed at influencing reporting earnings numbers, often with the goal of placing management in a favorable light; the opportunistic use of accruals to manage earnings.

Earnings per share   The amount of income earned during a period per share of common stock.

Earnings surprise   The portion of a company's earnings that is unanticipated by investors and, according to the efficient market hypothesis, merits a price adjustment.

Economic depreciation   The change in the market value of capital over a given period.

Economic efficiency   A situation that occurs when the firm produces a given output at the least cost.

Economic exposure   The risk associated with changes in the relative attractiveness of products and services offered for sale, arising out of the competitive effects of changes in exchange rates.

Economic order quantity–reorder point   An approach to managing inventory based on expected demand and the predictability of demand; the ordering point for new inventory is determined based on the costs of ordering and carrying inventory, such that the total cost associated with inventory is minimized.

Economic profit   A firm's total revenue minus its total cost.

Economic rent   Any surplus—consumer surplus, producer surplus or economic profit. The income received by the owner of a factor of production over and above the amount required to induce that owner to offer the factor for use.

Economies of scale   Features of a firm's technology that lead to a falling long-run average cost as output increases. In reference to mergers, it is the savings achieved through the consolidation of operations and elimination of duplicate resources.

Economies of scope   Decreases in average total cost that occur when a firm uses specialized resources to produce a range of goods and services.

Effective annual rate   The amount by which a unit of currency will grow in a year with interest on interest included.

Effective annual yield (EAY)   An annualized return that accounts for the effect of interest on interest; EAY is computed by compounding 1 plus the holding period yield forward to one year, then subtracting 1.

Effective interest rate   The borrowing rate or market rate that a company incurs at the time of issuance of a bond.

Efficiency   In statistics, a desirable property of estimators; an efficient estimator is the unbiased estimator with the smallest variance among unbiased estimators of the same parameter.

Efficiency wage   A real wage rate that is set above the equilibrium wage rate and that balances the costs and benefits of this higher wage rate to maximize the firm's profit.

Efficient frontier   The portion of the minimum-variance frontier beginning with the global minimum-variance portfolio and continuing above it; the graph of the set of portfolios offering the maximum expected return for their level of variance of return.

Efficient portfolio   A portfolio offering the highest expected return for a given level of risk as measured by variance or standard deviation of return.

Elastic demand   Demand with a price elasticity greater than 1; other things remaining the same, the percentage change in the quantity demanded exceeds the percentage change in price.

Elasticity   A measure of sensitivity; the incremental change in one variable with respect to an incremental change in another variable.

Elasticity of supply   The responsiveness of the quantity supplied of a good to a change in its price, other things remaining the same.

Electronic funds transfer   The use of computer networks to conduct financial transactions electronically.

Elliott wave theory   A technical analysis theory that claims that the market follows regular, repeated waves or cycles.

Empirical probability   The probability of an event estimated as a relative frequency of occurrence.

Employment Act of 1946   A landmark Congressional act that recognizes a role for government actions to keep unemployment low, the economy expanding, and inflation in check.

Employment-to-population ratio   The percentage of people of working age who have jobs.

Enhanced derivatives products companies (EDPC)   A type of subsidiary engaged in derivatives transactions that is separated from the parent company in order to have a higher credit rating than the parent company.

Enterprise risk management   A form of *centralized risk management* that typically encompasses the management of a broad variety of risks, including insurance risk.

Enterprise value   A measure of a company's total market value from which the value of cash and short-term investments have been subtracted.

Equal weighting   An index weighting method in which an equal weight is assigned to each constituent security at inception.

Equitizing cash   A strategy used to replicate an index. It is also used to take a given amount of cash and turn it into an equity position while maintaining the liquidity provided by the cash.

Equity   Assets less liabilities; the residual interest in the assets after subtracting the liabilities.

Equity carve-out   A form of restructuring that involves the creation of a new legal entity and the sale of equity in it to outsiders.

Equity forward   A contract calling for the purchase of an individual stock, a stock portfolio, or a stock index at a later date at an agreed-upon price.

Equity method   A basis for reporting investment income in which the investing entity recognizes a share of income as earned rather than as dividends when received. These transactions are typically reflected in Investments in Associates or Equity Method Investments.

Equity options   Options on individual stocks; also known as stock options.

Equity risk premium   The expected return on equities minus the risk-free rate; the premium that investors demand for investing in equities.

Equity swap   A swap transaction in which at least one cash flow is tied to the return to an equity portfolio position, often an equity index.

Error autocorrelation   The autocorrelation of the error term.

Error term   The portion of the dependent variable that is not explained by the independent variable(s) in the regression.

Estimate   The particular value calculated from sample observations using an estimator.

Estimated (or fitted) parameters   With reference to regression analysis, the estimated values of the population intercept and population slope coefficient(s) in a regression.

Estimation   With reference to statistical inference, the subdivision dealing with estimating the value of a population parameter.

Estimator   An estimation formula; the formula used to compute the sample mean and other sample statistics are examples of estimators.

Eurodollar   A dollar deposited outside the United States.

European-style option (or **European option**)   An option that can only be exercised on its expiration date.

Event   Any outcome or specified set of outcomes of a random variable.

Excess kurtosis   Degree of peakedness (fatness of tails) in excess of the peakedness of the normal distribution.

Excess reserves   A bank's actual reserves minus its desired reserves.

Exchange for physicals (EFP)   A permissible delivery procedure used by futures market participants, in which the long and short arrange a delivery procedure other than the normal procedures stipulated by the futures exchange.

Exchange ratio   The number of shares that target stockholders are to receive in exchange for each of their shares in the target company.

Exchanges   Places where traders can meet to arrange their trades.

Ex-dividend   Trading ex-dividend refers to shares that no longer carry the right to the next dividend payment.

Ex-dividend date   The first date that a share trades without (i.e. "ex") the dividend.

Execution instructions   Instructions that indicate how to fill an order.

Exercise or exercising the option   The process of using an option to buy or sell the underlying.

Exercise date   The day that employees actually exercise the options and convert them to stock.

Exercise price (strike price, striking price, or strike)   The fixed price at which an option holder can buy or sell the underlying.

Exercise rate or strike rate   The fixed rate at which the holder of an interest rate option can buy or sell the underlying.

Exercise value   The value obtained if an option is exercised based on current conditions.

Exhaustive   Covering or containing all possible outcomes.

Expected value   The probability-weighted average of the possible outcomes of a random variable.

Expensed   Taken as a deduction in arriving at net income.

Expenses   Outflows of economic resources or increases in liabilities that result in decreases in equity (other than decreases because of distributions to owners); reductions in net assets associated with the creation of revenues.

Experience curve   A curve that shows the direct cost per unit of good or service produced or delivered as a typically declining function of cumulative output.

Expiration date   The date on which a derivative contract expires.

Exposure to foreign exchange risk   The risk of a change in value of an asset or liability denominated in a foreign currency due to a change in exchange rates.

External diseconomies   Factors outside the control of a firm that raise the firm's costs as the industry produces a larger output.

External economies   Factors beyond the control of a firm that lower the firm's costs as the industry produces a larger output.

External growth   Company growth in output or sales that is achieved by buying the necessary resources externally (i.e., achieved through mergers and acquisitions).

Externality   The effect of an investment on other things besides the investment itself.

Extra or **special dividend**   A dividend paid by a company that does not pay dividends on a regular schedule, or a dividend that supplements regular cash dividends with an extra payment.

Face value (also principal, par value, stated value, or maturity value)   The amount of cash payable by a company to the bondholders when the bonds mature; the promised payment at maturity separate from any coupon payment.

Factor   A common or underlying element with which several variables are correlated.

Factor risk premium (or **factor price**)   The expected return in excess of the risk-free rate for a portfolio with a sensitivity of 1 to one factor and a sensitivity of 0 to all other factors.

Factor sensitivity (also factor betas or factor loadings)   A measure of the response of return to each unit of increase in a factor, holding all other factors constant.

Fair market value   The market price of an asset or liability that trades regularly.

Fair value   The amount at which an asset could be exchanged, or a liability settled, between knowledgeable, willing parties in an arm's-length transaction; the price that would be received to sell an asset or paid to transfer a liability in an orderly transaction between market participants.

Federal budget   The annual statement of the outlays and tax revenues of the government of the United States, together with the laws and regulations that approve and support those outlays and taxes.

Federal funds rate   The interest rate that the banks charge each other on overnight loans.

Federal Open Market Committee   The main policy-making organ of the Federal Reserve System.

Federal Reserve System (the Fed)   The central bank of the United States.

Fibonacci sequence   A sequence of numbers starting with 0 and 1, and then each subsequent number in the sequence is the sum of the two preceding numbers. In Elliott Wave Theory, it is believed that market waves follow patterns that are the ratios of the numbers in the Fibonacci sequence.

Fiduciary call A combination of a European call and a risk-free bond that matures on the option expiration day and has a face value equal to the exercise price of the call.

FIFO method The first in, first out, method of accounting for inventory, which matches sales against the costs of items of inventory in the order in which they were placed in inventory.

Finance lease (capital lease) Essentially, the purchase of some asset by the buyer (lessee) that is directly financed by the seller (lessor).

Financial analysis The process of selecting, evaluating, and interpreting financial data in order to formulate an assessment of a company's present and future financial condition and performance.

Financial distress Heightened uncertainty regarding a company's ability to meet its various obligations because of lower or negative earnings.

Financial flexibility The ability to react and adapt to financial adversities and opportunities.

Financial futures Futures contracts in which the underlying is a stock, bond, or currency.

Financial leverage The extent to which a company can effect, through the use of debt, a proportional change in the return on common equity that is greater than a given proportional change in operating income; also, short for the financial leverage ratio.

Financial leverage ratio A measure of financial leverage calculated as average total assets divided by average total equity.

Financial reporting quality The accuracy with which a company's reported financials reflect its operating performance and their usefulness for forecasting future cash flows.

Financial risk The risk that environmental, social, or governance risk factors will result in significant costs or other losses to a company and its shareholders; the risk arising from a company's obligation to meet required payments under its financing agreements.

Financing activities Activities related to obtaining or repaying capital to be used in the business (e.g., equity and long-term debt).

Firm An economic unit that hires factors of production and organizes those factors to produce and sell goods and services.

First-differencing A transformation that subtracts the value of the time series in period $t-1$ from its value in period t.

First-order serial correlation Correlation between adjacent observations in a time series.

Fiscal imbalance The present value of the government's commitments to pay benefits minus the present value of its tax revenues.

Fiscal policy The government's attempt to achieve macroeconomic objectives such as full employment, sustained long-term economic growth, and price level stability by setting and changing tax rates, making transfer payments, and purchasing goods and services.

Fixed asset turnover An activity ratio calculated as total revenue divided by average net fixed assets.

Fixed charge coverage A solvency ratio measuring the number of times interest and lease payments are covered by operating income, calculated as (EBIT + lease payments) divided by (interest payments + lease payments).

Fixed costs Costs that remain at the same level regardless of a company's level of production and sales.

Fixed price tender offer Offer made by a company to repurchase a specific number of shares at a fixed price that is typically at a premium to the current market price.

Fixed rate perpetual preferred stock Nonconvertible, noncallable preferred stock that has a fixed dividend rate and no maturity date.

Fixed-income forward A forward contract in which the underlying is a bond.

Flags A technical analysis continuation pattern formed by parallel trendlines, typically over a short period.

Flip-in pill A poison pill takeover defense that dilutes an acquirer's ownership in a target by giving other existing target company shareholders the right to buy additional target company shares at a discount.

Flip-over pill A poison pill takeover defense that gives target company shareholders the right to purchase shares of the acquirer at a significant discount to the market price, which has the effect of causing dilution to all existing acquiring company shareholders.

Float In the context of customer receipts, the amount of money that is in transit between payments made by customers and the funds that are usable by the company.

Float factor An estimate of the average number of days it takes deposited checks to clear; average daily float divided by average daily deposit.

Float-adjusted market-capitalization weighting An index weighting method in which the weight assigned to each constituent security is determined by adjusting its market capitalization for its market float.

Floating-rate loan A loan in which the interest rate is reset at least once after the starting date.

Floor A combination of interest rate put options designed to hedge a lender against lower rates on a floating-rate loan.

Floor traders or locals Market makers that buy and sell by quoting a bid and an ask price. They are the primary providers of liquidity to the market.

Floored swap A swap in which the floating payments have a lower limit.

Floorlet Each component put option in a floor.

Flotation cost Fees charged to companies by investment bankers and other costs associated with raising new capital.

Foreign currency transactions Transactions that are denominated in a currency other than a company's functional currency.

Foreign exchange gains (or losses) Gains (or losses) that occur when the exchange rate changes between the investor's currency and the currency that foreign securities are denominated in.

Forward contract An agreement between two parties in which one party, the buyer, agrees to buy from the other party, the seller, an underlying asset at a later date for a price established at the start of the contract.

Forward integration A merger involving the purchase of a target that is farther along the value or production chain; for example, to acquire a distributor.

Forward price or forward rate The fixed price or rate at which the transaction scheduled to occur at the expiration of a forward contract will take place. This price is agreed on at the initiation date of the contract.

Forward rate agreement (FRA) A forward contract calling for one party to make a fixed interest payment and the other to make an interest payment at a rate to be determined at the contract expiration.

Forward swap A forward contract to enter into a swap.

Four-firm concentration ratio A measure of market power that is calculated as the percentage of the value of sales accounted for by the four largest firms in an industry.

Free cash flow The actual cash that would be available to the company's investors after making all investments necessary to maintain the company as an ongoing enterprise (also referred to as free cash flow to the firm); the internally generated funds that can be distributed to the company's investors (e.g., shareholders and bondholders) without impairing the value of the company.

Free cash flow hypothesis The hypothesis that higher debt levels discipline managers by forcing them to make fixed debt service payments and by reducing the company's free cash flow.

Free cash flow to equity The cash flow available to a company's common shareholders after all operating expenses, interest, and principal payments have been made, and necessary investments in working and fixed capital have been made.

Free cash flow to the firm The cash flow available to the company's suppliers of capital after all operating expenses have been paid and necessary investments in working capital and fixed capital have been made.

Free float The number of shares that are readily and freely tradable in the secondary market.

Free-cash-flow-to-equity models Valuation models based on discounting expected future free cash flow to equity.

Frequency distribution A tabular display of data summarized into a relatively small number of intervals.

Frequency polygon A graph of a frequency distribution obtained by drawing straight lines joining successive points representing the class frequencies.

Frictional unemployment The unemployment that arises from normal labor turnover—from people entering and leaving the labor force and from the ongoing creation and destruction of jobs.

Friendly transaction A potential business combination that is endorsed by the managers of both companies.

Full employment A situation in which the quantity of labor demanded equals the quantity supplied. At full employment, there is no cyclical unemployment—all unemployment is frictional and structural.

Full-employment equilibrium A macroeconomic equilibrium in which real GDP equals potential GDP.

Full price The price of a security with accrued interest.

Functional currency The currency of the primary economic environment in which an entity operates.

Fundamental analysis The examination of publicly available information and the formulation of forecasts to estimate the intrinsic value of assets.

Fundamental beta A beta that is based at least in part on fundamental data for a company.

Fundamental factor models A multifactor model in which the factors are attributes of stocks or companies that are important in explaining cross-sectional differences in stock prices.

Fundamental (or intrinsic) value The underlying or true value of an asset based on an analysis of its qualitative and quantitative characteristics.

Fundamental weighting An index weighting method in which the weight assigned to each constituent security is based on its underlying company's size. It attempts to address the disadvantages of market-capitalization weighting by using measures that are independent of the constituent security's price.

Future value (FV) The amount to which a payment or series of payments will grow by a stated future date.

Futures commission merchants (FCMs) Individuals or companies that execute futures transactions for other parties off the exchange.

Futures contract A variation of a forward contract that has essentially the same basic definition but with some additional features, such as a clearinghouse guarantee against credit losses, a daily settlement of gains and losses, and an organized electronic or floor trading facility.

Futures exchange A legal corporate entity whose shareholders are its members. The members of the exchange have the privilege of executing transactions directly on the exchange.

Gains Asset inflows not directly related to the ordinary activities of the business.

Game theory A tool that economists use to analyze strategic behavior—behavior that takes into account the expected behavior of others and the recognition of mutual interdependence.

Gamma A numerical measure of how sensitive an option's delta is to a change in the underlying.

Generalized least squares A regression estimation technique that addresses heteroskedasticity of the error term.

Generational accounting An accounting system that measures the lifetime tax burden and benefits of each generation.

Generational imbalance The division of the fiscal imbalance between the current and future generations, assuming that the current generation will enjoy the existing levels of taxes and benefits.

Geometric mean A measure of central tendency computed by taking the nth root of the product of n non-negative values.

Giro system An electronic payment system used widely in Europe and Japan.

Global depository receipt A depository receipt that is issued outside of the company's home country and outside of the United States.

Global minimum-variance portfolio The portfolio on the minimum-variance frontier with the smallest variance of return.

Global registered share A common share that is traded on different stock exchanges around the world in different currencies.

Golden cross A technical analysis term that describes a situation where a short-term moving average crosses from below a longer-term moving average to above it; this movement is considered bullish.

Good-on-close (market on close) An execution instruction specifying that an order can only be filled at the close of trading.

Good-on-open An execution instruction specifying that an order can only be filled at the opening of trading.

Good-till-cancelled order An order specifying that it is valid until the entity placing the order has cancelled it (or, commonly, until some specified amount of time such as 60 days has elapsed, whichever comes sooner).

Goodwill An intangible asset that represents the excess of the purchase price of an acquired company over the value of the net assets acquired.

Government debt The total amount that the government has borrowed. It equals the sum of past budget deficits minus the sum of past budget surpluses.

Government expenditure multiplier The magnification effect of a change in government expenditure on goods and services on equilibrium expenditure and real GDP.

Grant date The day that options are granted to employees; usually the date that compensation expense is measured if both the number of shares and option price are known.

Greenmail The purchase of the accumulated shares of a hostile investor by a company that is targeted for takeover by that investor, usually at a substantial premium over market price.

Gross profit (gross margin) Sales minus the cost of sales (i.e., the cost of goods sold for a manufacturing company).

Gross profit margin The ratio of gross profit to revenues.

Grouping by function With reference to the presentation of expenses in an income statement, the grouping together of expenses serving the same function, e.g. all items that are costs of goods sold.

Grouping by nature With reference to the presentation of expenses in an income statement, the grouping together of expenses by similar nature, e.g., all depreciation expenses.

Growth cyclical A term sometimes used to describe companies that are growing rapidly on a long-term basis but that still experience above-average fluctuation in their revenues and profits over the course of a business cycle.

Growth investors With reference to equity investors, investors who seek to invest in high-earnings-growth companies.

Growth option or expansion option The ability to make additional investments in a project at some future time if the financial results are strong.

Harmonic mean A type of weighted mean computed by averaging the reciprocals of the observations, then taking the reciprocal of that average.

Head and shoulders pattern In technical analysis, a reversal pattern that is formed in three parts: a left shoulder, head, and right shoulder; used to predict a change from an uptrend to a downtrend.

Hedge fund A historically loosely regulated, pooled investment vehicle that may implement various investment strategies.

Hedge funds Private investment vehicles that typically use leverage, derivatives, and long and short investment strategies.

Hedge ratio The relationship of the quantity of an asset being hedged to the quantity of the derivative used for hedging.

Hedging A general strategy usually thought of as reducing, if not eliminating, risk.

Held-for-trading securities (trading securities) Debt or equity financial assets bought with the intention to sell them in the near term, usually less than three months; securities that a company intends to trade.

Held-to-maturity investments Debt (fixed-income) securities that a company intends to hold to maturity; these are presented at their original cost, updated for any amortization of discounts or premiums.

Herding Clustered trading that may or may not be based on information.

Herfindahl–Hirschman Index A measure of market concentration that is calculated by summing the squared market shares for competing companies in an industry; high HHI readings or mergers that would result in large HHI increases are more likely to result in regulatory challenges.

Heteroskedastic With reference to the error term of a regression, having a variance that differs across observations.

Heteroskedasticity The property of having a nonconstant variance; refers to an error term with the property that its variance differs across observations.

Heteroskedasticity-consistent standard errors Standard errors of the estimated parameters of a regression that correct for the presence of heteroskedasticity in the regression's error term.

Hidden order An order that is exposed not to the public but only to the brokers or exchanges that receive it.

Histogram A bar chart of data that have been grouped into a frequency distribution.

Historical cost In reference to assets, the amount paid to purchase an asset, including any costs of acquisition and/or preparation; with reference to liabilities, the amount of proceeds received in exchange in issuing the liability.

Historical equity risk premium approach An estimate of a country's equity risk premium that is based upon the historical averages of the risk-free rate and the rate of return on the market portfolio.

Historical exchange rates For accounting purposes, the exchange rates that existed when the assets and liabilities were initially recorded.

Historical method A method of estimating VAR that uses data from the returns of the portfolio over a recent past period and compiles this data in the form of a histogram.

Historical simulation (or back simulation) Another term for the historical method of estimating VAR. This term is somewhat misleading in that the method involves not a *simulation* of the past but rather what *actually happened* in the past, sometimes adjusted to reflect the fact that a different portfolio may have existed in the past than is planned for the future.

Holder-of-record date The date that a shareholder listed on the corporation's books will be deemed to have ownership of the shares for purposes of receiving an upcoming dividend; two business days after the ex-dividend date.

Holding period return The return that an investor earns during a specified holding period; a synonym for total return.

Holding period yield (HPY) The return that an investor earns during a specified holding period; holding period return with reference to a fixed-income instrument.

Homogeneity of expectations The assumption that all investors have the same economic expectations and thus have the same expectations of prices, cash flows, and other investment characteristics.

Homogenization Creating a contract with standard and generally accepted terms, which makes it more acceptable to a broader group of participants.

Homoskedasticity The property of having a constant variance; refers to an error term that is constant across observations.

Horizontal analysis Common-size analysis that involves comparing a specific financial statement with that statement in prior or future time periods; also, cross-sectional analysis of one company with another.

Horizontal common-size analysis A form of common-size analysis in which the accounts in a given period are used as the benchmark or base period, and every account is restated in subsequent periods as a percentage of the base period's same account.

Horizontal merger A merger involving companies in the same line of business, usually as competitors.

Hostile transaction An attempt to acquire a company against the wishes of the target's managers.

Hurdle rate The rate of return that must be met for a project to be accepted.

Hypothesis With reference to statistical inference, a statement about one or more populations.

Hypothesis testing With reference to statistical inference, the subdivision dealing with the testing of hypotheses about one or more populations.

Iceberg order An order in which the display size is less than the order's full size.

Identifiable intangible An intangible that can be acquired singly and is typically linked to specific rights or privileges having finite benefit periods (e.g., a patent or trademark).

If-converted method A method for accounting for the effect of convertible securities on earnings per share (EPS) that specifies what EPS would have been if the convertible securities had been converted at the beginning of the period, taking account of the effects of conversion on net income and the weighted average number of shares outstanding.

Immediate or cancel order (fill or kill) An order that is valid only upon receipt by the broker or exchange. If such an order cannot be filled in part or in whole upon receipt, it cancels immediately.

Impairment Diminishment in value as a result of carrying (book) value exceeding fair value and/or recoverable value.

Impairment of capital rule A legal restriction that dividends cannot exceed retained earnings.

Implicit rental rate The firm's opportunity cost of using its own capital.

Implied repo rate The rate of return from a cash-and-carry transaction implied by the futures price relative to the spot price.

Implied volatility The volatility that option traders use to price an option, implied by the price of the option and a particular option-pricing model.

Implied yield A measure of the yield on the underlying bond of a futures contract implied by pricing it as though the underlying will be delivered at the futures expiration.

Imputation In reference to corporate taxes, a system that imputes, or attributes, taxes at only one level of taxation. For countries using an imputation tax system, taxes on dividends are effectively levied only at the shareholder rate. Taxes are paid at the corporate level but they are *attributed* to the shareholder. Shareholders deduct from their tax bill their portion of taxes paid by the company.

Incentive system A method of organizing production that uses a market-like mechanism inside the firm.

Income Increases in economic benefits in the form of inflows or enhancements of assets, or decreases of liabilities that result in an increase in equity (other than increases resulting from contributions by owners).

Income elasticity of demand The responsiveness of demand to a change in income, other things remaining the same. It is calculated as the percentage change in the quantity demanded divided by the percentage change in income.

Income statement (statement of operations or profit and loss statement) A financial statement that provides information about a company's profitability over a stated period of time.

Income tax paid The actual amount paid for income taxes in the period; not a provision, but the actual cash outflow.

Income tax payable The income tax owed by the company on the basis of taxable income.

Income tax recoverable The income tax expected to be recovered, from the taxing authority, on the basis of taxable income. It is a recovery of previously remitted taxes or future taxes owed by the company.

Income trust A type of equity ownership vehicle established as a trust issuing ownership shares known as units.

Incremental cash flow The cash flow that is realized because of a decision; the changes or increments to cash flows resulting from a decision or action.

Independent With reference to events, the property that the occurrence of one event does not affect the probability of another event occurring.

Independent and identically distributed (IID) With respect to random variables, the property of random variables that are independent of each other but follow the identical probability distribution.

Independent projects Independent projects are projects whose cash flows are independent of each other.

Independent variable A variable used to explain the dependent variable in a regression; a right-hand-side variable in a regression equation.

Index amortizing swap An interest rate swap in which the notional principal is indexed to the level of interest rates and declines with the level of interest rates according to a predefined schedule. This type of swap is frequently used to hedge securities that are prepaid as interest rates decline, such as mortgage-backed securities.

Index option An option in which the underlying is a stock index.

Indexing An investment strategy in which an investor constructs a portfolio to mirror the performance of a specified index.

Indifference curve The graph of risk–return combinations that an investor would be willing to accept to maintain a given level of utility.

Indirect format (indirect method) With reference to cash flow statements, a format for the presentation of the statement which, in the operating cash flow section, begins with net income then shows additions and subtractions to arrive at operating cash flow.

Induced taxes Taxes that vary with real GDP.

Industry A group of companies offering similar products and/or services.

Industry analysis The analysis of a specific branch of manufacturing, service, or trade.

Inelastic demand A demand with a price elasticity between 0 and 1; the percentage change in the quantity demanded is less than the percentage change in price.

Inflation premium An extra return that compensates investors for expected inflation.

Inflation rate The annual percentage change in the price level.

Inflation rate targeting A monetary policy strategy in which the central bank makes a public commitment to achieve an explicit inflation rate and to explain how its policy actions will achieve that target.

Inflationary gap The amount by which real GDP exceeds potential GDP.

Information ratio (IR) Mean active return divided by active risk.

Information cascade The transmission of information from those participants who act first and whose decisions influence the decisions of others.

Information-motivated traders Traders that trade to profit from information that they believe allows them to predict future prices.

Informationally efficient market A market in which asset prices reflect new information quickly and rationally.

Initial margin The amount that must be deposited in a clearinghouse account when entering into a futures contract.

Initial margin requirement The margin requirement on the first day of a transaction as well as on any day in which additional margin funds must be deposited.

Initial public offering (IPO) The first issuance of common shares to the public by a formerly private corporation.

In-sample forecast errors The residuals from a fitted time-series model within the sample period used to fit the model.

Instability in the minimum-variance frontier The characteristic of minimum-variance frontiers that they are sensitive to small changes in inputs.

Installment Said of a sale in which proceeds are to be paid in installments over an extended period of time.

Installment method (installment-sales method) With respect to revenue recognition, a method that specifies that the portion of the total profit of the sale that is recognized in each period is determined by the percentage of the total sales price for which the seller has received cash.

Instrument rule A decision rule for monetary policy that sets the policy instrument at a level that is based on the current state of the economy.

Intangible assets Assets lacking physical substance, such as patents and trademarks.

Interest coverage A solvency ratio calculated as EBIT divided by interest payments.

Interest rate A rate of return that reflects the relationship between differently dated cash flows; a discount rate.

Interest rate call An option in which the holder has the right to make a known interest payment and receive an unknown interest payment.

Interest rate cap or cap A series of call options on an interest rate, with each option expiring at the date on which the floating loan rate will be reset, and with each option having the same exercise rate. A cap in general can have an underlying other than an interest rate.

Interest rate collar   A combination of a long cap and a short floor, or a short cap and a long floor. A collar in general can have an underlying other than an interest rate.

Interest rate floor or floor   A series of put options on an interest rate, with each option expiring at the date on which the floating loan rate will be reset, and with each option having the same exercise rate. A floor in general can have an underlying other than the interest rate.

Interest rate forward   See *Forward rate agreement.*

Interest rate option   An option in which the underlying is an interest rate.

Interest rate parity   A formula that expresses the equivalence or parity of spot and forward rates, after adjusting for differences in the interest rates.

Interest rate put   An option in which the holder has the right to make an unknown interest payment and receive a known interest payment.

Interest rate swap   A swap in which the underlying is an interest rate. Can be viewed as a currency swap in which both currencies are the same and can be created as a combination of currency swaps.

Intergenerational data mining   A form of data mining that applies information developed by previous researchers using a dataset to guide current research using the same or a related dataset.

Intermarket analysis   A field within technical analysis that combines analysis of major categories of securities—namely, equities, bonds, currencies, and commodities—to identify market trends and possible inflections in a trend.

Internal rate of return (IRR)   The discount rate that makes net present value equal 0; the discount rate that makes the present value of an investment's costs (outflows) equal to the present value of the investment's benefits (inflows).

Interquartile range   The difference between the third and first quartiles of a dataset.

Interval   With reference to grouped data, a set of values within which an observation falls.

Interval scale   A measurement scale that not only ranks data but also gives assurance that the differences between scale values are equal.

In-the-money   Options that, if exercised, would result in the value received being worth more than the payment required to exercise.

Inventory   The unsold units of product on hand.

Inventory blanket lien   The use of inventory as collateral for a loan. Though the lender has claim to some or all of the company's inventory, the company may still sell or use the inventory in the ordinary course of business.

Inventory turnover   An activity ratio calculated as cost of goods sold divided by average inventory.

Inverse floater   A floating-rate note or bond in which the coupon is adjusted to move opposite to a benchmark interest rate.

Investing activities   Activities which are associated with the acquisition and disposal of property, plant, and equipment; intangible assets; other long-term assets; and both long-term and short-term investments in the equity and debt (bonds and loans) issued by other companies.

Investment banks   Financial intermediaries that provide advice to their mostly corporate clients and help them arrange transactions such as initial and seasoned securities offerings.

Investment opportunity schedule   A graphical depiction of a company's investment opportunities ordered from highest to lowest expected return. A company's optimal capital budget is found where the investment opportunity schedule intersects with the company's marginal cost of capital.

Investment policy statement (IPS)   A written planning document that describes a client's investment objectives and risk tolerance over a relevant time horizon, along with constraints that apply to the client's portfolio.

Investment strategy   A set of rules, guidelines, or procedures that is used to analyze and select securities and manage portfolios.

IRR rule   An investment decision rule that accepts projects or investments for which the IRR is greater than the opportunity cost of capital.

January effect (also **turn-of-the-year effect**)   Calendar anomaly that stock market returns in January are significantly higher compared to the rest of the months of the year, with most of the abnormal returns reported during the first five trading days in January.

Joint probability   The probability of the joint occurrence of stated events.

Joint probability function   A function giving the probability of joint occurrences of values of stated random variables.

Joint venture   An entity (partnership, corporation, or other legal form) where control is shared by two or more entities called venturers.

Just-in-time method   Method of managing inventory that minimizes in-process inventory stocks.

Keynesian   A macroeconomist who believes that left alone, the economy would rarely operate at full employment and that to achieve full employment, active help from fiscal policy and monetary policy is required.

Keynesian cycle theory   A theory that fluctuations in investment driven by fluctuations in business confidence—summarized in the phrase "animal spirits"—are the main source of fluctuations in aggregate demand.

Kondratieff wave   A 54-year long economic cycle postulated by Nikolai Kondratieff.

***k*-percent rule**   A rule that makes the quantity of money grow at a rate of k percent a year, where k equals the growth rate of potential GDP.

***k*th Order autocorrelation**   The correlation between observations in a time series separated by k periods.

Kurtosis   The statistical measure that indicates the peakedness of a distribution.

Labor force   The sum of the people who are employed and who are unemployed.

Labor force participation rate   The percentage of the working-age population who are members of the labor force.

Labor union   An organized group of workers whose purpose is to increase wages and to influence other job conditions.

Laddering strategy   A form of active strategy which entails scheduling maturities on a systematic basis within the investment portfolio such that investments are spread out equally over the term of the ladder.

Laffer curve   The relationship between the tax rate and the amount of tax revenue collected.

Law of diminishing returns   As a firm uses more of a variable input, with a given quantity of other inputs (fixed inputs), the marginal product of the variable input eventually diminishes.

Law of one price   The condition in a financial market in which two equivalent financial instruments or combinations of financial instruments can sell for only one price. Equivalent to the principle that no arbitrage opportunities are possible.

Lead underwriter   The lead investment bank in a syndicate of investment banks and broker–dealers involved in a securities underwriting.

Legal monopoly　A market structure in which there is one firm and entry is restricted by the granting of a public franchise, government license, patent, or copyright.

Legal risk　The risk that failures by company managers to effectively manage a company's environmental, social, and governance risk exposures will lead to lawsuits and other judicial remedies, resulting in potentially catastrophic losses for the company; the risk that the legal system will not enforce a contract in case of dispute or fraud.

Legislative and regulatory risk　The risk that governmental laws and regulations directly or indirectly affecting a company's operations will change with potentially severe adverse effects on the company's continued profitability and even its long-term sustainability.

Leptokurtic　Describes a distribution that is more peaked than a normal distribution.

Lessee　The party obtaining the use of an asset through a lease.

Lessor　The owner of an asset that grants the right to use the asset to another party.

Level of significance　The probability of a Type I error in testing a hypothesis.

Leverage　In the context of corporate finance, leverage refers to the use of fixed costs within a company's cost structure. Fixed costs that are operating costs (such as depreciation or rent) create operating leverage. Fixed costs that are financial costs (such as interest expense) create financial leverage.

Leveraged buyout (LBO)　A transaction whereby the target company management team converts the target to a privately held company by using heavy borrowing to finance the purchase of the target company's outstanding shares.

Leveraged floating-rate note or leveraged floater　A floating-rate note or bond in which the coupon is adjusted at a multiple of a benchmark interest rate.

Leveraged recapitalization　A post-offer takeover defense mechanism that involves the assumption of a large amount of debt that is then used to finance share repurchases; the effect is to dramatically change the company's capital structure while attempting to deliver a value to target shareholders in excess of a hostile bid.

Liabilities　Present obligations of an enterprise arising from past events, the settlement of which is expected to result in an outflow of resources embodying economic benefits; creditors' claims on the resources of a company.

Life-cycle stage　The stage of the life cycle: embryonic, growth, shakeout, mature, declining.

LIFO layer liquidation (LIFO liquidation)　With respect to the application of the LIFO inventory method, the liquidation of old, relatively low-priced inventory; happens when the volume of sales rises above the volume of recent purchases so that some sales are made from relatively old, low-priced inventory.

LIFO method　The last in, first out, method of accounting for inventory, which matches sales against the costs of items of inventory in the reverse order the items were placed in inventory (i.e., inventory produced or acquired last are assumed to be sold first).

LIFO reserve　The difference between inventory reported at FIFO and inventory reported at LIFO (FIFO inventory value less LIFO inventory value).

Likelihood　The probability of an observation, given a particular set of conditions.

Limit down　A limit move in the futures market in which the price at which a transaction would be made is at or below the lower limit.

Limit move　A condition in the futures markets in which the price at which a transaction would be made is at or beyond the price limits.

Limit order　Instructions to a broker or exchange to obtain the best price immediately available when filling an order, but in no event accept a price higher than a specified (limit) price when buying or accept a price lower than a specified (limit) price when selling.

Limit order book　The book or list of limit orders to buy and sell that pertains to a security.

Limit pricing　The practice of setting the price at the highest level that inflicts a loss on an entrant.

Limit up　A limit move in the futures market in which the price at which a transaction would be made is at or above the upper limit.

Line chart　In technical analysis, a plot of price data, typically closing prices, with a line connecting the points.

Linear (arithmetic) scale　A scale in which equal distances correspond to equal absolute amounts.

Linear association　A straight-line relationship, as opposed to a relationship that cannot be graphed as a straight line.

Linear interpolation　The estimation of an unknown value on the basis of two known values that bracket it, using a straight line between the two known values.

Linear regression　Regression that models the straight-line relationship between the dependent and independent variable(s).

Linear trend　A trend in which the dependent variable changes at a constant rate with time.

Liquid　An asset that can be easily converted into cash in a short period of time at a price close to fair market value.

Liquid market　Said of a market in which traders can buy or sell with low total transaction costs when they want to trade.

Liquidating dividend　A dividend that is a return of capital rather than a distribution from earnings or retained earnings.

Liquidation　To sell the assets of a company, division, or subsidiary piecemeal, typically because of bankruptcy; the form of bankruptcy that allows for the orderly satisfaction of creditors' claims after which the company ceases to exist.

Liquidity　The ability to purchase or sell an asset quickly and easily at a price close to fair market value. The ability to meet short-term obligations using assets that are the most readily converted into cash.

Liquidity premium　An extra return that compensates investors for the risk of loss relative to an investment's fair value if the investment needs to be converted to cash quickly.

Liquidity ratios　Financial ratios measuring the company's ability to meet its short-term obligations.

Liquidity risk　The risk that a financial instrument cannot be purchased or sold without a significant concession in price due to the size of the market.

Living wage　An hourly wage rate that enables a person who works a 40-hour work week to rent adequate housing for not more than 30 percent of the amount earned.

Load fund　A mutual fund in which, in addition to the annual fee, a percentage fee is charged to invest in the fund and/or for redemptions from the fund.

Local currency　The currency of the country where a company is located.

Lockbox system　A payment system in which customer payments are mailed to a post office box and the banking institution retrieves and deposits these payments several times a day, enabling the company to have use of the fund sooner than in a centralized system in which customer payments are sent to the company.

Locked limit　A condition in the futures markets in which a transaction cannot take place because the price would be beyond the limits.

Logarithmic scale　A scale in which equal distances represent equal proportional changes in the underlying quantity.

Logit model A qualitative-dependent-variable multiple regression model based on the logistic probability distribution.

Log-linear model With reference to time-series models, a model in which the growth rate of the time series as a function of time is constant.

Log-log regression model A regression that expresses the dependent and independent variables as natural logarithms.

London Interbank Offer Rate (LIBOR) The Eurodollar rate at which London banks lend dollars to other London banks; considered to be the best representative rate on a dollar borrowed by a private, high-quality borrower.

Long The buyer of a derivative contract. Also refers to the position of owning a derivative.

Long position A position in an asset or contract in which one owns the asset or has an exercisable right under the contract.

Long run A period of time in which the quantities of all resources can be varied.

Longitudinal data Observations on characteristic(s) of the same observational unit through time.

Long-lived assets (or long-term assets) Assets that are expected to provide economic benefits over a future period of time, typically greater than one year.

Long-run aggregate supply The relationship between the quantity of real GDP supplied and the price level in the long run when real GDP equals potential GDP.

Long-run average cost curve The relationship between the lowest attainable average total cost and output when both plant size and labor are varied.

Long-run industry supply curve A curve that shows how the quantity supplied by an industry varies as the market price varies after all the possible adjustments have been made, including changes in plant size and the number of firms in the industry.

Long-run macroeconomic equilibrium A situation that occurs when real GDP equals potential GDP—the economy is on its long-run aggregate supply curve.

Long-run Phillips curve A curve that shows the relationship between inflation and unemployment when the actual inflation rate equals the expected inflation rate.

Long-term contract A contract that spans a number of accounting periods.

Long-term debt-to-assets ratio The proportion of a company's assets that is financed with long-term debt.

Long-term equity anticipatory securities (LEAPS) Options originally created with expirations of several years.

Long-term liability An obligation that is expected to be settled, with the outflow of resources embodying economic benefits, over a future period generally greater than one year.

Look-ahead bias A bias caused by using information that was unavailable on the test date.

Losses Asset outflows not directly related to the ordinary activities of the business.

Lower bound The lowest possible value of an option.

M1 A measure of money that consists of currency and traveler's checks plus checking deposits owned by individuals and businesses.

M2 A measure of money that consists of M1 plus time deposits, savings deposits, and money market mutual funds, and other deposits.

M^2 A measure of what a portfolio would have returned if it had taken on the same total risk as the market index.

Macaulay duration The duration without dividing by 1 plus the bond's yield to maturity. The term, named for one of the economists who first derived it, is used to distinguish the calculation from modified duration. (See also *modified duration*.)

Macroeconomic factor A factor related to the economy, such as the inflation rate, industrial production, or economic sector membership.

Macroeconomic factor model A multifactor model in which the factors are surprises in macroeconomic variables that significantly explain equity returns.

Macroeconomic long run A time frame that is sufficiently long for the real wage rate to have adjusted to achieve full employment: real GDP equal to potential GDP, unemployment equal to the natural unemployment rate, the price level is proportional to the quantity of money, and the inflation rate equal to the money growth rate minus the real GDP growth rate.

Macroeconomic short run A period during which some money prices are sticky and real GDP might be below, above, or at potential GDP and unemployment might be above, below, or at the natural rate of unemployment.

Maintenance margin The minimum amount that is required by a futures clearinghouse to maintain a margin account and to protect against default. Participants whose margin balances drop below the required maintenance margin must replenish their accounts.

Maintenance margin requirement The margin requirement on any day other than the first day of a transaction.

Management buyout (MBO) An event in which a group of investors consisting primarily of the company's existing management purchase all of its outstanding shares and take the company private.

Managerialism theories Theories that posit that corporate executives are motivated to engage in mergers to maximize the size of their company rather than shareholder value.

Manufacturing resource planning (MRP) The incorporation of production planning into inventory management. A MRP analysis provides both a materials acquisition schedule and a production schedule.

Margin call A notice to deposit additional cash or securities in a margin account.

Margin loan Money borrowed from a broker to purchase securities.

Marginal cost The opportunity cost of producing one more unit of a good or service. It is the best alternative forgone. It is calculated as the increase in total cost divided by the increase in output.

Marginal cost pricing rule A rule that sets the price of a good or service equal to the marginal cost of producing it.

Marginal product The increase in total product that results from a one-unit increase in the variable input, with all other inputs remaining the same. It is calculated as the increase in total product divided by the increase in the variable input employed, when the quantities of all other inputs are constant.

Marginal revenue The change in total revenue that results from a one-unit increase in the quantity sold. It is calculated as the change in total revenue divided by the change in quantity sold.

Marginal revenue product The change in total revenue that results from employing one more unit of a factor of production (labor) while the quantity of all other factors remains the same. It is calculated as the increase in total revenue divided by the increase in the quantity of the factor (labor).

Market A means of bringing buyers and sellers together to exchange goods and services.

Market anomaly Change in the price or return of a security that cannot directly be linked to current relevant information known in the market or to the release of new information into the market.

Market bid–ask spread The difference between the best bid and the best offer.

Market float The number of shares that are available to the investing public.

Market model   A regression equation that specifies a linear relationship between the return on a security (or portfolio) and the return on a broad market index.

Market order   Instructions to a broker or exchange to obtain the best price immediately available when filling an order.

Market power   The ability to influence the market, and in particular the market price, by influencing the total quantity offered for sale.

Market price of risk   The slope of the capital market line, indicating the market risk premium for each unit of market risk.

Market rate   The rate demanded by purchasers of bonds, given the risks associated with future cash payment obligations of the particular bond issue.

Market risk   The risk associated with interest rates, exchange rates, and equity prices.

Market risk premium   The expected excess return on the market over the risk-free rate.

Market value   The price at which an asset or security can currently be bought or sold in an open market.

Marketable limit order   A buy limit order in which the limit price is placed above the best offer, or a sell limit order in which the limit price is placed below the best bid. Such orders generally will partially or completely fill right away.

Market-capitalization weighting (or value weighting)   An index weighting method in which the weight assigned to each constituent security is determined by dividing its market capitalization by the total market capitalization (sum of the market capitalization) of all securities in the index.

Market-oriented investors   With reference to equity investors, investors whose investment disciplines cannot be clearly categorized as value or growth.

Marking to market   A procedure used primarily in futures markets in which the parties to a contract settle the amount owed daily. Also known as the *daily settlement*.

Markowitz decision rule   A decision rule for choosing between two investments based on their means and variances.

Markowitz efficient frontier   The graph of the set of portfolios offering the maximum expected return for their level of risk (standard deviation of return).

Mark-to-market   The revaluation of a financial asset or liability to its current market value or fair value.

Matching principle   The accounting principle that expenses should be recognized when the associated revenue is recognized.

Matching strategy   An active investment strategy that includes intentional matching of the timing of cash outflows with investment maturities.

Materiality   The condition of being of sufficient importance so that omission or misstatement of the item in a financial report could make a difference to users' decisions.

Matrix pricing   In the fixed income markets, to price a security on the basis of valuation-relevant characteristics (e.g. debt-rating approach).

Maturity premium   An extra return that compensates investors for the increased sensitivity of the market value of debt to a change in market interest rates as maturity is extended.

McCallum rule   A rule that makes the growth rate of the monetary base respond to the long-term average growth rate of real GDP and medium-term changes in the velocity of circulation of the monetary base.

Mean   The sum of all values in a distribution or dataset, divided by the number of values summed; a synonym of arithmetic mean.

Mean absolute deviation   With reference to a sample, the mean of the absolute values of deviations from the sample mean.

Mean excess return   The average rate of return in excess of the risk-free rate.

Mean rate of return   The average rate of return on an investment over time.

Mean reversion   The tendency of a time series to fall when its level is above its mean and rise when its level is below its mean; a mean-reverting time series tends to return to its long-term mean.

Mean–variance analysis   An approach to portfolio analysis using expected means, variances, and covariances of asset returns.

Means of payment   A method of settling a debt.

Measure of central tendency   A quantitative measure that specifies where data are centered.

Measure of location   A quantitative measure that describes the location or distribution of data; includes not only measures of central tendency but also other measures such as percentiles.

Measurement scales   A scheme of measuring differences. The four types of measurement scales are nominal, ordinal, interval, and ratio.

Median   The value of the middle item of a set of items that has been sorted into ascending or descending order; the 50th percentile.

Merger   The absorption of one company by another; that is, two companies become one entity and one or both of the pre-merger companies ceases to exist as a separate entity.

Mesokurtic   Describes a distribution with kurtosis identical to that of the normal distribution.

Minimum efficient scale   The smallest quantity of output at which the long-run average cost curve reaches its lowest level.

Minimum wage   A regulation that makes the hiring of labor below a specified wage rate illegal. The lowest wage at which a firm may legally hire labor.

Minimum-variance frontier   The graph of the set of portfolios that have minimum variance for their level of expected return.

Minimum-variance portfolio   The portfolio with the minimum variance for each given level of expected return.

Minority active investments   Investments in which investors exert significant influence, but not control, over the investee. Typically, the investor has 20 to 50% ownership in the investee.

Minority interest (noncontrolling interest)   The proportion of the ownership of a subsidiary not held by the parent (controlling) company.

Minority passive investments (passive investments)   Investments in which the investor has no significant influence or control over the operations of the investee.

Mismatching strategy   An active investment strategy whereby the timing of cash outflows is not matched with investment maturities.

Mixed factor models   Factor models that combine features of more than one type of factor model.

Mixed offering   A merger or acquisition that is to be paid for with cash, securities, or some combination of the two.

Modal interval   With reference to grouped data, the most frequently occurring interval.

Mode   The most frequently occurring value in a set of observations.

Model risk   The use of an inaccurate pricing model for a particular investment, or the improper use of the right model.

Model specification   With reference to regression, the set of variables included in the regression and the regression equation's functional form.

Modern portfolio theory (MPT)   The analysis of rational portfolio choices based on the efficient use of risk.

Modified duration   A measure of a bond's price sensitivity to interest rate movements. Equal to the Macaulay duration of a bond divided by one plus its yield to maturity.

Momentum oscillators   A graphical representation of market sentiment that is constructed from price data and calculated so that it oscillates either between a high and a low or around some number.

Monetarist   A macroeconomist who believes that the economy is self-regulating and that it will normally operate at full employment, provided that monetary policy is not erratic and that the pace of money growth is kept steady.

Monetarist cycle theory   A theory that fluctuations in both investment and consumption expenditure, driven by fluctuations in the growth rate of the quantity of money, are the main source of fluctuations in aggregate demand.

Monetary assets and liabilities   Assets and liabilities with value equal to the amount of currency contracted for, a fixed amount of currency. Examples are cash, accounts receivable, mortgages receivable, accounts payable, bonds payable, and mortgages payable. Inventory is not a monetary asset. Most liabilities are monetary.

Monetary base   The sum of Federal Reserve notes, coins and banks' deposits at the Fed.

Monetary policy   The Fed conducts the nation's monetary policy by changing interest rates and adjusting the quantity of money.

Monetary policy instrument   A variable that the Fed can control directly or closely target.

Monetary/nonmonetary method   Approach to translating foreign currency financial statements for consolidation in which monetary assets and liabilities are translated at the current exchange rate. Nonmonetary assets and liabilities are translated at historical exchange rates (the exchange rates that existed when the assets and liabilities were acquired).

Money   Any commodity or token that is generally acceptable as the means of payment.

Money market   The market for short-term debt instruments (one-year maturity or less).

Money market yield (or CD equivalent yield)   A yield on a basis comparable to the quoted yield on an interest-bearing money market instrument that pays interest on a 360-day basis; the annualized holding period yield, assuming a 360-day year.

Money multiplier   The ratio of the change in the quantity of money to the change in the monetary base.

Moneyness   The relationship between the price of the underlying and an option's exercise price.

Money-weighted rate of return   The internal rate of return on a portfolio, taking account of all cash flows.

Monitoring costs   Costs borne by owners to monitor the management of the company (e.g., board of director expenses).

Monopolistic competition   A market structure in which a large number of firms compete by making similar but slightly different products.

Monopoly   A market structure in which there is one firm, which produces a good or service that has no close substitutes and in which the firm is protected from competition by a barrier preventing the entry of new firms.

Monopsony   A market in which there is a single buyer.

Monte Carlo simulation method   An approach to estimating a probability distribution of outcomes to examine what might happen if particular risks are faced. This method is widely used in the sciences as well as in business to study a variety of problems.

Moving average   The average of the closing price of a security over a specified number of periods. With each new period, the average is recalculated.

Moving-average convergence/divergence oscillator (MACD)   A momentum oscillator that is constructed based on the difference between short-term and long-term moving averages of a security's price.

Multicollinearity   A regression assumption violation that occurs when two or more independent variables (or combinations of independent variables) are highly but not perfectly correlated with each other.

Multiple linear regression model   A linear regression model with two or more independent variables.

Multiple *R*   The correlation between the actual and forecasted values of the dependent variable in a regression.

Multiplication rule for probabilities   The rule that the joint probability of events *A* and *B* equals the probability of *A* given *B* times the probability of *B*.

Multiplier models (or **market multiple models**)   Valuation models based on share price multiples or enterprise value multiples.

Multi-factor model   A model that explains a variable in terms of the values of a set of factors.

Multi-market index   An index comprised of indices from different countries, designed to represent multiple security markets.

Multi-step format   With respect to the format of the income statement, a format that presents a subtotal for gross profit (revenue minus cost of goods sold).

Multivariate distribution   A probability distribution that specifies the probabilities for a group of related random variables.

Multivariate normal distribution   A probability distribution for a group of random variables that is completely defined by the means and variances of the variables plus all the correlations between pairs of the variables.

Mutual fund   A professionally managed investment pool in which investors in the fund typically each have a pro-rata claim on the income and value of the fund.

Mutually exclusive events   Events such that only one can occur at a time.

Mutually exclusive projects   Mutually exclusive projects compete directly with each other. For example, if Projects A and B are mutually exclusive, you can choose A or B, but you cannot choose both.

_n_ Factorial   For a positive integer *n*, the product of the first *n* positive integers; 0 factorial equals 1 by definition. *n* factorial is written as *n*!.

Nash equilibrium   The outcome of a game that occurs when player A takes the best possible action given the action of player B and player B takes the best possible action given the action of player A.

Natural monopoly   A monopoly that occurs when one firm can supply the entire market at a lower price than two or more firms can.

Natural unemployment rate   The unemployment rate when the economy is at full employment. There is no cyclical unemployment; all unemployment is frictional, structural, and seasonal.

Needs-tested spending   Government spending on programs that pay benefits to suitably qualified people and businesses.

Negative serial correlation   Serial correlation in which a positive error for one observation increases the chance of a negative error for another observation, and vice versa.

Net asset balance sheet exposure   When assets translated at the current exchange rate are greater in amount than liabilities translated at the current exchange rate. Assets exposed to translation gains or losses exceed the exposed liabilities.

Net book value   The remaining (undepreciated) balance of an asset's purchase cost. For liabilities, the face value of a bond minus any unamortized discount, or plus any unamortized premium.

Net income (loss)   The difference between revenue and expenses; what remains after subtracting all expenses (including depreciation, interest, and taxes) from revenue.

Net liability balance sheet exposure   When liabilities translated at the current exchange rate are greater than assets translated at the current exchange rate. Liabilities exposed to translation gains or losses exceed the exposed assets.

Net operating assets   The difference between operating assets (total assets less cash) and operating liabilities (total liabilities less total debt).

Net operating cycle   An estimate of the average time that elapses between paying suppliers for materials and collecting cash from the subsequent sale of goods produced.

Net operating profit less adjusted taxes, or NOPLAT   A company's operating profit with adjustments to normalize the effects of capital structure.

Net present value (NPV)   The present value of an investment's cash inflows (benefits) minus the present value of its cash outflows (costs).

Net profit margin (profit margin or return on sales)   An indicator of profitability, calculated as net income divided by revenue; indicates how much of each dollar of revenues is left after all costs and expenses.

Net realizable value   Estimated selling price in the ordinary course of business less the estimated costs necessary to make the sale.

Net revenue   Revenue after adjustments (e.g., for estimated returns or for amounts unlikely to be collected).

Netting   When parties agree to exchange only the net amount owed from one party to the other.

New classical   A macroeconomist who holds the view that business cycle fluctuations are the efficient responses of a well-functioning market economy bombarded by shocks that arise from the uneven pace of technological change.

New classical cycle theory   A rational expectations theory of the business cycle that regards unexpected fluctuations in aggregate demand as the main source of fluctuations of real GDP around potential GDP.

New-issue DRP (scrip dividend schemes)   Dividend reinvestment plan in which the company meets the need for additional shares by issuing them instead of purchasing them.

New Keynesian   A macroeconomist who holds the view that not only is the money wage rate sticky but also that the prices of goods and services are sticky.

New Keynesian cycle theory   A rational expectations theory of the business cycle that regards unexpected and currently expected fluctuations in aggregate demand as the main source of fluctuations of real GDP around potential GDP.

Node   Each value on a binomial tree from which successive moves or outcomes branch.

No-load fund   A mutual fund in which there is no fee for investing in the fund or for redeeming fund shares, although there is an annual fee based on a percentage of the fund's net asset value.

Nominal rate   A rate of interest based on the security's face value.

Nominal risk-free interest rate   The sum of the real risk-free interest rate and the inflation premium.

Nominal scale   A measurement scale that categorizes data but does not rank them.

Nonconventional cash flow   In a nonconventional cash flow pattern, the initial outflow is not followed by inflows only, but the cash flows can flip from positive (inflows) to negative (outflows) again (or even change signs several times).

Non-cumulative preference shares   Preference shares for which dividends that are not paid in the current or subsequent periods are forfeited permanently (instead of being accrued and paid at a later date).

Noncurrent   Not due to be consumed, converted into cash, or settled within one year after the balance sheet date.

Noncurrent assets   Assets that are expected to benefit the company over an extended period of time (usually more than one year).

Non-current liability   An obligation that broadly represents a probable sacrifice of economic benefits in periods generally greater than one year in the future.

Non-cyclical   A company whose performance is largely independent of the business cycle.

Nondeliverable forwards (NDFs)   Cash-settled forward contracts, used predominately with respect to foreign exchange forwards.

Nonlinear relation   An association or relationship between variables that cannot be graphed as a straight line.

Nonmonetary assets and liabilities   Assets and liabilities that are not monetary assets and liabilities. Nonmonetary assets include inventory, fixed assets, and intangibles, and nonmonetary liabilities include deferred revenue.

Nonparametric test   A test that is not concerned with a parameter, or that makes minimal assumptions about the population from which a sample comes.

Non-participating preference shares   Preference shares that do not entitle shareholders to share in the profits of the company. Instead, shareholders are only entitled to receive a fixed dividend payment and the par value of the shares in the event of liquidation.

Nonrenewable natural resources   Natural resources that can be used only once and that cannot be replaced once they have been used.

Nonstationarity   With reference to a random variable, the property of having characteristics such as mean and variance that are not constant through time.

Nonsystematic risk   Unique risk that is local or limited to a particular asset or industry that need not affect assets outside of that asset class.

Normal backwardation   The condition in futures markets in which futures prices are lower than expected spot prices.

Normal contango   The condition in futures markets in which futures prices are higher than expected spot prices.

Normal distribution   A continuous, symmetric probability distribution that is completely described by its mean and its variance.

Normal profit   The return that an entrepreneur can expect to receive on the average.

Notes payable   Amounts owed by a business to creditors as a result of borrowings that are evidenced by (short-term) loan agreements.

n-Period moving average   The average of the current and immediately prior $n - 1$ values of a time series.

NPV rule   An investment decision rule that states that an investment should be undertaken if its NPV is positive but not undertaken if its NPV is negative.

Null hypothesis   The hypothesis to be tested.

Number of days of inventory   An activity ratio equal to the number of days in a period divided by the inventory ratio for the period; an indication of the number of days a company ties up funds in inventory.

Number of days of payables   An activity ratio equal to the number of days in a period divided by the payables turnover ratio for the period; an estimate of the average number of days it takes a company to pay its suppliers.

Number of days of receivables Estimate of the average number of days it takes to collect on credit accounts.

Objective probabilities Probabilities that generally do not vary from person to person; includes a priori and objective probabilities.

Off-balance sheet financing Arrangements that do not result in additional liabilities on the balance sheet but nonetheless create economic obligations.

Off-market FRA A contract in which the initial value is intentionally set at a value other than zero and therefore requires a cash payment at the start from one party to the other.

Offsetting A transaction in exchange-listed derivative markets in which a party re-enters the market to close out a position.

Oligopoly A market structure in which a small number of firms compete.

One-sided hypothesis test (or one-tailed hypothesis test) A test in which the null hypothesis is rejected only if the evidence indicates that the population parameter is greater than (smaller than) θ_0. The alternative hypothesis also has one side.

Open market operation The purchase or sale of government securities—U.S. Treasury bills and bonds—by the Federal Reserve in the open market.

Open-end fund A mutual fund that accepts new investment money and issues additional shares at a value equal to the net asset value of the fund at the time of investment.

Open-market DRP Dividend reinvestment plan in which the company purchases shares in the open market to acquire the additional shares credited to plan participants.

Operating activities Activities that are part of the day-to-day business functioning of an entity, such as selling inventory and providing services.

Operating breakeven The number of units produced and sold at which the company's operating profit is zero (revenues = operating costs).

Operating cycle A measure of the time needed to convert raw materials into cash from a sale; it consists of the number of days of inventory and the number of days of receivables.

Operating lease An agreement allowing the lessee to use some asset for a period of time; essentially a rental.

Operating leverage The use of fixed costs in operations.

Operating profit (operating income) A company's profits on its usual business activities before deducting taxes.

Operating profit margin (operating margin) A profitability ratio calculated as operating income (i.e., income before interest and taxes) divided by revenue.

Operating return on assets (operating ROA) A profitability ratio calculated as operating income divided by average total assets.

Operating risk The risk attributed to the operating cost structure, in particular the use of fixed costs in operations; the risk arising from the mix of fixed and variable costs; the risk that a company's operations may be severely affected by environmental, social, and governance risk factors.

Operationally efficient Said of a market, a financial system, or an economy that has relatively low transaction costs.

Operations risk or **operational risk** The risk of loss from failures in a company's systems and procedures (for example, due to computer failures or human failures) or events completely outside of the control of organizations (which would include "acts of God" and terrorist actions).

Opportunity cost The value that investors forgo by choosing a particular course of action; the value of something in its best alternative use.

Opportunity set The set of assets available for investment.

Optimal capital structure The capital structure at which the value of the company is maximized.

Optimizer A specialized computer program or a spreadsheet that solves for the portfolio weights that will result in the lowest risk for a specified level of expected return.

Option (or option contract) A financial instrument that gives one party the right, but not the obligation, to buy or sell an underlying asset from or to another party at a fixed price over a specific period of time. Also referred to as contingent claims.

Option price, option premium, or premium The amount of money a buyer pays and seller receives to engage in an option transaction.

Order A specification of what instrument to trade, how much to trade, and whether to buy or sell.

Order precedence hierarchy With respect to the execution of orders to trade, a set of rules that determines which orders execute before other orders.

Order-driven markets A market (generally an auction market) that uses rules to arrange trades based on the orders that traders submit; in their pure form, such markets do not make use of dealers.

Ordinal scale A measurement scale that sorts data into categories that are ordered (ranked) with respect to some characteristic.

Ordinary annuity An annuity with a first cash flow that is paid one period from the present.

Ordinary least squares (OLS) An estimation method based on the criterion of minimizing the sum of the squared residuals of a regression.

Ordinary shares (common stock or common shares) Equity shares that are subordinate to all other types of equity (e.g., preferred equity).

Organic growth Company growth in output or sales that is achieved by making investments internally (i.e., excludes growth achieved through mergers and acquisitions).

Orthogonal Uncorrelated; at a right angle.

Other comprehensive income Items of comprehensive income that are not reported on the income statement; comprehensive income minus net income.

Other post-retirement benefits Promises by the company to pay benefits in the future, other than pension benefits, such as life insurance premiums and all or part of health care insurance for its retirees.

Other receivables Amounts owed to the company from parties other than customers.

Outcome A possible value of a random variable.

Outliers Small numbers of observations at either extreme (small or large) of a sample.

Out-of-sample forecast errors The differences between actual and predicted value of time series outside the sample period used to fit the model.

Out-of-sample test A test of a strategy or model using a sample outside the time period on which the strategy or model was developed.

Out-of-the-money Options that, if exercised, would require the payment of more money than the value received and therefore would not be currently exercised.

Output gap Real GDP minus potential GDP.

Overbought A market condition in which market sentiment is thought to be unsustainably bullish.

Overnight index swap (OIS) A swap in which the floating rate is the cumulative value of a single unit of currency invested at an overnight rate during the settlement period.

Oversold A market condition in which market sentiment is thought to be unsustainably bearish.

Owners' equity The excess of assets over liabilities; the residual interest of shareholders in the assets of an entity after deducting the entity's liabilities.

Paired comparisons test A statistical test for differences based on paired observations drawn from samples that are dependent on each other.

Paired observations Observations that are dependent on each other.

Pairs arbitrage trade A trade in two closely related stocks involving the short sale of one and the purchase of the other.

Panel data Observations through time on a single characteristic of multiple observational units.

Parameter A descriptive measure computed from or used to describe a population of data, conventionally represented by Greek letters.

Parameter instability The problem or issue of population regression parameters that have changed over time.

Parametric test Any test (or procedure) concerned with parameters or whose validity depends on assumptions concerning the population generating the sample.

Partial regression coefficients or partial slope coefficients The slope coefficients in a multiple regression.

Participating preference shares Preference shares that entitle shareholders to receive the standard preferred dividend plus the opportunity to receive an additional dividend if the company's profits exceed a pre-specified level.

Partnership A business owned and operated by more than one individual.

Passive investment A buy and hold approach in which an investor does not make portfolio changes based on short-term expectations of changing market or security performance.

Passive strategy In reference to short-term cash management, it is an investment strategy characterized by simple decision rules for making daily investments.

Payables turnover An activity ratio calculated as purchases divided by average trade payables.

Payer swaption A swaption that allows the holder to enter into a swap as the fixed-rate payer and floating-rate receiver.

Payment date The day that the company actually mails out (or electronically transfers) a dividend payment.

Payment netting A means of settling payments in which the amount owed by the first party to the second is netted with the amount owed by the second party to the first; only the net difference is paid.

Payoff The value of an option at expiration.

Payoff matrix A table that shows the payoffs for every possible action by each player for every possible action by each other player.

Payout Cash dividends and the value of shares repurchased in any given year.

Payout policy A company's set of principles guiding payouts.

Payout ratio The percentage of total earnings paid out in dividends in any given year (in per-share terms, DPS/EPS).

Pecking order theory The theory that managers take into account how their actions might be interpreted by outsiders and thus order their preferences for various forms of corporate financing. Forms of financing that are least visible to outsiders (e.g., internally generated funds) are most preferable to managers

and those that are most visible (e.g., equity) are least preferable.

Peer group A group of companies engaged in similar business activities whose economics and valuation are influenced by closely related factors.

Pennants A technical analysis continuation pattern formed by trendlines that converge to form a triangle, typically over a short period.

Per unit contribution margin The amount that each unit sold contributes to covering fixed costs—that is, the difference between the price per unit and the variable cost per unit.

Percentage-of-completion A method of revenue recognition in which, in each accounting period, the company estimates what percentage of the contract is complete and then reports that percentage of the total contract revenue in its income statement.

Percentiles Quantiles that divide a distribution into 100 equal parts.

Perfect collinearity The existence of an exact linear relation between two or more independent variables or combinations of independent variables.

Perfect competition A market in which there are many firms each selling an identical product; there are many buyers; there are no restrictions on entry into the industry; firms in the industry have no advantage over potential new entrants; and firms and buyers are well informed about the price of each firm's product.

Perfect price discrimination Price discrimination that extracts the entire consumer surplus.

Perfectly elastic demand Demand with an infinite price elasticity; the quantity demanded changes by an infinitely large percentage in response to a tiny price change.

Perfectly inelastic demand Demand with a price elasticity of zero; the quantity demanded remains constant when the price changes.

Performance appraisal The evaluation of risk-adjusted performance; the evaluation of investment skill.

Performance evaluation The measurement and assessment of the outcomes of investment management decisions.

Performance guarantee A guarantee from the clearinghouse that if one party makes money on a transaction, the clearinghouse ensures it will be paid.

Performance measurement The calculation of returns in a logical and consistent manner.

Period costs Costs (e.g., executives' salaries) that cannot be directly matched with the timing of revenues and which are thus expensed immediately.

Periodic rate The quoted interest rate per period; the stated annual interest rate divided by the number of compounding periods per year.

Permanent differences Differences between tax and financial reporting of revenue (expenses) that will not be reversed at some future date. These result in a difference between the company's effective tax rate and statutory tax rate and do not result in a deferred tax item.

Permutation An ordered listing.

Perpetuity A perpetual annuity, or a set of never-ending level sequential cash flows, with the first cash flow occurring one period from now.

Pet projects Projects in which influential managers want the corporation to invest. Often, unfortunately, pet projects are selected without undergoing normal capital budgeting analysis.

Phillips curve A curve that shows a relationship between inflation and unemployment.

Plain vanilla swap An interest rate swap in which one party pays a fixed rate and the other pays a floating rate, with both sets of payments in the same currency.

Platykurtic Describes a distribution that is less peaked than the normal distribution.

Point and figure chart A technical analysis chart that is constructed with columns of X's alternating with columns of O's such that the horizontal axis represents only the number of changes in price without reference to time or volume.

Point estimate A single numerical estimate of an unknown quantity, such as a population parameter.

Point of sale Systems that capture transaction data at the physical location in which the sale is made.

Poison pill A pre-offer takeover defense mechanism that makes it prohibitively costly for an acquirer to take control of a target without the prior approval of the target's board of directors.

Poison puts A pre-offer takeover defense mechanism that gives target company bondholders the right to sell their bonds back to the target at a pre-specified redemption price, typically at or above par value; this defense increases the need for cash and raises the cost of the acquisition.

Pooled estimate An estimate of a parameter that involves combining (pooling) observations from two or more samples.

Pooling of interests accounting method A method of accounting in which combined companies were portrayed as if they had always operated as a single economic entity. Called pooling of interests under U.S. GAAP and uniting of interests under IFRS. (No longer allowed under U.S. GAAP or IFRS.)

Population All members of a specified group.

Population mean The arithmetic mean value of a population; the arithmetic mean of all the observations or values in the population.

Population standard deviation A measure of dispersion relating to a population in the same unit of measurement as the observations, calculated as the positive square root of the population variance.

Population variance A measure of dispersion relating to a population, calculated as the mean of the squared deviations around the population mean.

Portfolio performance attribution The analysis of portfolio performance in terms of the contributions from various sources of risk.

Portfolio planning The process of creating a plan for building a portfolio that is expected to satisfy a client's investment objectives.

Portfolio possibilities curve A graphical representation of the expected return and risk of all portfolios that can be formed using two assets.

Position The quantity of an asset that an entity owns or owes.

Position trader A trader who typically holds positions open overnight.

Positive serial correlation Serial correlation in which a positive error for one observation increases the chance of a positive error for another observation, and a negative error for one observation increases the chance of a negative error for another observation.

Posterior probability An updated probability that reflects or comes after new information.

Potential credit risk The risk associated with the possibility that a payment due at a later date will not be made.

Potential GDP The value of production when all the economy's labor, capital, land, and entrepreneurial ability are fully employed; the quantity of real GDP at full employment.

Power of a test The probability of correctly rejecting the null—that is, rejecting the null hypothesis when it is false.

Precautionary stocks A level of inventory beyond anticipated needs that provides a cushion in the event that it takes longer to replenish inventory than expected or in the case of greater than expected demand.

Preference shares (or preferred stock) A type of equity interest which ranks above common shares with respect to the payment of dividends and the distribution of the company's net assets upon liquidation. They have characteristics of both debt and equity securities.

Preferred stock A form of equity (generally non-voting) that has priority over common stock in the receipt of dividends and on the issuer's assets in the event of a company's liquidation.

Pre-investing The strategy of using futures contracts to enter the market without an immediate outlay of cash.

Prepaid expense A normal operating expense that has been paid in advance of when it is due.

Present (price) value of a basis point (PVBP) The change in the bond price for a 1 basis point change in yield. Also called *basis point value* (BPV).

Present value (PV) The present discounted value of future cash flows: For assets, the present discounted value of the future net cash inflows that the asset is expected to generate; for liabilities, the present discounted value of the future net cash outflows that are expected to be required to settle the liabilities.

Present value models (or **discounted cash flow models**) Valuation models that estimate the intrinsic value of a security as the present value of the future benefits expected to be received from the security.

Presentation currency The currency in which financial statement amounts are presented.

Pretax margin A profitability ratio calculated as earnings before taxes divided by revenue.

Price ceiling A regulation that makes it illegal to charge a price higher than a specified level.

Price discovery A feature of futures markets in which futures prices provide valuable information about the price of the underlying asset.

Price discrimination The practice of selling different units of a good or service for different prices or of charging one customer different prices for different quantities bought.

Price elasticity of demand A units-free measure of the responsiveness of the quantity demanded of a good to a change in its price, when all other influences on buyers' plans remain the same.

Price floor A regulation that makes it illegal to trade at a price lower than a specified level.

Price limits Limits imposed by a futures exchange on the price change that can occur from one day to the next.

Price multiple A ratio that compares the share price with some sort of monetary flow or value to allow evaluation of the relative worth of a company's stock.

Price priority The principle that the highest priced buy orders and the lowest priced sell orders execute first.

Price relative A ratio of an ending price over a beginning price; it is equal to 1 plus the holding period return on the asset.

Price return Measures *only* the price appreciation or percentage change in price of the securities in an index or portfolio.

Price return index (or **price index**) An index that reflects *only* the price appreciation or percentage change in price of the constituent securities.

Price taker A firm that cannot influence the price of the good or service it produces.

Price to book value A valuation ratio calculated as price per share divided by book value per share.

Price to cash flow A valuation ratio calculated as price per share divided by cash flow per share.

Price to sales A valuation ratio calculated as price per share divided by sales per share.

Price weighting An index weighting method in which the weight assigned to each constituent security is determined by dividing its price by the sum of all the prices of the constituent securities.

Price/earnings (P/E) ratio The ratio of share price to earnings per share.

Priced risk Risk for which investors demand compensation for bearing (e.g. equity risk, company-specific factors, macroeconomic factors).

Price-setting option The operational flexibility to adjust prices when demand varies from forecast. For example, when demand exceeds capacity, the company could benefit from the excess demand by increasing prices.

Price-weighted index An index in which the weight on each constituent security is determined by dividing its price by the sum of all the prices of the constituent securities.

Primary market The market where securities are first sold and the issuers receive the proceeds.

Principal The amount of funds originally invested in a project or instrument; the face value to be paid at maturity.

Principal–agent problem The problem of devising compensation rules that induce an *agent* to act in the best interest of a *principal*.

Principal business activity The business activity from which a company derives a majority of its revenues and/or earnings.

Prior probabilities Probabilities reflecting beliefs prior to the arrival of new information.

Private equity securities Securities that are not listed on public exchanges and have no active secondary market. They are issued primarily to institutional investors via non-public offerings, such as private placements.

Private investment in public equity An investment in the equity of a publicly traded firm that is made at a discount to the market value of the firm's shares.

Private placement When corporations sell securities directly to a small group of qualified investors, usually with the assistance of an investment bank.

Probability A number between 0 and 1 describing the chance that a stated event will occur.

Probability density function A function with non-negative values such that probability can be described by areas under the curve graphing the function.

Probability distribution A distribution that specifies the probabilities of a random variable's possible outcomes.

Probability function A function that specifies the probability that the random variable takes on a specific value.

Probit model A qualitative-dependent-variable multiple regression model based on the normal distribution.

Producer surplus The price of a good minus its minimum supply-price, summed over the quantity sold.

Product differentiation Making a product slightly different from the product of a competing firm.

Production quota An upper limit to the quantity of a good that may be produced in a specified period.

Production-flexibility The operational flexibility to alter production when demand varies from forecast. For example, if demand is strong, a company may profit from employees working overtime or from adding additional shifts.

Profitability ratios Ratios that measure a company's ability to generate profitable sales from its resources (assets).

Project sequencing To defer the decision to invest in a future project until the outcome of some or all of a current project is known. Projects are sequenced through time, so that investing in a project creates the option to invest in future projects.

Projected benefit obligation Under U.S. GAAP, a measure used in estimating a defined-benefit pension plan's liabilities, defined as "the actuarial present value as of a date of all benefits attributed by the pension benefit formula to employee service rendered prior to that date. The projected benefit obligation is measured using assumptions as to future compensation if the pension benefit formula is based on those future compensation levels."

Property, plant, and equipment Tangible assets that are expected to be used for more than one period in either the production or supply of goods or services, or for administrative purposes.

Proportionate consolidation A method of accounting for joint ventures where the venturer's share of the assets, liabilities, income and expenses of the joint venture are combined on a line-by-line basis with similar items on the venturer's financial statements.

Protective put An option strategy in which a long position in an asset is combined with a long position in a put.

Provision In accounting, a liability of uncertain timing or amount.

Proxy fight An attempt to take control of a company through a shareholder vote.

Proxy statement A public document that provides the material facts concerning matters on which shareholders will vote.

Pseudo-random numbers Numbers produced by random number generators.

Pull on liquidity When disbursements are paid too quickly or trade credit availability is limited, requiring companies to expend funds before they receive funds from sales that could cover the liability.

Purchase method A method of accounting for a business combination where the acquiring company allocates the purchase price to each asset acquired and liability assumed at fair value. If the purchase price exceeds the allocation, the excess is recorded as goodwill.

Purchased in-process research and development costs The costs of research and development in progress at an acquired company.

Purchasing power gain A gain in value caused by changes in price levels. Monetary liabilities experience purchasing power gains during periods of inflation.

Purchasing power loss A loss in value caused by changes in price levels. Monetary assets experience purchasing power losses during periods of inflation.

Pure discount instruments Instruments that pay interest as the difference between the amount borrowed and the amount paid back.

Pure factor portfolio A portfolio with sensitivity of 1 to the factor in question and a sensitivity of 0 to all other factors.

Pure-play method A method for estimating the beta for a company or project; it requires using a comparable company's beta and adjusting it for financial leverage differences.

Put An option that gives the holder the right to sell an underlying asset to another party at a fixed price over a specific period of time.

Put–call parity An equation expressing the equivalence (parity) of a portfolio of a call and a bond with a portfolio of a put and the underlying, which leads to the relationship between put and call prices.

Put–call–forward parity The relationship among puts, calls, and forward contracts.

Put/call ratio A technical analysis indicator that evaluates market sentiment based upon the volume of put options traded divided by the volume of call options traded for a particular financial instrument.

Putable common shares Common shares that give investors the option (or right) to sell their shares (i.e., "put" them) back to the issuing company at a price that is specified when the shares are originally issued.

***p*-Value** The smallest level of significance at which the null hypothesis can be rejected; also called the marginal significance level.

Qualifying special purpose entities Under U.S. GAAP, a special purpose entity structured to avoid consolidation that must meet qualification criteria.

Qualitative dependent variables Dummy variables used as dependent variables rather than as independent variables.

Quantile (or fractile) A value at or below which a stated fraction of the data lies.

Quantity theory of money The proposition that in the long run, an increase in the quantity of money brings an equal percentage increase in the price level.

Quartiles Quantiles that divide a distribution into four equal parts.

Quick assets Assets that can be most readily converted to cash (e.g., cash, short-term marketable investments, receivables).

Quick ratio, or acid test ratio A stringent measure of liquidity that indicates a company's ability to satisfy current liabilities with its most liquid assets, calculated as (cash + short-term marketable investments + receivables) divided by current liabilities.

Quintiles Quantiles that divide a distribution into five equal parts.

Quote-driven market A market in which dealers acting as principals facilitate trading.

Random number An observation drawn from a uniform distribution.

Random number generator An algorithm that produces uniformly distributed random numbers between 0 and 1.

Random variable A quantity whose future outcomes are uncertain.

Random walk A time series in which the value of the series in one period is the value of the series in the previous period plus an unpredictable random error.

Range The difference between the maximum and minimum values in a dataset.

Ratio scales A measurement scale that has all the characteristics of interval measurement scales as well as a true zero point as the origin.

Ratio spread An option strategy in which a long position in a certain number of options is offset by a short position in a certain number of other options on the same underlying, resulting in a risk-free position.

Rational expectation The most accurate forecast possible, a forecast that uses all the available information, including knowledge of the relevant economic forces that influence the variable being forecasted.

Real business cycle theory A theory of the business cycle that regards random fluctuations in productivity as the main source of economic fluctuations.

Real exchange rate The relative price of foreign-made goods and services to U.S.-made goods and services.

Real risk-free interest rate The single-period interest rate for a completely risk-free security if no inflation were expected.

Real wage rate The quantity of goods and services that an hour's work can buy. It is equal to the money wage rate divided by the price level and multiplied by 100.

Realizable value (settlement value) With reference to assets, the amount of cash or cash equivalents that could currently be obtained by selling the asset in an orderly disposal; with reference to liabilities, the undiscounted amount of cash or cash equivalents expected to be paid to satisfy the liabilities in the normal course of business.

Realized capital gains The gains resulting from the sale of an asset that has appreciated in value.

Rebalancing Adjusting the weights of the constituent securities in an index.

Rebalancing policy The set of rules that guide the process of restoring a portfolio's asset class weights to those specified in the strategic asset allocation.

Receivables turnover An activity ratio equal to revenue divided by average receivables.

Receiver swaption A swaption that allows the holder to enter into a swap as the fixed-rate receiver and floating-rate payer.

Recessionary gap The amount by which potential GDP exceeds real GDP.

Reference base period The period in which the CPI is defined to be 100.

Regime With reference to a time series, the underlying model generating the times series.

Regression coefficients The intercept and slope coefficient(s) of a regression.

Regulatory risk The risk associated with the uncertainty of how derivative transactions will be regulated or with changes in regulations.

Rejection point (or critical value) A value against which a computed test statistic is compared to decide whether to reject or not reject the null hypothesis.

Relative dispersion The amount of dispersion relative to a reference value or benchmark.

Relative frequency With reference to an interval of grouped data, the number of observations in the interval divided by the total number of observations in the sample.

Relative strength analysis A comparison of the performance of one asset with the performance of another asset or a benchmark based on changes in the ratio of the securities' respective prices over time.

Relative strength index A technical analysis momentum oscillator that compares a security's gains with its losses over a set period.

Renewable natural resources Natural resources that can be used repeatedly without depleting what is available for future use.

Rent ceiling A regulation that makes it illegal to charge a rent higher than a specified level.

Rent seeking The pursuit of wealth by capturing economic rent—consumer surplus, producer surplus, or economic profit.

Reorganization Agreements made by a company in bankruptcy under which a company's capital structure is altered and/or alternative arrangements are made for debt repayment; U.S. Chapter 11 bankruptcy. The company emerges from bankruptcy as a going concern.

Replacement value The market value of a swap.

Report format With respect to the format of a balance sheet, a format in which assets, liabilities, and equity are listed in a single column.

Reputational risk The risk that a company will suffer an extended diminution in market value relative to other companies in the same industry due to a demonstrated lack of concern for environmental, social, and governance risk factors.

Required reserve ratio The minimum percentage of deposits that banks are required to hold as reserves.

Reserve ratio The fraction of a bank's total deposits that are held in reserves.

Reserves A bank's reserves consist of notes and coins in its vaults plus its deposit at the Federal Reserve.

Residual autocorrelations The sample autocorrelations of the residuals.

Residual claim The owners' remaining claim on the company's assets after the liabilities are deducted.

Residual dividend approach A dividend payout policy under which earnings in excess of the funds necessary to finance the equity portion of company's capital budget are paid out in dividends.

Residual loss Agency costs that are incurred despite adequate monitoring and bonding of management.

Resistance In technical analysis, a price range in which selling activity is sufficient to stop the rise in the price of a security.

Retail method An inventory accounting method in which the sales value of an item is reduced by the gross margin to calculate the item's cost.

Retracement In technical analysis, a reversal in the movement of a security's price such that it is counter to the prevailing longer-term price trend.

Return on assets (ROA) A profitability ratio calculated as net income divided by average total assets; indicates a company's net profit generated per dollar invested in total assets.

Return on common equity (ROCE) A profitability ratio calculated as (net income – preferred dividends) divided by average common equity; equal to the return on equity ratio when no preferred equity is outstanding.

Return on equity (ROE) A profitability ratio calculated as net income divided by average shareholders' equity.

Return on total capital A profitability ratio calculated as EBIT divided by the sum of short- and long-term debt and equity.

Return-generating model A model that can provide an estimate of the expected return of a security given certain parameters and estimates of the values of the independent variables in the model.

Revaluation The process of valuing long-lived assets at fair value, rather than at cost less accumulated depreciation. Any resulting profit or loss is either reported on the income statement and/or through equity under revaluation surplus.

Revenue The amount charged for the delivery of goods or services in the ordinary activities of a business over a stated period; the inflows of economic resources to a company over a stated period.

Reversal patterns A type of pattern used in technical analysis to predict the end of a trend and a change in direction of the security's price.

Reverse stock split A reduction in the number of shares outstanding with a corresponding increase in share price, but no change to the company's underlying fundamentals.

Revolving credit agreements The strongest form of short-term bank borrowing facilities; they are in effect for multiple years (e.g., 3–5 years) and may have optional medium-term loan features.

Rho The sensitivity of the option price to the risk-free rate.

Ricardo-Barro equivalence The proposition that taxes and government borrowing are equivalent—a budget deficit has no effect on the real interest rate or investment.

Risk averse The assumption that an investor will choose the least risky alternative.

Risk aversion The degree of an investor's inability and unwillingness to take risk.

Risk budgeting The establishment of objectives for individuals, groups, or divisions of an organization that takes into account the allocation of an acceptable level of risk.

Risk governance The setting of overall policies and standards in risk management.

Risk management The process of identifying the level of risk an entity wants, measuring the level of risk the entity currently has, taking actions that bring the actual level of risk to the desired level of risk, and monitoring the new actual level of risk so that it continues to be aligned with the desired level of risk.

Risk premium The expected return on an investment minus the risk-free rate.

Risk tolerance The amount of risk an investor is willing and able to bear to achieve an investment goal.

Risk-neutral probabilities Weights that are used to compute a binomial option price. They are the probabilities that would apply if a risk-neutral investor valued an option.

Risk-neutral valuation The process by which options and other derivatives are priced by treating investors as though they were risk neutral.

Robust The quality of being relatively unaffected by a violation of assumptions.

Robust standard errors Standard errors of the estimated parameters of a regression that correct for the presence of heteroskedasticity in the regression's error term.

Root mean squared error (RMSE) The square root of the average squared forecast error; used to compare the out-of-sample forecasting performance of forecasting models.

Roy's safety first criterion A criterion asserting that the optimal portfolio is the one that minimizes the probability that portfolio return falls below a threshold level.

Rule of 72 The principle that the approximate number of years necessary for an investment to double is 72 divided by the stated interest rate.

Safety stock A level of inventory beyond anticipated needs that provides a cushion in the event that it takes longer to replenish inventory than expected or in the case of greater than expected demand.

Safety-first rules Rules for portfolio selection that focus on the risk that portfolio value will fall below some minimum acceptable level over some time horizon.

Sales Generally, a synonym for revenue; "sales" is generally understood to refer to the sale of goods, whereas "revenue" is understood to include the sale of goods or services.

Sales returns and allowances An offset to revenue reflecting any cash refunds, credits on account, and discounts from sales prices given to customers who purchased defective or unsatisfactory items.

Sales risk Uncertainty with respect to the quantity of goods and services that a company is able to sell and the price it is able to achieve; the risk related to the uncertainty of revenues.

Sales-type lease A type of finance lease, from a lessor perspective, where the present value of the lease payments (lease receivable) exceeds the carrying value of the leased asset. The revenues earned by the lessor are operating (the profit on the sale) and financing (interest) in nature.

Salvage value (or residual value) The amount the company estimates that it can sell the asset for at the end of its useful life.

Sample A subset of a population.

Sample excess kurtosis A sample measure of the degree of a distribution's peakedness in excess of the normal distribution's peakedness.

Sample kurtosis A sample measure of the degree of a distribution's peakedness.

Sample mean The sum of the sample observations, divided by the sample size.

Sample selection bias Bias introduced by systematically excluding some members of the population according to a particular attribute—for example, the bias introduced when data availability leads to certain observations being excluded from the analysis.

Sample skewness   A sample measure of degree of asymmetry of a distribution.

Sample standard deviation   The positive square root of the sample variance.

Sample statistic or **statistic**   A quantity computed from or used to describe a sample.

Sample variance   A sample measure of the degree of dispersion of a distribution, calculated by dividing the sum of the squared deviations from the sample mean by the sample size (n) minus 1.

Sampling   The process of obtaining a sample.

Sampling distribution   The distribution of all distinct possible values that a statistic can assume when computed from samples of the same size randomly drawn from the same population.

Sampling error   The difference between the observed value of a statistic and the quantity it is intended to estimate.

Sampling plan   The set of rules used to select a sample.

Sandwich spread   An option strategy that is equivalent to a short butterfly spread.

Sarbanes–Oxley Act   An act passed by the U.S. Congress in 2002 that created the Public Company Accounting Oversight Board (PCAOB) to oversee auditors.

Scalper   A trader who offers to buy or sell futures contracts, holding the position for only a brief period of time. Scalpers attempt to profit by buying at the bid price and selling at the higher ask price.

Scatter plot   A two-dimensional plot of pairs of observations on two data series.

Scenario analysis   Analysis that shows the changes in key financial quantities that result from given (economic) events, such as the loss of customers, the loss of a supply source, or a catastrophic event; a risk management technique involving examination of the performance of a portfolio under specified situations. Closely related to stress testing.

Screening   The application of a set of criteria to reduce a set of potential investments to a smaller set having certain desired characteristics.

Search activity   The time spent looking for someone with whom to do business.

Seasoned offering   An offering in which an issuer sells additional units of a previously issued security.

Seats   Memberships in a derivatives exchange.

Secondary market   The market where securities are traded among investors.

Secondary precedence rules   Rules that determine how to rank orders placed at the same time.

Sector   A group of related industries.

Sector indices   Indices that represent and track different economic sectors—such as consumer goods, energy, finance, health care, and technology—on either a national, regional, or global basis.

Sector neutralizing   Measure of financial reporting quality by subtracting the mean or median ratio for a given sector group from a given company's ratio.

Securities Act of 1933   An act passed by the U.S. Congress in 1933 that specifies the financial and other significant information that investors must receive when securities are sold, prohibits misrepresentations, and requires initial registration of all public issuances of securities.

Securities Exchange Act of 1934   An act passed by the U.S. Congress in 1934 that created the Securities and Exchange Commission (SEC), gave the SEC authority over all aspects of the securities industry, and empowered the SEC to require periodic reporting by companies with publicly traded securities.

Securities offering   A merger or acquisition in which target shareholders are to receive shares of the acquirer's common stock as compensation.

Security characteristic line   A plot of the excess return of a security on the excess return of the market.

Security market index   A portfolio of securities representing a given security market, market segment, or asset class.

Security market line (SML)   The graph of the capital asset pricing model.

Security selection   The process of selecting individual securities; typically, security selection has the objective of generating superior risk-adjusted returns relative to a portfolio's benchmark.

Segment debt ratio   Segment liabilities divided by segment assets.

Segment margin   Segment profit (loss) divided by segment revenue.

Segment ROA   Segment profit (loss) divided by segment assets.

Segment turnover   Segment revenue divided by segment assets.

Self-investment limits   With respect to investment limitations applying to pension plans, restrictions on the percentage of assets that can be invested in securities issued by the pension plan sponsor.

Sell side firm   A broker or dealer that sells securities to and provides independent investment research and recommendations to investment management companies.

Semideviation   The positive square root of semivariance (sometimes called semistandard deviation).

Semilogarithmic   Describes a scale constructed so that equal intervals on the vertical scale represent equal rates of change, and equal intervals on the horizontal scale represent equal amounts of change.

Semi-strong-form efficient market hypothesis   The belief that security prices reflect all publicly known and available information.

Semivariance   The average squared deviation below the mean.

Sensitivity analysis   Analysis that shows the range of possible outcomes as specific assumptions are changed.

Separately managed account (SMA)   An investment portfolio managed exclusively for the benefit of an individual or institution.

Serially correlated   With reference to regression errors, errors that are correlated across observations.

Service period   The period benefited by the employee's service, usually the period between the grant date and the vesting date.

Settlement date or payment date   The date on which the parties to a swap make payments.

Settlement period   The time between settlement dates.

Settlement price   The official price, designated by the clearinghouse, from which daily gains and losses will be determined and marked to market.

Settlement risk   When settling a contract, the risk that one party could be in the process of paying the counterparty while the counterparty is declaring bankruptcy.

Share repurchase   A transaction in which a company buys back its own shares. Unlike stock dividends and stock splits, share repurchases use corporate cash.

Shark repellents   A pre-offer takeover defense mechanism involving the corporate charter (e.g., staggered boards of directors and supermajority provisions).

Sharpe ratio   The average return in excess of the risk-free rate divided by the standard deviation of return; a measure of the average excess return earned per unit of standard deviation of return.

Shelf registration A registration of an offering well in advance of the offering; the issuer may not sell all shares registered in a single transaction.

Short The seller of a derivative contract. Also refers to the position of being short a derivative.

Short position A position in an asset or contract in which one has sold an asset one does not own, or in which a right under a contract can be exercised against oneself.

Short run The period of time in which the quantity of at least one factor of production is fixed and the quantities of the other factors can be varied. The fixed factor is usually capital—that is, the firm has a given plant size.

Shortfall risk The risk that portfolio value will fall below some minimum acceptable level over some time horizon.

Short-run aggregate supply The relationship between the quantity of real GDP supplied and the price level when the money wage rate, the prices of other resources, and potential GDP remain constant.

Short-run industry supply curve A curve that shows the quantity supplied by the industry at each price when the plant size of each firm and the number of firms in the industry remain the same.

Short-run macroeconomic equilibrium A situation that occurs when the quantity of real GDP demanded equals the quantity of real GDP supplied—at the point of intersection of the *AD* curve and the *SAS* curve.

Short-run Phillips curve A curve that shows the tradeoff between inflation and unemployment, when the expected inflation rate and the natural unemployment rate remain the same.

Short selling A transaction in which borrowed securities are sold with the intention to repurchase them at a lower price at a later date and return them to the lender.

Shutdown point The output and price at which the firm just covers its total variable cost. In the short run, the firm is indifferent between producing the profit-maximizing output and shutting down temporarily.

Signal An action taken by an informed person (or firm) to send a message to uninformed people or an action taken outside a market that conveys information that can be used by the market.

Simple interest The interest earned each period on the original investment; interest calculated on the principal only.

Simple random sample A subset of a larger population created in such a way that each element of the population has an equal probability of being selected to the subset.

Simple random sampling The procedure of drawing a sample to satisfy the definition of a simple random sample.

Simulation Computer-generated sensitivity or scenario analysis that is based on probability models for the factors that drive outcomes.

Simulation trial A complete pass through the steps of a simulation.

Single-payment loan A loan in which the borrower receives a sum of money at the start and pays back the entire amount with interest in a single payment at maturity.

Single-price monopoly A monopoly that must sell each unit of its output for the same price to all its customers.

Single-step format With respect to the format of the income statement, a format that does not subtotal for gross profit (revenue minus cost of goods sold).

Skewed Not symmetrical.

Skewness A quantitative measure of skew (lack of symmetry); a synonym of skew.

Sole proprietorship A business owned and operated by a single person.

Solvency With respect to financial statement analysis, the ability of a company to fulfill its long-term obligations.

Solvency ratios Ratios that measure a company's ability to meet its long-term obligations.

Sovereign yield spread An estimate of the country spread (country equity premium) for a developing nation that is based on a comparison of bonds yields in country being analyzed and a developed country. The sovereign yield spread is the difference between a government bond yield in the country being analyzed, denominated in the currency of the developed country, and the Treasury bond yield on a similar maturity bond in the developed country.

Spearman rank correlation coefficient A measure of correlation applied to ranked data.

Special purpose entity (special purpose vehicle or variable interest entity) A non-operating entity created to carry out a specified purpose, such as leasing assets or securitizing receivables; can be a corporation, partnership, trust, limited liability, or partnership formed to facilitate a specific type of business activity.

Specific identification method An inventory accounting method that identifies which specific inventory items were sold and which remained in inventory to be carried over to later periods.

Spin-off A form of restructuring in which shareholders of the parent company receive a proportional number of shares in a new, separate entity; shareholders end up owning stock in two different companies where there used to be one.

Split-off A form of restructuring in which shareholders of the parent company are given shares in a newly created entity in exchange for their shares of the parent company.

Split-rate In reference to corporate taxes, a split-rate system taxes earnings to be distributed as dividends at a different rate than earnings to be retained. Corporate profits distributed as dividends are taxed at a lower rate than those retained in the business.

Sponsored depository receipt A type of depository receipt in which the foreign company whose shares are held by the depository has a direct involvement in the issuance of the receipts.

Spot markets Markets that trade assets for immediate delivery.

Spread An option strategy involving the purchase of one option and sale of another option that is identical to the first in all respects except either exercise price or expiration.

Spurious correlation A correlation that misleadingly points towards associations between variables.

Stagflation The combination of inflation and recession.

Standard cost With respect to inventory accounting, the planned or target unit cost of inventory items or services.

Standard deviation The positive square root of the variance; a measure of dispersion in the same units as the original data.

Standard normal distribution (or unit normal distribution) The normal density with mean (μ) equal to 0 and standard deviation (σ) equal to 1.

Standardized beta With reference to fundamental factor models, the value of the attribute for an asset minus the average value of the attribute across all stocks, divided by the standard deviation of the attribute across all stocks.

Standardizing A transformation that involves subtracting the mean and dividing the result by the standard deviation.

Standing limit orders A limit order at a price below market and which therefore is waiting to trade.

Stated annual interest rate or quoted interest rate A quoted interest rate that does not account for compounding within the year.

Stated rate (nominal rate or coupon rate) The rate at which periodic interest payments are calculated.

Statement of cash flows (cash flow statement) A financial statement that reconciles beginning-of-period and end-of-period balance sheet values of cash; provides information about an entity's cash inflows and cash outflows as they pertain to operating, investing, and financing activities.

Statement of changes in shareholders' equity (statement of owners' equity) A financial statement that reconciles the beginning-of-period and end-of-period balance sheet values of shareholders' equity; provides information about all factors affecting shareholders' equity.

Statement of retained earnings A financial statement that reconciles beginning-of-period and end-of-period balance sheet values of retained income; shows the linkage between the balance sheet and income statement.

Static trade-off theory of capital structure A theory pertaining to a company's optimal capital structure; the optimal level of debt is found at the point where additional debt would cause the costs of financial distress to increase by a greater amount than the benefit of the additional tax shield.

Statistic A quantity computed from or used to describe a sample of data.

Statistical factor models A multifactor model in which statistical methods are applied to a set of historical returns to determine portfolios that best explain either historical return covariances or variances.

Statistical inference Making forecasts, estimates, or judgments about a larger group from a smaller group actually observed; using a sample statistic to infer the value of an unknown population parameter.

Statistically significant A result indicating that the null hypothesis can be rejected; with reference to an estimated regression coefficient, frequently understood to mean a result indicating that the corresponding population regression coefficient is different from 0.

Statistics The science of describing, analyzing, and drawing conclusions from data; also, a collection of numerical data.

Statutory merger A merger in which one company ceases to exist as an identifiable entity and all its assets and liabilities become part of a purchasing company.

Statutory voting A common method of voting where each share represents one vote.

Stock dividend (also **bonus issue of shares**) A type of dividend in which a company distributes additional shares of its common stock to shareholders instead of cash.

Stock grants The granting of stock to employees as a form of compensation.

Stock options (stock option grants) The granting of stock options to employees as a form of compensation.

Stock purchase An acquisition in which the acquirer gives the target company's shareholders some combination of cash and securities in exchange for shares of the target company's stock.

Stock-out losses Profits lost from not having sufficient inventory on hand to satisfy demand.

Stop order (or **stop-loss order**) An order in which a trader has specified a stop price condition.

Storage costs or carrying costs The costs of holding an asset, generally a function of the physical characteristics of the underlying asset.

Straddle An option strategy involving the purchase of a put and a call with the same exercise price. A straddle is based on the expectation of high volatility of the underlying.

Straight-line method A depreciation method that allocates evenly the cost of a long-lived asset less its estimated residual value over the estimated useful life of the asset.

Strangle A variation of a straddle in which the put and call have different exercise prices.

Strap An option strategy involving the purchase of two calls and one put.

Strategic analysis Analysis of the competitive environment with an emphasis on the implications of the environment for corporate strategy.

Strategic asset allocation The set of exposures to IPS-permissible asset classes that is expected to achieve the client's long-term objectives given the client's investment constraints.

Strategic groups Groups sharing distinct business models or catering to specific market segments in an industry.

Strategies All the possible actions of each player in a game.

Stratified random sampling A procedure by which a population is divided into subpopulations (strata) based on one or more classification criteria. Simple random samples are then drawn from each stratum in sizes proportional to the relative size of each stratum in the population. These samples are then pooled.

Stress testing A set of techniques for estimating losses in extremely unfavorable combinations of events or scenarios.

Strip An option strategy involving the purchase of two puts and one call.

Strong-form efficient market hypothesis The belief that security prices reflect all public and private information.

Structural surplus or deficit The budget balance that would occur if the economy were at full employment and real GDP were equal to potential GDP.

Structural unemployment The unemployment that arises when changes in technology or international competition change the skills needed to perform jobs or change the locations of jobs.

Structured note A variation of a floating-rate note that has some type of unusual characteristic such as a leverage factor or in which the rate moves opposite to interest rates.

Subjective probability A probability drawing on personal or subjective judgment.

Subsidiary merger A merger in which the company being purchased becomes a subsidiary of the purchaser.

Subsidy A payment made by the government to a producer.

Sunk cost A cost that has already been incurred.

Supply-side effects The effects of fiscal policy on employment, potential GDP, and aggregate supply.

Support In technical analysis, a price range in which buying activity is sufficient to stop the decline in the price of a security.

Support level A price at which investors consider a security to be an attractive investment and are willing to buy, even in the wake of a sharp decline.

Surprise The actual value of a variable minus its predicted (or expected) value.

Survey approach An estimate of the equity risk premium that is based upon estimates provided by a panel of finance experts.

Survivorship bias The bias resulting from a test design that fails to account for companies that have gone bankrupt, merged, or are otherwise no longer reported in a database.

Sustainable growth rate The rate of dividend (and earnings) growth that can be sustained over time for a given level of return on equity, keeping the capital structure constant and without issuing additional common stock.

Swap (or **swap contract**) An agreement between two parties to exchange a series of future cash flows.

Swap spread   The difference between the fixed rate on an interest rate swap and the rate on a Treasury note with equivalent maturity; it reflects the general level of credit risk in the market.

Swaption   An option to enter into a swap.

Symmetry principle   A requirement that people in similar situations be treated similarly.

Synthetic call   The combination of puts, the underlying, and risk-free bonds that replicates a call option.

Synthetic forward contract   The combination of the underlying, puts, calls, and risk-free bonds that replicates a forward contract.

Synthetic index fund   An index fund position created by combining risk-free bonds and futures on the desired index.

Synthetic put   The combination of calls, the underlying, and risk-free bonds that replicates a put option.

Systematic factors   Factors that affect the average returns of a large number of different assets.

Systematic risk   Risk that affects the entire market or economy; it cannot be avoided and is inherent in the overall market. Systematic risk is also known as non diversifiable or market risk.

Systematic sampling   A procedure of selecting every kth member until reaching a sample of the desired size. The sample that results from this procedure should be approximately random.

Tactical asset allocation   The decision to deliberately deviate from the strategic asset allocation in an attempt to add value based on forecasts of the near-term relative performance of asset classes.

Takeover   A merger; the term may be applied to any transaction, but is often used in reference to hostile transactions.

Takeover premium   The amount by which the takeover price for each share of stock must exceed the current stock price in order to entice shareholders to relinquish control of the company to an acquirer.

Tangible assets   Long-term assets with physical substance that are used in company operations, such as land (property), plant, and equipment.

Target balance   A minimum level of cash to be held available—estimated in advance and adjusted for known funds transfers, seasonality, or other factors.

Target capital structure   A company's chosen proportions of debt and equity.

Target company or **target**   The company in a merger or acquisition that is being acquired.

Target payout ratio   A strategic corporate goal representing the long-term proportion of earnings that the company intends to distribute to shareholders as dividends.

Target semideviation   The positive square root of target semivariance.

Target semivariance   The average squared deviation below a target value.

Targeting rule   A decision rule for monetary policy that sets the policy instrument at a level that makes the forecast of the ultimate policy target equal to the target.

Tax base (tax basis)   The amount at which an asset or liability is valued for tax purposes.

Tax expense   An aggregate of an entity's income tax payable (or recoverable in the case of a tax benefit) and any changes in deferred tax assets and liabilities. It is essentially the income tax payable or recoverable if these had been determined based on accounting profit rather than taxable income.

Tax incidence   The division of the burden of the tax between the buyer and the seller.

Tax loss carry forward   A taxable loss in the current period that may be used to reduce future taxable income.

Tax risk   The uncertainty associated with tax laws.

Tax wedge   The gap between the before-tax and after-tax wage rates.

Taxable income   The portion of an entity's income that is subject to income taxes under the tax laws of its jurisdiction.

Taxable temporary differences   Temporary differences that result in a taxable amount in a future period when determining the taxable profit as the balance sheet item is recovered or settled.

Taylor rule   A rule that sets the federal funds rate at the equilibrium real interest rate (which Taylor says is 2 percent a year) plus amounts based on the inflation rate and the output gap.

t-Distribution   A symmetrical distribution defined by a single parameter, degrees of freedom, that is largely used to make inferences concerning the mean of a normal distribution whose variance is unknown.

Technical analysis   A form of security analysis that uses price and volume data, which is often displayed graphically, in decision making.

Technological efficiency   A situation that occurs when the firm produces a given output by using the least amount of inputs.

Technology   Any method of producing a good or service.

Temporal method   A variation of the monetary/nonmonetary translation method that requires not only monetary assets and liabilities, but also nonmonetary assets and liabilities that are measured at their current value on the balance sheet date to be translated at the current exchange rate. Assets and liabilities are translated at rates consistent with the timing of their measurement value. This method is typically used when the functional currency is other than the local currency.

Tender offer   A public offer whereby the acquirer invites target shareholders to submit ("tender") their shares in return for the proposed payment.

Tenor   The original time to maturity on a swap.

Terminal stock value (or **terminal value**)   The expected value of a share at the end of the investment horizon—in effect, the expected selling price.

Termination date   The date of the final payment on a swap; also, the swap's expiration date.

Test statistic   A quantity, calculated based on a sample, whose value is the basis for deciding whether or not to reject the null hypothesis.

Theta   The rate at which an option's time value decays.

Time series   A set of observations on a variable's outcomes in different time periods.

Time to expiration   The time remaining in the life of a derivative, typically expressed in years.

Time value or speculative value   The difference between the market price of the option and its intrinsic value, determined by the uncertainty of the underlying over the remaining life of the option.

Time value decay   The loss in the value of an option resulting from movement of the option price toward its payoff value as the expiration day approaches.

Time value of money   The principles governing equivalence relationships between cash flows with different dates.

Time-period bias   The possibility that when we use a time-series sample, our statistical conclusion may be sensitive to the starting and ending dates of the sample.

Time-series data   Observations of a variable over time.

Time-weighted rate of return   The compound rate of growth of one unit of currency invested in a portfolio during a stated measurement period; a measure of investment performance that is not sensitive to the timing and amount of withdrawals or additions to the portfolio.

Top-down analysis With reference to investment selection processes, an approach that starts with macro selection (i.e., identifying attractive geographic segments and/or industry segments) and then addresses selection of the most attractive investments within those segments.

Total asset turnover An activity ratio calculated as revenue divided by average total assets.

Total cost The cost of all the productive resources that a firm uses.

Total fixed cost The cost of the firm's fixed inputs.

Total invested capital The sum of market value of common equity, book value of preferred equity, and face value of debt.

Total probability rule A rule explaining the unconditional probability of an event in terms of probabilities of the event conditional on mutually exclusive and exhaustive scenarios.

Total probability rule for expected value A rule explaining the expected value of a random variable in terms of expected values of the random variable conditional on mutually exclusive and exhaustive scenarios.

Total product The total output produced by a firm in a given period of time.

Total return Measures the price appreciation, or percentage change in price of the securities in an index or portfolio, plus any income received over the period.

Total return index An index that reflects the price appreciation or percentage change in price of the constituent securities plus any income received since inception.

Total return swap A swap in which one party agrees to pay the total return on a security. Often used as a credit derivative, in which the underlying is a bond.

Total revenue The value of a firm's sales. It is calculated as the price of the good multiplied by the quantity sold.

Total revenue test A method of estimating the price elasticity of demand by observing the change in total revenue that results from a change in the price, when all other influences on the quantity sold remain the same.

Total variable cost The cost of all the firm's variable inputs.

Tracking error The standard deviation of the difference in returns between an active investment portfolio and its benchmark portfolio; also called tracking error volatility, tracking risk, and active risk.

Tracking portfolio A portfolio having factor sensitivities that are matched to those of a benchmark or other portfolio.

Tracking risk (tracking error) The standard deviation of the differences between a portfolio's returns and its benchmark's returns; a synonym of active risk.

Trade credit A spontaneous form of credit in which a purchaser of the goods or service is financing its purchase by delaying the date on which payment is made.

Trade receivables (commercial receivables or accounts receivable) Amounts customers owe the company for products that have been sold as well as amounts that may be due from suppliers (such as for returns of merchandise).

Trading securities (held-for-trading securities) Securities held by a company with the intent to trade them.

Traditional investment markets Markets for traditional investments, which include all publicly traded debts and equities and shares in pooled investment vehicles that hold publicly traded debts and/or equities.

Transaction exposure The risk of a change in value between the transaction date and the settlement date of an asset or liability denominated in a foreign currency.

Transactions motive In the context of inventory management, the need for inventory as part of the routine production–sales cycle.

Translation exposure The risk associated with the conversion of foreign financial statements into domestic currency.

Treasury shares Shares that were issued and subsequently repurchased by the company.

Treasury stock method A method for accounting for the effect of options (and warrants) on earnings per share (EPS) that specifies what EPS would have been if the options and warrants had been exercised and the company had used the proceeds to repurchase common stock.

Tree diagram A diagram with branches emanating from nodes representing either mutually exclusive chance events or mutually exclusive decisions.

Trend A long-term pattern of movement in a particular direction.

Treynor ratio A measure of risk-adjusted performance that relates a portfolio's excess returns to the portfolio's beta.

Triangle patterns In technical analysis, a continuation chart pattern that forms as the range between high and low prices narrows, visually forming a triangle.

Trimmed mean A mean computed after excluding a stated small percentage of the lowest and highest observations.

Triple bottoms In technical analysis, a reversal pattern that is formed when the price forms three troughs at roughly the same price level; used to predict a change from a downtrend to an uptrend.

Triple tops In technical analysis, a reversal pattern that is formed when the price forms three peaks at roughly the same price level; used to predict a change from an uptrend to a downtrend.

Trust receipt arrangement The use of inventory as collateral for a loan. The inventory is segregated and held in trust, and the proceeds of any sale must be remitted to the lender immediately.

t-Test A hypothesis test using a statistic (t-statistic) that follows a t-distribution.

Two-fund separation theorem The theory that all investors regardless of taste, risk preferences, and initial wealth will hold a combination of two portfolios or funds: a risk-free asset and an optimal portfolio of risky assets.

Two-sided hypothesis test (or two-tailed hypothesis test) A test in which the null hypothesis is rejected in favor of the alternative hypothesis if the evidence indicates that the population parameter is either smaller or larger than a hypothesized value.

Type I error The error of rejecting a true null hypothesis.

Type II error The error of not rejecting a false null hypothesis.

Unbiasedness Lack of bias. A desirable property of estimators, an unbiased estimator is one whose expected value (the mean of its sampling distribution) equals the parameter it is intended to estimate.

Unbilled revenue (accrued revenue) Revenue that has been earned but not yet billed to customers as of the end of an accounting period.

Unclassified balance sheet A balance sheet that does not show subtotals for current assets and current liabilities.

Unconditional heteroskedasticity Heteroskedasticity of the error term that is not correlated with the values of the independent variable(s) in the regression.

Unconditional probability (or marginal probability) The probability of an event not conditioned on another event.

Underlying An asset that trades in a market in which buyers and sellers meet, decide on a price, and the seller then delivers the asset to the buyer and receives payment. The underlying is the asset or other derivative on which a particular derivative is based. The market for the underlying is also referred to as the spot market.

Underwritten offering   An offering in which the (lead) investment bank guarantees the sale of the issue at an offering price that it negotiates with the issuer.

Unearned fees   Unearned fees are recognized when a company receives cash payment for fees prior to earning them.

Unearned revenue (deferred revenue)   A liability account for money that has been collected for goods or services that have not yet been delivered; payment received in advance of providing a good or service.

Unemployment rate   The number of unemployed people expressed as a percentage of all the people who have jobs or are looking for one. It is the percentage of the labor force who are unemployed.

Unidentifiable intangible   An intangible that cannot be acquired singly and that typically possesses an indefinite benefit period; an example is accounting goodwill.

Unit elastic demand   Demand with a price elasticity of 1; the percentage change in the quantity demanded equals the percentage change in price.

Unit root   A time series that is not covariance stationary is said to have a unit root.

Uniting of interests method   A method of accounting in which combined companies were portrayed as if they had always operated as a single economic entity. Called pooling of interests under U.S. GAAP and uniting of interests under IFRS. (No longer allowed under U.S. GAAP or IFRS.)

Units-of-production method   A depreciation method that allocates the cost of a long-lived asset based on actual usage during the period.

Univariate distribution   A distribution that specifies the probabilities for a single random variable.

Unlimited funds   An unlimited funds environment assumes that the company can raise the funds it wants for all profitable projects simply by paying the required rate of return.

Unsponsored depository receipt   A type of depository receipt in which the foreign company whose shares are held by the depository has no involvement in the issuance of the receipts.

Up transition probability   The probability that an asset's value moves up.

Upstream   A transaction between two affiliates, an investor company and an associate company such that the associate company records a profit on its income statement. An example is a sale of inventory by the associate to the investor company.

Utilitarianism   A principle that states that we should strive to achieve "the greatest happiness for the greatest number of people."

Validity instructions   Instructions which indicate when the order may be filled.

Valuation   The process of determining the value of an asset or service.

Valuation allowance   A reserve created against deferred tax assets, based on the likelihood of realizing the deferred tax assets in future accounting periods.

Valuation ratios   Ratios that measure the quantity of an asset or flow (e.g., earnings) in relation to the price associated with a specified claim (e.g., a share or ownership of the enterprise).

Value   The amount for which one can sell something, or the amount one must pay to acquire something.

Value at risk (VAR)   A money measure of the minimum value of losses expected during a specified time period at a given level of probability.

Value investors   With reference to equity investors, investors who are focused on paying a relatively low share price in relation to earnings or assets per share.

Value stocks   Stocks that appear to be undervalued for reasons besides earnings growth potential. These stocks are usually identified based on high dividend yields, low *P/E* ratios, or low price-to-book ratios.

Value (market-capitalization) weighted index   An index in which the weight on each constituent security is determined by dividing its market capitalization by the total market capitalization (the sum of the market capitalization) of all the securities in the index.

Variable costs   Costs that fluctuate with the level of production and sales.

Variance   The expected value (the probability-weighted average) of squared deviations from a random variable's expected value.

Variation margin   Additional margin that must be deposited in an amount sufficient to bring the balance up to the initial margin requirement.

Vega   The relationship between option price and volatility.

Velocity of circulation   The average number of times a dollar of money is used annually to buy the goods and services that make up GDP.

Venture capital   Investments that provide "seed" or start-up capital, early-stage financing, or mezzanine financing to companies that are in the early stages of development and require additional capital for expansion.

Venture capital fund   A fund for private equity investors that provides financing for development-stage companies.

Venturers   The owners of a joint venture. Each is active in the management and shares control of the joint venture.

Vertical analysis   Common-size analysis using only one reporting period or one base financial statement; for example, an income statement in which all items are stated as percentages of sales.

Vertical common-size analysis   The most common type of common-size analysis, in which the accounts in a given period are compared to a benchmark item in that same year.

Vertical merger   A merger involving companies at different positions of the same production chain; for example, a supplier or a distributor.

Vested benefit obligation   Under U.S. GAAP, a measure used in estimating a defined-benefit pension plan's liabilities, defined as the "actuarial present value of vested benefits."

Vested benefits   Future benefits promised to the employee regardless of continuing service. Benefits typically vest after a specified period of service or a specified period of service combined with age.

Vesting date   The date that employees can first exercise stock options; vesting can be immediate or over a future period.

Volatility   As used in option pricing, the standard deviation of the continuously compounded returns on the underlying asset.

Vote by proxy   A mechanism that allows a designated party—such as another shareholder, a shareholder representative, or management—to vote on the shareholder's behalf.

Warehouse receipt arrangement   The use of inventory as collateral for a loan; similar to a trust receipt arrangement except there is a third party (i.e., a warehouse company) that supervises the inventory.

Weak-form efficient market hypothesis   The belief that security prices fully reflect all past market data, which refers to all historical price and volume trading information.

Weighted average cost method   An inventory accounting method that averages the total cost of available inventory items over the total units available for sale.

Weighted mean   An average in which each observation is weighted by an index of its relative importance.

Weighted-average cost of capital A weighted average of the after-tax required rates of return on a company's common stock, preferred stock, and long-term debt, where the weights are the fraction of each source of financing in the company's target capital structure.

White knight A third party that is sought out by the target company's board to purchase the target in lieu of a hostile bidder.

White squire A third party that is sought out by the target company's board to purchase a substantial minority stake in the target—enough to block a hostile takeover without selling the entire company.

White-corrected standard errors A synonym for robust standard errors.

Winner's curse The tendency for the winner in certain competitive bidding situations to overpay, whether because of overestimation of intrinsic value, emotion, or information asymmetries.

Winsorized mean A mean computed after assigning a stated percent of the lowest values equal to one specified low value, and a stated percent of the highest values equal to one specified high value.

Working capital The difference between current assets and current liabilities.

Working capital management The management of a company's short-term assets (such as inventory) and short-term liabilities (such as money owed to suppliers).

Working capital turnover A comparison of revenues with working capital to produce a measure that shows how efficiently working capital is employed.

Working-age population The total number of people aged 15 years and over.

Yield The actual return on a debt security if it is held to maturity.

Yield beta A measure of the sensitivity of a bond's yield to a general measure of bond yields in the market that is used to refine the hedge ratio.

Yield spread The difference between the yield on a bond and the yield on a default-free security, usually a government note, of the same maturity. The yield spread is primarily determined by the market's perception of the credit risk on the bond.

Yield to maturity The annual return that an investor earns on a bond if the investor purchases the bond today and holds it until maturity.

Zero-cost collar A transaction in which a position in the underlying is protected by buying a put and selling a call with the premium from the sale of the call offsetting the premium from the purchase of the put. It can also be used to protect a floating-rate borrower against interest rate increases with the premium on a long cap offsetting the premium on a short floor.